Praise for *Walking with the Wind*

"Publication of *Walking with the Wind* is a literary event, for sure. This is the definitive account of the civil rights movement.... A compelling history that promises to become a sensation and make [John Lewis] the country's most prominent black leader, the long-awaited successor to Martin Luther King Jr.... It is impossible to read this inspirational and hideous story of courage and cruelty without being moved."　—Mary McGrory, *The Washington Post*

"John Lewis is a true hero."　　　　　　　　　　—Ed Bradley, *60 Minutes*

"This dramatic autobiography doubles as a primer on the 1960s civil rights movement."　　　　　　　　　　　—*Chicago Tribune* (Editor's Choice)

"John Lewis evokes, with simplicity and passion, how the 1960s transformed the United States. Powerful...compelling...probing...full of dramatic stories, enriched with details that reflect Lewis's own perspective as a participant-observer."　　　　　　　　　　—*The New York Times Book Review*

"Powerful...a moving tale...deftly conveys the drama and the danger of those days."　　　　　　　　　　　　　　　　　—*Newsweek*

"An astute first-hand account of events that could be supplied only by a key player....Destined to become a classic in civil rights literature."　　　　　　　　　　　　　　　　—*Los Angeles Times*

"No other elected official in America embodies the grand legacy of Martin Luther King Jr. more than John Lewis. In other words, he is a national treasure. Read this book and see why!"　　—Cornel West, Harvard University

"Can be read not only for his insights into the movement, but for his insights into the human spirit. This is, in fact, social gospel."　　—*Detroit Free Press*

"A simple, fascinating chronicle of the South's modern freedom movement and its aftermath—a wise, moving and personal account that stirs with unusual honesty and directness."　　　　　—*The Philadelphia Inquirer*

"In a powerful new memoir, Georgia C̶o̶n̶g̶r̶e̶s̶s̶... his days as a brave civil-rights pioneer."　　　　　　　　　　　　　　—*People*

"John Lewis was not only a participant in this history, but was one of the founding fathers and key designers of the movement....For those too young to remember and those too old to forget, for everyone of race, we owe a debt of gratitude to this American hero, and the nameless, frightened (but ultimately fearless) multitudes that walked with him down those rugged roads of history."
—*Pittsburgh Post-Gazette*

"Of all the surviving saints of the civil rights movement, John Lewis...remains most committed to its original creed. A stirring portrait of the power of moral consistency and courage."
—*Time*

"A book of shrewd assessments. Though it is not a vainglorious book, nor a mean one, Lewis defends convincingly the stands he took....John Lewis is living proof that one can be uncompromising without being unforgiving."
—Garry Wills, *New York Review of Books*

"A classic invaluable blockbuster of the civil rights movement."
—*Kirkus Reviews* (starred review)

"Lewis notes that people often take his quietness for meekness. His book, a uniquely well-told testimony by an eyewitness, makes clear that such an impression is entirely inaccurate."
—*Publishers Weekly* (starred review)

"Distinguished by its honesty and insight—such as the role played by powerful black women in the South—*Walking with the Wind* inspires even as it acknowledges the road yet to be trod."
—*The Seattle Times*

"Superbly written, with Lewis's searing honesty showing through."
—*The Boston Globe*

"A detailed and stirring history of the U.S. civil rights movement that evolves as he does....A self-conscious journey to the past gives us both a front-row seat and some distance. It is a study in quiet, strong, dignified leadership."
—*The Viginian-Pilot*

"He may be a saint, but Lewis has the deadly aim of a true revolutionary. *Walking with the Wind* should electrify anyone who believes that society needs change....He not only gives history, he shows what it was like to live it."
—*Bay Area Reporter*

"Less compendious than the ongoing definitive history of the King years by Taylor Branch, *Walking with the Wind* is far better at giving a sense of the passions of the time.... "What...is...right"—that is the slogan of this book, written by a man who lived the words." —*The Atlanta Journal-Constitution*

"Long-awaited personal history.... Provides an insider's account of the movement that ended racial segregation in the South."

—*Free-Press,* Jacksonville, FL

"A good book, a powerful book. It's about a man who seems embarrassed about the significant role he played in this century's history. It's about an underdog who almost always comes out on top. It's about a brave man who helped change history." —*Huntsville Times*

"John Lewis's eloquent autobiography is also a powerful and inspiring record of one of the most significant periods of America's history. John tells it like it was—the sit-in movement, the Freedom Rides, the March on Washington, the walk across Edmund Pettus Bridge, and many other dramatic moments in the nation's conscience. This story of courage and hope should be read by Americans of all races and backgrounds, young and old. John Lewis spent most of his life walking *against* the wind of the times, but he was surely walking *with* the wind of history." —Senator Edward M. Kennedy

"There is something Lincolnesque about the life of John Lewis: the humble beginnings, the civil rights battles, the patriotic vision, the fearlessness. He emerges—though he would be the last to make such a claim—in this powerful autobiography as the conscience of a nation still grappling with right and wrong, justice and injustice."

—Wil Haygood, author of *King of the Cats: The Life and Times of Adam Clayton Powell, Jr.*

"*Walking with the Wind* is a beautiful, powerful book, not just about our past, but our future." —Senator Paul Wellstone

"Thrilling. A civil rights hero's fiercely honest look at himself and the nation. Lewis never went for the easy answers, the clichés or with the in-crowd. Now he bares his struggles with evil, history and himself in one of the great memoirs of black movement history." —Juan Williams

"A nuanced, insider's account of the pivotal role that young people played in that heroic effort."   —*The Dallas Morning News*

"No soldier has been braver or more patriotic than John Lewis. The brutal beatings he took at the Selma bridge, the Montgomery bus terminal and dozens of historic conflicts are vividly captured in *Walking with the Wind*. His rise from volunteer demonstrator to a mature leader in the final battle of the American Revolution ensures him a place as a national hero."
                                        —Morris Dees, Southern Poverty Law Center

"Captures the man and the movement with honesty and dignity."
                                        —*Post and Courier* (Charleston, SC)

"Moving...excellent memoir...A lesson in how the movement really worked and a clear-eyed explanation of why it fell apart, particularly after 1968."
                                        —*The Washington Monthly*

"Details the joys and sorrows of a life lived at the epicenter of the U.S. civil rights revolution....Filled with more than 50 years of vivid, often touching recollections."   —*Southern Voice*

"Without a doubt the best 'movement' autobiography yet published."
                                        —*Southern Changes*

Walking with

JOHN LEWIS *with Michael D'Orso*

the Wind

A MEMOIR OF THE MOVEMENT

SIMON & SCHUSTER PAPERBACKS
New York   London   Toronto   Sydney   New Delhi

Simon & Schuster Paperbacks
A Division of Simon & Schuster, Inc.
1230 Avenue of the Americas
New York, NY 10020

This Simon & Schuster trade paperback edition February 2015

SIMON & SCHUSTER PAPERBACKS and colophon
are registered trademarks of Simon & Schuster, Inc.

For information about special discounts for bulk purchases,
please contact Simon & Schuster Special Sales at
1-866-506-1949 or business@simonandschuster.com.

The Simon & Schuster Speakers Bureau can bring authors
to your live event. For more information or to book an event
contact the Simon & Schuster Speakers Bureau at
1-866-248-3049 or visit our website at www.simonspeakers.com.

Interior design by Kaelin Chappell

Manufactured in the United States of America

10 9 8 7 6

Library of Congress Cataloging-in-Publication data is available.

ISBN 978-1-4767-9771-7

To my beloved wife, Lillian, and our dear son, John-Miles,
and to the countless unsung heroes who cared deeply,
sacrificed much, and fought hard for a better America.

—J. L.

CONTENTS

ACKNOWLEDGMENTS

When I decided to write this book, I realized I could not rely on memory alone. During the winter of 1996, I set aside time from a very busy schedule to go back to Selma, Montgomery, Birmingham, and Nashville. This was more than a sentimental journey. It was a precious opportunity to thank all the brave and courageous men and women who participated in a freedom movement that changed our nation and the world. My visit to these places, crucibles where so much of the history of the struggle for civil rights was forged, reminded me in a way that mere memory could not of what it was like to have lived through those years. More important, it fortified my conviction that the story of my journey through this great period in our history had to be told.

My life as a participant in some of the most significant events in the twentieth century would not have been possible had it not been for the inspiration, influence, and friendship of Martin Luther King Jr. He will always have my gratitude and respect.

My participation in the movement afforded me an opportunity to meet and come in contact with hundreds and thousands of individuals whose lives shaped the arc of this story. To all of you—wherever life's journey has taken you—thank you, and don't give up the good fight. For those who have died, who lost their lives so others might be free, you should be honored by our country for your raw courage and patriotism. I honor you.

I am extremely grateful to members of my family: my brothers and sisters, who have helped me in more ways than they know; my father, Eddie Lewis, a remarkable man whose memory burns brightly within me; and my mother, Willie Mae Lewis, whose sweet spirit and abiding faith in God and her family have touched my life in so many ways. I cannot thank any of them enough.

I am deeply grateful to so many friends and colleagues for being so patient in seeing this effort through to its completion:

My editor, Alice Mayhew, who never gave up on me;

My agent, David Black, who kept telling me, "We are going to do this book, and it is going to be a book you will be proud of";

My friends Ronald Roach and Linda Chastang, who encouraged me from the beginning;

All of my colleagues and staff, who have been with me in all of my endeavors, for your support and patience;

Don Harris, Danny Lyon, Harriett Thornton, Ora Crawley, Ethel Tyner, Elizabeth Stein, Mildred Johnson, David Potvin, Rickey Wright, Earl Swift, and Larry Copeland; and so many other individuals—too many to name here—who offered their support, friendship, and advice.

I am more than grateful to Mike D'Orso for having patience with me. In the process of working on this book, we became more than friends—we became brothers.

Finally, I am forever indebted to the wonderful, powerful, magnificent Spirit of History. I was touched by that spirit long ago, and I have followed it ever since. I only hope and pray that my journey will continue to be blessed.

Atlanta, Georgia
January 27, 1998

I want to begin this book with a little story. It has nothing to do with a national stage, or historic figures, or monumental events. It's a simple story, a true story, about a group of young children, a wood-frame house and a windstorm.

The children were my cousins: Roy Lee and Jinnie Boy, Naomi and Leslie and Willie Muriel—about a dozen of them, all told—along with my older sister Ora and my brothers Edward and Adolph. And me, John Robert.

I was four years old at the time, too young to understand there was a war going on over in Europe and out in the Pacific as well. The grownups called it a world war, but I had no idea what that meant. The only world I knew was the one I stepped out into each morning, a place of thick pine forests and white cotton fields and red clay roads winding around my family's house in our little corner of Pike County, Alabama.

We had just moved that spring onto some land my father had bought, the first land anyone in his family had ever owned—110 acres of cotton and corn and peanut fields, along with an old but sturdy three-bedroom house, a large house for that part of the county, the biggest place for miles around. It had a well in the front yard, and pecan trees out back, and muscadine grapevines growing wild in the woods all around us—*our* woods.

My father bought the property from a local white businessman who lived in the nearby town of Troy. The total payment was $300. Cash. That was every penny my father had to his name, money he had earned the way almost everyone we knew made what money they could in those days—by tenant farming. My father was a sharecropper, planting, raising and picking the same crops that had been grown in that soil for hundreds of years by tribes like the Choctaws and the Chickasaws and the Creeks, Native Americans who were working this land long before the place was called Alabama, long before black or white men were anywhere to be seen in those parts.

Almost every neighbor we had in those woods was a sharecropper, and most of them were our relatives. Nearly every adult I knew was an aunt or an uncle, every child my first or second cousin. That included my uncle Rabbit and aunt Seneva and their children, who lived about a half mile or so up the road from us.

On this particular afternoon—it was a Saturday, I'm almost certain—about fifteen of us children were outside my aunt Seneva's house, playing in her dirt yard. The sky began clouding over, the wind started picking up, lightning flashed far off in the distance, and suddenly I wasn't thinking about playing anymore; I was terrified. I had already seen what lightning could do. I'd seen fields catch on fire after a hit to a haystack. I'd watched trees actually explode when a bolt of lightning struck them, the sap inside rising to an instant boil, the trunk swelling until it burst its bark. The sight of those strips of pine bark snaking through the air like ribbons was both fascinating and horrifying.

Lightning terrified me, and so did thunder. My mother used to gather us around her whenever we heard thunder and she'd tell us to hush, be still now, because God was doing his work. That was what thunder was, my mother said. It was the sound of God doing his work.

But my mother wasn't with us on this particular afternoon. Aunt Seneva was the only adult around, and as the sky blackened and the wind grew stronger, she herded us all inside.

Her house was not the biggest place around, and it seemed even smaller with so many children squeezed inside. Small and surprisingly quiet. All of the shouting and laughter that had been going on earlier, outside, had stopped. The wind was howling now, and the house was starting to shake. We were scared. Even Aunt Seneva was scared.

And then it got worse. Now the house was beginning to sway. The wood plank flooring beneath us began to bend. And then, a corner of the room started lifting up.

I couldn't believe what I was seeing. None of us could. This storm was actually pulling the house toward the sky. With us inside it.

That was when Aunt Seneva told us to clasp hands. Line up and hold hands, she said, and we did as we were told. Then she had us walk as a group toward the corner of the room that was rising. From the kitchen to the front of the house we walked, the wind screaming outside, sheets of rain beating on the tin roof. Then we walked back in the other direction, as another end of the house began to lift.

And so it went, back and forth, fifteen children walking with the wind, holding that trembling house down with the weight of our small bodies.

More than half a century has passed since that day, and it has struck me more than once over those many years that our society is not unlike the children in that house, rocked again and again by the winds of one storm or another, the walls around us seeming at times as if they might fly apart.

It seemed that way in the 1960s, at the height of the civil rights movement, when America itself felt as if it might burst at the seams—so much tension, so many storms. But the people of conscience never left the house. They never ran away. They stayed, they came together and they did the best they could, clasping hands and moving toward the corner of the house that was the weakest.

And then another corner would lift, and we would go there.

And eventually, inevitably, the storm would settle, and the house would still stand.

But we knew another storm would come, and we would have to do it all over again.

And we did.

And we still do, all of us. You and I.

Children holding hands, walking with the wind. That is America to me—not just the movement for civil rights but the endless struggle to respond with decency, dignity and a sense of brotherhood to all the challenges that face us as a nation, as a whole.

That is the story, in essence, of my life, of the path to which I've been committed since I turned from a boy to a man, and to which I remain committed today. It is a path that extends beyond the issue of race alone, and beyond class as well. And gender. And age. And every other distinction that tends to separate us as human beings rather than bring us together.

That path involves nothing less than the pursuit of the most precious and pure concept I have ever known, an ideal I discovered as a young man and that has guided me like a beacon ever since, a concept called the Beloved Community.

Let me tell you how I came to understand that concept, how it ushered me into the heart of the most meaningful and monumental movement of this American century, and how it might steer us all where we deserve to go in the next.

Let me tell you about my life.

Part I

COMING UP

1 / "THAT WAS SOME HARD TIMES"

I took a drive not long ago, south out of Atlanta, where I've made my home for the past three decades, down into Alabama to visit my mother and brothers and sisters. It's a drive I make several times a year, for a birthday, a holiday or simply whenever I feel drawn back to my roots.

On this particular occasion, the 104th session of Congress had just adjourned. It was late September 1996, little more than a month before election day. My Democratic colleagues in the House and I had done our best to hold Newt Gingrich's feet to the fire, trying to force Brother Newt to answer the questions raised by a committee's investigation into the ethics of some of his outside activities—specifically his role and rewards as a college instructor and as a writer of books.

The floor debate over that investigation had extended the session two days longer than it was scheduled. By the time I boarded a Saturday-night flight home from Washington to Atlanta—a commute I make almost every weekend—I was exhausted. My wife, Lillian, was waiting up for me when I arrived home from the airport. As usual, all it took was a good night's sleep and I was refreshed and ready to go, up at 5 A.M. By six I was behind the wheel of my Pontiac and headed south on Interstate 85 on a bright, gorgeous fall morning, the skyline of Atlanta growing smaller in my rearview mirror as the countryside around me turned rural and green.

An hour later I was approaching the Alabama state line, which I've crossed more times during the past forty years than I can count. Take away the six-lane interstate highway, the billboards, the occasional suburban development where a farm used to be and, of course, the fast-food restaurants, and not much has changed here since the 1950s. Pine trees, peanut fields and broken-down barns crawling with kudzu—this is the same scenery I saw when I was a teenager riding a bus north to Tennessee to begin college in 1957, the same scenery that, in the '60s, formed the backdrop for so many midnight drives from one small Alabama, Mississippi or Georgia town to the next, four or five of my SNCC brothers and sisters and I crammed into an old sedan, everyone but the driver asleep on each other's shoulders, soul music drifting out of the AM radio as we headed for a meeting the next morning. Or a march. Or a voter registration rally. Or, too tragically often, a funeral.

This is a drive I measure not just in minutes or miles, but in memories. When I finally exit the interstate, an hour or so into Alabama, turning toward the town of Tuskegee, I remember Sammy Younge, a SNCC colleague, a twenty-one-year-old veteran just out of the Navy who was shot to death here thirty years ago, shot in the back of the head outside a Standard Oil gas station for trying to use a "whites only" rest room.

That Standard Oil sign is long gone—it's a Chevron station now—but just about everything else in Tuskegee still looks much the same: the tired town square covered with weed-eaten grass and its statue of a Confederate veteran proudly facing south; the Goodwill Store with a hand-lettered sign in the window that reads THE POWER OF WORK—this in a county with one of the highest unemployment figures in the state; the tree-shaded antebellum homes at the center of town, once so grand but now mostly empty and boarded up; the Burger King off Route 29, with its painting of Booker T. Washington hanging above the front counter, honoring the man who founded Tuskegee Institute back in 1881 and who, by the turn of the century, had become vilified and ridiculed by his own people for working so closely with white America.

It's haunting to pass through Tuskegee, to cross the tiny two-lane bridge south of town and come upon a small wood-frame building by the side of the road, no more than a shack really, at the edge of a field, and to remember when that shack was a hot nightspot, Club 29 it was called, back in the '60s, when my fellow SNCC staffers and I would often stop in on one of our late-night trips for a cold drink and some music from one of the best jukeboxes in the state, a welcome break from the grind of our journey, our mission.

No one today would dream that that weed-covered hut was once a bright, happy place—not unless they had been there. The same with the Hardee's restaurant in downtown Union Springs, a half hour farther down the road, where a sign stuck in the grass outside lets customers know they can buy a hamburger and a milkshake *and* register to vote while they're at it. It seems like only yesterday that people my color were spat on and beaten if we even stepped into a restaurant like that. As for registering to vote, well, you were taking your life into your hands if you tried to do that back then. Who could have dreamed we would one day be able to do both at the same time, in the same place?

By the time I cross into Pike County, getting close to home now, the time warp is complete. Now the echoes reach back beyond the movement, to the years of my boyhood. I pass through a place called Saco—just a couple of dusty warehouses by the side of the road—and think back to forty years ago, in the early 1950s, when this was a busy center of commerce. Farmers from miles around would bring their cotton here to have it ginned. Every Saturday, during picking season, my father would put my brothers Adolph and Edward and me in the truck with him, drive a load of our cotton over to Saco, sell it, then hand us each a couple of coins so we could buy ourselves something sweet. Ike and Mikes were my favorite—little gingerbread men spread thick with marshmallow cream, named in honor of Dwight Eisenhower and Douglas MacArthur, or so I was told.

The landscape in this part of Alabama, once you get beyond the borders of the little communities scattered throughout these forests, looks not much different from the way it was two hundred years ago, when various Indian tribes passed through here on their way north to hunting grounds up in Tennessee. Drive the back roads, many of which were once Indian trails, and you cross over rolling hills thick with oak and hickory and chestnut trees. Small creeks and streams trickle through small valleys shaded by miles and miles of pine trees. Wild oats and peas are everywhere, feeding the Alabama deer that have been hunted in these woods for ages.

The county, strangely enough, is named for a man who never set foot here: General Zebulon Montgomery Pike, the early-nineteenth-century explorer for whom Pikes Peak in Colorado is also named. With all the exploration and expansion in this country at that time, there was much to be named, and Zebulon Pike apparently received his share. After he was killed in an 1813 battle in Canada, ten states honored him by establishing counties in his name—including Alabama, which created Pike County in 1821.

There were few, if any, black people in this section of the state at that time. But that changed drastically as cotton began to replace cattle as the county's main industry. By the middle of the century, one fifth of Pike County's 16,000 residents were black—all but ten of them slaves. Relatively speaking, there weren't many plantations in this part of the state—of 2,420 farmers listed in Pike County's 1850 census, only fourteen owned land worth more than $5,000. Most of the rest were what were called yeoman farmers—people who owned modest-sized pieces of land which they and maybe a couple of slaves worked. There were, however, enough of those farmers to account for a total of more than 2,000 slaves in Pike County just before the start of the Civil War.

After the war, rather than face the new social order, many of those middle-class farmers moved away—quite a few to Brazil, of all places. The ones who remained, most of whom were now almost as poor as the black people they had once owned, found themselves competing as sharecroppers with their former slaves. The plantation owners, of course, remained rich, controlling the tenant farmers by leasing them land and furnishing their supplies, then "settling up" each harvest season at rates that put the farmer—black or white—further in the hole each year. For most men and women working under this system, it was hardly better than slavery. Everyone worked for "The Man," and they were still working for him well into the twentieth century when I was born.

It's hard not to think about that as I drive the back roads of Pike County today. There is a lot of poverty in this county, and it's a poverty that is blind to color. Pass any of the rusted trailers or beat-up shacks back in these woods and you're as likely to see a white child playing in the dirt and weeds as a black one. It was the same when I was a boy, except that whites and blacks rarely saw one another. If you lived out in the country back then, you lived among your own kind. Until I took my first trip into the town of Troy with my father at age six, I had seen just two white people in my entire life—a mailman and a traveling merchant.

Much has been made over the years of the fact that a man named George Wallace was born and raised just a few miles east of where I grew up, in a little town called Clio, just across the Pike County line, over in Barbour County. I admit that there is a certain kind of symmetry, an odd sort of irony, in that fact. But the truth is that the world George Wallace grew up in as a white child living in an actual town, with a father who owned several farms in the surrounding countryside, was a universe away from mine. We might as well have been living on different planets, George Wallace and I. People who point out how close our birthplaces are usually fail to note that Wallace is twenty-one years older than I. By the time I was born, 1940, he was already a senior at the University of Alabama, making a name for himself in campus politics and on the Crimson Tide's boxing team. Our paths would eventually collide, but back then my world and George Wallace's were still far, far apart.

You can't miss the poverty as you drive through rural Pike County, and neither can you miss the churches. They're around just about every bend, modest little buildings, some of them wood, a few of them redbrick, but most of them cinder block. Their steeples are small, if they've got one at all. Many make do with a simple wooden cross mounted atop the front entrance. Needless to say, these churches are as segregated today as they were when I was a boy. And, in terms of the black community, they are still as central to the lives of their congregations as they were then.

I always know I'm nearing home when I pass the Macedonia Baptist Church, a beautifully plain, whitewashed, T-shaped structure perched on a knoll in the woods. The parking lot is all dirt and weeds, shaded by the pine and oak trees that run down the slopes on all sides. There's a graveyard out back where many of my relatives are buried: my uncle Rabbit, uncle Goat, uncle Edgar. Every summer there is a gathering on the grass around that graveyard, a picnic of sorts. But it's more than that, really. It's a reunion, a homecoming. All the parishioners are there, joined by the prodigal sons and daughters, the friends and family members who moved away a generation or two ago, to Buffalo and Detroit and Philadelphia. They all come back for this gathering, for this celebration. It is a revival, in the truest sense of the word, and it has been going on for the better part of a century now.

Macedonia Baptist is not my family's church anymore. There was a falling-out a few years back between my grandfather and the minister there, and my family wound up moving its membership to Antioch Baptist Church, not far from another church they once regularly attended: Dunn's Chapel AME (African Methodist Episcopal). Both Antioch and Dunn's Chapel are similar in appearance to Macedonia Baptist, with long histories of their own, including an attack by the Ku Klux Klan in 1904.

There was a practice in the early part of this century, common among the Klan, called whitecapping. Basically it was a variation of lynching. Property-owning blacks were terrorized, usually at gunpoint, run out of their homes and off their lands, which were then seized by the whites who had chased them away. The practice was common throughout the South, with the authorities typically looking the other way. In February 1904, it happened right here.

According to a newspaper account published that month in the *Troy Messenger,* five Pike County white men were indicted by a grand jury on charges that included burning two local black churches: Dunn's Chapel and Antioch Baptist. The two churches were targeted, stated the report, "because they were the houses of worship of Negroes." Rifles were fired into nearby homes as well, in an attempt to threaten the residents' "property and lives if they did not move."

There is no record of whether those five men were actually convicted, but Antioch Baptist still stands today, as does Dunn's Chapel, less than a mile from my mother's house.

It was mid-morning on this Sunday in September as I pulled into my mother's gravel drive. My brother Edward came hiking up from the edge of the woods, wearing a jeans jacket and a Harley-Davidson ball cap, waving and smiling, followed by a small parade of little animals: my mother's dog and four or five of her cats. Edward is deaf—he has been since he was born in 1938—but he is one of the most expressive people I know, as well as one of the most self-reliant. He lives alone in a trailer just across the road from my mother's house. He spends most of his time there or with her, taking care of odd jobs around both places. He left school in the fifth grade and spent the better part of his life working with his hands—farming, cutting timber, manning the machinery at a nearby pulp mill. Edward has always had a way with machinery; he can take apart a tractor or a truck and put it back together again, with no need for a manual or directions.

He was married briefly back in his twenties, but other than that Edward has always lived by himself, though never far from the family. After my father died in the late 1970s, Edward took over looking after my mother, although she really doesn't need much looking after, even today, at age eighty-four. Just having someone around is good enough, and that's the way my mother and Edward live, as companions, each with a place, but within a couple of hundred feet of each other's front door.

On this morning Edward had been picking up tree limbs and branches blown down by a recent windstorm. It had apparently been quite a storm, the way Edward described it. Most people probably would not understand him if they heard him speak. But I've been listening to Edward's voice my entire life, and like everyone else in my family, I have no problem understanding what to a stranger might sound like a series of grunts and moans. As he told me about the windstorm, he made huge sweeping motions with his arms to show the power of the wind and how it threw tree limbs against his trailer, rocking his small home with him inside it. Edward is deaf, but as he described the fury of that storm, he squeezed his eyes shut and covered his ears, and I could feel it myself.

None of my other brothers or sisters were around when I arrived that morning, although they often are. My younger brother Sammy lives within sight of my mother's house, as does my brother Grant. My brother Freddie, who lives and works in Detroit, moved his wife and children back here several years ago because he decided, as he watched his children approach their teenage years, that he would rather have them come of age in a setting like this than struggle with the challenges and influences they would face in a large city like Detroit. Freddie remains up north for the time being and commutes as often as he can to the small whitewashed, single-story home where his family now lives, right next door to my mother.

That's a lot of Lewises right there. Holidays often bring in the others: my sister Ora, from Detroit; my brother Adolph, from Fort Lauderdale; William, from Detroit; Ethel, who lives just across the county, south of Troy; and finally the youngest, my sister Rosa, who comes all the way from her home in Richmond, California.

It's quite a crowd when we all get together, along with our spouses and children. The energy, the closeness, the comfort—there really is nothing in the world like family. When I come home like this, I'm not a congressman anymore making speeches on national television. Nor am I a civil rights warrior quoted in history books. Or a "living saint," as *Time* magazine once called me years ago, to the unending amusement of my closest friends. No, by the time I step onto my mother's front porch, all those labels have faded away and I'm just plain Robert again, third oldest of Eddie and Willie Mae Lewis's ten children.

My mother has never been a large woman. And when she steps out onto the porch of her home to greet me, those soft eyes of hers smiling as warmly as her mouth, she looks smaller than ever. That's because the house she now lives in looks so large compared to where she had been living for years. It's a new house, built just the summer before last, against her protests. She was perfectly happy in the small, simple cinder-block place my father put up for the both of them back in the 1960s, after the house I was raised in was torn down to make way for a new county road.

For years after my father passed away, my brothers and sisters and I urged my mother to allow us to sell some of the timber on those 110 acres and use the money to build a new home for her. Every time we would bring it up my mother would shake her head. No, she would say, you all may need that wood someday. Besides, she would add, she was perfectly happy in the place my father had built. This was the home she knew. This was the life she knew. Why change it?

Change, as I learned back when I was growing up, was not something my parents were ever very comfortable with. And who could blame them? They, like hundreds of thousands—no, *millions*—of black men and women of their generation, worked harder than seemed humanly possible, under circumstances more difficult than most Americans today could possibly imagine, to carve out a life for themselves and their children in a society that saw them as less than fully human. Theirs was, as the Bible says, a straight and narrow way. There was little room for change in the world my parents knew, and what change there was was usually for the worse. It's not hard to understand at all the mixture of fear and concern they both felt as they watched me walk out into the world as a young man and join a movement aimed, in essence, at turning the world they knew upside down.

In the same way, it is not hard to understand why it took some doing to get my mother to allow us to build her this house. What finally turned the trick, I think, was pointing out how exceptionally large her family had grown, with all those children and grandchildren and great-grandchildren. There simply wasn't room in her old place for all these people to fit, so, finally, she relented. The house—a simple, well-built, brick ranch-style home—was finished in the early summer of 1996, and we had a gathering there, a christening of sorts, that Fourth of July...Independence Day.

My mother had been in her new house only two months when I arrived on this Sunday morning. The place still had a newness about it, though she had been doing her best to break it in. The kitchen, for example, is 1990s all the way, bright and sparkling, from the cabinets—more space there than she'd ever had before—to the appliances. But the food simmering in the pots on that shiny modern range was the same food I grew up on, the same food my mother has always had ready for whoever might drop in. Boiled short ribs. Collard greens. Sweet potatoes. Cornbread. Good food. Soul food, in every sense of the phrase.

It's fitting that we honored this house and my mother on Independence Day. No word better describes her than independent. She still cooks, cleans, tends her garden and cares for most of her needs herself. She still worships the ideal of good, hard work as if it were a religion. She picked her first cotton as a young girl, in the early 1920s, when Calvin Coolidge was president, and she was still picking it half a century later when Jimmy Carter was in the White House. Hard to believe, but at sixty-two my mother was still out in the fields, a sack over her shoulder, pulling those soft, white puffs with her long, hard fingers.

I hated picking cotton, and not just for what it was—literally backbreaking labor: planting, picking, chopping, fertilizing, row after row, often on your hands and knees, from one end of a field to the other, sunup to sundown, year in and year out, the blazing Alabama sun beating down so hard you'd give everything you owned for a little piece of shade and something cool to drink.

I hated the work itself, but even more than that, from a very early age I realized and resented what it represented: exploitation, hopelessness, a dead-end way of life. Imagine how much cotton must be picked to total a hundred pounds. Imagine a man picking a little over two hundred pounds in a day, and his wife, working right beside him, picking almost that much. Imagine that their payment at the end of that day is thirty-five cents per hundred pounds, or a total of $1.40 for four hundred pounds of cotton—a fifth of a ton for less than two dollar bills.

Now stop imagining. Those numbers are precisely what my mother and father were picking and earning at the time I was born.

We used to have arguments, my parents and I, about this kind of life, this kind of work. As soon as I was old enough to make sense of the world around me, I could see that there was no way a person could get ahead as a tenant farmer. One step forward and two steps back, that's what that way of life looked like to me. Every spring you would literally put your life—your *family's* life—on the line, looking at the coming year of planting and growing and harvesting crops, borrowing up front against the unpredictable disasters of disease, or bad weather, or dipping prices at the marketplace, or simply being cheated at the other end by the man who bought whatever crop you were finally able to harvest—the same man who loaned you the money to plant it in the first place. How could anyone get ahead in a system like that?

Working for nothing, that's what I would tell my mother we were doing. Gambling is what I would call it. I know it upset her and my father. My brothers and sisters, too, were bothered by my grumbling and complaining as we worked our way through each day in the fields that surrounded our house. I carried my load, I did my duties, but I also spoke my mind, and even today my mother shakes her head at what an irritating habit that was.

"I don't care how good a person can work" is how my mother puts it. "If he talks *against* work, that gets to be kind of an aggravating thing. It kind of affects your *spirit*."

My mother knows what she's talking about when she speaks about spirit. She's got more spiritual strength than any other person I have ever known, and that is no small statement, considering that this same strength of the spirit was at the center of the civil rights movement, fueling so many of the remarkable men and women with whom I became involved in that time of sweeping change. Nothing can break you when you have the spirit. We proved that in Nashville and Birmingham and Montgomery and Selma. But my mother and father and so many like them proved it long before my generation was even born. To understand the spirit that brought thousands of people just like me to those spotlighted stages of protests and marches, I am convinced it is necessary to understand the spirit that carried people like my mother—simple people, everyday people, good, honest, hardworking people—through lives that never made headlines but were the wellspring for the lives that did.

"Back in slavery times..."

That is the phrase my mother heard her grandfather Frank repeat over and over when she was a small girl. We don't know much more about Frank Carter's boyhood than that he was born into slavery, most likely somewhere not far from where my mother lives today. I've seen records that show Frank's parents, Tobias and Elizabeth Carter, briefly owned a small farm in Pike County which they bought in 1880 for $125 and sold five years later for more than six times that amount. They were ahead of their time in buying that land, and why they sold it so soon thereafter I'll never know. They might have been pressured to do so—the brief period of post-Civil War freedom and prosperity enjoyed by many Southern blacks was ending by then, as a white backlash symbolized by the creation of the Klan began to make itself felt through lynchings and other forms of terror meant to drive blacks back into "their place." Were Tobias and Elizabeth Carter pressured off that twenty-two acres of land they owned? Did they sell it willingly? If so, why? These are questions that will never be answered.

I do know that Frank Carter, their ninth child, was born at the turn of the 1860s, and that in 1882, at about age twenty, he married a young woman named Martha McNair. They had at least one child, my great-aunt Hattie, but the details of their marriage, and of its end, are sketchy. I've never been able to find any records of it, and my mother falls silent when the subject comes up, so I guess we'll never know.

What I do know is that Frank Carter married Betty Baxter—Grandma Bessie, as we always called her—in April 1885, and she is the great-grandmother I remember, the one I heard stories about as I was growing up, the one who was still alive when I was born, as was her husband, my great-grandfather Frank.

They were a striking couple—Bessie, tall and slim, dark-skinned, with soft, curly hair that fell to her shoulders, and Frank, a very light-skinned man with remarkably straight hair. Frank died in 1947, when I was seven years old, and I remember him being lighter than any other black person I had ever seen. My grandfather Dink, the first of Frank and Bessie's three sons, was light himself, but nothing like his father. And from what I understand, what I have heard from various older family members, including my parents, Frank Carter carried his light skin and his straight hair with a pride that bordered on arrogance.

My grandfather Dink inherited that skin and that hair, as well as the sense that he—that *all* the Carters—were just a little bit better than those around them, that they were somehow set aside, somehow special. I imagine every community develops its own pecking order, and I know there was one in the section of Pike County that came to be called Carter's Quarters. By the time I was born, Frank Carter's house, the biggest by far in the area, was a collecting place come holiday time for as many as three or four hundred of the Carter clan—sisters and brothers and cousins and children and grandchildren and great-grandchildren—all gathered around the patriarch, Grandpa Frank.

Still, Frank Carter was just a tenant farmer. He worked for "The Man," and like 125 other families in Pike County, the man he worked for was a white landowner named Josh Soules Copeland. Copeland had come over from Georgia before the start of the Civil War, and by the turn of the century, he and his son, also named Josh—Big Josh and Little Josh are what everyone called them—owned more of Pike County than anyone else. Walk through the town of Troy today and you will see the Copeland name emblazoned in letters as large as a full-grown man on the side of an old brick building downtown.

Early on, the Copelands hired Grandpa Frank to work a two-horse farm not far from Saco. They built Frank Carter a three-room wood-frame house and drilled him a well, loaned him the money and supplies to begin raising the typical Pike County cash crops—cotton, corn and potatoes—and come harvest season they kept half my great-grandfather's yield in exchange for what they'd given him up front. "Working on half"—that's what this arrangement, typical throughout the South, was called. "Working on fourth" meant you owed the landowner three fourths of your crop. And "standing rent," which was the rarest form of sharecropping, meant the farmer owned his own mules and equipment and paid a preset amount of money to rent the farm. By the time I was born, Frank Carter was standing rent, as was his son Dink and my father, Eddie. But it took a lifetime of literally backbreaking labor for them to get to that point, and they were among the lucky ones.

It wasn't just his business sense that helped Frank Carter rise to a level of relative success among his neighbors. He could also flat-out *work*. Frank Carter was known throughout the county as a man who could outplow and outpick any man or woman around. He was good and he was fast, not only behind a plow but also with a ledger book. He couldn't read or write, but he could do financial transactions in his head faster than the man on the other side of the desk could work them out with a pen and paper. That ability served him well on the first Saturday of each month, the day all sharecroppers knew as Draw Day. That was the day you went to meet the landowner to be advanced credit or to pay off loans. In Grandpa Frank's case, it was the day he would hitch his mules to the wagon, put Grandma Bessie in the seat beside him and one or two of their sons in the back, and drive into Troy to meet with the Copelands.

More than mere business was done on Draw Day. It was also a chance for the tenant farmers throughout the county to meet and catch up on each other's lives. Births, deaths, marriages—all the news of the previous month would be shared as husbands and wives and children gathered outside stores and around the central town square. For most farmers and their families, this was the one day a month they even saw anyone besides their own family and perhaps the family on the farm next to theirs. Distances between farms were large back then, and roads were very, very rugged. A trip of only a few miles could take an hour or two in a mule-drawn wagon or on foot. And with the demands of working the farm, there wasn't much time for visiting anyway.

So those Saturdays were a social event. The women and children would visit and play outside while the men took turns walking into the Copelands' "headquarters"—a combination office and general store one block from the county courthouse. Cash, receipts and records on all the Copelands' tenant farmers were kept in a massive black safe six feet tall and four feet wide with the letters J. S. COPELAND embossed across the top...in gold.

By the time Frank's oldest son, Dink, was eighteen, he was making his own trips into that office. And late that year, on December 28, 1904, he married a young Pike County woman named Della Ethridge. Dink and Della were my maternal grandparents. They went on to have ten children—eight boys and two girls. The second of those girls, born in 1914, was my mother, Willie Mae.

Ask my mother about what life was like when she was a girl, and she'll answer in much the same way she does when asked what her life is like today. It's about work, she'll say. First, last and in between, life on this earth—at least life as she has always known it—is about work. She doesn't say this in a sorrowful or complaining way, not at all. When she speaks of working, it is as if she is describing a sacrament, a holy act. Yes, work is hard, she'll say. And yes, it can seem thankless at times. But it is a pure thing, an honest thing. "I don't believe in depending on anyone," she says. "Work and put your trust in God, and God's gonna take care of his children. God's *gonna* take care of his children."

How many times did I hear those words when I was a child? I still hear them today.

All my mother remembers is working, she says with pride. She also says she does not remember ever feeling poor. "We never saw too much money," she says, "but we always had what we needed. Meat, vegetables, everything, we raised that for ourselves. All we ever had to buy were things like flour and sugar, that's all. And we weren't the only ones like that back there then. Moneywise, nobody had it. Maybe that's why we didn't *feel* poor. Because back there then, we were all in the same boat."

My mother left school in the eighth grade, and two years after that she met a young man at church, at Macedonia Baptist. He was twenty-one, five years older than she was. He was short and stocky, built very much the way I am today, but it wasn't his looks that attracted her.

"No, you don't do that, you don't go just by looks," my mother says. "You go by a person's attitude. And if you be in their company long enough and you watch how they talk and act, you get to know who it is exactly that you're meeting."

This young man my mother met that Sunday morning, this Eddie Lewis, apparently pleased her with his attitude and his words. She smiles even today at the memory before summing it up in a single, simple sentence: "We just fell in love."

They married the year after they met, in 1932. They had no honeymoon, couldn't afford one, not in terms of time or of money. My father was sharecropping on a farm not far from his mother's home. Sharecropping had run in his family's history just as it had in my mother's. The Lewises had come out of Georgia, from a place called New Albany, where they'd worked in the turpentine mills along with farming. Eddie's father and mother, Henry and Lula Lewis, were separated by the time Eddie met my mother, and Lula had only recently moved to Carter's Quarters from a little place called Rockford, on the other side of Montgomery. She made her living by "working out" on other people's farms—working in the fields by the day, along with most of her five children, including Eddie.

After Eddie married my mother, they both joined the Lewis family in Lula's house, and my mother began working with them in those fields, sometimes side by side with her husband, other times "working out" for one local farmer or another, chopping or picking cotton for fifty cents a day. Sometimes my mother would find a "house job" in Troy. A white family would hire her for several weeks to cook and clean house for them. The pay—typically about $3 a week—was basically the same as what she made in the fields. But the work—at least the physical strain of it—was definitely less demanding.

Shorty and Sugarfoot—that's what my parents called each other when no one else was around. Otherwise, most people knew my father as Buddy and my mother as just plain Willie. When the peak seasons of planting and picking came around, they would, like most couples at that time, spend their days together in the fields. Eddie would plow—"walking behind the mule," as my mother puts it. She would hoe. And when it came time to pick, they could bring in four hundred pounds together in a day. "For thirty-five cents a hundred," she recalls. "Yes," she shakes her head and smiles, "that was some hard times."

They didn't stay with Eddie's mother long. By 1934 they were renting their own house, a boxed wood-frame place built in the classic Southern rural "shotgun" style—one narrow hallway slicing straight from the front door to the back (if a gunshot were fired through the front door screen, it would sail right out the rear—thus the term "shotgun"), with small, square single-window rooms on each side of the hall—simple, bare, functional.

By 1936 they had their first child, my oldest sister, Ora. Two years later came Edward—"the one that can't talk so good," as my mother puts it. And then, on February 21, 1940, in that three-room shotgun house, with Grandma Bessie acting as midwife, I was born—John Robert Lewis.

2 / A SMALL WORLD, A SAFE WORLD

There is no trace left today of the house I was born in. There's not much left of any of the homes that once dotted those woods we called Carter's Quarters. The road through that section of forest is still unpaved, still the same hard red clay I played on as a boy. But there's barbed wire lining much of it now. "NO HUNTING" signs are nailed to some of the trees I once climbed. Yellow and blue wildflowers are growing through the broken windows of the shells of the few small homes still standing. They're long abandoned now, those homes. Their roofs are caved in. Ivy and weeds crawl up the outside walls. If you sit still long enough you'll see animals—raccoons and deer— edge out of the deep woods and approach this structure or that, poking their heads into the dark interiors, searching for something to eat.

I know these houses. I've been inside most of them, broken bread at their tables, slept in their beds. I can see them in my mind as they were fifty years ago, bright and solid and full of life. That burnt-out clearing back by that thicket of mulberry trees was where Uncle Edgar's house used to stand. Not far up the road is where Uncle Q.P.'s place used to be—it's gone now, and the ground is all overgrown with wild fig trees. Uncle Lem's home is gone now, too. And the house of Uncle J.D.—the one we all called Goat—is nowhere to be seen. Uncle Fox and Aunt Lyzanka's cottage is still standing, but there are trees growing through the front porch these days, breaking through the roof, letting in the sky and the rain. Aunt Lyzanka was my mother's sister, her closest friend. The other children and I used to climb up on that porch, and she'd bring us out a snack—tea cakes and syrup bread, her specialty. The truth is Aunt Lyzanka wasn't much of a cook. Those cakes were pretty bad, but we appreciated the gesture. And we forced them down, so we wouldn't hurt her feelings.

More people were living in Pike County the year I was born than at any time before or since. The 1940 census shows 32,500 residents of the county—roughly double the number living there at the end of the Civil War.

That figure has dropped by a couple thousand every decade since I was born, not a good sign at all, but easily explainable. Over the years, most of those who could get out, especially the younger generation, have gotten out. They did what so many of the rising generations of rural Southern blacks have been doing for the past half century: moved to a city where jobs might be more plentiful—Montgomery or Birmingham or Atlanta—or left the South completely and gone north to urban areas like Detroit or Chicago or Philadelphia.

The northward migration of Southern blacks through much of this century has been well documented. Studies in recent years have shown signs of a reversal, as large numbers of blacks with Southern roots seem to be returning to the communities their parents and grandparents left behind in Georgia and Mississippi and Alabama. I see some hope in that movement, in the belief that the better life so many dreamed of when they left the ugliness and oppressiveness of the South and headed north thirty and forty and fifty years ago might now be found in the place they left behind, in a South that has changed—or *been* changed—for the better in terms of its treatment of *all* humans.

There is no question about the beauty of the place, at least not in my mind. For all the wounds and scars and pain that surround it, this is still home to me. My earliest memories are not of drudgery and labor, oppression and inequality, exclusion and neglect. Those memories would take shape later, as I grew up. But the world I knew as a little boy was a rich, happy one. In the same way that my mother never felt poor as a little girl, I didn't know the meaning of the word when I was small. We were poor—dirt poor—but I didn't realize it.

It was a small world, a safe world, filled with family and friends. There was no such thing as a stranger. I never ventured out of the woods of Carter's Quarters—there was no reason and no means. And outsiders rarely ventured in—especially white people. I knew the man who owned our house and land was named Josh Copeland—I would hear the grownups talk now and then about Little Josh. But I didn't know what he looked like. As I said, until I was six years old, I saw only two white people in the flesh—the mailman and a traveling merchant who regularly came through Carter's Quarters. I never saw Little Josh Copeland. In my mind, he was a figure like Santa Claus or the tooth fairy—not quite real.

I can't say I recall anything about the house I was born in other than what I was told by my parents. But I do remember moving in the spring of 1944, not long after my fourth birthday, into the house where I would spend the next ten years of my life. It was about half a mile up the road from the place where I was born. I remember riding in the back seat of a car, which Daddy must have borrowed because this was long before he owned his first automobile. Our big old radio—I mean *old*, a piece of furniture in itself, battery-powered, with tubes as big as Coke bottles and a dial that slowly lit up and glowed when you turned it on—was wedged in the seat beside me, along with our little white dog, Riley.

The bulk of our belongings were loaded and strapped on our family's mule-drawn wagon—the same wagon and the same mules my father used for farming. The house we were moving into, along with the 110 acres of wooded, gently rolling land around it, had been bought by my father from a white grocer in Troy, A. M. Hickman, for $300. I know now, much more than I realized then, what a monumental move this was for my parents. My mother still looks back on that day with a mixture of pride and sentiment. "It was good to get to have something you could call yours," she says. "Working for somebody else all your days, and then to have a little something you could call your own, it was *bound* to make you feel good."

What struck me most about our new house was the ceilings. They were high, higher than any I'd ever looked up at. The house had only three rooms—the same as the one I'd been born in, but these rooms were much, much larger. And the place had a porch, a wonderful front porch, with an old pecan tree spreading its canopy above it and the property's well built right at one end of it. You could draw water from that well from right off the porch, which we did, several times a day.

Inside the front door were the house's two main rooms, with a fireplace for heat. There was no running water, no electricity and no insulation to speak of. We'd burn oak in that fireplace in the dead of winter, and I remember how uneven that heating system was, how ragged and loosely constructed the house was—you could look down through the cracks between the floor-boards in places and see the ground below, feel the cold air coming up through those cracks. I remember how you'd just burn up in the front of the room, near the fireplace, but move back just a few feet and you'd be freezing. Nothing in between.

The third room, of course, was the kitchen, which was in the rear of the house. The odd thing about that kitchen—and this was just the way the house had been built—was that you couldn't get to it from the front without walking outside and around onto the back porch. There was no interior door connecting the kitchen to the rest of the house. I realized only in later years how odd that arrangement was. Growing up, I saw it as just a natural part of life to walk back and forth outside, in all kinds of weather, at all times of day and night, to get from the kitchen to our rooms, or vice versa.

Behind the house there were three buildings, each vital to the rhythm of our lives. One was the barn, where we stored animal feed and our assorted farm equipment—from the plow, to hoes and shovels, to the wagon. Near the barn was the smokehouse, shaped like an undersized log cabin and filled, in the best of times, with cured meat, seasoned sausage and thick bunches of homegrown hot peppers, all hanging from the ceiling like big sleeping bats.

Finally, there was the outhouse, which was a nasty place anytime of the year. In winter, it was bitter cold, with the wind cutting through the cracks between the wood planks that made up the walls. You might as well have been outside for all the good those walls did. In the summer, it was the smell that did you in, with the heat turning that little hut into a tiny oven. Year in and year out we kept a bucket of lye by the door—Red Devil lye, I'll never forget that brand name—to battle the smell a bit and to keep the pit moderately sanitized. Inside, we kept a stack of old Sears, Roebuck catalogs, whose pages served as toilet paper. If no catalogs were on hand, there were always some dried corncobs around—which, let me tell you, was incentive enough to keep those catalogs in stock.

The yard encircling our house was nothing but dirt—no grass, no weeds. We weren't allowed to let weeds grow out there. My mother made us clean that yard every Saturday. My brothers and sisters and I all had to get out there and pull every weed, pick up every leaf and every pecan that had dropped from those trees—hundreds of pecans. Finally, we had to take out the brooms—homemade brooms fashioned from small bunches of slim tree branches—and sweep the entire yard. When we were done, the place looked immaculate, as manicured in its own way as the finest gardener-tended lawn.

The pecans we gathered were absolutely inedible—Rusty Jennies is what we called them, or Nasty Jennies. They were so bitter even the hogs wouldn't eat them. But just about everything else that grew out of that ground around our house became part of our diet, from the muscadine grapes that spread wild at the edge of the woods (during the summer months my mother would set aside some of that muscadine juice in the icebox, where it became one of the coolest, sweetest beverages I ever tasted; the rest of the juice she would cook down into a sweet jam or jelly) to the peaches, pears, figs and blackberries that my mother would can or turn into pies and cobbler, to the garden she kept behind the house, which was thick with the classic bounty of the South—green peas, okra, butter beans, cucumbers, turnips, tomatoes, collards, sweet potatoes, watermelons, green beans, peppers. That's one of the very visible differences between being poor in the city and poor in the country—country poor almost always have the option of growing at least a little something to eat from the ground around them; city poor rarely have that choice.

The backyard was also where my mother did the laundry, filling a massive black cast-iron pot with water we'd fetch from the well, getting a good wood fire going under it, dumping in a measure of soap made from a blend of that lye and some old cooking grease, bringing the mixture to a rolling boil, then dropping in the clothes and stirring them with a long, smooth stick. By the time there were ten of us, my sisters did as much of the laundry as my mother, and the clothesline out back was perpetually hung with breeze-drying shirts and pants and dresses and skirts.

That is, when there *was* a breeze. There is really no way to describe how hot and heavy the summer months can get in a place like south Alabama. You work all day, outside, under that broiling sun, the air as still as death, then you come home to a house that is hardly cooler inside than out, even with the shade, even at nighttime. We had no fans; we had no electricity. Air-conditioning would have sounded like something out of science fiction—if we had even heard of it, which we had not. Still, again, it's hard to miss what you have never known. What might sound like hardship today still holds a happy, sentimental place in my memory. The kerosene lamps we lit each evening cast a dull, uneven glow and emitted a steady plume of smoke that darkened the ceiling above them, but I remember that glow as a comfort, an embrace. The tin tub we bathed in, a mere three feet wide and a foot and a half deep, which was filled with boiling water off the stove, then cut to a bearable temperature with cool well water, was hardly large enough to fit a body into. Most times we didn't bother, choosing instead to sit on the rim with our feet in the tub and bathe by hand, what we called a bird bath. Still, I remember bath time the way any child does, with my mother sitting beside me and scrubbing and rinsing and drying my willing, eager skin.

Nighttime we would listen to that radio, its huge old battery pulling in the sounds of the world "out there." Weeknights we'd tune in the country station, WLAC, out of Nashville, which played the music of singers like Hank Snow, Eddy Arnold, Lefty Frizzell and, of course, everything it could get its hands on by Montgomery's native son, Hank Williams. Saturday nights we'd listen to the Grand Ole Opry. My mother and father always got the biggest kick out of Minnie Pearl coming on with that *"How-deeeeeeee!!!"* of hers. They just thought that was great.

Sundays we would listen to WRMA, the gospel station. The Pilgrim Travelers, the Soul Stirrers, the Five Blind Boys of Mississippi—groups like these were all over gospel radio in the 1940s. A decade later their upbeat, wall-rocking sounds would evolve into something called rhythm and blues. A decade after that it would become the music they called soul. But Sunday afternoons in our house there in Carter's Quarters in the '40s, we didn't put any labels on any of it. We just loved it.

There wasn't much to read in our house. Until I went to school and discovered the world of books, the only reading material I had was the family Bible, an occasional copy of the *Montgomery Advertiser* newspaper—usually a few days old, passed on from a neighbor or friend—and those Sears, Roebuck catalogs, which I would leaf through so often I would fall asleep with their pencil drawings of merchandise drifting through my brain. Most of the essentials that we had to buy—winter clothing, long johns, shoes, even the wagon my father used for farming—came out of that Sears catalog.

The mailman who delivered most of those Sears items was one of the very few outsiders I saw during my early boyhood years. Another we called the Rolling Store Man, a vendor who drove through Carter's Quarters in an old truck from which he sold flour, sugar, baking soda, baking powder—the kinds of goods that people couldn't grow on farms. The best thing about the Rolling Store Man, as far as we children were concerned, was that he sold treats. You'd hear him coming down the road from a distance, just the way kids hear the neighborhood ice cream truck today, and you'd run out there with your nickel or your dime and buy a little wrapped cake—a Moon Pie or an Ike and Mike. Or a Coke. Or an Orange Crush. Or a grape Nehi.

More than anything else—besides work, of course, which became the center of my life as soon as I was big enough to join my parents in the fields—the most important thing in my family's life, and in almost every family's life around us, was church.

Church met once a month, and we went to two of them—Macedonia Baptist the third Sunday of each month, and Dunn's Chapel AME every first Sunday. That's an indication of how rural this area was—traveling a distance of merely a few miles over those rough roads, roads that turned into impassable quagmires with just a little bit of rain, was a difficult task. And these were people who worked their fingers to the bone week in and week out. Making it to church every Sunday would have been simply another load in already overloaded lives. But once or twice a month, that was a joy. That was a relief. That was sweet inspiration.

I remember the whole family piling into our wagon—each of us boys dressed in our only pair of slacks and a clean white shirt, the girls wearing dresses you never saw the rest of the month—and riding to church along a road crowded with other families in their own wagons. We'd arrive near the church, park, and my mother would always hook up with two of her aunts, my great-aunts Ella and Julie. They were both retired schoolteachers, and they always dressed very well, each in an outfit that included a very sharp hat. Both their homes were filled with nice things, lots of knickknacks on the shelves and sideboards, glass figurines and vases, the kinds of objects that make people drool in antique stores today. As I look back, the lives of Aunt Ella and Aunt Julie were probably the closest to a middle-class lifestyle that I saw during my childhood.

They never missed church, and they never ceased to be amazed by a curious habit of mine. At an early age—and to this day I don't know why I did this—I began calling my mother Mrs. Lewis. It's become a joke in my adulthood; I still ask if Mrs. Lewis is there when she answers the telephone. But back then I was dead serious. I remember Aunt Ella and Aunt Julie hearing me address my mother this way as we walked toward the church, and they would turn to each other with puzzled looks, glance back at me, and Aunt Ella would say to my mother, "Baby, *what* did he say? *What* is he calling you?" They thought it was the strangest thing, and I guess it *was* a bit odd. But then there were plenty of things yet to come that would set me apart as an odd child.

Church was an exciting place, a colorful, vibrant place. For people whose lives were circumscribed by the rhythms and routines of hard, hard work, with relatively little time or opportunity for contact with others beyond their immediate neighbors, church was literally a time of congregation, a social event much like going into town, a chance to see and spend time with friends you might not see at all the rest of the month. You could feel the energy in the air as people arrived from all directions and gathered in groups outside the church building, everyone talking and laughing and hugging, just getting together.

Inside, the atmosphere was almost festive. The children held colorful cards, used in our Sunday school classes to help learn the Scriptures. The cards had drawings of biblical figures or scenes on one side and a verse on the other. I guess you would call them flash cards, and our Sunday school teachers used them just that way, drilling us as we recited and memorized those verses.

There were no hymnbooks in either church I attended as a child. Neither were there musical instruments. No piano. No organ. But there was music, music richer and fuller and sweeter than any I've ever heard since. I'm talking about pure singing, the sound of voices fueled by the spirit, people keeping rhythm with a beat they heard in their hearts, singing songs that came straight from their soul, with words they felt in every bone of their body. These people sang with no self-consciousness and no restraint. Young and old alike, all of whom lived the same hard life, toiling in the fields, struggling with poverty and doing their best to make the best of it, found joy and meaning in the midst of hardship and pain. Is it any wonder that come Sunday their voices were lifted so strongly and so openly to God?

Each Sunday service began with a song-filled prayer meeting conducted by the church deacons. They would lead the congregation in hymns: "Leaning on the Everlasting Arms," "Father, I Stretch Out My Hand to Thee" and, of course, "Amazing Grace." Then someone would come up from the pews, kneel in front of the pulpit and begin praying aloud. It might begin as a verse or two from the Bible, but then he or she would add something spontaneous, heartfelt and very inspirational. For example, this worshipper might recite the Lord's Prayer, but then at the end, instead of simply saying "Amen," they would flow into a personal entreaty, such as:

This morning, our heavenly Father, it's once more and again that we come before You with knee bent and body bowed in humble submission, thanking You for last night's slumber and this morning's rising, finding that our bed was not our cooling board and our last night's cover was not our winding sheet. Our bodies *was* not wrapped up in the clay of the grave and the four walls of our *room* was not the walls of our *grave*. We stopped right here to say thank You and that You *abled* us to look out our *winder* and see Your darling sun rise in the east and make its way across the blue and settle behind the western hills. Thank You, Lord.

We thank You, Lord, that the fowl of the air are Thine, the fish that swim the mighty deep are Thine, and the cattle of the hills. We thank You for putting food on our table, shoes on our feet and a place to lay my head. Lord, if we haven't been too mean, we ask forgiveness of our sins that they will not rise against us in the world or the next.

Sweet Jesus, when we come to the end of life's journey, give our souls a resting place somewhere in Your kingdom where we can praise Your name forever, where every day will be Sunday and Sabbath will have no end. This is Your servant's prayer in Jesus' name. Amen.

While that person prayed, the congregation would hum softly. When the prayer ended, the whole church would swing into another hymn. And so it would go for half an hour or so. Then the minister would step forward to preach his sermon, and the deacons would take up the collection, and then the service would be dismissed.

But church was not over, not really, because after the service we would always go, as all the families did, to one of our relatives' homes, where the adults would gather and socialize—maybe with one of the deacons in attendance or even the minister himself—and the children would play.

Most Sundays we wound up at Grandpa Frank's house. Grandma Bessie would always have something out for us to eat—some pieces of cheese, some tea cakes or gingerbread or a couple of slices of pound cake. I remember that cake often having some mold on it. Stuff spoiled easily in those days because there were no preservatives. Everything was homemade, all natural, and, naturally, it didn't keep that well. But we didn't mind. We'd just scrape off the mold and have at it.

My memories of Grandma Bessie stand out from those Sunday afternoons. She was a beautiful woman—not elegant, but just naturally attractive.

During the week she wore her hair pulled back in a head rag, and she was always chewing on a little twig. Sundays she'd have a dress on and the head rag would be gone, but when she came out on her porch to greet us, that twig would still be there.

My Grandma Bessie had a little ritual she'd put us through every time we arrived. She and Grandpa Frank had a big chinaberry tree in their front yard. About ten feet or so up in the trunk of that tree was a hollow, a large hole. One of Grandma Bessie's hens used that hole as a nesting spot, and the first thing Bessie would do when we pulled up would be to holler from the porch to us children, "Would one of y'all check the nest and bring the eggs in?" As soon as I was old enough to climb, I was always the one who shinnied up there and fetched those eggs. No way could my sisters or brothers beat me up that tree. It wasn't that I was bigger or faster than they, not at all. It was simply that I *wanted* it more.

Which brings me to my chickens.

If there is a single point in my childhood that provided an early glimpse into my future, a first indication of what would come to shape my character and eventually guide me into the heart of the civil rights movement—qualities I certainly could not name at the time, such as patience, compassion, nonviolence, civil disobedience and not a little bit of willful stubbornness—it would be the year my parents gave me the responsibility of taking care of our family's chickens.

There were about sixty of them at the time filling the small henhouse that sat back near the barn behind our home. They roamed their wire-fenced dirt yard during the day and slept on their shelved roosts at night. I never had any feelings one way or the other about the rest of the animals that came and went on our farm—the horses, cows, mules, hogs, dogs and cats. But I was always drawn to the chickens. I know now that the reason was their absolute innocence. They seemed so defenseless, so simple, so pure. There was a subtle grace and dignity in every movement they made, at least through my eyes. But no one else saw them that way. To my parents and brothers and sisters, the chickens were just about the lowest form of life on the farm—stupid, smelly nuisances, awkward, comical birds good for nothing but laying eggs and providing meat for the table. Maybe it was that outcast status, the very fact that those chickens were so forsaken by everyone else, that drew me to them as well. In any event, for whatever the reasons, from the first day I was given charge of those chickens—the spring of the year I turned five—I felt as if I had been trusted to care for God's chosen creatures.

The henhouse itself seemed a holy place to me. It was built of wood, of course, about six feet square and five feet high, little more than a shed, really, with a tin roof. There were no windows, so each time I entered, pulling open the little latched door, it would take a minute or so for my eyes to adjust to the darkness inside. Thin shafts of sunlight came in at different angles through cracks in the pine-plank walls, providing just enough light for me to see.

Anyone who's ever raised chickens knows what I'm talking about when I say that the smell hit me each time I stepped into that shed. Few odors in this world are as powerful as that of chicken manure, especially when it's trapped inside an unventilated space like that, *especially* in the summer, when the air in that space is cooked to the temperature of a furnace.

It didn't bother the chickens, though. Each morning, as I pulled open that door, about five or six o'clock, as the sun was rising, it would be dead silent inside, the rows of birds sleeping like babies, roosting line by line on the straw-padded shelves that ran the length of each side of the shed. There were Rhode Island Reds, the same color as their name; dominiques, with their bright yellow legs and dull gray plumage; and bantams, small Cornish hen– like birds that could fly. It would be still as death in there—until I reached for the door. Then, in an instant, the silence would be shattered, and the place would burst with clucking and cackling. I liked to think they were excited to see me, but the fact is they were simply ready for breakfast.

From the beginning, though, I never took the chickens straight out to the yard to feed them. For some reason, I felt a need to talk to them first. And for some reason, they listened. I'd speak softly, gently, as if I were hushing a cry-ing baby, and very quickly the cackling would subside, until finally the shed was as silent as a sanctuary. There was something magical, almost mystical, about that moment when those dozens and dozens of chickens, all wide awake, were looking straight at me, and I was looking back at them, all of us in total, utter silence. It felt very spiritual, almost religious. I could swear those chickens felt it, too.

I took that communal time with my chickens very seriously. I treated *everything* I did with them seriously. I spent hours carefully shelling dried ker-nels of corn off cobs in the barn, filling the pails out of which I'd feed those birds. I tended the straw in their nests as a mother tends a baby's bed, and when the hens began laying their eggs, I'd mark each one with a lightly pen-ciled number, to help me keep track of its progress during the three weeks it took to hatch. The numbers were always odd, never even. Somewhere along the way I had been told that you never put an even number under a setting hen, that that was bad luck, and I took that bit of wisdom to heart.

Springtime quickly became my favorite time of year because that was the only season we could get baby chicks. In the winter they would die from the cold; in the summer, from the heat. Come spring I would spend every spare minute in that henhouse, obsessing over those eggs. I think most of the hun-dreds—maybe even thousands—of eggs hatched in that henhouse during my boyhood were warmed as much by my hands as by the mother hens.

A trick I learned early on in order to pump up the production of my chickens was to redistribute the eggs beneath them, taking a few from under the hens that were setting on a large number and slipping them beneath the ones that didn't have that many. This cut down on the number of unhatched or "bad" eggs. My pencil markings were crucial to this procedure, allowing me to keep track of which eggs were which. The strategy also allowed me to keep those hens setting for longer than they normally would. As long as a hen has eggs underneath her, she will continue to set. Under normal circumstances, that setting time is three weeks, the length of time it takes an egg to hatch. But by slipping more eggs under my hens, I was able to keep them setting for as much as another three weeks.

I was cheating Mother Nature, and it took its toll. During a normal setting period a hen seldom if ever leaves her nest. She might get up and go just a few feet away to get some water or to peck for a little bit of food, but that's it. Consequently, she loses weight and her feathers thin out. It's part of the stress of the process. It's natural. Stretching that process out an extra three weeks, however, is not natural. During that time I made a point of paying close attention to each setting hen. If they were thirsty, I brought them water. If they were hungry, I brought them food. I even built a makeshift incubator to help ease some of the hens' burden. I put a small kerosene lantern in a box, lined the bottom with soft pine needles and placed some of the eggs in there, counting on the lantern's glow to give off the same heat a hen's body does. It worked. I used that system for years. I always hoped I could save enough money to buy an actual incubator, one like the $18.95 model advertised in the Sears, Roebuck catalog. We called that catalog our Wish Book, and there was nothing I wished for more during my childhood than that incubator. I fell asleep many nights dreaming about it the way other children dreamed about bicycles and dollhouses. But I never was able to afford it.

I don't think there's any way to estimate how much that experience of tending those nesting hens taught me about discipline and responsibility, and, of course, patience. It was not a struggle, not at all. It was something I *wanted* to do. The kinship I felt with these other living creatures, the closeness, the compassion, is a feeling I carried with me out into the world from that point on. It might have been a feeling I was born with, I don't know, but the first time I recall being aware of it was with those chickens.

Of course my family thought it was the strangest thing, the amount of time and energy and affection I spent on those birds. No one else could tell those chickens apart, and no one cared to. But I knew every one of them, by appearance and personality. They were all individuals to me. Some I even named. Big Belle, for instance—she was the one that fell down into the well one afternoon, and it took us five days to get her out. We finally put some bread crumbs in a basket, lowered it down, and darned if she didn't climb right into that basket. Then there was Li'l Pullet, my favorite. She was a big, golden brown hen who lived longer than any other bird I had. Everywhere I went around that chicken pen, Li'l Pullet would be right there behind me, like a pet.

Of course anyone can figure out the danger of making pets out of farm animals, especially chickens. You get attached emotionally to an animal destined for the dinner table, and you're asking for a broken heart. But I couldn't help it. Routinely—more often than I liked—a chick or even a grown hen would catch one disease or another and die, and I would conduct a funeral for it. This was not child's play. It was not mere "acting out." I was genuinely grief-stricken, and the services I held were painstakingly precise.

I would find an old lard can and gently place the body of the dead bird inside it. This was the coffin. I would find some wildflowers and place them beside the can, then I would gather whichever of my sisters and brothers and cousins I could and seat them in a row. Then I would deliver a eulogy. An uncle gave me a Bible for Christmas when I was four, and I'll never forget my mother reading aloud to me the first words in that book: "In the beginning God created the heaven and the earth." By the time I was five I could read it myself, and one phrase that struck me strongly, though I couldn't comprehend its full meaning at the time, was, "Behold the lamb of God, which taketh away the sin of the earth." There was something about that image that hit me in my heart. I felt it literally—for lambs, and for chickens, too.

I preached to my birds just about every night. I would get them all into the henhouse, settle them onto their roosts, and then stand in the doorway and speak to them, reciting pieces of the Bible, the same verses I memorized for Sunday school. They would sit very quietly, some slightly moving their heads back and forth, mesmerized, I guess, by the sound of my voice. I could imagine that they were my congregation. And me, I was a preacher.

That's what my family took to calling me early on: Preacher. My parents would watch me perform one of my funerals, then see me lead a procession of children down to our ever-growing chicken cemetery, where the newest tiny coffin would join a neat row of small dirt-mounded graves, and they had to wonder what kind of son they had here. I even went through a period of performing baptisms, filling an empty syrup can with water and conducting the ceremony with each tiny chick I could get my hands on. I was truly intent on saving the little birds' souls. On one occasion I was too intense. I was holding a small, brown-feathered chick underwater, praying aloud as always, and I guess I misjudged the time. When I pulled the dripping bird up, it was limp and lifeless. I was shocked, absolutely terrified. I had taken one of my innocent babies and actually killed it. I didn't know what to do. In my panic I shook the little thing and laid it out on the dirt, hoping somehow the sun's heat might dry its feathers and maybe revive it. Incredibly, it did. The little thing stirred, then stood up and waddled back toward the coop. I never felt more guilt than I did that day. I can still feel the pang of it right now.

All these aspects of my chicken play tickled my parents at first, but their amusement vanished as I began seriously protesting their own treatment of the birds. From time to time they would have no cash to pay the Rolling Store Man for some sorely needed sugar or flour, so they would offer a bird in barter instead—one of *my* chickens. I'd cry, refuse to speak to them for the rest of the day, even skip that evening's meal.

Worse, though, was watching my mother or father kill one of the chickens for a special Sunday dinner. They would corner one of the squawking birds and carry it off to the chopping block, where they would either break its neck with their hands—spinning it around until the bone snapped—or simply chop the head off with a blow from an axe. They would then drain the blood out of its body and dip it in boiling water, scalding it, as we called it, to loosen the feathers for plucking. Needless to say, I was nowhere to be seen at those family meals.

Where my parents truly began to lose their amusement with my childish principles, however, was when I turned old enough to join them in the fields. Chickens might be child's play, but farming was dead serious business.

I had just turned six the first spring my parents brought me with them out to the fields. That was when the cycle of each year's field work began, in the spring. From then until the fall, there was no line drawn between the lives of the crops in those fields and our own lives. Those fields *were* our lives. What happened in them, down to the tiniest detail, became as familiar to me as the beating of my own heart. Year in and year out, from March to October, there was a rhythm to each day, the same rhythm of soil and sun and seeds and wind and rain that any farmer, anywhere, at any time, has always understood.

If that farmer was black and living in Alabama in the middle of this century, the rhythm he understood better than any other was the tedious, grinding, monotonous rhythm of cotton. He might have raised other crops— maybe some corn, probably some peanuts—but nothing came close to the amount of his land and his time and his energy that was devoted to cotton. For better and for worse, cotton, as the saying went, was truly king.

Planting season came first, of course, and it always began with the plow. Ours was a massive, twin-handled, solid oak contraption with a heavy steel spade on the end. My father would haul it out from the barn, where it had spent the winter. He'd pull out a short, thick chain and hitch it to our mule. Then he'd harness a long rope to each side of the mule, forming the reins with which he'd steer the animal. "Gee!" meant go right. "Haw!" meant left. And "Giddy up!," of course, meant to get moving.

Holding both a rein and a plow handle in each hand, my father would set the spade into the winter-hardened soil, shout to the mule to start pulling, and the three of them—mule, plow and my father—would move as one toward the far end of the field, leaving a fresh-dug furrow behind them. The furrow might be the length of a football field. Or two. Or sometimes even three. Then my father would shout, "Come here!" and the mule would turn, and they would head back in the direction they'd come, opening another furrow a foot or so away from the first. Back and forth they would go like that until an entire field was opened up with fresh, perfectly parallel lines of newly dug dirt.

Breaking new ground, we called it, and that's how our family would spend the first weeks of planting season, my father digging the furrows and my mother and we children following behind him, each of us carrying a sack of seeds. Every foot or so we'd drop a handful of seeds into the furrow. Then my father would follow back around, setting his spade between the now-seeded rows and digging yet another fresh furrow, which would turn up the dirt to cover those seeds.

It wasn't until I turned twelve that I was strong enough to do some of the plowing myself. It took a good amount of strength just to deal with that unwieldy tool. Even more than that, it took skill. I never knew how much skill until I got behind it myself. Only then did I realize how much the mule had a mind of its own—as, it seemed, did the plow. I had watched my father dig his razor-straight lines for years, and I expected to do the same. Instead, my furrows looked like crazy squiggles. My father would watch me veer off and plow up some seeds that had just been planted, and he'd shake his head and softly say, "Bob, you're plowing up the cotton." Then he'd take the reins himself and replow the row, straight as a ruler.

I have to say I enjoyed plowing, though. There was something about planting and springtime and new life that made me feel almost reverent. I would stop often and pick up a handful of dark, moist, fresh-turned dirt, study the tiny, threadlike roots, watch the little insects scrambling to get back into the safety of the darkness, and it would make me feel good, like breathing fresh air.

But that feeling didn't last long. A few weeks after planting, the fields would begin turning green as thousands of tiny cotton shoots started breaking through the soil. That meant the time had come for what is generally considered the most despised, backbreaking phase of cotton farming: chopping. Each of us would carry a hoe out into the fields and, walking slowly through the furrows, under a sun that was getting higher and hotter every day, with endless swarms of tiny biting black gnats nipping at the sweat around our eyes and mouths, we would stop at each group of shoots and chop away all but the tallest, healthiest-looking one. It was painstaking work, carefully digging around each selected plant, removing the unwanted seedlings while taking great care not to damage the chosen one. We would also dig out the weeds, which would grow back throughout the summer, making chopping seem like a never-ending task.

As bad as chopping was, though, I always felt that fertilizing was even worse. Dropping soda is what we called it because the white powder we used to feed the plants had the consistency of baking soda. At least that's how it looked when we filled our pails with it each morning. We'd spread the stuff by hand, walking back and forth along the rows, stopping at each plant to drop a fistful of fertilizer around it. It was hot, sweaty, sticky work, and it didn't take long for the perspiration from our arms and hands to turn the powder in those pails into a gooey paste. That paste would then harden into grainy, crystalline lumps, which you'd have to break up with your fingers before you could grab a handful. By the end of the day your hands would be swollen and sore, sliced with tiny cuts. Breathing the fumes of those chemicals for hours on end couldn't have been healthy, but who even thought of that in those days? All I knew was I hated dropping soda, just as much as I hated chopping cotton.

But I probably hated picking most of all.

It was always late summer, around the end of August, when the cotton bolls would begin popping from their pods. The fields we had worked so hard to keep green since the spring would finally turn white with what should have been our reward. I saw it instead as our punishment, both in terms of picking and of payment.

Each cotton stalk stood about waist-high to a full-grown man. There were four to ten stems to a stalk, and on the end of each stem grew four pods, each producing a single puff of cotton. A good picker could pull the puffs from all four pods in one swipe. He or she could finish an entire stalk in mere seconds. You could tell the good pickers by the fact that they carried two bags, one slung on each shoulder, instead of the single bag most of us wore into the field. And they didn't just work a single row at a time; they'd pick from two rows at once, pulling cotton with their left hand from one row even as their right was picking from another.

You had to bend down to pick cotton. Eight to ten hours of stooping like that and your back would be on fire. It would ache all night, and it would still be aching when you got up the next morning to go out and do it all over again. There were some who beat the bending by wrapping makeshift padding around their knees and *crawling* up and down those rows all day long. But they then had to deal with a different kind of pain—a sharp stabbing in their legs and knees. And we all came home each night with fingertips chewed ragged and bloody by the sharp edges of those cotton pods.

The cotton itself would pile up in big baskets placed at each end of the field. As your bag would fill, you'd empty it into one of those baskets. At the end of the day, we'd load those baskets onto the wagon, haul them to the house and dump the cotton out near the barn. We were taught that it was best to pick cotton early in the morning, when it was still wet with dew. Wet cotton weighed more than dry, and weight is what cotton was all about. You were paid by the pound, so it only made sense to get as much of that wet, heavy cotton as you could into the bottoms of those baskets and to keep it there, where it would not dry out in the sun.

When we had collected enough cotton to make a bale, my father would let the Copelands know, and they'd come to carry it off to be ginned, or we'd take it over to Saco ourselves. The Copelands would take half the bale right off the top for themselves, as part of the tenant arrangement. Then, from the other half, they would subtract whatever my father might owe them for the supplies they might have fronted him earlier in the year—seed, fertilizer, equipment. What was left after all that was ours.

It was never enough. I could see that from the beginning. Even a six-year-old could tell that this sharecropper's life was nothing but a bottomless pit. I watched my father sink deeper and deeper into debt, and it broke my heart. More than that, it made me angry. There was no way to get ahead with this kind of farming. The best you could do was do it well enough to *keep* doing it. That looked like no kind of life to me, and I didn't keep my opinion to myself. Early on, to the dismay of the rest of my family, I would speak out against what we were doing right there in the fields.

"*Gambling,*" I would proclaim. "This is nothing but gambling. We're betting on getting ahead, but there ain't no way. We're gonna lose. We're *always* gonna lose. The Bible says gambling is a *sin,* and that's what we're doing."

My mother would look up and draw a deep breath, her hands still pulling cotton even as she spoke.

"Well, Robert," she'd say, "what *else* are we going to do? You got to *work* to make a living."

"Not like this," I would answer. "Nobody should have to work like this."

My father would ignore me. My brother Adolph would get so tired of hearing me complain that he'd offer to do my share of the picking just so I'd shut up and go on back to the house. Of course I never did that. Despite my carping, I always carried my load. But Adolph was serious. That's how irritating my griping was.

It was just so obvious to me, though. There was no way up with this way of life. And as far as I could see, there was no way out.

Not, that is, until I started school.

*I*n a way, my first day of school was like any other child's. I was up before dawn, already fully dressed by the time the sun rose, much too excited to eat my breakfast. My blue denim overalls—the same pair I'd worked in all summer—were clean and pressed. I was wearing my favorite red flannel shirt. And on my feet were a pair of well-worn black brogans, the work boots I wore just about everywhere I went.

Other than that boyish anticipation, however, there was not much about my introduction to elementary school that most Americans would recognize. There was no bus. It would be six years before I would ride a bus to school. Until then I, along with the seventy or so other students who attended Dunn's Chapel Elementary School, walked.

It was only a half mile hike, downhill to the AME Church, beside which sat a small whitewashed wood building with a roof painted green—our school. The paint on that roof, as well as on all the exterior walls, was peeling. The wooden steps leading up to the front door were crooked and cracked. The whole structure seemed about to tip over. This was the same school my mother attended, as well as the generation before her, and it looked it. It had been built at the turn of the century with money provided by a man named Julius Rosenwald, a Northern philanthropist who traveled through the South in the late 1890s and early 1900s establishing one-room schoolhouses for the training and education of black children.

Our school had been sectioned by an interior wall into two rooms, one for the first three grades and the other for the rest. There was a single potbellied stove in each room, which we fed with wood during the winter months. Setting out into the surrounding forest on a firewood-gathering expedition was a regular part of our schoolweek routine. So was gathering straw to bundle into brooms that we'd use to sweep the dusty classroom floor, as well as the red clay yard outside.

We had no running water. We had no well either. Nor did the church. There was a farmhouse about three blocks up the road that allowed us to use their well, and we would take turns walking back and forth to that house to fill our schoolroom's bucket. We each kept our own cup or glass with our name taped on it on a shelf by a window, above the bucket and dipper.

It's funny, but the thing I remember most about that classroom was the huge Alabama state flag mounted up by the blackboard, right next to the teacher's desk. The flag was white, with two bold red lines forming an X across it. I was thrilled when I first saw it—I'd never seen anything quite so majestic—and that feeling of respect never went away, even when I began to learn what that flag actually represented. It was what it was *supposed* to stand for—a people, a community, a society united by a common bond—that I felt in awe of. I still have that feeling.

Oddly, there was no American flag in that room, but we did begin each day by reciting the Pledge of Allegiance. We said the Lord's Prayer as well. We would finish up with a patriotic song—"God Bless America" or "My Country 'Tis of Thee"—and then we would start our day.

There was one teacher for the entire room, all three grades. She was, like each of us, black. Her name was Miss Williams. Her salary was paid by the county—the only government money that came our school's way. Everything else we needed, we—or, more accurately, our families—provided. As I look back, it is shameful how little Miss Williams had to work with in terms of books and supplies. That flag, I soon learned, was handmade. Our desks, worktable, maps, paper and pencils all had to be bought piecemeal with cash raised by community events. Fish fries were always good moneymakers. So was the occasional picnic, with a mini-carnival and homemade games. My favorite of these games was one we called fireball. A fireball was a small, tightly wrapped bundle of rags, about the size of a baseball, soaked in kerosene. You'd light it on fire and quickly—*quickly*—fling it toward the sky. You did this at night, and the thing would make a bright, colorful arc as it rose and fell, trailing sparkling bits of flame all the way. Five for a dollar, that's what fireballs cost.

I loved school, loved everything about it, no matter how good or bad I was at it. My penmanship was poor—it's gotten a little better over the years, but just a little—yet the thrill of learning to write was intense. Public speaking, or playacting of any sort, terrified me—ironic, considering my performances at home with my chickens. Still, despite my discomfort, some of my sweetest memories are of standing in front of my classmates, having finished reciting a poem or reading a short essay, and hearing the teacher tell me I'd done a good job. Maybe that's because I always expected so little when I first stepped forward. I was so shy, so self-conscious, but that always vanished once I got going. By the time I was done, I didn't want it to be over. I could feel that connection with my classmates, I guess, just as with my birds.

Most of all, though, I loved reading, especially about real people and the real world. Biographies were my favorite, stories that opened my eyes to the world beyond Carter's Quarters. By the time I was in third grade, I had learned that there were actually black people out there who had made their mark on the world—Booker T. Washington, Joe Louis, Mary McLeod Bethune, George Washington Carver. I'll never forget my first field trip. It was a day's outing to Tuskegee Institute, my first journey out of Pike County. We walked through the museum there, touring a lab like the one in which Carver had done his pioneering work with peanuts. I came home that night to a front room piled with peanuts picked from our fields, waiting for us to shell and store them for the winter, and all I could think of were the specimens I'd seen that afternoon, scientifically sorted and labeled in clear jars of solution.

My parents knew education was important, and it was clear to them how hungry I was for it. They hadn't gone far in school themselves, and they certainly wanted better for me. But when there was work to be done in the fields, that came first. Farming season and the school year would overlap, and when they did, I was expected to stay home and help pick the cotton or gather the peanuts or pull the corn. I wasn't the only one, of course. This was true for almost every child in our school. It was a Southern tradition, just part of the way of life, that a black child's school year was dictated by the farm rhythms of planting and harvesting. You went to school when you could.

I resented that. It wasn't a question of falling behind my classmates; we were all in the same boat. But it was clear that all these days we were missing—a couple here, three or four there, sometimes an entire week—interfered with our learning. We were playing catch-up, not just with ourselves, but with children in other schools who didn't have to work in their families' fields to survive.

I didn't know about children like that when I began elementary school, but I knew about them by the time I finished. I knew that the names written in the fronts of our raggedy secondhand textbooks were white children's names, and that those books had been new when they belonged to them. I began to hear my parents talk a little bit about white people—not my father so much as my mother. She worked now and then in Troy, doing laundry and cooking and cleaning in white families' homes, and she would speak sometimes about how there were certain things you did and didn't do around white people, how there were certain things you could say and certain things you could not. It was all pretty vague to me at the time, but basically her message was you just don't get in white people's way. You must be very, very careful not to get out of line with a white person. I wondered a lot about why it was so. By the time I was nearing the end of elementary school, however, I could see for myself—because by then I had been to Troy.

The place looks today much as it did back then. There are some things that are new, of course—a shopping center here and there, plenty of convenience stores, a few small neighborhoods, but most of those are around the edges of town. Downtown itself remains pretty much the same as it was in the late 1940s and early '50s, when I'd ride in with my father and siblings on a Saturday afternoon.

There's the town square, of course, dominated by its statue of a Civil War soldier. LEST WE FORGET reads the inscription on the statue's base, beside a brass plate inscribed with the names of dozens of Confederate dead.

Troy was always a town that knew how to fight. One of the first buildings erected in the late 1830s, when the town was created, was a jail. For years Troy remained little more than a backwoods crossroads, a clump of "grocery shacks and lawless saloons," as one local history book puts it. The major form of entertainment on weekends was outdoor, all-comers wrestling matches there on the town square. When it came time to send its sons off to fight for the South in the Civil War, the boys from Troy went with names that reflected their violent roots: Raccoon Roughs was the name of one Confederate company from Pike County; Rough and Ready Pioneers was the name of another.

When they came back home, beaten and wounded, many of their best friends dead, they still refused to surrender. After Lincoln was assassinated in April 1865, a Troy businessman named Joseph Pinckney Parker wasted no time designing a monument. It was made of white marble and placed in the front yard of his home on Madison Street, where it stood until his death, its inscription printed clearly for all passersby to see:

IN MEMORY OF JOHN WILKES BOOTH
WHO KILLED OLE ABRAHAM LINCOLN

That monument is long gone, moved out to the cemetery where Parker is buried. But the sentiment hasn't vanished. You still see plenty of Confederate flags on shirts and hats and on bumper stickers fixed to the backs of pickup trucks parked in front of the county courthouse.

The storefronts surrounding the town square are typical of most small Southern towns: a florist; a shoe store; two banks; two jewelers; a couple of hairstyling salons; three empty spaces, all FOR LEASE; and a drugstore on the corner, Byrd's Drugs, with the same Formica counter soda fountain I used to walk up to to order what we called a combination—a hand-mixed Coca-Cola. I could buy a combination there, just like anyone else, but I had to take it outside to drink it. Blacks were allowed to buy anything they wanted in Byrd's— their money was as welcome as white folks'—but they could not sit down at those wrought-iron tables and chairs and have a sandwich or relax up at that counter with a nice, cool drink. That was simply not allowed. It was unthinkable.

Along the wall outside Byrd's sat an old wooden bench, and that's where the men from Carter's Quarters would congregate. It was an unofficial meeting place, the spot where my father and Grandpa Dink and the rest of their farm buddies would sit or lean or stoop, sometimes for hours, talking among themselves, watching the Saturday traffic pass through, just "getting a feel," as my father would put it, "getting a sense of what's happening." Which, it seemed to me, was never much.

They called that spot Carter's Corner, and the bench is still there, looking as tired and beaten down as the faded bricks of the buildings around it. I noticed not long ago that there's a slogan painted on those bricks outside Byrd's Drugs: SERVING SINCE 1940—the same year I was born. I guess you could say we grew up together, that drugstore and I.

Just up the street, a block off the town square, sits a movie theater, the same one I went to as a boy. I remember a lot of westerns: Hopalong Cassidy, The Lone Ranger, Billy the Kid. And I remember Tarzan—my friends and I would all cheer for the natives whenever they came on screen. But most of all, I remember that we had to sit upstairs, in a balcony section set aside for "Coloreds." We called it the Buzzard's Roost, and I hated it. I didn't go to too many movies before I decided I would never go again. It was an insult to have to sit up there. I felt it intensely. To this day I rarely go out to the movies. The memory of sitting up in that balcony is just too strong.

I have a lot of memories about Troy that remain painfully strong. Like the washrooms at the bus station, the nice clean one marked "WHITE," and the dirty, run-down one marked "COLORED." And the drinking fountains at the five-and-dime store, one a modern, chrome-spouted water cooler, the other nothing more than a rusty spigot—and I don't need to say which was which.

Then there was the public library, where I longed to go, but through whose doors I was not allowed to set foot. That killed me, the idea that this was a *public* library, paid for with government money, and I was supposedly a U.S. citizen, but I wasn't allowed in. Even an eight-year-old could see there was something terribly wrong about that.

There was a black commercial section of Troy a couple of blocks from the center of town, along a thoroughfare called Love Street. That was actually its name, *Love* Street. I now know that it was named in honor of one of the most eccentric characters in Pike County history, an illiterate widow named Ann Dowdell Love, who settled in Troy in the late 1830s and used to roam the dirt streets of town with a whip and a butcher knife, "urging" the drunks lying around the courthouse square to get up and go to church.

I didn't know about any of that back when I was a boy. All I knew was my mother would have whipped our bottoms raw if she had caught any of us anywhere near what she called the dives on Love Street. Never mind that there were beauty parlors and barbershops and plenty of other respectable black-owned businesses along that three-block stretch of town. All my mother saw were the couple of small nightclubs located there, and that was enough to make it a place of sin. I'll never forget her warning my older sister Ora time and time again, "I better not *catch* you over on Love Street." My mother never did catch Ora there, though I'm not sure Ora never went.

Love Street is as run-down today as so much of the rest of Troy. The businesses that were so busy when I was a boy are boarded up now. One building that still stands strong, with its doors still open for customers, is a big brick, warehouse-sized store at the very top of the street, a buffer between the white center of town and the stretch of black shops that once flourished here. COPELAND BROS. reads the lettering on one wall of the building. JOSH COPELAND reads another. Yes, these are the same Copelands my family farmed for.

By the turn of the 1950s, the lines between black and white in the place where I lived were becoming painfully clear to me. I paid attention now, more than ever, to the grownups' conversations, to the talks my mother and father would have with relatives and neighbors out on the porch, on weekends, in the evenings, when they would speak about some of our family members who had left, who had moved north, people like my mother's brothers Dink Jr. and O.C. They both lived up in Buffalo, where they'd gone during the war for the factory work they'd heard they'd find. They found it, and now we saw them once a year, the third Sunday in July, when they'd come back to Carter's Quarters for the annual reunion over at Macedonia Baptist.

I was beginning now to see all these scattered relatives coming in from places like Detroit and Newark in a new light. The North was no longer just a foreign, faraway place to me. Now I was sensing that it was a *different* place, different specifically in terms of race. I wondered what it would be like to live in a place like that, where the lines between whites and blacks weren't so sharply drawn as they were in Pike County. It was no dream world up north, I could tell that. I'd listen to my aunts and uncles from up there complain about a lot of things. But I would also hear them talk about schools where white and black children sat in the same classes. And buses where blacks sat beside whites. And stores where people shopped together *and* shared a lunch counter. All I had to do was merely look at these relatives from the North, wearing their city clothes, driving their big, shiny cars, and I could see that they lived in a different world than I did.

I started obsessing about it, about what it would be like to live up north.

I thought about it all the time. I would be out in the field, leaning on a plow handle, picturing in my mind one of these big, bustling cities where black people were not programmed from birth to be nothing but field hands, and suddenly my father's voice would snap me out of it. "*Bob!*" he'd shout from a couple of cotton rows away, and it was back to reality.

I remember distinctly how one afternoon my cousin Della Mae and I got this grand scheme into our heads. We couldn't have been more than nine years old. We were talking about this and that, just daydreaming out loud, and the next thing you know we had grabbed a handsaw out of the barn and were hiking into the woods, searching for the biggest, tallest pine tree we could find, because we were going to build ourselves a bus. We were going to saw down a tree, and somehow we were going to make it into a bus. And then we were going to roll right out of Alabama, leave the place behind for good and forever.

It wasn't too long after that, in the summer of 1951, that I took my first trip north, not in a homemade bus, but in my uncle Otis's car. He was the one who arranged that journey, planned it completely for my sake—Otis Carter, another one of my mother's brothers. He lived in Dothan, sixty miles south of us, where he was a teacher and a principal, in a black school, of course. Uncle Otis had always taken a special interest in me, especially as I began to grow and stand out a little bit, not just with my devotion to my schoolwork, but with the way I generally acted. I was so serious, very earnest, still sermonizing with my chickens, still protesting when that white meat went on the table. I wore a tie often, and some of the grownups would tease me about that, telling me I dressed like a preacher. I know now that Uncle Otis saw something in me that I hadn't yet seen. I think he sensed somehow that I was destined for a life different from my parents'. No telling what that life might be, but it would be different, and someday it would get me out of Troy.

That, I know, is why we took that trip in June of '51. I remember getting up early in the morning, meeting Uncle Otis out front of our house, and helping my mother pack his car with my clothes and with food—lots of food. There would be no restaurants for us to stop at until we were well out of the South, so we carried our restaurant right in the car with us—boxes and boxes of my mother's fried chicken. And biscuits. And pound cake. And sandwiches. And sweet potato pie.

Stopping for gas and to use the bathroom took careful planning. Uncle Otis had made this trip before, and he knew which places along the way offered "colored" bathrooms and which were better to just pass on by. Our map was marked and our route was planned that way, by the distances between service stations where it would be safe for us to stop.

Alabama. Tennessee. Kentucky. These were the states we had to be careful in as we made our way north. Black drivers we passed going the other direction, from north to south, faced an added danger: The out-of-state license plates on their new Northern cars made them visible targets as they crossed into the South. "What are those niggers from the North doing with a car like that?"— that's the kind of comment, and sometimes worse, that they had to face.

It wasn't until we got into Ohio that I could feel Uncle Otis relax, and so I relaxed, too. By the time we reached Lake Erie—that looked like the *ocean* to me, more water than I'd ever dreamed of—and turned east toward Buffalo, I was about ready to burst with excitement.

And I was not disappointed. Arriving in Buffalo—seventeen hours after we'd left the front yard of my Alabama home—was like stepping into a movie, into a strange, otherworldly place. It was so busy, almost frantic, the avenues filled with cars, the sidewalks crowded with people, black and white alike, mixing together as if it was the most natural thing in the world. What a contrast to sleepy, segregated little Troy. When we reached my uncle O.C.'s and Dink's house, I couldn't believe it—they had white people living next door to them. On *both* sides.

My aunts—Aunt Leola and Aunt Mae Charles—took me shopping downtown one day at a department store called Sattler's, and there, for the first time in my life, I rode an escalator. I had never even heard of an escalator. I found my way to the candy counter, of course, and it was like magic, standing there and beholding the variety of sweets laid out behind that glass. I remember I bought a bag of Brach's Neapolitan candy, each little cube with a layer of white coconut, red strawberry and brown chocolate. I made that bag last forever, savoring each piece as if it were made of pure gold.

We went to the outdoor market and I watched my aunt Leola shop for a chicken. There were rows of wooden crates lined up, filled with live hens, just like the ones I raised back home. But city people didn't raise chickens. They did what my aunt did—study those crates for a while, finally point her finger at her selection and tell the shopkeeper, "I want that one," and the man would pull that chicken out, kill it, clean it and dress it right before our eyes. That amazed me. It was so different from back home. I wasn't even bothered by the fate of these chickens. Maybe the fact that I didn't know them had something to do with it, I don't know. I do know that I joined my aunts and uncles for the meal that evening and had no problem cleaning my plate.

I saw Niagara Falls that summer and felt swept away by the power and majesty of that roaring water. I spent a lot of time just walking the streets of the city, soaking up the sights and sounds and smells. By the end of August, though, when it was time to go back to Alabama, I was more than ready. I missed my brothers and sisters. I missed my parents. When I finally arrived home, climbing out of my uncle Otis's car and giving him a hug goodbye, I was crying, it felt so good to be back.

But home would never feel the same as it did before that trip. And neither would I. Now, when I went into Troy on a Saturday afternoon, I was more acutely aware than ever of how black men and women—the grownups of my world—addressed all white people, even white *children*, as "Mr." or "Mrs." or "Miss," always adding "Sir" or "Ma'am" and never receiving any of those courtesies in return. The signs of segregation that had perplexed me up till then now outright angered me. I began junior high school that fall, which meant riding a school bus for the first time in my life, an experience that on the face of it should have been exciting and fun. Instead, it was sad, just another reminder of how different my life was from those of white children.

Our roads weren't paved. The county didn't bother blacktopping roads into "colored" communities unless it was necessary for white traffic to pass through. Few whites ever needed to come through Carter's Quarters, so our roads remained nothing but red clay until the year I left for college. Until then we were at the mercy of the elements, specifically rain. Rain turned those clay roads into impassable nightmares. They would become slick as ice in some spots, the bus spinning its tires in vain as it strained to climb a hill, or sliding sideways off the road and into a ditch on the slightest turn. I can't count the number of times we had to empty our seats in the midst of a downpour, all of us children climbing out into the rain and putting our shoulders to that huge vehicle to help get it back onto the road. In other spots the clay would soften into a tire-sucking quagmire, and we'd have to climb out there, too, stepping into that red mud to help get the bus free. We were picked up each day at 7 A.M., with our first class scheduled to start at eight, and many a wet morning we did not reach the school until noon.

The bus itself was a rattling, rusty jalopy, an old hand-me-down, just like our schoolbooks. I realized how old it was when we finally climbed onto the paved highway, the main road running east from Troy, and passed the white children's buses, so new and shiny. We went past their schoolhouse as well, very sleek, very modern, with nice playground equipment outside, nothing like our cluster of small cinder-block buildings, with the dirt field on which we played at recess and the privvies out back.

We would drive past prison work gangs almost every day, a dozen or so convicts picking up paper or doing road maintenance under the watchful eye of an armed guard or two. And those prisoners were always black. As were the folks working in the fields beyond them, chopping or picking cotton. You couldn't help but notice that.

The old school is still there today, right off Route 29, eight miles east of my mother's home, at a spot on the highway called Banks. The school is still surrounded by the same wide open fields that used to turn snow white with cotton each September. The railroad tracks across the road, where the trains used to pass by and we'd run outside and holler to the engineers to blow their whistles and they would, are still there. The school is for elementary-aged children now, but it was a junior high back when I attended there: Banks Junior High School.

Despite all the inequities that confronted me on the way to those classrooms, I was in heaven once I stepped inside them. This was an actual school compared to little Dunn's Chapel. It had multiple classrooms and teachers, and a principal as well. Her name was Mrs. Horton, and she brooked no nonsense. She was known for putting children across her lap, no matter how old or how large. We all lived in fear of crossing Mrs. Horton.

Our teachers, all of them women, were trained, most of them as dead serious about the process of education as Mrs. Horton. No one needed to convince me about the value of learning. By then I was absolutely committed to giving everything I had to bettering myself in the classroom. I had no doubt that there was a way out of the world I saw around me and that this was the way. My parents, like most poor black parents of that time, agreed. To them as well, education represented an almost mythical key to the kingdom of America's riches, the kingdom so long denied to our race. More than once they said to me, "Get an education so you won't have to do what we're doing. Get an education so you won't have to work like this."

But when planting and harvesting seasons arrived, the reality of those fields displaced any dreams about the future. My parents needed my hands and my muscles, and as much as it hurt them, knowing how I adored school, they insisted I had to stay home at those times to help with the crops. I'd plead with them to let me go. I'd point out how far behind I'd fall if I missed those days of classwork. They understood, but they still said no. They needed me.

And so I'd hide. I would get up and eat breakfast, not saying much. Then, as the others made their way out toward the fields and the day's work, I would slip around the front of the house, duck under the front porch and wait there, my heart pounding, for the school bus to pull up. After a while I would hear my mother calling, and still I'd stay put. When I could hear the familiar whine and groan of the approaching bus, I'd dash out, climb on and be off.

When I got home my father would be furious, but he never whipped me. I always expected that, was certain he would tan my hide. But he never did, not over that. He scolded me, just reamed me out, told me never to do it again. I did, of course, and he would scold me again. But deep inside I think he knew there was no stopping me, that this was a decision I had made about my life and that once I made a decision, it was just about impossible to turn me away from it. That's something that would remain true about me my entire life, that I take a great deal of care in weighing an important choice. I'm not impetuous. But once I make a decision, I stay the course. I was that way when I was eight, and I'm that way today, at fifty-eight. I am not without passion; in fact, I have a very strong sense of passion. But my passion plays itself out in a deep, patient way. When I care about something, when I commit to it, I am prepared to take the long, hard road, knowing it may not happen today or tomorrow, but ultimately, eventually, it will happen. That's what faith is all about. That's the definition of commitment—patience and persistence. People who are like fireworks, popping off right and left with lots of sound and sizzle, can capture a crowd, capture a lot of attention for a time, but I always have to ask, where will they be at the end? Some battles are long and hard, and you have to have staying power. Firecrackers go off in a flash, then leave nothing but ashes. I prefer a pilot light—the flame is nothing flashy, but once it is lit, it doesn't go out. It burns steadily, and it burns forever.

That's how I was about school. I was going to school, no matter what. And that's how I became about something else as well, something that was sparked by the voice of a man named Martin Luther King.

It was the beginning of 1955, midway through my second year at Pike County Training School—the county's only high school for black students who lived beyond the city limits of Troy. PCTS was located in a little town called Brundidge, about four miles up the railroad tracks beyond Banks. Drive down Brundidge's main street today and you'll see more antique shops than anything else. The town itself is kind of an antique, with its Pride of Dixie barbecue joint sitting just up the street from the pulp-wood sawmill that provides much of the town's employment. The last weekend of each October, Brundidge decks itself out for its annual Peanut Butter Festival, highlighted by a nice parade. Not long ago I was invited to ride as the grand marshal. I brought my mother along with me, and she really enjoyed it, waving at all her friends from the back seat of that convertible. They waved back, and you could hear them saying, "Hey, that's Willie Mae! And look, that's her son beside her!" I love that about a place like Pike County. No matter how old you are or how far you roam, you will always remain, first and foremost, your mother's son.

There is no Pike County Training School anymore. A small ballfield now sits where the school used to be. The dirt infield is covered with bits of broken beer bottles. There are trailers beyond the outfield, and beyond them, up near the railroad tracks, stand a couple of rows of small wood-frame houses, many of them rotting with age. This is still the black section of Brundidge, as it was back when I went to school here.

Like the junior high in Banks, the high school in Brundidge was a collection of buildings between which we walked from class to class. The buildings were bright white, built from wood, with black tarpaper roofs. Most of the students lived in or around Brundidge and had been classmates since first grade. Kids like me, bused in from the rural parts of the county, were outsiders and were treated that way. That, coupled with my natural shyness, kept me from getting involved in anything much beyond my schoolwork. My only extracurricular activity was a club called the New Farmers of America, something like a Four-H Club. I was raising turkeys as well as my chickens by then, which made me a natural for the New Farmers. But then, almost every student at PCTS was a natural for a club like that—we almost all lived on farms. In fact, the primary focus of the school's entire academic program was something called Vocational Agriculture—preparing kids to become farmers. College was something you hardly heard mentioned. The word "training" in the school's name was there for a reason. Basically, we were being trained to go right back out into the fields from which we had come.

But some teachers there wanted us to aim higher. Almost the entire staff were graduates of Alabama State College. Most of the Pike County students who managed to go on to college went to Alabama State, and many returned as teachers at PCTS. I knew I didn't want to be a teacher. I wanted to preach, or possibly study the law. I remember an uncle of mine teasing me about that. "What do you want to be?" he asked me. "A lying lawyer preacher!"

Whatever I was going to do, I was determined to do it beyond the bounds of Pike County. I was obsessed with learning all I could about the world beyond the one I knew, and that's why the school library became like a second home for me. Until I got to high school, the only newspapers I'd ever read were those back issues of the *Montgomery Advertiser* that my mother occasionally brought home from her work trips to Troy. But in the training school library I was exposed to shelves and racks of newspapers and magazines from across the country—*black* newspapers and magazines with names like *Jet* and *Ebony*, the *Pittsburgh Courier*, the *Baltimore Afro-American*, the *Chicago Defender*. The librarian, a tall, light-skinned woman named Coreen Harvey, became a daily presence in my life. She was beautiful—she looked a lot like Lena Horne—and she was regal in a firm but soft-spoken kind of way. "My dear children," she would say, putting her finger against her lips to shush the loud ones, "read. Read *everything*."

I did. Near the end of my freshman year, on a May morning in 1954, I read something that stunned me, just absolutely turned my world upside down. The U.S. Supreme Court had finally handed down its decision in the school desegregation case of *Brown* v. *The Board of Education of Topeka*. The ruling declared that the "separate but equal" doctrine, on which almost the entire institution of segregation was based, was unconstitutional. I remember the feeling of jubilation I had reading the newspaper story—*all* the newspaper stories—that day. Everything was going to change now. No longer would I have to ride a broken-down bus almost forty miles each day to attend classes at a "training" school with hand-me-down books and supplies. Come fall I'd be riding a state-of-the-art bus to a state-of-the-art school, an *integrated* school.

All that spring I searched the papers for news of Alabama's plans for desegregating its schools. Instead, what I saw were stories quoting state politicians derisively referring to the day of that Supreme Court decision as Black Monday and making clear that they had no intention of obeying the ruling. I read about branches of something called White Citizens Councils—coat-and-tie versions of the Ku Klux Klan—forming in Georgia and Mississippi. As for the Klan itself, there were reports of hooded marches and midnight cross burnings across the state of Alabama. I heard talk that summer of black men being beaten and even castrated—not in Pike County, but in places just like it. I didn't know if that talk was true, but I didn't doubt it was possible. Things felt as if they were starting to get stirred up a little bit throughout the South. And I was glad they were.

Not everybody was so glad, however. My parents, despite their enthusiasm about the Supreme Court ruling, were disapproving of people trying to push things, no matter how justified the cause. Right or wrong didn't matter to them as much as reality. We heard stories all the time about black men being arrested in Troy for one offense or another and being physically manhandled, even beaten. As far as my parents were concerned, anyone who was arrested for any reason was "riffraff," and that was that. "Decent" black folks stayed out of trouble. It was that simple.

My parents' attitude toward injustice didn't bother me nearly as much as the attitude I saw among the ministers at church. Our minister at Macedonia Baptist lived in Montgomery and traveled out to preach to us once a month. It always bothered me that he knew, as we all did, how sharecroppers were cheated by our landlords right and left, underpaid and overcharged every year, but not once did he ever speak about this in his sermons. Sunday after Sunday he'd talk about an eye for an eye, a tooth for a tooth, how the soul must be saved by and by for that pie in the sky after you die, but hardly a word about *this* life, about *this* world, about some sense of salvation and righteousness right *here*, between the cradle and the grave. It also did not escape my notice that that minister arrived and departed in a pretty nice automobile, and that he went back to a very comfortable home in Montgomery, more comfortable than the homes any of us lived in.

Naturally there was no talk in our church of that Supreme Court decision. Nor was there any mention of the acts of violence that followed it throughout that summer. I wondered why. I wondered if God might not be wondering why as well. It seemed to me that the Lord had to be concerned with the way we lived our lives right here on earth, that everything we did or didn't do in our lives had to be more than just a means of making our way to heaven. My thoughts on this subject weren't too sophisticated or developed—I was only fourteen—but they were earnest, and they were in my head almost all the time, even more so as I began my sophomore year in the fall of 1954 by climbing onto the same beat-up school bus and making the same twenty-mile trip to the same segregated high school I'd attended the year before. *Brown v. The Board of Education* notwithstanding, nothing in my life had changed.

And then, on a Sunday morning in early 1955, I was listening to our radio, tuned to WRMA out of Montgomery, as always, when on the air came a sermon by a voice I'd never heard before, a young minister from Atlanta. I didn't catch his name until the sermon was finished, but the voice held me right from the start. It was a strong voice, a deep voice, clearly well trained and well schooled in the rhythmic, singsong, old-style tradition of black Baptist preaching we call whooping. There's a creative pacing to that style of sermonizing, a cadence, with lots of crescendos and dramatic pauses and drawing out of word endings as if holding a note in a song. It's so much like singing. He really could make his words *sing*.

But even more than his voice, it was his message that sat me bolt upright with amazement. His sermon was titled "Paul's Letter to the American Christians." He'd taken it from Paul's letter to the church at Corinth, in which Paul criticized complacent Christians for their selfishness and failures of brotherhood. He adapted it to what was happening here, right now, on the streets of Montgomery, Alabama. I listened, as this man spoke about how it wasn't enough for black people to be concerned only with getting to the Promised Land in the hereafter, about how it was not enough for people to be concerned with roads that are paved with gold, and gates to the Kingdom of God. He said we needed to be concerned with the gates of schools that were closed to black people and the doors of stores that refused to hire or serve us. His message was one of love and the Gospel, but he was applying those principles to *now*, to today. Every minister I'd ever heard talked about "over yonder," where we'd put on the white robes and golden slippers and sit with the angels. But this man was talking about dealing with the problems people were facing in their lives right now, specifically black lives in the South.

This was the first time I had ever heard something I would soon learn was called the social gospel—taking the teachings of the Bible and applying them to the earthbound problems and issues confronting a community and a society. I was on fire with the words I was hearing. I felt that this man—his name was Martin Luther King Jr.—was speaking directly to me. This young preacher was giving voice to everything I'd been feeling and fighting to figure out for years. When I got to school that Monday, I went straight to the library to find out anything I could about this man. There wasn't much, but I did come across a small newspaper article describing his appointment the previous September as resident pastor at Dexter Avenue Baptist Church in Montgomery. The story mentioned that he had graduated from Morehouse College in Atlanta, and so I decided right then and there that that was where I was going to go to school.

That year, 1955, was a watershed not just for me but for the movement as well. Actually, no one was using the term "movement" quite yet, but they would be before the year was out, because the nearly century-old struggle for black Americans' civil rights, spurred by the *Brown* v. *Board* decision, was now finally coming to a head. Things were truly beginning to "move," both for bad and for good. Lines were starting to be drawn, and blood was beginning to spill.

In May of that year, in response to Southern states' defiance of the 1954 decision, the Supreme Court issued an "implementation ruling" on *Brown,* ordering lower courts to require "a prompt and reasonable start toward full compliance." Southern political leaders—avowed segregationists such as U.S. Senators James Eastland of Mississippi and Strom Thurmond of South Carolina and U.S. Representative James Davis of Georgia—swore that they would defy the Court to the death. That summer there seemed to be an increase of racial incidents—attacks on blacks. Some you would read about in the newspapers, others you'd hear about through the word-of-mouth grapevine by which black people in the South have long gotten much of their news—news not necessarily reported or even known of by the white mainstream press.

That August an incident took place that no one could ignore. The body of Emmett Till, a fourteen-year-old boy from Chicago who was spending the summer with relatives near a tiny Mississippi town called Money, was pulled from the bottom of the Tallahatchie River. He had been shot through the head, one eye had been gouged out, and a seventy-five-pound cotton gin fan was wired around his neck. The day before, on a dare from some friends, as he was leaving a country store in Money, he said, "Bye, baby" to the white woman behind the counter. Now he was dead. "What else could I do?" one of the men who killed him subsequently explained to a magazine writer. "He thought he was as good as any white man."

That man, along with the white woman's husband, was found not guilty of Emmett Till's murder, despite the testimony of a sixty-four-year-old black farmer named Moses Wright, who witnessed the two men drag Emmett Till out of bed the night he was killed. Moses Wright actually pointed to the two

men in a Mississippi courtroom filled with white reporters and white spectators, a white judge and a white jury, and said, simply and straightforwardly,
"Thar' he."

We read about Moses Wright's testimony, my family and I, and we marveled at his bravery, to do what he did in that time, in that place. My parents
shook their heads sadly at what had happened to this "colored boy" over in
Mississippi. My parents often used the word "colored" back then, as did most
of their generation.

As for me, I was shaken to the core by the killing of Emmett Till. I was fifteen, black, at the edge of my own manhood, just like him. He could have
been me. *That* could have been me, beaten, tortured, dead at the bottom of a
river. It had been only a year since I was so elated at the *Brown* decision. Now
I felt like a fool. It didn't seem that the Supreme Court mattered. It didn't
seem that the American principles of justice and equality I read about in my
beat-up civics book at school mattered. The messages I heard in church, the
songs we would sing—"In Christ there's no east or west, no north or
south"—declarations of absolute equality in God's eyes, didn't seem to matter either. They didn't matter to the men who killed Emmett Till. They didn't
matter to the jury that deliberated for a mere hour before delivering its verdict
of not guilty. Nor did they matter to the county that continued to send me to
a school separate from white children and forbade me to eat at the same drugstore lunch counter or even use the same public rest room as they.

By the end of that year, I was chewing myself up with questions and frustration and, yes, anger—anger not at white people in particular but at the system that encouraged and allowed this kind of hatred and inhumanity to exist.
I couldn't accept the way things were, I just couldn't. I loved my parents
mightily, but I could not live the way they did, taking the world as it was presented to them and doing the best they could with it. In a lot of ways I saw
them as far stronger than I would ever be. It's simple to criticize people of another time for not acting as we would today. It's easy to judge the past, looking through the filter of the present. But that is a mistake. No one can truly
know what it was like to be faced with the challenges and realities of a certain
time and place unless he or she has actually lived through it. There was no
weakness in the way my parents and others of their generation shouldered the
burden of their time and made the best of it. Fighting back was hardly an option for them. Fight back against whom? With what? My parents, and millions
of other black men and women just like them, bore their load through an age
of unbelievable oppression with a grace and a dignity I could only hope to
come close to. Theirs was not a time nor a place for turning and facing the
system.

But as I began to come of age in the mid-1950s, the landscape had begun to shift. The time had come. I could feel it. I could *see* it. I saw it up north, in the rulings that were coming down from the courts. I saw it at home, in the South, where the lines of white backlash and violence were being drawn in response to those rulings. And, in December of that landmark year, 1955, I saw it just up the highway, in Montgomery, where that man, the Reverend Dr. Martin Luther King Jr., took the words I'd heard him preach over the radio and put them into action in a way that set the course of my life from that point on. With all that I have experienced in the past half century, I can still say without question that the Montgomery bus boycott changed my life more than any other event before or since.

My parents didn't know Rosa Parks, but they knew plenty of women like her. More than a few of the wives and mothers in Carter's Quarters often worked in Montgomery, doing the same kinds of domestic work Rosa Parks did. Some of them may well have occasionally ridden the same bus Mrs. Parks regularly rode, the one on which she was arrested the first day of that December for refusing to give up her seat to a white man. But whether any of us knew her or not before that day, we all felt that we knew her after it.

Montgomery was just fifty miles away. I'd been there only once myself, on a day trip I took by train with an uncle my seventh-grade year. But my parents and my neighbors knew Montgomery. Our minister lived there. Most of my teachers were from there. Even though we lived far out in the Alabama woods, we were connected to Montgomery in many ways. We were part of the place. And when that young minister, the Reverend King, in his role as the president of a group called the Montgomery Improvement Association, launched a black boycott of those buses, we felt we were a part of that as well.

It went on for more than a year, and I followed it almost every day, either in the newspapers or on radio. This was riveting. This was real. I'd hear firsthand accounts of what the mood was like over in Montgomery from the grownups who lived or worked there. They'd describe buses normally full of black passengers now riding up and down the city streets with no one inside them. This wasn't just talk. This was action. And it was a different kind of action from anything I'd heard of before. This was a fight, but it was a different way of fighting. It wasn't about confrontation or violence. Those 50,000 black men and women in Montgomery were using their will and their dignity to take a stand, to resist. They weren't responding with their fists; they were speaking with their feet.

There was something about that kind of protest that appealed to me, that felt very, very *right*. I knew nothing about the philosophy of nonviolence or passive resistance—not yet—but I'd always had a visceral aversion to violence of any sort. I was just born that way. It had nothing to do with fear or cowardice. The only things I was afraid of in this world were lightning and snakes. But violence of any sort sickened me. One of my earliest memories—I couldn't have been older than four—was of my mother pleading with my father one afternoon not to leave the house. He had a shotgun in his hand, his face was full of anger, and he was trying to push past my mother toward the door. I don't know to this day what it was about, what had happened out there, beyond that door. But I knew what I saw in my mother's face. It had anguish and terror written all over it. "Don't do it!" I remember watching her plead with my father as she pushed her body full-up against his. "Buddy, *please* don't do it!"

I have never heard my mother beg for anything from anyone my entire life, but she was begging my father that day. And I've never forgotten it. My brothers all grew up hunting, just like my father. They still love to hunt, every one of them. But I have never been hunting in my life, never fired a gun, never even held one in my hands until I visited the Middle East in 1993. The reason, I'm sure, has much to do with my inborn nature. But there's no question that that scene between my parents had a profound impact as well.

Just as profound was watching the Montgomery boycott play itself out. My parents would talk about "that young preacher" who was leading this thing, and I could sense a mixture of both awe and disapproval in their voices. As for me, there was no question. I saw 50,000 black people refusing to ride segregated buses, and the reason, more than any other single factor, was the words and inspiration of one man, that young preacher Martin Luther King.

More than ever I wanted to be a preacher, too. My life was centered around school, our farm and the church, with the church dominating my thoughts about the other two. I had hardly any social life to speak of, largely because of sheer geography. There were girls I was attracted to at school. We'd write letters—love notes, I guess they were—back and forth sometimes. I even recall two girls actually having a fight over me once on the bus. Somehow a note one girl had written to me wound up in the hands of the other. The driver had to stop the bus to break it up.

But I didn't date. First of all, I had no driver's license. I got as far as taking the driving test in Troy the month I turned sixteen. It consisted of driving around the block and parking. I was so nervous I messed up on my first try, and that was it. There was no second chance. Not only that, but the official riding with me, a middle-aged white man, yelled at me unmercifully when the test was over. "Boy!" I remember him shouting, right there in front of the courthouse, with people all around us, "don't you come back here till you learn how to *drive!*" I was mortified and angry and embarrassed, all at once. I didn't go back, not that year. Not the next year, either. In fact, it would be twenty-six years before I finally got my driver's license. That became a running joke among my friends for most of my life, how I traveled all over creation, from one town or city to another, throughout the South and eventually across the country, all through the '60s during the height of the movement, through the '70s as an organizer and activist, and into the '80s as a politician—and I did not drive. I've been down just about every road there is in the state of Alabama, and most of them in Georgia and Mississippi as well, but I was never behind the wheel until the spring of 1982. When the Georgia state trooper who gave me the test that April—a female trooper—told me I had passed, I kissed her on the cheek. "Free at last," I told her. "Free at last." And I drove home, forty-two years old, with my first driver's license in my wallet.

But I had no license when I was sixteen. The girls I knew lived halfway across the county, and they may as well have been halfway around the world. Beyond that, even if I had been able to date, there would not have been much to it. There was no place for a teenager to go in rural Pike County, certainly not for a *black* teenager. And the church was exceedingly strict and exceedingly specific about what was and was not allowed in terms of socializing or entertainment. No dancing. Definitely no drinking. Physical intimacy was, of course, out of the question. Naturally, all these rules were violated at one time or another by almost every member of our church. But that didn't mean they weren't taken seriously. I remember when I was in tenth grade, a young girl, a third cousin of mine, about my age, became pregnant. The church put her out, called her right up front on a Sunday morning and told her she had to leave and could not return. She was no longer a member in good standing of the "Christian Fellowship." That's how they put it. I'll never forget. I felt so sorry for this girl, seeing her face, so sad and ashamed and afraid. I couldn't understand how these people who preached love and tolerance could be so harsh and judgmental, and to a *child!* Where was their forgiveness? Their compassion? Their fairness? And speaking of fairness, I wondered why the boy or man who helped get her pregnant wasn't made to stand down front alongside her, to face what she faced.

I had problems with the church. On the one hand, I was absolutely committed to my faith, to the Lord, to the stories and lessons I read in the Bible— beautiful stories and deep, deep lessons. On the other hand, I was torn and confused, full of questions about why so many people treated one another so cruelly sometimes, often in the name of the same Bible I was reading. That kind of question didn't curb my desire to become a minister. In fact, it increased it. Seeing what the Reverend King was doing showed me there were more ways to be a minister than the ones I had seen in my own church.

It was with all those feelings that I preached my first public sermon. The date was February 16, 1956, five days before my sixteenth birthday, two days past Valentine's Day and just twelve days after riots had broken out among whites in Tuscaloosa in the wake of a court order forcing the University of Alabama to admit the first black student in the school's history, a young woman named Autherine Lucy. She never did make it to a class that semester; she was suspended, then subsequently expelled from the university in the wake of those riots—"for her own safety," according to the college administration. But reading about her walking through those crowds of taunting onlookers and thinking about the courage that must have taken, I became even more convinced that I had to make myself part of all this, that I had to *do* something.

The subject of my sermon that Sunday morning—my "trial sermon," as the Macedonia Baptist elders who allowed me to take the pulpit called it— came from the First Book of Samuel, in which Hannah, who is supposed to be beyond the age of childbirth, prays for a son, promising God that if He gives her one, she will give Him back the boy for life, and that her boy will become a man of moral courage. "A Praying Mother," I called my talk. Certainly I was nervous, but it didn't take long to warm up, and pretty soon I could feel it. Pretty soon the congregation felt it, too. There was shouting, cries of "Amen!" and "Praise the Lord!"—all the wide-open emotions of the black church, everyone just extremely happy about the whole thing, including me. Someone must have called the *Montgomery Advertiser* about it because later that week I went into Troy to have my photograph taken in a studio—a white photographer's studio—posed in my Sunday suit with a Bible in one hand and making a dramatic gesture with the other. That photo, along with a story about my sermon, was published in what they called the Negro Section of the newspaper. That was the first time I ever saw my name in print, as the "boy preacher" from Pike County.

Two days after I preached that sermon, the rising tide of racial violence I'd been reading so much about in the newspapers struck close to home. One of my uncles, "Fox" Thomas—my aunt Lyzanka's husband—had an uncle named Thomas Brewer who lived in Columbus, Georgia. Dr. Brewer was very active in that area's NAACP leadership—he had led the fight to allow black people to vote in Georgia's Democratic primary in 1946, which made him both visible and none too popular with many white people in that region. He visited Troy often to see his sister, who lived right near Dunn's Chapel. We saw Dr. Brewer many times and knew he was an important, respected man.

On the night of February 18, he was shot seven times by the owner of a department store located just beneath his office. The store owner, who admitted the shooting, was never indicted. A grand jury ruled that the shooting was justifiable homicide. But among the black community the belief was that Dr. Brewer had been murdered by the Klan because of his NAACP activities.

That killing jolted me even more than the others I'd read about. This was a man I knew. I was horrified by what happened, and I was enraged at a system that could condone and encourage such hatred. Curiously, at least to many people with whom I have shared my feelings about racism at that time—and my feelings have in essence not changed at all since then—I did *not* feel anger or ill will toward white people in general. I did not really know any white people. And I refused to believe that all white people acted or felt like the ones I read about. I know it might sound simplistic, but then some of the most basic truths in this world are just that when you boil them down—basic. I truly felt with all my heart that it made no more sense for me to generalize about all white people being one way or another than it did for white people to generalize about blacks. That attitude would become more refined and developed in the years to come as I was introduced to and began studying the formal philosophy of nonviolence.

But those years were still to come in 1956. All I knew then was that I believed that most people, regardless of race or any other distinction, were kind and had a conscience—or were *capable* of being kind and having a conscience. I guess I was born with that belief, and I feel blessed because of it. I have never hated anyone in this world. I hurt for them sometimes. I feel sadness about them. In a way I pity those filled with anger and hate because they are victims just as much as the people they attack—victims of the forces that nurture the kind of hatred they feel. That kind of hatred does not spring from nowhere. The development of those thoughts would come when I got to college, but those feelings were already inside me.

I didn't hate the librarian at the Pike County Public Library who turned me away—very politely—when I walked up to her desk in the spring of that year and said I would like to apply for a library card so I could check out a book. I knew I would be refused. But that was the first step of the first formal protest action of my life. I went home and wrote a petition stating that the library must be opened to black people—public tax-paying black people. I then passed it around to my friends and classmates at school. They were as angry about the segregation we saw all around us as I was. We talked about it all the time. But they had also read the same newspaper stories I had, stories about black people being castrated and killed. They all knew about Dr. Brewer. And they were understandably nervous and afraid. A few of them—not many, mostly some of my cousins—did sign the petition, and I went ahead and mailed it to the library, but that was the end of it. We got no response, and we did nothing further. But it was a start. It was an *act,* and that meant something, at least to me.

The next "action" I took involved the NAACP. That summer the state's attorney general, a man named John Patterson—who would soon become governor by running a racially charged campaign against George Wallace, a campaign that prompted Wallace to vow that he would never be "outniggered" again—obtained a court order banning the NAACP in Alabama. I immediately found the address of the NAACP national headquarters and mailed away an application and $1.50 for my youth membership card. It arrived in a matter of days, and I carried that blue and white card in my wallet for years, until it finally crumbled apart with age.

The fall of my senior year it was time to apply to college. I had no counselor to advise me. Pike County was a training school. We weren't supposed to go on to college, though more of us did than anyone would have expected. Of the thirty-seven students in my senior class—the Class of '57—ten went on to college. No one in my family had ever gone. My parents were proud of me for aiming that high. They had given up long before on any hopes of my becoming a farmer. Now they saw me becoming a minister, and they knew college was a step in that direction. But there was next to nothing they could do for me in the way of money. I understood that. And when I studied the catalog Morehouse College mailed to me, I could see there was absolutely no way I could afford to go there. My grades were nowhere near good enough for a scholarship—I was an earnest student, but not an exceptional one. And so, as the year turned to 1957 and I began my last semester of high school, I still didn't know where I was going to go to college. I only knew it would not be where Dr. King had gone.

Then, out of nowhere, as if by Providence, my mother came home from work one day with a brochure in her hand. She'd picked it up at an orphanage in Troy where she did laundry part-time, mostly washing sheets. The orphanage, the Alabama Baptist Children's Home, was operated by the white Southern Baptist Convention, which also owned, in partnership with the National Baptist Convention, a small theological seminary for black ministerial students in Nashville, Tennessee. The brochure my mother handed me that day described this school, the American Baptist Theological (ABT) Seminary. The place was small, with fewer than a hundred students. It seemed far away—I'd never been to Nashville and wasn't quite sure exactly where it was. I knew the Grand Ole Opry was located there, and that was about it.

What I learned, however, as I read the ABT brochure, was that there was no tuition required to attend this school, that students worked at on-campus jobs in exchange for their education and room and board. And that was all I needed to know. I wrote away for an application, mailed it back with my transcript, and within a matter of weeks I received a letter in the mail—my acceptance at American Baptist.

Now it was real. I was actually going away, leaving my family and Pike County, leaving everything I knew. It was frightening and exhilarating and unnerving all at once. I graduated from the training school that spring, spent the summer working on the farm, and as fall approached I was getting ready to leave. By the first week in September, my uncle Otis had given me a foot-locker, and now it was packed with everything I owned, which was not much—basically my clothing and my Bible.

Uncle Otis came out to our house the morning I left, gave me a few words of encouragement, then handed me a hundred-dollar bill. I'll never forget that as long as I live. A hundred dollars, *solid*. I'd never held that much money in my hand before.

My brothers and sisters all gave me a hug. My mother cried a little. "Be particular," she said, then went back in the house.

My father and I climbed in the pickup truck, and he drove me into Troy, to the Greyhound bus station, where we bought a ticket to Montgomery and one from there on to Nashville. We shook hands, neither of us saying much more than "Goodbye."

I watched the baggage handlers—two older black men—load my trunk in the bottom of the bus. Then I climbed aboard, showed my ticket to the driver—a white man, pleasant and polite—and made my way to a seat in the back.

As the bus pulled out, I pushed my face against the window, looking for my father somewhere on the platform, wanting to wave goodbye to him.

But he was already gone.

Part II

NASHVILLE

4 / "THE BOY FROM TROY"

*I*t was a week before Christmas 1996 that I most recently returned to Nashville. The nighttime skyline twinkled with holiday lights as I approached from the west on Interstate 40—a highway that didn't exist when I was a student here.

There was a lot of controversy when this interstate was built in the 1970s because of what it did to Nashville's downtown black community. The road cut straight through the heart of black Nashville, taking out churches, bisecting established neighborhoods, essentially separating blacks in north Nashville from those in the center and southern parts of the city. Students at Fisk University, accustomed to walking the eight or so blocks over to Tennessee State, suddenly had their way blocked by an eight-lane interstate highway. Groups of black community activists and businesspeople organized and filed a lawsuit in an effort to stop the construction. Their case made it all the way to the U.S. Supreme Court, where they lost. And so, today, most traffic approaching Nashville from the west shoots directly through—or more accurately, *over*—the heart of the black section of the city.

It was eighteen degrees the night I arrived, Nashville's coldest night of the year. Floodlights shot beams of light into the sky above the center of the city, where a brand-new 20,000-seat entertainment arena was opening that evening with a Christmas concert. The marquee outside announced a show featuring singers Amy Grant and CeCe Winans. Hundreds of men, women and children, bundled against the cold, streamed through the doors of this gleaming, glass-and-steel building as I drove past in the direction of a downtown I hoped I would recognize.

I did not. When I first came here forty-one years ago, the city had just one structure worth calling a skyscraper—the thirty-one-story Life & Casualty Insurance Building. Today there are half a dozen high-rises at least that tall. Some of the city's historic sites—the state capitol, the state supreme court building, the Davidson County courthouse—still stand where they were when I lived here, but little else looks the same. The department stores are gone. The dime stores are gone, replaced by banks and office buildings. People don't shop downtown much anymore. They don't eat here much anymore, either, except for lunch. They work here during the day, then go home at night to their neighborhoods outside the city, leaving the center of the city essentially empty, except for scattered locations like that new arena and a strip of neon nightclubs—honky-tonks, a Planet Hollywood, a Hard Rock Cafe—built for the out-of-town visitors who come to Nashville for its country-and-western flavor.

I hadn't expected to see so much gone of the Nashville I knew. Especially the places I had helped integrate.

Cain-Sloan department store. Gone.

Kress's five-and-dime. Gone.

Woolworth's. Gone.

McClellan's. Gone.

Grant's. Gone.

As I drove up Church Street, a downtown thoroughfare that forty years ago would have been lined with pedestrians doing their last-minute holiday shopping on a wintry night like this, it was eerie to see it so empty and to see all those businesses—battlefields in a nonviolent campaign that was every bit as strategic as a war—gone. The one store still standing from that time, a Walgreen's, no longer has a lunch counter, as I learned from one of its managers. "There *used* to be a lunch counter here, I think," explained a pleasant young man, too young to have been born when I first sat on one of those stools in the spring of 1960, "but they tore it down about twenty years ago."

By the time I checked into a motel that night, planning to drive out to my old college campus the next morning, I half wondered if the campus would still be there.

It was. And it looks almost exactly as I remembered it. Two long brick buildings on a lonely hilltop—The Holy Hill, we used to call it. Oak trees all around. And behind the buildings, a broad, open field sloping down to the Cumberland River. We used to sit in that field for hours, my classmates and I, watching the river flow past, gazing beyond at the Nashville skyline to the south, and talking about God and justice and society.

An NBC television camera crew came to this very field in November 1960 and spent an afternoon filming me and two of my closest classmates and friends, James Bevel and Bernard LaFayette, as we sat in the grass and talked about the desegregation movement we had helped launch a year earlier. The hour-long NBC White Paper report that eventually aired, narrated by Chet Huntley, was titled "The Nashville Sit-In Story." It was a powerful piece of television, broadcast nationally in prime time, something rare in those days for a program featuring black people doing anything besides singing or dancing. Andy Young, in a book he recently wrote about his life, described watching that broadcast with his wife, Jean, in their home in Queens and being so affected by it that they decided right then and there to move back to Georgia. "When the television program ended," wrote Andy, "Jean and I knew that it was time to return home, to the South."

It was bitter cold on this December morning as I walked down that field to the river. The water ran broad and brown, as always. And as always, I kept my distance from the riverbank. I couldn't swim when I was a student here, and I still cannot swim today. I love rivers—the serenity of all that slow-moving water—but at the same time I have always respected, even feared, the power and danger that lies beneath the surface. I felt the same way when I went back to Selma in 1995 and recrossed the Edmund Pettus Bridge on the thirtieth anniversary of our march to Montgomery. Peering over the railing of that bridge down at the deep, wide Alabama River scared me to death, just as it had when I first crossed it along with six hundred other marchers on that awful Sunday afternoon back in 1965.

That afternoon—"Bloody Sunday"—still lay far ahead of me in September 1957, the day I arrived in Nashville to begin college. I was just a boy from the woods, nervous and unsure as I climbed out of the taxicab that had carried me from Nashville's downtown bus station out to the American Baptist campus. The trunk my uncle Otis had given me was lashed with rope to the top of the cab, and the driver—a black man, of course—helped me wrestle it down. That trunk was all I arrived with, that and the hundred dollars Uncle Otis had given me, seven of which I now handed to the taxi driver.

As I hauled my trunk up to the second floor of Griggs Hall, which would become my home for the next four years, I felt very alone, very out of place. Some of the men I passed were just that—*men,* in their thirties, forties and even older. Quite a few had been in the military and now felt called by the Lord to preach the Gospel. Some were married, living in a small section of cinder-block bungalows down near the river.

Most of the seventy or so men who made up the student body—there were fifteen or twenty women as well, living in their own small dormitory—were my age, but even then I felt different. I was small, five feet six and about 135 pounds—the same height I am today, though I now weigh half again as much as I did then. I was shy. And I was very conscious of having grown up on a poor, rural farm. Never mind that many of my classmates came from the same kind of setting in Tennessee or Georgia or Mississippi. I still felt different.

It felt odd now, almost forty years later, to walk into that same dormitory building on this December morning, up those same narrow stairs, past the same communal bathroom with its three open shower stalls, its two sinks and its one urinal. Most of the doors on the hall were locked. The college had closed down for Christmas break, and many of the students had gone home.

But not all of them. The sound of a radio came from one of the rooms, and when the hall phone rang, a large, sleepy young man who looked to be in his early thirties stumbled out of that room to answer it. When he hung up I introduced myself.

"John Lewis," he said, rubbing his chin and squinting his eyes. "Yeah, the civil rights. All those sit-ins."

He told me his name was Mike Flippin. He said that he was thirty-three, a junior, and that he had preached in San Antonio for eight years before coming to American Baptist. He wore a T-shirt inscribed with the logo of Hoi Adelph Hoi, a national preachers' fraternity. He admitted he didn't recognize my name at first, but he knew about the movement that had begun here four decades before.

"I don't know if we today would *have* that kind of courage," he said. "We might talk the talk, but people like you all, you walked the *walk.*"

My old room, Room 202, was locked, but the one next to it was open, and it looked just as mine had. Square, sixteen by sixteen, with two narrow single beds, each bearing a hard blue-and-white-striped mattress. Two battered five-drawer bureaus separated by a pair of equally battered desks. Two tiny closets. Four slim windows.

Spartan, cramped, yes. But back on that September afternoon in 1957, through my seventeen-year-old eyes, these dorm rooms looked palatial. I'd never had a bed of my own. Back home, I had always slept with two or three of my brothers. As I unpacked the green-khaki Army-issue underwear and long johns my uncle Otis had given me, along with two secondhand suits, I felt I was starting a whole new life.

My roommate was an ex-GI from Illinois named Ellis Toney, a serious student whose nose was always in one book or another. He, like so many of my classmates, intended to return home after graduation to become pastor of his church.

Toney was my roommate, but it was a guy across the hall who became one of the biggest influences in my entire life. To say he was loud would be an understatement. To say he was extreme would not say enough. This person was like no one I had ever met before. Wild. Crazy. Nuttier than a nut. Brilliant. Passionate. Eccentric. A man who revered women as much as he revered the Scriptures—and he worshipped the Scriptures so much that he took to wearing a skullcap to honor the prophets of the Old Testament.

His name was James Bevel. He was a semester ahead of me, a Navy veteran born in Itta Bena, Mississippi. Bevel's parents were divorced, so he grew up splitting time between his mother's home in the Mississippi Delta and his dad's place in Cleveland. As a teenager, he spent his summers working in Cleveland's steel mills. He tried his hand at rock and roll, too, singing in a doo-wop group with his brothers and actually signing a contract with a record label. But about that time the Lord called him, and he answered, enrolling at American Baptist, where, in his own words, he set about becoming the classic "chicken-eating, liquor-drinking, woman-chasing Baptist preacher."

I ran into him my first day, his booming voice preceding him as he emerged from the bathroom singing a hymn at the top of his lungs. He always sang or preached in the shower, practicing a sermon aloud, his "whooping" echoing off the bathroom's tiled walls for the whole dorm to hear. We used to laugh and tell him he needed a shower after his shower, he worked so hard in there.

Balding, light-skinned, as short as I was but much taller-acting, wide open in every way, he looked me up and down that first day we met—him standing there in the hallway buck naked and dripping, not a trace of self-consciousness about him—and the first words out of his mouth were a challenge:

"Can you *preach*, boy?"

That was the question that mattered most at ABT. It was the center of our existence from the moment we awoke till we turned out the lights at night. In our classes, at chapel, which we attended three times a week, at lunch and dinner, in our dorm rooms at night, where we'd gather in groups to hear bits of each other's sermons, pieces of improvisation of which we were particularly proud—always the question was, Can you *preach?*

James Bevel could preach. And he could make you think. He loved nothing more than stirring the pot, rubbing somebody the wrong way just to see what would happen. He loved nothing better than a good argument, and it didn't really matter what it was about. It was like push-ups for the brain to him, a workout that made the mind sharper and stronger.

There was no question who the leader was among us that first year. Bevel always set the tone. Years later all that fire and passion would turn him inside out, just the way the movement itself eventually lost its bearings and its balance. But back in those Nashville days, James Bevel had it all together. And he took to me immediately, always calling me Lewis, always trying to tutor me in the ways of the world, always urging me to go with him to pursue women, which I never did. That was a game I simply did not play, not the way Bevel did. He was not particularly attractive, but he had an irresistible confidence about him that gave those around him—men and women alike—no choice but to pay attention and even follow him. He was so sure of himself, he could tell you he had the Cumberland River to give to you and you'd believe it was yours. A great quality for a leader. A great quality for a salesman.

But Bevel could never sell me on joining him when he traveled across town to Fisk or Tennessee State to chase skirts. First, that was just not my style. And second, I had no time. My contract with the college included working for my room, board and tuition. And that meant *working*. Three times a day—breakfast, lunch and dinner—I positioned myself at the cafeteria kitchen sink, where my job was to scrub and clean the biggest, heaviest pots and pans I'd ever seen. I was a skinny kid, but by no means was I weak. Back home I routinely lifted hundred-pound sacks of fertilizer or cornmeal without any problem. But these industrial-sized, cast-iron pots filled with hot water to soak off the food caked inside them just about did me in.

And that was just the lifting. The scrubbing was something else. I spent hours scraping and scrubbing that dried food off the insides of those pots: dried eggs, potatoes and liver—liver was the *worst;* that stuff just did not want to come off. I thought I knew what hard work was after growing up on a share-cropper's farm, but this was the hardest work I'd ever done. My first couple of months I fell into bed each night so sore and tired I thought I'd never get up again.

For that I was paid $42.50 a month, $37 of which went back to the school for my costs. I could hardly afford a social life on the little cash I was able to keep. Books and supplies had to come out of that money. My mother sent me $4 or $5 when she could, and my uncle Otis sent a couple of bills here and there, but money was always a problem. Not that I fretted about it; it was just a fact of life.

Socially, I was probably behind most of my classmates. But beyond the exception of a James Bevel or two, most of us had neither the time nor the inclination to spend much time "romping." We were, after all, ministers-in-training. We were Baptists. We were forbidden to go out dancing. Drinking anything stronger than soda was out of the question. We did have a small student center where you could have a Coke and maybe some cookies, but the music was religious and the conversation was almost always about the Bible.

There were girls, and I can't say I wasn't interested. In fact, I had my first girlfriend, if you can call it that, my freshman year. Her name was Helen Johnson. We spent a lot of time together, walking down by the river, talking. We even had our picture taken together—I still have that picture. I was very taken with her, just a classic case of puppy love. But to her, I was more a little brother than a boyfriend. Helen felt very protective of me—a response I would encounter from women during all the years of my young adulthood. I always looked and acted younger than I was, and women tended to want to mother me, to shield me, to keep the big, bad wolves away. Even after I became chairman of SNCC, there were young women who attached themselves to me simply to protect me, to keep me from getting hooked up with the wrong men...or the wrong women.

I was a square, a real square. I have no problem admitting it. I missed out on a lot of things when I was growing up. In most ways it was a hard life, a serious life, and I was a serious child. When it comes down to it, I don't really feel I ever had a childhood. I feel childhood just passed me by. Which is not all a bad thing. It's probably one reason I often act so childish even today.

Girls, dating, going into Nashville to mix with the students at Fisk or Tennessee State or Meharry Medical School—these were all tangential parts of my life at best. The center of my world was school, and I dove into it with a vengeance. The universe of philosophy and religion was opened to me, and I took to it like a fish to water.

Plato, Socrates, Aristotle, Kant—I devoured their thoughts.

Heraclitus, who said that everything in the universe is in a constant state of change, that nothing stands still—I would walk down to the river, look at that rushing water and feel that truth humming in my blood. *Nothing stands still.*

St. Augustine, who said that man is innately restless, forever restless, until he makes contact with God—his words were music to my soul.

And Kant, asking the rock-bottom question, "What is God?"

And Hegel, whose theory of thesis and antithesis seemed so completely and absolutely *right* to me. It was a professor named Powell—John Lewis Powell—who introduced me to Hegel. Professor Powell would run around the classroom—actually *run*—scribbling ideas along the length of the blackboard, spelling out the dynamics of thesis and antithesis and the process of synthesis. Segregation, he would explain, is a thesis. Its antithesis would be the struggle to destroy segregation. Out of that struggle would come the synthesis: integration. Birth, death and rebirth. Out of a creative conflict—a creative schism, a division and a tension between what is and what should not be—comes the process that results in what *should* be.

I had never heard anything like this. Except for Dr. King's speeches, I had never been exposed to religion beyond the bounds of the Good Book. Now my brain was crackling as it strained to assess and absorb these new ideas. Now I saw philosophical and theological underpinnings for what I'd sensed and deeply felt all my life—that there was a contradiction between what was and what ought to be. This contradiction extended even to training people to preach the Gospel. For the most part, white Southern Baptist churches didn't even want black people to step inside their buildings. Yet within these very institutions, people were being taught that Jesus Christ says to love thy neighbor as thyself. How could that be? How could people reconcile that belief with the way they lived? It was illogical. It was contradictory. I was more convinced than ever that Dr. King was right and the white South was wrong.

It was at this time that I began believing in what I call the Spirit of History. Others might call it Fate. Or Destiny. Or a Guiding Hand. Whatever it is called, I came to believe that this force is on the side of what is good, of what is right and just. It is the essence of the moral force of the universe, and at certain points in life, in the flow of human existence and circumstances, this force, this spirit, finds you or selects you, it chases you down, and you have no choice; you must allow yourself to be used, to be guided by this force and to carry out what must be done. To me, that concept of surrender, of giving yourself over to something inexorable, something so much larger than yourself, is the basis of what we call faith. And it is the first and most crucial step toward opening yourself to the Spirit of History.

This opening of the self, this alignment with Fate, has nothing to do with ego or self-gratification. On the contrary, it's an absolutely selfless thing. If the self is involved, the process is interrupted. Something is in the way. The self, even a *sense* of the self, must be totally removed in order to allow this spirit in. It is a process of giving over one's very being to whatever role history chooses for you.

I had no way of knowing it then, but that sense of being in tune with my destiny would very shortly bring me face-to-face with Dr. King. And in the years ahead, time and again—more times than I could count—it would place me in the center of the crucible of the struggle for civil rights.

Those first months at American Baptist, though, my eyes were on my books. My mind was awhirl with this torrent of new ideas, and my goal in life was to become the best preacher I could. Which meant working night and day on my "whooping."

We all worked on it. Sunday nights we'd gather around a radio in someone's room and listen to the best in the nation—the Reverend C. L. Franklin, for example, out of Detroit. His daughter Aretha would soon make a pretty big name for herself, but in the fall of 1958 it was Aretha's father, the Reverend Franklin, who was the most famous member of that family. He was perhaps the best-known black preacher in the nation, a whooper beyond compare. What made him stand out was his ability to put words together in a way that reached both the Ph.D.s and the "No D."s. He was not just a fire and brimstone guy. He could, as we used to say, "pull it." You could hear his congregation shouting the sweetest words a preacher can hear: "Make it *plain*, brother!" they would shout. "Make it *real!*" He was a master at building his sermon, pacing it, layering it, lifting it level by level to a climax and then, finally, bringing it *home*. No one could bring it home like the Reverend Franklin.

There were others, revivalists like Caesar Clarke out of Dallas, who would travel the country with their sermons. When shows like that came through Nashville, and they often did, we were there.

And then, of course, there was Dr. King. He was everything I wanted to be. But not everyone shared my enthusiasm. In fact, most of my fellow students at American Baptist were at best lukewarm when it came to Martin Luther King. I remember one night a group of us were in someone's room shooting the bull, and Bevel suddenly turned to me and said, "Lewis, why you always preaching this *social* gospel and not the *Gospel* gospel?"

"Well," I said, parroting the words I'd heard Dr. King speak in Montgomery, "I think we need to be less concerned with getting people up to those streets paved with gold and more concerned about what people are dealing with right down here on the streets of Nashville."

"John," one of the others said, shaking his head, "you gotta stop preaching the gospel according to Martin Luther *King* and start preaching the Gospel of Jesus *Christ*."

That feeling right there—that the role of the church was to save souls, to convert people and to guide them to the land of milk and honey—was strong among a lot of religious people at that time. The kind of trouble that a man like Martin Luther King was stirring up, the tension and conflict and chaos he was creating, was not a good thing. In fact, the thinking went, it was in defiance of the Scriptures. If something was supposed to happen here on earth, the Lord would make it happen. Who did King think he was? Did he think *he* might be the Lord?

I wasn't alone in my belief in the social gospel. There were a few others among my fellow students who continued to probe the writings and philosophy of men like Walter Rauschenbusch, a German Baptist preacher who worked in New York's Hell's Kitchen tenements at the turn of the century. Rauschenbusch was deeply concerned with the proper Christian response to the kind of urban suffering he witnessed and dealt with every day. He went on to become widely regarded as the first American to preach the social gospel.

Bevel and most of the others could not care less about Walter Rauschenbusch or Martin Luther King. But that didn't deter me. I was sold on the social gospel, and I began to feel a sense of obligation to *do* something. I began to feel a sense of shame if I did not. Professor Powell liked to quote Horace Mann on the shame one ought to feel if one lives a life making no contribution to humanity. Be ashamed, he said, to leave this world having done nothing to improve the human condition. I take that message with me to this day when I go out to speak to student groups. Do some good, I tell them. Do *something* out of a sense of community, something that is aimed beyond yourself. And be ashamed if you do not.

It was that sense of mission, of involvement, of awareness that others were putting themselves on the line for the cause—the high school showdown in Little Rock, Arkansas, was happening the fall of my freshman year—that moved me to do my part. I remember praying for those brave children in Little Rock as I gathered the courage to go to the president's office at American Baptist and tell him I wanted to start an on-campus chapter of the NAACP.

I had been surprised to learn that the school had no such chapter. One of my classmates, an older student named Harold Cox, had taken me with him into Nashville to several meetings of a local youth chapter of the group. It seemed so natural for there to be a branch right on campus.

But the president disagreed. His name was Turner—Dr. Maynard P. Turner Jr. He had come from Kansas City only a year or so before, and he was in a tough position, very beholden to the white Southern Baptist Convention, which had a strong hand in both funding and directing the college. ABT could ill afford to lose the support of that organization; the college was operating on a shoestring budget as it was. It has *always* operated on shoestrings, ever since its creation in 1924. It still operates that way today.

Dr. Turner was very gracious with me, polite and attentive, but my notion was out of the question. Taking such a step would make it appear that the school was sanctioning the civil rights movement, and that, Dr. Turner told me, was something the college could simply not afford to do.

Looking back, I don't know where I thought I was going to find the time to bring the NAACP to ABT. Dr. Turner's refusal was enough to discourage me that fall, but by the end of that first semester I was stirred even more to take action, to put myself in the path of history. I wanted to be involved. I didn't want to stand on the sidelines anymore.

That was when I decided to apply as a transfer student to Troy State University.

I didn't particularly want to go to Troy State. I was happy at ABT. But I had thought of Troy a lot. Ever since I had watched Autherine Lucy attempt so courageously to integrate the University of Alabama, I had thought about the fact that Troy State, the closest college to where I was raised, to where my family still lived, allowed no black students inside its doors. Just as I had chafed during my entire childhood at the sight of white schoolchildren enjoying facilities and opportunities so far beyond what was available to me, now I felt a searing sense that it was simply, inherently wrong that a black student could not attend Troy State. Call that the thesis. And the antithesis? I would become the first black student to step through those doors.

And so, during that Christmas break of 1957, I sent an application along with a copy of my transcripts to Troy, by registered mail.

I got no reply. One month passed, then two, so I took another step. I wrote a letter to Dr. King.

No one knew what I was doing. I didn't discuss it with any of my classmates. Nor did I mention it to my parents or my sisters and brothers. There was nothing to discuss. This was something I simply had to do. I had no doubt about it.

Soon after I mailed that letter, in which I introduced myself and described my situation, I received a reply from a man named Fred Gray. I knew who Fred Gray was. Everyone knew Fred Gray. He had represented Rosa Parks during the bus boycott and now he was Dr. King's attorney. Mr. Gray asked me for more details. Over the course of the next several weeks I exchanged a series of letters with both him and with the minister of Montgomery's First Baptist Church (Colored), the Reverend Ralph David Abernathy. We spoke on the telephone as well.

Finally, late that spring, Gray and Abernathy wrote to tell me that Dr. King wanted to meet with me. We set a date at the beginning of the summer, when I would be home from school. They mailed me a Greyhound ticket to make the trip.

I was overwhelmed. I was actually going to meet Martin Luther King Jr. I kept telling myself to be calm, that Fate was moving now, that I was in the hands of that Spirit of History. But I was still nervous. I had only just turned eighteen. I was a baby, really. And now I had an appointment with destiny.

The weeks leading up to that meeting seemed to crawl by. I finished my final exams, packed my trunk, said goodbye to my friends at ABT and boarded the bus home to my family.

Soon thereafter, late on a Saturday morning, I climbed onto another bus, this one bound for Montgomery. My father had driven me to the station in Troy, and though he knew what I was doing and where I was going, he didn't say a word about it. No mention of Montgomery. No mention of Dr. King. My father was never much of a talker. I know I picked up some of my quietness and shyness from him. The only words he spoke that morning were before we left home. "Bob," he said, "I think it's time for me to take you to the station." That was all. We rode in silence.

During that bus ride to Montgomery I thought of what I would say to Dr. King. I rehearsed this sentence and that, but nothing stuck. I was anything but calm.

Mr. Gray had given me directions to his office, which was a short walk from the Montgomery station. I'd written the address, 113 Monroe Street, on the piece of paper I held in my hand.

When I knocked on the door, a slender man, about five ten, wearing a nice suit, answered.

"And I presume you're John Lewis?" he said, offering his hand.

"Yes, sir," I answered. "Attorney Gray?"

He nodded, grabbed his hat and his briefcase, stepped out, shut the door behind him and strode past me toward the street. I was excited. I'd never met a black attorney before. I'd never met a white attorney either.

"We're going to drive over to the church," he said.

That would be First Baptist, the Reverend Abernathy's church. When we arrived, Mr. Gray led me down a long staircase to the basement pastor's office. The room was paneled, with one window high up near the ceiling. Sitting inside were two men, one large and dark—the Reverend Abernathy—the other younger, very relaxed, very congenial—Dr. King.

It was King who spoke first, rising behind the desk and smiling across it at me.

"So you're John Lewis," he said, lifting an eyebrow. "The boy from Troy."

Gray and Abernathy chuckled softly.

"I just want to meet the boy from Troy," King said again.

Then Abernathy joined in.

"Who is this young man who wants to desegregate Troy State?" he asked.

I didn't say a word. I was petrified. These men, this moment, this whole thing that was happening, was bigger than life to me. They were checking me out, clearly, and I had no idea what they saw. I had no sense of myself at that moment. I was mesmerized, just listening, just trying to take it all in.

Dr. King and Abernathy did almost all the talking. I don't recall Fred Gray saying a word. King sat behind the large pastor's desk, Abernathy sat to the side, and I sat beside Gray, facing both of them. They questioned me about my background, where I came from, how I'd been raised, who had raised me, and I told them. They asked whether I was truly aware of what I was getting into here. They wanted to know how prepared I was for what I would face, and how committed I was to stick it out. If I took this step, they told me, it was imperative that I stay the course. Better to not begin this at all, they told me, if there was a chance I might quit. There could be no backing out.

I understood, I told them. And I was ready.

"You know, John," said Dr. King, "if you do this, something could happen to you."

He seemed genuinely concerned, troubled even. I remember wondering at that moment—and this was something I would think about again many times over the coming years—how heavy, how terrifying the responsibility must have felt to him for all the people he inspired to take up this struggle.

"It's not just you who could be hurt, John," he continued. "Your parents could be harassed. They could lose work, lose their jobs. They could be assaulted. Your home could be attacked. The farm could be burned."

I nodded.

"All right," said Dr. King. "If you really want to go to Troy State, we will do what we can to help you. We will get the money to fight the legal battle. All that will be taken care of.

"If you really want to do it," he said, "we will see you through."

Abernathy was just watching now, along with Gray. Dr. King did all the talking. He told me I needed to go home and talk this through with my family. Being a minor, I would need my parents' permission to file a lawsuit. He explained it all, and when he was done, we stood and shook hands. I shook the Reverend Abernathy's hand as well.

"We'll be in touch, John," said Dr. King.

Then Fred Gray led me out, back up the stairs and into what had become night in Montgomery.

I was exhilarated. I could have floated back to Troy. The bus ride home that evening was like a dream. Total darkness swallowed the fields outside and I was lost in a swirl of feelings. No thoughts, really. Just sweet, delicious feelings.

My father was there to meet me in Troy, and we drove home in silence. He didn't ask me one question, and I didn't think anything of it. That was his way. But the next morning he and my mother called me into the kitchen and sat me down, and now they both had something to say.

They asked me what had happened yesterday afternoon. I told them. It was what they had expected, what they were afraid of. And they *were* afraid, deathly afraid, not just for me or for themselves, but for the people around us, our neighbors. They were proud, though, as well. They knew who Dr. King was, and he was as large a figure to them as he was to me. They were worried, they told me, but they were willing for me to go ahead with this lawsuit if that's what I really wanted to do.

I was ecstatic, but my joy did not last long. Shortly after that meeting in Montgomery, I returned to Tennessee, where I had arranged, through the college, to teach vacation Bible school in the town of Jackson. I moved in with a host family there—black, of course—and began thinking about the coming fall. Entering Troy State was going to change my life.

But something else changed before that. As the weeks passed that summer, my mother became more and more afraid that they would lose their land, or that their credit at the feed and seed store would be canceled. My father was driving the county school bus by then—the same bus I'd ridden to school each day as a boy—and my mother was afraid he might lose that job. I think she was also concerned about the bombings in Montgomery during the boycott, though she didn't mention them.

She did share her fears about the farm and my father's job. Basically, she had changed her mind. She did not want me to sue. Seeing how she felt, my father changed his mind, too.

I was heartbroken, but I didn't argue. This was their decision, not mine. I needed their blessing, and they couldn't give it. As disappointed as I was, I understood. It was one thing to decide that this was my fight, but I had no right to make it theirs. And so, late that summer, I wrote Dr. King a letter explaining that I had decided to return to Nashville. That was a hard letter to write. I was leaving behind the man in Montgomery whom I thought would change my life. Little did I know that the man who would truly turn my world around was waiting for me in Nashville.

His name was Lawson. Jim Lawson.

5 / SOUL FORCE

When I came back to Nashville in the fall of 1958, it felt like a different place than it had been the year before. There was a sense of urgency and awareness spreading among my classmates and friends, and indeed, among black students throughout the city. There was a growing feeling that this movement for civil rights needed—no, *demanded*—our involvement. This wasn't even just an American movement anymore. Amazing changes were happening in Africa, where Ghana had won its independence a year earlier, opening the door to a black African liberation movement that would soon sweep away much of the centuries-old colonial rule by European powers like Britain, Belgium, Portugal and France.

Zaire, Somalia, Nigeria, the Congo—freedom was stirring in all these places, and we couldn't help being thrilled. Thrilled, but also a little bit ashamed. Here were black people thousands of miles away achieving liberation and independence from nations that had ruled them for centuries, and we still didn't have those rights in a country that was supposed to be free. Black Africans on their native continent were raising their own national flags for the first time in history, and we couldn't even get a hamburger and a Coke at a soda fountain. Here we were, in the capital of the state of Tennessee, and there was only one movie theater that would allow us to enter, and *that* was by way of the balcony. There was something wrong with that, something terribly wrong.

By the fall of '58 my eyes were opening in many ways. Like most college freshmen, I had spent my first year focused primarily on the campus itself, on acclimating myself to life at ABT, to my job and my studies. But now, as I came back for my second year, I started seeing and understanding the city that surrounded me, a city that was already beginning to tremble with the same racial tension that was rising throughout the South.

Nashville at that time was an odd mix of racial progressiveness on the one hand and conflict and intolerance on the other. Its geographic location—at the northern edge of the Confederacy—reflected its split personality. The city changed hands nearly a dozen times during the Civil War. During the ensuing century it established itself as a national center for music, religious publishing and higher education—thirteen colleges and universities were located there at the time I attended ABT. Some people, mostly Nashvillians themselves, called the city the Athens of the South. Compared to other cities in the South, it was a truly progressive place in terms of race. Blacks had seats on the city council. The police force had black officers. Blacks and whites sat beside each other on the city's buses.

But this was still the South, so there was still segregation. In the libraries and theaters, in public schools, in hotels and restaurants, at the lunch counters in department stores, blacks were kept apart from whites or were entirely excluded. There were ongoing attempts to respond to such segregation. Nashville had a significant black middle class, and there had been gestures since World War II from both blacks and whites in the city to establish at least a dialogue among the races. Fisk University, long one of the leading black colleges in the country, annually hosted a gathering of scholars—both black and white—for a conference on the racial situation in the New South. A local group called the Nashville Community Relations Conference, composed mostly of whites, met regularly to discuss and respond to the problems facing the city's blacks. The NAACP, Dr. King's Southern Christian Leadership Conference (SCLC) and the Southern Regional Council all had strong chapters in Nashville. The year I arrived, the city launched what was called the Nashville Plan, aimed at desegregating its schools.

Of course, "eventually" was the operative term. The fact was, despite its relatively progressive stance compared to other Southern cities, Nashville remained rooted in racial division, hatred and even violence. The same year that school desegregation plan was announced, a bomb ripped open a section of the Hattie Cotton Elementary School on the east side of town. Not long after that another bomb exploded at the city's Jewish Community Center, which was known for its efforts toward integration.

All this was in the air the fall of my sophomore year. On campus, in the dorms, in the dining room, wherever you went, it seemed, the talk was of the movement. "Free by '63"—you heard that slogan everywhere. My friend Harold Cox picked right up where he'd left off the year before, bringing me with him into Nashville, mostly to Fisk, to hear every speaker who came through town. There were so many—Fred Shuttlesworth; Daddy King, Dr. King's father; Roy Wilkins; Thurgood Marshall. One day Harold and I were walking across the Fisk campus when W.E.B. Du Bois strolled right past us. I was awed, dumbstruck—but not so paralyzed that I couldn't backtrack, introduce myself and shake that man's historic hand.

A huge event that fall was a mass rally sponsored by the Nashville branch of the SCLC. Dr. King himself was scheduled to speak, but just before the event he was attacked in New York at a book signing for his just-published *Stride Toward Freedom*. A woman stepped out of the crowd gathered around him at a Harlem department store, pulled a letter opener and stabbed him in the chest, shouting, "I've been after him for six years! I'm glad I done it!" Dr. King nearly died from that attack. The blade grazed his aorta. Two ribs had to be removed before doctors were able to pull out the letter opener. In the ensuing weeks, as he recovered at his home in Montgomery, we all wondered what would happen if Dr. King died.

His wife, Coretta, came to that SCLC rally in Nashville, taking Dr. King's place as the keynote speaker. I had never seen her before, and I was struck, not just by her beauty, but by the pure grace of her presence. She was captivating, the way she stood, her hands cupped as she talked about the boycott days in Montgomery. And she sang, all alone on the stage, spirituals like "Steal Away" and "There's a Great Camp Meeting in the Promised Land," and some old slave songs. She recited a poem or two as well. It was mesmerizing, just her by herself, a one-woman show.

Watching Coretta King that day, I felt even more certain that this thing that was swelling around me, this movement, was not going to be stopped. Not by a madwoman wielding a letter opener. Not by men throwing bombs in the night. Not by a government committed to keeping an entire people apart from the country to which they belonged.

Each Sunday that fall I attended services at the First Colored Baptist Church, Nashville's oldest black church. Its roots went back to the 1830s, to slavery, when the blacks sat in the upper balcony while the whites sat below—just the way the movie theater in Troy was shared when I was growing up. The seminal moment in the church's history was the day in 1873 that First Baptist's black congregation, most of them former slaves, jubilantly marched out of that balcony and down the street to a brand-new church they had built for themselves. Frederick Douglass came to speak there, as did many other black leaders during the course of the next half century. By the 1950s, First Baptist had established itself as the church of choice for the upper crust of Nashville's black middle class. Students and faculty from the surrounding universities, doctors, lawyers, private businessmen and -women all filled the church's old wooden pews each Sunday to hear the words of one of the most impressive speakers I had ever listened to, the Reverend Kelly Miller Smith.

This man was not a whooper. He was dignified and sophisticated, an intellectual who made his case with very reasoned, very compelling arguments. Tall and brown-skinned with aristocratically wavy hair, he had come to First

Baptist in 1951 with a degree in divinity from Howard University. In seven short years he had established himself as a progressive force in Nashville. Like Dr. King, he was committed as much to the needs of the community around him as to the disposition after death of the souls of his congregation. When a group of Southern black leaders gathered in Atlanta early in 1957 to form what would become the SCLC, the Reverend Smith was there. And when, a year after that, a Nashville branch of the organization was created, Kelly Miller Smith became its first president, writing in the chapter's initial Statement of Purpose and Principles:

> If we are to see the real downfall of segregation and discrimination it will be because of a disciplined Negro Christian movement which breaks the antiquated methods of resolving our fears and tensions and dramatically applies the gospel we profess.

It wouldn't be long before the Reverend Smith acted on those words, offering his church as the staging area for the waves of student demonstrators who would eventually topple the segregated barriers of downtown Nashville.

But in the fall of '58, the Reverend Smith was simply an inspiration to me, a model, someone we all looked up to. He occasionally taught classes at local colleges, including ABT, where I was one of his students. The subject was homiletics, the art of writing and preaching sermons. This was Reverend Smith's forte—how to organize a sermon, how to build it, brick by brick, testing and stretching concepts and ideas, using logic and dialogue for the purposes of power and persuasion. For my final exam in that class, I created a sermon that questioned the authenticity of Jesus Christ. It was titled "Is He the One, or Should We Look for Another?" I began by building Jesus up, then I tore him down, explaining why he was *not* the messiah. Finally, at the end, I brought him back to his original place. The Reverend Smith loved it. He gave me an "A."

It wasn't Kelly Miller Smith's teaching, though, nor his fine example as a minister and a man that had as much of an impact on my life as a visitor he brought into his church one Sunday that fall. This man had passed through Nashville earlier that year, in his role as a field secretary for a group called the Fellowship of Reconciliation (FOR)—the same group that had published a wildly popular comic book–style pamphlet titled *Martin Luther King and the Montgomery Story,* which explained the basics of passive resistance and nonviolent action as tools for desegregation. The pamphlet wound up being devoured by black college students across the South. I'd read a copy of it myself the year before.

This idea of nonviolent direct action was at the root of the FOR, which actively opposed nuclear weapons testing and war as well as such domestic issues as racial segregation. The group's field secretaries traveled from city to city, teaching the principles and practice of passive resistance in churches and on college campuses. On this particular Sunday, announced the Reverend Smith, an FOR workshop would be held that evening.

I said to myself, This is something I should really attend. And so, about six-thirty that night, I walked into a small room at the church, took a seat along with seven or eight other young men and women, all of us college students, all of us black—I was the only one from ABT—and watched a man named James Lawson introduce himself.

Even before he began speaking, I could see that there was something special about this man. He just had a way about him, an aura of inner peace and wisdom that you could sense immediately upon simply seeing him. He was tall, bespectacled, and about to turn thirty. He'd grown up in Ohio, where he had a life-changing experience when he was eleven: He slapped a white boy who called him nigger. When he went home and told his mother what had happened, she proceeded to give him the first lecture he had ever heard about the concept of Christian love. It was like a conversion experience, said Lawson. From then on he was committed to what he called New Testament pacifism.

He practiced what he preached. When he was twenty-two the Korean War began, and he filed for conscientious objector status rather than register for the draft. This was in 1951, when such protests were extremely rare. Lawson spent fourteen months in jail for his refusal to serve. Upon his release, he traveled to India as a Methodist missionary and became consumed by the teachings of Mohandas Gandhi. When he returned to America in 1956 to study theology in Oberlin, Ohio, he became equally consumed by the work Martin Luther King was doing. The two had so much in common—they were about the same age, they were both black, both ministers—it was only natural that they should meet, which they did in 1957, when King visited Oberlin to make a speech. Soon after that meeting Lawson left school to join the FOR, where he hooked up with a white minister named Glenn Smiley, with whom he began traveling throughout the South, conducting workshops on nonviolence. The two had passed through Nashville early in 1958, and now, come the fall, Lawson had settled in the city with his wife and two children, enrolling as a student at Vanderbilt's School of Divinity and continuing to conduct his workshops for the local community.

That September evening in the back room at First Baptist was more or less just an introduction. Lawson gave a very general talk, an overview of the great religions of the world—Judaism, Buddhism, Hinduism, Islam, Christianity—and he offered the suggestion that all these religions share a fundamental tenet: the concept of justice. This, he told us, would be the theme we were going to explore in the workshops that would begin that Tuesday night—and every Tuesday night thereafter—at a little church over near the Fisk campus called Clark Memorial United Methodist.

Clark Memorial is still there today, a modest redbrick chapel two blocks away from the Gothically imposing structures of Fisk. There are no plaques, no monuments, nothing to suggest that anything historic happened there. It's just a little church on a sleepy street lined with paint-peeled bungalows, dirt yards and barking dogs. But from the autumn of 1958 into the following fall, that little building played a major role in educating, preparing and shaping a group of young men and women who would lead the way for years to come in the nonviolent struggle for civil rights in America.

Those Tuesday nights in the basement of Clark became the focus of my life, more important even than my classes. I'd finally found the setting and the subject that spoke to everything that had been stirring in my soul for so long. This was stronger than school, stronger than church. This was the word made *real,* made whole. It was something I'd been searching for my whole life.

I was an eager student for this stuff, just voracious, and I couldn't have found a better teacher than Jim Lawson. I truly felt—and I still feel today— that he was God-sent. There was something of a mystic about him, something holy, so gathered, about his manner, the way he had of leaning back in his chair and listening—really *listening*—nodding his head, saying, "Yes, go ahead," taking everything in before he would respond. Very patient. Very attentive. Very calm. The man was a born teacher, in the truest sense of the word.

And we learned. We learned about Reinhold Niebuhr and his philosophy of nonviolent revolution. We read Thoreau. We studied ancient Chinese thinkers like Mo Ti and Lao-tzu. We discussed and debated every aspect of Gandhi's principles, from his concept of ahimsa—the Hindu idea of nonviolent passive resistance—to satyagraha—literally, "steadfastness in truth," a grounding foundation of nonviolent civil disobedience, of active pacifism.

We talked a lot about the idea of "redemptive suffering," which from the first time Jim Lawson mentioned the phrase made me think of my mother. Often, when I was growing up, I would hear her groan and moan while she was praying. "The seeds of the righteous must never be forsaken...," she would recite. I didn't know what she was talking about then, but now I was beginning to understand. What my mother was saying, in her Old Testament phrasing, was that we must honor our suffering, that there is something in the very essence of anguish that is liberating, cleansing, redemptive. I always understood the idea of the ultimate redeemer, Christ on the cross. But now I was beginning to see that this is something that is carried out in every one of us, that the purity of unearned suffering is a holy and *affective* thing. It affects not only ourselves, but it touches and changes those around us as well. It opens us and those around us to a force beyond ourselves, a force that is right and moral, the force of righteous truth that is at the basis of human conscience. Suffering puts us and those around us in touch with our consciences. It opens and touches our hearts. It makes us feel compassion where we need to and guilt if we must.

Suffering, though, can be nothing more than a sad and sorry thing without the presence on the part of the sufferer of a graceful heart, an accepting and open heart, a heart that holds no malice toward the inflictors of his or her suffering. This is a difficult concept to understand, and it is even more difficult to internalize, but it has everything to do with the way of nonviolence. We are talking about *love* here. Not romantic love. Not the love of one individual for another. Not loving something that is lovely to you. This is a broader, deeper, more all-encompassing love. It is a love that accepts and embraces the hateful and the hurtful. It is a love that recognizes the spark of the divine in each of us, even in those who would raise their hand against us, those we might call our enemy. This sense of love realizes that emotions of the moment and constantly shifting circumstances can cloud that divine spark. Pain, ugliness and fear can cover it over, turning a person toward anger and hate. It is the ability to see through those layers of ugliness, to see further into a person than perhaps that person can see into himself, that is essential to the practice of nonviolence.

One method of practicing this approach, when faced with a hateful, angry, aggressive, even despicable person, is to imagine that person—actually *visualize* him or her—as an infant, as a baby. If you can see this full-grown attacker who faces you as the pure, innocent child that he or she once was—that we *all* once were—it is not hard to find compassion in your heart. It is not hard to find forgiveness. And this, Jim Lawson taught us, is at the essence of the nonviolent way of life—the capacity to forgive. When you can truly understand and *feel,* even as a person is cursing you to your face, even as he is spitting on you, or pushing a lit cigarette into your neck, or beating you with a truncheon—if you can understand and feel even in the midst of those critical and often physically painful moments that your attacker is as much a victim as you are, that he is a victim of the forces that have shaped and fed his anger and fury, then you are well on your way to the nonviolent life.

And it *is* a way of life. This is something Lawson stressed over and over again, that this is not simply a technique or a tactic or a strategy or a tool to be pulled out when needed. It is not something you turn on or off like a faucet. This sense of love, this sense of peace, the capacity for compassion, is something you carry inside yourself every waking minute of the day. It shapes your response to a curt cashier in the grocery store or to a driver cutting you off in traffic just as surely as it keeps you from striking back at a state trooper who might be kicking you in the ribs because you dared to march in protest against an oppressive government. If you want to create an open society, your means of doing so must be consistent with the society you want to create. Means and ends are absolutely inseparable. Violence begets violence. Hatred begets hatred. Anger begets anger, every minute of the day, in the smallest of moments as well as the largest.

Dr. King would often say that we've got to love people no matter what. Most of all, he would say, we must love the unlovable. Love the *hell* out of them, he would say. And he meant that literally. If there is hell in someone, if there is meanness and anger and hatred in him, we've got to *love* it out.

I had no doubt that this could be done. Gandhi showed it could be done. This one little man, armed with nothing but the truth and a fundamental faith in the response of human society to redemptive suffering, was able to reshape an entire nation without raising so much as a fist. And he did it not by aiming high, at the people in power, but by aiming low, at the downtrodden, the poor, the men and women and children who inhabited the streets and the fields of his country. It is an ancient theme, as old as the Christian Bible: "Blessed are the meek; for they shall inherit the earth.... Blessed are they who are persecuted for righteousness' sake; for theirs is the kingdom of heaven."

Heaven *and* earth. This was the social gospel in action. This was love in action, or what we came to call in our workshops soul force. Jim Lawson knew— though we had no idea when we began—that we were being trained for a war unlike any this nation had seen up to that time, a nonviolent struggle that would force this country to face its conscience. Lawson was arming us, preparing us, planting in us a sense of both rightness and righteousness—"soul force"—that would see us through the ugliness and pain that lay ahead, all in pursuit of something both he and Dr. King called the Beloved Community.

This idea, beyond any other, was the fulcrum of all that Jim Lawson was teaching us. It was at the center as well of everything that Dr. King was working toward. As both men understood it, and as we were taught to believe in our workshops, the Beloved Community was nothing less than the Christian concept of the kingdom of God on earth. According to this concept, all human existence throughout history, from ancient Eastern and Western societies up through the present day, has strived toward community, toward coming together. That movement is as inexorable, as irresistible, as the flow of a river toward the sea. Wherever it is interrupted or delayed by forces that would resist it—by evil or hatred, by greed, by the lust for power, by the need for revenge—believers in the Beloved Community insist that it is the moral responsibility of men and women with soul force, people of goodwill, to respond and to struggle nonviolently against the forces that stand between a society and the harmony it naturally seeks.

This was eye-opening stuff for me, learning that the feelings I'd had as a boy, the exclusion and unfairness that I had witnessed growing up in Alabama, the awful segregation that surrounded all of us there in Nashville and throughout the South—throughout this entire nation—was nothing new. It was mind-blowing to learn that the tension between what was right and what was wrong that had torn at me since I was old enough to think had a historical context, that people of all cultures and all ages had struggled with the same issues, the same questions, the same brutal realities that were facing 1950s America in terms of race, and that their responses, across thousands of miles and thousands of years, had much in common and much to show us about how to deal with the wrong we faced—the wrong of racial hatred and segregation.

These were incredibly powerful ideas, and their beauty was that they applied to real life, to the specifics of the world we walked in. They applied to Byrd's drugstore and to the Troy theater. They applied to the buses I rode to high school and to the all-black classes in which I sat. They applied to the men and women who refused to serve black people at the lunch counters of downtown Nashville. They applied to the admissions office at Troy State University.

There were fewer than ten of us at those first meetings, but soon the number began to grow, including one of my classmates at ABT, a freshman from Florida who would become my best friend. His name was Bernard LaFayette. Tall, slim, talkative—though nowhere near as talkative as Jim Bevel—Bernard quickly became like a brother to me. His mother would send him care packages, typically a pound cake, and the first thing he'd do was walk over to my room and offer me half. I'd do the same with the pies or pecans my mother mailed me. Bernard was outgoing, but he wasn't pushy or aggressive the way Bevel was. In fact, he was one of the few people who could handle Bevel and hold his own in a debate with that human hurricane. Where Bevel would typically bulldoze anyone who tried to verbally tangle with him, Bernard was able to deflect and actually engage him.

I always thought Bernard deliberately tried to come across as a teacher, a professor, but I never imagined that forty years later, today, Bernard LaFayette's life would bring him full circle, back to American Baptist, where his name is now on the door of the president's office. I dropped in to see him during that December 1996 visit, and he was as bright and upbeat as ever, still teasing me about taking everything he owns—we used to share all we had, from clothing to books to, yes, food. His office is the same one the president sat in when we were students. The linoleum floors in the hallways outside are the same ones I mopped and waxed as a student janitor during my junior and senior years.

Truth be told, that redbrick administration building, the grounds outside, the entire campus—save for a new chapel/student center built a few years ago—looks tired, beaten down, near collapse because of lack of support. But Bernard doesn't see it that way. The man is so bright, so positive, so patient, so hopeful. The day I dropped in, it wasn't but a few minutes before a reporter from the local newspaper showed up with a camera. Bernard had called her. He made sure there was a picture of the both of us in that week's paper, a little publicity for the college, any opportunity to maybe raise a few dollars.

I admire that stick-to-it-iveness so much, that willingness to be *out* there, to sacrifice, that belief that somehow, some way, things *will* get better. It was that kind of faith that fueled the movement, but in a way I believe what Bernard is trying to do today at American Baptist is even harder. In the movement, we had tangible, well-defined targets: the lunch counters in Nashville, the bus stations in Birmingham and Montgomery, the courthouse voting registration offices in Selma and Jackson. The entire nation was watching our every step. But Bernard toils in obscurity on that lonesome hilltop above Nashville—no glamour, no glory. He could be doing something else for much more reward, but instead he is there, hanging in, day in and day out. Honestly, I don't know if I could do that. I don't know if I'd have it in me to be the president of a small, struggling black college in the 1990s.

Back in that fall of '58 we were just kids, totally mesmerized by the torrent of energy and ideas and inspiration washing over us every Tuesday night in those Jim Lawson workshops. And when, late that autumn, Lawson told us there was going to be a weekend retreat at a place in the Tennessee hills called the Highlander Folk School, Bernard and I immediately signed up.

I knew about Highlander. We all did. It was created back in the early 1930s by a man named Myles Horton, a liberal white activist who'd spent his entire life working for social justice in every arena from labor unions to racial equality. What Jim Lawson was doing that fall in the basement of Clark Methodist, Myles Horton and his staff had been doing for decades up in those wooded mountains. Dr. King had spent time at Highlander. So had Rosa Parks. Now we were going, and, even more amazing, so was Bevel. I hadn't been able to convince him to come to Jim Lawson's gatherings, but I was able to talk him into taking this weekend trip up to Highlander. Who knows, he probably saw it as an opportunity to meet some women.

And there *were* women there. That was one of the hallmarks of Highlander's reputation, that women were as involved as men in all the seminars and workshops, and were treated with as much respect. In fact, the single person who most impressed me that weekend was a woman—a sixty-year-old organizer named Septima Clark. Her father had been a slave in South Carolina. Her specialty was working with grassroots people—sharecroppers, common folk, black men and women who had little or no schooling—teaching them basic literacy as a first step toward becoming voters. What I loved about Clark was her down-to-earth, no-nonsense approach and the fact that the people she aimed at were the same ones Gandhi went after, the same ones I identified with, having grown up poor and barefoot and black. I sensed then, and this belief would grow as the years went on, that the lifeblood of the movement was not going to be the spokesmen—the schooled, sophisticated, savvy upper crust who might be best at speechmaking and press conferences. They would be the leaders, naturally, but it was going to be the tens of thousands of faceless, nameless, anonymous men, women and children—men like my father, women like my mother, children like the boy I had been—who were going to rise like an irresistible army as this movement for civil rights took shape. Septima Clark was one of those people. Her name might be generally unknown today, but she was a powerful influence on many of us at that formative time.

Myles Horton was just as impressive in his own way. About fifty or so, he'd spent half his life establishing and keeping Highlander going, facing constant attacks on his patriotism and his character from critics who saw the school as nothing more than a breeding ground for Communists. The very fact that Horton's staff and students were racially mixed (this was the first time in my life that I saw black people and white people not just sitting down together at long tables for shared meals, but also cleaning up together afterward, doing the dishes together, gathering together late into the night in deep discussion and sleeping in the same cabin dormitories—men and women separated, of course) was enough to invite investigations and continual attempts by politicians and local authorities to shut the place down.

Horton had seen it all, working for almost thirty years to enlighten and organize a huge range of "students," from Appalachian whites to Alabama blacks. So he was more than prepared to deal with a young guy with a chip on his shoulder, a kid as brash as James Bevel. Bevel was used to challenging everybody and everything. The idea of the social gospel, of nonviolent revolution, was all basically hogwash to him. Which made it all the more amazing to watch Horton—a *white* man—bring Bevel around to the point where he actually listened, where he was actually reconsidering a lot of these ideas. I think the setting had a lot to do with that. There was no arguing with the fact that this place was established, that all these people were here for a strong reason, that there was an undeniable, infectious energy running through this collection of simple whitewashed buildings and well-manicured lawns. It was an energy even James Bevel couldn't resist.

Besides the workshops and the speakers and the discussions, we did a lot of singing at Highlander. It didn't matter whether you could carry a tune or not, everyone sang. Even me, and I *cannot* sing. The song leader was a man named Guy Carawan. He was a regular at Highlander, sort of the resident musician. Tall and lanky, he played a banjo and taught his audiences the tunes he'd learned over the years, including a lot of old folk and protest ballads, as well as spirituals and hymns. He was the first person I ever heard sing "We Shall Overcome," which was actually an old Baptist hymn ("I'll Overcome Someday") combined with a work song used by black union laborers in the 1940s ("We Will Overcome"). It was Pete Seeger, I believe—another regular at Highlander—who adapted the two and fit them together, and the song quickly became a favorite among us all. It perfectly fit the movement we were becoming a part of.

Before we left that weekend, Myles Horton delivered a warning of sorts which turned out to be very wise, very prophetic. Most of us were young, and Horton, a generation older than we, told us never to let any organization or group capture our spirit. He warned us not to allow ourselves to become the slaves of any of the old, established civil rights organizations. And he told us not to ever lose hope, but to keep on going, keep on doing our thing.

Of course I left Highlander on fire. That was the purpose of the place, to light fires and to refuel those whose fires were already lit. Back in Nashville, the Reverend Smith, through the Nashville Christian Leadership Council (NCLC), had been organizing in his own way, inviting local black leaders—men and women like J. F. Grimmet, Mrs. C. H. Fitzgerald, C. T. Vivian and Mrs. C. M. Hayes—to visit our workshops and talk to us about some of the hands-on problems facing the community. Early in 1959, a group led by Smith and including most of these leaders approached the owners of several downtown Nashville department stores and asked them to voluntarily open their lunch counters to blacks. There was little hope that the store owners would comply—and they did not—but the request was a significant first step toward events that would quicken in the coming months.

That summer there was an important gathering at Spelman College in Atlanta. It was called the Institute on Nonviolent Resistance to Segregation. The speakers included Bayard Rustin, whose combination of Quaker and Communist influences earlier in his life had led him in the direction of radical pacifism. Rustin was a colorful character, with his high-pitched singsong voice and circle of Greenwich Village bohemian artist and musician friends. His former Communist connections, along with the well-hidden fact that he was homosexual, were stigmas that would burden him throughout his career. But they didn't stop him from staying centrally involved in the movement. He helped Dr. King organize the Montgomery bus boycott, and he was completely committed to applying Gandhian methods to America's struggle for civil rights, enduring more than his share of jailings and beatings long before any of us experienced ours.

Another speaker at that conference was Ella Baker, who had become a legend of sorts during the previous twenty or so years for her knack of relating to young people. She had single-handedly organized dozens of youth chapters of the NAACP throughout the South, and it would not be long before she became involved with the work that was taking shape in Nashville.

Joining Baker on a panel at that conference was a white minister and writer named Will Campbell. He, too, would become a voice in our Nashville campaign.

And, of course, there were Glenn Smiley and James Lawson, partners as always in preaching and teaching the philosophy and tactics of nonviolent action. "The New Gandhians," that's what they were coming to be called, and we—Lawson's students in Nashville—would soon be called that as well, as our workshops that fall stepped up the pace and began turning toward action.

When school began that fall semester of '59, it became clear that word of our Tuesday night gatherings had spread. A year earlier we rarely had ten people in that room. Now there were often more than twenty, black and white alike, women as well as men, students from Fisk and Vanderbilt, Tennessee State, Meharry Medical School and ABT. Bernard was now joining me every week. Bevel started coming now and then, though he was still holding back, still reluctant.

Among the whites was a Fisk student named Paul LaPrad. He had recently transferred from a school in the Midwest, where he had strong Quaker roots. Slim, tall, blond and soft-spoken, Paul was more a listener than a participant in the meetings. But he was always there. And it would soon become clear, once we began moving in on those downtown lunch counter stools, that he was listening well.

Another student who became a regular that fall was a tall, lanky, cool— very cool—chemistry major from Fisk. His name was Marion Barry. He was older than most of us, a graduate student, and he had the confidence that comes with those couple of extra years. Suave, very suave, from his nicely pressed shirts down to his sleek calf-length socks, Marion would claim his corner of the room and spread himself out, everything about his presence saying, Here I am. He wasn't arrogant, and he wasn't loud or pushy. He was simply relaxed, confident and comfortable with himself.

But the one person who made more of an impact than anyone else on our meetings that fall was a young woman named Diane Nash. The first thing you have to say about Diane—the first thing anyone who encountered her noticed, and there was no way *not* to notice—is that she was one of God's beautiful creatures, just about the most gorgeous woman any of us had ever seen. Small and shapely, with honey brown skin and bright green eyes, she had won more than her share of beauty pageants as a young teen. She was from Chicago, had spent a year at Howard University and had transferred that fall to Fisk, where she was shocked to find so much segregation surrounding her in Nashville. She wasn't used to any of that.

It was Paul LaPrad who told Diane about our workshops, and she came with a lot of doubt at first. But she quickly absorbed all that Jim Lawson had to share, and she soon emerged as the leader in our group, which was an extraordinary thing, considering the role of women in society at large at that time. The role of women in the movement was not much different. There were a lot of black women in visible positions across the board working for civil rights, from Coretta King to Ella Baker and on down the line to so many others. But there persisted an attitude of chauvinism among many of the men that was expressed pretty succinctly a few years later when Stokely Carmichael stated that the only position for females in the movement was a prone position. That was in the mid-'60s, after a feminist groundswell had formed within the ranks of SNCC's women, some of whom staged what they called a "pussy strike," refusing to have sex with any of their boyfriends (or men) in the group until they were treated with more respect.

Stokely was not speaking just for himself. Many other men in the movement felt the same way about women. But that attitude did not infect our Nashville workshops, which is not to say there were not some natural feelings running through our group. Plenty of fellows attending those sessions gave a go at hitting on Diane. You saw resentment among some guys because they thought another guy was making an inroad with her. Early on, everyone wondered why Diane Nash was at these workshops at all, why a beautiful woman like her wasn't out on a hot date with a rich medical student from Meharry. The cliché at the time was that middle-class mothers sent their daughters to Fisk so they could meet and marry a doctor from Meharry.

There seemed to be some jealousy as well among the other young women in the group, like Angela Butler and Peggy Alexander, who were also from Fisk and who couldn't help being envious in the beginning at all the attention Diane was getting. But none of this turned Diane's head. She was dead serious about what we were doing each week, very calm, very deliberate, always straightforward and sincere. As time passed, she came to be seen more as our sister than as an object of lust. We all became brothers and sisters, a family. In the years to come, as the young arm of the movement took shape in the form of SNCC, there would be bickering, head-butting, clashes of ideology and tactics among competing factions. But there in Nashville, in the beginning, we were completely together, totally solid, a unit bound by trust and devotion. We really were our own Beloved Community.

And now we were preparing for action. As that semester went on, we began moving beyond theory and philosophy and started asking ourselves how we could apply these historic and universal principles to the situation we faced right then, right here in America, right there in Nashville. Now that we understood a concept like soul force, our question became how do you *use* soul force? How do you *use* ahimsa? How do you *use* satyagraha?

With Jim Lawson's guidance, we began answering these questions. We started mostly with talk, then we began acting out the kinds of situations we might be confronted with during an actual protest. Lawson taught us specific tactics to protect our bodies during an attack. He showed us how to curl our bodies so that our internal organs would escape direct blows. He told us how important it was to try to maintain eye contact with our assailant even as the blows were raining down because that eye contact could be a viscerally disarming thing. He showed us how to help one another, how if one person is taking a beating, others could put their bodies in the way, diluting the force of the attack.

We role-played, teaching ourselves how to respond to verbal and physical assaults. We staged little sociodramas, taking turns playing demonstrators and antagonists. Several of us would sit in a row of folding chairs, acting out a sit-in, while the others played waitresses or angry bystanders, calling us niggers, cursing in our faces, pushing and shoving us to the floor. Always, Jim Lawson would be there, hovering over the action, pushing, prodding, teaching, cajoling. It was not enough, he would say, simply to endure a beating. It was not enough to resist the urge to strike back at an assailant. "That urge can't *be* there," he would tell us. "You have to do more than just not hit back. You have to have no *desire* to hit back. You have to *love* that person who's hitting you. You're *going* to love him."

It was intense. Things were moving now. The group was growing. By the end of October we had formalized ourselves, taking the Nashville Student Movement as our name. A central committee was created, a core group of us who would represent the others in terms of decision-making and speaking for the group. The chairmanship of that committee, we agreed, would continually rotate—Myles Horton's warning about not trusting established organizations extended as well to the dangers of passing power into the hands of individual "leaders." We were determined that our leadership would be shared. No one person would own that title. There would be no power in that position, not if we could help it. This was about group effectiveness and responsibility, not individual power.

That idea alone weeded out a few people right there at the beginning. Among the people showing up at the workshops that fall were some student government leaders, people very involved in campus politics. For them, this sort of activity—*any* kind of organized activity—represented an opportunity to take control, to direct, to lead. That seemed to be almost a mindset among many of the people involved in traditional student politics. It was almost like a game to them, a contest of dominance and control, personality and popularity.

Well, the notion that we would have no leader in that traditional sense, that we would share our leadership among one another, did not go over well with some of those campus politicians. Two of them—a couple of guys named Luther Harris and Earl Mayes—were able to maneuver themselves into position as our first two central committee chairs, but they wound up serving only a week apiece before resigning from the group.

Our third chairman was Diane, who would hold that position several times in the months to come. So would I. We would all take turns in the coming campaign, at everything from chairing the committee, to being beaten, to going to jail.

By November we were itching to get started. We had our training, and toward the end of that month we established our target. Jim Lawson spent as much time out in the community visiting local church and business groups as he did with us, and the black women of Nashville had made it clear to him which specific form of segregation in the city bothered them the most. It was no contest. They all pointed to the downtown department stores and five-and-dimes where they shopped alongside white women and children, bought the same items at the same prices, but were forbidden in most cases to try on clothing and were barred in all cases from resting their feet and those of their children at the stores' lunch counter seats. It was humiliating, they said. It was insulting.

This, we decided, was where it would begin.

The last Saturday of that month, November 28, about a dozen of us gathered at First Baptist, the Reverend Smith's church. Marion Barry was there, as was Diane. The men among us wore coats and ties, the women skirts and blouses. Our plan was simple. Today would be a test, nothing more. We would simply enter a store, ask to be served, and if—or *when*—we were refused, we would leave. No issues would be forced, no confrontations created. Our aim was simply to establish the issue, and in the process to dip our toes in the water, to get a taste of the setting in which things would soon get real—very, very real.

Our target that Saturday morning was a downtown department store called Harvey's. With its reasonable prices and its "customer is king" approach, Harvey's was one of the most popular stores in the city. A lot of black people shopped there. Its clerks had a reputation for treating all shoppers, black or white, with courtesy.

I had been in Harvey's many times, and I always felt that familiar sting each time I walked past the lunch counters located at the back of the store on both the first and second floors. I was always reminded of having to carry my combination outside Byrd's drugstore to drink it. I felt a similar pang every time I passed the Harvey's rest room marked "COLORED MEN."

Jim Lawson, the Reverend Smith and a handful of other adults were at the church to see us off. Three cars were ready, each driven by a First Baptist member. I climbed in the one driven by Mrs. H. B. John, who was very active in the NAACP.

I was nervous. We were all nervous. We didn't know what to expect. All my life I'd heard, seen and obeyed the rules. You can't use that library. You can't drink at that fountain. You can't go in that bathroom. You can't eat in that restaurant. I hated those rules, but I'd always obeyed them. Until now.

It was a short drive, just a few blocks, to Harvey's. The sidewalks were crowded with weekend and Thanksgiving shoppers. So was the store. No one paid much attention as we walked in. The plan was to purchase something—it didn't matter what—and then, after establishing ourselves as legitimate paying customers, sit down at the lunch counter for a bite to eat.

I bought a hanky. Then I joined the others and walked to the end of the counter they called the Monkey Bar—a fast-food section of the store's restaurant where you could get a quick sandwich or hamburger.

No one seemed to notice us take our seats, not immediately. We spaced ourselves along the counter, in groups of two and three. We'd been there a minute or so—it seemed like an hour to me—when a waitress turned and saw us. She was middle-aged, dressed in white and very polite.

"I'm sorry," she said. "We can't serve you here."

She was very nice about it, not nasty at all. I'm sure she thought we were students from someplace up north, someplace where blacks were allowed to eat in a restaurant like this. We just didn't know any better.

"May we speak to the manager?"

That was Diane's voice. Calm, firm. Part of the discipline, part of the plan, was that one and only one person would speak for the group. On this day, we had designated Diane.

The waitress looked a little confused. She hadn't expected this. As she left to go find the manager, she glanced back at us and said something to another woman in white.

We waited.

Shortly, a middle-aged white man wearing a suit approached. He identified himself as the manager. He was very polite—all Harvey's employees were very polite.

"It is our policy," he said, "not to serve colored people here. This is the policy of our store."

Diane nodded, then asked about the white students among us. Could *they* be served?

No, said the manager. Because they were with us, they could not.

Then we all stood. Diane thanked the man, and we left.

No harsh words. No violence. No one even paid much attention. Just a ripple of whispers and comments among a handful of shoppers who happened to see what had just happened.

When we got back to the church, Lawson and the others were waiting. We detailed what had happened, step-by-step. He told us we'd done superbly. I came back to my dorm that afternoon elated, just about ready to burst. I told a few of the guys what had happened. Some seemed interested, but most really didn't care. They had sermons to work on.

So did I. But I was in no state of mind to get any schoolwork done, not that night, not that entire week. Every day, beginning the next evening, we met with Lawson, planning another test for the following Saturday, and even more importantly, planning our course of action beyond that. These tests were a prelude to a massive assault, a series of sit-ins that would involve hundreds of students. How many sit-ins for how long a time would depend on the response of the stores and the city. We would not stop until the policy of segregation at those counters was ended. It was that simple.

And it was that complicated. We had yet to organize and train those hundreds of students in the philosophies and tactics Jim Lawson had spent months teaching us. We had yet to plan our "attack." Which stores would we target, and when? We had to decide what we would do if we were arrested. Would we post bail? If so, where would that money come from? If not, who would steer the effort while the others sat behind bars?

Word of this impending student campaign began spreading through black Nashville. Words of encouragement and moral support came from adults like Mordecai Johnson, the president of Howard University and a frequent visitor to Nashville, and Z. Alexander Looby, a highly regarded West Indian–born attorney who had become one of the first black elected officials in the South when he was elected to the Nashville City Council in 1951.

They were all behind us as we staged our second test sit-in the following Saturday, December 5. This time the target was a department store called Cain-Sloan, which was a bit more upscale than Harvey's, with higher prices and a much smaller black clientele.

About eleven-thirty that morning we arrived, a racially mixed group of eight students.

This time we were expected. I can't say for certain, but I'm convinced to this day that Harvey's manager—Greenfield Pitts was his name—must have called some of his colleagues during the week, warning them of what had happened in his store.

In any event, before we could even sit down, a white woman in a green-and-white waitress uniform confronted us and said, "We don't serve colored people."

This time I was the spokesman.

"May I speak to the manager, please?"

The manager appeared and gave us a replay of the previous Saturday. He too was polite. He too recited his store's policy.

I thanked him, and again we walked out without incident.

Again Lawson debriefed us back at the church. Again I came back to ABT excited, very pumped. The semester was coming to an end. It was time to turn to my classes, take my final exams, then head home for Christmas. The next semester, I knew, we would be taking the last step. No more tests. Now the stakes would be raised. Now it would be real.

That was all Bernard and I could talk about a week before Christmas as we boarded a bus at the Greyhound station in Nashville for the holiday ride home. I was bound for Troy; Bernard was going on all the way to Tampa.

No sooner were we settled into our seat, right behind the driver, than the man turned around and told us to move.

"To the back," he said. "You can't sit there. You sit in the back."

The last thing in the world we were going to do was move from that seat. We didn't say a word. And we did not budge.

The man looked furious.

"I'm going to get off and go inside," he said, just about spitting out the words. "When I come back, you better be out of there."

He did. And we weren't.

So he slid into his seat, pulled a lever on the side and jammed the seat back as far as it could go.

Our legs were shoved up against us, our knees raised toward our chins.

And that's the way we rode, all the way to Birmingham, where another driver came on, then on to Montgomery, where I got off for the transfer to Troy and Bernard switched buses for Tampa.

Our legs were sore, but our spirits were sky-high. Christmas lay ahead, and then the New Year, which would be new in ways neither of us could imagine.

6 / "NIGRAS, NIGRAS *EVERYWHERE!*"

January 1960 was not just the beginning of a new year, it was the start of a new decade. And America as a whole seemed to feel that freshness, that optimism that comes with turning a corner and taking a new direction. The ugliness of the McCarthy era was gone, though the threat of the Soviet Union still loomed large. There were no major crises overseas, though brushfires were crackling in Cuba and Vietnam. The economy was booming—at least for mainstream Americans—and the impending presidential race gave people plenty to talk about: Would the Democrats nominate the Southerner Lyndon Johnson or the luckless Adlai Stevenson, the liberal Hubert Humphrey or the young Catholic from Massachusetts, John Kennedy? And who would the Republicans offer to replace President Eisenhower—his vice president, Richard Nixon, or the wealthy governor of New York, Nelson Rockefeller?

All these issues were in the air, but the only news that mattered to me as I returned to school early that month and resumed my habit of reading each morning's edition of the *Nashville Tennessean* at the ABT library was news of the movement. That term "movement" was beginning to look as if it might actually apply to American society at large, to the nation's attitude about and response to the struggle for racial equality. Three years earlier the first civil rights bill since Reconstruction had been passed by Congress, and now another was being discussed, not just in Washington but by newspaper and television commentators across the country. Whoever ran for president was going to have to deal with this issue. It wasn't something the politicians could afford to ignore any longer.

Which did not mean that any of us in Nashville intended to simply sit back and wait for change to take place. Forces were gathering in this country in terms of civil rights—there was a general sense that momentum might be beginning to mount—but we weren't about to just sit on the sidelines and see what happened. There were issues to be forced, and we were going to do what we could to force them.

Throughout that January the numbers at our weekly workshops swelled. Dozens of students, black and white, joined us and began taking crash courses in nonviolent action. Blacks played white roles in our training socio-dramas, and whites played black. It was strange—unsettling but effective, and very eye-opening as well—to see a black student pushing a white off a chair, screaming in his or her face, "Coon!" and "Ape!" and "Nigger!," or to see a white student shoving a black, yanking his or her hair, yelling, "White trash!" and "Nigger lover!"

We had moved to a larger upstairs room at Clark now, and we sometimes met on Thursdays in addition to our standard Tuesday evening gatherings. We were getting all kinds of involvement and all kinds of responses from those who came. There were medical students from Meharry who couldn't commit to putting themselves on the line in public—they were planning to become doctors and were understandably worried about what an arrest record might do to their careers. There were athletes unwilling to risk their scholarships. There were participants who knew themselves well enough and were honest enough to admit that they just did not have it in them to endure taunting and spitting and beating without either fleeing or fighting back.

Many of these people stepped aside, and no one held it against them. Many more offered behind-the-battle-lines help—maybe driving carloads of student demonstrators from pickup points on the various campuses to First Baptist Church, which we had decided would be our launching area; maybe working at the church itself, helping handle the logistics of processing what could be as many as several hundred students moving on downtown Nashville; or maybe helping with communication, getting messages and updates from one place to another, from churches to campuses, from the Student Central Committee to the Nashville Christian Leadership Council (NCLC). There was the simple matter of keeping everyone fed. There was the need to develop a plan for dealing with the press to achieve the most favorable publicity. Even something as simple as painting protest signs wouldn't just happen by itself.

There was so much to organize, so much to prepare for. That was what we were doing as January drew to a close. We were close to ready, though no specific date had yet been set for our first sit-in. And then, on Monday, February 1, as fate—or the Spirit of History—would have it, someone else made the move for us.

They were four guys in Greensboro, all of them freshmen at North Carolina A&T College. They had no plan, no preparation. One of them had read that FOR comic book about King and Montgomery, they had begun talking about the process of nonviolent action, and on this particular afternoon they simply decided it was time for them to do something. Which they did, taking four seats late that day at the whites-only lunch counter of Greensboro's downtown Woolworth's store and touching off what would come to be called the sit-in movement across the South.

It happened so spontaneously, so suddenly, that the next morning's newspapers contained no accounts of the incident. It was not until Wednesday, two days later, that the names of those students—Joe McNeil, Ezell Blair, Frank McCain and David Richmond—were published and word of what had happened in Greensboro began to spread.

I first learned about it reading our dorm mother's copy of the *Tennessean* that Wednesday morning. I felt a rush—not one of those "I can't believe it" responses, but rather a feeling of "Well, of *course.*" I *could* believe it. I wasn't surprised at all. Sit-ins had happened here and there over the previous three years in more than a dozen Southern cities. In every case they had been isolated incidents, small splashes hardly noticed by the press or the general public. But this one would turn out to be different. This one would start a wave, and we in Nashville would soon find ourselves on top of it.

That same Wednesday, Jim Lawson got a telephone call from an old friend of his in Durham, North Carolina, a Methodist minister named Douglas Moore. Moore, like Lawson, had been working for some time teaching students about the philosophy and practice of nonviolence. When he heard about what had happened in Greensboro, fifty miles from Durham, Moore had rushed there to find the number of protestors swelling almost by the hour. On Tuesday, nineteen students, black and white, had joined the original four at Woolworth's. Wednesday, the number had ballooned to eighty-five, and "sympathetic" sit-ins were taking shape in Durham and Raleigh. Moore knew about our preparations in Nashville, and he was calling now to ask Lawson if we were ready to go.

We discussed that question that evening at a mass meeting in Fisk's chemistry building auditorium. More than five hundred students filled the seats and spilled into the aisles to hear Jim Lawson announce that we would be staging sit-ins at all of Nashville's major department stores and that volunteers would be needed. What we had in mind, what we had been planning for months, was something on a far larger scale than any such protest that had ever taken place before. Now, with the pace quickening, we did not want to act impulsively. We were speeding up our schedule, yes, but we remained determined to do this right. We did not want to unleash hundreds of eager, emotional college students without properly preparing them in the ways of restraint. But we no longer had weeks to do our teaching. Now it was a matter of days.

We spent the next week in daily gatherings, briefing everyone who could attend on the essentials of sitting in, on the behavior that would be demanded as they entered those downtown stores. No aggression. No retaliation. No loud conversation, no talking of any kind with anyone other than ourselves. Dress nicely. Bring books, schoolwork, letter-writing materials. Be prepared to sit for hours. Study, read, write. Don't slouch. No napping. No getting up, except to go to the bathroom, and then be sure there is a backup to fill your seat while you're away. Be prepared for arrest. Be prepared to be taken to jail.

Finally came the evening of Friday, February 12. The next morning we would begin. A crowd of close to six hundred students and adults filled the pews and aisles of First Baptist Church. News of bomb scares and Klansmen in Greensboro and mass arrests in Raleigh had many people—mostly the adults—worried. Jim Lawson presided over a discussion that immediately turned into a debate. Some of the adults argued for a delay. The Reverend Smith was worried about the fact that the NCLC had a mere $87.50 in its treasury—nowhere near what it would cost to cover the bail of those of us who were bound to be arrested. Other NCLC members stood to support Smith, saying we should wait a couple of weeks so money could be raised in the churches. Even Jim Lawson stood on the side of caution, warning that too many in the crowd that night had yet to be trained for what we were about to do the next day.

But there was no stopping this thing now. The hundreds of students in that room were dead set to sit in the next day. We weren't about to wait. We were young, we were ready. We had nothing to lose. We didn't owe anybody anything. We weren't tied to the community the way Kelly Smith and the other adults were. We were young, free and burning with belief—the perfect foot soldiers for an assault like this.

And so Lawson wound up giving yet another short course in nonviolence right there from Kelly Smith's pulpit, detailing everything from the dress code—coats and ties for the men, stockings and heels for the women—to the pickup points at campuses across the city where we would need to gather the next morning to be transported to the church. Finally, we sang. Then we prayed. Then we went home to sleep, if we could.

I couldn't. In the years to come I would have dozens of nights like this—before a sit-in, or a march, or a protest of one sort or another—and they would always be the same. You feel a mixture of fear and excitement. There's a stirring inside as well, the sense of a power beyond you, of a calling, a mission. That's a strong feeling, and it does help calm the soul.

But doubt lingers, the feeling of not knowing what to expect. There is never a way to know what will happen that next day. I don't care how many times you do something like this, how many times you sit in, or march, or in any way put yourself in the path of those who might do you harm, you can never know what's going to happen and you can never become complacent.

Never do you have the feeling, Ho hum, here we go again. It's different every time. It's dangerous every time. It's more real and more vividly gripping than any experience I can imagine. And it's totally unpredictable. You can prepare and make plans, but in the end you have to hand it over to the spirit, just let the spirit take control.

That's why the song came along, the one we would sing over and over during the demonstrations:

> *I'm gonna do what the spirit says do,*
> *If the spirit says sit in, I'm gonna sit in,*
> *If the spirit says boycott, I'm gonna boycott,*
> *If the spirit says go to jail, I'm gonna go to jail,*
> *I'm gonna do what the spirit says do.*

The spirit. That's what I thought about as I finally slipped off to sleep in my dorm room late that night.

And when I awoke that morning and went to my window, I couldn't believe what I saw.

Snow.

A half foot of snow. A deep blanket of white covering everything in sight. I'd seen a little bit of snow growing up in Alabama, but never anything like this.

I really believed it was an omen, something to do with the order of the day. Everything felt so soft, so hushed, almost holy. Pure as the driven snow. Clean. Innocent. That was the setting. That was us.

I had my outfit laid out—a white shirt, print tie and the same light blue suit I'd bought for my high school graduation. That would become a trademark of sorts for me in the years to come, the light blue suit. I still wear one now and then today on the floor of the House.

When I arrived that morning at the staging area, First Baptist, dozens of others were already there. The atmosphere was intense but calm. Very sober, very serious. No one was goofing around. Very few were even talking. We knew what we had to do. We were ready. We had each been assigned to a group, twenty-five or so people per group. One or two groups had been assigned to a particular store, depending on the number of lunch counters inside. A central committee member had been assigned to each group as the designated spokesperson.

Eleven o'clock came. A few of us prayed together—nothing massive, nothing formal. And then it was time to go.

We walked out of the church, 124 of us, two abreast, quiet, solemn, into the snow and toward downtown Nashville. Passersby didn't know what to make of us. They thought it might be some sort of Saturday morning parade. Or maybe a funeral.

Several city blocks away we arrived at a place called the Arcade, an old mall of sorts, an open-air marketplace built back in the 1920s. The building was a couple of stories high, but the ground floor was open at both ends. You walked in one end, past vendors and small shops, and when you came out the other side, you were on Fifth Avenue, Nashville's busiest shopping street. Kress's, Woolworth's, McClellan's—all the five-and-dime stores were right there on Fifth Avenue.

My group headed to Woolworth's. As we entered we drew looks from the shoppers inside but nothing more. No comments. No confrontations. No one there had any idea what was going on. No one knew how to react.

There were two lunch counters, one on each of the store's two floors. Our target was upstairs.

The first thing we each did was make a small purchase—a notebook, a handkerchief, whatever. No one tried to stop us.

Then we went up. The counter ran along one mirrored wall. Behind the long row of seats was a railing over which you could look down on the first floor below.

As we took our seats, we were careful to leave empty stools among us. This allowed regular customers an opportunity to be served and to sit beside us if they so chose.

A few people were already there eating lunch. No one got up. No one said anything. A waitress came out from the kitchen, stopped when she saw us, then picked up a cloth and began wiping the counter. She didn't say anything, but the next waitress who came out stopped dead in her tracks.

"Oh my God," she said to no one in particular, "here's the niggers."

These were middle-aged women, pleasant enough in their white uniforms and delicate hairnets. There was no anger in them, just bewilderment, nervousness and maybe a little bit of fear.

As that day's designated leader, I asked if we could be served.

"We don't serve niggers here," one of the women said. A couple of the customers left then. The others soon followed.

Then a woman came out from the back with a sign in her hand, a crude, handwritten sign:

COUNTER CLOSED

Minutes later the lights in that section of the store were shut off, and the waitresses left. And there we sat, in semi-darkness, alone.

There was natural light enough to read by, and that's what some of us did. Others pulled out schoolbooks and binders and did their homework. Every once in a while I got up and walked the length of the counter, asking everyone if they were okay, making sure everyone stayed calm.

The afternoon passed. Groups of shoppers downstairs gathered and stared up at us, whispering among themselves. One witness later told a reporter it was like a scene from a science fiction movie, where a stunned city is laid siege by aliens or giant grasshoppers.

As the hours went by there were some taunts from a group of young white men who came upstairs and stood behind us.

"*Niggers,*" they said. "Go home."

"What are y'all *doing* here?" one of them asked.

We kept our eyes straight ahead. No response. Those men soon left. And then, finally, at about six that evening, word came that it was time to go. We had set up a system of runners to deliver messages from the church to the groups in the stores and to bring news back to the church about what was happening downtown. When our runner said it was time to go, we stood and walked out in as orderly and silent a fashion as we had arrived.

It couldn't have gone any more smoothly. When we got back to First Baptist, it was like New Year's Eve—whooping, cheering, hugging, laughing, singing. It was sheer euphoria, like a jubilee. The other sites had gone just as well as ours. Kress's had closed just like Woolworth's. McClellan's took a little longer but wound up shutting down its counters as well. Diane described watching a jittery waitress drop dish after dish on the floor. Two girls from another group told how they left to use the "whites only" ladies' room and walked in on an elderly white woman who exclaimed, "Oh! Nigras, Nigras *everywhere!*" before fleeing.

No one wanted to leave the church. Everyone was so up, so elated and eager to keep going. What next? they wanted to know. What do we do next?

I went back to First Baptist during that Christmas 1996 visit and found nothing but a gravel parking lot where the church used to be and a plaque telling passersby that this was where Kelly Miller Smith's church once stood, the site where the Nashville sit-ins began. The church was razed in 1972 and rebuilt about a quarter mile down the hill. A low-slung modern building, the new sanctuary sits today near the interstate and the railroad tracks. On a Friday morning I could hear the rumble and clanks of a passing freight train as I walked through the front doors.

A group of three women sat at a back room table, collating and stapling a stack of church mailings. I started to introduce myself, but one of the ladies smiled and waved me silent.

"Oh, I'm *up* on you, John Lewis," she said, coming around the table to give me a hug. "I'm up on *all* of our young men."

Her name was Beulah Hardge. She'd lived in Nashville all her seventy-nine years, she said, most of it over on Jefferson Street. She'd been coming to

First Baptist since she was a young girl, and she was right here, "right in the middle of it," she told me, during that spring of 1960.

"My children were too young to take part," said Mrs. Hardge, "but I did what I could. We all did. Making sandwiches, raising money, we *all* did whatever we could."

I looked at Mrs. Hardge—white-haired, stout, still going strong at seventy-nine—and I thought that her name should be on that plaque up the hill, hers and the names of hundreds of thousands of others in cities throughout the South who made the movement what it was. Yes, we marchers and demonstrators filled the streets and went to jail. But beyond us, *behind* us, were the people nobody ever saw, the Beulah Hardges of the world.

It's hard to believe it was thirty-eight years ago—nearly half Mrs. Hardge's life and two thirds of mine—that I sat with the others in those pews on that snowy Saturday night, soaking in the sweet sensations of our first sit-in and asking ourselves what was next.

Next was that Thursday, the eighteenth. This time there were close to two hundred of us. My group went to W. T. Grant's. Again the counter was closed. Again we stayed the afternoon, this time about four hours. Again there was minimal response from employees or onlookers. White Nashville was just not ready for this. It had never had to deal with black people this way. These waves of well-dressed, well-behaved young black men and women were something no one had seen before.

We *wanted* them to see us. We planned each sit-in to begin around lunchtime because we wanted people to be there when we arrived. We wanted white people, everyday citizens, everyday customers to be exposed to us, to see us as we were, not as something in their minds, in their imaginations. We wanted them to watch how we responded to the people who refused to serve us. And we wanted them to watch those people as well. Among so many other things, this was about education, pricking consciences, teaching one race about another, and, if need be, about itself. If some of these white onlookers went back to their own homes, their own jobs, their own churches, and began talking about this in heartfelt terms, about what they had seen, then we had achieved one of our main objectives.

Two days later, on Saturday, the twentieth, we marched 340 strong to the same four five-and-tens we'd been to before. We also added Walgreen's to the list. Now there were hecklers inside the stores and small angry crowds outside, complaining to reporters that they now had no place to eat lunch.

The stores were now beginning to counterattack. The managers at Kress's and McClellan's ordered employees to stack goods—wastebaskets, blankets, lampshades, pots and pans—on the lunch counters to keep us from studying.

There was no violence, but temperatures were rising. This could not go on for-ever. Sooner or later the city would have to respond in one way or another.

That night the store owners asked for a moratorium, promising to come up with a response, what they called a proposal. Jim Lawson met with us, the central committee, and we agreed to wait. But by the end of that week, when we'd heard nothing, we said enough. Saturday we would sit in again.

This time, though, the city was set to respond. Late that Friday afternoon we got word from Nashville's chief of police, a man named Hosse, that any-one involved in further protests would be arrested for disorderly conduct and trespassing. There were also rumors of planned attacks by groups of young whites, attacks which the police would do nothing to stop.

This was what we had prepared for. That night Bernard and I let ourselves into the ABT administration building—as a janitor, I had my own set of keys—and "liberated" a ream of mimeograph paper. Though many of the stu-dents who would be sitting in the next day had been trained, our numbers were swelling so fast that there were hundreds who had not. So I wrote up a basic list of dos and don'ts to be distributed the next day:

DO NOT: 1. Strike back nor curse if abused.
             2. Laugh out.
             3. Hold conversations with floor walker.
             4. Leave your seat until your leader has given you permission to do so.
             5. Block entrances to stores outside nor the aisles inside.

DO: 1. Show yourself friendly and courteous at all times.
             2. Sit straight; always face the counter.
             3. Report all serious incidents to your leader.
             4. Refer information seekers to your leader in a polite manner.
             5. Remember the teachings of Jesus Christ, Mahatma Gandhi and Martin Luther King. Love and nonviolence is the way.

MAY GOD BLESS EACH OF YOU

Bernard and I, with the help of a young administrative secretary, made five hundred copies of the leaflet that night. Then we locked up and left.

The next morning there were fewer than a hundred of us gathered in the pews at First Baptist as we listened to Will Campbell, the white minister I'd first met at Highlander, warn us of the danger waiting for us downtown. Campbell, who had been run out of Oxford, Mississippi, a couple of years earlier for playing Ping-Pong with a black janitor, had come to Tennessee to work with the religious community. He was also a member of the Nashville Council of Churches, as well as one of the few white members of the NCLC. He'd been to a few of our meetings, supported us completely and had come down this morning to tell us he'd heard from some of Nashville's white community leaders that the police did indeed intend to make arrests that day. He said there might be violence as well, attacks from onlookers.

There was no question we would continue, no debate, no protest from any of the adults. We knew that sooner or later the stakes would be raised. It was a natural step in the process, a step we had practiced and prepared for. Our workshops had been like little laboratories in human behavior and response to nonviolent protest. Now we were seeing real humans respond in almost exactly the ways Jim Lawson had taught us they would. The danger waiting for us this day was to be expected, which didn't mean I wasn't a little bit nervous. But by now I was so committed deep inside to the sureness and sanctity of the nonviolent way, and I was so calmed by the sense that the Spirit of History was with us, that the butterflies were gone by the time we left the church and headed downtown.

To the five stores we'd already struck, we added a sixth target this day—Cain-Sloan. As we walked en masse toward the Arcade, we faced the typical taunts we'd come to expect from white onlookers, mostly teenagers. But this time there was some pushing and shoving, which was new, and which the police, who were in sight along the way, did nothing to stop. I learned later that after we'd passed through the Arcade, a black teenager who worked at one of the stores there and had nothing to do with our group was badly beaten by some of those young white toughs. It was sickening to hear that.

As soon as my group entered our target store, Woolworth's, we were confronted with a group of young white men shouting, "Go home, nigger!" and "Get back to Africa!" They jabbed us as we passed and chided us for not fighting back. "What's the matter? You *chicken?*" they teased, trying to force the situation onto terms they were comfortable with—fists and fighting.

We weren't playing by those rules, of course, and that infuriated them even further. No sooner did we take our seats at the upstairs counter than some of these young men began pushing the group at the downstairs restaurant off their stools, shoving them against the counter, punching them.

We immediately went down to join our brothers and sisters, taking seats of our own. I was hit in the ribs, not too hard, but enough to knock me over. Down the way I could see one of the white men stubbing a lit cigarette against the back of a guy in our group, though I couldn't tell who it was in the swirl of the action.

I got back on my stool and sat there, not saying a word. The others did the same. Violence does beget violence, but the opposite is just as true. Hitting someone who does not hit back can last only so long. Fury spends itself pretty quickly when there's no fury facing it. We could see in the mirror on the wall in front of us the crowd gathered at our backs. They continued trying to egg us on, but the beating subsided.

At the same time, we would learn later, the same thing was happening in the other stores. Yellow mustard was squeezed onto the head of one black male student in Kress's while the crowd hooted and laughed. Ketchup was poured down the shirt of another. Paul LaPrad, being white, attracted particularly brutal attention over at McClellan's. He was pulled off his stool, beaten and kicked by a group of young whites with the word "Chattanooga" written on their jackets—a reference to recent white-on-black attacks in that city that had followed a series of sit-ins there.

A television camera crew was at McClellan's, recording the scene as LaPrad's attackers spent themselves. It filmed Paul—bloody and bruised and silent—pulling himself back on to his chair. When the footage aired that night on national television, it marked one of the earliest instances where Americans were shown firsthand the kind of anger and ugliness that the peaceful movement for civil rights was prompting in the South. Many viewers were sickened by what they saw. They would see more in the years to come.

We didn't sit there long before the police, conspicuous by their absence during the attacks, arrived. I didn't imagine they had come to arrest anyone for assault, and I was right. As the young men who had beaten us looked on and cheered, we were told that we were under arrest for "disorderly conduct."

It was strange how I felt as a large, blue-shirted Nashville police officer stood over me and said without emotion, "You're under arrest." A lifetime of taboos from my parents rushed through my mind as the officer gripped me by the bicep of my left arm. *Don't get in trouble. Stay away from Love Street. Only bad people go to jail.*

I could see my mother's face now. I could hear her voice: *Shameful. Disgraceful.*

But I felt no shame or disgrace. I didn't feel fear, either. As we were led out of the store single file, singing "We Shall Overcome," I felt exhilarated. As we passed through a cheering crowd gathered on the sidewalk outside, I felt high, almost giddy with joy. As we approached the open rear doors of a paddy wagon, I felt elated.

It was really happening, what I'd imagined for so long, the drama of good and evil playing itself out on the stage of the living, breathing world. It felt holy, and noble, and good.

That paddy wagon—crowded, cramped, dirty, with wire cage windows and doors—seemed like a chariot to me, a freedom vehicle carrying me across a threshold. I had wondered all along, as anyone would, how I would handle the reality of what I had studied and trained and prepared for for so long, what it would be like to actually face pain and rage and the power of uniformed authority.

Now I knew. Now I had crossed over, I had stepped through the door into total, unquestioning commitment. This wasn't just about that moment or that day. This was about forever. It was like deliverance. I had, as they say in Christian circles when a person accepts Jesus Christ into his heart, come home. But this was not Jesus I had come home to. It was the purity and utter certainty of the nonviolent path.

When we got to the city jail, the place was awash with a sense of jubilation. With all these friends, these familiar faces piling out of those wagons, it felt like a crusade, as if we were prisoners in a holy war. We sang as we were led into cells much too small for our numbers, which would total eighty-two by the end of the day. Cubicles built for three or four prisoners were jammed with fifteen to twenty of us each. The police could hardly keep up with the waves of students who were replacing one another back at those lunch counters. No sooner would one group be arrested than another would take its place. Once word spread back to the campuses what was happening downtown, students arrived at First Baptist literally by the hundreds, angry, outraged, and ready to put their own bodies on the line. Even the adults stood ready to join. C. T. Vivian, an ABT graduate who was now pastor of a small church near Fisk, urged his fellow NCLC members to join him on the sit-in line. "We'll let our vacant pulpits be our testimony tomorrow morning," he proclaimed.

But by then word had come that the police had stopped the arrests. They couldn't deal with the numbers they were facing. And there was no more room at the jail.

I learned later that among those hundreds of students who responded to word of our arrests that afternoon was Jim Bevel. Until then Bevel had refused to have any part of this campaign. He came to one or two of the workshops, more out of curiosity than anything else, but he refused to sit in. Now, though, this thing had become personal. When he heard that Bernard and I were in jail, Bevel rushed downtown and tried everything he could to get arrested. Unfortunately, the police weren't taking anyone else in at that point, and Bevel, in a kind of comical way, wound up free—free and very, very frustrated.

Meanwhile, those of us in jail faced the issue of bail. The NCLC had now raised more than $50,000 in bail money for us—a mind-boggling leap from the $87.50 they'd had in their treasury two weeks earlier. The police, wanting nothing more than to be rid of us, dropped the bail from the required $100 per person to $5 apiece. But it didn't matter. We weren't about to pay bail. We were in jail because of racial segregation in Nashville. Until that segregation was ended, we had nowhere else to be—we *belonged* nowhere else—but in those lunch counter seats or behind bars.

We were happy to be in jail for this cause. We welcomed it. If the authorities chose to release us, fine. We would walk out freely and resume the task at hand. But we were not about to *pay* our way out. We were not about to co-operate in any way with a system that allowed the discrimination we were protesting. Instead, we sang. We sang, and we chanted: "Jail without bail!"

It didn't take Nashville's powers-that-be long to realize it was fruitless to try forcing us to pay our way out. At eleven that night, after about six hours behind bars, we were released into the custody of the president of Fisk, Dr. Stephen J. Wright. With him were reporters and about two hundred cheering students.

We were exultant. Those six hours had been an act of baptism for all involved. We felt as if we'd won a huge victory. We felt that way the next day when we saw newspapers trumpeting the violence and arrests with huge headlines. A rally was staged late that morning, Sunday morning, with more than a thousand students from across the city jammed into Fisk Memorial Chapel to hear President Wright wholeheartedly endorse what we were doing. This was a big step. Up to that point Dr. Wright had been cautious, as anyone in his position might be. He had to answer to a board of trustees. He had parents calling from all over the country complaining about the trouble their sons and daughters were getting into, children they had trusted him to take care of. Not just racial lines were being drawn here. There were also generational lines *within* our race—lines that separated the older, conservative blacks from their offspring. We, the younger generation, were saying, in effect, we are moving on now. You can be with us and come, or you can stay and be left behind, but we are *moving* on.

Dr. Wright announced that morning that he and many others in Nashville's established black community were with us. He was the first black college president in the country to take such a stand. We were euphoric.

The next day we went to court—the eighty-two who had been arrested, along with more than two thousand supporters. We marched as a group from First Baptist to the downtown Davidson County Courthouse. With us walked Z. A. Looby, the attorney. He, along with his partners, Avon Williams and Bob Lilliard, had offered to represent us, free of charge, of course.

What we faced that day was almost as predictable as what we had faced in those downtown lunchrooms. The judge, a man named Harris, began by announcing his intention to try us in groups of half a dozen or so each. Part of his aim was to demonstrate a conspiracy on our part. Looby immediately objected, making a motion that we be tried individually. Harris would have none of it. He hardly seemed to be listening.

So we were tried group by group. Looby—dark-skinned, in his early sixties, a Trinidad native with a captivating West Indian accent—stood to make our case. He explained that far from disturbing any peace, we had been completely peaceful customers completely compliant with the laws, that it was the mob that had moved in and beaten us and had disturbed the peace. Not only did Harris appear not to listen, he actually turned his back on Looby, swung his chair around and faced the wall as our lawyer made his argument.

Finally Looby threw up his hands. "What's the *use!*" he said, cutting short his comments and returning to his seat.

The judge then found us all guilty. He gave us the option of paying a $50 fine each or serving thirty days in the county workhouse.

That's when Diane Nash stood and spoke for all of us.

"We feel that if we pay these fines," she said, "we would be contributing to and supporting the injustice and immoral practices that have been performed in the arrest and conviction of the defendants."

This was big. This was historic. It wasn't just Nashville that was looking on. The whole nation was watching as we were led back to jail.

It seemed that almost every move the city made backfired. No one had ever had to deal with this situation before. There was no model, no map, no blueprint for the Nashville authorities to follow. They had to make their own mistakes, and they were making them. The sight of many of Nashville's— many of the *nation's*—finest young men and women being led off to jail was bad enough. But when the city followed through with its workhouse routine, sending these students out into the streets to shovel snow and pick up trash, it prompted outrage from all over the country. Telegrams of support arrived from Ralph Bunche, Eleanor Roosevelt and Harry Belafonte.

Meanwhile the sit-ins went on. Two days after we were jailed, we got word that there had been sixty-three arrests at the Nashville bus terminal. Among those arrested: Jim Bevel. After Bernard and I were taken to jail, Bevel had come to the next meeting and insisted on not just joining a group targeting the bus station, but *leading* it. Classic Jim Bevel. And, of course, he *did* wind up leading that group, first to the bus station and then into jail. Now he was with us all the way.

The following day, March 3, the mayor of Nashville, Ben West, ordered our release. Like the city itself, he had a relatively progressive reputation on race. He seemed a pleasant enough man, always wearing a bow tie. You often heard the phrase "a friend of the Negro" used with his name—which could simply have meant he was not as openly hostile to blacks as many of his counterparts in other Southern cities. It did not necessarily mean he was ready to reach out and risk his job and his reputation to help.

What West did was name a biracial committee to study the situation of segregation in the city. He asked us to halt the sit-ins while the committee looked into the problem, and we agreed. Again we came out of jail with a sense of triumph. Bevel, in particular, was near rapture. As intense as he normally was, now he was almost in an altered state. Now he had a specific place to funnel all his energy. He became a true believer. I really think Jim Bevel changed that day. You no longer saw him trying to make it with every woman who walked by. He just seemed more focused after this.

That same day, while Mayor West was announcing his plan to defuse the sit-ins, something just as significant was happening across the city, on the Vanderbilt campus. The chancellor and trustees of the university ordered the dean of the Divinity School to dismiss James Lawson. Two days earlier Lawson had been among a group of local black leaders who met with the mayor. During the meeting Lawson had stepped forward to say that an ordinance used by the store managers to justify closing their counters was "a gimmick to manipulate the Negro." None of the whites at the meeting knew who Lawson was. Neither did the reporters covering it for their newspapers. Until then, as far as white Nashville knew, Jim Lawson did not exist.

But when he was confronted by the press after that meeting and calmly answered their questions, telling them of the work he had been doing with us over the past year and a half, the authorities suddenly had a target. An instigator. A rabble-rouser. A "flannel-mouthed agitator," as the *Nashville Banner* put it in an editorial published the next day.

The day after that Lawson was dismissed. Cut off the head, the thinking went, and the body would fall. But again, things did not work out as the powers-that-be had planned. First, there was a backlash among the Vanderbilt faculty and staff, four hundred of whom temporarily resigned in protest of Lawson's dismissal. The case got national coverage, including a front-page story in *The New York Times,* and the college wound up with more than a little bit of egg on its face.

Meanwhile, we continued our work, Lawson or no Lawson. The authorities underestimated us and the training we'd received. When they learned of Lawson's role, they assumed we were nothing more than easily influenced college kids under the sway of a mesmerizing adult. But they soon found out differently.

We honored the March 3 moratorium on downtown sit-ins, but on March 16, Diane and three other students went to the Greyhound terminal to test not a local law but a federal one. A 1955 Interstate Commerce Commission ruling had established that public facilities in interstate transportation terminals had to be integrated. No one had tested the ruling until recently, when lawsuits had been filed in several Southern cities. On this day Diane and the others meant to do the same thing we'd done with the downtown stores—push the issue.

Surprisingly, when they sat down at the bus terminal restaurant, they were served. When the manager was asked why by a reporter, she said it was because of "this ICC thing."

The ICC, however, had no sway over Nashville's department stores, whose lunch counters continued operating as always while the mayor's committee kept meeting. By the last week of the month, we decided we'd waited long enough. On the twenty-fifth, a Friday, more than a hundred of us marched from First Baptist to nine downtown stores, dramatizing our displeasure with the slow movement of the mayor's group. There were no arrests. When footage of that day's protest aired on national television, Tennessee governor Buford Ellington was irate. "These sit-ins," he told reporters, "are instigated and planned by and staged for the convenience of the Columbia Broadcasting System."

CBS. Another outside agitator. But there was no way the governor or the mayor or anyone else could complain that outsiders had anything to do with the stories being written almost daily by a young *Tennessean* reporter named David Halberstam. When we had first begun, he had been the only one covering us. This was his beat, and we always made sure he knew what we were doing. We realized from the beginning how important media coverage was. We knew we needed the press to get our message out, and early on this tall, skinny guy with his big brown eyeglasses *was* the press. The *Tennessean* was, by Southern standards, a moderate, even liberal newspaper, and Halberstam was allowed by his editors to cover us fairly and accurately. If he had any problem with being objective, it might have been that he was sympathetic to us, and it showed. He was *like* us in many ways—about the same age, young and idealistic. Beyond that, I think he sensed the historic importance of what he saw happening. I think he felt as fortunate to be in that place at that time doing what he was doing as *we* felt about what *we* were doing. Like so many journalists in the coming years, I think he felt lucky to be there to tell our story.

No one could accuse David Halberstam of being an outside agitator. And no one could say outsiders had anything to do with the next stage of that spring's siege to desegregate Nashville—a black community boycott of all downtown stores.

It had begun quietly, almost invisibly, in late March. No one knew quite where it started, but it became organized and communicated through the churches. "Don't Buy Downtown" was the simple slogan, and it was amazingly effective. Estimates were that black Nashville spent as much as $60 million a year in the city, a figure which meant even more to downtown merchants who had seen many of their white customers move to the suburbs in recent years and were depending increasingly on the black buyers who remained.

By the beginning of April, those stores stood virtually empty. One leader at a local black Baptist church asked every person in the congregation who had not spent a penny downtown in the previous two weeks to stand. Everyone in the room rose.

White people, too, were staying away. Some were wary of the violence and disturbances caused by the sit-ins. Others joined the boycott as a sign of support for our cause. A few white women went down to their favorite Nashville stores and made a visible show of turning in their credit cards as their own act of protest.

Easter was approaching, normally a boom time for the clothing stores. Everybody wants to get a new outfit for Easter. A new dress, a new hat, a new pair of shoes, something to show off at church on Easter morning—it's a tradition, certainly among the black community. But black Nashville's motto that month was "No Fashions for Easter," and it had its effect. One downtown store owner stood staring out his door at the deserted sidewalks and said to a reporter, "You could roll a bowling ball down Church Street and not hit anybody these days."

It was those empty streets—and empty cash registers—that brought an offer from the mayor's committee on April 5. The downtown businesses had agreed to set up a system of "partial" integration, a three-month trial period during which they would serve blacks separately in designated sections of the formerly whites-only restaurants.

We couldn't believe that *this* was their proposal. All it showed was how little they understood what we were doing and why we were doing it. Their suggestion smacked of the "separate but equal" doctrine that had been struck down six years earlier by the Supreme Court's *Brown* v. *Board* decision. Couldn't they see that this was not about sandwiches and salads? It was not about being allowed to sit separately at a counter. It was about nothing less than being treated exactly the same as the white people with whom we shared citizenship in this country.

Worse than the inability of the white members of that committee to recognize that "partial" integration was the same as partial *segregation* was the endorsement of the proposal by the committee's two *black* members—Fisk president Wright and the president of Tennessee State University, W. S. Davis. This felt like a betrayal of sorts to us, more evidence of the differences between the generations.

And if even more evidence was needed, it came the next night, as Thurgood Marshall, who was seven years away from becoming the nation's first black U.S. Supreme Court justice, arrived at the Fisk gymnasium to address an audience of more than four thousand. The atmosphere was intense as Marshall began by praising what we had accomplished with our sit-ins. But then he told us we were making a mistake by staying in jail and refusing bail. The way to change America, Marshall maintained, was the way the country's black power structure had been doing it since the 1940s—through the courts. Take a single case, put the power of the NAACP's lawyers—of whom Marshall was one of the best—behind it and force the issue legally. "Once you've been arrested," he told us, "you've made your point. If someone offers to get you out, man, get out."

It was clear to me that evening that Thurgood Marshall, along with so many of his generation, just did not understand the essence of what we, the younger blacks of America, were doing. It was clear a year later, when I wound up on a panel with Marshall at a conference on race relations sponsored by Fisk and heard him say we were wrong to continue taking our Freedom Rides to such dangerous places as Montgomery and Birmingham, where our young people were beaten, and Jackson, where they were imprisoned. It's a waste, he said. You'll get people hurt, he told us. You'll get people killed.

Maybe so, I answered. And I made clear that I did not want to discredit all that had been achieved by the process he believed in, the path of the courts. But that path was a slow, laborious one. And there are times in history—and this was such a time, I said—when more immediate, more dramatic means are called for, when the people themselves must be asked to put their own bodies and hearts and spirits on the line. That is what we believed in, what we were all about—a mass movement, an irresistible movement of the *masses.* Not a handful of lawyers in a closed courtroom, but hundreds, *thousands,* of everyday people—disciplined, peaceful people—taking their cause and their belief to the streets.

Thurgood Marshall was a good man, a historic figure, but watching him speak on that April evening in Nashville convinced me more than ever that our revolt was as much against this nation's traditional black leadership structure as it was against racial segregation and discrimination.

Five days after Marshall's speech, we resumed our sit-ins. A week after that—Easter weekend—a conference organized by the SCLC's Ella Baker was held at Shaw University in Raleigh. The SCLC in general, and Dr. King in particular, wanted to pull together and harness some of this student energy that was sweeping the South. Our central committee in Nashville met to discuss who would make that weekend trip. We couldn't all go. Some of us needed to stay behind to help guide the sit-ins which were still in progress. I offered to stay. Diane, Bernard and Marion went, along with Jim Lawson, whom Baker had asked to give a keynote address.

The organizers expected about a hundred or so students to show up. Three times that many arrived. They listened to Dr. King urge them to become part of the SCLC, but his request didn't get a lot of enthusiasm from this young crowd seeking a new direction. Jim Lawson's words were more to their liking. He spoke to the very issue Thurgood Marshall had addressed in Nashville two weeks earlier, but he, of course, took the other side, criticizing the NAACP as "too conservative," taking it to task for not tapping into "our greatest resource, a people no longer the victims of racial evil, who can act in a disciplined manner to implement the Constitution."

The gist of his speech, summarized in a subsequent student report on the conference, was that the movement had moved beyond traditional avenues. Laws had been changed, but society—at least in the South—was not responding. "Unless we are prepared to create the climate," the report stated, "the law can never bring victory."

Baker herself, in a speech titled "More Than a Hamburger," praised our success so far but warned that our work had just begun. Integrating lunch counters in stores already patronized mostly by blacks was one thing. Breaking down barriers in areas as racially and culturally entrenched as voting rights, education and the workplace was going to be much tougher than what we had faced so far. She had another warning as well, the same one Myles Horton had given us at Highlander: Don't let anyone else, especially the older folks, tell you what to do. Think and act for yourselves. Hold onto your energy and your vision. Keep it pure. Keep it real.

The weekend ended with the creation of a formal student-run group that would coordinate and organize the entire sit-in movement, as well as whatever lay beyond. The name they gave themselves—*ourselves*—was the Continuations Committee, which was shortly changed to the Student Nonviolent Coordinating Committee, or SNCC. Or, as we quickly came to pronounce it, simply *snick*.

Diane and the others got back to Nashville late Sunday evening. I couldn't wait to hear what had happened. Monday morning I was up early, preparing to head over to Fisk for our 6:30 A.M. central committee meeting. We always met early on Mondays so the undergrads among us would be able to get to our 8 A.M. classes. And then there were the med students, who would walk over from Meharry, still wearing their surgical scrubs, with stethoscopes stuffed in their pockets, and take part in the meetings, then hurry back to their shift at the hospital, exhausted but energized.

I was just heading out that morning when the hall phone rang. To this day

I can't recall who was on the other end of the line. I guess that's because I was so stunned by the message.

There had just been a bombing. At Mr. Looby's house.

I couldn't believe it. I grabbed Bernard and we caught a ride over to Clark. By the time we arrived, the place was crawling with students. The phone was ringing. Rumors were flying. The facts quickly took shape.

At five-thirty that morning someone in a passing car had thrown dynamite at the Looby home. The blast blew away the front of the house and shattered 147 windows at Meharry's Hubbard Hospital a block away. Mr. and Mrs. Looby, whose bedroom was in the back, were miraculously unharmed. No one was injured.

The intent was clear. At first we students had been a target. But there were too many of us. Then it was Lawson, our visible leader. Now it was Looby.

If the blast was meant to scare us, however, it had the opposite effect. By noon, nearly two thousand students, faculty and townspeople had gathered at Tennessee State to march on city hall. We—the central committee, along with Lawson and C. T. Vivian, who had hurried over to Clark at first word of the bombing—had decided that morning to march and had sent the mayor a telegram telling him we were on our way.

I had never seen anything like the scene as we moved toward city hall that day. The nation had never seen anything like it. This was the first such mass march in the history of America, the first civil rights assault on such a scale. People kept coming and coming. The newspapers said there were three thousand of us, but I think that figure is low. I'm certain the number was closer to five thousand.

We walked three and four abreast in complete silence, blacks and whites, ten miles through the heart of Nashville. People came out of their homes to join us. Cars drove beside us, moving slowly, at the speed of our footsteps. The line looked as if it went on forever. Everyone was very intense, but very disciplined and very orderly. It was a stupendous scene. There was some singing at first, but as we neared city hall it stopped. The last mile or so, the only sound was the sound of our footsteps, all those feet.

Diane and C. T. Vivian were at the very front. I was a row or two back from them. When we reached city hall, Mayor West, in his bow tie and hat, came down the steps out front to meet us.

Vivian spoke first, saying how outraged we were that such a thing could happen in this city. The crowd exploded with applause at that. When West began to respond, Vivian cut him off and the two argued for a minute or two. Then West made a plea with us to be peaceful.

"You all have the power to destroy this city," he said. "So let's not have any mobs."

He went on to say he would enforce the laws without prejudice, but that he had no power to force restaurant owners to serve anyone they did not want to. Then he said, "We are all Christians together. Let us pray together."

To which one of our students shouted, "How about *eating* together?"

Then Diane stepped forward. She held a typed list of questions, which we'd come up with that morning. When she asked West if he would use "the prestige of your office to appeal to the citizens to stop racial discrimination," his answer was succinct.

"I appeal to all citizens," said the mayor, "to end discrimination, to have no bigotry, no bias, no hatred."

Then Diane asked the million-dollar question, pushing the mayor to be specific.

"Do you mean that to include lunch counters?"

Now West was rankled.

"Little lady," he said, "I stopped segregation seven years ago at the airport when I first took office, and there has been no trouble there since."

Diane didn't budge.

"Then, Mayor," she said, boring in, "do you recommend that the lunch counters be desegregated?"

"Yes," said West.

The crowd exploded, cheering and applauding.

"That's up to the store managers, of course," West added, a little awkwardly. But those words were drowned out. All anyone had heard was the word "Yes." That's the word that rang out in the next morning's *Tennessean*, which ran a front-page banner headline:

INTEGRATE COUNTERS—MAYOR

The downtown store owners, most of whom were tired of the sit-ins and ready to open their lunch counters but none of whom wanted to go first, read that headline. Now they could make the move and put the blame on the mayor.

A measure of the importance of that march was the arrival of Dr. King in Nashville the next night. When I heard he was coming, I felt a rush inside. The last time I had seen him was in that basement office in Montgomery two years earlier, when I'd met with him and Abernathy and Gray. Now he was coming here to salute us.

Again the Fisk gym was packed. Loudspeakers were set up outside for the hundreds who could not get in. I was inside, squeezed in the crush of the crowd, when an announcement was made that the gym had to be cleared. There had been a bomb threat.

It took a long time for everyone to move outside, and even longer to move back in. But nobody left. No one wanted to miss this. And Dr. King did not disappoint. He called our movement "the best organized and the most disciplined in the Southland." It was like a dream, really, hearing this same voice I'd listened to on the radio as a boy, now praising Diane, Bernard, Bevel, me and all the others for the work we'd done.

"I came to Nashville not to bring inspiration," he told the crowd, "but to gain inspiration from the great movement that has taken place in this community."

The place erupted.

"No lie can live forever," said King as he drew to a close. "Let us not despair. The universe is with us. Walk together, children. Don't get weary."

Twenty days later, after several meetings with city officials and store owners, we agreed on a carefully orchestrated series of test servings downtown. We would arrive only in small numbers, on specified days, at specified times. The press agreed to limited coverage. No one would claim victory, which was no problem for us. A fundamental principle of nonviolence is that there is no such thing as defeat once a conflict is justly resolved, because there are no losers when justice is achieved.

At 3:15 on the afternoon of May 10, 1960, the six downtown Nashville stores we had marched on, sat in and been arrested at during the previous three months served food to black customers for the first time in the city's history.

This, of course, was just a beginning. We still had miles to go before Nashville could be called a desegregated city. Sit-ins, marches, arrests and beatings would continue for the next four years as our student movement turned to hotels, movie theaters and fast-food restaurants across the town. I would be part of many of those demonstrations, but there was something else waiting in my immediate future, something that would carry me far beyond Nashville and even deeper into the movement.

That something else was a bus.

Part III

FREEDOM RIDE

7 / "THIS IS THE STUDENTS"

I lost my family that spring of 1960. When my parents got word that I had been arrested—I wrote them a letter from the Nashville jail explaining what had happened and that I was acting in accordance with my Christian faith— they were shocked. Shocked and ashamed. My mother made no distinction between being jailed for drunkenness and being jailed for demonstrating for civil rights. "You went to school to get an education," she wrote me back. "You should get out of this movement, just get out of that mess."

My parents were in no danger themselves, nor were their jobs. Nashville was worlds away from Carter's Quarters. But still there was talk around them, not among the white community, who neither knew nor cared about someone like me, but among our neighbors. *"Y'all hear about Eddie and Willie Mae's son gettin' in all that trouble up in Tennessee?"* That's the sort of thing my mother and father were hearing. And then there was the fact that I had lost any desire to be a preacher. That bothered them just as much—if not more—than the shame of my arrests.

It all added up to a schism that would take years to close. I continued to go back to Alabama for a couple of days each summer and for holidays, but starting in 1960, Nashville—and later Atlanta—became my home. And the movement became my family.

That spring and summer, further sit-ins in Nashville were suspended while we carried out the orchestrated integration of the city's downtown lunch counters. We—the central committee—began mapping out a campaign that would begin the next school year, aimed at the restaurants beyond downtown, at movie theaters, at segregated hotels and grocery stores. We also launched a local voter registration drive that May—a seedling compared to the massive campaigns that would grow in the coming years in Mississippi and Alabama and Georgia. I was still a year shy of voting age myself, but that didn't keep me from helping to canvass Nashville's black churches and neighborhoods, joining my student movement colleagues as we made speeches, passed out instructional leaflets and wore large lapel cards that read:

WE SAT IN FOR YOU
NOW STAND UP FOR US

Nearly four hundred black citizens responded and registered that spring as a result of our drive. That might not sound like many, but at that time, in that place, it was a significant number.

I also spent that spring and summer traveling to college campuses up north and out west. The University of Wisconsin, the University of Michigan, the University of Minnesota—places like that began inviting me, Diane, Bernard, Marion, Bevel, Angela Butler, Curtis Murphy, Kenneth Frazier and other Nashville Student Movement members to visit their campuses, meet with student organizations, guide discussion groups and conduct workshops. Typically we'd travel alone. We'd arrive at a campus, stay at a dorm or fraternity house and meet with the students there. Our expenses were paid either by the groups themselves or, in some cases, by local civil rights organizations in those areas.

The benefits of those trips ranged from the educational aspect—sharing and spreading the knowledge and experience of nonviolent resistance that we'd gathered in Nashville—to building a national, networked student movement. There was also the benefit of financial support, as groups on these campuses and in these cities began sending us money. Starting that summer, the student movement in Nashville became one of the best financed in the country, second only to SNCC headquarters in Atlanta.

But there were drawbacks to this outreaching as well. Kids from these campuses up north—in most cases they were white students—started coming down to Nashville, just dropping in, itching to get involved, to be part of what was happening here, to see what this sitting-in was all about. They were swept up by the excitement, which was not a bad thing in itself. Early on we had seen—and Jim Lawson had reiterated—that what we were doing in Nashville was not just about desegregating one city, but about desegregating the entire South. We needed the kind of national support that was starting to stir that summer.

But when these students started coming south on their own, with no plan or direction, dropping in on us totally unannounced, they presented problems. Often there was simply nothing going on for them to be a part of. That summer of 1960, for example, was basically a silent period in Nashville. We'd take the time to walk some of these visiting students around and give them a little show-and-tell about what had happened here and there in February and March and April. Some of them would be carrying cameras and taking pictures, like tourists. But most were more serious than that, chomping at the bit to *do* something, which presented problems as well. What were we supposed to do, manufacture a demonstration for the benefit of these undergraduates from the University of, say, Illinois, or these kids from up in Oshkosh?

When the demonstrations resumed that fall, some of these students became liabilities. They would come down on their own and charge right in, getting themselves arrested on traffic violations, whatever, and bringing accusations from local authorities that our campaign was riddled with "outside agitators." I can recall one group from the University of Minnesota that came down and did just that, got themselves arrested—for something that had nothing to do with our carefully planned demonstration—and prompted charges of "outside conspiracy" from a city spokesman.

This entire issue of who exactly should be involved in this student movement, as well as the debate over white involvement, would continue to grow and fester in the coming years. Eventually it would split the entire civil rights movement at its core. But at that time, at the dawn of the decade, these questions were still just minor issues, a nuisance, nothing more.

That fall was the beginning of my senior year at ABT. I'd kept up with my classwork, though it didn't mean nearly as much to me as it had my first two years. I was also the student body president, a position to which I'd been elected the previous spring. It was interesting stepping into that position at a time when a *real* presidential race was taking place, one that would have a direct impact both on the movement and on my own life.

Nixon and Kennedy had become the candidates for the White House. Neither was taking any kind of significant stand on civil rights, though both wanted the black vote, which had become a big factor up north, where blacks were registered and actually voted in numbers far beyond blacks in the South. Going after those Northern black votes meant risking the white votes of the South, which neither candidate was apparently willing to do.

Politically, Kennedy was in a complicated position. He had spoken out— at least more than Nixon—on the plight of the Negro in America. In their first debate, Kennedy expressed sympathy for the issue of civil rights, though it was revealed later that his words came from a careful briefing with his advisors rather than from any strong personal feelings. He did promise to end discrimination in federally supported housing and to appoint more blacks to government positions. But he was a Democrat, and the Democrats were the party of the white South. The Southern bloc controlled not only their own states and most of the popular votes that went with them, but they controlled Congress and most of its committees as well. Kennedy could not afford to lose them, and so he was stuck, as they say, between a rock and a hard place, having to court the support of an avowed racist like Alabama governor John Patterson, who had recently defeated George Wallace, thanks to the open support of the Ku Klux Klan. Even Kennedy's choice of a running mate—Lyndon Johnson of Texas—was a concession to the power of the South and an affront to most black voters.

Nixon, on the other hand, had little going for him with the black electorate other than the fact that he was identified with the current president Dwight Eisenhower, who had sent troops into Little Rock to enforce school integration there.

I didn't care much for either man, nor did most of my friends. In fact, none of us cared much about the presidential race at all. Marion, who had been selected as SNCC's first chairman at the April gathering in Raleigh, had testified about civil rights on SNCC's behalf that summer before the platform committees at both the Republican and Democratic conventions. But his words had been basically ignored. The mainstream political process seemed distant and irrelevant compared to the direct action we were involved in. You saw no black students in Nashville campaigning for either Kennedy or Nixon in the early fall of 1960. Nothing about either candidate connected directly to what we and other students were doing throughout the South—nothing, that is, until the middle of October, when Dr. King decided for the first time to join us in direct action, got himself arrested, and in the process forced Kennedy and Nixon to respond to his situation.

It happened in Atlanta, at SNCC's fall conference. About a dozen of us from Nashville drove down, arriving at the Atlanta University campus on a bright Friday afternoon. Over two hundred students were there, from Northern college campuses as well as from the South. But the two groups who had the most influence and respect were our Nashville contingent and the Atlanta chapter, which called itself the Atlanta Committee on Appeal for Human Rights. Although a founding principle of SNCC had been a mistrust of concentrated leadership, a rivalry of sorts had grown between our two groups. It's human nature, I guess. We did our best to control it, but there was a bit of a power struggle from the beginning between Nashville and Atlanta. After Dr. King had come up that spring and given his blessing to our campaign in Nashville, the Atlanta group had insisted that SNCC headquarters, which had not yet been established, be based in their city, as a sort of balance of power. We agreed, and now, on this October weekend, they were hosting the first groupwide gathering.

Among the leaders of the Atlanta branch, some of whom I had met but most of whom I had not, was a guy named Julian Bond. He was, like most of the Atlanta members, more upper crust than those of us from Nashville. Bond was a Morehouse man. His father had been a college president. Julian had grown up in an environment of books and thoughts, but he didn't let any of that get in the way of his humanity or his heart. We came face-to-face for the first time that weekend and I liked him immediately. We are the same age—he is little more than a month older than I—and he struck me as charming and delightful. Tall and boyishly handsome, he seemed open and interested in everyone around him. I could tell right then that we were going to become friends, good close friends.

Capitalizing on the momentum of the sit-ins that were continuing to sweep the South, the planners of the conference had decided that this would be an "action-oriented" weekend. During the eight months since Greensboro, student-led sit-in demonstrations had been staged in more than 110 Southern cities. We wanted to extend that activism and energy to the presidential race and agreed to stage election day demonstrations come November. The workshops that weekend were hands-on, focusing on the nitty-gritty details of desegregating a public facility and on the ramifications of the attitude of "Jail, No Bail."

Jim Lawson spoke, as did a man named Amzie Moore, a black filling station owner from Mississippi who had been trying to register voters in that state for several years and had come to Atlanta to urge SNCC to send students down to help him with his work. Mr. Moore, a middle-aged man with a soft steady voice—clearly a blue-collar, hardworking man—impressed me very much. His request didn't get much response that weekend—everyone was too swept up with sitting in to get excited about the drawn-out, ground-pounding work of house-to-house voter registration—but it wouldn't be long before many of us joined him in the heat and the hatred of that most deeply Southern of Deep South states: Mississippi.

The speaker who captured the most attention that weekend, though—and not all that attention was positive—was Dr. King. He was living in Atlanta by then, pastoring at Ebenezer Baptist Church along with his father, Daddy King. And he was running the SCLC from its Atlanta headquarters. The same rift that had developed in Nashville between the older, more cautious NCLC leadership and the young Turks, as some called us, in the Nashville Student Movement had spread by that fall into the broader relationship between SNCC and the SCLC. SNCC was just six months old, but in that brief time we'd built an impressive head of steam. The organization's confidence had rocketed with the spread of the sit-ins, and now, on this weekend, that confidence, combined with a rooted mistrust of the older SCLC's middle-class values and its criticism of some of our actions, resulted in a showdown of sorts between King and the young arm of the movement.

Until then, King, though supportive of our efforts, had not actually joined us in any of our actions. More than a few students criticized him for this, and he knew it. We knew it, too, though our Nashville core group never joined in the attacks. We learned during our early days with Lawson—and he imbued us with this idea—that there were roles for everyone to play in this movement and not everyone's role was the same. If a person felt that he or she could go only to a certain point in terms of active demonstration, that was okay. That went for the med students over at Meharry and the football players at Fisk. And it went for Martin Luther King Jr. as well.

But there was plenty of carping coming from other quarters, especially in Atlanta. The SNCC contingent there was much better financed and equipped than we—they had everything from walkie-talkies to laminated rainproof picket signs. But we had gotten started sooner in Nashville and had received more attention for our efforts than they. They were eager to act that October, and they were insistent that Dr. King join them. Some of the leaders of the Atlanta group, including Lonnie King (who was not related to Dr. King), A. D. King (who *was* related—he and Dr. King were brothers) and Herschelle Sullivan, a student leader at Spelman College, met with King that weekend and pressed on him the urgency of joining them in a sit-in.

King could see SNCC's power and influence growing by the month—along with our independence. He knew that if he stayed on the sidelines much longer, he and the SCLC risked losing us. Basically he knew it was time for him to stick his neck out, as so many of us had been doing for months. Still, it wasn't easy for him. His father was dead set against his joining the sit-in line, and Daddy King was no small influence on his son. "This is the students," Daddy King told Martin after Martin met with some of the Atlanta contingent late that weekend, "not you."

But King decided it *was* he. I wasn't in on those talks between Dr. King and the Atlantans, but I heard about them. By the time we headed back to Nashville Sunday evening, we all knew something big was brewing. Wednesday we found out exactly what.

I heard the news on the radio. That morning, October 19, eighty demonstrators, including Dr. King, were arrested for taking seats in the sixth-floor restaurant of Atlanta's Rich's Department Store. Beyond a charge of trespassing, King was charged with violating the terms of his probation for an earlier driving infraction. When he refused to pay $500 bail, he was sentenced to four months hard labor at a Georgia state penitentiary known for its brutal treatment of black inmates.

It was one week now before the presidential election. The race looked like a toss-up, with Nixon narrowly ahead in the polls. Neither candidate could afford a controversy, but now they had one, and how they dealt with it might determine who the next president would be.

The best Nixon could come up with when asked about the King case was

"No comment." He later explained that he didn't think it was proper for a lawyer (himself) to try influencing a judge (the man who had sentenced Dr. King).

Kennedy didn't call the judge either. He called Coretta King to offer his moral support, but he issued no public statement. His brother Robert, however, who was managing his campaign, *did* call the judge who had sentenced King and urged the man to let King go.

King was released the next day, and when word of Bobby Kennedy's call was made public, Daddy King told a cheering crowd waiting in Atlanta for Martin's return that he had "a suitcase full of votes, and I'm going to take them to Mr. Kennedy and dump them in his lap."

With only days till the polls opened, the Kennedy campaign seized the moment, printing 2 million pamphlets titled *"No Comment" Nixon vs. A Candidate with a Heart—Senator Kennedy.* The brochures went out to black churches and schools across the country. That Sunday, hundreds of black ministers from coast to coast took to their pulpits to praise John F. Kennedy. Two days later, in one of the narrowest presidential elections in American history, Kennedy beat Nixon by less than one percent of the popular vote. Those pamphlets and sermons must have had some effect—roughly 70 percent of the country's black vote went Kennedy's way, a fact the new president would not be able to ignore easily.

Meanwhile, we swung back into action in Nashville. It was November now, and we had kept our part of the bargain with the city leaders. No sit-ins had been staged since the truce was declared in the spring. The department stores we had targeted were now desegregated, but the rest of the city's businesses remained as racially divided as ever. Now it was time to move, and this time our targets became the fast-food grills and cafeterias sprinkled across the city, places with names like Burger Boy, the B&W, Tic-Toc, Candyland...and Krystal.

You'll still find Krystals in cities throughout the South, certainly in Nashville. They still serve the same little hamburgers they did back then, tiny rectangular slabs of meat smothered with chopped onions. They cost six cents apiece back in 1960. Or you could buy three at a time and save a penny on each one.

That November afternoon—the tenth, to be exact—we weren't there for the burgers. Bernard and two young women from our group, Elmyra Gray and Maryann Morgan, walked into a Krystal on Church Street around lunchtime, took seats at the whites-only counter and asked to be served. Instead, the waitress emptied a bucket of water over their heads and poured detergent powder down their backs. When Bernard and the women didn't budge, the waitress pulled out a hose and turned it on them. Still no response. Angry and frustrated, the waitress then cut on the air-conditioning full blast to try freezing them out.

I was back at First Baptist when we got a call from one of our spotters that there was trouble at the Krystal. I grabbed Bevel, and the two of us rushed out, sprinting the four blocks up Church Street to the restaurant.

As soon as we arrived, the manager came out from the back, wearing his white uniform and chef's hat. Bernard and the women left, and Bevel and I took two seats.

"I'm closed," the manager told us. "You'll have to leave."

Bevel and I glanced at each other. I looked at my watch, a gesture that said it was mid-afternoon, nowhere near closing time.

The man pulled out a mop, went over the floor with a couple of swipes, then walked to the front door and locked it. By then the two or three other employees in the place were gathered behind the counter. The manager told them to head out the back and he followed, stopping for a moment to flip on a machine before he left.

The machine was a fumigator.

A white cloud of insecticide began filling the room. Within seconds it was so thick we could not see out the front window.

I tried the front door. It was locked. The back was now locked as well. The fumes were getting thicker by the minute.

I didn't panic. I was frightened, but I wasn't frantic.

Then I heard Bevel's voice, which I knew so well from the dorm, from the showers, from the pulpit on Sundays. It was his preaching voice, raised even louder than the machine churning out that poison. Bevel had begun to whoop, reciting the words from the Book of Daniel, where an angel appears before the kingdom of Nebuchadnezzar and warns the people to bend before God or be thrown into the fire and smoke of hell.

"*And whoever falleth not down and worshipeth,*" Bevel chanted, his eyes squeezed shut, "*shall the same hour be cast into the midst of a burning fiery furnace.*"

Then he started singing. Then he chanted some more, about the three Hebrew children—Shadrach, Meshach and Abednego—who were saved from that furnace.

I could hear other sounds now, from outside. Someone was banging on the window. We were both coughing, gasping for air. I had wet my handkerchief and pressed it over my face, but it hardly helped. It was all I could do now to draw a breath.

We're going to suffocate, I thought. We're going to die. Could that man have really left us here to die?

Then, suddenly, the front door burst open. A rush of cool air came through, along with the shapes of bodies—firemen dressed in full gear.

They helped us out into the street, where a crowd of more than a hundred people had gathered. The manager was among them. He'd stepped forward to unlock the door when he saw the Nashville city firefighters about to break in the window. A passerby had called the fire department after seeing what looked like smoke rising from the roof of the Krystal.

Ella Baker had been right. The stakes were going to keep rising in this struggle. It was one thing to challenge segregation in a setting like Nashville's department stores, where blacks were already welcomed and needed in many ways. It was going to be quite another to face entrenched racism in places where we were neither wanted nor needed—places like that Krystal.

A week after that incident, I was jailed for the third time that year—the third of what would eventually total forty arrests in my lifetime. This one happened at a Tic-Toc restaurant not far from the ABT campus. As always, my belongings were taken and placed in a brown envelope, which would be returned to me upon my release. I still have one of those envelopes. "Contents," it is labeled. Scrawled beneath the label are the words "Belt, Keys and Wallet." Beside the word "Money" is written "none." The fact of the matter is that I rarely had more than a dollar or two in my pocket during those early sit-ins. If I had actually been served at any of those restaurants, I wouldn't have had the money to pay. But that was a problem I never had to deal with.

A couple of weeks after that Tic-Toc arrest, just before Christmas break, a ruling came down from the U.S. Supreme Court on a case called *Boynton* v. *Virginia*. There aren't many people today who can recall the name of this case or what it was about. It's not in as many history books as a landmark decision like *Brown* v. *Board of Education*. But for us in the movement at that time, and particularly for me, this ruling would become earthshakingly important.

Clearly and concisely, the *Boynton* decision extended the federal ban on segregation to all terminals for interstate travel. This meant that every train and bus station in the nation would have to remove its signs for "colored" and "whites only" rest rooms, water fountains and snack bars. No more segregation of any kind in an interstate travel facility. Period.

Issuing this decision was one thing, of course. Carrying it out, as I would soon learn firsthand, was another.

Come that new year, January 1961, questions of racial justice and government action—or inaction—were pressing in on the nation's new president-elect from all sides. Kennedy had to satisfy the status quo segregationists, who were demanding to know where he stood on these rising issues of civil rights, and he could not ignore an increasingly aggressive and visibly organized array of black movement groups—the SCLC, SNCC, CORE, the NAACP—who were demanding to know the same thing.

What Kennedy did was begin to backpedal. He appeased the Southern bloc of Congress by assuring them that he did not intend to propose any new civil rights legislation. He was suddenly saying nothing about the federally supported housing legislation that he had promised during the campaign to push through with "the stroke of a pen." *Where's the PEN, Mr. President?* That's what we were asking. *Why don't you use the PEN?* In a glaring omission no one could ignore, Martin Luther King Jr. was not invited to the inauguration.

Still, I've got to say I watched Kennedy's inaugural address that January with a great sense of hope. Here was this young, vibrant man who seemed to represent the future just by his energy and his age. He didn't mention race or civil rights in his speech, but I assumed that was simply a matter of political expediency. I believed that *he* believed in what we all believed in—the Beloved Community.

Even as Kennedy was making that speech, our central committee was in the process of planning a campaign that would be the next comprehensive step in our movement in Nashville. The demonstrations we'd staged during November and December at the Krystals and Tic-Tocs around the city were basically hit-and-run actions. Now, as February 1 approached, the first anniversary of the Greensboro sit-in—Freedom Day, as SNCC officially called it—we were ready to launch another full-scale nonviolent assault, a sustained demonstration on the order of the department store sit-ins we had staged almost a year earlier.

Our target this time was the movie theaters, and this time we would not be sitting in. This time we would be standing.

Just as the movie theater in Troy had done when I was a boy, the theaters in Nashville forbade blacks to sit among whites. Not only were we relegated to the balconies, but to get there, black customers in some instances actually had to walk outside, go into a dark alley and climb an exterior fire escape. It was more degrading than I can put into words. I had never been to a movie in Nashville, but I was familiar with the theaters. There was a string of them running down Church Street for several blocks, all within walking distance of First Baptist Church—the Paramount, Loew's, several theaters belonging to the Martin chain. I often read the movie titles lit up on their marquees, but I never considered going inside. Not until that month.

One of the films playing that first week of February 1961 was Cecil B. De Mille's *The Ten Commandments*. Bevel, in one of our final planning meetings, pointed out the irony that this film about freedom and the Promised Land was being shown in places that forced men and women to walk out into the cold and rain, past garbage cans and up rickety metal steps, in order to see it.

Our tactic was one borrowed from students at the University of Texas in Austin who had staged a "stand-in" outside some businesses there. We set up "revolving" lines of picketers in front of each theater, ten or fifteen people to a line, each line moving from one theater to the next, working its way down one side of the street, then back up the other.

Starting on the first of that month, and every night for the next two weeks, we would leave from the church at about six—the same time most moviegoers were arriving at the theaters to buy their tickets. We would approach the ticket window of each theater, form a long line and, one by one, ask for a seat inside. When refused, we would either return to the end of the line or move to a line at the next theater. Not only were we visibly demonstrating against the segregationist policies of these theaters, but we were tying up their ticket lines as well.

The first few nights were uneventful. As with the department stores a year earlier, the theaters were not prepared to respond to something like this. They were, however, seeing many of their white customers turn away, some because of the trouble it was taking them to work their way through these long lines, and others because they sympathized with our cause.

Soon, though, small groups of whites began showing up who were anything but sympathetic. This was wintertime, it was dark outside by six, and the cover of that darkness, combined with the unwillingness of the Nashville police to protect us from attackers, invited roving gangs of young white hoodlums out for some evening "sport."

It began as taunting. "Hup, two, three, four!" they would shout, these teenaged boys with their ducktail haircuts. They would laugh and spit in our direction. Now and then, one of them would throw a rotten egg or a tomato. When we didn't react, things predictably turned more violent. By the second week, an occasional rock or bottle or brick would fly through the air.

Then these young men got even bolder. There was some hitting and kicking. People were picked off the end of the lines and attacked. One night, on the way back to First Baptist by himself, a young man from one of our groups was pinned up against a stone wall and beaten by a gang of white hoodlums.

And they didn't go after just us. One night a small mob of these teenagers turned on some of the newspeople covering the scene and knocked a couple of them down, an incident that was reported more fully in the next day's newspaper than any attack we had experienced. The police, some of whom were as eager to get at us as these gangs, became more aggressive, too, as the days went by. When Fred Leonard, a student at Tennessee State, refused to move away from a ticket booth one night after being ordered to do so by a police officer, the policeman cracked Leonard's rib with a blow from his nightstick. When LeRoy Wright, a friend of Fred's from Fisk, saw this, he confronted the police officer and wound up with a serious head wound himself, for which he was treated in the same emergency room as Fred.

Again, the grownups began to get worried. Some in the NCLC began suggesting we suspend our stand-ins for a period of cooling off. In the middle of that month, not long after Valentine's Day, Kelly Smith called an evening meeting at First Baptist to discuss what we should do next. Will Campbell, the white minister, was there, and he spoke at length on the violence that was growing each day and on whether this was a morally as well as physically healthy direction for us to be going. That started a long debate among the student leaders in the room—Bevel, Bernard and others—and the NCLC representatives—mainly Smith and Campbell.

I just listened. I didn't say a word. As far as I was concerned, there was nothing to say. One of the most fundamental principles of the Gandhian notion of satyagraha—nonviolent action—is that it is not merely a technique of achieving specific goals. It is not simply a means to attaining political independence or racial desegregation. It is not just a tool to achieve unity and freedom in the world around us. True satyagraha, as Gandhi taught it, is about a fundamental shift inside our own souls. It is rooted in the achievement of *inner* unity, of *inner* freedom, of *inner* certainty. It is a place we find within ourselves—a calm, sure place. And once found, that place is not swayed or disturbed or affected in any way by the thousands of details of the world around us that bombard us every day.

I listened to the debate that night. I considered everything that was said. And I heard nothing fundamental enough to shift the sureness I had felt inside about what we were doing. I did not have a shred of doubt about what our next step should be.

"We're gonna march," I said, when Will Campbell asked my opinion.

He turned away and went on with the discussion. Someone else asked what I thought about something that was said, and my answer was the same.

"We're gonna march," I said, as simply and softly as before.

At that point, Campbell lost his temper with me.

"John," he said, "you're agreeing with everything everyone in this room is saying. But all *you* say is, 'We're gonna march.'

"There's very apt to be some serious violence if there's another demonstration," he continued. "You agree with that, and still you say, 'We're gonna march.'

"What it comes down to," he went on, "is that this is just a matter of pride with you. This is about your own stubbornness, your own sin."

The room was absolutely silent. Everyone turned to me.

I looked straight at Will.

"Okay," I said. "I'm a sinner."

The room remained still.

"But," I added, "we're gonna march."

And that was that.

The demonstrations went on, with no increase in the violence but no decrease either. Less than a week after that meeting, on the night of February 20, a group I was leading decided to push things further, to try something we hadn't done so far. Rather than simply stand in line, we deliberately blocked the entrance to the Loew's Theater. Bevel was there, as was Bernard. It had snowed that day, and I remember noticing how the whiteness sparkled under the streetlights as the police vans pulled up.

Twenty-six of us were arrested that night. We refused, as always, to post bail, and so, the next day, my birthday, I turned twenty-one behind bars. Not only that, but I was scheduled to deliver my senior sermon that afternoon. It was going to come from the tenth chapter of Saint Matthew, where Jesus says, "Think not that I come to send peace on earth; I came not to send peace, but a sword." The subject was discipleship, commitment, sacrifice. It was about the kind of faith Jesus describes when he says in that same chapter, "Fear not them who kill the body but are not able to kill the soul."

I was not concerned about my body. No one was going to kill my soul. And as for my senior sermon, it was just going to have to wait.

It did, until early March, when I successfully delivered what amounted to my final exam. Not long after, the theaters in Nashville relented and opened their seating to blacks. This was another significant step forward. Bernard and I were talking about that one evening late that month, about where all this was headed. Somehow we got on the subject of that Christmas bus ride we had taken home together, where the driver jammed us with his seat. We started discussing the bus station in Nashville and how it compared to the one in, say, Birmingham, where black people were treated as if they were another species. The next thing we knew, we were drafting a letter to a man named Fred Shuttlesworth.

The Reverend Shuttlesworth was a longtime minister in Birmingham who had emerged during the 1950s as a leader for civil rights in that city. When the NAACP was banned in Birmingham following the Montgomery bus boycott, Shuttlesworth had created a replacement organization called the Alabama Christian Movement for Human Rights. That made him a target of Birmingham's segregationists, who bombed his home twice and chain-whipped him when he tried to enroll his daughter in a white grammar school.

This was a tough guy, raised in the same kind of Alabama woods as I was—though I was never convicted for running a family still, as Fred Shuttlesworth was back in 1941. This was a man who seemed to have no fear, which is why Bernard and I decided he was the person to contact with a proposal we outlined in a letter we mailed him late that month.

Our idea was to have a core group of us ride the bus down to Birmingham and test the waiting areas, rest rooms and eating facilities in the Greyhound station there—perhaps the most rigidly segregated bus terminal in the South—applying the same tactics we'd used with our sit-ins and stand-ins in Nashville.

It didn't take long before a letter came back from Shuttlesworth. He said this was not a good idea. Not only would it be too dangerous, he said, but the situation in Birmingham was already volatile enough without giving the authorities a group of "outsiders" to target and blame for the racial climate that seemed to be getting stormier in that city every day.

It was getting on toward April now. My time at ABT was nearing an end, and I wasn't sure what I'd be doing next. I had mailed an application to the American Friends Service Committee (the Quakers) for a two-year program helping to build homes in either Africa or India. I was also thinking about applying to graduate school, though I wasn't sure what I might study or where. Graduation itself was on my mind—despite my parents' unhappiness about my extracurricular activities, they were still excited about coming up to see the first member of our family get his college degree. I myself was looking forward to walking down that aisle.

All this was in the air when a friend of mine, J. Metz Rollins, came up to me one afternoon with some papers in his hand. "John," he said, "you might want to take a look at this."

It was a copy of a newsletter called *The Student Voice,* a monthly publication put out by SNCC. Rollins had it opened to a page carrying an ad placed by the Congress of Racial Equality (CORE). The ad announced that the group was seeking volunteers for a campaign to test desegregation in interstate transportation facilities—the *Boynton* decision—by sending black and white passengers on buses into the South. The campaign had a simple title: "Freedom Ride 1961."

I couldn't believe it. This was just what Bernard and I had written to Fred Shuttlesworth about. Somehow, the Spirit of History was putting its hands on my life again.

I immediately wrote for an application. When it arrived, it contained detailed warnings about violence and arrests, which were nothing I hadn't faced already in Nashville. This would be more dangerous, no doubt. This was the Deep South we were talking about, the belly of the segregated beast. But I wasn't frightened. On the contrary, I was elated. And eager.

I said as much in my application.

"At this time," I wrote, "human dignity is the most important thing in my life. This is the most important decision in my life, to decide to give up all if necessary for the Freedom Ride, that Justice and Freedom might come to the Deep South."

I asked Jim Lawson to write me a recommendation, which he gladly did. I told no one besides my closest friends what I was doing. My professors didn't know. My family didn't know. This would interfere with my graduation, but I hardly even thought about that. Graduation seemed trivial compared to the importance of this venture. Marching down that aisle meant nothing compared to getting on that bus.

Within days of mailing off my application, I received an envelope from CORE. I remember how nervous I was as I climbed the dorm stairs from the basement mail room up to my hall, clutching that unopened letter. I didn't want to open it until I was alone.

I shut my door, sat on my bed and thought about how long it had been since I first walked into that room. I could hardly remember the boy I had been. So much had happened. And yet I was still a boy, twenty-one years old, with my whole life ahead of me.

But all that mattered at the moment was the contents of that envelope I held in my hand.

I opened it.

Inside was an acceptance letter, an itinerary and a one-way bus ticket from Nashville to Washington, D.C.

No graduation present could have been sweeter than this.

I was about to become a Freedom Rider.

This Freedom Ride I was bound for was not the first of its kind. There had been one before, back in 1947.

It was called the Journey of Reconciliation, a response to a 1946 Supreme Court ruling that made segregation on interstate buses illegal. Bayard Rustin, James Farmer and several other early leaders of CORE—which was only five years old at the time—decided to dramatize this new federal law by testing it. They gathered sixteen well-trained pacifists, eight black and eight white, and bought seats on a bus traveling south. They were careful to confine their route to Virginia, Kentucky and North Carolina—"Upper South" states that presented less danger than more violent Deep South sections of America like Alabama and Mississippi. Because this law applied only to segregation *on* interstate buses, they did not approach the segregated facilities in any of the terminals along the way. Even with that, there was opposition to this "journey" among the black leadership of the time. The NAACP was dead set against it. Thurgood Marshall warned black men and women in the towns these riders would pass through that they should stay clear of the "well-meaning radicals" coming their way.

In fact, that two-week trip turned out to be more symbol than substance. The expedition ended with a whimper when twelve of the riders, including Rustin, were arrested in North Carolina for violating a state segregation law and wound up serving twenty-two days on a chain gang.

Fourteen years had passed since then. It was late April 1961, and I had my bags packed for a far different and potentially deadlier trip. I had read and reread the itinerary CORE had mailed me until I just about had it memorized. After three days of training in Washington, we would leave on May 4, stopping at terminals in Virginia, North Carolina, South Carolina, Georgia, Alabama, Mississippi and Louisiana, before finally arriving in New Orleans on May 17—the anniversary of the Supreme Court's 1954 *Brown* v. *Board* decision.

Or so it was planned.

From the beginning, though, things did not go quite as intended, beginning with my bus from Nashville to D.C.

I missed it.

When I arrived at the Nashville terminal the last morning of that month, ticket and suitcase in hand—Bevel had driven me over in his car, and Bernard had come along to see me off—I was told the bus bound for Knoxville had already pulled out. The clerk said it had left only fifteen or so minutes earlier, so we threw my bag back in Bevel's car, floored it east and caught up at Murfreesboro, where my friends bid me goodbye and I climbed aboard.

The next morning, after an all-night ride through Tennessee and Virginia, we pulled into the noisy, crowded Greyhound terminal in downtown Washington, D.C. As I stepped off the bus, got my suitcase and moved out to the sidewalk along busy New York Avenue to find a cab, I could see the U.S. Capitol just up the street. The top of the Washington Monument rose high in the distance. I'd been in big cities before, but this was more than big. This was the seat of the nation's government, the place where laws were made, the center of all that this country stood for. That, combined with the purpose for which I had come, made the moment overwhelming, truly magical.

It was a short drive to the address CORE had given me. The cab pulled up in front of an old Victorian row house on a tree-shaded street—the Fellowship House, run by the Quakers as a headquarters and dormitory of sorts for a variety of pacifist organizations. Inside was room after room filled with books and posters and pieces of art, all centered around the themes of peace and community. By the mid-1960s, houses like this—movement-oriented urban communes of one sort or another—would be common in every city in the country, on or near every college campus, the decorations and the furnishings and even the food in the refrigerator declaring the politics of the inhabitants.

But this was early. This was 1961, and places like the Fellowship House were rare. I'd never been in a building like this. I'd never been among people like this.

The twelve others who had been chosen for the ride had already arrived. They were all older than I, each selected for his or her involvement in nonviolent activity of one sort or another.

There was Albert Bigelow, a big, rugged-looking guy from New England who looked as if he belonged on a sailing ship a century ago. In fact, he *had* been a sailor, a Navy captain during World War II, and that experience had turned him into a committed pacifist—so committed that he was arrested in 1958 for steering a skiff he called *The Golden Rule* into a nuclear testing zone in the South Pacific as a protest against the use of the atomic bomb.

There was Jim Peck, who looked to be about the same age as Bigelow, in his late forties, though I couldn't be sure—these guys all looked pretty old through my twenty-one-year-old eyes. Peck had actually been on CORE's Journey of Reconciliation ride in 1947, during which he was beaten by an angry cabdriver. Pacifism, protest and civil disobedience had been a way of life for him for almost thirty years. He'd shocked his classmates at Harvard back in 1933 by bringing a black date to a freshman dance. He'd spent several years in prison during World War II as a conscientious objector. And he was now one of the most committed white members of CORE.

Other whites in the group included a sixty-year-old professor from the University of Michigan named Walter Bergman; Dr. Bergman's wife, Frances; a journalist from New York named Charlotte DeVries; a CORE field secretary named Genevieve Hughes; and another CORE staffer named Ed Blankenheim.

With one exception, the black members of our group were younger than the whites. I was the youngest. Then there was Jimmy McDonald, a folksinger from New York, a very playful, bohemian, Greenwich Village kind of guy. There was Elton Cox, a young minister from North Carolina who was one of the most devout men I've ever met—he almost always wore his clerical collar. There was Joe Perkins, a CORE field secretary from the University of Kentucky; and Hank Thomas, a Howard University senior from St. Augustine, Florida. Besides me, Hank was the youngest among us. Like me, he'd come off a poor farm, and like me he'd been deeply involved in the sit-in movement, taking part in demonstrations in Washington.

Finally, there was the man who had brought us all together, the architect of this ride as well as its leader: James Farmer.

Farmer had been one of the founders of CORE back in 1942, and he served as its first national chairman. He'd left the group around the end of the war, after a falling-out with Bayard Rustin. After a few years working with union causes and studying Gandhian philosophy, Farmer was hired by the NAACP, where he spent most of the 1950s before rejoining CORE and resuming its national chairmanship on February 1, 1961—the same day we launched our stand-ins at the movie theaters in Nashville.

It was that very day, his first day back in his old position, that Farmer and several CORE staff members began discussing the idea of replicating the '47 Journey of Reconciliation, this time in response to the 1960 *Boynton* decision. This ride, Farmer and his colleagues—most notably Marvin Rich, CORE's executive secretary—decided, would reflect the more aggressive, confrontational climate of the times. The situation down south was clear: The federal government was not enforcing its own laws in that section of the country because of fear of political backlash from those states. If, in some way, it might become more politically dangerous for the federal government *not* to enforce those laws than to enforce them, things would begin to change. If, for example, those states were forced to visibly—even violently—defy the law, with the whole nation looking on, then the federal government would be forced to respond in ways it had not so far.

And so the idea of a ride was reborn. It would be bolder and reach farther into the South than before. It would need a bolder title as well—nothing so tame and accommodating as "reconciliation"—which is how Farmer came up with the phrase "*Freedom* Ride." There was a tone of demand in that phrase, a sense of proclamation, of no more waiting.

Freedom. As in "Freedom *Now.*"

We wasted no time getting down to business, and Farmer wasted no time letting us know that this was a CORE undertaking and that he was in charge. He was a big, tall man with an unbelievably powerful voice, a rich deep baritone that grabbed you in your gut when he spoke. In the smallest, simplest conversation, he spoke as if he were onstage. And in a way, he was. Everything he did and said seemed to be in the interest of CORE. He was completely committed to the organization, as if it had a life of its own. And that was understandable. The group had almost faded out of sight during the early 1950s, due to a variety of problems—primarily internal divisions among its leadership. But toward the end of the decade, with the wave of the civil rights movement rising, CORE's membership had surged. At the time Farmer took over in 1961, the number of CORE's financial contributors had almost tripled from 4,500 in 1958 to more than 12,000. Among his responsibilities was to make sure numbers like that continued to rise.

It didn't bother me that Jim Farmer came across as ambitious and even overbearing at times. I understood that that ambition was in the name of CORE. He continually reminded us during the three days we spent training and preparing for our trip that we had come together because of CORE, that the journey we were about to embark on was created by CORE, and that we should always be aware of CORE's pivotal role in the history we were about to make. We were, however, each required to sign statements absolving CORE of any responsibility should we be injured or worse on this trip.

Those days of training in Washington went by like a blur. We began by covering much of the ground I'd already spent years learning from Jim Lawson. We read and discussed Gandhi, Thoreau and the like. Then we moved on to the specifics of our trip. We studied the structure of the Jim Crow system, learned about the local and state laws we would encounter in the places we were headed, listened to lawyers brought in by Farmer to lecture us on our rights under the *Boynton* decision and our legal recourses should those rights be denied, heard a sociologist describe the racial attitudes and socioeconomic backgrounds of the people we would likely cross paths with on our trip, and listened to a social activist describe in detail the kind of clubbing and punching and kicking and worse that we would probably receive from some of those people. We practiced enduring those kinds of attacks in intense role-playing sessions much like those I had gone through back in Nashville.

There was almost no downtime during those three days, but still there were opportunities for personalities to show through. Once or twice Jimmy McDonald would pick up his guitar and sing a song—one of those old labor tunes—and Farmer would join in with that deep, booming voice of his:

Which side are you on, boy?
Which side are you on?

Watching Walter and Frances Bergman together, sharing each other's food at our communal meals, gave you all the faith in the world about the possibilities of lifelong love between a man and a woman. You could see how much these two elderly people enjoyed and simply *liked* each other.

Charlotte DeVries, though she was a journalist and surely intended to write about this experience, was clearly with us first and foremost as a committed participant.

Genevieve Hughes, who was as graceful and gentle as her name, turned out to be a person who was not at all afraid to speak up when she had strong feelings about something.

And Elton Cox, naturally, was always the one to say grace before meals, though prayer at all other times was done silently and individually, in deference to the agnostics and atheists in the group.

As the time to board the buses drew near, everything was in place. In accordance with the Gandhian principle of informing authorities about a planned act of civil disobedience, Farmer had written a letter describing in detail the plans for our ride. He had mailed copies to President Kennedy; to the attorney general, Robert Kennedy; to the director of the FBI, J. Edgar Hoover; to the chairman of the Interstate Commerce Commission; and to the presidents of both the Greyhound and Trailways bus companies.

Farmer knew that most of the people he had written to had probably never even heard of CORE. They had almost certainly never heard of James Farmer. He sent the letters by standard U.S. mail a week before we began our training. They were not certified. They were not registered. And they were not answered, not one of them. As of the day before we were to leave, there was no acknowledgment from the government nor from the press that we even existed. Later, when the ride literally exploded into the national spotlight, Bobby Kennedy would furiously shout to his staff, "How could something like this come about without our knowing about it in advance?" There would be tales that Farmer's letter had been lost in the attorney general's "IN" box. There would be stories that Bobby Kennedy had indeed been told by a reporter from *Jet* magazine that this ride was impending but that he had not paid much attention.

In any event, as we gathered on the evening before our departure, the only outsiders who seemed to know we were there were two black journalists: the writer from *Jet*—and *Ebony* as well—a man named Simeon Booker, and a reporter from the *Baltimore Afro-American* newspaper. They had each called to tell us they'd be at the bus station to meet us in the morning.

Farmer decided to make that last evening meal together a special occasion. He reserved a large table at a Chinese restaurant in downtown D.C. I'd never been in a restaurant like that, other than to protest for my right to be served. This was different. The atmosphere was pleasant and relaxed. The food was delicious, unlike anything I'd ever eaten before. The conversation and the company were delightful.

I was, for the first time in my life, actually dining out.

As we passed around the bright silver containers of food, someone joked that we should eat well and enjoy because this might be our Last Supper. Several in the group had actually written out wills in case they didn't come back from this trip. It was that serious. It was that real. As for me, just about all I owned was packed in my suitcase. There was no need for me to make out a will. I had nothing to leave anyone.

The next morning, a bright clear Thursday, we arrived downtown, where the Greyhound and Trailways terminals sat across the street from each other. Six of us walked over to the Greyhound ticket window and the rest lined up over at Trailways. We bought our tickets, no problem, checked our bags, then boarded the buses. The two reporters were there to record the scene, but other than that no one paid us much mind.

My seatmate was Albert Bigelow. He was on the aisle. I sat by the window, watching the scenery as we pulled out of the terminal, wound through the city, then rolled across the Potomac and south into the open fields and farmland of Virginia. Ahead stretched thirteen days and 1,500 miles of Deep South highway.

Under my seat sat my carry-on bag, which contained several books—one by Thomas Merton, another about Gandhi and the Bible. The bag also contained my toothpaste and toothbrush. We were advised to keep our toothpaste and toothbrush with us at all times since we never knew when we might be arrested, and it was not likely that we'd have a chance to fetch our suitcases.

Our first stop was in Fredericksburg, an hour or so south of D.C., where we stepped off to see that the "WHITE ONLY" and "COLORED ONLY" signs had been removed from the terminal bathrooms and restaurant. "Looks like they knew we were coming and baked us a cake," someone said. There was no disruption as we used rest rooms traditionally designated for another race and ordered drinks at a counter that never would have served us before.

It was the same when we pulled into Richmond. No signs. No trouble. Nothing but a few cold stares.

We arrived in Petersburg late that afternoon and deboarded, as planned, for the evening. We were met by a group led by a local minister and SCLC leader named Wyatt Tee Walker. Walker was a flamboyant guy. He was about ten years older than I, from New Jersey, where he had become an activist early in his life, joining the Communist Party while he was still in high school. He made a name for himself in the movement when he walked into the Petersburg Public Library in 1958 and asked to check out a biography of Robert E. Lee. His arrest, in front of a crowd of reporters who didn't miss the irony of the book Walker had chosen, became a small legend.

I had heard of Wyatt Walker, but I had never met him. I knew that he didn't have much patience with this rising student arm of the movement, that he wanted nothing to do with SNCC, and that he considered himself one of the privileged few who were keepers of the gate.

He was dressed very sharply, in a tailored suit, no hat. Tall, slim and fair-skinned, with a neatly trimmed moustache, he greeted us warmly, introduced five or six of the people beside him, then led us to a line of cars, which took us to dinner. Then it was on to a mass meeting at Walker's church.

This was the planned routine for each of our stops along the way. Farmer's former boss, NAACP director Roy Wilkins, had promised the support of NAACP branches in almost every community in which we stopped. The white people in many of these towns and cities might have had no idea we were coming, but the black men, women and children certainly did. We would meet with them, typically in a church, tell them what we were doing and urge them to get involved, to join their local organizations and test the segregation in the towns and cities in which they lived. No place was too small and no people were too powerless to do what we on those buses were doing. That was our message.

We selected different spokespeople at each stop, but I was not eager to be one of them. Besides my natural shyness, I was keenly aware of my position as the youngest in our group. I just didn't feel that it was my place to speak up. I was more than ready to speak through action, but words, well, I would just as soon leave them to others.

As I recall, it was Albert Bigelow who spoke that night in Petersburg. Afterward we split up for sleep in the homes of various host families. Then, in the morning, it was back to the bus, this one bound for a town called Farmville.

Farmville is located in south-central Virginia's Prince Edward County, which had closed its public schools two years earlier rather than obey the

Brown v. *Board* order to integrate. Virginians proudly called their defiance "massive resistance." Since then the white children in Prince Edward County had attended private schools while the county's black children had gone without formal education. We couldn't help noticing that the "WHITE" and "COLORED" signs at the Farmville terminal had not only not been removed, but they had been freshly painted on our behalf. That, however, was as far as the Virginians' defiance went that day. We used the bathrooms and were served at the snack bar without incident.

Then it was on to Lynchburg. Then Danville. Then across the border and into North Carolina, where things got a little rougher. Joe Perkins, who was riding in our bus, asked for a shoeshine at the barbershop in the Charlotte Greyhound station and was promptly arrested for trespassing. Joe went to court the next day, where his case was immediately thrown out, but by then we were pulling into Rock Hill, South Carolina, where I could tell we were in real trouble as soon as I stepped off the bus.

Rock Hill's white community had been shaken during the previous year by a series of sit-ins staged by students from the town's Friendship Junior College. Back in January, as our Nashville stand-in was beginning, nine Friendship students had been arrested at a McCrory's lunch counter in downtown Rock Hill and wound up doing thirty days of hard labor on a road gang. In response to that conviction, four SNCC leaders, including Diane Nash, drove down to Rock Hill, got themselves arrested and joined the group already in jail for a visible and publicized "jail-in" that brought this little South Carolina town the kind of attention its residents were not especially eager to receive.

That jail-in was an important stage in galvanizing the student arm of the movement. It demonstrated that SNCC was organized and aggressive enough to send members from one or more cities to respond to a situation in another. It also had the effect of angering the citizens of Rock Hill, which was the climate we stepped into when we deboarded our bus the morning of May 9.

As Al Bigelow and I approached the "WHITE" waiting room in the Rock Hill Greyhound terminal, I noticed a large number of young white guys hanging around the pinball machines in the lobby. Two of these guys were leaning by the doorjamb to the waiting room. They wore leather jackets, had those ducktail haircuts and were each smoking a cigarette.

"Other side, nigger," one of the two said, stepping in my way as I began to walk through the door. He pointed to a door down the way with a sign that said "COLORED."

I did not feel nervous at all. I really did not feel afraid.

"I have a right to go in here," I said, speaking carefully and clearly, "on the grounds of the Supreme Court decision in the *Boynton* case."

I don't think either of these guys had ever heard of the *Boynton* case. Not that it would have mattered.

"Shit on that," one of them said.

The next thing I knew, a fist smashed the right side of my head. Then another hit me square in the face. As I fell to the floor I could feel feet kicking me hard in the sides. I could taste blood in my mouth.

At that point Al Bigelow stepped in, placing his body between mine and these men, standing square, with his arms at his sides.

It had to look strange to these guys to see a big, strong white man putting himself in the middle of a fistfight like this, not looking at all as if he was ready to throw a punch, but not looking frightened either.

They hesitated for an instant. Then they attacked Bigelow, who did not raise a finger as these young men began punching him. It took several blows to drop him to one knee.

At that point several of the white guys by the pinball machines moved over to join in. Genevieve Hughes stepped in their way and was knocked to the floor.

That finally brought a reaction from a police officer who had stood by and witnessed the entire scene. He stepped in, pulled one guy off us and said, "All right, boys. Y'all've done about enough now. Get on home."

Within minutes more police arrived, including a sympathetic officer who asked if we wanted to press charges. I was back on my feet by then, woozy and feeling stabs of sharp pain above both eyes and in my ribs. My lower lip was bleeding pretty heavily. I've always had very sensitive lips. They cut easily.

We said no to the offer to press charges. This was simply another aspect of the Gandhian perspective. Our struggle was not against one person or against a small group of people like those who attacked us that morning. The struggle was against a *system*, the system that helped produce people like that. We didn't see these young guys who attacked us that day as the problem. We saw them as victims. The problem was much bigger, and to focus on these individuals would be nothing more than a distraction, a sideshow that would draw attention away from where it belonged, which in this case was the sanctioned system of segregation in the entire South.

The attack that day—the first time blood was drawn on the Freedom Ride—did exactly what we wanted it to do. It drew attention. The next morning's newspapers across the country carried a small story about the beating of these Freedom Riders in South Carolina. There's no telling, though, how many Americans paid attention to that little story, considering that the day's big headline was the flight of NASA's first manned rocket, which was circling the earth above us with an astronaut named Alan Shepard aboard.

I had no idea that history was being made up in space while I was being beaten in Rock Hill. It was only later that I learned about that. At the time, my entire world was framed by the windows of that Greyhound bus and by the towns and terminals we stepped into. Nothing else existed. Nothing else mattered.

By the time we were driven over to Friendship Junior College that afternoon by several students, somebody had found a first-aid kit and put Band-Aids over both my eyes. I was asked if I wanted to go to a hospital, but I said no. I was sore, but that was all. Nothing felt broken. Al gave the same response.

Later that day the other riders, who had left Charlotte two hours behind us, arrived in Rock Hill to find the Trailways terminal closed and locked. Their alarm turned to relief once we were reunited, but we all realized that morning was probably just the beginning, a warning shot of even worse to come.

For me, though, there was even more to think about that night than the beating I'd just experienced. As soon as we had gotten to the Friendship campus I was told there was a telegram waiting for me. I couldn't imagine who would be sending me a telegram. Who even knew where I was?

It was from the American Friends Service Committee—the Quakers. They'd tracked me down by calling Nashville. My application for foreign service had been accepted. I was a finalist. Included with the telegram was a money order for a plane ticket to Philadelphia, where I was scheduled for an interview the next day at the group's national headquarters.

This was a tough decision, and I didn't have much time to make it. Since first learning of the Friends program, I'd often imagined actually living in Africa, reconnecting to my heritage, to the native land. Who could have dreamed someone like me, a sharecropper's son from a poor farm in Alabama, could have an opportunity like that?

Now that opportunity had arrived, but the timing was terrible. I had to decide that night. My stay in Philadelphia, should I go, would keep me at least three days. If all went as scheduled, that would allow me to rejoin the ride the following Sunday in Birmingham—May 14, Mother's Day. The heart of the journey would still lie ahead of us.

I decided to go to Philadelphia. I told the others, and not only did they understand, but they were excited for me. The following morning I said my goodbyes, got in a car with one of the students from Friendship and left for the Charlotte airport, about an hour away, where my flight to Philadelphia was waiting.

The interview went well. So did the physical, though the doctor had some questions about the cuts and bruises on my head and torso. After two days and nights in Philadelphia, I was told I'd been accepted—but not for Africa. My assignment was India. Should I agree to go, I'd be leaving late that summer. I was a little disappointed, but India, too, would offer an enriching experience. This was, after all, the home of Gandhi. Jim Lawson had had his own life-changing experience there.

I accepted the assignment, then rushed to the airport for an Eastern Airlines flight down to Nashville, where I planned to then go by car to Birmingham to rejoin the group. The Freedom Ride was once again all I was thinking about.

It was Saturday night when I landed in Nashville, and jubilation was in the air. After fourteen weeks of our stand-ins, the city's theater owners had finally agreed that very day to desegregate. A big picnic, a "victory" celebration of sorts, was planned for the next afternoon. After that, I would head down to Birmingham to rejoin the riders, who were having dinner in Atlanta that evening with Dr. King and Wyatt Walker. After the attack at Rock Hill, both buses had rolled on through South Carolina and into Georgia without any further violence. At the meal that night with Dr. King, the group raised toasts honoring the completion of the first seven hundred miles of the journey. I learned later that after those toasts, Dr. King took aside Simeon Booker, the reporter from *Jet* magazine who was traveling on the Trailways bus, and whispered to him, "You will never make it through Alabama."

He was right.

That next afternoon, as several dozen of us sat outside in Nashville's gorgeous spring sunshine, eating and laughing and listening to Bevel make a passionate speech about our stand-in campaign, how we had staged forty demonstrations outside those theaters during the past three months and how the Bible's Great Flood had lasted exactly that long—forty days and forty nights—a report came over the radio that stunned us all to silence.

A Greyhound bus carrying nine Freedom Riders (a handful of new volunteers had joined the ride in Atlanta) was in flames in Anniston, Alabama.

The bus had been bombed.

I felt shock. I felt guilt. That was my bus, my group. It was devastating to hear this news, and it was torture to hear it only in the sketchiest terms. There were no details—no reports about injuries or deaths. I could only imagine, and imagination coupled with fear is a torturous thing.

Later I would learn what had happened. The next morning every newspaper in the nation, and many more around the entire world, would carry a front-page photograph of the Greyhound bus in Anniston, Alabama, flames licking out its exploded windows, a column of thick black smoke billowing toward the sky. Even now, thirty-seven years after the fact, the picture is stunning to look at. It's like a scene out of Bosnia. Or the aftermath of a tank battle in World War II. Or the carnage of Verdun. Or Antietam.

But this was America in 1961. Those were American men who had clutched pipes and clubs and bricks as they surrounded that bus when it had pulled into the Anniston terminal that day. Those were Americans shouting and cursing and beating on the windows with their crude weapons. It was all the driver could do to gun the engine and hurriedly back the vehicle out. And even then, someone got to the rear tires and slashed them before the bus managed to pull away.

It had sped west, its back tires flattened, with an army of fifty cars and pickup trucks in hot pursuit. It was like something out of a horrible movie.

After six miles the bus had rolled to a stop, its tires worn down to the rims. The driver threw open the door and ran, as one witness later described it, "like a rabbit."

Meanwhile the mob arrived, two hundred of them, circling the bus and smashing the windows. They tugged at the door, which had been pulled shut. They screamed at the riders, who were sprawled on the floor of the bus, avoiding the flying glass.

Then someone in the crowd hurled a firebomb, a Molotov cocktail, through the back window. As thick smoke and flames began to fill the bus, the riders rushed to the door and found they couldn't open it. The mob was now pushing the door shut, trapping the people inside.

At that point a passenger in the front of the bus pulled a pistol and waved it at the crowd outside. He was a white man. His name was Eli Cowling. He was an Alabama state investigator who had been traveling undercover to keep an eye on the riders. Now it was no longer a priority for him to keep his identity secret. His life was on the line along with everyone else's on that bus.

The crowd backed off. Out the emergency exit door, led by Al Bigelow, tumbled the riders, choking and coughing. One by one they fell to the grass, the last one climbing out just as the bus was rocked by a blast—the fuel tank exploding.

Now the mob moved in, still cautious because of Cowling's pistol, but pecking around the edges, like birds darting at a wounded animal. Henry Thomas, whose large size was usually a deterrent, was clubbed as he staggered away from the bus; somebody swung a baseball bat into the side of his head. Genevieve Hughes had her lip split open. Rocks and bricks were heaved from people in the crowd too afraid to come closer.

Finally, Alabama state troopers arrived with their weapons pulled. The mob was dispersed. No arrests were made. Twelve riders were taken to a nearby hospital, most for smoke inhalation. Only Genevieve Hughes, because she was white and female, was admitted.

When James Farmer, who had left the ride in Atlanta to attend his father's funeral in Washington, saw the photo of the burning bus the day after the Anniston attack, he ordered his staff in New York to superimpose the image on the torch of the Statue of Liberty, and that became the symbol of the Freedom Ride.

The first news reports had hardly crackled out of our radio that Sunday afternoon before we packed up our picnic and rushed over to First Baptist for an emergency meeting. Diane, Bernard, Bevel—our whole core group, the central committee—gathered to talk about what to do. Already reports were coming in that the Trailways bus, too, which had pulled into Anniston an hour after the Greyhound, had been attacked. Jim Peck had been beaten badly. So had a Morehouse student named Charles Person. Walter Bergman—sixty-year-old Dr. Bergman—was beaten to the floor of the bus and stomped on.

By the time we heard reports of that attack, the Trailways bus had managed to pull away and head on south to Birmingham. Those riders, forced to the back of the bus by the mob, several of whom stayed aboard to keep them there, felt relieved to be clear of the danger in Anniston. They had no way of knowing that what awaited them in Birmingham would be even worse. Who could have imagined that that day's horror was only just beginning?

None of us in Nashville knew. We were scrambling to figure out how to get down to reinforce the riders who had already been hurt. The Greyhound group was somewhere in Anniston, we knew that, though we didn't know exactly where. The Trailways riders, half of them beaten and bloody, were bound for Birmingham. Diane was on the phone, trying to track down Jim Farmer in Washington.

And then came yet another news report.

All hell had broken loose at the Trailways terminal in Birmingham. An on-the-scene report from Howard K. Smith, a CBS radio correspondent, sounded like something out of a war zone:

> ... toughs grabbed the passengers into alleys and corridors, pounding them with pipes, with key rings, and with fists. One passenger was knocked down at my feet by twelve of the hoodlums, and his face was beaten and kicked until it was a bloody pulp.

That was Jim Peck's face. He and Charles Person had stepped off at the Birmingham terminal into a furious, club-wielding crowd of men, including local members of the Ku Klux Klan. There was not a policeman in sight, though the whole world knew the riders were coming. The newspaper and radio reporters waiting at the scene certainly knew, and several of them became targets of the violence that erupted as the riders deboarded. A photographer for the *Birmingham Post-Herald* was beaten with a club and had his camera smashed. A radio reporter making a live broadcast from his car was dragged into the street by a mob that then ripped his microphone from the dashboard and kicked in the windows of his vehicle.

Dr. Bergman, already bloody from the attack in Anniston, was beaten to the terminal floor and kicked repeatedly in the head. His bravery matched anyone's on the ride, but his body was not up to the beatings he took that day. He sustained permanent brain damage and a stroke that would paralyze him for the rest of his life.

As for Jim Peck, the gashes in his head would eventually take fifty-three stitches to close. His broken teeth were another matter.

For fifteen minutes this unchecked mayhem went on. It was a wilding—a sanctioned wilding. We all would learn later that word about the Freedom Riders' arrival had been circulating around Birmingham for more than a week and this had been a planned attack. Testimony presented before the U.S. Congress years later described local Klan leaders conferring with the Birmingham police in advance of the riders' arrival and actually receiving a promise that their mob would be given enough time to freely attack the passengers before the police moved in.

That day, though, when Birmingham's chief of police—a man named Eugene "Bull" Connor—was asked why there were no police at the station when the bus arrived, he answered that it was Mother's Day. "We try to let off as many of our policemen as possible," he said to the reporters gathered around him, "so they can spend Mother's Day at home with their families."

By the end of that afternoon, the Freedom Ride looked splintered and in disarray. The Birmingham group had finally found safety at Fred Shuttlesworth's house—those who weren't in the hospital. Shuttlesworth himself had led several cars up to Anniston to pick up the Greyhound riders and bring them back to Birmingham. All that evening and into the early hours of Monday morning, we discussed and debated what to do. Should we reinforce the ride? If so, how many of us would go? When? And where would the money come from to pay our way? There were dozens of details to iron out, and just as many opinions on each one.

Then, Monday morning, came news that Jim Farmer had decided to call off the rest of the ride altogether. Plans were being made for the riders gathered in Birmingham to be taken to the airport and flown out of Alabama, on to safety in New Orleans.

I couldn't believe it. I understood the thinking behind this decision, but it defied one of the most basic tenets of nonviolent action—that is, that there can be no surrender in the face of brute force or any form of violent opposition. Retreat is one thing; surrender is another. Backing down in a situation like that means that other values matter more than the issues or principles that are at stake—values such as personal safety. The definition of satyagraha is "holding on to truth." Truth cannot be abandoned, even in the face of pain and injury, even in the face of death. Once the truth has been recognized and embraced—in this case, the truth of the absolute moral invalidity of racial segregation and the necessity of ending it—backing away is not an option. It is simply not a choice.

On this everyone gathered in that First Baptist meeting room agreed. The ride would go on, and we would be the ones to continue it.

Diane immediately called Jim Farmer in Washington to let him know our intent and to ask for his support—not his permission, but his support. This would become a Nashville Student Movement–guided ride now, not a CORE ride.

Farmer was caught off guard by the call. He cautioned Diane to think hard about what awaited us in Alabama. He used the words "suicide" and "massacre." We were all a bit irritated by that kind of warning. It was a little insulting to assume that we hadn't already considered the brutal reality that lay ahead of us. Farmer wanted to back down from that brutality. We felt there was no choice but to face it, to push on. To back down would effectively end the entire civil rights movement as we saw it. It would tell those in the South and anywhere else in the nation who respond with their fists and weapons to opposition that violence *can* put an end to peaceful protest. And it cannot. The danger we faced was not, as many people, including Jim Farmer, saw it, the continuation of this ride. Quite the opposite. The danger, as we saw it, was in ending it. Farmer, with reservations, agreed. He told us to go ahead and pick up the reins.

Jim Farmer wasn't the only person alarmed, appalled and afraid of the horror that had exploded in Anniston and Birmingham. Early that Monday morning, in the White House, President Kennedy—still wearing pajamas—met with his brother Robert and with the new assistant attorney general for civil rights, a man named Burke Marshall, to talk about what to do. Marshall's job was a relatively new one—his position had been created by the Civil Rights Act of 1957. He was new at dealing with racial conflict, as were the Kennedys. None of them had had to deal with a racial situation of this magnitude before. They had no map, no directions, not even a sure sense of the scope of what was unfolding in the South. Years later Burke would admit as much. "The Freedom Ride was an education to me, to the Attorney General and to the White House," he acknowledged. "When it started, we were still too ignorant of our jobs to recognize its implications and its dangers."

One thing the White House did know was that the stakes of this crisis were high in terms of the effect it would have abroad, of all things. President Kennedy was preparing for a meeting in two weeks with Soviet chairman Nikita Khrushchev in Vienna. At a time when he was trying to establish his strength in Europe and to show the Soviets his resolve—the disastrous Bay of Pigs invasion had happened just a month earlier—the young president did not need a domestic crisis indicating weakness and division in his own backyard.

It had become clear that the Kennedys could not count on cooperation from state or local authorities. Alabama governor Patterson, when asked that Monday about the safety of the riders, answered that "the citizens of the state are so enraged that I cannot guarantee protection for this bunch of rabble-rousers." When President Kennedy tried to reach him by telephone that same day, Patterson neither answered nor returned the call.

It was time for federal intervention. Bobby Kennedy sent a personal representative named John Seigenthaler—a native of Nashville, oddly enough—down to Birmingham, where he joined the riders at the Birmingham airport, boarded their flight with them and accompanied them to New Orleans.

Meanwhile, we were well into our second day of around-the-clock discussion in Nashville. We'd tracked down Jim Lawson in Ohio, spoken to him by telephone, and he had wholeheartedly endorsed our plan. Not only that, he said, but as soon as he could—in a couple of days at the most—he promised to join us on those buses.

Others weren't so enthusiastic. As always, there was caution and resistance from several of the older NCLC members taking part in our meetings. We needed their support, at least in terms of money, and they were using that as a lever for their position. As far as I was concerned, it was time to go. The money and everything else we were debating were trivial, tedious. Time was wasting. This was a crisis, and we needed to act.

Late that Tuesday the NCLC board yielded and agreed to give us $900 to pay for our expenses on the road. By then, Seigenthaler, who had been alerted upon landing in New Orleans of our plans, was trying to track us down by phone. Word of Diane's calls to Farmer and SNCC headquarters in Atlanta had spread quickly.

"All hell is going to break loose," Seigenthaler told a friend in Nashville. "She [Diane] is going to get those people killed."

He never was able to reach us.

We spent that Tuesday evening deciding who would make this ride. As chairman at the time, it was up to Bevel to choose, but the entire central committee was in on the decision. The $900 we'd been given would allow ten of us to make the trip. The group we settled on consisted of six black men (William Harbour, Charles Butt, Paul Brooks, William Barbee, Allen Cason and me), two black women (Lucretia Collins and Katherine Burke) and two whites—one male (Jim Zwerg) and one female (Selyn McCollum).

Finally, Diane called Fred Shuttlesworth to let him know we were on our way. Because Shuttlesworth's phone was tapped by the Birmingham police (the FBI had told him so), he and Diane spoke in a makeshift code, referring to a shipment of "chickens" that would be leaving Nashville at dawn the next day.

And so, the next morning, May 17, a Wednesday—the anniversary of the *Brown* v. *Board* decision—I found myself once again climbing aboard a Greyhound bus, this one bound for Birmingham.

The Birmingham Greyhound terminal sits today in the same spot it did back in 1961. Its front doors still open onto downtown Nineteenth Street. Its rear doors still lead to a loading platform and a line of buses painted red, silver, blue and white, their engines idling, the destination tags above their windshields reading:

TUSCALOOSA
SHREVEPORT
NEW ORLEANS
MERIDIAN
JACKSON

Inside, the floor of the waiting room is the same worn patchwork of yellow and cream-colored tiles I walked across many times as a college student traveling back and forth from school to home for the holidays. Sunlight still slants down through the windows high up near the ceiling, just as it did back then. And though they now sit together instead of separately, there are still many more black men and women than whites lined up at the ticket counter and resting in the rows of hard plastic seats.

"No, that hasn't changed a bit," a man named Joe Cavanaugh told me when I visited the terminal not long ago and we stood looking at the room full of travelers, mostly elderly couples and young soldiers in uniform. "If it wasn't for black people," Mr. Cavanaugh said with a little smile, "Greyhound wouldn't *have* no business."

Mr. Cavanaugh is black. I met him the winter before last in the terminal's baggage-handling area, where he works five days a week loading luggage, just as he did back in 1961. Mr. Cavanaugh is sixty-nine years old, and he's been working for Greyhound since he was twenty-three. He was on the job that Sunday in 1961 when a crowd of Klansmen gathered in this terminal to wait for the bus full of Freedom Riders scheduled to arrive from Atlanta—the bus that never made it because it was bombed up in Anniston. He watched that afternoon as someone rushed in and shouted that another load of riders had arrived at the Trailways terminal four blocks away. He remembers the Klansmen running out the door and down the street, waving their clubs and pipes in the air. "They *whooped* those people down there," he told me, shaking his head. "I remember that. They gave them a real ass-whipping."

Mr. Cavanaugh was on the job the following Wednesday as well, when word spread through the Greyhound employees' area that yet another group of Freedom Riders was headed their way, this time from Nashville. "I never will forget," he told me, recalling the words of one of the white drivers standing out on the loading platform that day. "That man said he was *not* gonna drive no niggers out of here."

We didn't know what was waiting for us in Birmingham that day. We had no idea whether anyone in that city besides Fred Shuttlesworth knew we were coming. We suspected they might, but we couldn't be sure. As we crossed the state line from Tennessee into Alabama that morning, everything seemed serene. No one, not the white passengers nor the driver, seemed to mind that Paul Brooks, a black man, and Jim Zwerg, a white man, were sitting side by side in a front-row seat. It was not until we reached the Birmingham city limits, two hundred miles south of Nashville, that the trouble began.

Several Birmingham police cruisers were parked alongside the highway and an officer stood in the road to wave us over. As we came to a stop, the police climbed aboard and immediately arrested Zwerg and Brooks for violating the state law by sitting together. We were all then told to produce our tickets. One look at our destinations, which were the same, and the policeman chuckled.

"Y'all are Freedom Riders," he said, waving to his colleagues to shut the door and instructing the driver to head on into the city, which he did, escorted by a squadron of police cars.

Once we pulled into the terminal, the other passengers were allowed to leave. Among them was Selyn McCollum, who had missed our departure in Nashville that morning, had caught up to us in Pulaski and, because her ticket showed her boarding there, was not identified by the police as one of us. Selyn immediately rushed to a phone and called Diane back in Nashville to tell her what had happened.

As spokesman for our group, I stood and told the police that we had a right to get off this bus. We had tickets for Birmingham. We had friends and relatives in this town.

One of the policemen stuck his billy club into my stomach and shoved me back into my seat.

"Sit down," he said, "and stay there."

We could see a crowd collecting outside. I couldn't tell if they were just curious or worse. Before any of us had a chance to figure that out, the interior of the bus began to turn dark. The police were taping newspapers over the windows and across the front windshield to keep the crowd from seeing in and us from seeing out. It was strange. Very eerie.

We could hear crowd noise building outside—shouts and jeering. We tried talking to the policemen, a tactic we'd learned in our workshops—humanize your enemy, break down the barriers, try to connect with him as a person, make him see you as an individual and you him. It didn't have much effect. For the most part, the officers stayed silent.

This went on for three hours. Finally, the door was opened and we were told to step off.

The crowd, huge now, many of them shouting obscenities, tried closing in, but they were held back by two rows of policemen who created a funnel through which we were able to walk from the bus into the terminal. There we were met by Selyn McCollum and Fred Shuttlesworth. We were allowed to use the rest room, but that was it. There was no food—the restaurant was closed, the entire terminal cordoned off. That was fine, though. There was a five o'clock bus scheduled to leave for Montgomery, a bus for which we had bought tickets back in Nashville, and we intended to be on it.

So we waited. And we sang. Freedom songs. Songs of the movement. The songs we'd been singing for years now and would keep singing for years to come.

Then, as the time drew close for the bus to Montgomery to arrive, a man walked in whom I recognized immediately, though I'd never seen him before in my life. He was short, heavy, with big ears and a fleshy face. He wore a suit, his white hair was slicked straight back above his forehead, and his eyes were framed by a pair of black, horn-rimmed glasses.

Bull Connor.

"Ole Bull," his friends called him. He had a lot of friends around Birmingham. He was in his early sixties and had been a local legend nearly all his life, first as a radio announcer for minor-league baseball games back in the 1930s, and then as the city's police commissioner from the '40s onward. His deep, croaking voice was well known to reporters, who could always count on Bull to give them a good quote, especially when it came to the subject of race. He had long made it his personal mission to stop any attempts to "inta-grate" his city. "Long as I'm po-leece commissioner in Birmingham," he told one reporter, "the niggers and white folks ain't gon' segregate together [sic] in this man's town." When the *Brown* v. *Board* decision was announced in 1954, Commissioner Connor warned that "blood would run in the streets."

Now, on this spring afternoon in 1961, I was hearing that well-known voice for the first time, and it was telling us we were under arrest.

"For your own protection," he said with a little smile, before his officers stepped forward and led us off to a waiting paddy wagon. When Fred Shuttlesworth tried to step in and protest, he was arrested as well. This was not the first time Bull Connor had arrested Shuttlesworth. The two had butted heads many times over the years.

So once again I was in a paddy wagon, this one headed for the Birmingham jail. We sang all the way. When we arrived, the one white person in our group, Selyn McCollum—Jim Zwerg had already been arrested along with Paul Brooks—was taken to another part of the building from which she was subsequently released to the custody of her father, who flew down from Buffalo. The rest of us were separated by gender, and we men were put in a cell that looked like a dungeon. It had no mattresses or beds, nothing to sit on at all, just a concrete floor.

We went on singing, both to keep our spirits up and—to be honest—because we knew that neither Bull Connor nor his guards could stand it. Later on Connor would tell reporters that was one of the worst things about this experience for him—listening to the sound of our singing.

We refused to eat or drink. Our noncooperation extended to the food and water we were offered. We hadn't eaten since leaving Nashville that morning. We didn't eat that night, or the next day. We sang. No one came to see us, though we were told Fred Shuttlesworth, who was in another part of the jail, had already been taken out and tried. When Bull Connor himself showed up late that second evening with a group of police officers, my first thought was that we were being taken to trial, too. But it was eleven-thirty at night. No one goes to court at that hour.

Once again Connor told us he was putting us under "protective custody," this time by taking us all the way back to Nashville, where, as he put it, "you belong." To make sure we got there, he added, he was going to ride along.

This was strange. A midnight ride in the Deep South with a man like Bull Connor? The fact that he had brought along a couple of newspaper reporters did not make it feel any safer.

We refused to cooperate. We let our bodies go limp, forcing the officers to drag us from the jail and out into the night to three black, unmarked police station wagons. The girls had been taken out as well. Our luggage was put in one of the cars, and we were loaded into the others. Bull Connor was the last to get in, sliding behind the wheel of the station wagon in which I sat.

He tried being friendly, making small talk as we drove through dark empty streets and out of the city, headed north toward Tennessee. None of us responded, except Katherine Burke, who told Connor he'd be welcome to join us for breakfast in the Fisk cafeteria when we got to Nashville. He said it would be his pleasure.

I really thought that was where we were going, to Nashville. As we rolled through the night, and Katherine and Connor chatted on, my initial thoughts that this might be a lynching faded away. I can't say I was comfortable, but relatively speaking, considering the situation, I got pretty relaxed. We all did. Which made it all the more shocking when we reached the Tennessee state line and the convoy suddenly pulled to a stop at the edge of a tiny little town called Ardmore.

"This is where you'll be gettin' out," said Connor, as our doors were opened by a couple of his officers. He wasn't being chatty anymore. I could see a pair of policemen unloading our luggage from a car in front of us, stacking our bags on the side of the road, in the moonlight.

"Y'all can catch a train home from here," Connor said, nodding toward some railroad tracks and a small, dark depot off in the distance. "Or maybe," he added with a chuckle, "a bus."

Then he drove away, back toward Birmingham, the other two cars behind him, leaving us in the middle of nowhere, in the middle of the night, seven of us standing all alone on the border of Alabama and Tennessee.

This was Klan territory. We knew that. There wasn't a soul in sight. Just a couple of silent little streets, dark, with no lights on anywhere, not even streetlights. There was not much chance that any of the homes we could see had black people living in them. Little towns like this were always where the white people lived; you had to go out into the surrounding countryside to find the homes of the blacks.

And so we did. A mile or so up and across the tracks—railroad tracks are always a safe bet to be a dividing line between blacks and whites in a community like this—we knocked on the door of a small, weather-beaten little house, and an elderly black man opened the door. He looked very puzzled, very frightened. Here were seven young men and women standing on his front step with suitcases in their hands at three in the morning.

"We're the Freedom Riders," I told him. "We are in trouble, and we need your help. Would you help us?"

He shook his head.

"I can't let you in," he said. He looked sad and scared. "I'm sorry. I can't."

"Please, sir," I said. "We really need your help. If you could just let us make a telephone call."

The door opened wider and a small woman stepped up beside him. Like him, she looked to be in her seventies. They reminded me of so many older members of my family in Pike County. You could tell they had both worked very hard all their lives.

"Honey," she said to her husband. "Let them in."

It was warm inside. And with seven of us, it was very crowded. I called Diane, told her what had happened and described as best I could where we were. She told me eleven other "packages" had already been "shipped" down to Birmingham. That was code for eleven other riders who had been sent down by train to take our place. There was a good chance the FBI had Diane's phone tapped, and so the caution was necessary. She was ready to send a car down for us, she said. The question was, where should it take us? Home to Nashville? Or back to Birmingham?

There was no question as far as I was concerned. The others felt the same way. To a person, we believed there was no choice but to go back to Birmingham. We had a mandate, a moral obligation. Those words came up in our discussion, which was a short one. Okay, said Diane, a car would be there to get us by mid-morning.

Meanwhile the couple who owned the home—we never did learn their names—brought two small tin tubs filled with hot water into the tiny back room where we sat so we could wash up. When daybreak came, the man of the house, with money we gave him, went into Ardmore and, taking care to go to several stores rather than making a single, suspiciously large purchase at one, bought bread and baloney and cheese and some eggs for our first meal in two days.

Near noon a tan Studebaker pulled up in front of the house. At the wheel was Leo Lillard, a recent Tennessee State graduate—today he's a member of the Nashville City Council. Leo had been right there during our 1960 sit-ins and during the '61 stand-in campaign as well. We should have known he'd be the one Diane would send down to get us. First, he owned a car; and second, Leo could *drive*. He told us he'd covered the hundred miles from Nashville to Ardmore in under an hour.

It was all we could do to cram our bags in the trunk and our bodies into those seats—four in the front and four in the back, counting Leo. We thanked the old man and woman for risking so much to help us. Then we pulled out, squeezing ourselves down in the seats, out of sight, whenever another vehicle passed—eight young black men and women crowded in a single automobile would not have been a normal sight.

On the way a report came over the radio from a Birmingham station that the Nashville students, the Freedom Riders—we—were back at their college campuses. We loved it. We laughed, imagining Bull Connor's face when we showed up. But we didn't laugh long. Within minutes another bulletin, this one from United Press International, came over the air, announcing that the riders were *not* in Nashville. They were on their way back to Birmingham. Somehow word of our approach had gotten out.

And somehow we made it to Fred Shuttlesworth's house without being detected. We were soaked with sweat when we got there. We'd kept the windows rolled up all the way—somehow that made us feel safer—and this was a hot day in May. The other eleven "packages"—Bernard LaFayette among them—had already arrived at Shuttlesworth's, along with Jim Zwerg and Paul Brooks, who had been released from jail. Ruby Doris Robinson from Spelman joined us. That made twenty-one of us altogether, ready to board the 3 P.M. bus for Montgomery.

After a meal of chicken and sandwiches we were driven downtown in several cars arranged by Shuttlesworth. It was no surprise to see a crowd waiting for us at the Greyhound station. The police were there, as were reporters. There was no sign of Bull Connor. He had to be furious. This was the third time in less than a week that he and his city's segregation laws had been defied by the Freedom Riders.

The crowd, which was larger than any I'd seen so far—estimates later put it at three thousand—was loud and angry. They pushed in at us as we entered the terminal, but no one touched us. I truly was not frightened, partly, I guess, because I'd been through so many situations like this already, and partly, I know, because I had internalized that Gandhian perspective that Jim Lawson had taught us.

We walked back to the loading area, where our bus sat, engine idling. But there was no driver in sight. Before we could even climb aboard, we were told that that bus had been canceled. The next one out would leave at five.

The crowd cheered and jeered as we walked back into the terminal and took our seats on the long benches—those benches have been replaced by seats since then—to wait. The presence of the police kept the mob from outright attacking, but still our feet were stepped on and drinks were "accidentally" spilled on our legs or squirted in our faces by whites walking past. To keep our courage, we sang— "We Shall Overcome"—and I led several of the others in prayer.

At five we again went out to the platform. Again there was a bus, but no driver. Again we reentered the terminal to wait for the next bus. We were not going to give up, even if we had to wait for days. That night it looked as if we might. As the sun went down the police moved the crowd outside. With darkness the mob grew bolder and more violent. We could see them through the glass doors and streetside windows, gesturing at us and shouting. Every now and then a rock or a brick would crash through one of the windows up near the ceiling. The police brought in dogs and we could see them outside, pulling at their leashes to keep the crowd back.

We tried sleeping, but it was hard. There was nothing to eat. The terminal restaurant was shut down. So were the telephones, denying us the comfort of calling family or friends. Under Bull Connor's orders, the police were making sure our stay here was as uncomfortable as possible. And no one knew how long that stay might last.

Late that night a reporter told us he'd heard that Attorney General Kennedy was negotiating with Greyhound to have a bus take us out of Birmingham. We weren't sure what to believe. The only reality we were sure of was the crowd of hateful faces outside those windows. What was happening in Washington or even down the road in Montgomery was a world away from us.

But something was indeed happening in both those places. Earlier that afternoon, about the time we had arrived at the terminal, John Patterson finally returned the White House's phone call from five days earlier. The Alabama governor told the U.S. attorney general that he could not "guarantee the safety of fools"—us. But he agreed to meet with Kennedy's staff member, John Seigenthaler, who had come back to Alabama earlier in the week after escorting the original riders to New Orleans.

When Seigenthaler got to the governor's mansion in Montgomery late that afternoon, he was met by an angry John Patterson and his entire cabinet. Patterson told Seigenthaler he was sick of people backing down in the face of what he called "the goddamned niggers." He told Seigenthaler he believed he was better liked in America at that moment than President Kennedy.

It was basically a showdown, the same "states rights" versus federal control face-off that George Wallace would use so effectively as he rose to power in the coming years. Seigenthaler let Patterson have his say, then made it clear that the Justice Department intended to step in fully and with all its force wherever the state of Alabama ignored its responsibility to ensure our passage and protect our safety.

Having stated his position, for the benefit of posterity and the press if nothing else, the governor grudgingly agreed to cooperate. Throughout that night, while we sang and tried to sleep on those bus station benches, state and federal lawyers traded phone calls and injunctions between Montgomery and Washington, setting the stage for our departure in the morning. Those calls included a conversation between Bobby Kennedy and the manager of the Birmingham Greyhound terminal on the subject of finding a driver. Kennedy told the manager that if he couldn't find a driver there in Birmingham, he should call the company headquarters and "get in touch with Mr. Greyhound."

Whoever Mr. Greyhound was, they must have tracked him down because at sunrise the next morning, we were told that a bus was ready. This time there was a driver waiting. But as we approached, the man stepped forward instead of onto the bus and made a short statement. "I have one life to give," the driver told us and everyone else looking on, "and I'm not going to give it to CORE or the NAACP."

Then he walked away.

I understood that man's fear. After all, a bus had been bombed just a few days before. But for some reason, what struck me the most at that moment was the fact that this white bus driver knew enough to mention CORE by name. The NAACP I could understand. Everyone had heard of the NAACP. But CORE? A lot of *black* people in America didn't know what CORE was.

The fact that this white man knew—and I would be willing to bet that he didn't know a month earlier—was proof in itself that the Freedom Ride was broadening minds, even if it wasn't changing them.

Now everything was up in the air yet again. Bull Connor arrived at the terminal in a huff. So did several high-ranking Greyhound officials, along with leaders of the local bus drivers' union. They all met in a back office and came out shortly, along with the driver who had made the speech. Without a word the driver got on the bus, along with a couple of the officials, and we were told to climb aboard.

It was 8:30 A.M., Saturday, May 20, six days since the bombing in Anniston and the beatings in Birmingham, eighteen hours since we had walked into this terminal to continue the ride. Now, finally, we were moving on, south to Montgomery.

It was a surreal trip. We were the only passengers on that bus. A squadron of Birmingham police cars drove ahead and behind us, their lights flashing and their sirens wailing as we wove through downtown. Several carloads of reporters followed behind. When we reached the city limits, the police dropped away, and the Alabama Highway Patrol took over. Arrangements had been made for a state patrol car to be stationed every fifteen miles between Birmingham and Montgomery, and the highway patrol provided our escort, handing us off along the way. Overhead, a highway patrol airplane pointed the way as we raced down the highway, doing about ninety miles an hour.

I could see that plane out the window of my front-row seat. I was directly behind the driver. Jim Zwerg was beside me. No one on the bus said much. The mood was very relaxed. A couple of our group actually dozed off. It was a pleasant ride, a nice Saturday morning drive.

In less than two hours we reached the Montgomery city limits, and suddenly, as if on cue, the patrol cars turned away, the airplane banked off toward the horizon, and we were on the road alone. There were no Montgomery police cars to meet us. There was nothing on the road but our bus. As we slowed to the city speed limit and began turning toward the downtown station, it felt eerie, very strange.

The Montgomery Greyhound terminal looked almost deserted as we pulled up to the loading dock. The only people I could see were a couple of taxi drivers sitting in their cabs, a small group of reporters waiting on the platform and a dozen or so white men standing together over near the terminal door.

"This doesn't look right," I said to William Harbour as we stepped off the bus. I didn't like the looks of those men by the door.

The journalists moved in. An NBC reporter and his cameraman stepped up to speak to me and Katherine Burke. Norm Ritter, a writer from *Life* magazine, started to ask me a question, but I didn't hear it. I was looking past Ritter, to those white men, who were suddenly coming toward us fast.

Ritter saw the look on my face, I guess, and turned around. I remember how he lifted his arms, holding them out wide, as if to protect us, as if he could hold these men back by himself.

There was a low wall behind us, with about an eight-foot drop to a concrete ramp below. I backed the others toward the wall. "Do not run," I told them. "Let's stand here together."

And then, out of nowhere, from every direction, came people. White people. Men, women and children. Dozens of them. Hundreds of them. Out of alleys, out of side streets, around the corners of office buildings, they emerged from everywhere, from all directions, all at once, as if they'd been let out of a gate. To this day I don't know where all those people came from.

They carried every makeshift weapon imaginable. Baseball bats, wooden boards, bricks, chains, tire irons, pipes, even garden tools—hoes and rakes. One group had women in front, their faces twisted in anger, screaming, *"Git them niggers, GIT them niggers!"*

It was the press, though, who got it first. The NBC cameraman, a guy named Moe Levy, was kicked in the stomach by a fat man with a cigar in his teeth. Levy's camera—a big, heavy piece of equipment, not one of those small minicams they use today—fell to the ground and someone picked it up and began beating him with it. A *Life* photographer named Don Urbrock had his camera yanked from his neck and it, too, became a weapon, swung at his face. The scene quickly became a blur as the crowd moved in. One reporter— I don't know who he was—had blood just gushing from his head.

Now the mob was moving toward us, and Jim Zwerg became their target. They shouted *"Nigger lover!"* as several men clutching axe handles grabbed Jim and pulled him into the mob. All I could see were his legs as his body disappeared into this mass of people.

Behind me, several of our group—Bernard, Fred Leonard, Allen Cason— leaped the wall and dropped down to the ramp, which, it turned out, led to the basement mail room of the federal courthouse building next door. The mail workers, sorting letters on their Saturday morning shift, had no idea anything was happening outside. They were stunned when these three men burst through their doors and sprinted down the hall.

None of the mob bothered chasing them. I'm not sure anyone even noticed they'd escaped. The crowd's focus had been on Jim Zwerg. And now they turned to us, this sea of people, more than three hundred of them, shouting and screaming, men swinging fists and weapons, women swinging heavy purses, little children clawing with their fingernails at the faces of anyone they could reach.

It was madness. It was unbelievable. I could see some of our group trying to climb a nearby tree to get away. Others were scrambling to get up the wall of a building, which was impossible. Everywhere this crowd was screaming and reaching out and hitting and spitting. It was awful. They were like animals.

I tried shouting directions about the way to get out of the lot and up the street. I knew Montgomery. I knew this terminal. But there was no way anyone could hear me. And there was no way to get through the crowd, which had now closed all around us.

There was still a way clear to the cabs, though, and we tried getting the women among us over there. They managed to reach one of the taxis, which had a black driver sitting at its wheel, but when the two white women among us began to climb in, the driver said no, he could not carry them. "It's the law," he said, referring to the city's segregation statutes. Katherine Burke yelled at him to move over then, that *she* would drive. But the man would not budge. So the two white women, Susan Wilbur and Sue Harmann, were left behind as the cab pulled away with our five black women inside.

This was all happening at once, all within seconds, really. I could see Jim Zwerg now, being horribly beaten. Someone picked up his suitcase, which he had dropped, and swung it full force against his head. Another man then lifted Jim's head and held it between his knees while others, including women and children, hit and scratched at Jim's face. His eyes were shut. He was unconscious.

So was William Barbee, a classmate of mine at American Baptist, who was now lying on the pavement, a crowd of men stomping on his head and shoulders.

And now they were all around me. Someone grabbed my briefcase, which I'd been holding in my right hand since stepping off the bus. I pulled back but it was ripped from my fingers. At that instant I felt a thud against my head. I could feel my knees collapse and then nothing. Everything turned white for an instant, then black.

I was unconscious on that asphalt. I learned later that someone had swung a wooden Coca-Cola crate against my skull. There was a lot I didn't learn about until later.

The two Susans—Wilbur and Harmann—were cornered by a group of men and women who began taunting and hitting them. A white man drove up on that scene and yelled at them to get in his car. It was John Seigenthaler, who had driven behind us from Birmingham and, thinking our bus was going to make its normal stops along the way rather than running straight through, had stopped for gas and coffee before coming to the terminal.

Seigenthaler was shocked by the scene he came upon. He could see our luggage being thrown in the air, the contents flying out. As he got out of his car to help Wilbur and Harmann, the mob moved in on him. He yelled at them to back away, that he was a federal agent. No sooner did he get those words out of his mouth than he was hit in the head with a pipe and knocked unconscious. For twenty minutes he lay there, a personal aide to the attorney general of the United States, clubbed to the parking lot pavement of an Alabama bus terminal.

By the time I regained consciousness, the scene was relatively under control. Floyd Mann, Alabama's state public safety director, had pushed his way into the mob, tried pulling some men off William Barbee's body, then raised a pistol and fired it in the air, warning the crowd away.

Montgomery police commissioner L. B. Sullivan and his men had finally arrived—Sullivan had reportedly sat in his car around the corner from the terminal during the worst of the attack, calmly waiting while the mob had its way.

Also now on the scene was the attorney general of Alabama, a man named MacDonald Gallion. As I got to my feet, he stood over me and read aloud an injunction forbidding "entry into and travel within the state of Alabama and engaging in the so-called 'Freedom Ride' and other acts or conduct calculated to promote breaches of the peace." The words had been written by Montgomery judge Walter Jones the previous night, during Governor Patterson's negotiation with Robert Kennedy.

I hardly listened to those words. My head was spinning, both with thoughts about the carnage that had occurred and with pain. I was bleeding pretty badly from the back of my head. I couldn't believe how much blood there was.

I looked around. Pieces of our belongings were scattered on the asphalt—a shoe here, a composition book there. I could see only two other riders—Barbee and Zwerg. The others, I later learned, had made their way into the surrounding black community, many to a nearby Presbyterian church.

Zwerg looked horrible. Barbee looked almost as bad. They clearly needed to get to a hospital right away. But when I tried getting Zwerg to his feet and asked a police officer for help in finding an ambulance, he shrugged. "He's free to go," the policeman said, glancing at Zwerg, but it was up to us, he said, to find our own transportation.

Barbee and I were able to find a black cabdriver who would give us a ride, but the man refused to carry Zwerg, again because of the segregation statutes. Zwerg was eventually driven to a local hospital, St. Jude's, by another driver, a black man, who chose to ignore those laws.

Barbee and I were taken to the office of a local doctor, who treated us both. He shaved, cleaned and bandaged the gash on the back of my head. My coat, shirt and tie were splattered with blood. I hadn't had time till then to think about the $900 in cash I had carried since leaving Nashville—the money the NCLC had given us for expenses. When I reached into my coat pocket, I didn't know if the money would still be there.

It was.

By the time the doctor was done, a volunteer driver had arrived to take me to the home of a local minister named Solomon Seay. The Reverend Seay, like Fred Shuttlesworth in Birmingham, had emerged in recent years as a visible and outspoken leader of Montgomery's black community. Barbee was nowhere near well enough to come with me. We didn't know it then, but his injuries would leave him paralyzed for life.

At Seay's house, I was greeted with cheers and hugs—the same reception each of the riders received as we all arrived there that afternoon. The phone was ringing constantly, with news of response from the world beyond Montgomery. Jim Lawson was on his way down from Ohio. Diane was coming in from Nashville. Dr. King was reportedly on his way. And the Kennedys were livid. Patterson had promised to protect us, then turned around and not only allowed us to be ambushed, but then sent his attorney general to the scene to serve us with injunctions. Warrants were now out for our arrest, even as the mob back at the bus station, which had grown to over a thousand, was still rioting—setting parked cars on fire, roaming the surrounding neighborhood and beating any black person they could find (one man had his leg broken, another was soaked with kerosene and set aflame).

As the violence and the afternoon wore on, Police Commissioner Sullivan leaned on a car, chatting with reporters who asked him to sum up the situation. "I really don't know what happened," he told them. "When I got here, all I saw were three men lying in the street. There was two niggers and a white man."

That would be us—Barbee, Zwerg and I.

By that night—Saturday night—we got word that Dr. King was indeed coming in from Chicago, where he was in the midst of a speaking tour. Federal marshals were also on their way, sent by Bobby Kennedy. And Jim Farmer was flying down from Washington. With the whole world's eyes now on the Freedom Ride, he wanted to make sure CORE was not forgotten.

We slept in various homes that night, the other riders and I, and the next day we were taken to Ralph Abernathy's church, First Baptist, where a mass meeting was planned for that evening, at which Dr. King would speak. Technically we were fugitives from the law—those warrants were still out for our arrest—so we arrived at the church hours early and spent the afternoon in the basement library, essentially in hiding. This was the same room in which I had met with Dr. King and the Reverend Abernathy in the summer of '58, when we had discussed my enrollment at Troy State. Now, here I was again, preparing for another meeting with those two men, under entirely different circumstances, and not so privately.

By five o'clock that afternoon, black residents of Montgomery began arriving by the dozens. The meeting was still three hours away, but already the pews were filling up. Outside a crowd was growing as well—a loud restless mob of white onlookers, many of them waving small Confederate flags, some of them letting loose with Rebel yells. The presence of federal marshals spaced around the church kept the crowd across the street, at a safe distance.

By sunset the church was jammed with nearly 1,500 people, including reporters from the three national television networks, AP and UPI, *The New York Times,* and state and local newspapers. Outside, the crowd of whites had grown to at least that size, and they were growing louder and angrier, shouting and occasionally hurling small rocks at the church walls.

The people inside, these black men and women of Montgomery, were unfazed by the uproar outside. It was not easy to intimidate them, not after what they had already gone through with the bus boycott. They had been through fire. They knew what it felt like. They answered that ominous noise outside with their own sound, the sound of hymns.

I was sitting in the upstairs balcony, the choir loft. We riders had decided earlier that day to scatter ourselves among the congregation, to make it difficult for us to be identified in case the authorities arrived and tried to single us out. Then again, it would not be too hard to pick me out—the bright white X-shaped bandage on top of my head was a giveaway.

Downstairs, in the basement study, Abernathy and Wyatt Walker and Dr. King, who had arrived earlier in the day, were waiting for Shuttlesworth, who had gone to the airport to pick up Farmer. When Shuttlesworth left, he was pelted with small stones and stink bombs by the mob, which was restrained only by the presence of the massively outnumbered federal marshals.

While Shuttlesworth was gone, Dr. King came upstairs and stepped outside to see for himself how bad things really were. I think he wanted to show the mob he wasn't afraid—and to show the people who had come to hear him speak that he wasn't afraid as well. The mob didn't recognize him at first. As soon as they did, rocks were thrown in his direction. When the door was opened to let him back in, we could hear shouts of "Nigger King!" behind him.

It was close to eight when Shuttlesworth returned with Farmer. A block from the church, their car was surrounded by the mob, which began rocking it back and forth. Shuttlesworth and Farmer were able to get out and push toward the back of the church on foot, with Shuttlesworth leading the way, waving his thin arms and screaming at the startled crowd, which actually backed away to let him and Farmer through. Big, hulking Jim Farmer followed behind little Fred Shuttlesworth like a lamb, amazed by the thin man's fearlessness. Later, Farmer would explain the crowd's obedience in the face of Shuttlesworth's screaming by calling it the "crazy nigger" syndrome—"as in 'Don't mess with that nigger, he's *crazy.*'"

When Farmer arrived, Dr. King brought him out to introduce him to the congregation. They asked me to come down as well, and Farmer gave me a big hug—the remaining two original Freedom Riders reunited.

Now it was eight o'clock, and there was an upsurge in the noise outside. Rocks began banging off the church windows. Someone shouted that a car was on fire. The mob had moved closer. A car was turned over.

I had seen this so many times now, the rhythm of a mob, how its temperature rises as the hours pass, how it is timid and careful at first but then grows bolder as its size and restlessness increase. And then the sun sets, bringing the twisted kind of courage that comes with the cover of darkness.

It was happening now, the mob moving in, forcing the marshals to answer with tear gas. Small Molotov cocktails began sailing toward the church from the crowd, bouncing off the walls and landing on the ground, flaming and smoking.

The riders among us no longer felt the need to hide ourselves. Now we stood and led the congregation in more singing—not hymns, but music of the movement: "Ain't Gonna Let Nobody Turn Me 'Round" and, of course, "We Shall Overcome."

The Reverend Seay took to the pulpit and told the congregation to stay calm. His steadiness was unbelievable. So was the congregation's. There was no panic, none at all. Not that there wasn't fear in that church, but the people took their fear and mixed it in with faith and put it into their singing. Some of them were also fully prepared to fight back. We riders were nonviolent, steeped and trained in the teachings of Gandhi, but most of the people of Montgomery were not. They were simply men and women, husbands and wives, mothers and fathers and children, and now, as that mob began literally beating on the church, some of those fathers moved toward the doors, with knives and pistols in their hands, ready to fight back for their families.

Downstairs, Dr. King was on the phone with Bobby Kennedy. Kennedy could hear the mob through the telephone, and he tried making a joke, to lessen the tension, I guess. "As long as you're in church down there," he told Dr. King, "you might as well say a prayer for us." Dr. King did not find that amusing. No one did.

The marshals outside were doing all they could to keep the crowd back. At one point a door was actually pushed open, and several marshals came running through the church to force it back shut.

Then a brick came crashing through one of the stained-glass windows, and now there was some alarm. Women and children screamed as broken glass flew through the air. Tear gas began drifting in, and people started coughing, covering their faces.

But no one lost control. The children were hurried downstairs. Everyone else dropped to the floor, to avoid flying glass and the gas now hovering in the air.

Then there was another noise from outside, a different noise, the sound of boots and metal and moving men. The Alabama National Guard had arrived. Bobby Kennedy and John Patterson had had yet another crisis conversation, a shouting match from the governor's end of the phone, and Patterson had finally declared martial law. The guard, wearing white combat helmets and carrying rifles with fixed bayonets, had arrived to relieve the small squadron of weary, terrified federal marshals.

It was ten o'clock, two hours since the siege had turned into a full-scale attack. The aisles and pews were sprinkled with broken glass. Wisps of tear gas still hung in the air. The children, who were being led back upstairs now, were whimpering. Our mass meeting, finally, was set to begin.

Wyatt Walker spoke first. Then Abernathy. Then Farmer. And then up stepped Dr. King. He praised the congregation's courage. He criticized John Patterson. He encouraged the people to remain confident. He told them that they would triumph, that there could be no other way.

"Alabama will have to face the fact," he said, "that we are determined to be free."

There were shouts of "Amen!" and "Praise God!"

"Fear not," he said, "we've come too far to turn back."

There was singing and celebration.

And then it was over. The time was near midnight, seven hours since the seats had started to fill. The audience began moving toward the doors, some carrying sleeping children, everyone drained, ready to go home.

But the doors were blocked. The troops, which had been facing the crowd across the street, now turned to face *us*. There was no way to get us out through that mob, we were told. No transportation had been arranged. It was too dangerous.

There were words of anger from some among the congregation. Those soldiers didn't look like protectors now. Their rifles were pointed our way. They looked like the enemy.

As we pulled back into the church, there was talk that this was what Patterson really intended, to imprison us. There was no reason to put that beyond him. Bull Connor had done the same sort of thing up in Birmingham, putting us in jail "for our own protection," then trying to literally run us out of the state.

So now we settled in for the night. The children were taken back down to the basement to sleep. The elderly were given the cushioned pews. And the rest of us slept as best we could on the floor.

Kennedy and Patterson argued all night on the phone. The governor railed against "Communists" and "outside agitators." He said the Freedom Riders were nothing but "mobsters." He blamed Kennedy and the federal government for everything that had happened and for anything that was *going* to happen.

Again, it was all mostly words. The tangible result of their conversation was the arrival, at four-thirty that morning, of National Guard trucks and jeeps, a convoy of them, in front of the church. Group by group, the 1,500 people inside that building were led out under armed guard and loaded into military vehicles, which took them home to their neighborhoods around Montgomery.

I was taken by jeep to the home of a man named Dean Harris, a black pharmacist whose house was a haven of sorts for many, many people in the movement—SCLC people, SNCC people, CORE people, dozens and dozens of people. Whenever the foot soldiers of the movement came to Montgomery, Dr. Harris's house is where they would stay. It was a big house, with a dozen or so rooms. Plenty of space, with a tree-shaded yard. A very comfortable place. Very relaxing, very refreshing. Dr. Harris's wife and mother and relatives and friends were always around to make you feel comfortable and welcomed. In fact, it was at this house that I had my first beer. I've never much cared for alcohol, and I don't have it at all anymore, but now and then, during those years, I would occasionally enjoy a cold beer with my friends, and it was at Dr. Harris's house in Montgomery that I had my first.

Dr. King was there that morning, along with Farmer and Walker and Diane. Bevel and Lawson arrived during the day, which the other riders and I spent at the federal building— right next to the bus station—in the courtroom of a U.S. federal judge named Frank Johnson Jr.

A day earlier, in the wake of the attacks that week, which had clearly involved the Klan, Judge Johnson had signed a federal restraining order against Klan groups in Montgomery. Now, as he sat on his bench to consider both lifting the injunctions against our ride and issuing an injunction guaranteeing our protection as we continued our journey, there were federal marshals in the courtroom assigned to protect the judge's life.

We had a team of NAACP lawyers there to speak for us, including Fred Gray—the man who had taken me to my first meeting with Dr. King and Abernathy—and Arthur Shores, one of Birmingham's best-known and bravest attorneys. Shores's home would be bombed more than once in the coming years, earning that section of his Birmingham neighborhood the title of "Dynamite Hill."

I had been in court before, but this was the first time I had actually testified. Judge Johnson asked me to explain what I had experienced during the Freedom Ride so far and why we wanted to carry this ride on into Mississippi. I was nervous. This was an imposing setting, this room with its enormously high ceilings and arched windows, its dark oak benches, its massive doors covered with brown leather, and a huge state seal—a ring of gold stars over a background of blue—on the wall behind the black-robed judge.

This was different from a press conference, or a crowd massed for a rally, or a church filled on a Sunday morning. This was a courtroom, the seat of the law, and it was the law itself, come down from the Supreme Court in Washington, that was at issue this day. That was how I answered the judge's question, by stating that we had begun this ride to see that the law was carried out, and we wanted to continue it for the same reason.

That, apparently, was good enough for Judge Johnson, who lifted the injunctions against us and allowed us to leave the courtroom without the shadow of arrest over our heads. As for the continuation of our journey into Mississippi, the details were unclear. By the time we gathered that night, in a room at the downtown Montgomery YMCA, we weren't sure what kind of protection we'd be offered, if any, should we go on with the ride.

We sat on the floor that night, Diane and Bevel and the others and I, while the elders—King, Walker, Abernathy, Farmer—sat in folding chairs. Diane and I did most of the speaking for the students. Farmer started out speaking for the others, and just as he had done during our training in Washington, he took center stage with pronouncements about CORE's importance, and his own. By now, though, I guess I was not as much in awe of him as I was before. Neither were the others. Many people in the room that evening were rubbed the wrong way by Farmer's apparent showmanship and bravado. He talked loud and big, but his words sounded hollow to me. His retreat after the attacks in Anniston and Birmingham had something to do with it, I'm sure, but he just struck me as very insincere. It was clear to everyone that he wanted to take the ride back now, when we all knew that without our having picked it up, there would have been no more Freedom Ride. It didn't matter to me at all who got the credit; that wasn't the point. But from where Farmer stood, that seemed to be all that mattered. He saw this ride in terms of himself. He kept calling it "CORE's ride," which amazed everyone.

So there was Farmer to deal with. And then there was the issue of Dr. King's participation. He had faced this before with the sit-ins, and now Diane, true to form—fearless and straightforward—confronted him with the question of whether he would join us, whether he would climb on the bus and ride with us into Mississippi.

No, Dr. King said, he could not go. He was on probation, he explained, from his arrest in Atlanta.

"I'm on probation, too," one of our group shouted.

"Me, too," yelled another.

"We're all on probation," said someone else.

Dr. King did not budge.

"I think," he answered, with some irritation in his voice, "*I* should choose the time and place of my Golgotha."

That did it. Several of our group stood up, shook their heads and moved toward the door. The rest followed. On the way out I heard for the first time a phrase that would be repeated often in the coming years, a phrase used to mock Dr. King for his loftiness in the movement and for quoting the Scripture, invoking God and Jesus in terms of his own situation.

"*De Lawd!*" That's what someone muttered as we left the YMCA room that night. There was anger in the phrase, criticism of Dr. King for somehow comparing himself to Christ. There couldn't have been a more concise way to capture the split that was widening between the generations in the movement than that simple phrase: *De Lawd.*

It was really not fair. Dr. King felt terrible about having to say no. It was very important to him not to encourage people to do anything that he himself was not prepared to do. Six months in prison for a parole violation, though, what would that mean to the movement? Four or five years earlier his decision might have been different, but now his position and his responsibilities had grown so incredibly large that his every step, his every word, had to be measured for its impact. That's a great burden for any man. I could feel Dr. King's quandary. And I also felt that no one had the right to force another person into making a moral decision. That was something Gandhi taught, that in the end people must each decide for themselves what they will and will not do, and no one else should try to force them or shame them into acting.

By the following morning, we got word that Bobby Kennedy was calling for a "cooling-off" period, making clear that he wanted the ride to stop. He and the President were sick of John Patterson, but they were sick of us, too, for resuming this ride after the violence on Mother's Day. And Roy Wilkins, who had originally offered the NAACP's support during our trip, was now warning us against going into Mississippi, which promised to be even more dangerous and violent than Alabama. One of Wilkins's field secretaries in Mississippi, a young man named Medgar Evers, agreed. Evers told reporters he was against our coming. He felt it was too soon. Mississippi, he said, was not ready for us. It was too dangerous. In his opinion, there was much work still to be done there before a confrontation like the one we might bring should be forced.

But we had to go. To stop now would be a disaster. There was too much commitment, too much momentum. This Freedom Ride had taken on a life of its own. For the same reasons that we had picked up the reins after Farmer and CORE set them down, we all agreed that we had to carry on now. We considered the adults' advice, but the decision was in our hands, the students' hands, and there was no question. We were moving on.

That afternoon, Tuesday, we called a press conference. Farmer, Dr. King,

Abernathy and I sat at a long table facing a room full of reporters. I still had the big patch on my head—it looked like a large white cross. Dr. King's comments focused on the brutal reality of this situation, of the danger we faced. Even as he spoke, a "hate bus" sponsored by the American Nazi Party was heading south from Washington, D.C., bound, like ours, for New Orleans. Even as we sat at that table, Mississippi governor Ross Barnett was wiring words of support to John Patterson, hailing him for holding his ground against us and the federal government. Dr. King's comments spoke directly to and about such resistance.

"Freedom Riders must develop the quiet courage of dying for a cause," he told the reporters. "We would not like to see anyone die, but we are well aware that we may have casualties.

"I'm sure," he said, "these students are willing to face death if necessary."

It was no longer just us, the core group from Nashville and the volunteers we'd picked up in Atlanta. Now students were flooding into Montgomery from all across the South, from as far west as New Orleans and as far north as D.C. The nature of the ride had shifted now, with control moving from CORE to the students. It had become a more spontaneous event, less like a precise, military-like assault and more like an organism with a life of its own, a thing that seemed to be growing of its own accord, with students arriving by the scores even as we met with the press, all of them piling into Dr. Harris's house, eager to get on the bus, ready to fill Mississippi's jails, if need be.

But we would go first, the two dozen or so of us who were set to board a pair of buses the next morning, Wednesday. We left Dr. Harris's house at dawn that day, in cars escorted by National Guard troops. The city was still under martial law. There were still outbreaks of violence in various neighborhoods where small groups of whites were attacking black people or property.

When we arrived at the terminal, there were troops everywhere, inside the building and out. Dr. King, Abernathy, Walker and others were there to walk with us through the waiting room and into the snack area, where orders were placed for cups of coffee and a bite to eat. We were, according to the manager, who addressed the reporters witnessing the scene, the first blacks ever served at that counter.

Then we walked out to the bus, where a dozen or so reporters and photographers were already aboard, waiting to record the trip.

Twelve of our group stepped aboard, including Jim Lawson. Out on the platform, Dr. King reached up to shake hands with the riders through the windows. And then the bus pulled out, escorted by a convoy of National Guard jeeps and trucks, highway patrol cruisers and carloads of reporters—forty-two vehicles in all, plus two helicopter spotters and three U.S. Border Patrol airplanes flying overhead to check bridges and trouble spots ahead of the bus for signs of booby traps, bombs or snipers. A thousand guardsmen were stationed along the route between Montgomery and the Mississippi state line. All normally scheduled stops during the seven-hour ride were canceled.

Four hours after that first bus pulled out, the rest of us boarded the second. Hank Thomas was among us. So was Lucretia Collins. As we got set to leave, we could see Jim Farmer out on the loading platform waving goodbye. Up to that point we had assumed he was coming along. One of our group, a young CORE member from New Orleans named Doris Castle, leaned out her window and said, "Jim, you're going with us, aren't you?"

Farmer said something about having paperwork and CORE obligations. He would admit later on that he was, in his own words, simply "scared shitless." After he was done answering Doris, she just stared at him.

"Jim," she pleaded. *"Please!"*

That was it. Shame got the better part of Farmer. He had his luggage put on the bus, climbed aboard, and we pulled out of the terminal, headed west to Jackson.

The military escort provided for the first bus was not given to ours. Kennedy's agreement with Patterson had been based on one vehicle. But the troops lining the road were still there as we headed west. They were there all the way to the state line, where we were met by Mississippi state patrol cars and several units of National Guard troops commanded by an officer named Sonny Montgomery. Who could have dreamed that thirty years later, Sonny Montgomery and I would be colleagues in Congress? That day Sonny Montgomery was just another helmeted, holstered Mississippian to me. I'd never been to Mississippi before. All my life I had heard unbelievably horrible things about the place, stories of murders and lynchings, bodies dumped in rivers, brutality and hatred worse than anything I'd ever heard of growing up in Alabama or attending college in Tennessee. Now I was here, and it was unsettling seeing crowds of onlookers standing by the roadside, held back by those armed troops, some of whom wore big bushy beards that made them look like Confederate soldiers. It turned out that they *were* Confederate soldiers, in a way—they were members of a Civil War reenactment group that had been preparing to stage one of their gatherings when they were called up for duty by the guard.

Our anxiety began to rise as we approached Jackson, and so, as we always did when the tension increased, someone started a song, and we all joined in:

> I'm taking a ride on the Greyhound bus line,
> I'm riding the front seat to Jackson this time.
> Hallelujah, I'm a-traveling,
> Hallelujah, ain't it fine.
> Hallelujah, I'm a-traveling
> Down freedom's main line.

Upon our arrival at the Jackson bus station, we learned that the first bus-load of riders had already been arrested and taken to jail. Now would be our turn. As we walked into the station and moved toward the white bathrooms and lunch counter, a police officer pointed toward the "colored" facilities on the other side of the room. We continued on, and the officers followed. One of the officers caught up with me in the "white" men's room, where I was arrested as I stood at a urinal.

"Move," said a deputy, poking me in the ribs.

"Just a minute," I said. "Can't you see what I'm doing?"

"I said *move! Now!*"

So I zipped up and moved out, on my way to yet another cell, this one in the Hinds County jail, where a total of twenty-seven Freedom Riders were incarcerated that day. As always, we refused bail. As always, we were separated by race and gender. And as always, Jim Bevel took center stage with his voice and his passion, preaching to whoever was within earshot while we sang in between his impromptu sermons. The jailers couldn't stand it. They tried stopping it by taking cigarettes from the smokers among us and then by cutting out the afternoon snack.

But we weren't eating anyway—most of us, at least. We immediately launched a hunger strike as a form of noncompliance. Not everyone among us was eager to take part. Our campaign had grown to include riders who came with all their heart and soul and courage to put their bodies on the line for the cause of racial and human justice, but who were not necessarily familiar with nor committed to the way of nonviolence. This caused some tension among us during our stay in Mississippi. There were arguments and near fights among factions in our jail cells over the decisions to stage such protests as hunger strikes.

An example was a guy named LeRoy Wright, who was among the first group in the Hinds County jail. He seemed to be fighting or arguing with someone constantly, until it finally got to the point that we decided it would be better for all of us if he were bailed out. And so that was done. We got him bailed out early, for the good of the group.

Two days after we were arrested, we went to court, where the judge treated our attorney exactly as Judge Harris back in Nashville had treated Z. A. Looby at our trial during the sit-ins—he turned his back to our attorney, ignored our lawyer's comments, then wheeled around, smacked his gavel on the bench and gave us each a $200 fine and sixty days in jail.

Three days after that, we were transferred to the Hinds County prison farm, where we were crammed into cells even smaller than the jail's. There were not enough beds for all of us, and so we slept on the floor, on tables, on benches, anywhere we could stretch out our bodies. Unlike the other prisoners, we were not taken out to work. The only exercise we got was cleaning our cells, which we did religiously with the mops and brooms brought by the guards.

For two weeks we were kept at that prison farm, confined to our cells, day in and day out. We were eating now, but only enough to survive. And that's all we were fed, just enough to survive—biscuits and syrup and streaks of "lean" (thin pieces of hard, tough meat), and burnt black coffee in tin cups. Occasional bits of news would trickle in, including word that the Freedom Ride had burst wide open now, mushrooming and multiplying into Freedom *Rides,* dozens of them, buses filled with literally hundreds of Freedom-Riding Northerners arriving in Jackson each day from every direction. Quakers, college professors, rabbis, pacifists, unionists, communists, conscientious objectors, clergymen—they were flooding in from Minnesota, Wisconsin, California, as well as from points east and south, merging with the students of SNCC and CORE and overflowing the jail cells of Jackson.

Only a handful, two dozen or so, were sent out to join us at the farm, though. And on the fifteenth of June, well past midnight, we were marched out into the darkness, forty-five of us, and put into windowless truck trailers—herded like horses, like cows, into these airless, seatless containers. The doors were closed, locked, and in utter darkness we were driven away, bracing ourselves against one another as the trucks lurched around turns, the drivers doing the best they could to slam us into the walls. We had no idea where we were going.

And then, after about two hours, we were a hundred miles northwest of Jackson, in the middle of nowhere. The doors were opened, and we stepped out in the light of dawn to see a barbed-wire fence stretching away in either direction. And armed guards with shotguns. And beyond the guards, inside the fence, a complex of boxy wooden and concrete buildings. And beyond them, nothing but dark, flat Mississippi delta.

This was Parchman Farm, the state penitentiary of Mississippi.

I'd heard about Parchman in the same way I'd heard about Mississippi—in tones of horror and terms of brutality. In a South filled with nightmarishly inhuman prisons and work farms, Parchman Penitentiary was infamous for being the worst. It was essentially a 21,000-acre twentieth-century slave plantation owned by the state and farmed by hundreds of stripe-suited black convicts who were goaded by bullwhips and cursing, kicking guards to turn out a daily quota of cotton or other crops. The dark legend of Parchman Farm has made its way onto the pages of some of the South's most famous writers, from Eudora Welty to William Faulkner to John Grisham. The farm still stands today, though in a much more benign form than the place it was that June morning in 1961. At that time it was basically a state unto itself, with its own laws, administered by its superintendent, a planter named Fred Jones.

It was Fred Jones who greeted us as we climbed out of those trucks. "We have some bad niggers here," he told us, chewing on an unlit cigar and welcoming us to his home. "We have niggers on death row that'll beat you up and cut you as soon as look at you."

One of the guards began pushing us toward the gates. "Go ahead and sing your goddamn freedom songs now," he said. "We got niggers here that will eat you *up*. So you go and sing your songs inside now."

Behind us, two of our group—two young white men whose names I did not know—began kicking and resisting, forcing the guards to drag them from the truck by their legs. "What you actin' like that for?" chuckled one of the guards. "Ain't no newspapermen out here."

He was right. There was nothing out there but them and us—and, oddly, a small flock of ducks and geese waddling around near the barbed-wire fence. I imagined the birds as some form of barnyard warning system, quacking and honking at the sound of escapees in the night.

We were led into a cement building where deputies with cattle prods stood by while we were ordered to strip naked. For two and a half hours we stood wearing nothing, while we waited for...well, we didn't know *what* we were waiting for. I could see that this was an attempt to break us down, to humiliate and dehumanize us, to rob us of our identity and self-worth. I had read that such methods were used by oppressors throughout history. When we were finally led, two by two, into a shower room guarded by a sergeant with a rifle, I thought of the concentration camps in Germany. This was 1961 in America, yet here we were, treated like animals for using the wrong bathroom.

Those of us with facial hair were ordered to shave in the shower. I had none, but I felt fear, real fear, as I watched my friends, some with visibly shaking hands, cut off their moustaches and beards. Finally we were led to a maximum-security wing and put in cells, two to a cell, segregated by race. We were here, we were told, for our own protection from the inmates who would "kick our asses." Again we waited naked, this time for an hour and a half, until we were issued our prison uniforms: an olive green T-shirt and shorts. That was it. No socks. No shoes. No long pants. No change of clothes. Simply a T-shirt and shorts.

Someone among us complained. And then came Bevel's voice, loud and angry.

"What's this hang-up about clothes?" he proclaimed. "Gandhi wrapped a rag around his *balls* and brought down the whole British *Empire!*"

My cellmate was a guy named William Harbour, who had been among our group of reinforcement riders from Nashville. Bill was a Tennessee State student, from poor roots—though not as poor as we ABT guys. He was small, even smaller than I, and very open, very talkative. He and his sister Liz were both very active in our Nashville movement, and though they were only a year or two younger than Diane, Bevel, Bernard and I, Bill and Liz treated us almost with awe. Through their eyes we were the veterans, the leaders. Bill particularly looked up to me. If John Lewis said go, Bill Harbour was ready to go.

And now here we were in Parchman. I didn't know it at the time, but Governor Barnett had instructed the superintendent to be careful with us. The press outside that fence was paying too much attention to the fate of the Freedom Riders for us to be treated the way Parchman's prisoners were normally treated. I wondered at first why we did no work, why we were confined to our cells throughout each day, never going outside, not even for exercise. I later learned that this was by order of the governor.

The monotony was tremendous. We had no reading material other than the Bible, a palm-sized copy of the New Testament, which was given to each of us by the local Salvation Army. I didn't read my Bible; I didn't feel like reading it. But I kept it. I still have that Bible today, with the date June 11, 1961, inscribed inside its cover.

We each had our own metal-frame bed with a mattress made by the inmates. That, a commode and a small washbowl completed the cell's furnishing. There were walls between the cells, so we could not see one another. Only when we were taken out to shower, which was twice a week, did we see anyone but our cellmate and the guards. Once a week we could write a letter, which I always made as long as I could.

One of the letters I wrote was mailed to the registrar at American Baptist, where I was due to graduate that month. In it, I explained to the ABT administration why I was missing my graduation. It was unreal in a way to be sitting in a Mississippi penal farm's maximum-security cellblock while many of my classmates were marching in procession in their commencement caps and gowns. But I really felt that there was no better place for me to be than right where I was. It was that feeling, more or less, that I expressed in my letter.

The guards had been ordered by the governor to be careful with us, prompting complaints from some of the deputies. "Guv'nor," one of the guards reportedly asked, "how we gon' stop their singin' if we cain't go upside their heads?"

The fact that physical punishment was prohibited forced them to be creative. On one occasion a fire hose was brought in and we were blasted with jets of water. Giant fans were then set up and turned on full blast, freezing us in our flooded cells.

On especially hot days—and there were many, this being summer in Mississippi—the windows were kept closed and we baked in the airless heat. Ceiling lights were kept on around the clock, making it difficult to sleep. One of the women, who were kept in another building, miscarried while a prison guard watched and did nothing.

One day our singing and preaching prompted a deputy to threaten to take our mattresses away. Hank Thomas hollered from his cell, *"Take* my mattress! I'll keep my *soul!"* With that, everyone—or almost everyone—threw his mattress against his cell bars. Two who did not were Fred Leonard and his cellmate, a tall, lanky, outspoken student from Howard University named Stokely Carmichael. Neither Carmichael nor Leonard had much interest in Gandhi or the principles of nonviolence or even the Bible, which was so often preached by Jim Bevel. Stokely and Fred were both totally committed to our cause, but they didn't necessarily agree with us on tactics. And they did not want to yield their mattresses. Leonard wound up clinging to his even when a guard began pulling it out into the hall. I will never forget the sight of that guard dragging Fred Leonard's mattress down that hallway, with Fred firmly attached, singing "I'm Gonna Tell God How You Treat Me," accompanied by a chorus of our cheers.

The same kind of bickering that had broken out among our ranks in the Hinds County jail surfaced during our stay at Parchman, and Stokely Carmichael in particular showed a knack both for starting an argument and for winning it. He had an amazingly sharp mind and a quick tongue as well. He was as different from me as night from day, both in personality and in philosophy, but for some reason I liked him. Maybe because he made no pretense to be anything but what he was. There was no guile about Stokely, and I liked that. What you saw was what you got. Not everyone liked Stokely, but I did, at least in the beginning.

We had no idea how long we'd be kept at Parchman. A week passed, then two. One day an elderly round-bellied white man in a suit and tie came down our hallway with a group of visitors behind him, showing us off as if we were attractions in a zoo. It was Governor Barnett, demonstrating for a group of his colleagues what happened to "outside agitators" in his state.

Barnett was mirroring the attitude of more than a few Mississippians. During our time in Parchman, as the jails back in Jackson continued to overflow with riders pouring in from all directions, the *Jackson Daily News* published a stark bulletin, a tongue-in-cheek warning with a message that was no joke:

Editor's note—The following is offered as a facetious editorial cartoon for the benefit of potential "tourist" traffic from the North and East:

ATTENTION: RESTLESS RACE-MIXERS
WHOSE HOBBY IS CREATING TROUBLE

Get away from the blackboard jungle. Rid yourself of fear of rapists, muggers, dopeheads, and switchblade artists during the hot, long summer.

FULFILL THE DREAM OF A LIFETIME

HAVE A "VACATION" ON A REAL PLANTATION

Here's All You Do

Buy yourself a Southbound ticket via rail, bus or air.

Check in and sign the guest register at the Jackson City Jail. Pay a nominal fine of $200. Then spend the next 4 months at our 21,000-acre Parchman Plantation in the heart of the Mississippi Delta. Meals furnished. Enjoy the wonders of chopping cotton, warm sunshine, plowing mules and tractors, feeding the chickens, slopping the pigs, scrubbing floors, cooking and washing dishes, laundering clothes.

Sun lotion, bunion plasters, as well as medical services free. Experience the "abundant" life under total socialism. Parchman prison fully air-cooled by Mother Nature.

(We cash U.S. Government Welfare Checks.)

Finally, on July 7, three weeks and a day after we'd been driven to Parchman—and three days after Independence Day, which we spent behind bars—our cell doors were opened, we were handed the clothes we'd been wearing when we arrived, and we were walked to the prison's front gate, where a small group of lawyers and friends were waiting to greet us. There were hugs, but no tears. A line of cars was waiting to drive us away.

On the trip back to Jackson, I thought about the fact that we had just about literally been through hell, first in Anniston, then in Birmingham, then in Montgomery, and now here at Parchman. Freedom Riders were flooding the South now, scores of buses filled with black and white passengers bound to break down the walls of segregation in these states. Before the summer was over, dozens of buses would pass through Georgia and Alabama and Mississippi and Louisiana, carrying riders who would continue the work we began that May.

But that work was just beginning. I knew that now. As I boarded a train in Jackson to carry me back to Nashville, I knew that my calling was not to go on to India. If there was anything I learned on that long, bloody bus trip of 1961, it was this—that we were in for a long, bloody fight here in the American South.

And I intended to stay in the middle of it.

Part IV

SNICK

10 / RAISE UP THE RUG

Though it took turns we never imagined—Parchman Penitentiary was not on our original itinerary; nor was St. Jude's Hospital or the Birmingham jail—our Freedom Ride of 1961 wound up doing exactly what we intended. It dramatized the situation of segregation in the South. It took the movement into places it had not been before. And it forced the federal government to respond with might to carry out the laws its own courts had passed. By the end of that summer of '61, more than three hundred riders—one fourth of them female—would be thrown into Jackson's jails, and Robert Kennedy would have no choice but to push the Interstate Commerce Commission to actively enforce the *Boynton* decision in bus terminals throughout the South, which it did that September.

But the real significance of the Freedom Rides went far beyond bus station snack bars and bathrooms. The rides marked a shift in the temperature of the movement, an upsurge in our aggressiveness. We were no longer content to simply wait for the government and courts to respond on their own terms and their own timetable. When Bobby Kennedy asked for a "cooling-off period" at the height of the rides, Jim Farmer just about snorted. "We've been cooling off for a hundred years," he answered. "If we get any cooler, we'll be in a deep freeze."

We now meant to push. We meant to provoke. We had done it in Nashville, in an orderly, disciplined, almost textbook-perfect nonviolent manner. Now we had carried that method south, bringing the Gandhian way into the belly of the Black Belt. The outrage generated by the ugly resistance we met that May—precisely the resistance we had hoped to elicit—swelled the movement with new members, hundreds of young men and women eager to put their own bodies on the line. The movement was no longer playing itself out on scattered local stages—in Nashville, Atlanta, Birmingham, Montgomery. It was no longer even limited just to the South. We had a national stage now. Segregation was a *national* problem now. And the nation—or at least its sons and daughters—was beginning to respond.

Unfortunately, many of those sons and daughters were unschooled in the techniques of nonviolent action. Worse, most of them had little or no interest in learning those techniques. This, it would turn out, would become the most significant result of the Freedom Rides: the turning toward radicalization of the movement, a militancy that would surge and swell month by month over the coming years, building pressure and tension from within until finally it would blow, bursting the civil rights movement apart and leaving it in scattered disarray.

I could see signs of that change when I returned that summer to the streets of Nashville. After the success of our spring campaign to desegregate the city's movie theaters, we decided for the first time to shift our focus from the issue of access and accommodation to the broader question of fair employment. There were many businesses in Nashville that owed their success to black customers but hired no black employees other than janitors or maids. A prime example was the city's grocery stores, most notably those owned by the H. G. Hill family, one of Nashville's wealthier white families. We—the Nashville Student Movement and the NCLC—decided to boycott and picket those stores that summer, urging them to adjust their hiring practices. At the same time we went after hotels, libraries, every business or public service in the city that practiced racial segregation.

We called the campaign Operation Open City, and for the first time we were joined on the picket lines by large numbers of non-Nashvillians—students, mostly Northerners, coming or going from the Freedom Rides. Nashville had become kind of a way station, a stop-off point, for many of these students. They were eager to be involved in what we were doing in Nashville, and they jumped right in, which would have been a good thing except for the fact that many of them were untrained in our practices and procedures.

I had no question then, and I have no question now, that the unique success of what we had achieved in the city of Nashville up until then, and what we would continue to achieve there in the coming years, was due to the discipline and care with which we approached our demonstrations. That summer, though, I could see that discipline eroding, crumbling a little at the edges where the outsiders were stepping in. You could see it in the clothing people wore. We Nashville students had always dressed carefully, the men typically in ties, the women in dresses or skirts. Now there were jeans and T-shirts on line. When confrontations occurred, as we knew they would—the Hills actually hired young thugs to harass us when we picketed—there was name-calling and taunting and cursing coming from some of the new faces on our lines. I can't count the number of times I had to step in and take someone aside and say, "This is not the way we conduct demonstrations here." But it kept happening.

One of the worst offenders, I have to say, was Stokely Carmichael. He'd come up to Nashville after our release from Parchman, and he settled in that summer, intent not just on joining us but on putting himself in a leadership role. Stokely was, as always, very visible. He loved nothing more than to scare the hell out of people, especially white people. And he was good at it. He had a sharp tongue, and he knew how to use it, to poke and prod and provoke. It was interesting to watch Stokely and compare him to Bevel. Both loved to speak. Both loved working an audience. But Bevel was a listener as well as a talker. He was open, eager to hear what you had to say, hungry to absorb new concepts and ideas. Stokely, on the other hand, was someone who had the answer and you were going to listen to it, period. He knew the way, and it was up to you to follow. He either mesmerized you or irritated you; there was no middle ground. And early on that summer in Nashville, he irritated more people than he attracted.

As soon as he stepped into those H. G. Hill's picket lines, Stokely began outright daring the white hecklers to attack him. He was threatening to disrupt and undo everything we were trying to achieve. I wasn't the only one who felt that way. At a meeting of our central committee early that July, we agreed that Stokely needed to be "invited" to leave Nashville. Jim Lawson himself delivered the message to Stokely, who left shortly thereafter, returning to D.C. There had to have been some hard feelings on his part, though I didn't see or hear about them. We obviously had our philosophical differences, Stokely and I, but I respected his passion and his conviction, and I still considered him my friend.

Another outsider who joined us in Nashville that summer was a schoolteacher and writer from Chicago, a black journalist named James Forman. He'd done some reporting for the *Chicago Defender,* covering Little Rock in 1957, and he had gone in 1960 to southwest Tennessee's Fayette and Haywood Counties, where three hundred black sharecroppers were thrown off their land that year and forced to live in a squalid tent city after daring to try to register to vote.

Now Forman was on his way to Monroe, North Carolina, where a local NAACP chairman named Robert Williams was making his reputation by advocating "self-defense" when faced by attacks from whites. "Meeting violence with violence" is how Williams put it, and Forman was on his way to see what this new attitude was all about. During his visit with us in Nashville that summer of '61, Forman was not shy about stating his differences with our views about violence.

I wasn't quite sure what to make of Jim Forman. I think I've always had a pretty good instinct about people, I've always been able to read them pretty well, and I felt right from the start with Forman that he was always holding something back, that he wasn't quite upfront. There was something about the man that was just not *real*. I never felt that Jim was showing all his cards, and that's something that's very important with me. I've said it all my life; I still say it today to my friends and colleagues in Congress: "Put your cards on the *table*. Put them on the table face *up*, so we can see them all." I never felt that Jim Forman was willing to put all his cards on the table. He always seemed to have motives and agendas and strategies that he wasn't sharing.

From the start, though, he made no secret of his questions about nonviolence. And he wasn't alone. Forman and Stokely, and so many of the new people we were seeing coming through Nashville were jaded, outraged at the brutality they had seen or, in many cases, experienced during the Freedom Rides. Many of these young men and women were not veterans of the sit-ins. They had never been exposed to the kind of sustained nonviolent demonstrations we had orchestrated in Nashville. All they had seen was the horror and violence flashed on television screens and newspaper front pages during the Rides. *That* was what they were responding to. That was what had brought them south. They were outraged. They were angry. And they were at best merely tolerant of the notion of nonviolence.

This wave of anger and outrage alarmed the Kennedys. They were sickened by the hatred and brutality of the whites who had attacked and imprisoned us in South Carolina and Alabama and Mississippi, but they were just as upset with *us*. They felt we were instigators, stirring up more trouble than was necessary. Their priorities at that point were keeping the peace, quelling crises, positioning the President politically, both in the South and abroad. Bobby Kennedy admitted in later years that in 1961 he "did not lay awake at night worrying about the problems of Negroes." That would change. He would change. There would come a point where he would tell me personally that we changed him. But back then, still early in the game, it was the problems of the Kennedys that were the Kennedys' major concern, not the problems of black America.

Which was why Bobby Kennedy met with a small delegation of SNCC and CORE members, including Diane Nash, early that June, while I was still imprisoned down in Parchman. The group had gone to Washington seeking more federal help for the rides. Instead they got a counteroffer from the attorney general. Rather than focusing on provocation and confrontation, Kennedy suggested, we would be more effective in the long run to concentrate on registering black voters. He didn't mention that all those black votes could only help the President, but he didn't have to. That was obvious.

The "long run," of course, was something we were fed up with. The phrase itself struck a raw nerve. So did the notion of an outsider, especially a white outsider, telling young black people what they should or shouldn't be doing. One of the group at that meeting, a SNCC member from Virginia Union Seminary named Charles Sherrod, was so incensed at what he considered Kennedy's gall that some people present were afraid he would attack the attorney general right there in his office.

But the White House was not the only place where the idea of voter registration as the focal point of the movement had taken hold. Before the year was out, Dr. King would give it his full endorsement. "The central front," he would say, "is that of suffrage. If we in the South can win the right to vote, it will place in our hands more than an abstract right. It will give us the concrete tool with which we ourselves can correct injustice."

Voting versus marching, registering versus "riding," moving beyond the direct action of protests and demonstrations to the mainstream political process of voter registration—this was the central subject at a SNCC leadership workshop held that July in Nashville. And the debate was intense.

Jim Forman was there. So was Charles McDew from South Carolina State College in Orangeburg—McDew would soon replace Marion Barry as the chairman of SNCC. He, along with Charles Jones of Johnson C. Smith College in Charlotte and Charles Sherrod, was strongly in favor of shifting our focus from direct action to registration, as was Tim Jenkins, a Howard University graduate who was vice president of a group called the National Student Association. Jenkins had the ear of the White House—he and Civil Rights Division director Burke Marshall were friends—and he was completely committed to Bobby Kennedy's vision of building the black vote. Jenkins considered himself a little more sophisticated, more politically savvy than the students who had been filling stools at snack counters and riding buses into Birmingham. He didn't think much of the "pain and suffering school" of martyrdom. He saw power in politics through representation, through the ballot box.

There was no question that we could use the money being promised by the Kennedy administration if we shifted our focus their way. SNCC had no money to speak of. We had one full-time staffer, a student from Kentucky State named Ed King, who manned a tiny, dingy one-room office directly across Atlanta's Auburn Avenue from the SCLC's comparatively spacious and well-furnished headquarters. The White House had money lined up for us—from the Field Foundation, the Taconic Foundation, the Edgar Stern Family Fund and even Harry Belafonte, who was a personal friend of the Kennedys and who had invited several SNCC members up to Washington in late June to discuss fund-raising for a national voter registration campaign.

I didn't take that trip to meet with Belafonte, but I heard all about it. And

I didn't like it. Neither did Diane, or Marion, or Bevel or Bernard, all of whom spoke firmly in defense of sticking to our roots. As far as we were concerned, the very future of SNCC was on the line here. Direct action was what had gotten us this far; SNCC had been created and built on the foundation of confrontation—disciplined, focused, aggressive, nonviolent confrontation.

Diane was adamant about not forsaking those roots. And she was vocal about not trusting the government's motives. The money we were being offered could be seen as an effort to buy us out, to make us beholden to the very government we were confronting. Diane, and many of the others in our camp, felt that this voter registration plan was nothing more than a device to "get the niggers off the streets," as more than one of our group put it.

To me the matter was simple. We had gotten this far by dramatizing the issue of segregation, by putting it onstage and *keeping* it onstage. I believed firmly that we needed to push and push and not stop pushing. Raise up the rug and pull out the dirt and force people to look at it, to *see* it. I believed in drama. I believed in *action*. Dr. King said early on that there is no noise as powerful as the sound of the marching feet of a determined people, and I believed that. I *experienced* it. I agreed completely with Diane and the others, at least at that time, that this voter registration push by the government was a trick to take the steam out of the movement, to slow it down.

Nothing was decided at that Nashville gathering. A month later, at a conference at Highlander, the debate continued, and this time it came to a head. Ella Baker, who was completely committed to the utter necessity of keeping this student movement independent and in control of itself, suggested a compromise solution. Two wings of SNCC would be created, a direct action wing headed by Diane and a voter registration wing directed by Charlie Jones. Nobody turned cartwheels over the idea, but it was the best we could do. Bernard put a nice spin on the decision with a comment at the end of the weekend. "A bird," he observed, "needs two wings to fly."

As we would soon learn, there was no separation between action and voter registration. Southern states were riddled with legal obstacles to keep black men and women from voting—poll taxes, literacy tests. But those states were perfectly willing to resort to terrorism as well. We had to look only as far as that tent city over in Fayette County, or at the 1958 beating of a Louisiana farmer named Izell Henry for daring to try to vote (he suffered permanent brain damage), to understand how far the white powers-that-be would go to keep black people away from the ballot box. Dozens of scattered episodes of brutality like this were just hints of what was to come, of the violence we would be met with as we journeyed south to organize the vote. We would learn almost immediately that voter registration was as threatening to the entrenched white establishment in the South as sit-ins or Freedom Rides, and that it would prompt the same violent response. As far as the staunch segregationists were concerned, there was no difference at all between direct action and voter registration, none whatsoever.

By that fall, SNCC memorandums were going out labeling voter registration as our top priority. A new, privately funded Voter Education Project was being set up in Atlanta under the direction of a group called the Southern Regional Council. A plan was taking shape to send "field secretaries" into communities throughout the South, men and women who would set up offices and prepare for the arrival of a projected 200,000 volunteer workers, all aimed at bringing America's invisible black vote out of the darkness of fear and repression.

Small handfuls of organizers were already out in the field that fall, ahead of the voter registration machinery still taking shape back at the offices of SNCC and CORE and the SCLC and the NAACP. Bevel and Bernard had gone down to Jackson, trying to organize demonstrations there as part of SNCC's direct action wing. Charles Sherrod, who at twenty-two was a year older than I, and an eighteen-year-old SNCC staffer named Cordell Reagon had gone down late that summer to Terrell County, Georgia—Terrible Terrell, as it was called. Their intent was to establish a base of operations in what was probably the most racially oppressive section of the state of Georgia. They would be there only a few weeks before they would narrow their focus to a city called Albany, a former slave-trading center, a racially repressive community of 60,000 where these two young guys, Sherrod and Reagon, would soon risk their lives to register voters.

Lives were on the line. There was no question about that. Later on a reporter would describe these first field workers as "nonviolent guerrilla fighters," and that's exactly what they were, slipping quietly and unnoticed deep behind enemy lines during that late summer and fall of 1961.

Deepest behind those lines was a man named Bob Moses, a serious, soft-spoken twenty-six-year-old Harlem native with a graduate degree in philosophy from Harvard. When Amzie Moore, the filling station owner and local organizer from Cleveland, Mississippi, had come to our SNCC meeting in 1960 and asked us to send help, Bob Moses wound up being the help that eventually arrived. Now, with our plans for a massive voter registration project taking shape, Moses and Moore were on the move in a place where any out-of-the-ordinary move by a black man could be deadly. Cleveland was not far from Money, Mississippi, where just six years earlier Emmett Till's mutilated body had been pulled up from the waters of the Tallahatchie.

There was no state that showed us what we were up against more than Mississippi. Statistics there made the rest of the South look progressive by comparison.

Nearly 90 percent of Mississippi's black families lived below the poverty level.

The average annual income of Mississippi's blacks was less than $1,500 —the lowest in the nation.

Seven percent of Mississippi's black students finished high school—one sixth of the state's number of white graduates.

And finally, 5 percent of the state's eligible black voters were registered; in many counties, there were none. Zero.

To white Mississippians, this was the way it *should* be. Governor Barnett, the man who had paid us a visit at Parchman, made no bones about the sanctity of segregation. "The good Lord," he proclaimed, "was the original segregationist. He put the Negro in Africa, separated him from all other races."

This was the attitude Bob Moses was up against in Mississippi—"the middle of the iceberg," as he called it after one of his many jailings there. He set up his base of operations late that summer down in the southwest corner of the state, in Pike County (Mississippi's Pike County, as opposed to the one I was born in in Alabama), in a town called McComb. By the end of the year, Moses would be directing a team of about fifteen SNCC workers running Freedom Schools throughout the state, knocking on doors of farmhouses and shacks, explaining voting requirements to elderly men and women one step away from slavery, preparing them for the questions they would find on literacy tests, then escorting them to county courthouses that had never seen a black person walk up the steps to register to vote. White Mississippians had never seen it, and they didn't like it. Beatings, arrests and deaths would begin that fall, and things would get much worse before they would begin to get better.

Meanwhile, after spending my summer on the picket lines in Nashville, with a couple of more visits to the city jail, I returned to school that fall of '61, this time enrolling at Fisk, where I registered for a degree in philosophy. I was hungry for a secular liberal arts education to supplement the Bible-focused education I had received at American Baptist. I wanted to delve more deeply and thoroughly into the teachings and ideas Jim Lawson had introduced me to in his workshops. And I also wanted a degree that was not as limited as the one from ABT, which certified me only to become a preacher.

I entered school that fall with a measure of fame as a Freedom Rider. That had become an almost magical phrase among black communities all over the country. If you'd been on the Freedom Rides, you were treated almost like royalty. It was pretty heady stuff. We—the first wave of riders—were invited late that summer up to Pittsburgh, where a "Salute to the Freedom Riders" mass rally was held to raise funds for the upcoming voter registration campaign. Dr. King spoke. Mahalia Jackson sang. And not long after, I, along with the other nine riders who had picked up the gauntlet in Nashville after the attacks in Anniston and Birmingham, received a $500 Freedom Award scholarship from the SCLC. Dr. King presented the awards at a ceremony in the Grand Ole Opry auditorium. Without that money, I could not have afforded to enter Fisk. It was a godsend.

It also came with a note from Dr. King telling me how valuable I had been to the movement and how much I could contribute in the future. He wrote that the SCLC was looking for someone to head its operation in Alabama, and perhaps after I finished my studies at Fisk, I might consider taking that position. Dr. King and the SCLC leadership were constantly trying in one way or another to pull many of us more visible members of SNCC into their fold. As more and more arguments and disagreements began surfacing at our SNCC meetings, some of us did accept King's entreaties. Jim Bevel, for example, would, by the following spring, be the SCLC's field secretary for the state of Mississippi.

Personally, I never considered leaving SNCC. SNCC was where I belonged. SNCC was who I was. I acutely felt the difference between us and the older, established "black bourgeoisie groups," as I described them in a column I wrote that fall for the Fisk student newspaper. Those words looked pretty radical at the time, which is ironic considering that even then I was beginning to be labeled "square" by the more militant elements emerging within the student end of the movement, within SNCC.

I took a light load of courses that fall, to leave room for my priority, which was the movement. I was elected to the chairmanship of our Nashville Student Movement that September. Diane had left by then to join Bevel down in Jackson. By the end of the year, they would be man and wife, which truly surprised no one. Bevel had lost none of his passion and charisma. The fact that he had turned so much of it toward the cause couldn't help but make him even more attractive to Diane. For his part, Bevel's commitment to the cause did not make him any less attracted to attractive women, and there was no woman more attractive than Diane Nash. I think just about every guy who joined the Nashville movement had a crush on Diane at one time or another. But no one could have hooked her besides Bevel.

I really believe Diane and Bevel were fated to come together, but I hated to see them go. Bernard, too, was gone. In fact, most of the group that had first gathered on those Tuesday nights with Jim Lawson had moved on. I had become an oddity, a holdover of sorts. Many of the professors at Fisk, as well as many of my fellow students, thought I was some sort of weird character, that I was not really in school but was just using Fisk as a base of operations, that I was some sort of transient activist, just passing through.

I did take my studies seriously, but I took just as seriously the fact that there were things that needed to be done in this country, and somebody had to do them. I could have made better grades if I had focused entirely on school—especially in German; Lord, I had trouble with German. But I didn't do that. It all mattered to me, school *and* the movement.

The movement in Nashville actually shrank that year. It wasn't as "mass" as it had been a year earlier. We had to work hard to keep it going, which we did by developing a small, hard-core, dedicated group to recruit freshmen and younger students, who were typically more eager and, frankly, more ready for action than older students. We called our core group the Horrible Seven— Fred Leonard was one of them; and Bill Harbour and his sister Elizabeth; and this young kid from New York, David Thompson; and Rick Momeyer, an exchange student from Allegheny College up in Pennsylvania. We spent that fall and winter "marching through the Yellow Pages," as one reporter put it.

I will never forget gathering one afternoon that November to go downtown for a demonstration. We were over near Fisk's Jubilee Hall, a cornerstone of the campus. It was a week or so before Thanksgiving. Autumn was in the air. We were getting set to drive over to First Baptist when we heard a commotion and a group of fraternity guys came running around a building, thirty or forty of them, wearing dog collars around their throats and carrying their Greek paddles. They ran past us, barking like hounds, hollering and whooping and going through their fraternity ritual. I was stunned. I really was. It struck me as completely distasteful, very disappointing, very distressing, to see these young black men swept up in this trivial silliness at the very moment that people their own age, young men and women just like them, were risking their lives down in Mississippi, standing up for the future of all of us. What these young guys were doing had so little meaning compared to that. It was almost an affront. It was just so irrelevant, so insulting. It was hard to believe. I still haven't reconciled to it.

And those young men and women south of us *were* risking their lives. Things were rapidly turning even more violent as that year drew toward a close.

That September, down in McComb, a man named Herbert Lee, a local black farmer who had hooked up with Bob Moses to help register voters, was shot dead by a member of the Mississippi state legislature, a man named E. H. Hurst. Hurst claimed Lee had attacked him with a tire iron and so he had shot him through the head. The coroner's jury ruled "justifiable homicide" after the testimony of three witnesses, one of them black. But when Moses visited that black witness, the frightened man said he had lied at the inquest because he was scared for his own life. He said he had watched Hurst outright murder Herbert Lee, who was unarmed and attacked no one.

A subsequent protest march, led by Moses and Charlie McDew and a white member of SNCC from Alabama named Bob Zellner, resulted in those three being beaten by a mob as they were arrested along with 119 local students. The three were sentenced to four months in prison, and the McComb movement, for the time being, was brought to a halt.

At the same time, trouble erupted in Albany. Sherrod and Reagon had hardly begun their work before broadening their focus from just getting out the vote to mobilizing and confronting segregation in Albany in the same way we were doing in Nashville. They called it the Albany Movement, but they faced a far more educated and sophisticated reaction than anything we had encountered in Nashville.

The police chief in Albany, a man named Laurie Pritchett, had actually read Dr. King's *Stride Toward Freedom*, which outlined the Gandhian method of protest. Pritchett was determined not to make the same mistakes as, say, Bull Connor. What he did was take the basic ideas from Dr. King's book and strategically counterattack with a divide-and-conquer method of arrests and jailings. Pritchett and his men made more arrests in Albany than had been made anywhere else in the movement's history thus far—more than five hundred men, women and children would eventually be imprisoned around Albany. But Pritchett spread those prisoners out in jails all through the surrounding counties, so there was never a central focal point for either the demonstrators or the reporters to fix on. Bill Hansen, one of our SNCC staffers in Albany, summed up the cleverness of Pritchett's tactic. "We ran out of people," said Hansen, "before he ran out of jails."

Pritchett's men were no less violent than Connor's—a pregnant woman was clubbed by one police officer so badly that she had a miscarriage; another woman was pulled into court by her hair; a man was dragged into court by his gonads; and one man was hanged by his thumbs in a jailhouse—but on the whole they were much more careful than the police had been in Birmingham or Montgomery.

Comparatively speaking, Laurie Pritchett was a cunning man, as deceitful as he had to be. When Dr. King came down to Albany that December, was arrested and vowed to stay in jail until the city accepted the demands for desegregation, Pritchett and the city leaders agreed to a settlement, promising to make concessions. Dr. King came out of jail, and, to his embarrassment, most of the concessions were simply never made.

It was confusing. The rules were changing every day, and resentment was growing. Some of the SNCC workers in Albany vocally objected to Dr. King coming there in the first place. When he held a press conference after his release from jail and excluded SNCC volunteers from the proceedings, a lot of them felt the way Cordell Reagon did. "I don't think," said Reagon, "that any-body appreciates going to jail, getting their balls busted day in and day out, and then you don't even get to speak on it."

The press put a lot of focus on this kind of dissension in the ranks. And that played right into Pritchett's hand. He crowed in the newspapers about "meeting nonviolence with nonviolence," the flip side of Robert Williams's formula up in North Carolina. By the end of the year, the Albany Movement looked as paralyzed as McComb's.

Still, the voter registration drive continued to take shape. In January 1962 the Southern Regional Council's Voter Education Project was formally begun. At the same time, a coalition of civil rights groups called the Council of Federated Organizations (COFO), an alliance of SNCC, SCLC, CORE and NAACP organizers in Mississippi, was created to harmonize all the voting rights activity springing up in that state. The director of COFO naturally became Bob Moses, who was getting more and more attention and liking it less and less. He was very wary of what he called the cult of personality. And he tried as hard as he could to avoid the spotlight, partly because of his personal philosophy and partly because in that part of the country, at that time, doing what he was doing, any attention at all from the white community could mean danger or even death.

Bringing organizations together in the way we tried doing with COFO was not easy. In the best of times, there were always small egos and turf battles to deal with, both within the various civil rights organizations and be-tween them. That's human nature. You can't escape it. We didn't want—we didn't *need*—competition among us, but it was always there, to one degree or another. In 1962, as the movement on Mississippi began to take shape, some of those rivalries intensified. When the Kennedy administration first men-tioned sending money to groups like SNCC for voter registration work, some leaders of the NAACP, which had virtually monopolized the cause of civil rights for decades and had always been first in line to receive federal funding, were alarmed that more money for another organization might mean less for them.

As for the SCLC, our differences were primarily philosophical. From the beginning we at SNCC had believed in moving away from the cloistered set-tings of colleges and universities, away from the town and the gown, and going out on the byways and highways to connect with the people, the true masses. Unlike the members of the old-guard civil rights organizations, espe-cially the SCLC, who tended to look down through a telescope at the little people, who met with one another and conducted membership drives and membership meetings and big fund-raisers and rallies but did not step down and suffer the kinds of indignities and injustices that the local people were suffering on a daily basis, we *did* go out and live and suffer with the everyday people. That was the key to whatever success we were able to achieve.

I really felt then, and I still feel, that we in SNCC were a lot like members of the early Christian church, going out with virtually nothing but the clothes on our backs to bring the gospel of Freedom to the people. We went out into these tiny little towns and hamlets in Sunflower County, Mississippi, and Lowndes County, Alabama, not knowing where we were going to stay from one night to the next, where or what or *if* we were going to eat. We couldn't be certain we were even going to return.

There was a great deal of faith involved with this. We were venturing out basically on our own, becoming missionaries in a sense. But not missionaries in a traditional sense, because we were meeting the people on *their* terms, not ours. If they were out in the field picking cotton, we would go out in that field and pick with them. If they were planting squash, we planted, too. Whatever the people were doing, we were there with them, *really* there. We lived with them in their homes, held hands and prayed with them, shared their food, shared their beds, shared their worries and their hopes. We listened to them. Before we ever got around to sharing what we had to say, we *listened*. And in the process, we built up both their trust in us and their confidence in themselves. Essentially we were out to spread faith and courage, and naturally we had to find those things in ourselves first.

One group of people who helped us find our own courage in these communities were the local women, the matriarchal heads of so many of these households. Over and over again we found that it was these women—wives and mothers in their forties and fifties, hardworking, humorous, no-nonsense, incredibly resilient women who had carried such an unimaginable weight through their own lives and had been through so much unspeakable hell that there was nothing left on this earth for them to be afraid of—who showed *us* the way to mobilize in the towns and communities where they lived. No one was more ready, eager and willing to climb on the Freedom Train in these little towns and on these little farms than the women.

A prime example was a stout, soulful forty-four-year-old sharecropper in Sunflower County named Fannie Lou Hamer. Mrs. Hamer came from a family of twenty children. She knew nothing but hard work all her life, but her spirit was far from extinguished. She'd never dreamed of doing something as daring as registering to vote—she didn't even know a black person *could* register to vote in Mississippi—until one evening in 1962 when she went to a local SNCC meeting and heard Jim Bevel speak. Inspired and awakened by that evening, she went down to the county courthouse in a little town called Indianola to register, and was subsequently fired from her job, arrested and beaten badly while in jail. That made her all the more resolved to join SNCC as a field organizer. From that summer on Fannie Lou became a tireless voice for our cause, putting herself out front as an organizer, a speaker and, eventually, an actual political candidate—always an outspoken image of a poor, black woman who was simply out of patience.

Most people today have never heard of Fannie Lou Hamer, but she is a legend to anyone who knows anything about what was happening in Mississippi in the early 1960s. Without her and hundreds of women like her, we would never have been able to achieve what we did.

Faith, hope and courage—these were all essential ingredients for the work SNCC was doing in the Deep South in those early years. And anger, too. Yes, there was anger among us in SNCC, but it was a good anger, a healthy anger, at least in that early stage. It was a positive, constructive type of anger. We were rebels, absolutely. We were all about rebellion, but it was rebellion against an evil thing, the whole system and structure of segregation and racial discrimination. If the old guard leadership of our own black community was holding us back, then we were rebelling against them, too.

We found that most of the people—the *people,* not the leaders—were hungry for what we had to offer. They felt things were moving too slowly, just as we did. We were telling them, "You don't have to wait until Roy Wilkins comes to Jackson. You don't have to wait until Martin Luther King comes to McComb. You can do it *yourself.* There is no more powerful force than *you.* There is no leader as powerful as *you,* if you pull together."

This is a very noble concept, the idea of a leaderless movement, of a truly indigenous, nonviolent revolution. This is what we set out to create in the early years in Nashville, it is what we believed in at the dawn of SNCC, and it is what I still believe in today, that the leaders should follow the people, and the people can and should lead themselves. People talk often these days about empowerment. Well, empowerment is exactly what we were trying to share through SNCC in the early 1960s in small towns and cities throughout the American South.

This was all on the table in April 1962, when SNCC observed its second anniversary with a conference in Atlanta. It was incredible to see how drastically the complexion of the organization had changed in such a short time. So many faces were gone—Bernard, Bevel, and Diane (who was pregnant with their first child) and many others who had been there in the beginning. In their place had risen new voices—Stokely, Forman, Sherrod, Ruby Smith—as well as a wave of white activists from various leftist groups. These included Carl and Anne Braden of the Southern Conference Educational Fund; Bob Zellner, also of the SCEF; and a guy from Students for a Democratic Society (SDS) named Tom Hayden. Hayden had gone down to McComb that winter and been pulled from a car and beaten. He had been affected deeply by this

experience, and he and his wife, Casey, came to Atlanta that spring with an almost religious commitment to our cause.

Our cause remained the same, of course, but our methods were all in
question. You heard the term "revolution" more than the word "integration."
The spirit of redemptive love was being pushed aside by a spirit of rage. And
the whole idea of nonviolence was up for debate. Jim Forman was not alone
in embracing the "self-defense" argument—more than a few of the 250
SNCC representatives in Atlanta that weekend argued that it should be ac-
ceptable to strike back if you're hit. Jim Lawson would never have accepted
such a position, but he wasn't there to offer his own. For the first time, Lawson, who had been so crucial to the creation of SNCC, was not invited to its
conference.

It was ironic to see Jim Lawson spurned by the same organization whose
original "Statement of Purpose" was still printed in the organization's hand-
book:

> We affirm the philosophical or religious ideal of nonviolence as the
> foundation of our purpose, the presupposition of our faith, and the
> manner of our action. Nonviolence as it grows from the Judaic-
> Christian tradition seeks a social order of justice permeated by love.
> Integration of human endeavor represents the crucial first step to-
> wards such a society.
>
> Through nonviolence, courage displaces fear; love transforms
> hate. Acceptance dissipates prejudice; hope ends despair. Peace
> dominates war; faith reconciles doubt. Mutual regard cancels enmity.
> Justice for all overthrows injustice. The redemptive community su-
> persedes systems of gross immorality.
>
> Love is the central motif of nonviolence. Love is the force by
> which God binds man to Himself and man to man. Such love goes to
> the extreme; it remains loving and forgiving even in the midst of hos-
> tility. It matches the capacity of evil to inflict suffering with an even
> more enduring capacity to absorb evil, all the while persisting in love.
>
> By appealing to the conscience and standing on the moral nature
> of human existence, nonviolence nurtures the atmosphere in which
> reconciliation and justice become actual possibilities.

It was Jim Lawson who had guided the writing of those words in May 1960.

Everyone knew I stood where Jim stood when it came to the philosophy
of nonviolence, but the fact that I'd been at the forefront of so many actions,
that I'd been arrested and beaten and jailed so many times, held a lot of
weight with my SNCC colleagues, old and new. Whether or not they embraced the idea of nonviolence, they respected those who had been through

the battles, as it were. So it was not surprising, I guess, that at the same time as Jim Lawson was shunned, I was elected to SNCC's executive coordinating committee.

A month later, at an SCLC meeting in Chattanooga, I was elected again, this time to the board of the SCLC. Dr. King had urged my nomination, against the objections of some of the more entrenched SCLC leaders. He wanted "young blood" among the SCLC leadership, and I was one of several new board members chosen for that reason. I was happy to do it, to contribute whatever I could, anything to help the cause. The way I saw it, we were all, in the end, on the same team. If our eyes were on what really mattered, then there was no question of divided loyalty. There could be many paths to the same end—I really believed that. My own path was that of SNCC, of taking the movement to the people, but that didn't stop me from helping others along their chosen paths.

My path took me that summer to a tiny town called Cairo, at the southernmost tip of Illinois, where the Mississippi and Ohio Rivers come together. Though Illinois is considered a Northern state, Cairo, bordered by Kentucky and Missouri, was Southern in every way—very small, very rural, very segregated. It, along with the nearby town of Charleston, Missouri, became a target that summer of a direct action campaign much like the one we had going in Nashville. Theaters, restaurants, hotels, bus station, the city swimming pool—they were all segregated, and I spent that summer getting to know them all very well. I also became familiar with the interior of the Cairo city jail.

What we faced in Cairo that summer was more harassment than outright brutality. It was nothing like what was happening in Mississippi, where violence, as we knew it would, was increasing almost daily. When Sam Block, a SNCC organizer down in Greenwood, set up his office there, it was soon attacked by a group of armed whites. Sam and two staffers were able to flee through a second-story window and slide down a television antenna to safety.

Guns were the most obvious weapons, but they weren't the only ones used by the people who wanted to stop us. A particularly cruel tactic used in Leflore County, where Greenwood is located, was the cutoff by authorities of a federal program that supplied surplus food to the county's impoverished black residents, thousands of whom depended on this food to supplement their meager income from cotton farming and get them through the winter.

Another terrorist tactic was to print the names of all voter applicants in local newspapers—the publishers fully cooperated—which made the new black voters visible targets for everything from getting fired from their jobs, to having loans denied, to seeing their rents increased, to being evicted. All this, besides of course the ever-present danger of being physically attacked.

The same ugliness was surging in Albany, where Dr. King's return that

July for sentencing in connection with his arrest the previous December rekindled the violence there. When King was given a jail term and put behind bars, subsequent rallies and marches erupted into brick-throwing from demonstrators as police moved in for arrests. Chief Pritchett made hay of the brick-throwing, mocking the "nonviolence" of the marchers, and he arrested even more of them.

Scattered beatings continued. C. B. King, a black Albany attorney and civil rights leader, had his head split open by an elderly cane-wielding sheriff when he presented himself at a local jail to represent Bill Hansen, one of our white SNCC staffers, who had been arrested during a demonstration. In another confrontation, Marion King, the wife of C. B. King's brother Slater King, was slapped to the ground and kicked by a police officer during a gathering outside a local jailhouse. She was six months pregnant at the time and suffered a miscarriage a few weeks later.

The violence in Albany did not stop with fists and canes and feet. There were shootings as well—four homes of Albany area voter registration organizers were riddled with bullets in late August, and four nights later three shotgun blasts were fired into a home where Charles Sherrod was sleeping.

Through all this, in Mississippi and in Georgia, where our voter registration efforts were concentrated and where the backlash of violence was most brutal, the federal government was conspicuous by its absence. There were few words of support from Washington, and no physical support in the way of federal marshals. Pleas were pouring in to the White House for the government to step in and help. But those pleas were ignored. Chuck McDew sent a telegram to Robert Kennedy late that summer concerning the violence in Greenwood and warning that "there is a great possibility of more Emmett Till cases." Soon thereafter, there was just such a case—the unidentified body of a black man was found in the small Mississippi town of Goodman.

"Where are the Kennedys?" That was the question we were all asking. The only federal presence was occasional FBI agents who did nothing but watch and take notes while these attacks went on. Of course this was not surprising. The agents' boss, J. Edgar Hoover, was known to be unsympathetic to our cause.

Near the end of that summer, an enduring image of our pleas for federal help came out of Cairo, where I was leading a demonstration of students and young children one afternoon at the city's swimming pool, which had remained segregated despite our weeks of protest. During this particular vigil outside the pool, I gathered our group and we knelt to pray in support of our brothers and sisters in Albany. Danny Lyon, a new staff photographer for SNCC—we called him Dandelion—was there that day. He'd approached Jim Forman one day and asked him if there was any way he could help us with his photography skills. Forman told him if he wanted to do something, he should take his camera and go to Cairo and shoot what was going on up there. Danny became one of my closest friends; eventually we would become roommates.

Danny Lyon was with us that day outside the swimming pool, and as we knelt and prayed, he snapped a photograph. That picture, captioned "COME LET US BUILD A NEW WORLD TOGETHER," became probably the most popular poster of the movement. Ten thousand copies were printed and put on sale for a dollar apiece, and they sold out.

What a lot of people don't know is that moments after that photo was taken we moved into the street to sing, and a white man in a pickup truck came driving straight at us. He slowed down as he got near us, but he didn't stop. He kept inching forward. We cautiously moved aside, all of us but one young teenage girl, who defiantly stood her ground, just like the Chinese student who stared down the line of tanks at Tiananmen Square. Unlike those tanks, which stopped, this truck kept coming. The driver kept moving forward until his truck's bumper nudged the girl and pushed her body aside.

It was a very symbolic moment, that little showdown. It reflected the resistance we faced, the fact that we would have to stand our ground and be knocked down many times before those trucks would finally stop.

That fall I returned to Fisk for my second year and to the streets of Nashville, where we were now staging a series of "sleep-ins" in the lobbies of the city's segregated hotels, places like the Hermitage and the Andrew Jackson. It would not be long before *Jet* magazine would come out with a cover story naming Nashville the "Best City in the South for Negroes." The story made much of the success we had accomplished, especially in light of the frustration and failure the movement had experienced in Albany:

> Negroes in Tennessee's capital city have earned for themselves more desegregation in more diverse areas than is enjoyed by their brothers of color in any other major Old South community....
>
> For at least five years, whites and Negroes stood eyeball-to-eyeball in bitter confrontations over segregation in Nashville. There were times when brushfire violence threatened to reduce the city to smoldering ashes. An eyelash before it was too late, the white power structure blinked. When their eyes had adjusted to the new light of the revolution, they became more color blind. They watched their city desegregate in direct ratio to the pressures exerted by the Negro community.

The success we were tasting in Nashville, though, meant less and less to the more radical factions in SNCC, who were understandably deeply disturbed by the seething violence that was increasing by the day down in Mississippi. That September the whole country watched as federal marshals sent in to protect James Meredith, the first black student ever to enroll at the University of Mississippi, were attacked and overwhelmed by a mob of 2,500 white rioters carrying clubs and guns and screaming, "Kill the nigger-loving bastards!" and "Give us the nigger!" By dawn the next day, more than half of the 320 marshals were wounded, and two bystanders—a French journalist and a jukebox repairman—were killed.

Compared to a vicious battle like that, our success at desegregating movie theaters and grocery stores in Nashville could seem almost quaint. I was told as much at a SNCC conference that November, where, as part of the gathering, we staged a demonstration at a downtown restaurant called the Tic-Toc. The same problems I'd seen a year earlier on the H. G. Hill picket lines recurred, with most of the out-of-town SNCC staffers not understanding why we needed to have a briefing before going out to march, or why I was walking the line, asking several people to put out the cigarettes they were smoking. "Young man," I'd say, "we don't allow smoking here." Or, "Young lady, please stand up straight." I was hardly older than these kids I was talking to, but I *felt* much older. And some of them scoffed. I heard the term "square" again and again, along with laughter. It didn't bother me personally, but this insulting of one another was not a good sign. Unity and mutual respect were utterly essential to what we were doing, whether it was in those deadly woods down in Mississippi or on a harmless picket line there in Nashville (not so harmless that particular day, as it turned out—I was beaten to the floor inside the lobby of that Tic-Toc that afternoon by a group of young whites who wound up with my blood on their fists).

Unity was becoming an issue as well in terms of the role of whites in SNCC. There were voices starting to question whether SNCC should be an interracial organization at all. Never mind that Jane Stembridge and Bill Hansen, Bob Zellner and Dotty Miller, Casey Hayden and Mary King, and so many other white men and women had been with us almost from the beginning. Now there was talk that they might somehow be liabilities—talk I wanted nothing to do with. I spoke out loudly and often on this issue. We're all in this together, I said. The Beloved Community isn't just an idea. It's real, and it begins with us. If you were committed to the idea of seeing the spark of the sacred in every human being, no matter how vile or how violent, how could you hold yourself apart from someone else simply because he or she was white? This so obviously embraced the very concept of racial discrimination that we were fighting against. How could we ask others to look beyond race if we weren't able to do it ourselves?

Even beyond that, there was the matter of our shared experience. We had stood side by side for years now with young white men and women in

Nashville. During the Freedom Ride, I'd seen people like Jim Peck, Al Bigelow and Jim Zwerg stand and suffer *with* us. We had become brothers and sisters in the struggle. We bled together. We suffered together. How could you look at something like race after experiences like that?

There were also concerns about where a lot of these white students were coming from, about what political philosophies and ideologies they were bringing with them. Some of our people were afraid of what labels might get attached to us because of this group from California or that one from Wisconsin. "Communist," of course, was the big one. We had many long, intense discussions about whether someone coming into SNCC had been a member of the American Communist Party, or whether someone had been on the House Un-American Activities Committee list, or whether this person was gay, or whether that one from SDS was too radical. This kind of talk had been going on even back during the Freedom Rides, when some of the SNCC and CORE people considered some of the lawyers sent down by the National Lawyers Guild to represent us in court possibly too "radical." They were talking about attorneys like William Kunstler, who came down to defend us in Jackson and who I thought was a great guy—as well as brilliant in the courtroom.

None of these labels meant a thing to me. All that ever mattered to me was whether a person was committed to the ideal of an interracial democracy and to the philosophy of nonviolent activism as a means to that end. If you had a committed heart and were willing to put your body on the line alongside us, then as far as I was concerned, you were welcome to march and ride and sit in with us.

The racial or political composition of SNCC was in no way an issue for me. It couldn't be. But it was beginning to be for some, and it would become more so as time passed.

And time *was* passing. The first month of 1963 a new governor of Alabama, a man who had vowed after his 1958 defeat by John Patterson that he would never be "outniggered" again in a political race, stepped forward on the capitol steps in Montgomery and delivered his inaugural address, cobbled together by one of his closest advisors, a local leader of the Ku Klux Klan:

> Today I have stood where Jefferson Davis stood, and took an oath to my people. It is very appropriate then that from this Cradle of the Confederacy, this very heart of the great Anglo-Saxon southland, that today we sound the drum for freedom as have our generation of forebears before us time and again down through history.
>
> Let us rise to the call of freedom-loving blood that is in us and send our answer to the tyranny that clanks its chains upon the South.

In the name of the greatest people that ever trod this earth, I draw the line in the dust and toss the gauntlet before the feet of tyranny. And I say: Segregation now! Segregation tomorrow! Segregation forever.

This was George Wallace.

Even as Wallace was speaking that day, Dr. King and several SCLC leaders were meeting to decide what to do after the confusion and anticlimax of events in Albany. They needed a new target. They "needed a victory," as Fred Shuttlesworth put it. And he offered his own city to stage that victory. Shuttlesworth made a promise that afternoon to King. "I assure you," he said, "if you come to Birmingham, this movement will not only gain prestige but it will really shake the country."

And so, they decided, the movement would now set its eyes on Birmingham.

Except for a shift in the city's leadership, nothing had changed in Birmingham in the two years since we'd come through on the Freedom Rides. The dynamite attacks on black homes, churches and businesses—sixty such bombings since the end of World War II—had continued. Birmingham continued to earn its label as the "most segregated city in the South," with parks, playgrounds, swimming pools, restaurants, theaters, hotels, even *elevators,* all separated by race. There were no black clerks in white-owned stores, no black policemen or firemen on the city payroll. And the man in charge of the city's police and firefighting forces was none other than Bull Connor, who had been named Birmingham's commissioner of public safety during a shake-up of the city government.

Shuttlesworth and King and Ralph Abernathy all knew that Bull Connor did not have the restraint or savvy of a Laurie Pritchett. And, unlike in Albany, where Sherrod and Reagon and our SNCC people had essentially come into a completely unorganized community, there was already a solidly entrenched activist infrastructure in black Birmingham, spearheaded over the years by Shuttlesworth.

And so the Birmingham movement began that first week of April 1963, with the first of what would become sixty-five consecutive nightly mass meetings. These were powerfully emotional gatherings, with singing like nothing anyone had ever heard before. The massive Birmingham Movement Choir and the Albany Freedom Singers took the power of movement music to a near-celestial level, literally rocking the walls of the churches in which they and the people lifted their voices.

The SCLC brought in leaders from all corners of the movement, including Diane and Bevel, who set about organizing student contingents. All the tools we had used in Nashville—sit-ins, boycotts, mass marches, rallies, mass meetings—were put into place in Birmingham, but on a much more massive scale. Literally tens of thousands of people were positioned to take part.

Naturally with numbers like those, the discipline of nonviolence was harder to maintain. And Bull Connor's men, with their dogs and their hoses, were just itching for an excuse to unleash themselves.

The actions and reactions were tame at first, with demonstrations and arrests occurring in an orderly fashion. But there was fear from many quarters that ugly violence was right around the corner. When Dr. King was arrested on Good Friday, he was criticized by some of the area's liberal and moderate white leadership for stoking the fires of conflict by leading these demonstrations. His response, written on scraps of paper and smuggled out of his cell, was the now-famous "Letter from Birmingham Jail," and in it was a passage that pointed directly to a growing impatience in the movement with some of its white supporters. The passage was addressed to local clergymen in the Birmingham area, but it could easily have been aimed directly at the White House:

> I must make two honest confessions to you, my Christian and Jewish brothers. First, I must confess that over the last few years I have been gravely disappointed with the white moderate. I have almost reached the regrettable conclusion that the Negro's great stumblingblock is not the White Citizen's Council-er or the Ku Klux Klanner, but the white moderate who is more devoted to "order" than to justice, who prefers a negative peace which is the absence of tension to a positive peace which is the presence of justice... Shallow understanding from people of good will is more frustrating than absolute misunderstanding from people of ill will. Lukewarm acceptance is much more bewildering than outright rejection.

Dr. King, increasingly criticized for kowtowing to the white establishment, was drawing his own line of sorts in the sand, and it both surprised and delighted the more radical arms of the movement, including many of my colleagues in SNCC.

While King was in jail, Bevel was busy organizing and training a huge army of Birmingham's children. He went into local black schools and churches, using the NBC White Paper documentary "The Nashville Sit-In Story"—the one for which we had been interviewed back in 1960—to teach hundreds of teenagers the techniques of nonviolence.

What Bevel was doing in Birmingham was little different from what we had done from the beginning in Nashville and, indeed, what we would do later in Selma. We considered it natural and necessary to involve children—adolescents—in the movement. We weren't far from being teenagers our-

selves, and we shared many of the same basic feelings of adolescence: unbounded idealism, courage unclouded by "practical" concerns, faith and
optimism untrampled by the "realities" of the adult world. Young people
identify more strongly than anyone else with the whole concept of freedom.
They are free in the fullest sense of the word—free of major responsibilities
that might hold them back. They have no mortgage, no marriage, no family,
no children of their own, no job. They are, as we assumed ourselves to be,
willing to risk everything for something noble and deserving, for the cause.

There was a black high school in Nashville not far from Fisk, a school
called Pearl High, and many of the foot soldiers of our Nashville Movement
came out of that school. Critics, of course, charged exploitation. Our response was the same as Dr. King's answer when similar cries of alarm rose up
as Bevel began assembling the children of Birmingham. Where did all this
concern for the black children of America suddenly come from? Where had
this concern been for the past two hundred years? Who had spoken up for
black children born in slavery, and later living in utter poverty, virtually ignored in terms of social services and schooling, treated as less than human
from the day they came into this world? The stance of nonviolent action
is that of one soul appealing to another, confronting the powers-that-be with
the faces and hearts, with the sheer *humanity*, of the oppressed. As far as we
were concerned, this included, very powerfully, the faces and hearts of the
children.

They began marching in Birmingham at the beginning of May, hundreds
and hundreds of teenaged and even younger children, stepping out from the
Sixteenth Street Baptist Church, singing and clapping, striding together toward the center of the city, where Bull Connor's officers stopped them and
steered them into waiting paddy wagons and patrol cars. By the end of that
first day, nearly a thousand of Birmingham's black children were in jail. It was
an embarrassment for the city, an outrage. Connor was determined not to let
it go on, and so, the next day, when the children marched again, he swore he
would make no arrests. His duty was to keep these black protestors out of the
city's downtown district, and if arrests wouldn't do it, he decided something
more forceful might—dogs and fire hoses.

I watched the images on television that night and, like the rest of America, was absolutely stunned by what I saw. Snarling German shepherds loosed
on teenaged boys and girls, the animals' teeth tearing at slacks and skirts. Jet
streams of water strong enough to peel the bark off a tree, aimed at twelve-
year-old kids, sending their bodies hurtling down the street like rag dolls in a
windstorm.

It was absolutely unbelievable. It looked like battle footage from a war.
Those images, like the bombed bus in Anniston, or the photos of Jim Zwerg

and me after the bus station attack in Montgomery, became timeless. They went out to the world, and no one who saw them would ever forget them.

We in Nashville made sure they were seen. We took photos from the front pages of the *Tennessean*, pasted them on poster board and tacked them to trees and poles all over campus, as well as out in the surrounding community, along with announcements to come to a mass meeting, to march in support of the people in Birmingham. We were still in the process of desegregating Nashville, still marching on our own, and now there was Birmingham as a backdrop, as a context, a frame of reference. This stuff was going on just down the road from us. A lot of those kids being blasted by Bull Connor's fire hoses were students at Birmingham's largest black high school, Parker High. A lot of the kids attending Fisk and Tennessee State were *from* Parker. A lot of them *knew* some of the young men and women they saw being bitten by dogs on the TV news. It was all very, very immediate. It hit very, very close to home.

And our ranks began growing immediately because of it. The attitude was, Hey, if they are standing up to fire hoses and dogs down there, the least we can do is march outside a restaurant up here. Where at the time we might have had seven or eight people on a picket line, now we were seeing fifteen, or twenty, or thirty. All because of Birmingham.

A week after the attack on the children, an accord was reached in Birmingham. The city promised to take steps toward desegregation and fair hiring practices—the same goals we were working toward in Nashville—and the demonstrations ceased. But as a reminder that changes among people require far more than a simple handshake among leaders or a stroke of a pen among lawmakers, the day after that accord the Klan staged a rally where the children had marched, and one of the speakers proclaimed, "Martin Luther King's epitaph can be written here in Birmingham." That night the motel where Dr. King was registered was dynamited, setting off a riot, with beatings of several whites in various sections of the city. Clearly, things were going to get far worse before they would begin to get better, not just in Birmingham but throughout the South.

By this time, President Kennedy could no longer drag his feet in response to the issue of civil rights. He had watched that footage of dogs and hoses, just like the rest of the country, and in response, on June 11, exactly a month after the truce in Birmingham, the President appeared on television to make a national address. Just five months earlier, at a meeting in early January with Dr. King, Kennedy had told King that the administration had no plans to propose any civil rights legislation in 1963. Now here he was, on national television, announcing his intention to send to Congress the most sweeping civil rights bill in the nation's history. I'll never forget watching him that night and hearing his words:

> Now the time has come for this nation to fulfill its promise. The events in Birmingham and elsewhere have so increased the cries for equality that no city or state legislative body can prudently ignore them. The fires of frustration and discord are burning in every city, North and South....
>
> We face, therefore, a moral crisis as a country and a people. It cannot be met by repressive police action. It cannot be left to increased demonstrations in the streets. It cannot be quieted by token moves or talks. It is time to act in the Congress, in your state and local legislative bodies, in all of our daily lives....
>
> A great change is at hand, and our task, our obligation, is to make that revolution, that change, peaceful and constructive for all.

Earlier that very same day, George Wallace made his "stand in the schoolhouse door," making a big show of blocking a young black man and woman—James Hood and Vivian Malone—from entering the University of Alabama's Foster Auditorium in order to register for that semester. Wallace's "stand" was carefully scripted, orchestrated and arranged in cooperation with the federal authorities, who let him make his speech before he stepped aside and allowed Hood and Malone to enter.

It was head-spinning, in a way, to watch Wallace's stand and the President's speech on the same day. It was even more mind-boggling to wake up the next morning to the news that just a little past midnight the evening before, Medgar Evers, returning home from an NAACP meeting in Jackson, had been shot through the back, killed outside his front door by a sniper's bullet.

It was hard to keep up with events and emotions at the pace they were tumbling that week, and they began swirling even more when, on June 14, I received a telegram from SNCC headquarters saying Chuck McDew was resigning as chairman and telling me to hurry to Atlanta for an "emergency" meeting of the coordinating committee. Not long after I got the telegram, Jim Forman called to tell me McDew was stepping down and there was the "possibility" that I might be elected as his replacement.

I didn't have any real reaction to that. I had no dream, no ambitions, certainly no designs for such a position. I never really saw myself as a leader in the traditional sense of the word. I saw myself as a participator, an activist, a *doer*. My talent, if I had one, was in mobilizing—organizing and inspiring people to come together and act to create that sense of community that would bring us all together, both ourselves and those who stood against us.

I had no thoughts, ever, of being chairman of SNCC. There were too many other things to think about, especially that week. The murder of Medgar. The President's speech. Our SNCC campaigns in Arkansas and Mississippi and Georgia and Alabama, and up in Cambridge, Maryland, as well. A swirl of thoughts went through my mind as I sat in the back seat of Sue Thrasher's car late that afternoon, looking out the window at the darkening sky as we raced down the highway toward the SNCC meeting in Atlanta.

There were five of us in that automobile—Sue, Lester McKinney, Paul LaPrad, David Kotelchuck, and I. Lester was driving. Not far from Murfreesboro it began to rain. We were rounding a curve just outside town when Lester lost control. I'll never forget the car leaving the road, turning over and throwing us through the windshield. There were no seat belts, or at least we weren't wearing them—this was 1963. Incredibly, none of us was seriously injured. Maybe we were meant to make it to that meeting, I don't know.

And we did make it. The car was demolished, but another was sent from Nashville to pick us up and carry us on. No sooner did we arrive than the meeting began. McDew wasn't there. The official explanation was that he was ill, but many of us at the meeting suspected that Chuck was simply tired, worn out, absolutely exhausted. Ever since replacing Marion Barry as chairman, McDew had focused on fund-raising, which meant constant traveling all over the country, mostly through the Northern states, drumming up interest and money to help our broadening efforts. All that traveling had taken its toll. And the organization was ready at that point to shift its primary focus from fund-raising to our actual campaigns. The discussion that night centered on choosing a more action-oriented chairman.

No decision was made that evening, but I knew by then that I was probably going to be the choice. The reason, I think—and I don't want to sound arrogant or boastful or presumptuous—wasn't my commitment to nonviolence so much as my actual experience, the fire that I had been through. At that point I had been arrested twenty-four times—seventeen in Nashville. That fact alone carried a lot of weight with my colleagues.

I heard later that there was some behind-the-scenes campaigning by a couple of people who were interested in the position. Charles Sherrod was one name I heard mentioned. But I didn't know about any of that at the time. When we met the next day, it was as if the decision had already been made. Forman nominated me, the motion was seconded and approved with almost no discussion, and so I became chairman of SNCC, elected to serve out McDew's term, which would expire the following April.

Again, as I had already felt so many times in my life, I sensed a power at work that was much larger than any of us. It was no coincidence that so many events were cascading that week. I truly believed it was the Spirit of History at work.

I felt that spirit as I watched Medgar Evers's body arrive in Atlanta, his casket passing through by train on its way to Washington, where he would be buried in Arlington National Cemetery.

I felt so much as I returned to Nashville and packed to move to Atlanta, my first move since leaving my family for college. It had been a whirlwind of a week. But there was even more to come, and soon. Almost lost in the swirl of events that week was Dr. King's announcement on June 11—the same day as Kennedy's speech and Wallace's stand—of plans for a march, a *massive* march, perhaps the biggest march of its kind in history. It would take place later that summer, he announced, and this march would not be in Birmingham, or Montgomery, or Atlanta.

It would be in Washington, D.C.

When I moved in June 1963 from Nashville to an apartment in Atlanta, it marked the first time in my life that I had a place of my own. Until then I had always made my bed with my family, in a college dormitory, in the homes of host families in towns and cities across the South during one campaign or another... or in a jail cell.

Now I had my own address, a small second-floor walk-up in an old brick apartment building on Gordon Road, in the southwest section of the city—a black neighborhood, of course. It was a quiet section of town, with a bus stop on the corner, which was convenient—just a fifteen-minute ride to the SNCC offices. My salary was $10 a week, which wasn't much, even then. But my rent was covered by SNCC as well—$54 a month—and there was little else that I needed. I owned hardly more than the shirt on my back—six shirts, to be exact, along with three pairs of pants, two suits, two pairs of shoes, several neckties, some socks and some underwear. That and some books were all I had to pack when I moved that summer.

If your life was in the movement at that time, as mine was, the concepts of home and belongings were different from most people's. You spent very little time in your own home. You traveled constantly, and you traveled light. When you were on the road, which was much more often than not, home was wherever you found a bed and a blanket for the night. Which was fine. Sometimes you found nothing, and that was all right, too. I certainly preferred a soft mattress to the seat of a car, but there were many times when I had no choice. It would have been unthinkable to complain, or to even think of complaining. This was nothing less than a revolution we were involved in. Nonviolent, yes, but a revolution nonetheless. Comfort was simply not a concern.

I had hardly unpacked my bags that first week in Atlanta when word came that there was to be a meeting June 22 at the White House. President Kennedy was concerned about the march Dr. King had announced and wanted representatives from various civil rights organizations, including SNCC, to come discuss it with him.

John Kennedy probably did not know, nor did most Americans at the time, that this march was not Dr. King's idea. It originated with a man named A. Philip Randolph, an elder statesman of the movement who, in 1925, had founded the Brotherhood of Sleeping Car Porters, one of the most effective civil rights and labor organizations of its time. With his distinguished bearing and his rich bass voice, Randolph was, at seventy-four, still a commanding presence. People respected him for both his appearance and his achievements.

Among those achievements was a showdown with Franklin Roosevelt back in 1941. The country was gearing up for war, black workers remained unemployed in shameful numbers, and Randolph responded by announcing plans for an unprecedented mass march of black labor on Washington. A week before the march was to take place, President Roosevelt invited Randolph to the White House. The two talked, and Roosevelt agreed to issue an executive order forbidding discrimination in defense industry hiring if Randolph would cancel the demonstration—which, it turned out, was more a bluff than reality, with far fewer numbers and far less organization in place than he pretended.

But it worked. Randolph called off the march, FDR signed the order, and tens of thousands of black workers were hired by factories that had turned them away until then. Now, however, more than two decades later, the disparity in the nation's black and white employment remained outrageously grim. From jobs to average income, black America was in essence a country within a country—one modernized and affluent, the other undeveloped and destitute. And by raising their voices for justice, America's black communities in the South were under attack as well. The year before had been like a second Civil War, with bombings, beatings and killings happening almost weekly. A march would be met with violence, which would cause yet another march, and so on. That was the pattern. Justice Department figures showed nearly eight hundred demonstrations in almost two hundred cities in the ten weeks following President Kennedy's announcement that he planned to send a civil rights bill to Congress. During that ten-week period alone there were 20,000 arrests. And ten deaths.

Kennedy had been moved to introduce the civil rights legislation by the ugliness he saw in Birmingham. But he immediately met resistance from political leaders in the South, and within days he was already showing signs of backing off from the bill. He had no easy way out, though. Black America was not about to back off from its demands for racial and human justice and civil rights. If nothing was done, the situation in the South, as ugly as it already was, was only going to get worse. Bob Moses, testifying that summer of 1963 before a House subcommittee on the civil rights bill, warned that the situation he saw every day in Mississippi would become "ten times worse than Birmingham" if the federal government did not respond.

It was in this swelling storm that Randolph and his longtime friend and associate Bayard Rustin had begun talking early that year about a mass demonstration in Washington. Rustin had worked with Randolph on the 1941 march plans. He was a gifted organizer, and he was as concerned about black economic power as Randolph, who was now chairman of a group called the Negro American Labour Council. Randolph and Rustin's initial focus was black employment; their working title for the demonstration was "March on Washington for Jobs and Freedom." But as time passed and more people became involved in the planning for this event, the primary focal point shifted from jobs to civil rights in general. By mid-June, when the President called for this gathering of black leaders, the slogan for the march was already shifting from "For Jobs and Freedom" to "Pass the Bill."

The bill was what brought Kennedy to ask for this meeting. Essentially, he wanted the march canceled, just as Roosevelt had twenty-two years earlier. But unlike Roosevelt, Kennedy had to deal with more than one person, as well as with a very awakened national black citizenry. In the seven months since Randolph and Rustin had hatched this idea, a coalition of black leaders had become involved. The President's invitation list included the most visible of these. King, of course, as the White House saw it, was at the top. Then there was Randolph, Roy Wilkins of the NAACP, Jim Farmer of CORE, Whitney Young of the National Urban League and ... someone from SNCC.

Nobody knew who that someone would be. We at SNCC had heard rumblings about this march since the beginning of the year. After the assassination of Medgar Evers telephone calls began going back and forth between SNCC headquarters and Dr. King's office, as well as with Randolph and Rustin up in New York. When the President put out the call for this meeting, and SNCC was invited to be represented, there was some question if we would even accept.

From the first mention of this march, a good number of SNCC people wanted nothing to do with it. Their feeling was that this would be a lame event, organized by the cautious, conservative traditional power structure of black America, in compliance with and most likely under the control of the federal government. At SNCC we had little patience with meetings and talk and inflated, empty gestures. That had been the standard procedure for the previous one hundred years. We were about something different—aggressive action. More than any of the other groups invited to meet with Kennedy, we were the one with our people out on the front lines, being beaten and jailed and killed all across the South with little response or protection from the federal government. Why should we sit down and talk with that government about a nice, orderly march in D.C.?

The feeling among most of the rank and file of SNCC was that if we did take part in this march, we should do it *our* way, which would be to turn this demonstration into a protest rather than a plea. Stage sit-ins all across Washington. Tie up traffic. Have "lie-ins" on local airport runways. Invade the offices of southern congressmen and senators. Camp on the White House lawn. Cause mass arrests. *Paralyze* the city.

These were ideas that came up as we met that week to decide whether we should attend this meeting. In the end there was simply not a lot of enthusiasm about this trip to Washington. Someone should go, we decided, simply so we would have a presence. Forman, in his position as our executive secretary, would have been the natural choice, but he deferred to me. He just didn't think it was going to be that big a deal.

As for me, I thought the march was a good idea. I felt that *any* form of action, any form of drama of this kind, was helpful and effective. I think that whenever you can get a large group of people together, whether it's to march, or to have a prayer vigil, or to sit in, you should. Whenever people have an opportunity to dramatize their feelings, to point out an issue, to educate others and alert them and open their eyes, I think they should *do* those things.

That's how I saw this march. I never saw it as something to support a particular political position or a particular piece of legislation or even a particular issue. I saw it as an opportunity to highlight what we were doing and facing with our direct action all throughout the South, a chance yet again to call the nation's attention to the ugliness and violence and suffering. The other leaders might or might not focus on those things, but *we* could focus on them. We could certainly make our voice heard, the voice of SNCC.

So it was decided that I would be that voice.

One leader who was expressly *not* invited to that meeting, though he was certainly a force to be reckoned with in the black community, and was becoming more so every day, was Malcolm X of the Nation of Islam, or, as they were better known, the Black Muslims.

I respected Malcolm. I saw him as a very articulate, very forceful spokesperson for what he believed in. But I never accepted his ideas. I didn't—and I don't—have any sympathy with black nationalism, separatism, the attitude of an eye for an eye or violence of any sort. I can respect a person and understand what he's saying and still not be sympathetic to it. As far as I was concerned, Malcolm was not a civil rights leader. Malcolm was not part of the movement. The movement had a goal of an integrated society, an interracial democracy, a Beloved Community. What Malcolm X represented were the seeds of something different, something that would eventually creep into the movement itself and split it apart. He was not about integration, not about an interracial community, and he was not nonviolent. To his credit, he preached personal independence and responsibility, self-discipline and self-reliance. But he also urged the black man to fight back in self-defense—"by any means necessary," as he famously put it. And I just could not accept that.

But there were many that summer of '63 who did—more, it seemed, every day. I could see Malcolm's appeal, especially to young people who had never been exposed to or had any understanding of the discipline of nonviolence—and also to people who had given up on that discipline. There was no question Malcolm X was tapping into a growing and understandable feeling of restlessness and resentment among America's blacks. Earlier that year, when Dr. King delivered a speech in Harlem, a section of the audience jeered him, chanting, "We want Malcolm! We want Malcolm!"

The President, however, did not. Neither did the other black leaders who arrived at the White House that June afternoon—the "Big Six," as we were collectively called by the press.

It was mind-blowing for me to be there. Exactly one week after being elected chairman of SNCC, here I was, at the White House, meeting with John F. Kennedy, meeting Bobby Kennedy, meeting Lyndon Johnson. The President was due to leave for Vienna the next day to meet Khrushchev—their first meeting since the previous October's Cuban Missile Crisis—and he came into the room in somewhat of a rush. He shook hands all around the table, greeting us each with a "Hello." No names. Bobby sat over by a wall, with one of his daughters in his lap. There were other people around, watching over the proceedings and taking notes.

The President got right to the point. He was concerned about all the violence and unrest he was seeing in the South. He was mightily concerned about the success of this civil rights bill, and he didn't see how this march was going to help anything.

"We want success in Congress," he told us, "not just a big show at the Capitol."

He said this bill stood a much better chance of passing if black people stayed off the streets.

"The Negroes are already *in* the streets," answered Randolph, who had been face-to-face with a president before and showed no fear whatsoever. There would be a march, he told Kennedy. The only questions were what form it would take. And those questions, Randolph made clear—politely, respectfully, but firmly—would be answered by us, not the government.

King did not speak until near the end of the two-hour meeting. He held the preeminent role in black America at that point in time, no question. But in that meeting we all deferred to Randolph, King included. Randolph was the dean. Although he was getting up in age, the man still had so much dignity and pride. He was so impressive, such a wonderful, decent human being, with so much bearing, so much grace. I've said this many times: If he had been born in another time, in another place, or of another race, A. Philip Randolph would have been a prime minister, or a president, or a king.

The talk went back and forth in a generally pleasant way. I listened, taking everything in. It was not my place to talk. Not here. My time—*our* time— would come later. When Wilkins noted that we would have problems with our own organizations and memberships if we did *not* march, the President stood up, sighed and said, "Well, we all have our problems. You have your problems. I have my problems."

Then he shook hands all around again, wished us well and turned the meeting over to his brother and Vice President Johnson.

Minutes later the meeting broke up.

As soon as I got back to Atlanta, I briefed Forman and the rest of the central committee on what had occurred. This march was going to happen, and we were going to be part of it. Now there was suddenly a lot more interest and desire for involvement, at least on the part of the committee, and certainly on the part of Forman. When word came that there would be a gathering of the march planners on July 2 in New York City, Forman was not about to miss this one. He and I flew up together.

This was my first trip ever to New York City. The one thing I will never forget about that trip was the great sense of anger and hopelessness I felt in Harlem. It was very different from the South, where we were moving and marching and acting with a sense of community and purpose. In Harlem I saw boarded-up buildings, metal grates on store windows, a different kind of poverty from the poverty we had in the South—a starker, dismal, urban kind of poverty. I felt a great sense of despair. I passed a crowd of people on a corner, listening to a speaker chant and rave about what they were going to do with "Whitey," and it seemed very sad, very hopeless. The whole situation seemed to lack a sense of direction, a sense of vision.

There was a tremendous need then, and there remains a need today, for someone to take hold of the urban centers in the North and give them that sense of direction. Despite the setbacks of recent years, there remains in the South an inherent sense of purpose, of belief, of people pulling together and actually effecting change. Despite all the failures and frustration of the past three decades, there is still a *spirit* in the South, a spirit instilled by the civil rights movement that is still felt and remembered today, a spirit that was not and *is* not felt in the same way in the North. That, I believe, is the huge difference between the legacy of the civil rights movement in the North and the

South. All the great battlegrounds of the civil rights movement were in the South. That fact is cherished and remembered by the people there. In the North there seem to be a great many people with little faith, people who have almost given up, people who feel that they have little to hold on to or believe in. They never went through what we went through. They never tasted directly what we tasted. So they simply do not believe.

I saw this for the first time during that July 1963 trip to New York. Our meeting took place at the Roosevelt Hotel, and it provided my first real look at the personality of Roy Wilkins. I can't say I liked what I saw. He had held himself back when we met with the President, but now, here, among just us, Wilkins was really asserting himself. We met in one of the hotel's private dining rooms, and from the moment Wilkins entered the room he came across to me as some sort of New Yorker who thought he was smarter than the rest of the group. He seemed to assume that because he was the head of the largest organization among us in terms of sheer membership—the NAACP—he was the master and we were nothing but a bunch of upstarts. He clearly assumed that we were naive—all of us, including Dr. King. He didn't trust us young people in SNCC, and that was not surprising. But he didn't trust Dr. King either. He seemed to feel that King was basically a careless, unsophisticated country preacher, and to envy the power and position Dr. King had attained. He didn't think King deserved it.

What was memorable about the meeting that day, much more than the details of planning the upcoming march, was watching the dynamics among the participants. It was a real exercise in power and positioning and political rivalry. When Wilkins entered the room, about a dozen or so people were there chatting, waiting to take their seats around the large dining table. Wilkins immediately shook his head and began walking through the room, tapping people on the shoulder, saying who would stay and who had to leave. These were powerful people he was ordering around, and he was not very polite about it. He was particularly nasty to Bayard Rustin—very hostile. And he was hardly more cordial to the others. He didn't suggest that anyone leave the room; he *demanded* it.

It was amazing to me that he would do that. Even more amazing was the fact that the others obeyed. Fred Shuttlesworth. Ralph Abernathy. Forman. And, yes, Rustin. They all did as Wilkins said. They weren't happy about it, but they left.

When Wilkins was done, only six people remained—the group that had met with the President, the "Big Six."

To be honest, I was surprised from the beginning to see the Urban League represented at all. It was not an activist organization per se. And Whitney Young was certainly not an activist. He was not, in my estimation, movement-oriented at all. He was more a teacher, an administrator, the director of a so-cial agency. The Urban League took care of the social and economic needs of people, doing good work, necessary work, but they were not known for being out in the streets and fighting. Having Whitney Young at that table was like having a college president in a room full of soldiers. But he was very close to Wilkins, so he was there.

It was no coincidence that Wilkins and Young seemed to agree on every issue that came up that day. And it made sense that, in an unspoken lan-guage, a coalition developed among King, Farmer and me. We were, after all, the ones who had actually been out there fighting. It was as if the others were coming with an appetite to a meal that had already been prepared, and we were the ones who prepared it. It was the SCLC, SNCC and CORE that had, for the most part, laid the foundation, created the climate, gone into the streets and set the stage for this march. Randolph and Rustin had done their time as well. They had fought their battles in the past. But you could sense that Wilkins and Young had lost the high ground before we even began. They had lost the moral authority on who should direct this march. We were all ready to work together for the sake of unity and for the success of this demon-stration, but Roy Wilkins was in no position to tell us what to do.

None of this was said openly. It was just something that was sensed, and I think Wilkins sensed it, too. He was much more polite and deferential once the others had left the room and the meeting began.

It was interesting to watch Jim Farmer that day. He was usually a little louder than everyone else, but during this meeting he was almost subdued. This was partly because he was in the presence of Randolph, who was every-one's elder and had everyone's respect, and partly because Farmer was in the presence of Wilkins, the man who had been his boss when Farmer worked for the NAACP. It was one thing for Farmer to throw his weight around with a bunch of young kids, as he had done with us during the Freedom Rides. But it was quite another for him to be at a table with men like these.

As for Dr. King, he was very quiet. I think he was entirely comfortable and secure in the role he knew he had. He didn't have to say anything to assert or establish himself. He was the undisputed leader, the undisputed symbol of what the movement had come to, at least at that point in time. His very pres-ence spoke for itself.

And me? I was just a young kid, one week into the chairmanship of a na-tional organization, still getting a sense of where I was and what my respon-sibilities were. My natural inclination is to listen—to listen *well*—before I speak. In this case, I knew my time to speak would come later, but right now my job was to watch, absorb and learn. I was there to represent SNCC, the young arm of the movement, which was taken seriously now. We were included in this so-called coalition in the first place because there was no way *not* to include us. Rustin put it best during one of our early meetings, when he snorted, "I guess we *got* to deal with the Snickers."

Rustin quickly became the central topic of the day's discussion. Wilkins was adamantly opposed to Rustin's having anything at all to do with this march. He was very nervous about Bayard's homosexuality—though Wilkins never used that word. This was 1963, and no one openly used the word "gay" or "homosexual" or any such straightforward term. The phrase I think Wilkins used included the term "morals." And it was not just Rustin's sexual orientation that disturbed Wilkins. There was also his status as a conscientious objector, and his controversial involvement over the years with the Communist Party. To his credit, I don't think Wilkins had a personal problem with any of these issues, but he was concerned about how they might be used by our adversaries and critics, people like South Carolina's adamantly segregationist senator Strom Thurmond, who did indeed attack Bayard later that summer on these very issues in a speech delivered before Congress.

Wilkins considered Rustin a huge liability, and we didn't deny that might be so. But we also respected the man for all he had done for the movement, and we valued his organizational skills. We *needed* them. This was going to be a massively complex undertaking, and there was no one more able to pull it together than Bayard Rustin. The consensus was that he be involved, and Wilkins relented. That was probably the most important decision made that day—to name Randolph the march director and Rustin his deputy.

There were other broad issues, most of which left Farmer and me feeling skeptical. We basically felt that this event was not going to be dramatic enough for our tastes or our colleagues in SNCC and CORE. As for Wilkins and Young, they seemed afraid at every turn that the march might be *too* dramatic.

In the end, though, the course was set. Randolph and Rustin would run this show. And it would happen on August 28, a Wednesday.

The press, of course, besieged us as we came out of the meeting. The reporters were hungry to get each of our opinions on this event. For my part— for SNCC's part—I told them our intention was to keep the pressure on by continuing with the same demonstrations that had brought the President to the table in the first place.

"We do not want violence and we do not advocate it," I told one reporter. "But we will not slow down because of the possibility. Violence represents the frustration of the Negro community and the slow pace of progress in achieving real democracy; the only way to avoid this is to show tangible proof to the American Negro that his life is getting better."

Dealing with the press was suddenly a central part of my life, much more than it had ever been before. I understood when I took the position as chairman that I was no longer involved in just a particular community, that the entire South, the entire country, was my concern and my focus now. Emotionally, intellectually, socially, I think I was prepared for this very visible role. But politically—among the various factions and forces of SNCC itself—I'm not sure I was ready, or even aware of, what I was in for.

From the beginning, people were coming at me from all sides, trying to force me into a more politically active role, to be more conscious and forceful in dealing with other civil rights organizations. Forman and Marion Barry kept pushing and saying, "Take on this person, take on that organization." Infighting and one-upmanship was the game, they told me. "Don't take a back seat," they'd say.

When I returned from that July meeting in New York, Forman took me aside and pointed at a newspaper photo where I'm at the end of the group, almost out of the frame. "You've got to get out *front*," he said. "Don't let King get all the credit. Don't stand back like that. Get out *front*."

I just never thought that way. Trying to get out front and worry about who's getting the credit, that's just never been my concern. Let's get the job done—that's how I feel. That's how I've always felt. Don't worry about the limelight. Get the job done, and there will be plenty of credit to go around.

I realize that attitude has sometimes—some would say often—resulted in my being overlooked now and then through the course of my life. I've never been the kind of person who naturally attracts the limelight. I'm not a handsome guy. I'm not flamboyant. I'm not what you would call elegant. I'm short and stocky. My skin is dark, not fair—a feature that was still considered a drawback by many black people in the early '60s. For some or all of these reasons, I simply have never been the kind of guy who draws attention.

And I'm thankful for that. It's always seemed to me that the people who are fed by and who focus on visibility and notoriety and getting the credit don't have what you might call staying power. They rise and fall in the public eye, here today and gone tomorrow. Too often they become flashes in the pan, winding up in those "Where Are They Now?" columns. It's sad. Dr. King used to talk about this. He said individuals who fall in love with public attention are not worthy of it. People who hunger for fame don't realize that if they're in the spotlight today, somebody else will be tomorrow. Fame never lasts. The work you do, the things you accomplish—that's what endures. That's what really means something.

But I understood Jim Forman's concern. Back when we started, during the sit-ins, SNCC had the stage almost entirely to itself. But by the time of the Freedom Rides, and certainly in Albany and later in Mississippi and Selma, a pattern developed in which our SNCC people would come in first, do what you might call the dirty work, the tough, hands-on, dangerous and largely unseen organizing work, and then other organizations would arrive—just about the time the press rolled in—and they would join the effort and, in many cases, receive more of the credit than they might have deserved.

With credit came money, funding from groups and individuals who were eager to support the movement. The feeling among our SNCC leadership was that we weren't getting the credit or the support that we deserved. Fundraising had been the primary focus of Chuck McDew's chairmanship, and though I was elected for a different purpose, the fact was that money was still a top priority. Which was one reason Forman and Marion were constantly urging me to push myself into the public eye, get out front, be a symbol, in effect. There is no question that part of my appeal as chairman was that I was a symbol of the student movement. I was a walking example of the things that SNCC stood for, the things SNCC was trying to do. When people saw me, they saw arrests and beatings and nonviolence.

That summer was a whirlwind for me. SNCC was seemingly everywhere, and so was I. From one town to another, wherever we had a campaign, I would visit, take stock, gather information on what was needed, give a speech, take part in a march or demonstration, perhaps talk to a reporter or two, then move on to the next place.

Wherever I went, Julian, in his capacity as our communications director, did his best to make sure the press knew I was there. Often he went with me. If he didn't, he'd keep in constant touch with me, collecting information to pass on to reporters like Claude Sitton of The New York Times or Karl Fleming of Newsweek, writers who, like us, used Atlanta as a base of operations to cover the South. Julian would call me in West Helena or Forrest City, Arkansas, wherever I was on the road, and he'd ask what had happened that day, what we were planning to do tomorrow, how many people would be marching, and then he would pass that information on to the press, who knew they could depend on what he told them. Julian loved his job, and he was good at it— very, very good. A big reason that this period of the civil rights movement— the early '60s—is so well documented in stories and photographs is that Julian Bond made sure the national press knew what was happening, and when, and where.

My itinerary that summer of '63 was dizzying.

I visited Greenwood, Mississippi, where Bob Moses, Sam Block and Stokely were staging clinics and classes and mass meetings, as well as setting up community libraries with hundreds of donated books.

I went to Pine Bluff, Arkansas, where Bill Hansen, Ben Gringe and Bob Whitfield were canvassing the community, urging voter registration and collecting poll taxes.

I stopped in at Somerville, Tennessee, where a SNCC staffer named Walt Tillow was organizing a cadre of non-SNCC volunteers to help conduct a massive voter registration drive.

I went up to Danville, Virginia, where the police were as openly brutal as Bull Connor, using fire hoses and clubs on marchers, sending dozens to the hospital and even breaking down the doors of the city's High Street Baptist Church to arrest local protest leaders. The mayor of Danville promised to "fill every stockade" with marchers rather than relent to their demands. I spoke at several rallies there that summer, conducted some workshops and was amazed by the spirit and raw courage of the people of Danville.

There were so many hot spots that summer—Chapel Hill, North Carolina; Columbia, South Carolina; Helena, Arkansas; Tehula, Mississippi—that sometimes I had to check to make sure where I was.

Late that July, I went over to Selma to visit Bernard LaFayette and his new wife, Colia, who had been running a series of voter education clinics there since February. They'd begun with one student attending their classes—a brave sixty-seven-year-old man named Major Washington. The next week Mr. Washington brought a friend. The week after that the friends brought friends, and so on. This was a familiar pattern wherever we set up these projects. By June, with the help of local high school and college students, Bernard and Colia were drawing an average of forty people to their clinics. More than seven hundred Selma area men and women attended a mass rally that month at which—who else?—Jim Bevel spoke.

Soon—and this was a pattern as well—the success of Bernard's clinics aroused the attention of the local authorities, including county sheriff James G. Clark, a man whom I and the rest of the nation would eventually come to know very, very well. Clark and his men had begun harassing Bernard and his staff early that summer, arresting them on the vaguest of charges and ignoring the beatings our people were suffering at the hands of local whites. Bernard himself took a blow to the head that June that sent him to the hospital for two days.

The nation—and history—would, of course, come to know Selma forever two years later, in 1965. But as in so many towns and cities across the South, the dirty work, the unseen work, was already being done years earlier by people like Bernard and Colia and so many others.

I had just spoken at a mass rally in Selma late that July when I got a call to come to Cambridge, a community in Maryland on what is called the Eastern Shore of the Chesapeake Bay. A wave of demonstrations there had focused on public accommodations, employment and housing—the housing problem in particular was horrific in Cambridge, with very bad slums that were virtually ignored by the city. The demonstrations had resulted in several serious clashes with police, the most recent prompting the governor of Maryland to call in four hundred National Guard troops. Maybe it was because of Cambridge's proximity to Washington, D.C., maybe it was the fact that this was the first indigenous grassroots civil rights campaign to occur beyond the Deep South, but whatever the reason, the Justice Department—Bobby Kennedy himself—was openly concerned about Cambridge and was preparing to step in to find a solution.

When I got to Cambridge, I met a woman I'd heard a lot about already—Gloria Richardson, director of the Cambridge Nonviolent Action Group. Gloria was older than the typical SNCC member. She was a mother, and she was fiercely independent, very militant, very articulate and very outspoken. She had what some people might call an attitude, and understandably so. In Cambridge, as in so many other spots where the movement took root, it was primarily women who had gotten out and done the grunt work, then men stepped out front, filled the visible positions and took most of the credit. This is also true in most political campaigns, although things have changed some in recent years.

That discrimination was what alienated Ella Baker from the SCLC early on—not necessarily from Dr. King, but from Wyatt Walker and Ralph Abernathy and the male structure of that organization in general. Ella had all the qualities of a successful leader—she was intelligent, savvy, charismatic, an organizer. But she was a woman, a woman born at the wrong time. I don't know what exactly happened with her inside the SCLC, but something poisoned her with the men there, and it set the course for the rest of her life. Long before people began using the term "male chauvinism," Ella Baker was describing it and denouncing it in the civil rights movement, and she was right. There were very, very few women getting credit for their work, and even fewer emerged into leadership positions. Daisy Bates was one, out in Arkansas. There was Diane Nash, of course, in Nashville. And there was Gloria Richardson in Cambridge.

It was Gloria's leadership that forced the crisis that finally brought the attorney general to step in that July in an unprecedented way. A meeting was called at the Justice Department building, in Bobby Kennedy's office, to hammer out and sign an accord. Gloria, the mayor of Cambridge, a representative from the Maryland governor's office and I were invited. It was not a happy occasion for Gloria. She was very cynical by then. She didn't trust this scene. She felt it was an empty ritual, staged more for the Kennedy administration's public relations purposes than anything else. Gloria felt no sense of relief, no sense of happiness or joy. It was written all over her face. At one point Bobby Kennedy tried to get her to loosen up. "Mrs. Richardson," he said, gently teasing her, "do you know how to smile?" She did, but it was a weak one.

The moment I recall most about that meeting was during a break in the discussions. There was a television on in another room, and it was broadcasting the Floyd Patterson–Sonny Liston heavyweight fight. Bobby Kennedy invited us to come with him and see how it was going. As we stood there, he took me aside and said something I will never forget, an astounding statement, really.

"John," he said, "the people, the young people of SNCC, have educated me. You have changed me. Now I understand."

That was something to hear, coming from the man who had been reviled by so many of us—including me—for his foot-dragging in response to our needs in the South. That showed me something about Bobby Kennedy that I came to respect enormously—the fact that, though he certainly could be stern, firm, even ruthless, in some people's opinion, he was willing to listen, and learn, and *change*. The same Bobby Kennedy who had resisted responding to so many of our pleas early on in the movement wound up out front later on, leading a one-man crusade across the country, speaking out against hunger, against poverty, going into Mississippi, into the Southwest, going to the Indian reservations, going into the coal-mining sections of West Virginia, standing up and speaking out for the dispossessed of all races—blacks, Hispanics, Native Americans, Appalachian whites. The man really grew. You could *see* him growing.

It was July 23 when the Cambridge Accord, as it was called, was signed, ending the demonstrations in that city in exchange for a promise by local white leaders to desegregate the public schools, construct low-rent public housing for blacks and appoint a biracial commission on human relations— promises that were not, as it turned out, and as Gloria rightly sensed, all kept.

Now it was time to turn to the March on Washington. There was still plenty of resistance among the SNCC membership to taking part at all. President Kennedy had come back from his trip to Europe and immediately announced his support of the march, hailing it as a "peaceful assembly for the redress of grievances." His emphasis was on the word "peaceful," which quickly became the focal point of the administration, of the many government planners and agencies involved in coordinating the event, and of the many white liberal organizations that had signed on to become part of this day.

All this arranging and orchestrating was alarming to many of us at SNCC. The sense of militancy, which was so central to most of our efforts, which was so much a part of our definition of ourselves, was being deflated. Civility had become the emphasis of this event. It was becoming a march *in*, not *on* Washington. The whole thing seemed to have been co-opted by the government—co-opted very deftly. What we had hoped would be a protest against government neglect was being turned into a propaganda tool to show the government as just and supportive. The Kennedy administration seemed to be trying to silence us in a way, to cool us off, to take the steam out of the movement, to get rid of the *drama*.

That dismayed many of my SNCC colleagues, and it dismayed me, too.

But I also felt that no matter what tone this day might have, no matter what attitude others might bring to it, we needed to be there, to have our voice heard, in our own words, with our own tone. The eyes of the entire world were going to be on this event. The culmination of the day would be speeches by each of the leaders who planned it—including me. And so, in the middle of that month, about a week before the march was to take place, I began drafting what I would say.

I started with one of the staff people in our office in Atlanta, a young white woman named Nancy Stern. She typed while I talked, hashing out a rough shape of the points I felt we needed to make.

I wanted a strong speech, one that went beyond supporting a particular piece of legislation. I wanted a civil rights bill, certainly—a *strong* bill. We all wanted that. But we weren't going to beg for it. And besides, there was a much larger picture to address here. We wanted to send as strong a message as possible to the Kennedy administration that we felt the President was being too cautious, doing far too little when it came to meeting the needs of black Americans. Ever since his campaign in 1960 he had been talking about how he was going to do this and that in terms of civil rights legislation, and in actuality he had done virtually nothing. Meanwhile we were out in the streets across the South, taking a whipping.

My words needed to be forceful—I knew that. I didn't want to be part of a parade. I wanted to see discipline and organization on this day, but I wanted it to have an air of militancy as well, even some disruption if necessary—*disciplined* disruption. I have never stopped believing in the power of creative disruption. I have always believed in aggressive nonviolence. I've always believed in putting some *sting* into it. I wanted this march to have some sting, and if the only place for that sting would be in my speech, then I needed to make sure my words were especially strong.

I worked through several early drafts in Atlanta, with the help and consultation of Julian, Forman, Prathia Hall, Ruby Doris Smith and a few others, all of whom made suggestions and recommendations about certain phrases and ideas.

C. B. King, for example—it was Forman's idea to refer specifically to the beating of King and of Slater King's wife down in Albany. Forman was good at recognizing the need for details, the need not to get lost in a lot of general philosophizing and rhetoric. We were all very alarmed about the situation in southwest Georgia, which had gotten even worse early that month with the arrests of three SNCC staffers—Don Harris, Ralph Allen and John Perdew—during a demonstration in a town called Americus, near Albany, in Sumter County (the home county, by the way, of Jimmy Carter—Plains, Georgia, is located there).

As the arrests were being made, Harris had lain on the ground in a non-violent posture and was jolted by a policeman's electric cattle prod, which prompted brick-throwing from the crowd, gunshots from the police and mass arrests. Harris, Allen and Perdew, along with a CORE worker named Zev Aelony, wound up being charged with "seditious conspiracy"—a capital offense—and now they were sitting in an Americus jail facing the real possibility of execution.

This was unbelievable, just outrageous. Our colleagues, my friends, were facing a Deep South state's death penalty for nothing more than civil disobedience, and the federal government was not stepping in to stop it. I had wanted to go down to Americus as soon as those arrests were made, but other staffers, especially Forman, urged me not to go. I couldn't afford to wind up in a jail cell myself, they said, not with the march so close at hand. But I could make the Americus situation part of my speech, and I did.

The weekend before the march, I went up to New York, where an old four-story church building on West 130th Street in Harlem had been turned into command central for the "MARCH ON WASHINGTON FOR JOBS AND FREE-DOM," as a hand-painted banner flapping outside the third-floor window proclaimed it.

More than a hundred civil, labor and religious organizations from across the country had committed themselves to supporting and participating in this event, and several white labor and religious leaders had signed on as sponsors—people ranging from Rabbi Joachim Prinz of the American Jewish Congress to Walter Reuther of the AFL-CIO. Randolph called it a "coalition of conscience." But basically this was Bayard Rustin's show. And this building in Harlem was where he was making it happen.

This was Bayard at his best, seemingly everywhere, with that gray bushy hair, those high cheekbones and an ever-present cigarette dangling from the corner of his mouth. He, along with "transportation director" Rachelle Horowitz, directed dozens of volunteers who were working around the clock, swarming over lists and charts and telephones, passing updates back and forth to an army of organizers in virtually every major city in the nation. Estimates were that 100,000 people were going to descend on D.C. by bus, train, airplane and any other way they could get there. But there was really no way of knowing how many people would actually come.

Most of us had no doubt there would be many more than that, and the logistics and preparations were dizzying. Doctors, drinking water, food, getting the march route to the crowds that would be pouring into the capital that morning, a sound system to accommodate an audience the size of a small city, press passes to the three thousand members of the media expected to arrive to cover the event... and toilets. Toilets were a major concern. I will never forget Bayard proclaiming, in that rich British accent of his: "Now we *cawn't* have any disorganized *pissing* in Washington."

There was not one detail that Bayard missed. The staffers rushing in and out of those offices each wore a small button displaying a black and a white hand clasped together in a show of solidarity—Bayard had commissioned the buttons to help raise money. They sold for a quarter apiece, and by the weekend I arrived 175,000 had been bought, with 150,000 more on order.

That last Friday night before the march, a fund-raiser Bayard helped arrange was staged at the Apollo Theatre, with Quincy Jones, Tony Bennett, Thelonious Monk, Carmen McRae, Billy Eckstine and others donating their performances for the cause.

By then I was working through the final drafts of my speech. Courtland Cox, who was in New York representing SNCC at the march headquarters, and another SNCC member named Joyce Ladner read through what I had so far, as did a young law student named Eleanor Holmes and one of Rustin's assistants, Tom Kahn, a young Jewish man who, like Courtland, had been a student at Howard University.

Courtland suggested saying something about both political parties abandoning our cause, about the fact that a racist such as Mississippi senator James Eastland was a Democrat, just like President Kennedy, and that a Republican like Barry Goldwater, who was mounting a run for the White House and was adamantly opposed to any civil rights bill, was a party colleague of a liberal like New York's Jacob Javits. "Where is *our* party?"—it was either Courtland or Tom who came up with that question, and we put it in the speech.

We added more teeth as well to my references to the pending civil rights bill. Not only did the bill offer too little, as far as we were concerned, but there were parts of it that we outright opposed. Most disturbing was a section of the bill that required men and women to have at least a sixth-grade education to be able to register to vote. We were outraged at that. Here were these Southern states that had for so long denied black children the right to a decent education, and now, beyond that denial, these children were to be *punished* for that neglect when they reached voting age. The only qualifications to vote, we believed, should be age and residence, period. That would become a part of this speech as well.

During that weekend I saw a photograph in *The New York Times* showing a group of Rhodesian women holding signs that said, "ONE MAN, ONE VOTE." I liked that. Somewhere in the speech, I would use it.

The text I had brought with me to New York already made clear our resolve to stay in the streets, to keep on pushing, that this was a *revolution* taking place in the American South—the word "revolution" was woven throughout the speech. But Courtland and Tom felt that we needed something to make that idea even stronger—an image, an analogy. We batted around several ideas, and then Tom came up with the notion of using General William Sherman's "March to the Sea" during the Civil War. Like Sherman, we were an army—a nonviolent army—bent on nothing less than destruction—the destruction of segregation. I liked that.

And so, finally, I had a finished draft of my speech, the words that would speak for SNCC in Washington:

We march today for jobs and freedom, but we have nothing to be proud of, for hundreds and thousands of our brothers are not here. They have no money for their transportation, for they are receiving starvation wages, or no wages at all.

In good conscience, we cannot support wholeheartedly the administration's civil rights bill, for it is too little and too late. There's not one thing in the bill that will protect our people from police brutality.

This bill will not protect young children and old women from police dogs and fire hoses, for engaging in peaceful demonstrations. This bill will not protect the citizens in Danville, Virginia, who must live in constant fear in a police state. This bill will not protect the hundreds of people who have been arrested on trumped-up charges. What about the three young men in Americus, Georgia, who face the death penalty for engaging in peaceful protest?

The voting section of this bill will not help thousands of black citizens who want to vote. It will not help the citizens of Mississippi, of Alabama and Georgia, who are qualified to vote but lack a sixth-grade education. "ONE MAN, ONE VOTE" is the African cry. It is ours, too. It must be ours.

People have been forced to leave their homes because they dared to exercise their right to register to vote. What is there in this bill to ensure the equality of a maid who earns $5 a week in the home of a family whose income is $100,000 a year?

For the first time in one hundred years this nation is being awakened to the fact that segregation is evil and that it must be destroyed in all forms. Your presence today proves that you have been aroused to the point of action.

We are now involved in a serious revolution. This nation is still a place of cheap political leaders who build their careers on immoral compromises and ally themselves with open forms of political, economic and social exploitation. What political leader here can stand up and say, "My party is the party of principles?" The party of Kennedy is also the party of Eastland. The party of Javits is also the party of Goldwater. Where is *our* party?

In some parts of the South we work in the fields from sunup to sundown for $12 a week. In Albany, Georgia, nine of our leaders have been indicted not by Dixiecrats but by the federal government for peaceful protest. But what did the federal government do when Albany's deputy sheriff beat attorney C. B. King and left him half dead? What did the federal government do when local police officials kicked and assaulted the pregnant wife of Slater King, and she lost her baby?

It seems to me that the Albany indictment is part of a conspiracy on the part of the federal government and local politicians in the interest of expediency.

I want to know, which side is the federal government on?

The revolution is at hand, and we must free ourselves of the chains of political and economic slavery. The nonviolent revolution is saying, "We will not wait for the courts to act, for we have been waiting for hundreds of years. We will not wait for the President, the Justice Department, nor Congress, but we will take matters into our own hands and create a source of power, outside of any national structure, that could and would assure us a victory."

To those who have said, "Be patient and wait," we must say that "patience" is a dirty and nasty word. We cannot be patient, we do not want to be free gradually. We want our freedom, and we want it *now*. We cannot depend on any political party, for both the Democrats and the Republicans have betrayed the basic principles of the Declaration of Independence.

We all recognize the fact that if any radical social, political and economic changes are to take place in our society, the people, the masses, must bring them about. In the struggle, we must seek more than civil rights; we must work for the community of love, peace and true brotherhood. Our minds, souls and hearts cannot rest until freedom and justice exist for *all people*.

The revolution is a serious one. Mr. Kennedy is trying to take the revolution out of the streets and put it into the courts. Listen, Mr. Kennedy. Listen, Mr. Congressman. Listen, fellow citizens. The black masses are on the march for jobs and freedom, and we must say to the politicians that there won't be a "cooling-off" period.

All of us must get in the revolution. Get in and stay in the streets of every city, every village and every hamlet of this nation until true freedom comes, until the revolution is complete. In the Delta of Mississippi, in southwest Georgia, in Alabama, Harlem, Chicago, Detroit, Philadelphia and all over this nation, the black masses are on the march!

We won't stop now. All of the forces of Eastland, Barnett, Wallace and Thurmond won't stop this revolution. The time will come when we will not confine our marching to Washington. We will march through the South, through the heart of Dixie, the way Sherman did. We shall pursue our own "scorched earth" policy and burn Jim Crow to the ground—nonviolently. We shall fragment the South into a thousand pieces and put them back together in the image of democracy. We will make the action of the past few months look petty. And I say to you, WAKE UP AMERICA!

I felt satisfied. It was a good speech, a strong one. I put it to bed that Sunday night and got ready to go down to D.C. the next day. Randolph, Rustin, King—everyone had rooms at the Statler Hilton, where we would spend the final hours preparing for Wednesday's march.

I checked in Monday night, ready for a Tuesday morning private meeting and public press conference with the other march "leaders." Early Tuesday morning, as I waited in the lobby for the others, I was amazed to see Malcolm X walk past. He had loudly and thoroughly condemned this event, calling it a "sellout," but there he was, with a small crowd trailing behind him like smoke behind a fire. I don't know if the others saw him that day, but the primary topic of that morning's meeting was a fear of disorder and violence—the kind of violence Malcolm X might encourage. Randolph and Wilkins, especially, were deeply concerned. The city was very tense. Every police unit in the District of Columbia was on duty—all leaves were canceled—along with backup units from surrounding suburban communities. For the first time since Prohibition, liquor sales were banned throughout the nation's capital that day. The Washington Senators, in the middle of a home stand, canceled two games. Fifteen thousand Army paratroopers had been put on alert. Later, we would learn that the D.C. police had gone so far as to rig our sound system so they could take it over instantly if trouble arose.

Despite all that anxiety we felt fairly calm, thanks to Bayard's attention to details. All in all, things looked well in hand. Which is how we wrapped up the day, and which was how I felt as I returned to my room late that night. That's why I was surprised to find a handwritten note that had been slipped under the door while I was out.

"John," it read, "come downstairs. Must see you at once."

It was signed by Bayard.

Almost as soon as I read it, the phone rang. Bayard's voice was on the line.

"We have a problem," he said.

"A problem?" I asked. "What problem?"

"It's your speech," he replied. "Some people are very concerned about some of the things you're going to say in your speech. You need to get down here. We need to talk."

My speech? Who had a problem with my speech? Who had *seen* my speech? I went downstairs wondering what in the world was going on here.

When I got to the room, Bayard was there, along with Walter Fauntroy from the SCLC and a couple of other people I didn't know. None of the other "leaders" were there. Basically, this was between Bayard and me, and quickly I learned what had happened.

Earlier that evening, apparently, Courtland Cox had walked past a table stacked with copies of Whitney Young's prepared text for his speech the next day. Someone had put it out for the press. Courtland got excited. He wanted the press to see my speech—*our* speech—too. So he got Julian to run off a bunch of copies and put them out on the table beside Whitney's.

Someone picked up a copy and rushed it over to Washington's Archbishop Patrick O'Boyle, who was to deliver the event's opening invocation the next day. O'Boyle was so horrified by what he considered the inflammatory tone of my words that he contacted the White House—Burke Marshall, specifically. Then O'Boyle called Rustin and said he would have nothing to do with this event if I was allowed to deliver this speech.

Bayard was surprisingly calm. Unlike most of the others, who had thrown in their lot in support of the President's bill and had accepted this march as a show of solidarity with the administration's civil rights proposal, Bayard agreed with most of the things my speech had to say about the bill. He had no problem with the word "revolution," or the phrase "cheap political leaders," or even the reference to Sherman. What bothered him right then, and what O'Boyle was apparently most alarmed by, amazingly, was, of all things, the word "patience." Apparently, my calling patience a "dirty and nasty word" had sent O'Boyle through the ceiling.

"This is offensive to the Catholic Church," explained Bayard.

"Why?" I asked. I honestly had no idea.

"*Payyyy...tience,*" Bayard said, drawing the word out, as if that would make it clear to me. "Catholics *believe* in the word 'patience.'"

So this was an eternal issue we were talking about here, a theological theme. Okay. I had no problem with that. I could take that out.

Good, said Bayard. It was late, he said. This was enough for now. There would be more the next day, he warned, once the others had looked my speech over. For now, though, he said, we needed to get to bed. We had a big day ahead of us.

By the time I got back to my room, I was incensed. This was a good speech, maybe a great one. That's how everyone who had seen it felt—everyone with SNCC. That's why Courtland and Julian had rushed to pass it out. And now, because someone with the church objected to a simple word, the whole thing was up for inspection. That made me furious. I had told Bayard I would listen to the others the next day, but I made no promises. And the more I thought about it as I fell asleep that night—yes, I could sleep; I had learned long before how to find calm and necessary rest the night before a march or a demonstration or an arrest—the less inclined I was to change one word.

The following morning we met for breakfast, then went as a group to Capitol Hill to pay a call on congressional leaders. No one mentioned my speech, not yet. There was business to take care of, short meetings with House Speaker John McCormack and Senate leaders Mike Mansfield, Everett Dirksen and Hubert Humphrey. These were quick, cordial sessions, nothing substantial, simply courtesy calls arranged early in the morning so we would have plenty of time to make it over to the Lincoln Memorial for the beginning of the event.

But while we were still at the Capitol, word came that the march had begun without us. The crowds, we were told, had already begun surging up Independence and Constitution Avenues toward the reflecting pool and the Lincoln Memorial.

"My God, they're *going,*" said Rustin, as we stepped outside the Capitol to see masses of people moving down the streets. "We're supposed to be leading *them!*"

We rushed down to join them. The cars that had carried us from the hotel attempted to get us over to the Lincoln Memorial, but the crowds were too thick. We were surrounded by a moving sea of humanity, tens of thousands of people just pouring out of Union Station, filling Constitution Avenue from curb to curb. It was truly awesome, the most incredible thing I'd ever seen in my life. I remember thinking, There goes *America.* We were supposed to be the leaders of this march, but the march was all around us, already taking off, already gone.

So we just climbed out of the cars, joined hands and began walking. This was the classic pose for so many marches, the leadership walking hand in hand or arm in arm in front of the people. It was always interesting to see the jockeying that often took place, the push to be in the middle, to be next to this person or that. It's natural, I guess. People want to be seen, to be photographed. In this case, some people wanted to be as close as possible to Randolph, who was the focal point this day. Even Dr. King was pushed toward the side. As for me, I wound up off at the end, which I'm sure made Jim Forman furious.

A spot was cleared so the photographers could shoot pictures, and some of those photos ran in newspapers the next day as if we were in front of the march. But we couldn't even *see* the front. As people turned and recognized us, they began clearing the way and sweeping us along from behind, and that's how we came to the Lincoln Memorial, the leaders being pushed along by the people—as it should be.

The number-one song on the nation's radios that week was Martha and the Vandellas' "Heat Wave," and D.C. typically was broiling at that time of year. But this day was amazingly balmy—eighty-four degrees, clear skies, a slight breeze. God could not have made the weather more perfect.

By the time we arrived at the Lincoln Memorial, there were people everywhere, as far as the eye could see. And still they were coming, streaming in from all directions. Besides the tens of thousands who had come on hundreds of chartered buses and trains, some had arrived on foot (fifteen members of CORE's Brooklyn chapter left thirteen days early and walked the entire 230 miles to D.C.), many had used their thumbs, one cyclist had pedaled in from South Dakota, and there was even a guy who had roller-skated 698 miles from Chicago.

I was stunned as I climbed the steps up to the speakers' platform. My thought, looking out at that vast scene, was, We are here. We, the people, are *here*. It was fascinating to see the collage of famous faces: Josephine Baker climbing up on the stage near me; Jackie Robinson over there telling a reporter, "We cannot be turned back!"; Paul Newman turning away from the celebrity section, preferring to watch from the crowd; Marlon Brando sitting on stage, twirling an electric cattle prod in his hands as a symbol of police brutality; Dick Gregory ushering around a woman named "Scarlet Mary," a prostitute from Chicago who had asked him to help find her a housecleaning job a week before the march because she wanted "to come to Washington with clean money."

Sidney Poitier. Lena Horne. Ossie Davis. Charlton Heston. Sammy Davis Jr. Diahann Carroll. Harry Belafonte. It was interesting to see the stars, but what blew me away was the mass of the audience itself, the enormous size of the crowd, the nameless, faceless, everyday men, women and children who were what we were all about in the first place. The official count was a quarter million, but I swear there were even more. That figure was taken just before the program began at 1 P.M., and throngs of people continued to pour in long after that. I heard estimates as high as half a million by day's end.

In any case, I don't think anyone who was there that day would argue that the official figure was one of the great undercounts of all time. And the striking thing about this ocean of people was that this was truly a *human* rights demonstration. Four out of five people there were black, but there were whites as well. And a sprinkling of Asians, and Hispanics, and Native Americans. Protestants, Catholics and Jews. Liberals and labor. Hope and harmony—that was the music of the day, that was the message.

It began with music: Odetta; Joan Baez; Bob Dylan; Mahalia Jackson; Josh White; Peter, Paul and Mary; our own SNCC Freedom Singers—they each entertained as the crowd kept growing.

Word arrived around noon that W.E.B. Du Bois had just died halfway around the globe, in Ghana. Roy Wilkins made that announcement to the crowd, and you could feel the connection across time and space, that Spirit of History.

What none of the crowd saw—nor did any of the network television cameras mounted on platforms to beam the event live to a worldwide audience, thanks to the newly orbiting communications satellite Telstar—was what was happening back behind Lincoln's statue, where an emergency gathering of march leaders had been called in a security guard's small office. The subject of this small summit was my speech.

By now, word had come that alarms were sounding in all quarters. Walter Reuther was irate that I had dared to criticize the President's civil rights bill. Bobby Kennedy had talked to O'Boyle that morning and had then spoken with Burke Marshall about my speech. He, too, was upset.

Roy Wilkins was having a fit, saying he just didn't understand us SNCC people, that we always wanted to be *different*. He got up in my face a bit, saying we were "double-crossing" the people who had gathered to support this bill. But I didn't back down. I told him I had prepared this speech, and we had a right to say what we wanted to say.

"Mr. Wilkins," I told him, "you don't understand. I'm not just speaking for myself. I'm speaking for my colleagues in SNCC, and for the people in the Delta and in the Black Belt. You haven't *been* there, Mr. Wilkins. You don't *understand.*"

He started shaking his finger at me, and I shook mine right back at him. For a moment, it was getting to be a real scene.

Then Bayard pulled us apart. He could see that this was going nowhere. The music was finishing up out front, and it was getting near time to start the speeches. So Bayard suggested that a small "committee" decide what to do with me. Randolph, the Reverend Eugene Carson Blake of the National Council of Churches, Rustin and Dr. King stayed. The others were told to just get out of the way.

Archbishop O'Boyle, having been assured by the others that my speech would be changed, stepped up to give the invocation, even as our discussion continued back behind Lincoln.

Dr. King didn't have much to say. He was surprised, he told me, to see the section about Sherman and slicing a swath through the South. "John," he said, "that doesn't sound like you." But he knew it sounded like *us*, like SNCC. And he had used similar rhetoric himself in the past, words and images as strong as this or even stronger. So he had no problem with the content. He was just a little surprised that I was saying these words.

As for the Reverend Blake, he was very upset about the term "revolution," as well as the phrase "the masses," both of which he criticized as "Communist talk." But here, Randolph rose to the defense.

"There's nothing wrong with those two words," he said. "I've used them many times myself."

We were far from done, but Randolph had to leave. It was time for him to open the program. I could hear his voice echoing through the speakers mounted around the Lincoln Memorial as he addressed the massive crowd, many of whom had no idea who A. Philip Randolph was.

"Let the nation and the world know the meaning of our numbers," he told the audience, which erupted in cheers. He praised them for forming "the largest demonstration in the history of this nation... the advance guard of a massive moral revolution for jobs and freedom."

Revolution. It was nice to hear that word from someone else's lips.

Wilkins, Whitney Young and the Reverend Blake all stepped forward and made their speeches. James Farmer was conspicuous by his absence—he was in jail in Plaquemine, Louisiana, where he had been arrested a week earlier for leading a demonstration against police brutality.

As the time drew near for me to take the stage, there was still a battle going on over my address. Randolph had returned to the room. Rustin was there. A long list of objections and concerns had been scribbled. But now I wasn't the only one they were dealing with. Courtland Cox and Jim Forman had gotten wind of what was happening and had made their way back to the tiny office. They were hot. If one word of this speech was changed, they told Bayard, it would be over their dead bodies.

It looked as if no one was going to budge. Then Randolph stepped in. He looked beaten down and very tired.

"I have waited twenty-two years for this," he told us. "I've waited all my life for this opportunity. Please don't ruin it."

Then he turned to me.

"John," he said. He looked as if he might cry. "We've come this far together. Let us *stay* together."

This was as close to a plea as a man as dignified as he could come. How could I say no? It would be like saying no to Mother Teresa.

I said I would fix it. And so Forman sat down at a portable Underwood typewriter in that little room, and I stood beside him as we talked through every sentence, every phrase. We could hear the crowd beyond that statue as we worked through the changes and Forman typed them out.

Cut were the words that criticized the President's bill as being "too little and too late."

Lost was the call to march "through the heart of Dixie, the way Sherman did."

Gone was the question asking, "which side is the federal government on?"

The word "cheap" was removed to describe some political leaders, though the phrase "immoral compromises" remained, as did "political, economic and social exploitation."

I was angry. But when we were done, I was satisfied. So was Forman. The speech still had fire. It still had bite, certainly more teeth than any other speech made that day. It still had an edge, with no talk of "Negroes"—I spoke instead of "black citizens" and "the black masses," the only speaker that day to use those terms.

We all agreed—Forman, Cox and I—that our message was not compromised. We all felt it was still a strong speech, very strong. I was resolved and ready to deliver it with all the energy, vigor and passion I had in me.

And then it was my time. As I came around to the edge of the platform, Randolph was already finishing my introduction. "Brother John Lewis," he said, motioning at me as I made my way toward the microphone.

As I laid my papers on the podium and looked out at that sea of faces, I felt a combination of great humility and incredible fear. I could feel myself trembling a little bit. The sound of applause was immense. I looked over to my right and could see a little crowd of SNCC people hollering and yelling, cheering me on, and that helped loosen me up a little.

Standing directly behind my right shoulder, sucking on his cigarette, close enough, it felt, to yank me away if I got out of line, was Bayard.

As I began, I actually wondered if I'd be able to speak at all. My voice quavered at first, but I quickly caught the feeling, the call and response, just like in church. The crowd was with me, hanging on every word, and I could feel that. I soon had the rhythm, as the words went out and the sounds of support came back. These were *my* experiences I was sharing, and there were many in that crowd who knew that. These were *my* friends I was mentioning. The cities I was naming were cities in whose streets I had marched. Many among that sea of men and women knew these things, and they responded.

This speech itself felt like an act of protest to me. After going through what I'd been through during the previous sixteen or so hours, after feeling the pressures that had been placed on me and finally stepping out and delivering these words, it felt just like a demonstration, just like a march. It felt like defiance. I had been rubbed the wrong way, and I think it was evident in my tone that afternoon, even in my facial expression. I felt defiance in every direction: against the entrenched segregation of the South; against the neglect of the federal government; and also against the conservative concerns of the establishment factions, black and white alike, that were trying to steer the movement with their own interests in mind rather than the needs of the people.

By the time I reached my closing words, I felt lifted both by a feeling of righteous indignation and by the heartfelt response of those hundreds of thousands of men, women and children before me, who burst into cheers with each phrase:

> We will not stop. If we do not get meaningful legislation out of this Congress, the time will come when we will not confine our marching to Washington. We will march through the South, through the streets of Jackson, through the streets of Danville, through the streets of Cambridge, through the streets of Birmingham. But we will march with the spirit of love and with the spirit of dignity that we have shown here today.

> By the force of our demands, our determination and our numbers, we shall splinter the desegregated South into a thousand pieces and put them back together in the image of God and democracy.

> We must say, "Wake up, America. *Wake up!!!* For we cannot stop, and we *will* not be patient."

As I stepped away from the podium, every black hand on the platform reached out to shake mine.

Now, finally, for the first time that day, I was able to take my seat and soak in the spectacular scene. Until then, my day had been spent in a crisis mode, most of it back behind Lincoln's statue. Now I was able to relax while Rabbi Prinz delivered the speech after mine.

And then came the day's final speaker, Dr. King.

I had heard him speak many, many times by then. I knew his cadence, his rhythm, his favorite phrases and parables. As he delivered his prepared text that afternoon, I thought it was a good speech, but it was not nearly as powerful as many I had heard him make. As he moved toward his final words, it seemed that he, too, could sense that he was falling short. He hadn't locked into that *power* he so often found. I was not sitting near enough to hear her words, but apparently Mahalia Jackson, who was seated just behind King, leaned in as he was finishing and urged him out loud, "Tell them about the *dream*, Martin."

The dream. Many of us had heard Dr. King talk before about his "dream." It had become one of his favorite images, and he had used it several times recently, with variations depending on his audience. Just a week earlier, in Detroit, he had delivered the essence of his "dream" speech to a gathering of insurance executives.

"And so tonight I say to you," he had told that audience in Detroit, "as I have said before, I have a dream, a dream deeply rooted in the American dream...."

But this was a different audience, a different time, a different place. This was truly history, and Dr. King knew it. We all knew it. We'd known it with our own speeches, and he knew it with his. He was responding to the occasion. He was speaking not just to the massive audience before us, but to the President, to Congress, to the nation, to the world. He felt the immensity of the moment, and he delivered.

"...I have a dream that one day every valley shall be exalted and every hill and mountain shall be made low...."

It was not, in my opinion, the best speech he ever gave. I think his speech four years later at the Riverside Church in New York, in which he condemned the war in Vietnam and talked about the United States as the greatest purveyor of violence in the world, was by far the best speech of his life in terms of sheer tone and substance. But considering the context and setting and the *timing* of this one, it was truly a masterpiece, truly immortal. Dr. King spoke from the soul at that moment, and anyone who saw it—anyone who sees it today—could feel it.

"...Free at last! Free at last! Thank God Almighty, we are free at *last!*"

With those eternal words, the day was done. By nightfall there was little left on the sprawling lawn below the Lincoln Memorial but scattered litter. Almost all of those half million people had headed back home.

Those of us who had spoken that day were driven to the White House for a visit with the President, who had watched the entire event on television. Over cups of coffee and glasses of orange juice, we met briefly with Kennedy, posed for several photographs—again, to Jim Forman's dismay, I wound up in the back, obscured by Rabbi Prinz—and exchanged a couple of words each with the President. "I heard you speak," he said to me as we shook hands. His face gave no hint of how he felt about my speech, but I could guess. As for the subject at hand, the civil rights bill that was just beginning to battle its way through the legislature, the President was noncommittal about that as well. I think his overriding feeling about the day was relief that it was finally over, without crisis, incident or explosion, without any damage done.

In the days that followed, too much of the national press, in my opinion, focused not on the substance of the day but on the setting. Their stories portrayed the event as a big picnic, a hootenanny combined with the spirit of a revival prayer meeting. Too many commentators and reporters softened and trivialized the hard edges of pain and suffering that brought about this day in the first place, virtually ignoring the hard issues that needed to be addressed, the issues that had stirred up so much trouble in my own speech. It was revealing that the quotes they gathered from most of the congressional leaders on Capitol Hill dealt not with each legislator's stand on the civil rights bill but instead focused on praising the "behavior" and "peacefulness" of the mass marchers.

Meanwhile, as the days and weeks passed, the bill sank almost out of sight, mired deep in subcommittees. If it ever made it out, it would be in a horribly emasculated form. As for the jobs this day was supposed to hasten, they didn't happen either. Randolph's vision of economic change remained just that—a vision. The issue of jobs for black men and women still lay far beyond and much deeper than the scope of the civil rights movement at that moment. A mass march for "Jobs and Freedom" had, when the singing stopped and the cheering was over, done little to actually achieve either.

In spite of the shortcomings of the March on Washington, I felt fine about my own role in the event. I felt I had shared SNCC's position clearly and forcefully. The few journalists and commentators who addressed the substance of the day seemed to agree. While praising King for his inspirational words, most of them singled out my speech as the one that raised and addressed the key questions of the moment.

But there were plenty of critics of both King and me, especially among the more radical leaders of the black community. Malcolm X, of course, dismissed the entire event, calling it the "Farce on Washington." In a speech delivered not long after the march, he said, "They told those Negroes what time to hit town, how to come, where to stop, what signs to carry, what song to sing, what speech they could make, and then they told them to get out of town by sundown."

That was my speech he was talking about, of course. Some of my own colleagues in SNCC criticized me for agreeing to, as they put it, "sanitize" my text. Many of the same people criticized Dr. King as well for not taking the federal government to task for the suffering, injustice and violence inflicted on blacks, especially in the South. More than a few critics dismissed Dr. King's speech as a candy-coated, conciliatory gesture to white America. Some compared it to Booker T. Washington's Atlanta Compromise of 1895.

I understood at the time, and I understand today, the feelings behind those criticisms, both of my speech and of Dr. King's. But I've always felt that the critics missed the mark on both counts. My speech, although it was adjusted and changed, did what SNCC and I needed it to do. In its tone, it established and conveyed our firm and angry position on the hard issues of the day. As for content, it specified those issues and put them directly in the face of the government. It may have been less fierce than the original draft, but it still hit hard. It still had sting.

As for Dr. King's speech, I was not disturbed at all by its message of hope and harmony. I have always believed there is room for both outrage and anger *and* optimism and love. Many, many times in my life, in many situations and circumstances, I have felt all these emotions at once. I think this is something that separated me from many of my colleagues in SNCC—the fact that they saw this struggle as an either/or situation, that they believed it was impossible to feel hope and love at the same time as you felt anger and a sense of injustice. This difference in perspective would continue to push us further apart in the coming years.

But on that day in Washington, I really did feel hope. Yes, the march was a failure in terms of specifics, in terms of prompting meaningful action on the part of the government or moving the segregationists in the South from their entrenched positions. But it was a truly stunning spectacle in terms of showing America and the world the size and the strength and the spirit of our movement.

Dr. King's speech, despite its lack of substance, was magical and majestic in spirit. I felt immensely inspired and moved by his affirmation of brotherhood and community. It is the spirit of his words that has stood the test of time, even in the face of the darkness and pain and division that persist in America to this day. More than anyone else that summer afternoon in 1963, he captured the spirit of hope and possibility that so many of us wanted to feel.

There was no way we could have known then that that afternoon would represent the peak of such feelings, that the hope and optimism contained in King's words would dwindle in the coming years, that in a matter of mere days after he stepped down from that stage a bomb blast in Birmingham would kill four little girls and usher in a season of darkness for the movement...and for me.

12 / "KEEP YOUR STICK DOWN"

*I*t was a frigid December afternoon when I last stopped by to visit Birmingham's Sixteenth Street Baptist Church. The doors were locked. The sanctuary was empty. It was a weekday, and for a change there were no tour groups lined up beneath the Byzantine-style towers that flank the front steps of this stately old building. Spike Lee, who had just come several weeks earlier to shoot scenes for a film about the '63 bombing here, was packed up and gone. So was the crowd of reporters who had followed his every move.

Maybe it was the weather this day, but for some reason, although the church sits not far from downtown Birmingham, there was not a soul in sight. Across the street, at Kelly Ingram Park, where Bull Connor's dogs and hoses had torn into those marchers thirty-five years ago, the only human forms were the sculptures built to commemorate that long-ago attack—metal men, women and children forged in poses of singing and marching as a cast-iron dog bares its teeth and strains at its leash.

Another sculpture stands on the opposite corner, in front of the Birmingham Civil Rights Institute, which was opened in 1992 to honor all that happened here and throughout the South during the struggle against segregation. On the way in to that museum, visitors pass a bronze life-sized statue of Fred Shuttlesworth. But few of them know who Fred Shuttlesworth is, according to a minister named Christopher Hamlin.

Hamlin is the pastor of Sixteenth Street Baptist, a position that requires him to be a historian and tour guide as well as minister to the congregation of 1,600 members who fill the church's seats each Sunday. When I knocked on this wintry afternoon at the small office that sits beside the church, it was Hamlin who came to the door.

He is a young man, born in 1959—the year we staged our first test sit-ins in Nashville—but he knows all about what happened in Nashville. And in Montgomery. And in Mississippi. And, of course, in Birmingham. He studied the movement at Morehouse College, and he has spent years since then studying it on his own. Unfortunately, he says, too few of his generation have done the same.

"A lot of people just don't want to *touch* it," he says, grabbing his keys and leading the way next door, into the church. Most of the 80,000 visitors who come here each year, he says, are schoolchildren. He is happy to see them, but he is amazed at how little they often know about the story of the movement.

"They've all heard of Martin Luther King, of course," he says. "But Fred Shuttlesworth? The man is a living *legend,* especially here in Birmingham, and even the teachers sometimes don't know who he is. It's a shame, because without people like Fred Shuttlesworth, Martin would not have been able to do what he did."

The inside of the church is gorgeous, with rich red carpeting and massive stained-glass windows—several of which were installed that fall of 1963 to replace the ones blasted out by that terrible bomb. A memorial to that awful Sunday morning sits downstairs, in the church basement. It is a small shrine, featuring a glass case filled with photos and articles about that day, and a wall featuring portraits of each of the four young girls who died here.

I was home in Pike County that morning—September 15, 1963—visiting with my parents and my uncle Otis when a news bulletin came over the radio. A church had been bombed in Birmingham. The report was hardly finished when the phone rang. It was Jim Forman, on the line from our SNCC office in Atlanta, telling me to get over to Birmingham right away.

I took a bus, but not from Montgomery, where I'd been beaten two years earlier. Instead, Uncle Otis, who was worried something might happen to me there, drove me to the Greyhound station in Dothan, sixty miles south of Troy. Four hours later, I arrived at the same Birmingham terminal where we had spent that night under siege during the Freedom Ride. I caught a cab from there to the Gaston Motel—which had been bombed earlier that year—and joined Julian, who had already arrived from Atlanta. A short walk from there, and we were at the church.

I don't think I've ever seen so many people so silent. The police had cordoned off the area surrounding the building. Shattered glass covered the street. A crowd stood across the way, dozens of black men and women just staring at the gaping holes in the church windows, no one saying a word, everyone just standing there in shock, in total disbelief. Some were shaking their heads. There had been a lot of crying and wailing earlier in the day, but now it had settled into a vigil, a mourning, like people visiting a graveyard.

By then the details of what had happened that morning had emerged. The church had been celebrating its annual Youth Day, and the building was full of children. The theme of the day's Sunday school lesson was "The Love That Forgives." That lesson was in process when an explosion rocked the building. Once the smoke and the screaming settled, twenty-one children lay injured. And four young girls—Cynthia Wesley, Carole Robertson, Addie Mae Collins and Denise McNair—were dead.

It was unreal to stand there and try to absorb what had happened. I looked at the people standing on that sidewalk across the street, these black men and women of Birmingham, who had lived through so much, and I knew that they had to be asking themselves, How much *more?* What *else?* What's *next?*

There had been so many deaths by then. You never get used to death, you never get acquainted with it, you never really understand it. It's something I will never be able to understand, the concept of killing someone, of taking a life away. But this was beyond comprehension. Four children killed on a Sunday morning in church, in God's house. What *could* be next?

Three days later, exactly three weeks after the March on Washington, Dr. King spoke at the funeral for those little girls. Eight thousand mourners came together, the crowd outside pushing and pushing to get closer to the building. So many tears. So much grief. It was almost too much.

I remember being amazed at how peaceful that service was, that in spite of the pain, the people *still* seemed able to forgive. There were many who felt bitter, many who felt let down. There were some who were ready to take up guns, who were saying, "We *told* you this nonviolence would not work." But most shared Dr. King's attitude, the message he delivered in his eulogy that day, when he said, "You can bomb our homes, bomb our churches, kill our little children, and we are *still* going to love you.

"At times life is hard, as hard as crucible steel," he continued. "In spite of the darkness of this hour, we must not lose faith in our white brothers."

That was a powerful statement, and I don't think anyone else could have delivered it. Dr. King had an uncanny ability to comfort and calm when you would have thought it impossible, when people were so upset.

There were white people who felt terrible about this, too, and who voiced their feelings. I will never forget a man named Charles Morgan, a white attorney in Birmingham, who openly shared his own sense of shame and guilt on the part of the entire white community of the city for allowing this kind of hatred and violence to grow. "We all did this," he said of the bombing. After those words were publicized, he became such an object of scorn that he eventually had to leave Birmingham forever and move to Atlanta. I believe he's living in Washington today.

There were many, many white Southerners of conscience who dared to speak out at that time and who, like Morgan, had to leave the South. There was a conspiracy of silence back then, and if you broke it, it was very hard to stay. This was even true of journalists and writers. Many native Alabamians and Mississippians who wrote about the South during this time had to *leave* the South to do it. To this day, when I travel around the country and speak at universities in the North or the Midwest or out West, I come across professors and writers whose specialty is the South, who are *from* the South, but who had to move away during this time in order to write about it and who have never returned.

What happened in that church that Sunday was a particularly painful experience for all of us in the movement. It was a big blow to the hope and faith of many. The day after the bombing, Diane Nash and I talked to a young black reporter from the *Washington Post,* and we brought up the idea of a mass march on Montgomery, a nonviolent siege of the state capital. It was just a notion, a vague idea, but that story wound up in the *Post,* and then went into other newspapers around the country, and by the day of the funeral it had assumed a reality of its own. Diane had developed an outline of an actual plan. She called it a "Move on Alabama."

To see Diane there in Birmingham was a sign of the significance of this tragedy. Since marrying Bevel and having a baby, she had not been nearly as visible or involved in the movement as before. But this thing struck so close to home for her, not just as a member of SNCC but as a mother. She identified with those four women who had lost their daughters, and so she had come, intent on doing something.

The night of the funeral, after the girls had been buried, Diane, Bevel, some other SNCC and SCLC people and I went back to the motel and sat down with King. Diane did most of the talking, and she spoke for just about everyone in the room. Everyone felt that we had to do something, but *what?*

Diane described her idea to King—an assault, a nonviolent attack on Montgomery, the kind of siege many of our SNCC people had had in mind for the March on Washington. It was time, Diane told King, to literally drive the racists out of office, to throw waves of bodies at the state capital, surround the city, shut down the streets, railroads, airport runways—shut down *everything*—and refuse to leave until George Wallace vacated that statehouse.

King listened. He respected Diane. He agreed—though not as strongly as we—that we needed to strike back in a nonviolent way. But I don't think he ever took the idea of an "attack" on Montgomery seriously. And by the time we left the motel room that night, we knew there would be no massive move on Montgomery or on the state of Alabama, not as Diane had described it. The SCLC just wasn't ready for something that direct, something that aggressive, not after the campaign they'd just mounted in Birmingham. If we were going to launch a "move" anywhere, it was going to have to be essentially on our own, which was something we had understood as soon as we came home from the March on Washington.

Ideologically, SNCC had angered the established civil rights organizations during that day in D.C. The debate over our involvement in the march, the struggle over my speech—the entire Washington experience—had set us further apart from the movement's mainstream than we had ever been. In terms of funding, we were now set apart as well. After the march, a significant amount of money was made available from various Northern groups supporting the movement. A series of "civil rights breakfasts" were set up by a man named Stephen Currier, who was president of the Taconic Foundation. Currier was married to a member of the Mellon family, he was very wealthy and he was very enthusiastic about the cause of civil rights.

Forman and I went to the first of these breakfasts, and encountered the same tone of one-upmanship and infighting and political positioning that we'd witnessed during the planning for the march. Currier had raised $800,000, which was pledged to all our organizations collectively under the banner title of the Council on United Civil Rights Leadership. A formula was worked out, mainly by Roy Wilkins, that determined each group's share of the money based on its existing budget. This, of course, guaranteed that the groups that already *had* money—groups like Wilkins's NAACP—got the biggest chunks. As for us, well, we were at the bottom of the barrel. We were considered the kids, the upstarts, and we were given peanuts compared with what the others received. Every other group there, from the Urban League to the SCLC, wound up with at least $100,000. We, on the other hand, received $15,000.

Then again, there was always a current of distrust about money in SNCC. Along with an understanding that we needed it, there was always a concern about the strings that might be attached, about control over ourselves versus control by others. If it ever came to a choice between money or our independence, there was no question which we would choose. So we learned early on how to make do without money.

Diane's vision of a "move" that fall did not die after that meeting with King. And it did not fade for lack of funding. There would be a move, an all-out assault—we promised ourselves that. But it would not be that fall, and it would not be in Alabama.

Mississippi, we began to see, was where this massive "move" would take place.

Already those plans were taking shape, under Bob Moses's leadership. Earlier that summer Moses, along with a white activist named Al Lowenstein, had come up with the idea of staging a "mock election" in the fall, to coincide with the actual elections in Mississippi—elections from which virtually all black people were excluded. Lowenstein, who was a former dean at Stanford University, had arrived in Mississippi that summer after the murder of Medgar

Evers, and he had become aroused by conditions he compared to those in South Africa. This "protest vote," as he saw it, would be modeled after one that had taken place over there. As the idea took shape and our SNCC headquarters got involved, we gave it our own name: the Freedom Vote.

The plan was to have a full-scale election, with real candidates and real ballot boxes, an exercise to both give black men and women the sense of actually *voting* and to dramatize to onlookers the exclusion of blacks in the actual political process.

The campaign would be staffed by SNCC people, other members of COFO, and—extremely significantly, as it would turn out—a number of white students brought in from Northern and West Coast universities by Lowenstein.

By September, the stage was set. A slate of Freedom Party candidates was listed on Freedom Vote ballots beside the regular Democratic and Republican candidates running for state office. Our Freedom candidate for governor was Aaron "Doc" Henry, a druggist from Clarksdale and state chairman of the Mississippi NAACP. Ed King, a white minister at Tougaloo College in Jackson, was listed as Henry's running mate for lieutenant governor. And eighty of those white students, mostly from Yale and Stanford, were set to come down for the campaign.

Meanwhile, we did not ignore Alabama completely. While there would be no march on Montgomery—not yet—we decided after the church bombing in Birmingham to step up our activity, to turn up the heat... in Selma.

The reason we had targeted Selma in the first place earlier that year, with Bernard and Colia LaFayette moving in with their voter classes, was that this small city so typified the entire Black Belt. Half the voting age population of the county around Selma was black—about 15,000 men and women. But as of that fall, despite Bernard and Colia's efforts, only two hundred of those people—barely one percent—were registered to vote.

The black people of Selma, like the black citizens of so many Southern cities, had long lived under the heavy hand of local white authorities and citizenry. Lynchings were routine around this city at the turn of the century—twenty-one were reported in a particularly busy thirty-year period, and those were just the ones that were reported. Nighttime shootings, beatings and economic reprisals awaited any black person who tried to assert his or her rights in any way. Bernard's early memos to our SNCC headquarters described the black population of Selma as "fear stricken."

That September, just prior to the church bombing in Birmingham, Bernard and Colia returned to school at Fisk, leaving the local organization in Selma in the hands of the young people they'd been working with—college students and teenagers—as well as a local black businesswoman named Mrs.

Amelia Boynton. Two new SNCC representatives had been sent to replace Bernard and Colia: Worth Long and Prathia Hall. I knew Prathia well—she had been a great help with the early drafts of my Washington speech. I did not know Worth as well, but I was aware of his dedication as a SNCC field secretary in his native Arkansas, and I knew we would need that kind of focused commitment in a place like Selma.

There were demonstrations there the day after the Sixteenth Street bombing in Birmingham—sit-ins at several downtown Selma stores—and they brought a swift response from local and state police. Jim Clark, the sheriff of Dallas County, and Colonel Al Lingo, the director of Alabama's state troopers, arrived with almost two hundred of their men and arrested sixty-three people, and also beat several others. When local teenagers responded by picketing the Dallas County Courthouse—the first such open defiance in the history of the city—more arrests were made. And now, a movement was afoot.

The city's black citizens began holding mass meetings on a nightly basis in local churches. Local black leaders requested in mid-September that Selma be declared off-limits to military personnel from nearby Craig Air Force Base, since the city was defying federal law by enforcing segregation. This was a bold initiative, and it was totally ignored by the base commander. When, in my capacity as chairman of SNCC, I followed up that local request by telegramming Defense Secretary Robert McNamara with a description of the situation, his office at the Defense Department issued a curt reply: "The commander may not intervene in behalf of persons not under his command."

With that, it was time to personally go down to Selma, which Forman and I did late that month. I had just been down that July, but now it looked like a different place. Tensions were incredibly high. Armed troopers and police were everywhere, as well as squads of local white men who had been deputized by Sheriff Clark as "citizen's posses." They liked to call themselves "squirrel shooters," and, amazingly, they were actually authorized to make arrests.

The night we arrived, September 23, I attended a mass meeting at the town's Tabernacle Baptist Church and spoke to an audience of more than a thousand people. Outside, fifty of Colonel Lingo's troopers, armed with machine guns, surrounded the building. I envisioned another night-long shut-in siege, like the one in Montgomery during the Freedom Ride. For a time it looked as if I might be right. But eventually, late that evening, we were all allowed to leave, with no arrests.

The next day, though, thirty men and women were taken to the Selma city jail for demonstrating in front of the courthouse, which prompted an even larger gathering, which I took part in, along with a group of Selma University students. I carried a sign that read ONE MAN, ONE VOTE—the first

1. My maternal great-grandfather Frank Carter was a tenant farmer in Pike County, Alabama, the patriarch of Carter's Quarters, where I grew up. He died in 1947, when I was seven years old.

2. My mother, Willie Mae Carter Lewis, at my wedding. She taught me, "Work and put your trust in God, and God's gonna take care of his children."

3. My maternal grandfather, Dink Carter, was a very proud and hardworking man. He thought the Carters were just a little better than everyone else.

4. John Robert Lewis, "Preacher," at age eleven, about the time I took my first trip up north with my uncle Otis.

5. Eddie and Willie Mae Lewis and their children in 1969.

6. I had my first taste of politics as president of the student body at American Baptist Theological Seminary in 1961.

7. Jim Lawson, an early leader of the sit-in movement, turned my world around with his teachings on the philosophy and discipline of nonviolence.

8. Diane Nash, leader of the Nashville Student Movement and one of God's beautiful creatures, at age twenty.

9. James Bevel, a fellow student at American Baptist Theological Seminary and movement leader.

10. Protestors in the Nashville city jail after being arrested, February 1960. It felt like a crusade, as if we were prisoners of a holy war. A year later I would celebrate my twenty-first birthday behind bars.

11. The Greyhound bus carrying nine Freedom Riders, including several new volunteers, that was firebombed in Anniston, Alabama, in May 1961. I was supposed to be on that bus, but I had gone to Philadelphia at the last minute for an interview about the foreign service program into which I had just been accepted.

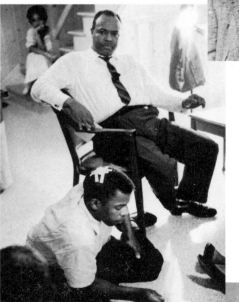

12. With my fellow Freedom Rider James Zwerg after we were both beaten by the mob that met our bus in Montgomery, May 20, 1961.

13. Mapping out plans to continue the Freedom Rides with James Farmer, head of CORE, after the attacks in Anniston and Montgomery, May 1961.

14. Buying a ticket for fellow Freedom Rider LeRoy Wright at the Greyhound bus station in Montgomery, May 1961.

15. Protesting a segregated swimming pool, I knelt and prayed with local residents in Cairo, Illinois, in August 1962. SNCC would later use this image in a recruitment poster with the appeal "COME LET US BUILD A NEW WORLD TO-GETHER."

16. Sitting down during an arrest was an act of civil disobedience.

17. Refusing to cooperate with evil, we let our bodies go limp, forcing the police officers to carry us to jail.

18. Bull Connor, pictured with fellow police officers, had taken us Freedom Riders into "protective custody" when we arrived in Birmingham. He would later escort us to the Tennessee state line in the middle of the night and leave us there, deep in Klan country.

19. Birmingham, May 1963. Powerful fire hoses, with streams of water strong enough to peel the bark off a tree, were aimed at children, sending their bodies hurtling down the street like rag dolls in a windstorm.

20. In July 1963, the "Big Six" of the civil rights movement discussed plans for the March on Washington: from left to right, John Lewis, Whitney Young, A. Philip Randolph, Dr. Martin Luther King Jr., James Farmer, and Roy Wilkins.

21. Bayard Rustin, the chief organizer of the March on Washington.

22. At the March on Washington, August 28, 1963, the leadership assumed the classic pose, walking arm in arm at the head of the crowd. In fact, the march had begun without us, but photographers had cleared a space to take pictures, so it looked as if we were at the front. But we couldn't even *see* the front.

23. At age twenty-three, I gave my controversial speech on the steps of the Lincoln Memorial. As I began, I wondered if I'd be able to speak at all. By the time I was finished, I felt lifted both by a feeling of righteous indignation and by the heartfelt response of those hundreds of thousands of men, women and children in the audience.

24. Civil rights leaders met with President Kennedy the afternoon of the March on Washington: from left to right, Whitney Young of the Urban League; Dr. Martin Luther King Jr. of the SCLC; John Lewis of SNCC; Rabbi Joachim Prinz of the American Jewish Congress; Dr. Eugene Carson Blake of the National Council of Churches; A. Philip Randolph of the Brotherhood of Sleeping Car Porters; President John F. Kennedy; and Walter Reuther of the United Auto Workers.

25. First Baptist Church, Nashville, Tennessee, spring 1964, with Lester McKinney, chair of the local Nashville Student Movement (center), and Paul Good of ABC News.

26. Reverend Fred Shuttlesworth, leader of the Birmingham Movement, spoke at the funeral of the four little girls killed at the Sixteenth Street Baptist Church in Birmingham, September 1963.

27. A meeting with Attorney General Robert F. Kennedy, July 1963.

28. *Above left:* In Rome with Don Harris, who would be best man at my wedding, on our way back from the 1964 trip to Africa Harry Belafonte had arranged for us.

29. *Above right:* With Fannie Lou Hamer, a grassroots civil rights and political leader. "Now, John Lewis," she would say, "let me tell you all, if you're going to come to Mississippi, you can't just come here and stay for one day or one night. You've got to stay here for the long haul."

30. *Below left:* Ella Baker, an advisor to the NAACP, SCLC and SNCC.

31. *Below right:* Trying to register voters in February 1965 with Mrs. Amelia Boynton at the Dallas County Courthouse in Selma. *The New York Times* described Mrs. Boynton's arrest: Sheriff Jim Clark "grabbed her by the back of her collar and pushed her roughly for half a block into a patrol car." Sixty-six other marchers were also arrested that day.

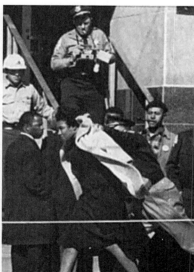

32. Amelia Boynton, Hosea Williams, Andrew Young, other SNCC and SCLC staff members and I gathered to sing and hold hands before the "attempted" march from Selma to Montgomery on March 7, 1965.

33. Leading the march with Hosea Williams across the Edmund Pettus Bridge in Selma on March 7, 1965.

34. Moments before the Alabama state troopers attacked us on the bridge.

35. Beaten by state troopers on March 7, 1965, a day that became known as "Bloody Sunday." I remember the clunk of the troopers' heavy boots, the whoops of rebel yells from the white onlookers, the clip-clop of horses' hooves hitting the hard asphalt of the highway, the voice of a woman shouting, "Get 'em! Get the niggers!"

36. Weary marchers, including Reverend Ralph Abernathy, Dr. Martin Luther King, Ponchita Pierce, Bernard Lee and Andy Young (back to camera).

37. Marching to Montgomery in March 1965 with, from left to right, Reverend Curtis Harris, Reverend G. K. Steele and Dr. and Mrs. King after Judge Johnson had ruled that Sheriff Clark and his deputies were guilty of harassment, intimidation, coercion, threatening conduct and brutal mistreatment of us two weeks earlier.

38. A rally after the march on the grounds of the state capitol in Montgomery. Those pictured include Dr. and Mrs. King, Ralph Abernathy, James Baldwin, Hosea Williams (at podium), Charles Evers and Bayard Rustin. Four and a half months later, on August 6, the 1965 Voting Rights Act was signed into law by President Johnson.

39. James Farmer and I met with President Lyndon Johnson and Major Hugh Robinson, a military aide to the President, on August 6, 1965.

40. A happy moment with my new bride, Lillian, and Daddy King after our wedding on December 21, 1968.

41. Getting a little advice from my good friend Julian Bond on my wedding day as Daddy King looked on.

42. With Julian and Alice Bond, SNCC supporter Harry Belafonte and my wife, Lillian.

43. Leading a voter registration tour with Julian Bond in the Mississippi Delta during the summer of 1971.

44. Campaigning in 1977 with then–Lieutenant Governor Zell Miller, John-Miles and Lillian for the Fifth District congressional seat vacated by Andy Young. My victory was supposed to be "part of God's plan," according to Reverend Abernathy, but Wyche Fowler was a formidable opponent, and he beat me in the runoff.

45. Our victory walk down Peachtree Street on September 2, 1986, after I won my first congressional campaign (with, from left to right, Love Sears Collins, Dewey Clark, Lillian, Quentin Watkins and Tyrone Albertey).

46. Savoring the victory with Lillian and our son, John-Miles.

47. Sharing a moment with freedom fighter Nelson Mandela on the day of his address to a joint session of the United States Congress, October 1994.

appearance of what was now SNCC's official slogan. The phrase had really struck a chord after my March on Washington speech, and now it was printed on the top of all our letterheads, as well as on most of our picket signs.

We weren't there long that afternoon before Lingo's men arrived and I experienced my first arrest, Selma-style—the first of many. The troopers had electric cattle prods, which concerned me. I knew what those things could do, how they burn, and how the men who used them enjoyed aiming for the genital area. As they waded in and began reaching out and arresting everyone they could put their hands on, pushing us toward a side alley where a school bus waited to take us to jail, I could see them reaching out with those weapons to herd us along. I was quick enough to dodge, but others weren't so lucky. I could hear sharp cries of pain here and there as we were loaded on the bus.

We were all charged with "unlawful assembly" that afternoon and were taken to the Selma prison farm, where the conditions were almost as bad as at Parchman. Our men's cell looked like a chicken coop, not much different from the one I had kept my birds in as a boy, only larger. It was a coop made for humans. Just a long hall with filthy mattresses on the floor. No tables. No chairs. One commode, one sink. When your food was brought in, you either ate off the tray standing up or, if you preferred, you could sit down on the filthy concrete floor. I chose to stand.

By the beginning of October, when I was released, more than three hundred arrests had been made in Selma, and no one was backing down. The registrar's office in the county courthouse was open the first and third Mondays of each month, and those became "Freedom Mondays," with hundreds of black men and women from both the city and the surrounding countryside standing in lines that stretched around the block. FBI agents and Justice Department attorneys were on hand to observe, and people like James Baldwin came from as far away as New York to help our SNCC volunteers deliver food and drinks to the people standing in line. Reporters from around the country stood taking notes.

But all those witnesses meant nothing to Sheriff Clark and his deputies, who roamed the line with their military helmets and their round angry faces, hounding and harassing our volunteers as they tried to do their jobs.

One of those volunteers was a SNCC worker from Tennessee named Carver "Chico" Neblett. Like me, he'd grown up on a sharecropper's farm. He had just joined SNCC earlier that year, and he had come to Selma that October to help in whatever way he could. On the first of those Freedom Mondays, October 7, Carver and another SNCC worker, Avery Williams, were surrounded by Sheriff Clark's men in full public view. Carver's report of that experience, filed with our SNCC offices, remains the most vivid first-person account I have ever seen of the beating and arrest of two civil rights workers in the 1960s:

> I, Carver Neblett, along with a friend of mine from Gadsden, Alabama, Avery Williams, started across Alabama Avenue, from the Federal Building to the Courthouse, with food for the Negro applicants. I was carrying a small open box containing approximately nine sandwiches, and a clipboard with voter registration applications, and a pencil. Avery Williams was carrying a clipboard with voter registrations, and a pencil. Our purpose was to feed the Negro applicants and to show them how to fill out the application forms. We thought, and still think, that this is legitimate voter registration business.
>
> Williams and I crossed the street at 2:00 P.M. and proceeded to the people. We were blocked by two state policemen. I said, "Excuse me."
>
> One of the officers said, "Nigger, if you want to get by you'd better go around."
>
> We went around two parked cars, and came within about four feet of the applicants who were standing on and alongside the Courthouse steps. There were four state policemen standing between the applicants and Williams and myself.
>
> I started to talk with the people. I said, "We have brought you food, and there is water across the street by the Federal Building."
>
> At this point, more state policemen had started to gather around me. I continued to speak. I said, "You know that you have the right to go across the street to get water and food."
>
> One lady that was in the line of applicants said, "We can't leave the line."
>
> I said, "There is no law that says that you can't leave this line to eat."
>
> The lady seemed very frightened, and the others appeared petrified as they stood there perfectly still, facing approximately 75 state policemen and a large number of the Sheriff's Possemen.
>
> The same lady said, under her breath, "You can't talk to us."
>
> I said, "There is no law that says that I can't talk to you about legitimate voter registration business."
>
> I started to approach the people to give them the sandwiches. A state policeman said, "You'd better get the hell out of here, nigger."
>
> I started to approach the people again, and a state policeman put his hands on me, and I fell to the ground to protect myself. Williams immediately fell on the ground beside me.

We were there on our backs, and about ten or fifteen state policemen surrounded us and began to beat us with their billy clubs. They lifted me from the ground and started around the corner. The policemen that had hold of my arms and legs were beating me in my stomach, on my head, shoulders, and punching at my groin with the billy clubs. The state policemen that surrounded me, to keep the spectators from seeing what was going on, also beat me with their billy clubs.

When one officer raised his billy club to hit me a second time, one officer said, "Keep your stick down, keep your stick down." (The press was there.)

The state policemen carried me up the side entrance steps of the Courthouse, on Lauderdale Street, head first. They bumped my back on the sharp concrete steps. The state policemen carried me back down the steps, feet first, and bumped my head on the steps. One of the state policemen said, "Put the nigger down and let him walk." They did not put me down.

When we had reached the bottom of the steps, one state policeman said, "Drop him, drop the nigger." The two state policemen that had hold of my arms let go of them. My back and head fell to the hard concrete street. One state policeman said, "Oops."

The state policemen lifted me again and threw me on the bus, feet first. One state policeman twisted my left leg around a bar that was on the bus. The state policemen jabbed me in the back with their billy sticks until I was in the front seat of the bus on the right hand side. While I was trying to help myself into the seat, a state policeman was hitting my hand with a billy stick.

After they had thrown Williams on the bus, a man in plain clothing came on the bus and asked me where I was from. I said, "I am from Illinois." He said, "Somebody give me a gun. I'm gonna shoot the nigger now."

The man in plain clothing left the bus, still begging for a gun. He returned shortly. He pointed his finger at me and said, "Nigger, you'd better get out of town, because if I see you on the streets anywhere, I'm going to kill you, do you understand that?"

I said, "I hear you."

The man left.

Another state policeman got on the bus and tried to take a billy stick from an officer that was sitting in the driver's seat of the bus, to hit me with. The officer was cursing and threatening my life. The officer in the driver's seat did not let go of his stick. The officer that was sitting in the driver's seat got up and moved to a seat in back of me. Another state policeman got on the bus and drove off.

As we turned the corner from Lauderdale onto Alabama Avenue, I waved to the people who were on the corner to let them know that I wasn't hurt too bad, and that I was still alive. One of the officers in back of me said, "Don't put your hand close to me, nigger. I'll beat you to death."

When we arrived at the Dallas County Jail, the three officers that were on the bus asked us to get off. I helped Williams to get off the bus, because he was having pains in his stomach. I helped him to walk to the elevator. The elevator door opened and the three officers asked us to get on.

We got on the elevator with the three state policemen. We were on our way up, and one officer said, "Ain't that that nigger from Illinois?"

One of the other state policemen said, "Yes."

One of the policemen stopped the elevator, and a state policeman, badge No. 8 (eight), started to beat me in the stomach with his billy club and asked me, "Are you going back to Illinois?"

I said, "No."

He continued to punch me in the stomach, and again he said, "Are you going back to Illinois now, nigger?"

I shook my head and said, "No."

Then badge No. 8 (eight) punched me in the groin. He missed my testes and hit my scrotum. This was very painful, and I slumped to the floor.

One of the state policemen said, "We'd better get going. They know that we are in here." The state policeman, badge No. 8 (eight), stopped beating me and we started up again.

When the door opened at the 4th floor, a county official said, "No wonder the elevator ain't workin' right." The county official laughed.

The officers told us to walk over to the window to get booked. As we were being booked, I leaned on the window. One of the state policemen punched me in the back with his night stick and said, "Stand up, nigger."

I stood up.

The booking officer started to ask Williams questions. He asked Williams if he had been arrested before. When Williams did not say "sir," the state policeman in back of him hit him in the back and said, "Can't you say 'sir,' nigger?"

When I was asked had I been arrested, I said, "I have been arrested." We proceeded with the regular booking procedure.

I was charged with Criminal Provocation and Resisting Arrest. I was released on 500 dollars appearance bond at 1:00 Tuesday morning. My trial is set for Thursday, October 10, 1963.

The beatings of Neblett and Williams that afternoon were briefly reported in the next day's newspapers—just another among the thousands of "routine" civil rights arrests going on all across the South.

I would continue to be in and out of Selma through that fall, and by the end of the next year the situation there would reach critical mass. But as that October drew to a close, it was Mississippi and its Freedom Vote that became our focus.

Fannie Lou Hamer, the grassroots activist down in Sunflower County who had joined the movement after hearing Jim Bevel speak, had become very visible by then. She had been arrested several times, along with her husband and one of her daughters. She had been beaten by policemen who called her a "nigger bitch," and she would pay for that beating every day for the rest of her life with constant pain in her back and hips and a permanent limp. Her family was continually harassed—they received a $9,000 water bill one month, and her house did not even have running water—but Mrs. Hamer refused to back down. Even the police who entered her home one night unannounced, without warrants, did not frighten her anymore.

Mrs. Hamer was a regular not just at local voting rights meetings in Sunflower County, but at our regional and national SNCC conferences as well. We became friends, and she was not afraid to speak up, not to white Mississippians, and not to black civil rights leaders either.

"Now, John Lewis . . . ," she would say. "Now, Jim Forman . . . let me tell you all, if you're going to come to Mississippi, you can't just come here and stay for one day or one night. You've got to stay here for the long haul.

"I know Mississippi . . . ," she would say, "and you'd better be ready to move in."

Well, now that we were beginning to make that move in the fall of 1963, she was enormously gratified. I don't think there was any man or woman more excited about that November's Freedom Vote than Fannie Lou Hamer.

The campaign was an incredible success. Hundreds of volunteers, including those eighty white students brought down by Al Lowenstein, went door-to-door in black communities to get out the vote. There were assaults and harassment, as word spread among local Mississippians of what was going on in the black neighborhoods and communities around them. But by election day, there were hundreds of ballot boxes in place throughout the state, at churches, in beauty parlors and grocery stores, on streetside tables, in makeshift meeting halls.

More than 90,000 black Mississippians "voted" that election day, the vast majority casting their ballots for the Freedom ticket. Those votes would have made a significant difference in the actual election, in who became the governor of Mississippi—if they had been counted.

But choosing the governor wasn't the goal, not in that election. What we demonstrated that November was that black people could and *would* actually vote in meaningful numbers. We had no doubt this would be the case. Now we had shown it, not just to the nation, which read about the heavily publicized mock election in newspapers and magazines, but also to Mississippi's black citizenry itself, which was emboldened by this experience. Those 90,000 voters who took part in that November's Freedom election were now committed to registering and voting for real. The 1964 national election was a year away, and now our Move on Mississippi had a focus: the selection of the next President of the United States.

There was little doubt about who that president would—and in my opinion, *should*—be. For all his reticence in terms of civil rights, I believed John Kennedy was the best hope we had for the White House. I criticized him, yes, and he deserved that criticism. He needed it. Every politician needs to be pushed and prodded by the people he represents. I had my differences with the man, but I liked John Kennedy. I admired him. He truly had ideals, which not all politicians do. He was a symbol of hope, of change. He represented a period of great expectations for this entire country, including us—*most* of us—in the movement.

Which was why I was devastated when he was shot dead that November 22.

I was in the midst of an extended speaking tour at the time, appearing at rallies and mass meetings across the country, sowing the seeds for the voter registration campaign we would be launching the following summer in Mississippi. That week my tour had been interrupted by a court appearance in Nashville, where I had to appear at a hearing for my appeal on a sit-in conviction from earlier in the year.

The hearing had ended that Friday morning, and I was on my way with Lester McKinney, the local SNCC leader in Nashville, from the Fisk campus to the airport when the news came on the radio. We pulled over, stunned, and listened to the report as a crowd of students gathered around the car to listen with us.

I felt sick. I didn't know what to do. I had a speech to make that night to a union group in Detroit, one the next day at the University of Illinois and another on Sunday in Cincinnati. But all I wanted was to go home to Atlanta. I felt lost—faint, really. I just wanted to go back to my apartment and forget about everything for a while. I've often felt like this at times of great crisis in my life. In such situations I want to go to a familiar place. I want to be home.

I called Atlanta, talked with Julian, and we decided I should go ahead with the trip. As I arrived at the Nashville airport and was on my way to my flight's gate, I heard a report on a radio at one of the ticket counters: The President had died.

My speech that night in Detroit became a eulogy for John Kennedy. I went through with the weekend, got home late Sunday night and spent Monday alone in my apartment in Atlanta, watching the funeral on television. I'd been on the run since Friday, and only now was I able to sit still and let this all soak in. Watching that black caisson move through that cold, clear Washington afternoon, from the Capitol, past the White House, to St. Matthew's Cathedral and then to Arlington National Cemetery, listening to the sound of those lonely muffled drums, I felt as if I was watching them all—Medgar Evers, the little girls in Birmingham and now this. So much death. So much sorrow.

I cried that afternoon. Many, many black Americans cried that day. It is not insignificant that even today, in the homes of many black people in this country—especially in the homes of poor black people—you will often find three portraits proudly displayed on the living room wall: Jesus Christ, Martin Luther King Jr. and John F. Kennedy.

Kennedy represented hope and possibility to most of America, white and black alike, and when he died, that flame of optimism in all of us flickered just a little bit lower. To this day I have a place in my heart for him. When the Kennedy half dollars came out, I collected them, and I still collect them to this day. I have a box at home filled with them.

But not everyone was as fond of Kennedy as I, especially not everyone in SNCC. In the days following the assassination there were heated discussions and debates among our top staff people about how we should officially respond to the President's death and about the effect that death might have on the movement in general and on SNCC's efforts in particular.

There was concern about the morale of our SNCC staffers out in the field. If Kennedy could be killed, they might easily reason, then so could *they*.

There was worry that the worst elements in Mississippi might consider this a go-ahead for even more brutality. "Will they think," asked Ivanhoe Donaldson at one of our committee meetings that week, "that liberalism is dead when the *man* is dead?"

There was concern that the killing of Kennedy might prompt a crackdown on "radical" organizations such as ourselves, that, as Forman put it at one meeting, "anyone left of center will be subject to a purge."

Then again, went another line of reasoning—one with which I happened to agree—Kennedy's death could be a unifying factor, bringing factions together in pursuit of the principles he believed in, beginning with a strong civil rights bill.

That bill was the focus of Lyndon Johnson's speech before a joint session of Congress five days after Kennedy's death. It was encouraging to hear the new president commit himself to this legislation, saying "no memorial or eulogy could more eloquently honor President Kennedy's memory than the earliest possible passage of the civil rights bill for which he fought."

But who knew what "earliest possible" might mean? And who knew where Lyndon Johnson stood on the issues that mattered most to us in the movement? I had several preconceived notions about Johnson, as most black people did. He was a Southerner, a Texan, which made him immediately suspect. He'd been raised on Jim Crow, and he had blocked his share of civil rights legislation during his time in Congress. I did not anticipate his being a friend of the movement, but I kept those thoughts to myself when the press began calling and asking for comments. I was guarded, I didn't say much. I took the position that you had to give the man a chance. Give him time, I said, and see what he will do.

I thought—I *hoped*—that the situation itself, the circumstances taking shape in the South, most prominently the campaign we were mounting in Mississippi, would help make some of Johnson's decisions *for* him, that the movement might guide and shape and develop the attitudes and reactions of the man, as it had begun to do with the Kennedy brothers.

Again, most of my SNCC colleagues were less hopeful about Johnson than I was. It didn't help that during the week after the assassination, Johnson invited several civil rights leaders to the White House, including Farmer, Wilkins, Young and King, but he did not invite anyone from SNCC. The snub caused a lot of grumbling and complaining around our offices. Those feelings were in the air when SNCC's annual conference was held at the end of that week in, of all places, Washington, D.C.

The theme of that gathering was the future of the movement and of SNCC. There were workshops on developing our relations with organized labor, and on economic development and training programs reflecting some of the themes from the March on Washington. But the most heated discussions were centered around whether SNCC should make an official visit to Arlington Cemetery, to pay its respects at Kennedy's grave.

Some thought it hypocritical, since many members did not consider Kennedy a friend of SNCC. Many outright opposed it. Forman and Stokely, especially, were against going. I, on the other hand, felt we should do it. It seemed small, almost childish, not to go. I believed the right thing to do was rise above our differences and honor another human being with dignity and with love.

The debate was intense. A suggestion arose that we visit both Kennedy's grave and Medgar Evers's grave, which sounded fair to me. But that idea was eventually voted down, and there was no visit at all. It would not be until 1968 that I went to Arlington National Cemetery for the first time—for the burial of John's brother Bobby.

Besides the question of whether to visit the cemetery or not, the most important topic on our agenda that weekend was Mississippi.

It had been nearly three years now since Bob Moses had begun his work there, and still the percentage of voting-age blacks who had actually registered remained the lowest in the nation—5 percent. This in the state that had the largest black population in America.

That month's mock election had been encouraging, but the task ahead of us was tremendous. Our SNCC research showed over 150 incidents of violence against civil rights workers and black residents in Mississippi since our work had begun there in 1961. The first month of 1964 brought yet another.

Louis Allen, the witness to the 1961 shooting of Herbert Lee, was found dead under his truck outside his house in Amite County on the last day of January, shotgunned three times in the head. Mr. Allen had been a marked man ever since coming to Bob Moses with the truth about Herbert Lee's murder.

Moses felt horribly guilty about that death. He had been the one who urged Mr. Allen to come forward with the truth. As with so many other such deaths, there was little response from local authorities and none from the federal government. Louis Allen's killers, like so many others, were not found. And personal responsibility hung heavy on Bob Moses's shoulders.

This was the climate that awaited as we mounted our Mississippi Summer campaign in early 1964. Our target was that August's Democratic National Convention in Atlantic City, New Jersey. The plan, worked out almost entirely by Moses, was to organize an insurgent party in Mississippi to challenge the state's regular Democratic Party—its segregated, whites-only delegates—for Mississippi's seats at that national convention. The mock election had been a test run. This time, black Mississippi was going after real votes with real candidates.

And a real party. That April, the Mississippi Freedom Democratic Party (MFDP) was officially created, with plans to participate in that June's precinct, county and state conventions of Mississippi's regular Democratic Party. There was no doubt that the MFDP would be barred from those conventions. But by going through all the proper procedures, the MFDP would then have legal grounds to challenge the party's claim to its seats at the national convention.

This was the plan, to spend that summer educating and organizing black voters across the state, to bring them into the MFDP and to have them choose their own delegates to descend on Atlantic City in August.

To get out those votes and those voters, however, we would need help. At that time, in early 1964, SNCC had roughly 120 field workers in the entire South, all doing dangerous work, all on their own, working for subsistence wages and priding themselves on their independence. We were as decentralized as an organization could be, and we felt good about that. We were almost entirely about the work. That was all that mattered. Not politics. Not money. Just the work, the people.

The people—the indigenous, local black populations in those little hamlets and dusty back-road communities throughout the South—were always our focus. We didn't go into those communities to lead anyone. We went in to help people learn how to lead themselves. That's what Bob Moses had spent years trying to do in Mississippi—build an organization based on local leadership.

But now, for this campaign, we knew we needed help. Moses knew it. And that help, we decided, should come from *white* America—not in the form of money, not in the form of moral support, but in the flesh-and-blood form of their own sons and daughters.

That mock election the previous November had showed the way. Those eighty white students who came down that month returned to their campuses eager and excited to do more. Al Lowenstein was excited, too. He told Moses he could deliver ten times that many students for the summer of '64. And Moses liked that idea. He felt, as I did, that the movement should not be about black against white, that it should be black *and* white, united against something that was simply wrong. I always felt that it was important that white people be involved with us, that they bear witness not just from a distance but by standing beside us, suffering with us and, ultimately, succeeding with us. The question of "Whose struggle is this?," which had been brewing for some time among the inner circles of SNCC and which would soon reach a fever pitch, was not a hard one for me to answer. It's *our* struggle, *all* of ours. I have never seen segregation as a black problem. Nor is it a white problem. It is *society's* problem, and we must solve it as a society—together.

Bob Moses felt that way, as well as many others. But just as many were adamantly opposed to the idea of bringing down this army of white volunteers. Yes, they said, those eighty white kids who had come down the previous November had created a lot of press, a lot of attention. But almost all that attention was focused on *them*. Dozens of magazine and newspaper stories featured Suzy Jones from Stanford or Jimmy Smith from Yale, working alongside poor, nameless, faceless blacks, as if those black people *had* no names or faces. That caused a lot of resentment. There was a strong current of feeling running through the SNCC membership that "Hey, we've been down here all these months, all these *years,* working our butts off day in and day out, and these white kids come down and stay a week or two and they get all the headlines, they get all the credit."

At an even more basic level, there was the question of perpetuating the image of racial dependence, that somehow black people need whites to get anything done. One of SNCC's founding principles was to nurture independence and self-reliance among the South's black citizenry. Having these privileged white kids coming in to teach skills to impoverished blacks seemed to contradict that principle.

And try as they might, even the most well-meaning whites often fell into the trap of taking their enthusiasm too far, pushing aside and often overwhelming the black people they were supposedly trying to help. We'd already seen this occasionally in some of our SNCC offices. A skilled, college-educated white volunteer would arrive from someplace like Smith College, a well-meaning coed just brimming with earnestness, and she would get right down to business, typing like the wind, cranking out newsletters, speaking at meetings, just shining, giving us everything we could want in terms of office and organizational and public relations skills.

All this, however, was at the expense of the self-esteem of the young black woman working in that same office who had not had the privilege of going to a place like Smith, who had in fact had to drop out of school in ninth grade to help her family at home, who had never been beyond the boundaries of the tiny Mississippi or Alabama or Georgia or Arkansas town she was born in, but who was now giving everything she had to this cause. It might be all she could do to tap out maybe thirty words a minute, and here comes this white college woman doing seventy-five with one hand tied behind her back. That was bound to cause resentment, and it often did.

Even more troublesome was the tendency of some white SNCC members to thrust themselves into leadership roles, pushing black members aside in the process. Many whites who joined SNCC early on were intelligent, intellectually aggressive men and women, eager to share their ideas and help make decisions. Sometimes, usually without realizing it, they went too far. This was always a sensitive area, and even the most self-aware whites sometimes had trouble knowing where the boundaries were.

About 20 percent of SNCC's staff by early 1964 was white, and there had been growing grumbling about that. The increasing violence and ugliness and hatred we had been experiencing at the hands of white Southerners were taking an increasing toll on many of our black SNCC staffers—especially those from Mississippi. Some of that frustration became directed at white staff members. It would come out in meetings, this anger and rage about whites in general, and white people in the room naturally became targets.

Lines of racial separation were already being drawn in SNCC by this time, lines that would widen rapidly in the coming year. You could see more identification with heritage and race among our members, more dress and hairstyles in the tradition of Africa. Racial integration remained our focus, but there was a growing sense of separation as well, of racial identity, of "blackness."

This issue of racial identity prompted a response that spring from some of our white members. The previous November, at that SNCC conference in Washington, Bayard Rustin had challenged white staffers to go into their *own* communities, just as we blacks were going into ours, and gather support for the movement. With that idea in mind, one of our white members, a young man named Sam Shirah, who, coincidentally, was born in Troy, created a spin-off group from SNCC, a group aimed to gather white student support in the South.

Sam was a very quiet, very intense guy. The son of a Methodist minister, he wore jeans, but they were always neatly pressed and usually worn with a shirt and tie. He had been at the center of the Danville demonstrations, and there was no question about his commitment. He was dedicated, almost to a fault. You had the sense with Sam that he was battling the collective guilt of the entire white South.

The group he created that spring was called the Southern Students Organizing Committee (SSOC). The very fact that it was formed was much more significant than anything the group ever accomplished (the SSOC soon drifted away from SNCC and toward the ranks of more predominantly white radical groups like the SDS). That an all-white shadow of SNCC was created in 1964 was an indication of the intensity of the racial issues that were brewing within our own organization.

For all the opposition to white involvement, however, there was one argument for bringing an army of Northern college students into Mississippi that appealed to even the most adamantly anti-white SNCC members:

The danger.

Mississippi was deadly, and it was getting worse each day. Our people were essentially being slaughtered down there. If white America would not respond to the deaths of our people, the thinking went, maybe it would react to the deaths of its *own* children.

Our strategy was the same as always—to pursue political power through the vote and, if impeded, force a confrontation between federal and state authorities. Now, however, we would have white middle-class college students standing with us, being beaten with us, possibly dying with us.

This was essentially the principle of the Freedom Ride, on a larger scale and concentrated on one state. Naturally, as soon as word of this plan began to spread, there was a howl of outrage that we were going to use these white students as sacrificial lambs, leading them to slaughter for our own ends. There were also cries of alarm about the dangers these whites would bring to the local black people they would be working with. For all the attacks and assaults our SNCC staffers had faced, at least we blended into the local communities to an extent—we were *black*. Bringing these white kids in would be like bringing in a spotlight—instant attention, instant visibility, instant targets—inviting attacks that would hurt not just them but the innocent people around them.

I did not feel that we were leading anyone to slaughter. I knew something could, and probably would, happen that summer, that these white students were going to be attacked, arrested, maybe worse. I also knew that if we had the sons and daughters of the executives of some of the nation's largest corporations and best colleges and universities by our side, people would pay attention if somebody got arrested or beaten or, God forbid, killed. I didn't *want* that to happen. I don't think anyone else wanted that to happen. But we knew it was a distinct possibility.

The white students knew it as well—we would make sure of that. And the black people in those Mississippi communities would know it—that, too, was certain.

No one was going to be "used." No one involved would have any illusions about the severity of what we were facing. With that, I had no doubt that bringing these young white people into the poorest and most isolated of Mississippi's black communities was a good thing, a healthy thing. It was a way of saying, "You're not *alone.*" It was a powerful way of encouraging and connecting with whole communities that didn't know what it was like to be connected to the courthouse in the town down the road, much less to the nation. This was a powerful way of saying to the black people of Mississippi that there were people throughout this country who were *with* them.

It said as well that not all white people are alike, and this was a crucial message for men and women who had known nothing but hatred, oppression or at best condescending affection from the few white people with whom they had contact.

I believed in bringing down this army of whites, and so did Bob Moses. He strongly argued against any form of segregation within SNCC. He refused to be part of an all-black organization. Without white involvement, he said, "we'll have a racist movement."

Fannie Lou Hamer, speaking for the people of Mississippi themselves, was eager to see the return of the students she had watched work so hard the previous November. She was now vice chairman of the MFDP. Her whole world was changing. Mississippi, finally, seemed to be changing. Fannie Lou didn't care what color those kids were. They were a big part of what was happening, and she wanted to see them come back.

Stokely, one of five district directors in the state—we had divided Mississippi along the lines of its five congressional districts, with CORE taking one district and SNCC handling the other four—insisted that he would *not* work with whites, that he would man his share of the Summer Project with blacks only. But he wound up relenting. There was no way to avoid it.

By the end of April, the plans for Mississippi Summer were in place, and SNCC recruiters, including me, were already spreading out across the country, visiting campuses from one coast to the other, talking to auditoriums full of Young Democrats, SDS types, Christian Fellowship types, all types of eager, earnest, dying-to-get-involved college students. Al Lowenstein had a network of recruiters, too, including a young guy up in the New England area named Barney Frank—later to become a colleague of mine in Congress.

And the volunteers came pouring forth. From Stanford and Berkeley, from Swarthmore and Harvard, from Mount Holyoke and Bryn Mawr. America's best and brightest. White, well-to-do students with high ideals, eager and able to afford to give up a summer to pay their own way South—besides being required to cover their own transportation and living expenses, each volunteer had to pledge a $500 bond against possible arrest. SNCC could hardly afford to bankroll this operation.

More kids than we could possibly have imagined were willing to come up with both the money and the time. The optimism and idealism into which John Kennedy had tapped was still high. Many of the applicants mentioned JFK in the essays on their questionnaires. They saw this in the spirit of a domestic Peace Corps. They were high on the concept of community, on the cause of civil rights, and like most young people that age, they were romantic, ready for high drama, out to change the world.

We screened them carefully, looking hard at their motives. Some were unintentionally patronizing. Others were out to alleviate racial guilt. A lot admitted this was a lark, an adventure. A few thought they'd feel holy by stooping to help the poor suffering blacks. One applicant wrote, "It is a pilgrimage to a foreign country; traveling there, I can leave my guilt behind and atone for someone else's." Many simply wanted to "find themselves."

An important question we asked every applicant was how willing they were to work under the leadership of blacks, blacks who in many cases did not have a formal education. This was asked right out front because we had decided that each community project would be directed by black workers—both SNCC staffers and local community members.

Late that April, I introduced our coming campaign—its purpose and our methods—in a speech to the American Society of Newspaper Editors:

...Any person who in any way interferes with the right of a Negro to vote in Mississippi commits a crime against the Federal Government. He commits as much of a crime as does the gunman who walks into a bank and robs it. Title 18, Section 594 of the United States Code makes it a crime to interfere with the right to vote. That law has been on the books since 1948, but nobody has ever been prosecuted under it. I doubt if there is a policeman of any sort in Mississippi who has not broken that law several times since 1948, but not one of them has been arrested and prosecuted for it.

...The Federal Government—the present administration, at any rate—has not helped the movement with the appointment of federal judges. For example, Federal Judge Harold Cox of Mississippi, who was appointed in 1961, called Negro voting applicants "a bunch of niggers," and said they were acting like "a bunch of chimpanzees." And so I say, the struggle is just beginning.

This summer, however, we are again presenting the Federal Government with an opportunity to act. With the cooperation of other civil rights groups, under the banner of the Council of Federated Organizations, we plan to install some one thousand summer workers in Mississippi. They will teach in the Freedom Schools, staff Community Centers, register as many as 400,000 Negroes on mock polling lists, and will do the often dangerous work of voter registration.

There are four congressional candidates in Mississippi today who are Negroes. If they lose, they plan to challenge the right of white Mississippians to choose who shall represent the state in Congress. There will be challenges at the Democratic Convention in August, and we will see whether the country is ready and prepared to allow full representation in Congress.

The Federal Government's challenge will come earlier. It will come as it is coming now, and has been, in the Black Belt areas of the Deep South. Will the government, at last, take action on the intimidations, threats, shootings, and illegal arrests, searches and seizures that are a direct result of voter registration activities?

Registering to vote is an act of commitment to the American ideal. It is patriotic. The Federal Government must decide whether it wants to let southern Negroes register. It must make that choice this summer, or make us all witnesses to the lynching of democracy....

Even as I was delivering that speech, the state of Mississippi was girding in its own way for what it saw as nothing less than an invasion, another "war of Northern aggression," as the Civil War is still called in some parts of the South. Local newspapers ran articles and ads warning of impending hordes of "beatniks." One paper warned its readers to be on the lookout for anyone "wearing blue jeans, sweat shirts, tennis shoes, badly in need of a haircut, perhaps with a fuzzy beard and carrying a guitar case."

Mississippi governor Paul Johnson doubled the number of state highway patrolmen on duty that summer, and Jackson mayor Allen Thompson did the same, doubling the size of his city's police force by deputizing dozens of local men. He also bought two hundred new shotguns, stockpiled supplies of tear gas and masks, set up troop carriers and searchlight trucks, and even bought a *tank,* on which he mounted a submachine gun. "This is it," Thompson told a newspaper reporter. "They are not bluffing, and we are not bluffing. We are going to be ready for them.... They won't have a chance."

Crosses were burned one night in sixty-four of the state's eighty-two counties—a warning from the Klan.

Our response to this rising tide of alarm in Mississippi was to move our SNCC headquarters there. Bob Moses had been telling us to do this for some time. He acknowledged the importance of our work elsewhere—in Georgia and Arkansas and Alabama—but there was no question Mississippi had become the priority, the focus. We needed to demonstrate that commitment, he said, and it made sense logistically as well.

But it wasn't easy. There was the issue of safety—moving our headquarters from Atlanta to Mississippi was like moving the U.S. Army headquarters in Vietnam from the relative security of Saigon out into the jungle. And there were the logistical challenges of setting up our communication network, installing a WATS line for national and statewide coordination, moving our press operation with everything from its darkroom to its mimeograph equipment, transferring our record-keeping facilities, organizing a transportation network, ensuring access to an airport—the difference between being in Atlanta and being in a little town like Greenwood was enormous. But we did it. By June, we had SNCC command centers set up both in Greenwood and Jackson, ready to coordinate the students who were scheduled to begin arriving late that month.

The issue of security became a sticky one. We were very vulnerable in that tiny two-story house in Greenwood and in that small building just off Lynch Street—the irony of *that* name, which came from a Civil War general, was lost on no one—in Jackson. It would be relatively easy to wipe out our entire organization and its records in one blow.

Early on, there had been guns in the Greenwood office. When Stokely arrived there, he was told to have those guns removed, and they were. But when our headquarters were moved there that June, Forman had a nightly armed guard placed around the office.

The issue of self-defense had continued growing within our organization. Forman was already committed to the idea of a coming armed struggle in America, and that idea was creeping into SNCC day by day. We were still an organization committed to nonviolence, but the edges of that commitment were crumbling.

There was good reason to have guards in Greenwood. Bob Moses, along with a SNCC worker named Jimmy Travis and a Voter Education Project consultant named Randolph Blackwell, had faced death firsthand in early 1963 when, during a nighttime meeting there, they saw several white men parked in a car outside. They broke up the meeting, and the three began driving north toward Sunflower County. When they saw the car full of white men following them, they sped up. So did the whites, who caught up and began shooting. Travis was wounded in the shoulder and neck, with one of the bullets penetrating his spinal cord.

Demonstrations in Greenwood following that attack elicited a quote from one local white resident to a reporter from *The New York Times*—I believe it was Claude Sitton. "We killed two-month-old Indian babies to take this country," said the local man, "and now they want us to give it away to the niggers."

This was what we were up against in Greenwood. I personally never supported the idea of armed guards. The people we were working with, share-croppers and their families, didn't have any armed guards out there on their homes and farms. But Forman insisted on this, and so the guards were put in place.

Now all that awaited were the students, who began arriving in Oxford, Ohio, on Saturday, June 13, for a week of training on the campus of the Western College for Women. We were able to rent the college's dorms and facilities thanks to funding from the National Council of Churches.

It was a very bucolic setting. Serene, tree-shaded, sleepy. Quite different from the places these students would be heading when their training was done.

There were three hundred that first weekend, with the remainder scheduled to arrive a week later. Three out of four were white. Nearly half were women. Their average age was twenty-one. The highest number came from New York State.

For publicity purposes, the volunteers provided Julian with the names and addresses of their local newspapers back home; each volunteer also provided four copies of a photograph of him- or herself for our press office to have on hand.

With more than one hundred of our staff people on-site, SNCC was at the center of everything. CORE had a significant presence with forty members, but the other members of COFO—the NAACP, the SCLC—were virtually absent. Roy Wilkins made no secret of his disapproval of this entire venture. "We're sitting this one out," he explained to one reporter.

There was some uneasiness on the part of our people about the CORE leadership—not about the CORE staffers themselves, who were much like us, but about Jim Farmer and some of his people, who had developed a reputation for coming in on demonstrations or actions with us, then trying to take more than their share of the credit by doing such things as issuing press releases on CORE letterhead about operations actually staged by SNCC. Relations between both groups had been sticky ever since the Freedom Rides.

But in Oxford we were in harmony. It was SNCC and CORE, along with several hundred ministers from a broad range of faiths, about a hundred medical personnel and 150 volunteer lawyers, primarily from the National Lawyers Guild—we knew we would have many arrests and trials ahead of us, and we would need all the legal representation we could get.

As for the volunteer training itself, it was intense. There were briefings from people like Moses and Rustin and Forman, and a session with R. Jess Brown, a Jackson lawyer—one of two black attorneys in Mississippi at the time—who five years earlier had defended Mack Charles Parker, a young black man accused of rape in the tiny town of Poplarville, Mississippi. Before that trial even began, Parker was dragged from jail by a lynch mob, shot to death and dumped in a river. No one was ever indicted for his murder. That, explained Brown, was what outsiders were up against in Mississippi.

"You're going to be classified into two groups in Mississippi," Brown told the students. "Niggers and nigger-lovers. And they're tougher on nigger-lovers."

John Doar, Bobby Kennedy's deputy chief of the Civil Rights Division at the Justice Department, who flew into Oxford to help out that week, echoed Brown. He told the students they might imagine they knew what they were in for, but, he assured them grimly, they had no idea.

Forman was blunt. "I may be killed," he told the volunteers. "You may be killed."

And Moses spoke about our mission.

"Don't come to Mississippi this summer to save the Mississippi Negro," he warned the students. "Only come if you understand, really understand, that his freedom and yours are one.... Maybe we're not going to get many people registered this summer. Maybe, even, we're not going to get very many people into Freedom Schools. Maybe all we're going to do is *live* through this summer. In Mississippi, that will be so much!"

Doar, when asked what the federal government would provide in the way of protection, said, ominously, "Nothing.

"There is no federal police force," he explained. "The responsibility for protection is that of the local police."

This was not reassuring. We prepared the students as best we could for the ugliness and danger they were certain to face. We put them through the same role-playing workshops we had used for years with our own SNCC staffers and volunteers. Many of these kids heard language and faced attitudes that week that they had never been exposed to. For some, long-held preconceptions and ingrained, unconscious attitudes were exposed and shattered.

Some of our SNCC guys, those who had been through the wars, took great pleasure in intimidating these kids. They strutted and swaggered and challenged these students on everything from race to politics to sexual attitudes. They explained the political structure of Mississippi, the creation of the MFDP and the ultimate fruits of our labor that awaited us in August in Atlantic City.

They emphasized again and again, as Moses had said, that we weren't going to change Mississippi in one summer or in one year, that this was the beginning of a long, protracted struggle, that there would be frustration and setbacks and often a feeling of more loss than success.

With all that, as the week came to a close and the time to leave for Mississippi drew near, there was a rising sense of exhilaration among these students, a feeling we in the movement called freedom high—almost an altered state of jubilation, a sense of being swept beyond yourself by the righteous zeal of the moment, whether it was a march or a sit-in or an arrest. There was a lot of singing, a lot of storytelling and soul sharing, a feeling of intimacy much like warriors might feel on the eve of a crusade.

But there was also a palpable sense of fear, an understanding that this was very, very real.

I felt that fear, along with many other things. I didn't know how our black and white workers would get along once they arrived and began their work. I didn't know how they would be received, black and white alike, by the local men and women in these towns and rural areas. I felt a huge personal responsibility for these young men and women, many of whom I had influenced myself during the countless campus recruiting visits I had made that spring.

We were surrounded by reporters that entire week. Everyone sensed history in the making here, though no one could say for certain what that history would be. A *New York Times* story, dated June 21, datelined Oxford, Ohio, described the departure of our first wave of Mississippi Summer volunteers:

> The first phase of one of the most ambitious civil rights projects yet conceived has ended here in an atmosphere of mixed hope and doubt, fear and determination....
>
> [The volunteers] will face white hostility in all the smallest cities, dusty county seats, farms and plantations of the countryside. They will attempt in two months to bring a lasting change in the pattern of segregation under which Negroes have lived for a century. No one can predict the outcome.

The very day those words were published, the outcome began to take shape—with the murders of three of those young people.

Part V

"*UHURU*"

13 / "FEEL ANGRY WITH ME"

I knew Mickey Schwerner. Most of us in SNCC knew him. He was a good man, a fun person and an extremely hard worker. He was from Brooklyn—"the Jew boy with the beard," as he was called by some of the Klansmen down around Neshoba County in central Mississippi, where he and his wife, Rita, were working as CORE field secretaries that summer of 1964.

Mickey was very visible. He was only twenty-four, but he was already a veteran of the movement, well known by local blacks and whites around that part of the state. And the whites did not like what he was doing, stirring up the blacks, teaching them how to vote. By that June there was apparently talk among some of the Klan down in that section of the state about dealing with this guy they called Goatee.

Andy Goodman, on the other hand, was a newcomer. Brand new. I had met him during a training session that week in Oxford. He was a twenty-year-old anthropology major from Queens College who had come south to spend his summer helping us out in Mississippi. I'll never know for sure, but Andy could well have been one of the students I spoke to during my recruiting swing through the Northeast that spring. I know I visited New York several times.

James Chaney I did not know. Like Schwerner, he was a CORE field worker. He was a native Mississippian, a plasterer by trade. And he was black, which might have been what caught the eye of the Neshoba County deputy sheriff who pulled the three of them over for speeding that Sunday afternoon—Schwerner, Goodman and Chaney.

Two white guys and a black, in a blue Ford station wagon. College-looking kids. Just the sort of "outside agitators" the entire state was on the lookout for. That could have been the reason the deputy arrested them. Or maybe he recognized Schwerner and saw this as a chance to get "Goatee."

Whatever the reason, Schwerner, Goodman and Chaney were taken to jail in the little Delta town of Philadelphia late that afternoon, June 21, 1964.

They were released that evening.

And no one ever saw them alive again.

The day they disappeared, I was at the funeral of an uncle, one of my mother's brothers. It seemed I was always at a funeral in those days, both my parents' families were so large. Someone always seemed to be passing away.

I got a call from Atlanta late that night telling me three of our people were missing. I couldn't believe it. Not already. We hadn't even gotten started yet. Half our eight hundred volunteers were still up in Oxford, getting set to board buses south for their assignments, and already we had three missing.

By the time I arrived in Atlanta the next morning, we had details. Schwerner, Goodman and Chaney had driven the previous afternoon from the CORE office in Meridian to a tiny Delta town called Longdale, to check into the burning of a church that had been functioning there as one of our Freedom Schools. They'd stayed in Longdale a couple of hours, talked with some of the local black residents, then left in mid-afternoon, headed back to Meridian, where they were due at four.

We were extremely strict about due times and check-ins, about keeping track of our people. By early that evening, when the three men had not yet shown up, our SNCC staff down in Greenwood knew something was wrong and set about calling every jail in Neshoba and its surrounding counties. Call after call, the answer was the same. No one had seen these men, not that night.

By the next day, Neshoba's deputy county sheriff, a man named Cecil Ray Price, acknowledged that he had arrested three men that Sunday afternoon, and that he had taken them to the Philadelphia city jail, where they were booked for speeding, fined $20 and, according to him, released late that evening and told to "leave the county."

Price's boss, County Sheriff Lawrence Rainey, dismissed the disappearance as a hoax. "If they're missing," he said, "they just hid somewhere, trying to get a lot of publicity out of it, I figure."

On Tuesday came word that a blue Ford station wagon—burnt, charred, gutted—had been pulled from the shallow, swampy, snake-infested waters of Bogue Chitto Creek, just outside Philadelphia. No bodies were found. Just the car.

I caught the first flight that afternoon from Atlanta to Montgomery, then boarded a small plane that took me to Meridian's Key Field, where I arrived late that day.

Downtown Meridian was swarming with police and state troopers. I checked into the black hotel in town, one of the very few black hotels in the state. Jim Farmer, who had flown down from New York, had a room next to mine. Mickey Schwerner's wife, Rita, was there, too, accompanied by one of our best SNCC people, Bob Zellner. She was very worried, naturally, but she was amazingly composed, very focused, which didn't surprise me. Anyone who had done this kind of work for any amount of time was well aware of the dangers to be faced every minute of every day. When Mickey Schwerner turned up missing that weekend, it was something Rita had probably imagined a thousand times. She had probably imagined it happening to herself as well. So in a sense, she was ready.

There was an armed guard outside our rooms that night, a black security man Farmer had brought down with him from New York. Wherever we went during the next several days, the guard was there, as were many, many other people. There was not an empty room in that motel that night, and many of the guests who had checked in were from out of state—movement people like myself who had come to respond to this crisis.

The next morning thirty-five of us, including Farmer, Dick Gregory, who had flown down from Chicago, a CORE secretary named George Raymond and I, left Meridian in a caravan of five cars, bound for Philadelphia. I remember looking out the window as we drove through that flat Mississippi countryside, having no idea of what exactly we were going to do when we arrived. I was amazed when we reached the city limits of Philadelphia and none other than Sheriff Rainey himself—a hefty man with a big wad of tobacco stuffed in his cheek—stepped out from a squadron of police cruisers to halt us and tell us we were going to be escorted into town by his deputy sheriffs, several of whom carried shotguns in their hands.

The town square looked like an armed camp. Dozens of men in short sleeves roamed around with guns and rifles in their hands—local men who had been deputized by Rainey. There were lots of reporters as well, including Claude Sitton and Karl Fleming—familiar faces to me by now. Stationed on the rooftops of buildings all around the square were state policemen with rifles. I wasn't sure who they were there to keep an eye on—us or all those armed white men around us.

Rainey stepped out of his car and announced that he would meet with no more than four of us. The rest would have to wait outside. Farmer, Gregory, Raymond and I followed him and his deputy, Price, into the old courthouse. We rode up an elevator in total silence and were then led into a hot, stuffy office with a slow-turning ceiling fan.

Three other men were there—two local attorneys and an officer with the state police. The atmosphere was tense. Rainey and Price did nothing to hide their contempt for us. They sneered. They smirked.

We told them we wanted to visit the site where the church had been burned, and we wanted to see the spot where the car was found.

One of the attorneys said we'd need a search warrant. Both sites, he said, were private property.

I said we had a right to see the car. The attorney answered that that was impossible because we might "destroy evidence."

Evidence! So, we said, that meant there *had* been a crime.

The attorney quickly backpedaled.

"*If* there has been a crime...," he said, carefully rephrasing his words.

"You know," he continued, "those boys may have decided to go up north or someplace and have a short vacation. They'll probably be coming back shortly."

By the time we left that room, I knew those men were lying. I had no doubt that Price and his boss, Rainey, knew who did this. I didn't imagine that they might have actually participated in it—that was inconceivable—but I had little doubt that they knew who killed our people.

And I had no doubt our people had been killed. It had been four days since anyone had seen them. None of us hoped anymore that they might be alive. What we were after now was the truth. And justice. For them. For their families. For all of us.

We actually went out that evening, a small group of us, all SNCC people, and searched for those bodies. Ivanhoe Donaldson, Charlie Cobb, Bob Moses's wife, Dona—a half dozen or so of us went out in the direction where the car had been found and walked around in the hot, sticky dusk, bugs buzzing around, out in the middle of nowhere, poking at scrub grass and bushes and dirt. It was really pretty useless, not to mention dangerous. We didn't expect to find anything, but it was better than sitting back in our motel rooms or staging yet another press conference. It made us feel that we were doing *something*.

We were so frustrated. We felt so helpless. We issued a formal appeal to President Johnson and to Attorney General Kennedy to do something. Johnson responded by ordering his defense secretary, McNamara, to send two hundred active duty Navy sailors to search the swamps and fields in the area. Kennedy had his FBI director, Hoover, send 150 agents into the state—ten times the number there at the time.

Meanwhile, up in Oxford, our SNCC staff and the students who had just completed their training, as well as the second wave of volunteers who had just arrived, were in shock. Bob Moses, who had gotten the news the morning after our three people disappeared, spent that entire Monday sitting on the steps outside the cafeteria on the campus in Oxford, silent, staring into space, not saying a word to anyone.

If there had been any doubt before, now we all saw clearly what John Doar had warned us about, that the only "protection" we would find in Mississippi would come from local law enforcement agencies—men like Lawrence Rainey and Cecil Price.

We also saw that we had been absolutely correct in assuming that America would respond in a different way once white people began dying alongside blacks. The disappearance of three civil rights workers in Mississippi was the lead story on television and in newspapers across the country that entire week. President Johnson met personally with the parents of Schwerner and Goodman, who flew from New York to Washington two days after their sons disappeared. The Chaneys, for reasons of money and the fact that they had no sympathetic congressmen from their home state to greet them in Washington and usher them to the White House, as the Schwerners and Goodmans did, were not there.

I spoke to those issues in a press conference that week. "It is a shame," I said, "that national concern is aroused only after two white boys are missing." The blood of those three missing men and any others who might follow them, I warned, would be on the federal government's hands if this case wasn't solved and any more violence prevented.

Meanwhile, the search went on. Rivers were dragged, woods were scoured, dirt was turned... and bodies were found. Old bodies, unidentified corpses, the decomposed remains of black people long given up as "missing." One torso, that of a young teenaged boy, was clad in an old CORE T-shirt.

It was ugly, sickening, horrifying. Here was proof—as if it was needed—that those woods and rivers in the heart of this state had long been a killing field, a dumping ground for the Klan. How many other bodies of black men, women and children lay on the bottoms of those rivers and beneath those bushes and trees?

If it was possible to be even more careful than we planned, the disappearance of our three colleagues made it so. No one went anywhere without saying exactly where he was going and exactly when he would be back.

No one went anywhere alone.

We installed two-way radios in all our staff cars, and because it was unsafe to travel in daylight (white and black passengers sharing the same vehicle were an easy target), we made most of our trips at night, driving dirt back roads from town to town in the darkness, always wary of headlights in the rearview mirror. We learned to drive without headlights ourselves. And we learned to drive fast, to get where we were going quickly, and if need be, to outrun the police or anyone else who might chase us. I have never seen anyone drive the way the guys in SNCC drove those cars. Whether someone was behind them or not, they always drove with the gas pedal to the floor. That was some of the greatest fear I felt that summer, not being chased by any Klansmen, but simply rocketing through those Mississippi woods in the middle of the night, doing eighty and ninety miles an hour down those dark dirt roads.

SNCC owned an armada of vehicles—sixty cars and a couple of pickup trucks, most of them donated by benefactors up north, almost all of them used. One businessman in Boston was particularly helpful in rounding up vehicles for us. We called our collection of automobiles the "Sojourner Fleet," in honor of Sojourner Truth, the nineteenth-century black female abolitionist. We kept a constantly updated list of each vehicle, of the driver to whom it was assigned and that driver's age. I still have a copy of the list from that summer of '64, a sampling of vintage cars—and vintage drivers:

'58 Chevrolet station wagon...Ruby Doris Robinson...23
'63 Valiant...Amzie Moore...52
'61 Nash Rambler...Bill Hansen...25
'64 Plymouth Savoy...Stokely Carmichael...23
'55 Chrysler Imperial...Cleveland Sellers...19

These, and dozens more like them, were our field generals, guiding and directing the hundreds of student volunteers who spread out across the state late that June and settled in for a long, deadly summer of getting out the vote.

It was hot, tiring, tedious work. Walking door-to-door, canvassing and convincing people to come to class at one of our Freedom Schools, to come to the courthouse to register to vote. Standing in unmoving lines outside those antebellum courthouses for hours on end, facing heat and hunger and profane harassment and worse.

Our Freedom Schools—nearly fifty of them, all told—were often hardly more than shacks, with hand-painted signs out front and classes held as often on the grass or dirt outside as in, where the heat was stifling and the small rooms too dark to see.

We reached people wherever we could, staging meetings and workshops in beauty parlors or barbershops, in storefront churches, even out in the fields where the people were plowing and chopping.

While our male volunteers did most of the door-to-door canvassing—this was considered the most dangerous of our duties—our schools were staffed and directed mainly by women. Besides civics and citizenship and the details of voting rights, our staff taught reading, African-American history (a subject children in Mississippi, black or white, knew nothing about), foreign languages, arithmetic, typing—skills and subjects not typically available to black students in Mississippi's public schools. It was truly like the Peace Corps in many respects, and it provided a prototype for future nationally administered education programs such as Head Start.

Besides organizing and educating, we provided volunteer doctors that summer, who set up a network of Freedom Clinics, offering health care to many children and grownups who had never seen a doctor before.

All of us—organizers, teachers, doctors and SNCC staffers—were extremely sensitive about how we approached the local people. The whites among us were made acutely aware that many of the black people into whose homes and communities they were coming had never been close to a white person in their lives. Some hands had never touched a white person's, and it was important to remember that when reaching out to shake those hands. Little things, such as being aware of body language, taking a seat on a stoop or a step or a chair rather than looming over someone you were talking to—were crucial.

As for our black volunteers and staffers, we had to be as sensitive and careful about our behavior and appearance as the whites. We knew we could easily be resented by the local blacks as outsiders, college-educated kids from a different class, really from a different *country* from the one in which they lived. We had to be extremely careful about any hint of condescension or superiority, from the way we acted to the way we dressed. Overalls became the standard outfit for our black volunteers. Blue denim bib overalls with a white T-shirt underneath became the symbol of SNCC. And it was practical. It fit our lifestyle of sleeping on sofas and floors and walking miles and miles of dusty back roads. It also identified us with the people we were working with—farmers and poor people. The more political members among us liked the fact that overalls symbolized the proletariat point of view, the worker, the masses. Some SNCC people felt uncomfortable in overalls but most of us had grown up poor ourselves, so wearing dungarees was nothing new. I had left my overalls behind when I moved from rural Alabama to go off to college, but that summer in Mississippi I put them back on.

I was all over the Delta that summer, spending a few days here, a few days there. Indianola. Ruleville. Belzoni. Greenwood. Clarksdale. I always stayed in local families' homes. We all did. Freedom Houses, we called them.

In Greenwood, the home I usually stayed in belonged to a family named Greene. Stokely stayed there, too—we spent more than one night sleeping in the same bed. Harry Belafonte stayed with the Greenes when he came to Greenwood. So did Sidney Poitier.

There was nothing fancy about the Greene home. It was solid middle-class. Both Mr. and Mrs. Greene had been schoolteachers, and both were completely committed to the movement. White people in Greenwood knew about the house, of course. There were several bullet holes in the front door—a reminder to us each time we came and went of what we were there for.

Blacks and whites alike stayed with the Greenes, as they did in most of the Freedom Houses throughout the state. We cooked together, ate together—often literally out of the same pot—and stayed up late talking together, all in a communal atmosphere in which a close sense of camaraderie developed. Several of the many formal communes that sprouted around America later in the decade were founded by men and women who had spent that summer of '64 working with us in Mississippi. These white kids brought a lot of the emerging counterculture south with them. Most were strait-laced, still in the clean-cut '50s, but there were some who arrived with woolly hair and bare feet and without bras. A bit of that had to be straightened out—what we were doing that summer was not about being overt or making your own personal statement, it was about the needs of the black people of Mississippi, period. So shoes were put on, as well as brassieres.

Still, there was no denying the influence of the times. You could feel it and hear it in everything from the ideas in those late-night discussions—arguments about Marx and Hegel, about Fidel Castro and Che Guevara, about revolutionary developments in African nations such as Malawi and Zambia, both of which achieved their independence that year—to the music we listened to, the songs that became the soundtrack of that summer.

The traditional freedom songs remained central to our lives, as they were from the beginning. They still had the power to lift our spirits and draw us together, those old slow-paced spirituals and hymns like "Come By Here, Lord," as well as updated, upbeat jubilee-type songs about Jim Crow and Uncle Tom. Bevel and Bernard were especially gifted at taking someone else's song and turning it into a movement tune. Little Willie John's rocker "(You Better) Leave My Kitten Alone," for example—they took that and turned it into "(You Better) Leave Segregation Alone." Or "I'm Movin' On," by Ray Charles—they turned *that* into a protest song:

> *Old Jim Crow's moving on down the track,*
> *He's got his bags and he won't be back.*

But beyond the freedom songs, we had the music on the radio to see us through that summer. All those hours driving all those miles in all those cars went a little bit easier with the rhythms coming out of those dashboard radios. Popular music always had its place right beside the protest songs we sang ourselves. Back when I was still in Nashville, I would listen late at night to a baritone-voiced deejay on WLAC named John Richbourg—"John R.," he called himself on the air. I remember returning from the Freedom Ride that summer of 1961 and lying in my bed listening to "Gee Whiz" by Carla Thomas. And to a new group called the Mar-Keys, playing a blues-riff instrumental called "Last Night." And to the Impressions, with a young lead singer named Curtis Mayfield, doing "Gypsy Woman." And, of course, there was Solomon Burke, a former boy preacher just like me, now a bluesman singing deeply and strongly with his big hit that year, "Just Out of Reach."

By the summer of 1964, something called soul music had arrived, and a record label out of Detroit called Motown was taking over the airwaves. Martha and the Vandellas' "Dancing in the Street" was all over the radio that summer, as were Mary Wells's "My Guy" and a song called "Where Did Our Love Go?" by a woman named Diana Ross. Within a year the soul sound would literally be a part of the movement, with politically overtoned songs like Sam Cooke's "A Change Is Gonna Come" and the Impressions' "People Get Ready" speaking directly to the work we were doing in the Deep South.

Some of the deepest, most delicious moments of my life were getting out of jail in a place like Americus, or Hattiesburg, or Selma—especially Selma—and finding my way to the nearest Freedom House, taking a good long shower, putting on a pair of jeans and a fresh shirt and going to some little Dew Drop Inn, some little side-of-the-road juke joint where I'd order a hamburger or cheese sandwich and a cold soda and walk over to that jukebox and stand there with a quarter in my hand, and look over every song on that box because this choice had to be *just* right... and then I would finally drop that quarter in and punch up Marvin Gaye or Curtis Mayfield or Aretha, and I would sit down with my sandwich, and I would let that music wash over me, just wash right *through* me. I don't know if I've ever felt anything so sweet.

For all the time I spent in Mississippi that summer, I still made it back to Atlanta now and then. My apartment there was basically just another Freedom House, a place I stayed in when I was passing through. It was sparely furnished, with just the basics: a bed; a couple of extra mattresses for whoever might be passing through, and there was *always* somebody passing through who needed a place to stay and would grab one of the mattresses or put a sleeping bag down on the floor; no sofa, just a couple of chairs from Goodwill or the Salvation Army; bookshelves fashioned with planks and cinder blocks; a refrigerator with nothing inside but some cold cuts and condiments—there was no time and no real desire for cooking.

It was a man's place, a typical bachelor's apartment, no doubt about it. Early on, Danny Lyon, SNCC's chief photographer, moved in as my roommate, who was from Forest Hills, New York. Slim, with dark curly hair, he was a wonderful human being, very gentle, very quiet, very intense about his work. He loved taking pictures. He *lived* to do that. Our bathroom was his darkroom, which meant every time you went to take a shower or use the toilet, you had to navigate through strips of film and prints hanging up to dry.

The neighbors didn't know what to make of us, these white and black guys coming and going from this apartment in one of the blackest sections of Atlanta. There were other races going in and out of my place, too. Tom (Tamio) Wakayama, a Japanese-Canadian photographer, lived with us for a while. I was always on Tom about his hair. He had this very long, jet black hair. Beautiful hair. But every time he'd take a shower, he'd leave behind this incredible tangle of hair in the tub. Tom was a good guy, but that *hair*...

A lot of people came and went in that apartment—friends, SNCC staffers, people involved in the movement who were on their way to or from Alabama or Mississippi. One person who did *not* spend much time there was Julian. We were close, close friends—the best of friends, really. But Julian, unlike me, was married. And his wife, Alice, kept a pretty tight leash on him, and probably for good reasons. Julian was a very handsome young man, striking, very boyish-looking, very attractive to women, and women did not mind showing him how attracted they were. There were always young women interested in Julian, and Alice, understandably, was not comfortable with that. So there was not much chance that she would be sending Julian off to my place to spend time hanging out with us bachelors.

In fact, there were very few women around that apartment. From time to time we would have a party—not often enough, as I look back on it. In retrospect, I wish we'd been able to lighten up a little bit more. The stress and tension of those years took a heavy emotional toll on a lot of people. Maybe if we'd been able to relax a little more here and there, we might not have wound up with so many casualties.

In any event, I do remember one party in particular where Shirley MacLaine showed up. A lot of Hollywood types and celebrities became involved in liberal causes in the '60s, and many of them were naturally attracted to the movement. Shirley was one. She eventually became a Bobby Kennedy–pledged delegate from California at the 1968 Democratic convention in Chicago, and in 1972 she would campaign hard and visibly for George McGovern. But in 1964 she was still relatively young—thirty—and her visibility was confined to being recognized as one of Hollywood's hottest actresses and dancers. She had received her third Academy Award nomination for *Irma la Douce* a year earlier, and she came down that summer to visit SNCC headquarters in Atlanta.

She described that visit in a book she wrote, an autobiography that came out in 1970. She recalled one of our staffers, someone she called Ralph in the book—I don't know who he actually was—asking her if she wanted to go to what he teasingly called a *"nigger* party." Shirley's account of that evening is just the way I remember it—what I *can* remember of it:

> We drove through the heart of Atlanta and into the ghetto to a small house. I could hear laughter. I touched Ralph's arm and he said, "It's cool," and I relaxed again as the back door opened and a spray of beer spewed out at us and somebody handed me a can of Schlitz.

A record player was going with what would soon be called soul music, and everybody in the living room (furnished with one chair and four orange crates) was gyrating. Their bodies jerked and undulated in movements unlike any dancing I had ever seen. The dancing the black kids was doing was free-form. At times it was an ugly movement—on-purpose ugly, I think—as though they were in love with ugliness—as though they were dancing the distortions they felt. Their heads jerked up and down, seeming to say, "Uh, huh, enough, enough—tell it, tell it—tell it like it is"—and then they'd stop moving altogether on some accented beat and wait—wait until some spirit moved them again and they had something else to say. The kids were watching each other; every gesture meant something and if you couldn't be sure of what their hips and elbows and strutting shoulders were saying you could look in their eyes and find it. It was soul dancing laid out bare, and every movement was full of protest. Some of the kids had bloodshot eyes from too much beer (there was only beer, no hard booze). There was a poker game going on at a long, wooden picnic table.

Ralph pulled a folding chair over to the table and took over the poker game as we sat down and he said, "This here's Shirley." If anyone recognized me they didn't acknowledge it. Ralph didn't introduce anyone to me. He knew I was too off balance to remember their names, so he didn't bother.

The dancing kids kept dancing. They were grooving to the records. . . .

Someone changed the record to a slower soul-grinding beat and I couldn't contain myself any longer. I didn't know what it would mean if I got up on my own and danced with whoever wanted to but I did it anyway. I could never resist dancing anywhere, any time.

The poker game continued as I moved away into the bare, hollow-sounding living room. One of the guys on the floor caught my eye and began to sway and bump his hips toward me. He had a rotund body with a great roly-poly fanny. He was John Lewis, the secretary of SNCC, and one day he would be castigated by his own people for not being militant enough. There was nothing militant about John; he was all love and soul and just to be with him made you smile inside, even though you knew he'd never make it because he was too sweet.

His dancing was laced with mischief. We grooved to the center of the floor and in two minutes were putting on a show. I had never met him before but felt I had known him all my life. Up and down, around and in and out we jerked and undulated and tripped out. I could see the others grin and nod as they watched us, lost in the movement. After an hour I was dripping with sweat and John was passed out cold on the one chair.

That's how big a drinker I was. Two beers, and I was fast asleep.

People often talk and speculate about all the wild, rampant sex that was supposedly going on within the movement back then. They joke about us *really* putting our bodies on the line. But the fact is that there was not nearly as much of that kind of activity as those stories would indicate. There was no time, no energy, no place for much of that. We were in a war. We were in dangerous, draining, dire settings and circumstances. In the movies, directors love to toss sex and action and violence together. That's what audiences like. But in real life, those things don't usually mix. When you're facing the razor-edge intensity of true life-and-death situations, the last thing on your mind is having sex with someone.

Of course there was *some*. I had several experiences myself. There were so many changes going on around us, changes that would spread and take root throughout society as the '60s developed. One of those changes was a more open, freer attitude toward sex. This was natural. It was part of the climate of the times, the stretching of limits, the opening of doors. If you felt you were in the right situation, with the right person, and there was a strong connection between you and the circumstances allowed, then you might act on those feelings.

When Shirley MacLaine talked about me being too sweet to "make it," she meant in a sexual way, as in "making a move." And she was right. I wasn't one to make a move. I was not a predator. But I did respond occasionally. It happened a few times when I was spending time in one place, sharing a lot of strong feelings with someone about life, about our problems and concerns as a people and as individuals. When you put your heart out like that with someone, and she puts hers out with you, those hearts are bound to touch sometimes. I didn't go out to make conquests. I didn't go out sowing my seeds throughout the South. I wasn't trying to replenish the earth. But I was certainly not a virgin when I married my wife.

I was married to the movement, as was almost everyone around me. There were things that went on, of course, most of which I didn't know about in detail. I didn't *need* to know. I'd hear about this person sleeping with that one and so on, and there were some serious relationships that developed as well. Diane and Bevel were, of course, a prime example. There were interracial couples, too, from the beginning. This was natural. We were a group of young men and women who were not hung up on racial differences, young men and women with natural attractions to one another, regardless of race. You saw it in Nashville early on, with couples like Paul LaPrad, who was white, and a young black woman named Maxine Walker. Paul and Maxine trained together back in '59 and '60, sat in at lunch counters together, were arrested together. And they fell in love.

Jim Forman wound up in an interracial relationship. He split up from his wife during those early years and began dating a young white woman named Constancia "Dinky" Romilly. They eventually married and had two wonderful kids.

Which did not make everyone in SNCC overjoyed. There was a current of resentment among some of our members about situations like that. It was that issue of separatism versus integration again, an issue that would always be a wedge for us. There were men and women in our organization who considered it a betrayal to our race, a denial of our identity, to become romantically involved with a white person. I think the people who had problems with that were louder than their numbers, but it *was* a problem for some. And like so many of our problems at that time, it would grow rapidly in the coming year.

Something I was not aware of in 1964 was the use of drugs. I didn't even know what marijuana smelled like, not back then. When I was in college, no one smoked dope, not in the circles I ran in. And even when I moved into SNCC, I didn't see it. People were smoking it, I'm sure, but never in my presence. That was partly out of respect for me and my values, and partly because this was still relatively early in the '60s and no one was smoking marijuana as openly then as they would be a few years later.

I know what marijuana smells like now, of course. There are sections of Washington, D.C., today where you can get a contact high just walking down the street. Even around the neighborhood where I live, a few blocks from the Capitol, I can smell marijuana now and then as I walk back and forth to my congressional office.

But back in 1964, if I did smell anything strange, I thought it was something like the homegrown tobacco we used to have around when I was growing up in Carter's Quarters, the stuff we kids used to call rabbit weed. I tried *that* once in high school, and once was enough.

That was a long summer, that summer of '64. Intense. Confusing. Painful. So hopeful in the beginning, and so heartbreaking by the end.

Less than two weeks after Schwerner, Goodman and Chaney disappeared, Congress passed the civil rights bill and President Johnson signed it into law, following through on the vow he had made in the wake of Kennedy's assassination. On paper, at least, it was indeed a strong piece of legislation, as Johnson had promised. It banned discrimination in places of public accommodation, it forbade discrimination in hiring practices by businesses with more than a hundred employees, it ended segregation in public schools, libraries and playgrounds.

Playgrounds. I was at a playground—a segregated playground in Greenwood—the day that bill was signed. I had been invited up to Washington for the ceremony, but I decided to stay in Mississippi instead. This was where I wanted to be, not on some stage someplace.

I was working with a group of young children and several black and white student volunteers when the news came over the radio. We felt glad, but not joyous. There was no sense of celebration. We were still in the middle of a war down there, a campaign that was just beginning. The news from Washington felt as if it were coming from another country, from a very distant place.

I was heartened by this new law, but I was worried, too, worried that with the signing of this act, a lot of people might think our work was done. And to a certain extent, I turned out to be right. Soon, after that summer was done, there was a marked falloff in the number of volunteers we were able to attract to our efforts. People just did not respond as they had up until then. It's hard to say how much of that reticence had to do with other factors, such as feelings of futility, frustration, anger and fear. But I know at least some of it had to do with a sense that now that we had this law, there was no need to push anymore, no need to protest. We had this act, and now we could just leave it to the Justice Department to enforce it. That was the assumption quite a few people made— an assumption, as we would all soon see, that was sadly mistaken.

We were steeled for a season of violence in Mississippi that summer, and we got it. Between June 15 and September 15 our people reported more than 450 "incidents," ranging from phone threats to drive-by shootings.

There were more than a thousand arrests.

There were eighty beatings.

There were thirty-five shootings.

There were thirty-five church burnings.

There were thirty bombings.

The Klan was quite simply running amuck. It was open season on civil rights workers, with very little response from local or federal authorities. And it would have been much worse if not for the press, which duly reported every incident. One of the many studies made of that Freedom Summer concluded that what we achieved in Mississippi could "be measured in column inches of newsprint and running feet of video tape...it provided summer-long nationwide exposure of the iniquities of white supremacy in the deepest of the Deep South states."

Claude Sitton, with *The New York Times*; Gene Roberts, Roy Reed and John Herbers, also of the *Times*; Karl Fleming, with *Newsweek* magazine; Dan

Rather, with CBS; Nicholas von Hoffman, with the *Chicago Daily News;* Bill Minor, with the *New Orleans Times-Picayune;* Herb Kaplow and Richard Valeriani, with NBC; Arlie Schardt of *Time* magazine; Jack Nelson, with the *Los Angeles Times;* and print photographers like Charles Moore and Ken Thompson all tried to remain objective, but there was no question that just as David Halberstam (who was in Vietnam by '64, trying to tell the truth about what was taking shape over there) had done with us in Nashville, the reporters covering Mississippi Summer became very sympathetic to the movement. They couldn't help it. Day in and day out, going into those backwoods communities as well as to the more visible towns and cities of that state, watching people singing and praying from the bottoms of their souls, seeing the sorts of conditions these people were living in, with nothing for a front step but an old metal bucket turned upside down, with front porches that were nothing but a couple of planks nailed over dirt and mud, with no plumbing or electricity or decent clothes for their children or themselves, just pure and utter poverty—these reporters *had* to be moved. They *had* to be touched. You couldn't be human and not be affected deeply by these kinds of experiences, in these kinds of settings.

And these reporters were right with us from the start, like the troops landing at Normandy. Plenty of others followed them in later, but the first ones in were with us when we were laying the foundation. They could see and understand what was really going on. In a sense, they were laying a foundation themselves, for the others who would follow *them* in.

They all faced danger, especially the TV guys, who were easily identified and easy targets because of their equipment. The print reporters could blend in with a crowd if they had to, but the TV cameramen, guys like Lawrence Pierce with CBS, were right out front. Pierce, in particular, is a man I will never forget. A lot of the civil rights scenes America saw each evening back then, with Walter Cronkite narrating, were footage shot by Pierce. Lawrence was there for the Montgomery bus boycott back in 1955, and he was on the scene at just about every major crisis from then on.

For a guy like Lawrence Pierce to get a story, he had to literally put himself right in the middle of it. He couldn't watch from a distance. And it had an effect on Lawrence. Toward the end, by the time of Selma in '65, he had taken to carrying a pistol and daring people to come near him. I watched him tell a small mob in Selma that if they so much as touched him or his equipment, he'd shoot them. And he meant it.

Lawrence Pierce could have just skipped the whole thing. Or he could have just shot what was safe, what the authorities wanted him to shoot. But he didn't. None of them did, not the good ones. And because they didn't, because they went after the truth and showed America what was really happening in a place like Mississippi, these men with their pencils and pads and cameras became referees in the struggle for civil rights—sympathetic referees.

As bad as the violence was that summer, God knows what it would have been without the presence of the press. And we used that weapon in every way we could, including organizing and publicizing boycotts and cancellations of virtually every planned appearance in Mississippi that summer by entertainers and celebrities.

Television actor Dan Blocker—Hoss in *Bonanza*—canceled an appearance at the Jackson Coliseum after I sent him a letter and Julian followed up with calls to reporters. James Webb, the director of NASA, canceled a speech at an all-white event in Jackson for the same reason. British author Stephen Spender bowed out of a literary festival. Classical pianist Gary Graffman canceled a concert appearance. Baseball player Stan Musial stayed away from a signing. The folk group the Journeymen refused to sing. Jazz trumpeter Al Hirt canceled an appearance, as did actor Theodore Bikel.

They all turned their backs on Mississippi that summer, a heartening show of support. But it was largely symbolic, increasing the sympathy for our cause from beyond the borders of the state, but with little effect on the grim realities that continued to exist within those borders.

Those realities slammed us yet again that first week of August—a mere eighteen days before the beginning of the Democratic National Convention in Atlantic City—when word came that the bodies of Schwerner, Chaney and Goodman had been found.

Someone had tipped the FBI, telling them to take a bulldozer to an earthen cattle pond dam southwest of Philadelphia. They did, and there, deep beneath the dirt, they found three bodies: Chaney, beaten badly, shot once in the head and twice in the body; Schwerner, killed by a single bullet; and Goodman, also murdered by a single shot.

I went to James Chaney's funeral three days later, at the First Union Baptist Church in Meridian. The church was packed, with more than seven hundred people. I can still see ten-year-old Ben Chaney, James's little brother, standing between his parents with tears streaming down his face. David Dennis, CORE's top person in the state—one of our first Freedom Riders, from New Orleans—spoke with a voice full of understandable anger:

> I've got vengeance in my heart tonight, and I ask you to feel angry with me. I'm sick and tired, and I ask you to be sick and tired with me. The white men who murdered James Chaney are never going to be punished. I ask you to be sick and tired of that. I'm tired of the people of this country allowing this thing to continue to happen....

If you go back home and sit down and take what these white men in Mississippi are doing to us...if you take it and don't do something about it...then God damn your souls!

To me, "doing something" meant to keep on keeping on. To others, however, it meant changing directions, taking another tack. Out of frustration, bitterness, outright hostility to the system, to the government, to white people in general, every day the more radical arm of the movement was swelling a little more. Every day there were some who said "To hell with it" and just dropped out of the movement altogether.

But the majority of us still remained resolved. Two days after Chaney's funeral, I was in New York for the separate burials of Goodman and Schwerner. At the service for Andy, held at the Ethical Culture Hall on West Sixty-fourth Street, with over a thousand people inside and hundreds more crowded on the sidewalk out front, Rabbi Arthur Lelyveld, a friend of the Goodman family who had actually gone down to Mississippi that summer as a representative of the National Council of Churches and was attacked while there, hit on the head with a pipe, delivered a eulogy that, in contrast to Dennis's words in Meridian, emphasized peace and hope and the enduring ideals of our Mississippi Summer volunteers:

Not one of those young people who are walking the streets of Hattiesburg or Camden or Laurel or Gulfport or Greenville, not one of them, and certainly neither Andy nor James nor Michael, would have us in resentment or vindictiveness add to the store of hatred in the world. They pledged themselves in the way of nonviolence. They learned how to receive blows, not how to inflict them. They were trained to bear hurts, not to retaliate. Theirs is the way of love and constructive service.

Those could have been my words. That night I spoke at Mickey Schwerner's funeral, at the Community Church on East Thirty-fifth Street. Jim Farmer spoke, too, as did Bill Kunstler and Dave Dennis, who repeated his sentiments of outrage. I repeated the sentiments shared by Lelyveld. And it was hard to tell which of our words reached more hearts. The hearts were so heavy. I myself wondered how long we could keep the faith. How long could we believe in a government that allowed things like this to happen? I had asked in my speech at the March on Washington which side the federal government was on. And now, a year later, the answer was no clearer.

The bodies of Schwerner, Chaney and Goodman were in the ground, but the government still had no suspects. Those 150 FBI agents who had been sent to Mississippi in the wake of the disappearance had, it turned out, spent more time investigating *us* than locating and identifying the people who were attacking and killing civil rights workers. We were only vaguely aware of it at the time, but years later we would learn how committed the FBI became during this time to linking the civil rights movement with the insidious force that seemed to dominate J. Edgar Hoover's every waking thought: Communism.

Hoover had been unleashed on Dr. King several years earlier, with the blessing of Bobby Kennedy, who was unhappy about King's refusal not to associate with people with "Communist" leanings. King's telephone was tapped, and the bureau learned all about his personal life, including his extramarital affairs, which made Hoover detest Dr. King even more than he did King's politics.

By the time of the March on Washington, Hoover was as concerned about us in SNCC as he was about King. He saw the entire young arm of the movement as an aggressive, alarming danger. As early as 1960, with our sit-ins, we had been labeled Communists in FBI files, though the label wasn't true, and the bureau knew it.

During the Birmingham movement in early 1963, the local FBI office informed Washington that no "CP activity," as they put it, could be found, try as they might to locate it. During the planning for the March on Washington, the FBI wiretapped the telephones of both Bayard Rustin and A. Philip Randolph, trying to decipher what the bureau's files called "communist plans for the Negro March." I didn't know about those files at the time, but I'm convinced now that the FBI fed a lot of information and details it gathered about Bayard's private life during that time to Wilkins and Young, to turn them against him. Where else could Roy Wilkins and Whitney Young have learned so much about Bayard Rustin's personal life?

By the summer of 1964, Hoover had set his sights directly on SNCC, focusing primarily, though not exclusively, on our association with the National Lawyers Guild. The guild had been labeled subversive back in the 1940s, when, largely because of its support of progressive labor, it was singled out as a front for Communists. That label stuck through the red-baiting hysteria of the 1950s and on into the '60s.

When we were making plans for Mississippi Summer and knew we would need legal representation, we had naturally gone first to the NAACP Legal Defense and Educational Fund. They turned us down, telling us they did not approve of our campaign. No one else would help us, certainly not the Justice Department. So we turned to the National Lawyers Guild, which upset many of our Northern supporters, including Al Lowenstein, who warned us that by allowing the guild—with its "radical" lawyers like Arthur Kinoy, Bill Kunstler, Victor Rabinowitz and Ben Smith—to represent us, we were making ourselves suspect, putting our patriotism in question.

Stephen Currier, who had steered so much money toward the movement through the Taconic Foundation, was also upset about our association with the guild. Whitney Young voiced his concern. Naturally, Roy Wilkins did, too. Dr. King, having experienced his own share of red-baiting, did not fall for any of it. Our association with the guild was fine with him. He refused to condemn it.

Not that it would have made any difference if he had. No matter who attacked us on this issue, we weren't about to be budged. This was a battle for civil liberties as well as civil rights, and we were as committed to one as we were to the other. We had always embraced certain fundamental attitudes about civil liberties, and among them was the position that we had certain friends, certain associates, with whom we worked toward the same goal, and we were not going to judge those people on the basis of philosophy or ideology. We judged them simply on the basis of what they did, how they supported us, how they worked with us in time of trouble. If you were willing to work with us for the cause of civil rights, then you were welcome. We did not care about your politics.

We made a conscious decision not to dissociate ourselves from any organization or group on the basis of what some other group might say or feel about them, or what the political ramifications might be, or how our funding might be affected. Much of the criticism of how we did things and whom we associated with came from the so-called liberal wing of the Democratic Party. Many of these people were afraid of SNCC. They thought we went too far, that we were too radical, that we came on too strong, too threatening. Basically, the problem was simply that we did not do things *their* way. We rocked their boat, and they did not like that. They may have been liberal, but they were political, too. And they didn't like the way we did politics.

Hoover was aware of all these divisions, and he tried his best to take advantage of them. Early that summer of 1964, around the time of the Senate vote on the civil rights bill, *The New York Times* ran a story headlined "HOOVER SAYS REDS EXPLOIT NEGROES." The focus of the story was SNCC's efforts in Mississippi. I responded to reporters that the director of the FBI should spend less time turning over logs looking for the Red Menace and more time pursuing "the bombers, midnight assassins and brutal racists who daily make a mockery of the United States Constitution."

But Hoover was relentless. He had his agents go through the files of every student volunteer who had passed through Oxford. Every resident of every Freedom House in Mississippi that summer wound up in an FBI file as well. One such Freedom House file contained a list of occupants that included a Catholic nun, the son-in-law of a Northern newspaper publisher, a newspaper reporter and "an oversexed Vassar girl."

The FBI also investigated the background of every lawyer who worked with us that summer, including the two attorneys who accompanied the parents of Schwerner and Goodman on that Washington, D.C., visit soon after their sons disappeared. Goodman's parents ran in what might be called leftist circles in New York. Martin Popper, one of the two attorneys who went with them to Washington, had been part of the "Hollywood Ten" defense team during the anti-Communist frenzy of the 1940s. He had also been a target of the House Un-American Activities Committee (HUAC) in the 1950s, which now made him a prime target of Hoover and his men.

Speaking of HUAC, I didn't help myself by speaking out in December 1963 on behalf of the National Committee to Abolish HUAC. I'm sure that was one of many strikes against me when my draft status came under investigation by the federal government that summer of 1964.

My draft status had been an issue ever since I turned twenty-one and applied for classification as a conscientious objector. My personal philosophy of nonviolence gave me no other choice but to seek CO status. I remember trying to explain this to my draft board in Pike County, which was a panel of men, all Methodists or Baptists, all white. When I began telling them about the history and philosophy of nonviolence, they had no idea what I was talking about. They were convinced that my request was somehow tied to the civil rights movement. They ignored my application and classified me 1-A.

I appealed that decision, and my appeal eventually wound up before the state draft board of Alabama. When the state board also denied it, I appealed again, this time to the federal level, which is where my case was that summer, when the Justice Department stepped in and began interviewing almost everyone I knew in and around Pike County, Nashville and Atlanta. Clearly my appeal was not being treated as a typical draft board review.

That September, I met with a hearing officer in Atlanta, a representative from the Justice Department, who told me they'd finished their investigation and would let me know when a decision was made. The following year I was notified that my request had been granted, making me, as I understood it, the first black man in the history of the state of Alabama to be classified a conscientious objector.

The fact that my military draft status became intertwined during that summer with my civil rights activity was a reflection of the many causes and issues in American society that were bubbling up and intersecting at that time. Many movements besides civil rights were taking shape, and several of those movements found both their roots and their future leaders in Mississippi that summer. The experience of standing up to the government in an active way opened the door to the student movement that swept college campuses in the middle to late '60s. The free speech movement, early demonstrations against the Vietnam War, the "teach-ins" of 1965, the Vietnam Summer Project of 1967—they were all modeled directly on Freedom Summer and were, in many cases, staffed by veterans of that experience.

The atmosphere of openness and breaking down barriers that we developed that summer extended far beyond issues of race. They extended into everything from sexuality to gender roles, from communal living to identification with working classes. And they live on today. I have no doubt that the Mississippi Summer Project, in the end, led to the liberating of America, the opening up of our society. The peace movement, the women's movement, the gay movement—they all have roots that can be traced back to Mississippi in the summer of '64.

For all the positive seeds that were planted that summer, however, the end result for most of the people who experienced it was pain, sorrow, frustration and fear. No one who went into Mississippi that summer came out the same. So many young men and women, children really, teenagers eighteen and nineteen years old, went down there so idealistic, so full of hope, and came out hardened in a way, hardened by the hurt and the hatred they saw or suffered, or both. So many people I knew personally, so many people I *recruited*, came out of that summer wounded, both literally and emotionally.

Dr. Robert Coles, a Harvard psychiatrist who conducted a formal study of the Freedom Summer staff and volunteers soon after the campaign was finished, concluded that the symptoms displayed by almost all these young men and women were those of shell-shocked soldiers:

> They are clinical signs of depression.... They constitute "battle fatigue." They indicate exhaustion, weariness, despair, frustration and rage. They mark a crisis in the lives of those youths who experience them, and also one in the cities which may experience the results, translated into action, of such symptoms.

Like the soldiers who would begin coming home from Vietnam within a year, the veterans of Mississippi Summer were affected for the rest of their lives by what they went through and what they witnessed. Their spirits, as well as many of their bodies, were broken. Some remained casualties from then on. Many simply dropped out of the system. Others surrendered to overwhelming anger and irrational behavior. Like the Vietnam veterans to come, the veterans of Freedom Summer received very little sympathy or understanding from the people they went home to. Get over it, their friends and families would tell them. Well, you don't just "get over" something like that. You need a lot of help and a lot of understanding. And here, the Freedom Summer veterans were even worse off than the Vietnam vets. At least the Vietnam veterans had hospitals and support groups to offer a measure of care and comfort.

And eventually, ultimately, they saw a nation turn and recognize what they had gone through. Their country finally gave them the sympathy, acknowledgment and respect they deserved. The veterans of Freedom Summer have never, to this day, received that kind of credit or compassion. Those who recovered had to do it essentially on their own. Those who did not remain virtually unknown and unacknowledged, casualties living ruined lives or lying in unmarked graves.

The crisis that Robert Coles pinpointed both in the people who came out of the Mississippi experience and in the cities to which they returned was a crisis of spirit, a crisis of faith in the fundamental promises and premises of the American system, and it extended into the entire black community of this nation. Riots that broke out that year in New York, Chicago, Philadelphia and several New Jersey cities were just a taste of what was to come as frustration began turning to fury in black America—the "results, translated into action," that Coles referred to.

Still, though, with all of that, we emerged from Mississippi Summer with a purpose, a goal, an object of hope. For all the opposition we faced that summer, all the fear and pain and anger, we did succeed in our objective of educating and organizing a significant number of black voters in Mississippi. More than 17,000 black men and women filled out registration forms, a testament to each of those souls' incredible bravery. Within the next decade more than 300,000 black Mississippians would be registered, and more blacks would hold public office in Mississippi than in any other state in the union.

But that would be later. More germane to our immediate objective at the time than those 17,000 registrants were the 80,000 black voters who registered as members of the Mississippi Freedom Democratic Party. They were now positioned to have their voices heard in Atlantic City at the Democratic National Convention, to challenge the white Democrats from Mississippi who pretended they did not exist.

Atlantic City.

That was what would make everything we had gone through that summer worth it. That was the prize our eyes had been on from the beginning of this campaign.

Now it was August, and time to go take it.

14 / FREEDOM FIGHTERS

*I*t was a bright, breezy Friday afternoon when I stepped out of the car that had driven me from the airport in Philadelphia to the boardwalk in Atlantic City. This was August 1964, long before Atlantic City became the gambling center that it is today. But even without the casinos, it was still a thriving resort, and its famous wooden oceanfront walkway was jammed that summer day with the typical crowds of tourists and conventioneers.

What was not typical were the dozens of black men and women talking and laughing and hugging outside the city's civic center, where the Democratic National Convention was set to begin the next day. I doubt this town had ever seen that many black people collected on its sidewalks at one time. And the purpose for which these men and women had gathered was something the nation had never seen before—to claim seats at a national convention.

These were the sixty-eight delegates of the Mississippi Freedom Democratic Party, all but four of them black, some of them sharecroppers and their wives, all dressed in their finest Sunday-go-to-meeting coats and ties and dresses, proud and strong and not at all weary despite the 1,200 miles they had ridden by bus to get here.

It was hard not to be stirred to tears by that sight. To me and all the families, friends and supporters who had traveled here to be part of this historic week, these men and women represented the very best of American democracy. They could have been a case study in grassroots politics, in the process of organizing local units of indigenous people, bringing them together and then watching them work their way through the steps necessary to finally climb onto a national platform.

During that long, hot summer of 1964, while our Freedom Summer staff and volunteers were doing the very visible work of educating and registering voters, the MFDP was going through the equally laborious, though much less publicized process of creating a valid and meaningful political party to represent those voters.

Late that summer, Roy Wilkins had called for a gathering in New York of essentially the same civil rights leaders who had met to plan the March on Washington. Like many people in the movement, Wilkins was worried that Barry Goldwater might become president. For all the concerns about Lyndon Johnson, there was no question that Goldwater had even less sympathy for the cause of civil rights. And the race riots that had broken out that year in Philadelphia, Chicago, New York and several New Jersey cities was creating a backlash of alarm among some of the white community, swinging a good number of on-the-fence voters toward Goldwater. Some national Democratic Party strategists, concerned over this trend, began calling civil rights disturbances "Goldwater rallies."

Roy Wilkins shared their concern. He had never approved of our Summer Project. He thought the civil rights bill was enough. He didn't understand why we had gone down to Mississippi in the first place. Once Goldwater officially received the nomination as the Republican Party candidate, Wilkins sent out a two-page telegram warning that further civil rights demonstrations could jeopardize the chances of the Democratic nominee, who would almost certainly be Johnson. Wilkins, backed by Young and Rustin and Randolph, was calling for a moratorium on all demonstrations.

This is what we came to New York to discuss. Again we met at the Roosevelt Hotel, and again the alignments were predictable, with the conservative camp—including Dr. King, which surprised me—supporting the moratorium, while Jim Farmer and I held fast against it.

I explained that SNCC had never seen its role as supporting any particular political candidate. We felt all along that black people—or any people, for that matter— should not be in the pocket of any political party or candidate. We had to keep ourselves free to choose any candidate or party at any given time, depending on what was in our best interest.

Beyond that, the right to demonstrate was, to me, something that must never, *never* be compromised. The right to challenge authority, to raise questions, point up issues, draw attention to needs, demand change, is at the basis of a truly responsive, representative democracy. People simply must never give up their right to protest. They must never cash in their right to dissent. They must never, ever deal that liberty away.

Almost all my SNCC colleagues felt the same way. We were created, in a way, to be a thorn in the flesh of the American body politic and of the established, traditional civil rights movement. Forming a consensus with other groups had never been a priority for us.

So Farmer and I stood at that meeting against the moratorium, which was nonetheless approved by the others. There were indeed no major demonstrations in America that summer, but not because SNCC honored the agreement. We continued staging small protests in Arkansas and southwest Georgia and Alabama—I myself was arrested that summer in Selma. But our focus was Mississippi, so that's where most of our resources and manpower went.

That's also where, that June, a man named Joseph Rauh arrived.

Rauh was a lawyer, a longtime behind-the-scenes political player in Washington and a man whose politics were quintessentially liberal. Back in 1941, when A. Philip Randolph convinced Franklin Roosevelt to sign that executive order forbidding discriminatory hiring practices by defense industry employers—the order that defused the first March on Washington—it was young Joseph Rauh who drafted the legislation.

In the 1950s, Rauh became counsel for the United Automobile Workers and was deeply involved in labor and civil rights. He butted up often against Lyndon Johnson during those years, and when Kennedy ran for president in 1960, Rauh pushed hard for Hubert Humphrey, not Johnson, to be JFK's running mate. It was no secret that Rauh was no friend of Johnson's, but he was deeply committed to the Democratic Party and its ideals, and he was equally committed to the cause of civil rights. Which was the reason he came down to Mississippi that summer in his capacity as general counsel for a group called the Leadership Conference on Civil Rights.

Joe Rauh believed in the MFDP, and he came to Mississippi to help guide the Freedom Democrats through the maze of precinct, county and state elections that marked the path to the national convention. The assumption was that the MFDP members would be excluded from each of these elections—which they were. That fact, supported by carefully documented legal briefs prepared by Rauh and his staff, would become the basis of the MFDP's claim that it should replace the regular Mississippi Democratic Party in Atlantic City and fill the state's seats at the national convention with its delegates.

I got to know Joe Rauh that summer, and I really respected the way he worked with people. On the surface he was an outsider in every way, with his lawyer-like bow tie and eyeglasses, his Northern accent and, of course, his white skin. But he was a serious, skillful, brilliant attorney, very polite and very passionate about basic human rights. From the middle of that June, when the MFDP sent out its first waves of local representatives to each of the more than 1,900 precinct meetings across Mississippi, through August, when everything came to a head in Atlantic City, Joe Rauh was right in the thick of it.

So was I. I traveled throughout the state during that time, from Hattiesburg to Biloxi, Vicksburg to Natchez, Gulfport to Yazoo City, attending and often speaking at MFDP rallies where the cry was always the same: *"Seat the Freedom Democratic Party!"* Dr. King was sometimes with me, and he would join the crowds in that chant, though with a bit of reluctance. He was concerned that the MFDP movement might cause Johnson to lose votes to Goldwater in the presidential election in both the South and the North. But it was impossible not to be swept up by the spirit of this party. The press really began paying attention when the delegate selection process moved from the precinct stage to the county level and the MFDP held its own conventions in nearly half of the state's eighty-two counties. By the weekend of its state convention, which the MFDP held in Jackson, the entire nation was looking on.

That was an electrifying event. More than 2,500 people were jammed into the Masonic Temple on Lynch Street, all chanting and cheering and waving placards as each speaker rose to address them. Lawrence Guyot, a Mississippi native, SNCC field director and chairman of the MFDP, spoke. So did the party's vice chair, Fannie Lou Hamer. Joe Rauh spoke. And so did I, with my SNCC overalls on. The atmosphere was electric. The optimism was unbounded. The sixty-eight men and women chosen that night to travel to Atlantic City represented much more than one state or one political party. They represented all of us, every American—black or white—who believed in the concept of interracial democracy. Those MFDP delegates truly carried the movement's hopes and dreams with them, and we didn't doubt that they would prevail.

I had no doubt. Rauh and a small army of attorneys, including some of the best from the American Civil Liberties Union and the Lawyers Guild— men like Bill Kunstler and Arthur Kinoy—had prepared seamless briefs detailing the legal violations committed by the regular Mississippi Democratic Party as it barred the MFDP from the state's due political process. Nearly two hundred attorneys had also worked to collect documentation of the attacks endured that summer by our civil rights workers. All of this evidence—documents, photographs, even a mock-up of the murder victims' charred Ford station wagon—were hauled to Atlantic City to help make the MFDP's case.

Meanwhile, both Rauh, through his deep political connections, and Ella Baker, through an MFDP office set up in Washington, D.C., were busy collecting commitments of support from other state Democratic Party delegations across the country.

How could we not prevail? The law was on our side. Justice was on our side. The sentiments of the entire nation were with us. I couldn't see how those convention seats could be kept from us.

That's how everyone felt. The sense of elation and excitement among the MFDP contingent outside that civic center when I arrived in Atlantic City that Friday before the convention began was palpable. Most of us had rooms at the Gem Motel, about a mile from the arena, but no one spent much time there. We didn't come to sit in a room, swim in a pool or lounge on the beach. The delegates were there to take those seats, and we were there to do all we could to help them.

I was not a citizen of Mississippi. I was not registered to vote in that state. Neither were Dr. King and the dozens of other movement people who arrived in Atlantic City that weekend to support the MFDP. While the Freedom Party delegates were inside the hall attending hearings, meetings and caucuses, we maintained a vigil outside, staging rallies, giving interviews to the press, pointing out the burnt carcass of the Ford, which had been towed all the way from Greenwood, and carrying placards bearing the photographs of Schwerner, Chaney and Goodman, whose killers were still at large.

The key to everything we hoped for with the MFDP was a hearing before the National Democratic Party's 108-member Credentials Committee on the convention's opening day. No one expected that committee to just hand over Mississippi's seats to our delegates. But party rules provided that a seating dispute could be taken from the Credentials Committee to the convention floor itself if as few as eleven committee members voted to send it there. At that point, if at least eight states requested it, there would then be a roll call vote of the entire convention to decide who would be seated—Mississippi's "regular" party delegates, or the MFDP. If they got that far, we had no doubt our people would be voted in by a landslide.

"Eleven and Eight." That was the strategy outlined by Rauh and the MFDP leaders. That was the rallying cry.

Saturday, August 22, the entire nation watched on live television as the Mississippi Freedom Democratic Party delegates gathered in a convention center hearing room to make their case before the Credentials Committee. The members of Mississippi's regular Democratic Party were there as well, white plantation owners and businessmen looking across the aisle at women whom they knew only as maids and cooks, and men they knew only as field hands.

It was riveting. I was in a crowded room down the hall, watching on closed-circuit television as Joe Rauh, who in his capacity as a delegate from the District of Columbia was on the Credentials Committee himself, introduced the MFDP's case. He told committee members that they would hear that day the "story of tragedy and terror in Mississippi." Then he called on Aaron Henry, Ed King and, climactically, Fannie Lou Hamer to testify.

It was Fannie Lou's testimony that everyone had been waiting for. Under the heat of the glaring television lights, with sweat rolling down her face, she began slowly, describing the murder of Medgar Evers and the riots at Ole Miss. Rita Schwerner sat beside Fannie Lou as she spoke, a reminder of the three deaths earlier that summer.

Finally Fannie Lou detailed her own experiences—the savage beatings she had endured in pursuit of the vote, the cruel humiliations, the violent violations of her basic rights as a human being and as an American citizen. With tears welling in her eyes—with tears filling the eyes of almost everyone watching—she asked, in the unrehearsed, down-to-earth, plain language of an everyday American, the question we all wanted answered:

> ...if the Freedom Democratic Party is not seated now, I question America. Is this America, the land of the free and the home of the brave, where we have to sleep with our telephones off the hooks because our lives be threatened daily because we want to live as decent human beings, in America?

It was a stunning moment. So dramatic. So riveting. Who could help being moved by this woman and those words? Lyndon Johnson, watching on television in the White House, was apparently thinking the same thing. And he was deeply disturbed. He could see the South slipping away before his eyes. John Connally, the governor of Texas, had warned him just days earlier, "If you seat those black buggers, the whole South will walk out." Johnson couldn't let that happen. And so, in a spur-of-the-moment move, he cut into the broadcast of Fannie Lou's testimony with a live address to the convention—a trumped-up announcement whose transparent purpose was to cut off this woman's powerful testimony before it did any more damage.

The networks complied, switching from Fannie Lou to the President, but not before she had captured the nation's attention. That evening highlights from her testimony led off the news broadcast of all three networks, prompting an avalanche of telegrams from across the nation to delegates from every state.

We had momentum now. It was working. Johnson's attempt to stem the tide had not stopped it. But he was far from finished. He saw he couldn't openly squash MFDP, but he had other options, and now he began to use them. The man was a seasoned politician, one of the best, and soon we would learn firsthand what power politics was all about.

First, LBJ appointed an emergency "subcommittee" chaired by Minnesota attorney general Walter Mondale to address the Mississippi situation. The subcommittee, under Johnson's instructions, produced a proposal to create two "at-large" seats which would be offered to the MFDP delegation with the specification that those seats go to Aaron Henry and Ed King, the party's two candidates in the previous year's mock election. The proposal, clearly aimed at the Mississippi regulars, who had already committed themselves to Goldwater, also required a loyalty oath by all delegates to the Democratic candidate. And the proposal forbade racial discrimination among delegates at future Democratic conventions, another point aimed directly at Mississippi.

Along with this proposal, Johnson let the MFDP delegation know that if we wanted Hubert Humphrey to be his vice presidential choice, which most of us did, the MFDP had better accept this compromise, or Johnson would select someone far less sympathetic to the cause of civil rights as his running mate.

Johnson made Humphrey himself responsible for carrying out this plan. Humphrey sent Mondale and Walter Reuther, the liberal United Auto Workers boss, to begin working the back rooms and corridors of the convention center, trying to sell the President's plan.

Meanwhile, a group of us met in the basement of Union Temple Baptist, a black church not far from the arena. It was an emergency summit meeting of sorts. SCLC, SNCC, NAACP and CORE people were there. The subject was political expediency, the art of the compromise. Half the room was urging that the MFDP accept Johnson's offer. I remember Andy Young, speaking for the SCLC, saying we should be satisfied with this, that those two seats were a victory. Jim Forman and Cleveland Sellers were furious, very much in Andy's face about even considering this compromise.

I agreed with them, though my words were more measured. The idea that Johnson was dictating everything here, from the number of delegates to who those delegates would be, was outrageous to me. But beyond that was the simple fact that too many people had worked too hard for too long to be told that they would now be treated as honorary guests and nothing more. That was too much, and that's what I told Andy.

"We've shed too much blood," I said. "We've come much too far to back down now." Anyone who had been in Mississippi that summer, I said, would feel the same way.

It's important to say here that we—the SNCC contingent there in Atlantic City—did not push our point of view on the MFDP delegates, and I think this is one place where we shined. We had a hands-off policy in terms of decision-making. We respected the fact that this was the Mississippi delegates' call, not ours. We stated what we thought were the pros and cons, then we stepped back and let people like Fannie Lou Hamer, Victoria Gray, Unita Blackwell, E. W. Steptoe, James Travis, Annie Devine and so many others speak for themselves, think for themselves and ultimately decide for themselves.

Not everyone took the same approach. The President's men, for example, did everything they could to steer the decision their way—including spying. We had no way of knowing at the time, but it was later revealed that Johnson's people had the advantage of FBI wiretaps on the MFDP office and on Dr.

King's and Bayard Rustin's hotel rooms. They knew the strategies and decisions being formed on our side even as they were taking shape.

Armed with a good idea of which people were leaning which way, Humphrey sent Dr. King, Rustin and Wilkins to meet with the delegates and convince them to go with Johnson's plan. Both King and Rustin preached practical politics. They talked about the "big picture," they emphasized the importance of Johnson winning this election, they explained that it was time now for the movement to begin shifting beyond protest and demonstration and climb into the arena of politics. And everyone needed to understand, they said, that there is no dishonor in compromise.

Even Joe Rauh was urging compromise at this point. Rauh was torn, really agonized about this thing. On the one hand, he wanted what was best for the movement. But on the other hand, he didn't want to jeopardize the chances of his friend Hubert Humphrey to become vice president.

So Rauh urged the MFDP people to accept the two seats, which would wind up as his eventual undoing. When the smoke finally cleared, Joe Rauh would be seen as a villain, a traitor, a back stabber. And that was a shame. He was a good man who worked incredibly hard to bring this moment about. It's ironic that the situation he had worked so hard to create wound up skewering his reputation, at least among the black community.

Once everyone on the outside had had their say, the MFDP delegates themselves hashed out their decision. Aaron Henry and Ed King both wanted to accept the compromise, but they were just about alone. When the vote was taken, and it didn't take long, all sixty-eight MFDP delegates unanimously rejected the President's offer. Wilkins, true to form, called them ignorant. Personally, I felt proud. If there's one thing I've believed in my entire life, it's taking a stand when it's time to take a stand. This was definitely one of those times.

That Tuesday night I watched from the convention hall gallery as the MFDP staged a sit-in on the convention floor. The white Mississippi regulars had already packed up and gone home rather than agree to a loyalty oath to Johnson. The MFDP's answer to Johnson's plan was to take the floor and fill those empty seats. It was a gesture of defiance, cut short by the security guards who arrived to remove them from the hall.

The next night, Wednesday, the delegation again took the floor, only now there were no seats in the Mississippi section. The chairs had been removed. And so they stood there in that vacant space, this tiny group of men and women, forlorn and abandoned, watching silently as Lyndon Johnson was nominated for president by acclamation and Hubert Humphrey was announced as the Democratic Party's vice presidential candidate.

The next morning, we all packed up and went home.

As far as I'm concerned, this was the turning point of the civil rights movement. I'm absolutely convinced of that. Until then, despite every setback and disappointment and obstacle we had faced over the years, the belief still prevailed that the system would work, the system would listen, the system would respond. Now, for the first time, we had made our way to the very center of the system. We had played by the rules, done everything we were supposed to do, had played the game exactly as required, had arrived at the doorstep and found the door slammed in our face.

I'm convinced that had the decision to seat the MFDP delegates reached a floor vote, especially after Fannie Lou Hamer's testimony, the Mississippi regulars would have been ousted and replaced. There is no doubt in my mind. It was power politics that did in the MFDP, politics at its worst, really. And it was Lyndon Johnson, the consummate power politician, who taught us a painful lesson.

What's tragic is that Johnson didn't have to do what he did. He was so afraid that he would lose the rank-and-file South. Well, he *did* lose it. That November, in the presidential election, Barry Goldwater carried the states of Mississippi, Alabama, Louisiana, Georgia and South Carolina. But those were the *only* states he carried besides his home state of Arizona. Despite being swept in the South, Lyndon Johnson still won by one of the most monstrous landslides in presidential election history.

But he lost something even more critical than the presidency, and it was something the whole nation would lose as the decade began to turn dark.

He lost the faith of the people.

That loss of faith would spread through Lyndon Johnson's term in office, from civil rights and into the issue of Vietnam. That loss of faith in the President would eventually grow into a loss of faith in the federal government as a whole, and it would extend out of the 1960s, into the '70s and '80s, and on up to today.

That crisis of confidence, the spirit of cynicism and suspicion and mistrust that infects the attitude of many Americans toward their government today, began, I firmly believe, that week in Atlantic City. Something was set in motion that week that would never go away. It was a major letdown for hundreds and thousands of civil rights workers, both black and white, young and old people alike who had given everything they had to prove that you could work through the system. They felt cheated. They felt robbed.

It sent a lot of them outside the system. It turned many of them into radicals and revolutionaries. It fueled the very forces of protest and discontent that would eventually drive Lyndon Johnson out of office. It was a classic tragedy—a man unwittingly bringing about his own downfall by what he thought was the right decision.

The ramifications of not seating the MFDP were immeasurable. They permeated the political climate for years to come. The same questions that were asked by all of us that August are still echoing today.

Can you trust the government?

Can you trust your political leaders?

Can you trust the President?

Through Johnson, through Nixon and on through to today.

Are we getting the truth?

Are they lying to us?

That was the turning point for the country, for the civil rights movement and certainly for SNCC. People began turning on each other. The movement started turning on itself. Fingers of blame and betrayal were pointed left and right.

The "white liberals" were not to be trusted—that was one lesson many said they had learned. Men like Joe Rauh were dismissed as manipulators, clever double-crossers. "Double crossers"—you heard that word a lot, along with "Uncle Tom." Anyone who trusted the white man at this point, who believed we could work together, was a fool, a Tom.

No one laid that label on me. Not yet. But people like Bob Moses, people who had insisted up until then that we must incorporate whites into the movement, that an interracial democracy must be pursued interracially, now began abandoning that belief. Atlantic City was the last straw for Moses. This was what he had worked for since going down to Mississippi in 1961. This was what he had sweated and suffered for, what he had watched so many suffer and die for. He had created this political party. He had planned the Summer Project. More than any other individual, he had personally steered this journey. And at the end he was shunned, slapped in the face, told in so many words that he was a fool.

It was a cruel lesson for Bob Moses, one from which he never recovered. He left Atlantic City vowing never to speak to a white man again. Within a year he would change his name and move to Africa.

So many felt like doing the same thing. Those who chose to stay were ready now to play by a different set of rules, their own rules. *"Fuck it."* You heard that phrase over and over among SNCC members that month. "We played by the rules, and look what it got us. So *fuck* the rules."

I was devastated. I realized how naive I had been to believe we could walk in there and be given those seats, just as I had been naive to believe that the federal government would come in and take over the state of Mississippi. I still believed in what we were trying to do in Atlantic City. But we needed more resources, more political power.

I was devastated, but I was not despondent. I refused to let myself become bitter. I've always refused to do that. I can get angry—I have gotten angry many, many times in my life—but I never let my anger overwhelm me. I made up my mind a long time ago that I would not let bitterness and hate engulf me, which they so easily can. When I first got involved in the movement as a teenager, I recognized that this struggle was going to be long, hard and tedious, and that I would have to pace myself and be patient where necessary, while continuing to push and push and push, no matter what.

But for the first time I could feel myself outnumbered by friends and colleagues who felt different. The physical and emotional toll taken by Mississippi Summer was crippling to the morale of SNCC. The disaster at Atlantic City was like a knockout punch. The movement in general, and SNCC in particular, was headed for a low point that August. Like soldiers who had been on the front lines too long, we were beat, burned out.

Everyone could see it, including Harry Belafonte, who had always been a behind-the-scenes supporter of SNCC. He could see us falling apart after the strain of that summer, and he wanted to do something to help. It happened that he was friends with the president of the newly independent African nation of Guinea, a man named Seaakou Toureaa. During a conversation sometime that summer, Toureaa told Belafonte he would like to host a group of young Americans who were involved in the civil rights movement, to bring them over to Africa and have them share ideas with young Guineans.

The timing couldn't have been more perfect. We needed a break, and this was a fruitful, educational way to take one. It was the chance of a lifetime, really, to meet young people like ourselves who were doing the same kind of work we were but in an entirely different setting, earning their independence from colonial rule. When Belafonte approached Jim Forman and me with the invitation for a SNCC contingent to take a three-week trip to Africa, we leaped at the chance. Within a matter of weeks we had raised the funds and selected the group that would go: Bill Hansen, Bob and Dona Moses, Prathia Hall, Matthew Jones, Ruby Robinson, Fannie Lou Hamer, Julian, Forman, Don Harris, and I.

By then, Don had become one of my closest friends. A year earlier, he had been facing a death sentence in that Americus, Georgia, jail. He stayed there almost one hundred days before he and the others were finally released. I began making regular trips to Americus after that and would always stay with Don when I was there. Like Julian, Don became closer to me than anyone else I knew. Like Julian, he would address me in a mock-formal tone, late at night, for example, as I rose to go into the kitchen. "Mr. *Chaiiiiiirman,*" he would say. "Mr. Chairman, would you be so kind as to get me a *beeeeer* while you're in there?"

Don would eventually be the best man at my wedding.

Unlike the rest of us, Don had actually been to Africa before, back in 1961, as a volunteer with a program called Operation Crossroads Africa. He had worked in northern Rhodesia, which became Zambia. Now, three years later, Zambia had finally won its independence from Great Britain. A massive celebration was planned for that October in the capital city of Lusaka, and Don badly wanted to be there. The SNCC trip to Guinea was set to leave in mid-September. While that group had plans to return in early October, Don and I made arrangements, thanks to a $500 contribution from an organization called America's Committee on Africa, to extend our stay another month and a half, during which we would visit several other African nations—including Zambia—and make contact with youth groups like ourselves across the continent. We'd be traveling by the skin of our teeth. Five hundred dollars would basically cover transportation; food and lodging would be up to the grace of God and the generosity of the friends we hoped we would make.

This was the trip of a lifetime for me, my first time out of the United States, my first visit to Africa, the land of my forebears. I had no idea what part of Africa my ancestors came from. I still don't. Over the years, friends have suggested, simply from looking at my physical features, that I probably have roots somewhere on the West Coast. I don't know.

But it wasn't my roots that excited me so much as my kinship with the young people there doing exactly what we were doing here. I had met with African students in America many times, on college campuses around the country. I'd read the newspapers and watched television reports, and had a basic sense of current events across Africa, the wave of liberation movements there. I felt a sense of communion, a sense of fellowship with these rising nations of Africa, and especially with the young men and women who were so much at the heart of it all.

My parents, on the other hand, couldn't understand why in the world I was making this trip. They were still getting adjusted to the dizzying swirl of my travels all over the United States. To them I was a civil rights leader, yes, but, more than that, I was their son—a son they wished would stay closer to home.

"Boy," my father said when I told him about the trip, "what are you going to do over *there?*"

"Robert," my mother said, shaking her head, "that's too far for you to go."

Pike County was essentially as far as my parents' world went. I had accepted that a long time before, just as they had accepted—even if they couldn't fully embrace it—the fact that my world would extend much, much farther than theirs. Now it was extending beyond anything even I had imagined—to Africa.

We left that September 11, on a Pan American flight from New York City to Dakar, Senegal. Belafonte and his wife were with us, and several Peace

Corps volunteers were on the flight, bound for their assignments in Africa. That seven-hour trip was like a family outing, with people roaming the aisles, laughing and eating and drinking. You could feel everyone letting go and relaxing almost immediately. We really were like battle-weary soldiers headed out for a little R&R.

When we landed at the Dakar airport, on the northwestern tip of the continent, we were met by a small group with signs that read: WELCOME SNCC TO SENEGAL. They gave us a little reception, where we toasted one another with glasses of banana juice and the word "*Uhuru*"—"freedom"—a word I would hear a thousand times over the coming weeks.

From Dakar we flew south aboard an Air Guinea jet piloted by two black men and staffed by black flight attendants. With all the flying I'd done in the United States, this was the first time I'd ever seen black pilots. And that was just the beginning. In every city I visited, I was struck by the sight of black police officers, black men behind the desks in banks, black people not just on bicycles but also behind the wheels of Mercedes. Black people in *charge*. Black people doing for *themselves*. I knew this was the situation over there, but knowing it was one thing; actually seeing it was another.

Our group stay in Guinea was basically a vacation. It was once the others left to return to America and Don and I moved on deeper into Africa that the real substance of our journey began. Now, instead of being a large group wined and dined by dignitaries, we were two young black men, Americans, encountering and meeting and conversing with young people like ourselves, young men and women swept up in the spirit of revolution, of change. As we moved deeper into the continent, into Liberia and Ghana and Ethiopia and Kenya, the young Africans we met were voraciously curious about all that was happening in the United States. And more than anything else, they wanted to know all about Malcolm X. He became the measuring rod in every one of our encounters. As soon as we were introduced to someone, the first thing he would ask was "What's your organization's relationship with Malcolm's?" The young Africans we met were extremely politically astute, and they were, for the most part, true revolutionaries, far more radical than we in SNCC. This was why Malcolm X struck such a chord with them. Wherever we went that month, all over the continent, people would tell us, "Look, you guys might be really doing something, we don't know. But if you are to the right of Malcolm, you might as well start packing right now, because no one will listen to you."

That was eye-opening. Back in America, we were considered radical by the mainstream elements of both the movement and society in general. Malcolm X was considered even further to the left than we—an extremist, a revolutionary. But here in Africa, among these young freedom fighters, we were dismissed as mainstream, and it was Malcolm who was embraced. We learned quickly how little the African students and activists we met knew about SNCC or about the civil rights movement in America. When we told them about our years of demonstrations and protests and campaigns, about the sit-ins, the arrests, the beatings and imprisonments, the March on Washington and the summer that had just concluded in Mississippi, they were enthralled, impressed and, in most cases, surprised. They had no idea of the intensity of the opposition we faced in America. Most knew very little about it. They were the victims of pro-American propaganda, newspaper stories and photographs showing American blacks and whites living together in supposed harmony, all of it arranged and orchestrated by U.S. government agencies, all of it meant to give the impression that everything was idyllic in America.

On our way south from Ethiopia to Zambia, our airplane developed mechanical trouble and we wound up spending three days in Nairobi, Kenya, while the plane was repaired. The airline put us up at the New Stanley Hotel, which the local Nairobians called the European because of its splendor and because of the nationalities of most of the guests on its registry. One of those guests surprised Don and me our first afternoon there. We were sitting in the hotel's courtyard cafe, having a cup of coffee, when up walked none other than Malcolm X.

"Hello," he said with a small smile, "what are you doing here?"

We were shocked. I was aware Malcolm was in Africa, but I thought he was up in the Egypt area, or over in Mecca. I had no idea he was this far down the East Coast.

He took a seat and we talked, then we went up to his room—our rooms were on the same floor—and we talked some more. It turned out he had just come from a conference of nonaligned nations in Cairo, where he had spoken about using a group called the Organization of Afro-American Unity to bring the problems of black people in America before the United Nations. He also wanted to raise the levels of awareness and involvement in Africa about the situation of black people and their struggle in America. Throughout his African journey, which had taken him to eleven nations, he had emphasized unity and talked about the dangers of factionalism and the kinds of rivalries he had seen among the various civil rights organizations in the United States. He was well aware of the various frictions that were continuing to grow within the movement, and he didn't mind sharing his observations with the Africans—or with us.

As Malcolm talked, it was clear that Africa was doing for him the same thing it was doing for us—providing a frame of reference that was both broadening and refreshing. The man who sat with us in that hotel room was enthusiastic and excited—not angry, not brooding. He seemed very hopeful. His overwhelming reception in Africa by blacks, whites, Asians and Arabs alike had pushed him toward believing that people *could* come together.

He talked to us about his impressions of Cairo, about various African leaders, but mostly he talked to us about what *we* were doing. He told us how happy he was to see SNCC reaching out like this to Africa, and how more black people in America needed to travel and see and learn what was happening with blacks outside our country, not just in Africa but all over the world.

I recall very well that he said he had been struck by how the majority of the black people in Cairo were light-skinned. That had been eye-opening for him, he said. The focus among blacks in America on the shading of skin, on race, was misdirected, he said. He talked about the need to shift our focus, both among one another and between us and the white community, from race to class. He said that was the root of our problems, not just in America, but all over the world. He saw the great powers, such as the Soviet Union and the United States, using the poor people, of whatever race, for their governments' own imperialistic ends. That was a word he kept repeating: "imperialistic."

He got most enthusiastic about his idea of bringing the case of African-Americans before the General Assembly of the United Nations and holding the United States in violation of the United Nations' Human Rights Charter. The civil rights voices in America, he said, were unable to think globally like this, to step outside the morass of their own situation and circumstances to seek help beyond the borders of our country and our culture.

Thinking globally. That was essentially the reason Don and I had made this trip. To see Malcolm X so swept up with such enthusiasm was inspiring. But there was something else I noticed about him both that afternoon and the next, as we continued our conversation in the hotel's restaurant. Beyond his excitement and blossoming optimism, there was fear in the man, a nervousness that was written all over him.

Earlier that year he had split away from Elijah Muhammad's Nation of Islam. Malcolm had begun to develop his own ideas about black-white relations, many of which he was now sharing with us. Something else he shared was a certainty that he was being watched, that he was being followed. When we went to his hotel room, he took a seat away from both the window and the door, explaining to us that he never sat with his back exposed. He did the same in the restaurant. I wouldn't say he was quite paranoid, but he had a great sense of alarm, a great sense of anxiety. In a calm, measured way he was convinced that somebody wanted him killed.

Before we left, Malcolm made a point of saying he supported what we were doing in America, in the South—something I couldn't have imagined hearing him say six months earlier. He even said he wanted to come visit us down there. This was clearly a man in the process of changing.

"Don't give up," he told us. "This is an ongoing struggle. People are changing. And there are people all over the world supporting you."

Little did I know that this would be the last time I would see Malcolm X alive.

The remainder of our trip took us to Lusaka, Zambia, for the independence celebration Don so badly wanted to see. That week-long event was truly epic, highlighted by a nighttime ceremony in the city's newly constructed Independence Stadium. More than 175,000 people packed the arena for a display of drill teams, native dancers, singers, acrobats, aircraft roaring overhead, bands, infantry and a flame much like the Olympic torch, a flame the people called *Kwacha*—"freedom"—burning high on a hillside, waiting for smaller torches to be lit and carried by runners to all parts of the country.

The climax of the evening was when Dr. Kenneth Kaunda, Zambia's newly elected president, arrived, along with a commissioner from Great Britain. Minutes before midnight, all the lights in the stadium went out except two spotlights, each trained on a single flagpole.

First the British national anthem was played, and the crowd roared as the British official drew his nation's flag down.

Then President Kaunda, dressed entirely in white, stepped forward and, very slowly, raised the Zambian flag, the crowd roar swelling as the flag climbed the pole, until, when it hit the top, the sky came alive with fireworks.

At that moment a woman burst from the crowd and ran straight at Kaunda. No one knew *what* she was going to do. She was too close to him for anyone to stop her. You could see that Kaunda had no idea what was coming. He just stood there as the woman fell at his feet and began wildly kissing the ground in front of him.

Everyone cheered and wept, and the aircraft roared overhead, and the fireworks exploded, and the flame of *Kwacha* burned on the hillside. I'd never seen anything like it in my life, this nation of black and brown people tasting their moment of history, celebrating their first step into liberation. I remember thinking that this needed to be felt in Alabama and Mississippi. This needed to *happen* in those places.

Don had been right to insist we make this trip. I wouldn't have missed it for the world. As we left Zambia, on the same airplane as Dr. Kaunda, I was awash with everything I'd seen there. Back through Kenya and on up to Ethiopia, Don and I wrote pages and pages of notes on our thoughts and feelings, on the ideas we would share with our SNCC colleagues upon our return. It was November 2 when we arrived in Addis Ababa, and it was unbelievably cold—thirty-six degrees. You don't think of temperatures like that in a place like Ethiopia, but Addis Ababa is 8,000 feet above sea level—half again the elevation of Denver.

We stayed at a Peace Corps house there for several days, including election day back in the United States. We listened to the returns on the Voice of

America. This would have been my first time voting in a national election, and I hated not being there to do it. After all I'd done in the name of the right to vote, it seemed crazy that I was halfway around the globe when it came time to do it myself. But I was pleased with the results. Johnson crushed Goldwater, and Bobby Kennedy defeated a man named Kenneth Keating to win a New York seat in the U.S. Senate.

Our last stop was Cairo, where Don and I climbed aboard a bus for the forty-five-minute ride to Giza. It was time to play tourist. We were not about to leave Egypt without seeing the Pyramids. We got to Giza as the sun was beginning to set. The desert sand was white and brilliant, like snow. The dunes were blowing in the early evening breeze. We rented two camels and took the long bumpy ride to the Pyramids themselves. We arrived just as the sun slipped below the horizon. I looked down at the Sphinx and out across all that empty sand. The only sound was the heavy breathing of our camels. I felt very sad, very lonely. Don felt the same way.

We rode back to Cairo in complete silence.

Then it was on to Rome. And to Paris, where we visited Hazel Scott, the jazz singer and former wife of Adam Clayton Powell. She was wonderful, so gracious, the epitome of the American expatriate living abroad. She introduced us to some of her circle of friends, who took us around for an evening of nightspots and clubs. Very sophisticated. Very hip.

And then we flew home, back to the United States, where we landed on November 22—the first anniversary of the assassination of President Kennedy.

We'd been gone two and a half months—seventy-two days, to be exact. There was a lot to catch up on and so much to share. Don and I wrote a long report on our trip for SNCC's official records. Then there were interviews with the press, a lot of opportunities to spread the lessons we'd learned from our journey. The gist of those lessons was contained in a quote from me that was carried in a *Washington Post* story published soon after our return:

> It matters not whether it is in Angola, Mozambique, Southwest Africa, or Mississippi, Alabama, Georgia, and Harlem, U.S.A. . . . The struggle is the same. . . . It is a struggle against a vicious and evil system that is controlled and kept in order for and by a few white men throughout the world.

Little did I know that a struggle just as vicious had begun erupting within SNCC itself. It had started while we were away, and by the time it was over, we—the SNCC that I knew and believed in, and my own role and purpose in it—would be finished.

*A*narchy and chaos.

Freedom and openness.

It's amazing how one set of values can slide almost imperceptibly into another, how principles that are treasured at one moment as positive and healthy can, with time and a shift in circumstances, become forces of destruction and divisiveness.

That was what had happened to SNCC by the fall of 1964. The precepts that had been so fundamental to us when we began—decentralization, minimal structure, a distrust of leadership—were now beginning to tear us apart. At the time I left for Africa that September, I knew these forces were at work, that issues of SNCC's identity and its direction were being called into question. Our people were upset. They were angry. They were frustrated. But I had no idea they would move so far and so fast in the mere ten weeks that I was gone. By the time I returned that November, SNCC was shaking at its very roots, fragmenting and threatening to fall apart under its own weight.

The "weight" of SNCC—the growth in size of our membership—had become a serious issue. After Freedom Summer ended, a large number of volunteers in Mississippi stayed on as SNCC field workers, swelling our staff to nearly two hundred, by far the highest number of full-time personnel we had ever had. And we weren't prepared to deal with it.

SNCC had begun as a group with its focus on college campuses. During the early sit-in period we were composed of representatives—mostly students—of each Southern state's sit-in movement structure, as well as an executive committee to steer the group as a whole. Once or twice a year our entire membership would gather for groupwide discussions and workshops and to make groupwide decisions.

Our decision-making, whether in committee meetings or in these larger gatherings, was always by consensus, never by edict or even by vote. We all knew one another. We considered ourselves a band of brothers and sisters, a circle of trust. We used that phrase often—"a circle of trust." Our meetings were "soul sessions"—freewheeling, wide-ranging, "anything goes" discussions through which we would finally arrive at a conclusion or decision accepted by everyone.

That type of process is workable when the participants all know and trust one another. But it becomes a problem when the participants are strangers. And that's what had happened by the fall of 1964—there were a lot of people in SNCC who simply didn't know one another.

It started, of course, that summer, when those eight hundred Northern students came into Mississippi. Our staffs in other states—Arkansas, Georgia, Alabama—bitched and griped about the focus on Mississippi, about who was getting what in terms of resources. There was a lot of grumbling in the field about decisions being made at our headquarters in Atlanta. There were a lot of complaints that not only were the staffers outside Mississippi being treated as stepchildren, but they were being ignored in favor of a bunch of outsiders. "Who *are* all those people in Mississippi? We don't even *know* them." I can't count how many times I heard that question. And the fact that the vast majority of those new people in Mississippi were white did not help.

In addition to the complaints from people in the field about the decisions we were making in Atlanta, there were concerns as well in Atlanta about the behavior of some of our people in the field. We had many reports that summer, both from staff people and from members of the local communities in which we were doing our work, that some SNCC staffers were misusing their position and status, that they were misspending money, that there was a significant amount of marijuana-smoking going on, mostly among the membership from Northern cities, black and white alike. When we tried to respond to these problems, we ran into classic SNCC-like objections: *You can't fire us. You can't tell us what to do. No one can be fired from SNCC. No one can be ordered to do anything within SNCC. SNCC is not an organization. It's not a union. It's not a club. It's a movement.*

The closeness and cohesiveness—the intimacy—that we had in the beginning was starting to disappear. Our campus representatives were virtually gone. Our membership now was more field-oriented. And those staffs of field workers were a blend of people with vastly different backgrounds, people who were starting to feel friction among themselves. On the one hand, you had large numbers of salt-of-the-earth Southern black men and women, local people who did not have much formal education but who were fiercely committed to the cause—people like Fannie Lou Hamer. And on the other, you had Northern, college-educated intellectuals like Cox and Carmichael, whose perspective was broader and more sophisticated in terms of politics and militancy and in terms of the emerging issue of black nationalism.

Normally an organization would depend on strong leadership to guide it through such tension and turbulence. But not SNCC. We had never been a group that trusted leaders. From the beginning we had just two leadership positions: the chairman, who was the visible representative of the organization; and the executive secretary, who was more the nuts-and-bolts, behind-the-scenes leader. I was the chairman. Jim Forman was the executive secretary. Both of us knew and respected the limits of our "leadership." Now, however, those limits had put us in a quandary.

I believed in consensus. I believed in a bottom-up system of direction. I thought it would be the death of SNCC if it became so highly organized and disciplined that it resembled the very governmental and traditional organizational structures that we were opposing.

On the other hand, I also felt—and I still feel—that in any movement or struggle there come times when you need some individual or some group of individuals to step forward and become the symbol of the struggle, the personification of its essence, the *face,* if you will, of what you are fighting for. Call it a leader, but it's not a leader in the sense of any kind of control. It's a leader in terms of inspiration and vision. It's a man or woman who doesn't see him- or herself as any larger than the movement itself.

Martyrs, champions, men and women of all kinds throughout time have stepped forward as this kind of figure, from Jesus to Joan of Arc. Gandhi played this role in the struggle for liberation in India. John F. Kennedy became it for many Americans at the turn of the 1960s. Martin Luther King played it for a large section of the civil rights movement. And if we in SNCC were going to reject King as such a figure, the time had come for us to find someone or something to replace him.

Ironically, the one person who might have become that symbol for us, the one man in SNCC who was respected and trusted enough to actually be embraced by most of our membership as a "leader," was the one man most repelled and alarmed by the notion of a leader of any sort. That was Bob Moses.

Just as the end of 1964 had become a terrible time for SNCC, it was also probably the low point of Bob Moses's life. He clearly felt crushed by the guilt and responsibility for all that had gone wrong that year, from the death and suffering in Mississippi to the debacle in Atlantic City.

Moses was aware of the godlike reverence he was accorded by others. He knew that many of our SNCC staffers saw him as a Jesus figure, all-knowing and all-holy. That made him so uncomfortable he felt like climbing out of his own skin. From his days as a student at Harvard on through the years he spent traveling every dirt path and back road in the state of Mississippi, Bob had always remained a true intellectual, a passionately and intensely deep thinker, reading and absorbing everything from the existential philosophy of

Albert Camus to the political theories of Mao Zedong, to the notions of black intellectuals like Frantz Fanon and John Hope Franklin. He would pick one idea from here, another from there, and over time he created a synthesis, a tapestry of personal philosophy with an underpinning of absolute, individual freedom. He had a near-religious attitude toward autonomy and self-direction. By the fall of 1964, he had become a fervent believer in people following their soul, their inner voice, their impulses. In the language of the time, we called it "doing your own thing." And by that fall, this attitude had crystallized into a concept that was embraced by the vast majority of SNCC staffers, a concept we all called Freedom High.

The Summer Project people really got into that attitude. It was just like the old song we used to sing when we marched: "Go where the spirit say go. Do what the spirit say do." No one is responsible to anyone or answerable to anything other than his or her own instinct, his own spirit—a spirit fueled by the righteous, sweeping sense of almighty *freedom*. Freedom High. It meant exactly what it said. You were *high* on freedom, literally carried away by the feeling, drunk with it. And whenever and wherever that feeling arose, you followed. If it was midnight and you were seized with the desire to pile into a car and drive from Selma to Montgomery and climb on the roof of the governor's mansion and sing a freedom song, then you did it. You just *did* it. It might not be a wise thing. It might have no point. But if you felt it, that was enough. If you felt it, you did it.

Bob Moses completely supported this attitude. If a SNCC staffer wanted to write a play or a poem, he believed the staffer should go and write that play or a poem. If the staffer felt like going off in the woods and singing a song with a guitar, the staffer should do that. And he or she should continue to be paid just like any other staffer. Writing that play or poem or song should be considered part of that staffer's job. Yes, there might be problems with accountability, with communication, with follow-through and organization, but those problems would just have to be worked out somehow. Personal instincts and the right to follow them were sacrosanct.

Freedom High. It contained all the elements that were tearing at the seams of SNCC that fall, the tension between the beauty of individual liberty and the instability of total anarchy. If there was one thread that might have held it all together, it would have been Bob Moses himself. He was the only person who could have drawn respect and support and attention from the various factions that had developed within our increasingly faction-riddled organization. But he absolutely refused to fill that role, and we would all suffer because of it.

I knew SNCC was facing some serious problems at the time I left for Africa that September. Not only were there pressures from within the organization, but there were pressures from without as well. In the wake of both Freedom Summer and of our actions at the Democratic convention, many white liberals who had previously supported us were now disturbed by our "extreme" and "aggressive" tactics. Red-baiting—unsupported charges of Communist influences— increased dramatically that fall, with people like Al Lowenstein, who had been so instrumental in helping shape our Freedom Summer campaign, now leading choruses of questions about the background of some of our volunteers in Mississippi. Some individuals or their families turned out to have ties to Communism. Our continued connection to the Lawyers Guild drew a lot of questions as well. It was red-baiting of the worst kind, and in that climate, with racial disturbances beginning to grow into full-scale riots in some urban areas—notably, Harlem and Watts—it had a dramatic effect. Just mention the word "Communism" and it became real. When people are afraid, they are ready to see bogeymen behind every door. They are ready to believe anything. By the fall of 1964, the American people were starting to become afraid.

One immediate effect on SNCC of these outside pressures was money—we were beginning to run out. After being flush with support for our Mississippi campaign that summer, we now saw our funds drying up. Contributors were no longer contributing. Our internal squabbles and dissent didn't help matters—efforts at fund-raising came almost to a halt. At a time when our growth in size required more money than ever for operating expenses—Forman estimated we needed about $40,000 a month by that fall—our bank account was shrinking.

Not only was the general public becoming wary of us, but we were being attacked by other civil rights organizations as well. We had peaked that summer, with the nation's spotlight focused on our efforts in Mississippi. We had established ourselves as the movement's most forceful, most effective, most action-oriented group. We had separated ourselves from the other civil rights organizations and acted essentially on our own, for which there were no apologies made and none necessary. Now, though, as we began to come under attack from some sectors of the American public, not only did we not receive support from our brothers in arms—the SCLC, the NAACP, CORE—but some of those groups joined in the attack.

This was all boiling up at the time I left for Africa. And while I was gone, unbeknownst to me, it exploded, first in October, at an "emergency" meeting for the entire SNCC membership called by Courtland Cox, who was in charge while Forman and I and the others were out of the country. Forman returned just in time for that meeting, held at Gammon Theological Seminary in Atlanta. It lasted five stormy days, with the issue of leadership being the central subject. People wanted to know who had set the agenda for this gathering, who was in charge and *why* they were in charge. There were plans to discuss something we called the Black Belt Summer Project, a campaign that would take the tactics we'd used in Mississippi that year and apply them to states throughout the South in the summer of 1965. But that discussion never took place. As soon as Forman mentioned the need for more organization and formal structure, some in the room saw this as simply a way for Forman to increase his own authority and control. There was finger-pointing and shouting, and several people, including Larry Guyot, who had rightly earned a lot of respect for his work with the MFDP in Mississippi, stormed out of the meeting.

People were upset. A lot of them turned to Bob Moses to see what he had to say. But Moses refused to speak. He felt it would not be fair for him to say anything because his words carried such weight. "Undue influence," he called it. He was so sensitive by then. At one meeting he complained out loud, "Nobody would ever call *me* a motherfucker." He said it with such lament, with sadness. He wished someone *would* call him a name like that. He wished he could just be another person, be treated like anyone else.

So he refused to assert himself. He refused to participate. He remained silent, and his very silence created even *more* reverence for him. It was maddening. You could see him almost starting to crack under all these pressures. It was as if all the strife and tension of the entire movement was playing itself out inside his skin, inside his soul and his head.

So, with no one voice to speak, all the voices spoke, and no one was really listening. There was no such thing as a consensus. The Black Belt Project was lost in the confusion and never addressed. It never took shape.

Forman made a prescient observation about the chaos of those five days, pointing out a growing trend that would eventually claim me as a victim:

> Since it was SNCC's practice to make decisions by consensus rather than by voting, that liberalism opened the door for meetings to be tyrannized by a minority. The vast majority of people present would, after hours of discussion, be ready to adopt a proposal; a very few would say they were not in agreement—and the meeting would bog down.

That's what happened at that October gathering. One faction, the Freedom High faction, was opposed to any increase in structure. They questioned whether we should have a central committee anymore, or a chairman, or an executive committee. There were suggestions that we disband the Atlanta office altogether, do away with a central headquarters and allow ourselves to be guided by a loosely knit, geographically scattered, rotating circle of "leaders."

Arguing for this position, in very forceful, articulate terms, were the Northern "intellectuals" like Stokely and Cox and Ivanhoe Donaldson and Charlie Cobb. Arrayed against them were the field staff from the South, the more rooted, indigenous members who, on the whole, *wanted* more structure and more organization, so they could get the help and support they needed, so they could feel that their voices were heard. They felt overwhelmed and intimidated by the aggressiveness and sophistication of these "intellectuals."

In a way, the lines in SNCC were beginning to be drawn as North versus South. The Northern faction was much more political, much more outspoken about many issues, including, increasingly, the subject of racial separation. Some people, mostly among the Northern group, were pushing harder than ever to do something about the large number of white staffers in SNCC. Again, the loudest voices were those of people like Stokely and Cox, which I always considered ironic, because of their backgrounds. When they first came south and joined SNCC, many of these guys had more white friends back where they came from than black. They grew up and lived, for the most part, in a white world—certainly whiter than the world many of the Southern blacks among us, people like me, grew up in. They went to some of the best schools and some of the best universities in the nation. When the sit-ins began, they saw young black students in the South facing situations totally unlike what they faced in Washington or New York, and they wholeheartedly responded. They wanted to identify with what we were facing in the South.

In the process, many of them felt compelled to throw off their past, in a sense. They disowned their own experiences with whites in the North, as they came south and were swept up by ugliness and anger. I saw it so many times. One young lady, Tina Harris, a very beautiful black woman, came out of a bohemian East Village environment where she had gone through a stage—very familiar to many young men and women of that time—of denying the fact that she was "Negro." She insisted she was "East Indian." She had white friends. She lived in a white world. But then she joined the movement, came south, became swept up in the wave of "black consciousness" and black nationalism, and suddenly she disowned everything and everyone that was white. Tina became one of the most bitter people I knew in the movement when it came to the subject of white people.

It's interesting that some of the people who were most outspoken in asserting their black identity and disassociating themselves from whites were the ones who had grown up among and been very close to whites and who had, in many cases, disowned their own background. It was fascinating to see people disowning their backgrounds and reinventing themselves. For a lot of the newer, Northern-raised members of SNCC, radicalism in terms of racial consciousness was almost inversely proportional to the degree to which they had, for one reason or another, kept down their "blackness" when they were younger. Roger Wilkins, who was a young black lawyer in the Johnson administration back during this time, later wrote about this very thing:

> Stokely and the other young intellectuals in the movement knew what they were doing. They were purging themselves of all that self-hate, asserting a human validity that did not derive from whites and pointing out that the black experience on this continent and in Africa was profound, honorable, and a source of pride.

You didn't see as much of that kind of swing from the Southern blacks among us. In terms of black consciousness or black identity, they saw less need to take on the trappings of Africa, or to assert their blackness through things such as clothing and appearance. They didn't feel the same need to discover and assert their black identity, I guess, because they had never lost it in the first place. I'll never forget Bob Mants, one of our staffers in Lowndes County, Alabama, down near Selma, standing up at one of our meetings and saying, "A Southern Negro doesn't need to wear a sign saying he's black. We don't need to wear Afros to show that we are black. We *know* we are black."

There's a pattern here that is not limited to the subject of race. I think people who feel lost, people who are searching for a place to belong, for something to believe in, often move from one extreme to another, first embracing something or someone at one far end of a spectrum, then forsaking that position or person for something entirely at the other end, all in the process of trying to find themselves.

That's what SNCC was struggling to do that fall of '64—find itself. On the heels of the October meeting, which didn't settle anything, there was a staff retreat in November in Waveland, Mississippi, a little town in the southeast corner of the state, down near the Louisiana border, on the Gulf of Mexico. It was another mass gathering, a week-long event with about 160 members in attendance. Don and I were still in Africa, so we didn't hear about this one either until we got back.

There were dozens of "position papers" written and presented, addressing every conceivable issue, from the interracial composition of SNCC's membership to the structure of the organization itself, to the subject of feminism. Mary King and Casey Hayden presented a paper comparing the struggle of poor black Mississippians to the struggle of women in the movement. "Assumptions of male superiority," they wrote, "are as widespread and deep-rooted and every much as crippling to the woman as assumptions of white supremacy are to the Negro." When asked his opinion on what they had written, Stokely made his famous response that the only position for women in SNCC was the "prone" position. He was half joking, but that hardly mattered. No one was in a mood to laugh.

All those papers presented at that November meeting, all the dialogue and arguments, all the breast-beating and the soul-sharing, *all* of it came down to the issue of how we felt about one another. There was no question that we had other important issues to settle, issues that cut to the very core of how we defined ourselves. But none of those issues mattered as much to me as how we felt about and related to one another. As long as we felt trust and security among ourselves, no issue was too big or too complicated for us to work out. I really believed that. The biggest problem we had, as I saw it, was the loss of that unity of spirit and purpose that we had shared in the beginning, the loss of faith in one another. We had become riddled with infighting and suspicion and rumors and behind-the-scenes politics—in other words, we were becoming much like the organizations we had opposed for so long.

By the end of that week in Waveland, most of our Southern field staff members had already gone home, disgusted and dispirited. That left the emotional and political momentum in the hands of those who remained—essentially the Northern contingent, those aligned with Stokely and Cox. When I got back late that month, rumors were swirling. There was talk of an impending "coup." Outsiders were whispering that SNCC had turned "Communist," and that Don and I had not traveled just to Africa, but had gone to visit Red China as well. It was crazy talk, but it was talk taken seriously by those who heard it, and so it became something I needed to address.

As soon as I got back, my friends—people like Charles Sherrod, Bill Hansen, Bob Mants, Laverne Baker and Julian—rushed to let me know what had happened while I was gone. They chastised me, telling me I had stayed away too long. I should have been more savvy, they said, more politically astute. "While the cat's away, the mice will play"—all that. I shouldn't have been so naive, they said. I shouldn't have been so trusting. But there was no other way I could be. There *is* no other way I can be. I always begin with an attitude of trust. I assume that your word is good until you show me otherwise. I refuse to be suspicious until I have *reason* to be. Yes, this sets me up to be burned now and then, but the alternative is to be constantly skeptical and distanced. I'd rather be occasionally burned but able to connect than always safe but always distant. "A circle of trust"—that's what it's all about.

As the end of that year approached, I began for the first time to have reason not to embrace everyone around me in SNCC with total trust. I learned that there were people stirring things up behind my back. I was told that

Stokely and a young guy named Lafayette Surmey were going around saying I was cut off, disconnected, that I was off in Africa playing the big cheese when I should have been back with them facing all these problems. It didn't worry me personally to hear talk like that, but I was concerned about the effect this kind of dissension was having on the organization.

It was a dark, dark month, that December. With the wounds still fresh from our summer in Mississippi and from the convention in Atlantic City, news came that December 4 that federal authorities had arrested twenty-one white Mississippians—including Sheriff Rainey and his deputy, Price—in connection with the deaths of Schwerner, Chaney and Goodman. Evidence and witnesses gathered by the FBI showed that a lynch mob had been allowed to remove the three from the Neshoba County jail that night and have their way with them before burying the bodies and dumping the car. Since murder was not a federal crime, and effective state prosecution for that charge was unlikely, the Justice Department decided instead to charge the mob members with conspiracy to deprive the dead men of their civil rights.

A week after those arrests, at a preliminary hearing in Meridian, the government's charges were dismissed by none other than U.S. District Judge Harold Cox—who had compared blacks to "chimpanzees" prior to our Freedom Summer campaign. The defendants, including Rainey and Price, filed out of Cox's courtroom laughing and congratulating one another.

That was devastating. Not until 1967, after an appeal to the U.S. Supreme Court and new testimony, would seven of those men—including Price, but not Rainey—finally be convicted and sentenced to prison for violating federal civil rights laws.

The same day Cox dropped those charges, December 10, Dr. King became the youngest person ever to receive the Nobel Peace Prize. In his acceptance speech, delivered in Oslo, Norway, he said he was receiving the award as "a trustee for the twenty-two million Negroes in the United States of America who are engaged in a creative battle to end the night of racial injustice."

I was overjoyed to hear those words and to see Dr. King be so honored. Only one other black American had ever received that prize—diplomat Ralph Bunche in 1950. But I was clearly in the minority among my SNCC colleagues, most of whom actually felt resentment and disdain. It was frightening. I could see us becoming more isolated every day, more cut off from those around us, black and white alike. In the middle of that month, after returning from a fund-raising trip to New York and Philadelphia, where rumors were rampant about the breakup of SNCC, I wrote an open letter to our entire membership:

From: John Lewis
To: All SNCC Staff

I have been back from Africa for more than two weeks. I hope by now that each of you has a copy of the report on the trip. I hope to talk with each of you about Africa and the movement for liberation throughout Africa and how it relates to the Civil Rights struggle in this country. I am convinced more than ever before that the social, economic, and political destiny of the black people of America is inseparable from that of our brothers of Africa.

On my arrival in Atlanta I was thoroughly informed about the questions and issues that were raised at both the staff meeting and the staff retreat. I have read the position papers and minutes, and talked with many members of the staff with great interest concerning the nature of your deliberations....

While in New York and Philly for four days, I had the opportunity to speak at five rallies and parties, and also attended two smaller meetings of supporters. At each of these gatherings some of the persons in attendance raised questions about the following:

The alleged coup in SNCC:

a: "Bob Moses is no longer Director of the Mississippi project, and he is out of the state."

b: "Jim Forman is no longer Executive Secretary of SNCC."

c: "John Lewis is no longer Chairman of SNCC."

The red-baiting of SNCC:

a: "SNCC has been taken over by the communists."

b: "Some of the key people in SNCC made a trip to Peking."

c: "Most of the volunteers that SNCC recruited were communists or communist sympathizers."

Now we all know that there is not a word of truth in any of this. We all should know that Bob Moses is still the Director of COFO, Jim Forman is still the Executive Secretary of the Student Nonviolent Coordinating Committee, and I am still SNCC's Chairman.

If I can further dispel the rumor that I am leaving SNCC or the Movement, let me say—and this is contrary to what some of the staff have said—that I have no plans for leaving the Movement to enter school in either January 1965 or September 1965. I will be involved in the struggle one way or another till every victory is won.

Our supporters and friends are confused and bewildered, for they feel a sense of uncertainty and instability about SNCC. It is hard to get people to invest in anything that is shaky, unstable, and without a sense of permanence, whether it be a country, the stock market, or a civil rights organization. I am of the opinion that these rumors are hurting SNCC financially and otherwise. In addition, we are under attack from many quarters—the press, and other civil rights groups. We must understand these rumors and the "red-baiting" as effective and destructive political gimmicks, and we cannot take this lightly. The situation demands that we reassure our friends, supporters, and the American public that we are a unified, effective, strong and vital force on the American scene for social, economic, and political change.

I am asking of all the staff to speak the truth of the work and programs of SNCC. We have nothing to make apologies for. Our projects and programs are worthy of support....As an organization SNCC does what SNCC must do and in SNCC's own way, that's that. What concerns me, however, is: that we do not let certain malicious and vicious rumors and attacks go unanswered. On the other hand we must never stoop so low as to engage in public slander or debate with any group.

I am asking Julian Bond and Betty Garman to use their respective departments to make a special effort to counter these rumors and attacks. Each of us must do our part to present the truth about SNCC.

During the next few days I will be visiting all of the projects and will be at your disposal. It is my hope that we will have some serious and honest discussions. My tentative schedule is as follows:

Dec. 17–18	Central Alabama
Dec. 19–24	Mississippi
Dec. 28–Jan. 5	Mississippi
Jan. 6–7	Eastern Arkansas
Jan. 9	Southwest Georgia

Hope to see each of you very soon.

Uhuru!
John Lewis

This was as close to desperate as I have ever felt. I was trying to do anything I could to put out the flames in our organization. I had never been much of a speechmaker. I had always believed much more in actions than in words. Keep on keeping on—that had always been my answer in a time of crisis. Always in the past—in Nashville, during the Freedom Rides—action pulled us back together when things seemed to be coming apart. I still believed, as always, that nothing would unify us, nothing would shore up our crumbling foundation, like another battle. We needed, that December, to turn our energy and passions not on one another but on a deserving target. And I had a good idea just where that target might be, just where we needed to turn: Selma.

After all our activity there in the fall of 1963—more than three hundred demonstrators were arrested outside the Dallas County Courthouse that October alone—Selma had settled down to a few scattered protests during the first half of '64. That July, after the passage of the civil rights bill, there was a burst of activity as groups of Selma teenagers went downtown to test the new law's provision that public accommodations be desegregated. The kids tried entering Selma's still-segregated movie theater and were arrested for trespassing. At a rally the next day protesting those arrests, Sheriff Clark's deputies shot tear gas into the crowd, and his "squirrel shooter" posse was turned loose and allowed to beat dozens of demonstrators.

That led to my coming down and joining yet another protest that July 6. I'll never forget Clark emerging from the courthouse that afternoon. I had seen his anger many times, but this day he looked more furious than ever. You could see the rage just building up in him. He was a huge man—about six feet five, 230 pounds, maybe 240—and it seemed as if he was going to burst out of his clothes. He was wearing a suit and a hat that day, not the military-style uniform and helmet he often had on. He was trembling, literally shaking with anger. The man really looked as if he was going over the edge. You could see it in his eyes.

"John Lewis," he sputtered, coming straight at me, "you are nothing but an outside agitator. You're the lowest form of humanity."

I looked him square in those eyes and I said, "Sheriff, I may be an agitator, but I'm not an outsider. I grew up ninety miles from here."

I paused.

"And," I continued, "we are going to stay here until these people are allowed to register and vote."

I was arrested, of course, along with the rest of our group. That led to an injunction by a local circuit judge named James Hare, forbidding public gatherings of more than three people in the city of Selma. It was an absurd restriction, obviously aimed directly at us. Our attorneys spent the rest of the year trying to have that injunction dissolved, but with no success. And so, with the combination of Judge Hare's regulation and SNCC's focus on Mississippi, protest activity in Selma came to a virtual standstill.

By that December, barely more than three hundred local blacks had registered to vote in Dallas County—only 156 in Selma itself. That was hardly a nudge of an increase from the two hundred voters who were on the rolls when Bernard and Colia LaFayette began their work there nearly two years earlier.

The vast majority of the county's 15,000 eligible black voters remained un-registered, held back by fear of repression and violence. The few who actually did reach the registrar faced an absurdly difficult "literacy test." Members of right-wing groups such as the White Citizens Council, the John Birch Society and an organization called the Alabama Sovereignty Commission—funded by state money directly ordered by Governor George Wallace—routinely visited registrars around the state, instructing them on how to impede black voter registration. One of their most effective impediments was these "literacy" tests, which typically required interpreting arcane sections of Alabama's state constitution, a task that would stump a graduate student in government, much less a poor sharecropper with a sixth-grade education. While black men and women sat struggling with that test, white people who could barely write their own name walked past and registered without having to take it.

By the end of that year, our efforts in Selma had come practically to a standstill. Meanwhile, the SCLC—Dr. King's organization—was deciding where they should turn their sights next. They'd launched a campaign earlier that year in St. Augustine, Florida, but they wanted something bigger, something like Birmingham. With the Civil Rights Act of 1964 now on the books, *voting* rights had become the focus of the entire movement. For all its signifi-cance, the Civil Rights Act made no provision to ensure the right of black Americans to register and vote. The SCLC was working toward that end in Alabama, as were we. They had Jim Bevel going all over the state with a grass-roots voter registration program he and Diane had created called G.R.O.W.— Get Rid of Wallace. That November, King and his staff decided it was time to turn the entire force of the SCLC back toward Alabama. They would depend heavily on Bevel. And Selma, they decided, was where they would set their sights.

Plans for an SCLC move on Selma were already being drawn up that De-cember when Dr. King met with President Johnson after returning from re-ceiving the Nobel Prize. The two men discussed the need for a voting rights act, and Johnson said in so many words that it was just impossible. Not right now, the president said. The votes in Congress simply were not there. John-son had his attorney general, Nicholas Katzenbach (the same man who had squared off against George Wallace in the schoolhouse door), putting together a piece of federal voting rights legislation, but they were moving slowly, care-fully. After the upheavals of 1964 the President felt the country was tired of civil rights, that the American people needed a rest from this subject. He told Dr. King he didn't know when this legislation might actually start moving. Maybe in late 1965. More likely in '66.

Dr. King told the President the people were not going to wait. And he was right. No sooner did he get back to Atlanta after that meeting in Washington

than a contingent of local Selma men and women representing a group called
the Dallas County Improvement Association arrived at the SCLC offices to
personally ask Dr. King to come help them.

That invitation clinched it. The people of Selma themselves had now in-
vited the SCLC in. If Dr. King and his staff had any concern about stepping on
SNCC toes in Selma, they vanished after that visit. This was the last green light
Dr. King needed.

As for our SNCC staff, we had known for some time that the SCLC was
planning a move on Selma. And there were feelings—*strong* feelings—that
toes were indeed being stepped on here. It was the same old story all over
again. We dug in early, did the groundwork, laid the foundation, then the
SCLC came in again with their headline-grabbing, hit-and-run tactics, doing
nothing to nurture leaders among the local community but instead bringing
in their own leaders, then leaving after they'd gotten what they needed out
of it.

These were the feelings of most of our staff, especially of the guys already
on the ground in Selma—Worth Long and a young staffer named John Love.
They'd been doing just what we at SNCC always did—digging in for the long,
hard haul, not just coming in for a day or a week or a month. They'd been
down there in Selma a long time—Worth for over a year—continuing the
work Bernard and Colia had begun. They, more than anyone, were upset that
Dr. King and his troops were now going to move in.

I had many different thoughts about this. On the one hand, I knew exactly how Worth and John felt. They already felt neglected by our own SNCC
leadership because of the emphasis we had put on Mississippi that year. And
now they were being pushed aside by the juggernaut of the SCLC. But I also
had more of a respect and understanding of what the SCLC was honestly and
earnestly trying to do than most of my SNCC colleagues. I was still a member
of the SCLC board, which put me in the peculiar position of having a foot in
both camps—something that did not sit well with many of my SNCC colleagues, but something I never apologized for. I had respected Dr. King and all
he stood for in the beginning. I respected him now. I would always respect
him. Simple.

Far outweighing the claims put on Selma by either the SCLC or SNCC, as
far as I was concerned, was the fact that the people of Selma themselves had
gone and asked King to come help them. How could we stand in their way,
no matter how valid our reasons or objections or concerns might be? We
might not like it. We might choose to be minimally involved—which turned
out to be the case, at least in the beginning. But we had no choice but to accept the fact that the Selma campaign was now going to officially become an
SCLC undertaking.

Which it did that December 28, with an SCLC announcement that Dr. King would kick off the organization's new campaign in Selma with a speech there on Saturday, January 2. This would be the first mass meeting of Selma's blacks since Judge Hare's injunction had gone into effect nearly six months earlier. That gathering, commemorating Lincoln's January 1 signing of the 1863 Emancipation Proclamation, was a fittingly symbolic occasion to defy the judge's order.

I was there that day. An overnight snowfall had dusted the streets white. It reminded me of the morning in Nashville five years earlier when I'd awakened in my college dorm room to go downtown for the first sit-in of my life.

As I headed to the church where Dr. King would make his speech that day—Brown Chapel African Methodist Episcopal Church—I felt I was walking through a town I knew almost as well as my hometown of Troy. I had spent so much time in Selma over the years, I was familiar with almost every one of its streets—the paved ones in the white section of the city, and the unpaved ones that ran past the white clapboard shanties and redbrick housing projects where the black people lived. I knew the buildings downtown, from the sleepy little five-and-dime stores to the old cotton warehouses perched on the steep bluffs that sloped down to the Alabama River.

Among the nicer buildings in town was a stately three-story structure off the steps of which as many as five hundred slaves a day were auctioned in the 1800s. Many of those slaves stacked the cotton on the riverboats that routinely arrived at the waterfront docks down below those warehouses.

I knew the bridge, too—the quaint, humpbacked Edmund Pettus Bridge, its steel framework arcing high across the river, an arched wrought-iron sign at its foot, with the words "SELMA WELCOMES YOU" spelled out above a Confederate flag, the entryway into Selma for all travelers arriving from the east.

Howard Zinn, an activist and a historian who was in and out of Selma during this time—Zinn was a lanky Spelman College professor in his thirties who joined us in some of our demonstrations in Atlanta during the fall of '64 and eventually became an informal advisor to SNCC—wrote of Selma's downtown in the mid-1960s:

> It is as if a movie producer had reconstructed a pre–Civil War Southern town—the decaying buildings, the muddy streets, the little cafes, and the huge red brick Hotel Albert, modelled after a medieval Venetian palace.

This was the town I walked through that January morning as I headed for Brown's Chapel to hear what Dr. King would have to say. There were already seven hundred people crushed into the church by the time I arrived. Police were there, but, curiously, they were directing traffic, not making arrests. That was because they were under the command not of Sheriff Clark, but of Selma's public safety director, a man named Wilson Baker.

Baker was a former police captain who had run for county sheriff against Clark in 1958 and lost. He was a hefty man with eyeglasses who always wore a suit and a dress hat. He was a comparatively reasonable and well-read man—he sometimes taught a criminology class at the University of Alabama. He was a segregationist, but a careful, smart one, more like a Laurie Pritchett than a Bull Connor.

Wilson Baker represented what there was of a white-collar Selma, and he was closely aligned with the city's newly elected mayor, a former washing machine salesman named Joe Smitherman. Smitherman was a young guy, skinny, crew cut, with big ears that even he made fun of. He was in his thirties, but he looked even younger—he looked as young I was. Like Baker, Smitherman was a segregationist but a moderate, especially when compared to his predecessor, a hardcore racist named Chris Heinz.

Smitherman had just been elected that October. He was still getting his feet wet as mayor, focusing on simple, basic issues like paving the roads and putting up streetlights. He leaned toward Baker in terms of dealing with the city's civil rights "troubles," but he had to please everyone. And so he wasn't above calling Dr. King "Martin Luther *Coon*," then chuckling at his slip of the tongue.

Positioned against Baker and Smitherman was Clark. If Baker was Laurie Pritchett, Clark was Bull Connor through and through. He had a violent temper, he took everything personally and he always retaliated physically, with the support of his "posse"—the deputized citizenry of Selma, which included not just poor whites, but well-to-do businessmen and landowners as well, many of whom answered his calls on horseback. When our demonstrations began in 1963, Clark had issued the call for all white males over the age of twenty-one to come to the courthouse and be deputized, creating an armed posse with one purpose—to keep the black people of Dallas County from voting. During Dr. King's '63 campaign in Birmingham, Clark had arrived with two hundred of his "possemen" from Selma—reinforcements for Bull Connor's men—and they busted heads with relish when they got there.

Clark took his orders not from Smitherman or Baker but from Judge Hare, the man who had issued the injunction the year before against gatherings of more than three people at a time. Judge Hare was a tightly wrapped, chain-smoking, dyed-in-the-wool segregationist. Like most of the judges we came up against throughout the state, he had studied law in Tuscaloosa, at the University of Alabama, and he was a traditionalist—which is to say, he liked his "nigras" obedient and kept in line. He and George Wallace saw eye to eye on that issue. And that was essentially the chain of command we faced in Selma:

Judge Hare as an extension of George Wallace, and Jim Clark as an extension of Hare.

With the judge and the governor behind him, Clark ran the county like a king. He really believed that the old racial order was the way things should be and that the black people of Dallas County were *happy* to have it that way. He stated over and over again that it was people like Martin Luther King and John Lewis—"outside agitators"—who were stirring up the county's "good colored people."

We in SNCC had known for a long time, and the SCLC learned quickly, that Clark's short fuse made him an easy target for provocation. And since he considered the county courthouse—where all voters were registered—his personal domain, it was inevitable that we would square off against him. That's what we prepared for. That's also what Baker and Smitherman did their best to prevent, knowing the damage Clark's temper and his violent reactions might do to the city's image and to its legal footing. In many ways the Selma campaign would come down to a tug-of-war between Baker and Smitherman on one side and Clark on the other, with us forcing things Clark's way, and with Judge Hare cooperating by pushing Clark out to stop us.

But the day that King first came to Selma to speak was calm. There was no march on the courthouse, not yet. There was no showdown with Jim Clark, not yet. This was a rally, a laying down of the gauntlet. Dr. King told the audience that if Governor Wallace and the Alabama state legislature didn't force Dallas County to begin registering its black citizens, "We will seek to arouse the federal government by marching by the thousands." He even threatened another March on Washington. "We must be willing to go to jail," he said, again, "by the thousands."

The actual demonstrations, he announced, would begin in about two weeks. Meanwhile, we—a coalition of SCLC, SNCC and Dallas County Voters League leaders—set about planning, preparing and organizing. SNCC had a small office downtown, on the corner of Alabama and Franklin Avenues, in a second-story room above a bail bondsman's office and the neon Budweiser sign of a barbecue restaurant, right across the street from the public safety building and the jail. Not far away was a little restaurant called Clay & Liston's—named for the heavyweight prizefighters. Clay & Liston's and a place called Walker's Cafe were the two main spots where black people in Selma could get something to eat. Both became informal meeting places for people in the movement, especially Walker's, which had a wonderful soul food menu with greens and pig's feet and cornbread and grits and sweet potato pie—and a great jukebox, to boot.

There was no SCLC office in Selma, so Dr. King and his staff turned Brown's AME and another local church just up the street, First Baptist, into command centers. Technically, the SCLC shared a small office with the county's Voters League in a little building down near the city's black upper school, Hudson High. But in reality, the churches were the headquarters. Both were located right beside the city's largest black housing project, the George Washington Carver Homes, a federally built community of two-story, redbrick apartment buildings. Living in those small, spare apartments were hundreds of the men, women and children who would become foot soldiers in the coming siege. These were salt-of-the-earth people—schoolteachers, beauticians, undertakers, housewives, men, women and children from every walk of black life in Selma. The "ground crew," I called them—nameless individuals to outsiders, faceless people to all but those of us who were there. Yet they *were* the face of the civil rights movement, these unidentified men and women with no titles in front of their names, no Ph.D.s after them.

They were the rank and file, in Selma, in Americus, in Little Rock, everywhere. You see their faces today in photographs in history books and nobody knows their names. That young guy sitting stoically at the lunch counter in Jackson with mustard streaming down his face and a mob of white hoodlums crowded around him taunting and laughing—who is he? Where is he today? The young man whose pants leg is being torn by a snarling German shepherd in Birmingham— what is his name? Where is *he?* Whatever happened to the little girl who was turned head over heels by those fire hoses?

Every one of our campaigns across the South was full of people like these, the *"maaaaasses,"* as A. Philip Randolph might have said. But Selma was even more a mass movement than any of the others, very different from, say, Birmingham, where there were lots of generals on the scene, lots of staff and leaders—the Fred Shuttlesworths and the Dr. Kings—carefully planning every move, all of it very organized from the top down. Selma was more of a bottom-up campaign, of the people acting with minimal direction from the leaders. We were there to guide and help carry out what the people wanted to do, but it was essentially the people themselves who pointed the way. People like Mrs. Amelia Boynton, who with her husband, Sam, had helped form the Dallas County Improvement Association and who had led the contingent that went to ask Dr. King to come to Selma. And Fred Reese, a high school science teacher and president of the local Voters League. And Marie Foster, a dental assistant. And Claude Brown, Ernest Doyle, J. D. Hunter, James Gildersleeve and Ulysses Blackman, all longtime civil rights soldiers in Selma.

These were the people who led the way in the almost-daily summit meetings and planning sessions held in the Brown Chapel Sunday school room, with its little tables and chairs, and drawings of Jesus and baby lambs on the walls. We—the SNCC and SCLC staffers who gathered for these meetings— took our lead from them. Besides Worth Long and John Love and Avery

Williams, who had been on the job in Selma before the SCLC moved in, SNCC was represented in those meetings by Silas Norman, our Alabama project director, brother of the opera singer Jessye Norman, and one of the calmest, steadiest young men I'd ever met. He wasn't much older than I, but he carried himself like a man in his forties.

Besides Bevel, who was the SCLC's point man on this project, and whose presence smoothed a lot of the ruffles among our SNCC people because of his ties to us—no matter where he went or what he did, Jim Bevel would always be one of us—Dr. King's contingent in Selma included one of King's own staff members, a guy from Georgia named Hosea Williams.

I knew Hosea from the SCLC board meetings. He was a very colorful person, a solid, beefy man, a World War II veteran who had joined the SCLC in Savannah in the early '60s and had rapidly moved up in the organization. He had a strong personality. He was a guy who wanted to be out there, who wanted to push. He was a doer, a man who was impatient with meetings and discussions, who tired quickly of analysis. Dr. King used to joke regularly about people getting bogged down in the "paralysis of analysis." Hosea did not have that problem. Quite the opposite. He was always the one who would throw up his hands and say people were just talking something to death here. What are we going to *do?* That's what Hosea always wanted to know. He saw himself as one of Dr. King's field hands, getting out there on the scene, organizing the troops, preparing the way for Dr. King to follow.

That's essentially what everyone was doing during those first two weeks of January, preparing for King to come pull the trigger. Bevel was the spearhead, wearing that skullcap and his SNCC-style overalls, preaching as much as speaking, gathering the masses, getting the people of Selma and the surrounding counties—hundreds of people, *thousands*—ready to be out in front of that courthouse every day beginning the middle of that month.

The Dallas County Courthouse. Those green marble steps, thirteen of them, leading up to that twin set of glass doors, the entranceway into that fortress-like three-story stone building inside which sat the keys to the kingdom, the office of the voter registrar—this would be our stage for the coming months. How many months, no one could say.

But it began on the eighteenth, when Dr. King and I led four hundred men and women from Brown's Chapel nine blocks to the white downtown section of the city and up to the courthouse steps, where we were confronted by a crowd of various right-wing figures who had flown in from across the country to make a show of their own positions against us. Among them was the founder and chairman of the American Nazi Party, a man named George Lincoln Rockwell. He looked like just another young tough from one of the many mobs I'd faced during the past five years. Slim, dark-haired, in need of a shave on this particular day, he was a former U.S. Navy commander who tapped into the same reactionary fear and hatred that fuels the neo-Nazi hate groups of today. It was Rockwell's followers, dressed in Third Reich–style uniforms, who staged the "hate bus" trip during our 1961 Freedom Ride. Later, wearing swastika armbands and "White Power" T-shirts (Rockwell wrote a book with that title), they would attack black demonstrators in the streets of Chicago. Eventually, in 1967, Rockwell would be shot to death by one of his own followers outside a Laundromat near his home in Arlington, Virginia.

On this day, in mid-January 1965, he was in his element, making a large show of standing against us outside the courthouse. Sheriff Clark was there as well, wearing his officer's cap with gold military braids and an Eisenhower-style waist jacket, and carrying a swagger stick. He was playing his role to the hilt, the commander in chief of his own special army.

His deputies stood behind him as Clark stepped forward and told us we'd have to clear the sidewalk out front and form a line in an alley beside the building, which we did. And we waited.

And waited.

And waited.

What tends to be forgotten among the dramatic photographs and news accounts of the moments of violence that erupted during so many demonstrations like this in so many cities across the South during the civil rights era were the days and days of uneventful protest that took place outside these courtrooms and jails. People silently walked a picket line for hours on end, or sang freedom songs from dawn to dusk, or simply stood in line at a door they knew would not be opened, hour after hour, day after day. The patience and persistence it took to endure those countless hours of weary boredom in stifling heat or bone-chilling cold, in driving rain and wet, slushy snow, is as admirable as the bravery it took to face the billy clubs of those deputies.

Waiting. Keeping the pressure on by simply maintaining a relentless presence. That would become the rhythm of our days in Selma. The courthouse workers would see the black people coming, and the registrar would put an "OUT TO LUNCH" sign in the window, and that "lunch" would last all day. Many days the people would stand out there from morning to night and not a single one would get through those doors. Other days, one or two might be let in, maybe a handful, and they'd be given the literacy test, fail it and come out empty-handed.

This day, the first day, Monday, January 18, was like that. None of us left that alley. No one was let into the courthouse. No one was registered to vote. But the line had been drawn, and that was enough. At the end of that afternoon, Dr. King went to the Hotel Albert—the ornate redbrick building that Howard Zinn compared to a Venetian palace—walked into the lobby and stepped up to the registration desk to sign in as the hotel's first-ever black guest. A good-sized group of us stood with him to watch. Also looking on were some white men and women, who did not look too happy.

What happened next was a blur.

Out of the group of white people lunged a tall, gangly man. He said, "You're Martin Luther King," and then, as if just saying those words pushed a button inside him, he began kicking and punching at Dr. King. It was weird. Very spontaneous, as if the man was just seized by some impulse.

I responded with an impulse of my own. I'm not a physical person. I've never been in a fight in my life. I've been hit—many, many times—but I've never hit back. At that moment, though, something shot up in me, something protective, something instinctive, and I jumped in and put a bear hug on the man. I wasn't even thinking about whether he might have a weapon or anything like that. It was just a visceral reaction. I didn't strike the man, though I thought about it. I don't think I've ever come as close to hitting someone as I did at that moment. Maybe it was because Dr. King meant so much to me, I don't know, but that moment pushed me as close as I've ever been to the limits of my nonviolent commitments. It made me realize there *were* limits, which was a humbling reminder of how human we all are.

It was all over in a few seconds. Wilson Baker, who was on the scene, stepped in and pulled the man away. The guy turned out to be one of those right-wingers who had been over at the courthouse earlier in the day, a man named Jimmie George Robinson, who belonged to a group called the National States Rights Party. Nobody was particularly upset about it, not even Dr. King. It was just a bizarre little incident, but one that got a lot of publicity, especially after the attack that had happened up in Harlem several years earlier, where the woman had stabbed Dr. King at his book signing.

That was the only violence that first day. The next, however, Sheriff Clark got his turn. We marched again to the courthouse, again Clark ordered us into the alley, but this time we refused to go. He and his deputies then moved in to push us off the sidewalk. Mrs. Boynton apparently moved too slowly for his tastes, and the next thing you knew he was manhandling her, really shoving and roughing her up. I couldn't believe it. You could hear the news photographers' cameras clicking, and I knew that now it was starting, that cycle of violence and publicity and more violence and more publicity that would eventually, we hoped, push things to the point where something—ideally, the law—would have to be changed. Sure enough, the next morning's newspapers across the country carried photos and descriptions of Clark's attack on Mrs. Boynton. As *The New York Times* described it, the sheriff "grabbed her by the back of her collar and pushed her roughly for half a block into a patrol car." Mrs. Boynton was taken to jail that day, as were sixty-six other marchers.

The next morning, Wednesday, came my turn. Our plan that day was to approach the courthouse in waves, three large groups of us, one after the other. I was in the first group, and when we got there Clark told us we had to line up in the alley and enter through a side door. I responded that we wanted to enter through the front door.

"You have one minute to move," he told me. Then he began counting out loud, the way a parent does with a child.

"One ... two ... three ..." All the way to sixty.

Then he arrested us. The next group had arrived by then, and they were arrested as well. Baker had arrived by then as well, and he was not happy. The night before, in the wake of the incident with Mrs. Boynton, Baker had complained to reporters that Clark was "out of control." Now the two men stood chin to chin, arguing, almost shouting, in full view of us and the reporters. It was a real scene. This was no laughing matter, but inside you had to chuckle a little at how comic these two men looked.

Clark wound up arresting all three groups that day. He locked us in a fenced outdoor compound next to the jail—the jail was already full—and he kept us there until buses arrived to take us to a county work farm, which had been vacated by the convicts already there, who were put out on road gangs to make room for us. And so I settled in for another series of nights in a setting I knew well. The smell of honeysuckle from the surrounding forest. The buzz of cicadas filling the air at night. The chicken coop pens in which we were kept, sleeping on the floor with blankets we had to share because there were more of us than there was "bedding."

While I was there, the marching continued. Dr. King, who had left town after that first day to honor a speaking engagement—that was his routine with all these campaigns; he was much too busy, too much in demand by too many people, to settle in for the duration of any one demonstration—returned that Friday to join a group of more than a hundred Selma schoolteachers led by Fred Reese, the Voters League president and a teacher himself. This was a significant demonstration because in the past teachers had been reluctant to take part in our protests. They were generally conservative, careful, wary of confrontation. They were also, however, among the upper crust of the local black community. They were among the best-paid and certainly the best-educated black professional men and women in every city. For *them* to be kept from voting was clearly outrageous. For them to step forward and face arrest in Selma was a big step forward for all of us. Their arrest that day inspired other groups of professionals in the city to stage their own marches in the days to come. The undertakers. The beauticians. It was beautiful.

The following Monday, a week after the demonstrations had begun, I was out of jail and on the line again, and again I watched Sheriff Clark's temper play right into our hands. Again it was a woman he confronted, and again the press delivered a blow-by-blow account of the fight.

And it *was* a fight—two heavyweights throwing punches at each other. One was Clark and the other was a large fifty-three-year-old woman named Annie Lee Cooper. Mrs. Cooper worked as a maid at the Torch Motel—the only black hotel in town. I'd met her several times in the past, and I liked her. She was up-front, pleasant and, as she showed on this particular day, absolutely fearless.

We were, as usual, lined up on the courthouse steps—the local men and women waiting to register and people like me and Hosea and other SNCC and SCLC people who were there to support and make sure these marchers had all that they needed. Clark and his deputies, as usual, were there to make sure they did not. As Clark's men moved in and began pushing people aside, Mrs. Cooper—all 235 pounds of her— confronted him.

"Ain't nobody scared around here," she said.

Clark wasn't one to stand for backtalk, especially from a woman. He shoved Mrs. Cooper, hard. But not hard enough. She came right back and punched the sheriff in the head, sending him reeling.

Three deputies then grabbed Mrs. Cooper and wrestled her to the ground, where she kept flailing and kicking even as they held her down. Clark looked out of his mind with anger. He had his billy club out and looked as if he was about to hit her with it. Then he hesitated. You could see his mind clicking in, his realization that everyone was watching. Us. The reporters. The photographers. Everyone.

What happened next was described in the following day's *New York Times* by reporter John Herbers:

> "I wish you would hit me, you scum," she snapped at the sheriff. He
> then brought his billyclub down on her head with a whack that was
> heard throughout the crowd gathered in the street.

It took two pairs of handcuffs to hold Mrs. Cooper as she was taken away to jail, blood dripping from a wound over her right eye. Photos of that, too, appeared across the country the next day.

I left several days later for the West Coast to raise some badly needed money for SNCC. Our involvement in Selma was minimal—except for our local field staffers already working there, I was the only one taking part in the campaign on a regular basis. As far as most SNCC people were concerned, this was an SCLC show, so they kept their distance.

While I was gone, Dr. King was arrested—by Baker, who peaceably inter-cepted King and the group he was marching with before they reached the courthouse and a confrontation with Clark. By now Clark had received rein-forcements with the arrival of nearly fifty Alabama state troopers under the command of George Wallace's state public safety director, Colonel Al Lingo. The manpower was needed, with literally hundreds of marchers now being arrested each day. As Bevel had done in Birmingham, the SCLC mobilized schoolchildren in Selma, and now they began marching as well. The same day Dr. King and the 250 men and women walking with him were taken to jail, 500 Selma schoolchildren, some carrying protest signs written in crayon, were arrested outside the county courthouse.

That was Monday, February 1. The next day, several hundred more children were arrested. The day after that came three hundred more, who sang "Ain't gonna let Jim Clark turn me around…" as they were taken off to jail.

Then came Thursday, and the arrival of Malcolm X.

Malcolm had promised Don Harris and me during our meeting in Africa that he would come south to visit "our" movement. Soon after our return from that trip, we—SNCC—sent a group of teenage students from Mississippi up to Harlem to meet with Malcolm, who told them essentially the same thing he had said to Don and me, that this was a *world* struggle we were engaged in here, not just an American struggle. "It is important for you to know," he told those children, "that when you're in Mississippi, you're not alone."

Now he kept his promise to come south himself. While I was out on the West Coast, Jim Forman contacted Malcolm in New York and arranged for him to come to Tuskegee to speak to the students at Tuskegee Institute. Because Selma was not far, Malcolm decided to make a side trip there, arriving Thursday, February 4, with a group that included Fred Shuttlesworth and Coretta King, sitting in for her husband, who was behind bars in the Selma city jail.

They all spoke that day—Shuttlesworth, Mrs. King, and Malcolm—at a rally at Brown's Chapel. I heard later that Malcolm was received politely though not enthusiastically by the audience of local Selmans. That didn't surprise me. These were Southern black people, used to the singsong preacherlike cadence and the God-and-heaven context of Southern black speakers. Malcolm was much more strident, much more fiery and much more political than what they were used to. Still, he struck a chord, including his use of the phrase "by any means necessary," referring to our struggle in the South to gain the right to vote.

At a press conference later that day, he elaborated:

I think that the people in this part of the world would do well to listen to Dr. Martin Luther King and give him what he's asking for and give it to him fast, before some other factions come along and try to do it another way. . . .

Those words were meant as a threat, and even as Malcolm X spoke them they were being taken to heart by SNCC sympathizers in cities across the North. A loose web of demonstrators and protestors called the Friends of SNCC had begun mobilizing that month in New York and Chicago and Washington, staging sit-ins at federal buildings to protest the lack of U.S. government intervention in Selma. They even staged a sit-in at the White House. These weren't actual SNCC members, and we often knew nothing about their actions until we read about them in the newspapers like everyone else. But as with our own staff members, we were happy to have these people join the cause, regardless of their personal politics or background. Some of them went so far as to help raise money, and we welcomed that as well. My only concern was when their methods violated our commitment to nonviolence. And that was beginning to happen that February. One clash at New York City's federal courthouse between fifteen SNCC sympathizers and the U.S. marshals who tried to block them from sitting in resulted in a fistfight described in *The New York Times*: "Hard punches were thrown and found their marks on both sides."

That bothered me a lot. This was just one more sign of the growing sense of impatience and militancy spreading throughout the movement, especially within SNCC. It did not bode well.

The day after Malcolm X spoke in Selma, I flew back from California. That same day—Friday, February 5—a contingent of fifteen U.S. congressmen, all liberals, of course, arrived from Washington to get a firsthand look at what was going on. Organized by Michigan's Charles Diggs (who had come south ten years earlier to watch the Emmett Till trial) and John Conyers, who like Diggs was black and a Democrat, the group was sprinkled with politicians whose reputations were already large but whose names would become even more well known in the decades to come: John Lindsay and Ed Koch of New York, both of whom would become mayors of New York City; Charles Mathias from Maryland; Ogden Reid from New York and Augustus Hawkins from California; and U.S. Assistant Attorney General Ramsey Clark, who would eventually step forward as one of the earliest and foremost opponents of U.S. involvement in the war in Vietnam.

They all came for a tour of Selma, which I joined and which Dr. King, who was released from jail that day, also took part in. While behind bars, King had written a "Letter from the Selma Jail," intended to arouse the same interest in a federal voting rights bill that his "Letter from Birmingham Jail" had inspired for the civil rights act. This new letter—published as an SCLC ad in *The New York Times*—aroused nowhere near the same interest as the one from Birmingham, but it did prompt President Johnson to announce at a news conference that week that "all of us should be concerned with the efforts of our fellow Americans to register to vote in Alabama."

Things were clearly stirring in Washington. But the President's words fell on deaf ears in Selma. The day those congressmen came to visit, Sheriff Clark arrested some five hundred more marchers at the courthouse. Several days later he put the city in national headlines again by arresting more than 160 teenagers and sending them on a forced run of more than two miles out into the countryside. His deputies used clubs and cattle prods to keep those kids going. "March, dammit, *march!*" one officer reportedly yelled. "You want to march so bad, now you can march. Let's *go!*" One fifteen-year-old boy said to a guard, "God sees you," and the deputy answered by clubbing him in the mouth. By the time they returned, several kids had lumps and cuts on their heads, and a few had been burned by cattle prods. One nine-year-old boy stood with tears streaming down his face—he had made the march barefoot.

I thought I had seen everything, but this was disgusting. I wrote a statement that afternoon, which was rushed to radio and newspaper reporters as soon as we could get it typed up. I still have that statement, hand-scrawled on notepaper:

> Sheriff Jim Clark proved today beyond a shadow of a doubt that he is basically no different from a Gestapo officer during the Fascist slaughter of the Jews....
>
> This is but one more example of the inhuman, animal-like treatment of the Negro people of Selma, Alabama. This nation has always come to the aid of people in foreign lands who are gripped by a reign of tyranny. Can this nation do less for the people of Selma?

Smitherman and Baker were just about beside themselves, and they weren't alone. A large number of white Selma residents were becoming embarrassed and concerned over the sheriff's actions. They weren't eager to give black people the right to vote, but they were certain there were more "civilized" ways of keeping us off the rolls. Unlike Birmingham, where an entire city essentially stood united against the black community, this was basically Sheriff Clark and his supporters against us, with the rest of Selma, including the mayor and the public safety director, looking on in distress.

It was important for us to hold the moral high ground, to maintain the principles of nonviolent action and response no matter what. Demonstrators may have begun fighting back elsewhere, some under the name of SNCC, but in Selma we were determined to stay the course that had gotten the movement this far. The second week of that February, when Sheriff Clark checked into the local hospital suffering from exhaustion—this thing was taking its toll on him as well—a group of black Selma schoolchildren went to the hospital and prayed outside for his recovery. They urged him to "Get well soon, in mind as in body," as one sign put it. Other signs read FREEDOM NOW. Clark was not moved. When he was released from the hospital, he wore a one-word message of his own on a badge pinned to his lapel: NEVER.

That Tuesday, February 16, Clark was back in front of the courthouse, standing with his deputies in the chilly rain as twenty-five of us, including C. T. Vivian, approached. The Reverend Vivian had become increasingly active in the movement since our Nashville days, rising to a top position in the SCLC. He was there with us on the Freedom Rides, he did time in Parchman, he was in Birmingham in '63, and Mississippi in '64, and now he was here.

When Clark stepped in front of our group that day, it was Vivian who squared off against him. He told the sheriff and his deputies that they reminded him of Nazis. "You're racists the same way Hitler was a racist!" he said, loud enough for the reporters to get every word. He then dared Clark to hit him. Even though deputies stepped in to try to stop him, the sheriff took the bait. He reached out and slammed his fist into Vivian's mouth, knocking him down the steps. He hit Vivian so hard he broke a finger in his hand. Vivian was then arrested.

That set up a march two days later up the road from Selma in the town of Marion, in neighboring Perry County. The people there had been demonstrating and being arrested by the hundreds, just as the Selmans had. On this night they held a rally protesting the arrest of an SCLC worker named James Orange. Vivian had been released from jail that day, and the people of Marion asked him and an SCLC staffer named Willie Bolden to come speak at their rally. By the time Vivian's speech was done, the people were eager to march, 450 of them, from their tiny local church—Zion Methodist—to the city jail, where they intended to sing outside Orange's cell. A half dozen or so reporters walked along with them, including John Herbers from *The New York Times* and NBC's Richard Valeriani.

This was a dangerous march, different because it took place at nighttime. We rarely staged marches at night. Too many things could happen. Too many things could not be seen.

The group had hardly stepped away from the church before they were stopped by the local police chief and state troopers. Jim Clark and some of his men were there as well. The marchers were instructed to turn around. One of them, a black farmer named James Dobynes, knelt and began praying.

Suddenly the streetlights went out. As if on cue, the police and troopers began beating the marchers while a crowd of white onlookers leaped on the press, spraying the TV camera lenses with paint and assaulting the reporters. Valeriani's head was gashed. A UPI reporter's camera was grabbed and smashed while he was beaten to the ground.

It was mayhem. The marchers broke ranks and tried fleeing back through the darkness to the church. There was screaming and blood on the pavement

from head wounds. One young black man, a twenty-six-year-old Army veteran named Jimmie Lee Jackson, veered off and ran with his grandfather, who
had been hit in the head, to a nearby cafe, a place called Mack's. A group of
state troopers followed them in, and a fight broke out. Jackson's mother was
hit and Jackson, pushing his way into the middle of it, was shot in the stomach. He staggered from the building, then collapsed in the street, where he lay
for half an hour before the local police picked him up and took him to the
county infirmary. Late that night he was transferred to the hospital in Selma,
where he was listed as critically wounded.

I got word the next morning, Friday, in Atlanta. This was serious. If Jimmie Lee Jackson died, no one could say what might happen. I left that day for
a meeting down in Americus and kept the radio on all the way, listening for
updates on Jimmie Lee's condition. What I heard instead was a statement
from Governor Wallace, banning all nighttime marches in Alabama and denouncing the incident in Marion as a setup staged by "professional agitators
with pro-communist affiliations."

Two days later, Sunday the twenty-first—my birthday—Jimmie Lee Jackson was still clinging to life in that Selma hospital. I was driving back late that
day from Americus to Atlanta with Cleve Sellers, the radio on again, when a
bulletin came over the air that took my breath away.

Malcolm X had been shot dead in New York, gunned down by assassins
in a ballroom in Harlem, in full view of his congregation.

I couldn't believe it. Malcolm had been killed, by his own people, as it
turned out, by Black Muslims. I had my differences with him, of course, but
there was no question that he had come to articulate better than anyone else
on the scene—including Dr. King—the bitterness and frustration of black
Americans. I was encouraged by the fact that Malcolm had begun taking that
frustration and rage into a broader perspective of hope and the future, into a
worldview, linking the struggle for human rights in Africa and other nations to
the movement here. He had begun looking beyond issues of race to issues of
class, and those ideas were intriguing and appealing. Malcolm, like the movement, was moving toward new horizons.

And now he was dead. That was deeply disturbing to me. When I flew up
with Cleve to the funeral later that week, I was struck by the severity, the
solemnity, the *silence* of the occasion. Ossie Davis, the actor, delivered the eulogy, and you really could just about hear a pin drop. No one showed any
emotions. No crying. No displays of grief, such as we always had at Southern
funerals. No singing. Everyone held their feelings in. It was very stoic. Very
grim.

Grim would describe the mood in Selma that week as well, with Jimmie
Lee Jackson lying close to death. We had meetings every day, at tables pulled

together in Clay & Liston's restaurant, or over in the Walker's Cafe, or in someone's home. No one was quite sure what to do next. The SCLC people—Hosea, Bevel and Young, mainly—were essentially calling the shots while we, the SNCC representatives—Worth Long, Silas Norman, John Love, and I—listened and didn't say much. I was in a strange position, caught between the cold distance of my SNCC colleagues, who had continued to grow increasingly resentful of the presence of King and his people, and my own connections with the SCLC. Overriding everything, of course, were my concerns about the people of Selma, many of whom were sitting in jail at that moment. I had come to know them well, especially the families in the Carver housing project, where I stayed many, many nights, in one household or another.

That's where most of our SNCC people stayed, in Carver. We had a Freedom House that we rented down a dirt road and across the tracks from Carver, but it didn't have a lot of space. It was a small shack, really, with several bunk beds, a shower and a refrigerator. It was good for emergencies, but if we had any time to plan, we preferred staying with one of the families in the community. That was part of our philosophy of being with the people, of bonding, and I loved that aspect of the experience, the spontaneity of it, the human connection. You'd have a meeting or a rally and you didn't know where you'd be spending the night when it began. At the end, as people were leaving, someone would walk up and say, "You can stay with me" or "My mother said it's okay for you all to stay with us." It was very informal, very touching.

I was staying in one of those apartments in Carver when word came Friday, February 26, that Jimmie Lee Jackson had died. I knew it was only a matter of time until we got that news, but nonetheless it was very emotional. A lot of people had suffered during the previous two months. A lot of people had been beaten and hurt and jailed. But no one had died. Not until now.

The funeral was extremely emotional, four hundred people—most of whom had been in that march the night Jimmie Lee was shot—squeezed into the tiny church in Marion, with six hundred more standing outside in the rain.

Dr. King spoke. Then Bevel. And then we all gathered and walked behind the hearse from the church to the cemetery, down a narrow dirt road turned to mud by the rain. Tree branches bent over us, hanging low with the weight of the rain on their leaves. It was overwhelmingly dreary. Very sad.

And it was during that procession that Bevel suggested we take Jimmie Lee's body to Montgomery. Walk the entire fifty-four miles from Selma and lay this young man's casket on the capitol steps. Confront the governor. Confront the state of Alabama. Give them something they couldn't turn their heads away from.

They went ahead and buried Jimmie Lee Jackson that day, but Bevel's idea of a march on Montgomery caught fire. The next four days our meetings were dominated by discussions of this march. The SCLC people, including Dr. King, were all for it. The SNCC people, especially Forman, were dead set against it. The feeling was that such a march would do more for King than it would for Selma. I disagreed. I knew the feelings that were out there on the streets. The people of Selma were hurting. They were angry. They needed to march. It didn't matter to me who led it. They *needed* to march.

This was one of the most difficult situations I'd had to deal with since becoming chairman of SNCC. The struggle over my speech at the March on Washington was different. There I had the support of my SNCC colleagues. Forman and Cox were right by my side. Here I was alone. Personally I might have favored this march, but as chairman of SNCC I had an obligation to represent the sentiments and decisions of my brothers and sisters in the organization. So when Bevel formally announced on March 3 that there would be a "massive" march that Sunday from Selma to Montgomery, a march led by Dr. King, Forman drafted a letter to King from SNCC, a letter that carried my signature at the bottom:

> We strongly believe that the objectives of the march do not justify the
> dangers . . . consequently the Student Nonviolent Coordinating Com-
> mittee will only live up to those minimal commitments . . . to provide
> radios and cars, doctors and nurses, and nothing beyond that.

That was a SNCC letter, not a John Lewis letter. It was settled that SNCC was going to have next to nothing to do with this march. As for me, well, one way or another, I intended to be there. During the next three days, while Governor Wallace held summit sessions with his staff in Montgomery to figure out how they should respond to this march—he finally slammed his fist on a table and pronounced, "I'm not gonna have a bunch of niggers walking along a highway in this state as long as I'm governor"—I was in a kind of limbo, not really a part of the SCLC group that was mapping out the details for this event, and not really with my SNCC colleagues either, who were setting themselves apart.

That Saturday, the day before the march would begin, a contingent of seventy white people, all Alabamians, all sympathetic to our cause, marched to the courthouse in Selma. They were led by a minister from Birmingham named Joseph Ellwanger, who was a Selma native and who chaired a group called the Concerned White Citizens of Alabama. They were taunted and attacked by a crowd of white Selmans, who sang "Dixie" while Ellwanger spoke. Ellwanger's group responded by singing "America the Beautiful." And a small group of local black men and women looking on broke out with a stanza of "We Shall Overcome."

You couldn't have scripted a scene that summed up the civil rights situation in the South any better than that.

As that scene was unfolding, I was four hours away, in Atlanta, in a back room of a restaurant called Frazier Cafe Society, coming to a decision that would change the course of my life.

Frazier's was a small soul food place, one of two favorite gathering spots in Atlanta for people involved in the movement. The other was a place called Paschal's. The SCLC people preferred Paschal's, which offered a big meeting room, while Frazier's was the main SNCC hangout—smaller and more intimate, with some of the best vegetable dishes you'd find anyplace in the South: early peas, green beans, fresh corn, turnips, collard greens…and yams that were out of this world. We'd often go there to eat, then move down to the basement for a meeting. Which is where we were that Saturday afternoon, talking hot and heavy about Selma.

There were about a dozen of us, primarily the executive committee. Forman, Marion Barry, Courtland Cox, Ivanhoe Donaldson, Ruby Doris Robinson and Julian were all there, along with Bob Mants, Silas Norman and Wilson Brown.

The decision had been made that SNCC would set itself apart from this march. But that decision could still be changed. This thing was going to be big, no question about it. It was going to attract a lot of attention. Did we really want to stand on the sidelines and not be a part of it?

That was one question. But there were so many others, such as the question of resources. Could we afford this in terms of manpower and money? And who would reap the benefits? King and the SCLC? And what about the danger? People could get hurt here, and where would King and his people be when that happened? Who would be left holding the bag?

All these questions and more flew around the room as that afternoon turned to night. After several hours it was clear that I was the only one arguing for joining this march. I felt that it was up to the people of Selma to decide whether to march or not, and we needed to support them, whatever their decision. If they wanted to march, we should march *with* them. This wasn't about us or our differences with the SCLC. It was about *them,* the people of Selma. They were the reason we had come in the first place. We had a moral obligation, a mission, to cast our lot with these people, wherever they wanted to go, whatever they wanted to do.

They were going to march, I said, and so it was just like the situation that morning of the March on Washington, when our leadership group had emerged from the Capitol to see that ocean of humanity heading to the Lincoln Memorial. "There go my people. Let me catch up with them." That had been my feeling in D.C., and that was my feeling now. I couldn't imagine living with myself if the people of Selma had marched and I had not been with them. If something was going to happen, I wanted to be there when it did.

It was getting close to midnight when I had my final say.

"I'm a native Alabamian," I told the group. "I grew up in Alabama. I feel a deep kinship with the people there on a lot of levels. You know I've been to Selma many, many times. I've been arrested there. I've been jailed there. If these people want to march, I'm going to march with them. You decide what you want to do, but I'm going to march."

And that was that. The only decision left to make was in what capacity I would march. It was decided that I would take part, but not as a member of SNCC. I would march simply as John Lewis.

That hurt me. I never imagined that my own organization, SNCC, would ever step aside and tell me to walk alone. It hurt personally, and it hurt in an even deeper sense to know that they were abandoning these people, the people of Selma. For the first time since I had become a part of the movement I was walking alone, in a sense. I would be walking with the people, but *my* people—the people of SNCC—would not be with me. The fact that those two could ever be separated—the people and SNCC— was something I had never imagined.

The meeting broke up just past midnight. Bob Mants and Wilson Brown and I headed for Wilson's car, a white Dodge, and took off for Selma, four hours away. We arrived close to dawn and went straight to the SNCC Freedom House for a few hours of sleep. It was close to noon when we woke up. I crawled out of my sleeping bag, took a shower, put on my clothes and threw a few things in my green Army backpack—an apple, an orange, a toothbrush, toothpaste, a couple of books.

And then it was time to go.

Part VI

GOING DOWN

16 / BLOODY SUNDAY

I've been back to Selma many times since that fateful Sunday afternoon. Normally I'm with a large crowd, gathered for one anniversary or another of that '65 march. The town is alive with noise and excitement on such days, but the rest of the time it remains today what it was back then: a sleepy, dying little Southern community. Many of the storefronts along its downtown Broad Street are boarded up, with handwritten FOR LEASE signs taped on the windows. The businesses that are left—Rexall Drugs, the El Ranchero cafe, Walter Craig Sportsman's Headquarters ("TONS OF GUNS" is its slogan)—point more to the past than they do to the future.

The Dallas County Courthouse is still there, its steps that same pale green, though the building itself has now been painted the color of cream. Brown's Chapel, of course, still stands as well, with the same arched whitewashed ceiling inside, the same rows of folding, theater-style seats up in its U-shaped balcony.

There's a monument in front of the church, a bust of Dr. King, which, on my most recent visit there, was coated with a thin dusting of snow. The unlikely snowfall had brought out children by the dozen in the dirt yards of the Carver projects, across the street from the church. They were hooting and hollering, trying valiantly to make snowmen out of the sprinkling of powder that lay on the ground. A couple of them were having a snowball fight, hiding from one another behind the streetside markers that commemorate the history that was written here in 1965.

None of those children were alive back then, but most of them know better than any historian the details of what happened on March 7 of that year. They've heard the story so many times, from parents and grandparents, from neighbors and friends—from the people who were there.

How could anyone ever forget a day like that?

It was brisk and breezy, a few puffs of purplish clouds scattered across the clear blue sky. By the time I arrived at Brown's Chapel, about half past noon, there were already close to five hundred marchers gathered on the ballfield and basketball courts beside and beyond the church. Some of the SCLC staffers were holding impromptu training sessions, teaching the people how to kneel and protect their bodies if attacked.

Hosea and Bevel were off to the side, huddled with Andy Young, the three of them talking animatedly, as if something was wrong. And there was something wrong. Dr. King, it turned out, had decided late the day before to postpone the march until Monday. He'd missed too many preaching commitments at his church in Atlanta, he explained. He needed to deliver his sermon that weekend. The march from Selma, he decided, would have to wait a day. That was the message Andy Young had been sent to deliver.

Hosea was clearly upset. So was Bevel. The people were here, and they were ready. There was no way to turn them back home now.

This was the first I'd heard of this news. Later I would learn that there were other factors that had affected Dr. King's decision, the most serious being a death threat, of which there had been several during the previous two months. Dr. King was initially leaning toward still coming, but his staff talked him out of it.

Or so the story goes. There is still disagreement and speculation today among many people about King's decision not to march that day. There is still resentment among a lot of people, especially SNCC members, who saw this as nothing but abandonment, a cop-out.

I don't feel that way. First of all, I can't imagine anyone questioning the courage of Martin Luther King Jr. Beyond that, in terms of the specific circumstances of that Sunday, no one in SNCC was in any position to criticize Dr. King. As far as I was concerned, they had lost the right to pass judgment of any kind on this march the moment they decided not to take part in it.

After seeing that the march could not be stopped, Andy Young went inside the church and called Dr. King in Atlanta. They talked over the situation, and King instructed Andy to choose one among them—Andy, Hosea or Bevel—to join me as co-leader of the march. The other two would remain behind to take care of things in case there was trouble.

Andy returned with that news, and the three of them proceeded to flip coins to see who would join me. The odd man would march; the other two would stay.

The odd man turned out to be Hosea, and so that little slice of history was settled—by the flip of a quarter.

It was mid-afternoon now, and time to assemble. A team of doctors and nurses from a group called the Medical Committee for Human Rights had arrived the day before on a flight from New York and set up a makeshift clinic in the small parsonage beside the church. We expected a confrontation. We knew Sheriff Clark had issued yet another call the evening before for even more deputies. Mass arrests would probably be made. There might be injuries. Most likely, we would be stopped at the edge of the city limits, arrested and maybe roughed up a little bit. We did not expect anything worse than that.

And we did *not* expect to march all the way to Montgomery. No one knew for sure, until the last minute, if the march would even take place. There had been a measure of planning, but nowhere near the preparations and logistics necessary to move that many people in an orderly manner down fifty-four miles of highway, a distance that would take about five days for a group that size to cover.

Many of the men and women gathered on that ballfield had come straight from church. They were still wearing their Sunday outfits. Some of the women had on high heels. I had on a suit and tie, a light tan raincoat, dress shoes and my backpack. I was no more ready to hike half a hundred miles than anyone else. Like everyone around me, I was basically playing it by ear. None of us had thought much further ahead than that afternoon. Anything that happened beyond that—if we were allowed to go on, if this march did indeed go all the way to Montgomery—we figured we would take care of as we went along. The main thing was that we *do* it, that we march.

It was close to 4 P.M. when Andy, Hosea, Bevel and I gathered the marchers around us. A dozen or so reporters were there as well. I read a short statement aloud for the benefit of the press, explaining why we were marching today. Then we all knelt to one knee and bowed our heads as Andy delivered a prayer.

And then we set out, nearly six hundred of us, including a white SCLC staffer named Al Lingo—the same name as the commander of Alabama's state troopers.

We walked two abreast, in a pair of lines that stretched for several blocks. Hosea and I led the way. Albert Turner, an SCLC leader in Perry County, and Bob Mants were right behind us—Bob insisted on marching because I was marching; he told me he wanted to be there to "protect" me in case something happened.

Marie Foster and Amelia Boynton were next in line, and behind them, stretching as far as I could see, walked an army of teenagers, teachers, undertakers, beauticians—many of the same Selma people who had stood for weeks, months, *years,* in front of that courthouse.

At the far end, bringing up the rear, rolled four slow-moving ambulances.

I can't count the number of marches I have participated in in my lifetime, but there was something peculiar about this one. It was more than disciplined. It was somber and subdued, almost like a funeral procession. No one was jostling or pushing to get to the front, as often happened with these things. I don't know if there was a feeling that something was going to happen, or if the people simply sensed that this was a special procession, a "leaderless" march. There were no big names up front, no celebrities. This was just plain folks moving through the streets of Selma.

There was a little bit of a crowd looking on as we set out down the red sand of Sylvan Street, through the black section of town. There was some cheering and singing from those onlookers and from a few of the marchers, but then, as we turned right along Water Street, out of the black neighborhood now, the mood changed. There was no singing, no shouting—just the sound of scuffling feet. There was something holy about it, as if we were walking down a sacred path. It reminded me of Gandhi's march to the sea. Dr. King used to say there is nothing more powerful than the rhythm of marching feet, and that was what this was, the marching feet of a determined people. That was the only sound you could hear.

Down Water Street we went, turning right and walking along the river until we reached the base of the bridge, the Edmund Pettus Bridge.

There was a small posse of armed white men there, gathered in front of the *Selma Times-Journal* building. They had hard hats on their heads and clubs in their hands. Some of them were smirking. Not one said a word. I didn't think too much of them as we walked past. I'd seen men like that so many times.

As we turned onto the bridge, we were careful to stay on the narrow sidewalk. The road had been closed to traffic, but we still stayed on the walkway, which was barely wide enough for two people.

I noticed how steep it was as we climbed toward the steel canopy at the top of the arched bridge. It was too steep to see the other side. I looked down at the river and saw how still it was, still and brown. The surface of the water was stirred just a bit by the late-afternoon breeze. I noticed my trench coat was riffling a little from that same small wind.

When we reached the crest of the bridge, I stopped dead still.

So did Hosea.

There, facing us at the bottom of the other side, stood a sea of blue-helmeted, blue-uniformed Alabama state troopers, line after line of them, dozens of battle-ready lawmen stretched from one side of U.S. Highway 80 to the other.

Behind them were several dozen more armed men—Sheriff Clark's posse—some on horseback, all wearing khaki clothing, many carrying clubs the size of baseball bats.

On one side of the road I could see a crowd of about a hundred whites, laughing and hollering, waving Confederate flags. Beyond them, at a safe distance, stood a small, silent group of black people.

I could see a crowd of newsmen and reporters gathered in the parking lot of a Pontiac dealership. And I could see a line of parked police and state trooper vehicles. I didn't know it at the time, but Clark and Lingo were in one of those cars.

It was a drop of one hundred feet from the top of that bridge to the river below. Hosea glanced down at the muddy water and said, "Can you swim?"

"No," I answered.

"Well," he said, with a tiny half smile, "neither can I."

"But," he added, lifting his head and looking straight ahead, "we might have to."

Then we moved forward. The only sounds were our footsteps on the bridge and the snorting of a horse ahead of us.

I noticed several troopers slipping gas masks over their faces as we approached.

At the bottom of the bridge, while we were still about fifty feet from the troopers, the officer in charge, a Major John Cloud, stepped forward, holding a small bullhorn up to his mouth.

Hosea and I stopped, which brought the others to a standstill.

"*This is an unlawful assembly,*" Cloud pronounced. "*Your march is not conducive to the public safety. You are ordered to disperse and go back to your church or to your homes.*"

"May we have a word with the major?" asked Hosea.

"*There is no word to be had,*" answered Cloud.

Hosea asked the same question again, and got the same response.

Then Cloud issued a warning: "*You have two minutes to turn around and go back to your church.*"

I wasn't about to turn around. We were there. We were not going to run. We couldn't turn and go back even if we wanted to. There were too many people.

We could have gone forward, marching right into the teeth of those troopers. But that would have been too aggressive, I thought, too provocative. God knew what might have happened if we had done that. These people were ready to be arrested, but I didn't want anyone to get hurt.

We couldn't go forward. We couldn't go back. There was only one option left that I could see.

"We should kneel and pray," I said to Hosea.

He nodded.

We turned and passed the word back to begin bowing down in a prayerful manner.

But that word didn't get far. It didn't have time. One minute after he had issued his warning—I know this because I was careful to check my watch—Major Cloud issued an order to his troopers.

"*Troopers,*" he barked. "*Advance!*"

And then all hell broke loose.

The troopers and possemen swept forward as one, like a human wave, a blur of blue shirts and billy clubs and bullwhips. We had no chance to turn and retreat. There were six hundred people behind us, bridge railings to either side and the river below.

I remember how vivid the sounds were as the troopers rushed toward us—the clunk of the troopers' heavy boots, the whoops of rebel yells from the white onlookers, the clip-clop of horses' hooves hitting the hard asphalt of the highway, the voice of a woman shouting, "Get 'em! *Get* the niggers!"

And then they were upon us. The first of the troopers came over me, a large, husky man. Without a word, he swung his club against the left side of my head. I didn't feel any pain, just the thud of the blow, and my legs giving way. I raised an arm—a reflex motion—as I curled up in the "prayer for protection" position. And then the same trooper hit me again. And everything started to spin.

I heard something that sounded like gunshots. And then a cloud of smoke rose all around us.

Tear gas.

I'd never experienced tear gas before. This, I would learn later, was a particularly toxic form called C-4, made to induce nausea.

I began choking, coughing. I couldn't get air into my lungs. I felt as if I was taking my last breath. If there was ever a time in my life for me to panic, it should have been then. But I didn't. I remember how strangely calm I felt as I thought, This is it. People are going to die here. *I'm* going to die here.

I really felt that I saw death at that moment, that I looked it right in its face. And it felt strangely soothing. I had a feeling that it would be so easy to just lie down there, just lie down and let it take me away.

That was the way those first few seconds looked from where I stood—and lay. Here is how Roy Reed, a reporter for *The New York Times,* described what he saw:

> The troopers rushed forward, their blue uniforms and white helmets blurring into a flying wedge as they moved.

The wedge moved with such force that it seemed almost to pass over the waiting column instead of through it.

The first 10 or 20 Negroes were swept to the ground screaming, arms and legs flying, and packs and bags went skittering across the grassy divider strip and on to the pavement on both sides.

Those still on their feet retreated.

The troopers continued pushing, using both the force of their bodies and the prodding of their nightsticks.

A cheer went up from the white spectators lining the south side of the highway.

The mounted possemen spurred their horses and rode at a run into the retreating mass. The Negroes cried out as they crowded together for protection, and the whites on the sidelines whooped and cheered.

The Negroes paused in their retreat for perhaps a minute, still screaming and huddling together.

Suddenly there was a report like a gunshot and a grey cloud spewed over the troopers and the Negroes.

"Tear gas!" someone yelled.

The cloud began covering the highway. Newsmen, who were confined by four troopers to a corner 100 yards away, began to lose sight of the action.

But before the cloud finally hid it all, there were several seconds of unobstructed view. Fifteen or twenty nightsticks could be seen through the gas, flailing at the heads of the marchers.

The Negroes broke and ran. Scores of them streamed across the parking lot of the Selma Tractor Company. Troopers and possemen, mounted and unmounted, went after them.

I was bleeding badly. My head was now exploding with pain. That brief, sweet sense of just wanting to lie there was gone. I needed to get up. I'd faded out for I don't know how long, but now I was tuned back in.

There was mayhem all around me. I could see a young kid—a teenaged boy—sitting on the ground with a gaping cut in his head, the blood just gushing out. Several women, including Mrs. Boynton, were lying on the pavement and the grass median. People were weeping. Some were vomiting from the tear gas. Men on horses were moving in all directions, purposely riding over the top of fallen people, bringing their animals' hooves down on shoulders, stomachs and legs.

The mob of white onlookers had joined in now, jumping cameramen and reporters. One man filming the action was knocked down and his camera was taken away. The man turned out to be an FBI agent, and the three men who attacked him were later arrested. One of them was Jimmie George Robinson, the man who had attacked Dr. King at the Hotel Albert.

I was up now and moving, back across the bridge, with troopers and possemen and other retreating marchers all around me. At the other end of the bridge, we had to push through the possemen we'd passed outside the *Selma Times-Journal* building.

"Please, *no,*" I could hear one woman scream.

"God, we're being *killed!*" cried another.

With nightsticks and whips—one posseman had a rubber hose wrapped with barbed wire—Sheriff Clark's "deputies" chased us all the way back into the Carver project and up to the front of Brown's Chapel, where we tried getting as many people as we could inside the church to safety. I don't even recall how I made it that far, how I got from the bridge to the church, but I did.

A United Press International reporter gave this account of that segment of the attack:

> The troopers and possemen, under Gov. George C. Wallace's orders to stop the Negroes' "Walk for Freedom" from Selma to Montgomery, chased the screaming, bleeding marchers nearly a mile back to their church, clubbing them as they ran.
>
> Ambulances screamed in relays between Good Samaritan Hospital and Brown's Chapel Church, carrying hysterical men, women and children suffering head wounds and tear gas burns.

Even then, the possemen and troopers, 150 of them, including Clark himself, kept attacking, beating anyone who remained on the street. Some of the marchers fought back now, with men and boys emerging from the Carver homes with bottles and bricks in their hands, heaving them at the troopers, then retreating for more. It was a scene that's been replayed so many times in so many places—in Belfast, in Jerusalem, in Beijing. Angry, desperate people hurling whatever they can at the symbols of authority, their hopeless fury much more powerful than the futile bottles and bricks in their hands.

I was inside the church, which was awash with sounds of groaning and weeping. And singing and crying. Mothers shouting out for their children. Children screaming for their mothers and brothers and sisters. So much confusion and fear and anger all erupting at the same time.

Further up Sylvan Street, the troopers chased other marchers who had fled into the First Baptist Church. A teenaged boy, struggling with the possemen, was thrown through a church window there.

Finally Wilson Baker arrived and persuaded Clark and his men to back off to a block away, where they remained, breathing heavily and awaiting further orders.

A crowd of Selma's black men and women had collected in front of the church by now, with SNCC and SCLC staff members moving through and trying to keep them calm. Some men in the crowd spoke of going home to get guns. Our people tried talking them down, getting them calm. Kids and teenagers continued throwing rocks and bricks.

The parsonage next to the church looked like a MASH unit, with doctors and nurses tending to dozens of weeping, wounded people. There were cuts and bumps and bruises, and a lot of tear gas burns, which were treated by rinsing the eyes with a boric acid solution.

Relays of ambulances sent by black funeral homes carried the more seriously wounded to Good Samaritan Hospital, Selma's largest black health-care facility, run by white Catholics and staffed mostly by black doctors and nurses. One of those ambulance drivers made ten trips back and forth from the church to the hospital and to nearby Burwell Infirmary, a smaller clinic. More than ninety men and women were treated at both facilities, for injuries ranging from head gashes and fractured ribs and wrists and arms and legs to broken jaws and teeth. There was one fractured skull—mine, although I didn't know it yet.

I didn't consider leaving for the hospital, though several people tried to persuade me to go. I wanted to do what I could to help with all this chaos. I was so much in the moment, I didn't have much time to think about what had happened, nor about what was yet to come.

By nightfall, things had calmed down a bit. Hosea and I and the others had decided to call a mass meeting there in the church, and more than six hundred people, many bandaged from the wounds of that day, arrived. Clark's possemen had been ordered away, but the state troopers were still outside, keeping a vigil.

Hosea Williams spoke to the crowd first, trying to say something to calm them. Then I got up to say a few words. My head was throbbing. My hair was matted with blood clotting from an open gash. My trench coat was stained with dirt and blood.

I looked out on the room, crammed wall to wall and floor to ceiling with people. There was not a spot for one more body. I had no speech prepared. I had not had the time or opportunity to give much thought to what I would say. The words just came.

"I don't know how President Johnson can send troops to Vietnam," I said. "I don't see how he can send troops to the Congo. I don't see how he can send troops to *Africa*, and he can't send troops to Selma, Alabama."

There was clapping, and some shouts of "Yes!" and "Amen!"

"Next time we march," I continued, "we may have to keep going when we get to Montgomery. We may have to go on to *Washington.*"

When those words were printed in *The New York Times* the next morning, the Justice Department announced it was sending FBI agents to Selma to investigate whether "unnecessary force was used by law officers and others." For two months we'd been facing "unnecessary force," but that apparently had not been enough. This, finally, was enough.

Now, after speaking, it was time for me to have my own injuries examined. I went next door to the parsonage, where the doctors took one look at my head and immediately sent me over to Good Samaritan. What I remember most about arriving there was the smell in the waiting room. The chairs were jammed with people from the march—victims and their families—and their clothing reeked of tear gas. The bitter, acrid smell filled the room.

The nurses and nuns were very busy. Priests roamed the room, comforting and calming people. When one of the nurses saw my head, I was immediately taken through and X-rayed. My head wound was cleaned and dressed, then I was admitted. By ten that night, exhausted and groggy from painkillers, I finally fell asleep.

It was not until the next day that I learned what else had happened that evening, that just past 9:30 P.M., ABC Television cut into its Sunday night movie—a premiere broadcast of Stanley Kramer's *Judgment at Nuremberg,* a film about Nazi racism—with a special bulletin. News anchor Frank Reynolds came on-screen to tell viewers of a brutal clash that afternoon between state troopers and black protest marchers in Selma, Alabama. They then showed fifteen minutes of film footage of the attack.

The images were stunning—scene after scene of policemen on foot and on horseback beating defenseless American citizens. Many viewers thought this was somehow part of the movie. It seemed too strange, too ugly to be real. It *couldn't* be real.

But it was. At one point in the film clip, Jim Clark's voice could be heard clearly in the background: "Get those goddamned niggers!" he yelled. "And get those goddamned *white* niggers."

The American public had already seen so much of this sort of thing, countless images of beatings and dogs and cursing and hoses. But something about that day in Selma touched a nerve deeper than anything that had come before. Maybe it was the concentrated focus of the scene, the mass movement of those troopers on foot and riders on horseback rolling into and over two long lines of stoic, silent, unarmed people. This wasn't like Birmingham, where chanting and cheering and singing preceded a wild stampede and scattering. This was a face-off in the most vivid terms between a dignified, composed, completely nonviolent multitude of silent protestors and the truly malevolent force of a heavily armed, hateful battalion of troopers. The sight of them rolling over us like human tanks was something that had never been seen before.

People just couldn't believe this was happening, not in America. Women and children being attacked by armed men on horseback—it was impossible to believe.

But it had happened. And the response from across the nation to what would go down in history as Bloody Sunday was immediate. By midnight that evening, even as I lay asleep in my room over at Good Samaritan, people from as far away as New York and Minnesota were flying into Alabama and driving to Selma, forming a vigil of their own outside Brown's Chapel. President Johnson, who had been contacted by the Justice Department almost immediately after the attack, watched the ABC footage that evening. He knew he would have to respond. Dr. King, too, was informed of what had happened as soon as the President—Andy Young called King in Atlanta, and the two agreed that now there *would* be a march. They made plans to file a request the first thing in the morning, asking for a federal injunction barring state interference in a massive Selma-to-Montgomery march.

That request arrived the next morning, Monday, in Montgomery, on the desk of Federal District Judge Frank Johnson—the same judge who had issued the injunction four years earlier providing us with safe passage out of Montgomery during the Freedom Ride.

Banner headlines, with four-column photographs—many showing the trooper clubbing me as I lay on the ground with my arm upraised—appeared that Monday morning in newspapers around the world. By midday I was receiving telegrams and cards and flowers from total strangers. A wreath arrived from an elderly woman in Southern California: "A FORMER ALABAMIAN," the card read. "WE ARE WITH YOU."

Dr. King and Ralph Abernathy came to see me. They told me what was going on outside, that people all across the country were with us, that they were going to have this march. "It's going to happen, John," Dr. King told me. "Rest assured it is going to happen."

John Doar, from the Justice Department, came to interview me about the attack, to take a deposition of sorts. The federal government was now very involved in this thing.

The hospital staff kept the press away from my room, except for a UPI photographer, who was allowed in to shoot a picture, I saw no reporters at all.

I was in a lot of pain that day. And I felt very strange lying in that bed. With all my arrests and injuries over the years, I had never actually been admitted to a hospital before. I'd been treated, but never admitted. And I did not like it. I felt very restless and a little bit frightened. Maybe it was the drugs, but I had visions of someone slipping into the room and doing something to me. I felt vulnerable, helpless.

Worst of all, though, was the sense of being cut off. I was hearing about everything secondhand, if at all. It was killing me not to know what was going on outside that hospital, because I knew there was plenty going on.

And I was right.

Several carloads, and a truckload as well, of SNCC field workers from Mississippi had rushed in that day, along with a chartered plane of staff people from Atlanta—Forman and others. All told, more than thirty SNCC people had arrived in Selma by that afternoon.

They came with a mixture of hurt and outrage and shame and guilt. They were concerned for the local people of Selma, and also for one of their own. I had been hurt, and they didn't like it. It made them mad. It got them excited, too. This was an emergency, a crisis, something to *respond* to. It was like firemen who hadn't had a fire to put out in a long time. Now everyone wanted to be the first to get to the blaze.

None of them came to see me in the hospital, except for Lafayette Surrney, whose purpose was to collect information for a press release. I really wasn't hurt about that. I guessed that they were probably very busy.

And I was right. Word came from Judge Johnson that Monday afternoon that he would not grant an injunction without a hearing, and he would not be able to hold a hearing any sooner than Thursday. That evening the SCLC and SNCC leadership—Dr. King, Andy Young and others of the SCLC; Forman, Willie Ricks and Fay Bellamy of SNCC, along with Jim Farmer, who'd come on the scene to represent CORE—argued over whether they should risk losing the judge's support by staging a march before getting his approval, or risk losing credibility and momentum by waiting patiently until he issued his injunction.

Unlike two days earlier, when he had been dead set against SNCC's participation, Forman was now pushing hard to march, and to march *now*. Hosea was with him, as was Farmer. Most of the others leaned toward accepting Judge Johnson's terms. If I had been there, I would have said we should march and let the courts do what they would—what they *should*. I wouldn't have gone as far as Forman, who was furious that this judge was telling us to wait—he called Judge Johnson's offer "legal blackmail"—but I would have said this was no time to stop and sit still.

Our SNCC people were even more fed up with the SCLC than they had been two days before. King's staff had prepared a fund-raising ad to be placed in *The New York Times,* showing a photograph of me being beaten on the bridge. That really bothered a lot of our people. The way Julian later put it to one reporter, "It was *our* chairman who was leading the march.... SCLC was hogging all the publicity and all the money and doing very little to deserve it.... We just resented SCLC's ability to capitalize on things we thought we were doing."

I understood that resentment. But again, I felt that SNCC had lost the upper hand completely, along with any right to complain, by not being part of that march. When Julian said it was "our chairman" leading the march, he was ignoring the fact that our leadership had pointedly decided the night before that I would march *not* as the chairman of SNCC but as myself. There was something wrong with trying to have it both ways now. I had played the role of a go-between up until this point, bridging my roles with both SNCC and the SCLC, but clearly that was going to be harder to do from here on out.

The final decision at that Monday night meeting was left up to Dr. King, and he decided there would be no march on Tuesday. Then he left with the others to attend a rally at Brown's Chapel. The place was packed; the atmosphere was overwhelmingly emotional, and apparently it overwhelmed Dr. King as well, who stunned everyone who had been at that meeting by announcing to the crowd that there *would* be a march the next day.

Late that night and on into the next morning, the SNCC and SCLC leaders met at the home of a local black dentist, Dr. Sullivan Jackson, to hash out the plans for the Tuesday march. State and federal authorities had issued official statements forbidding it. George Wallace actually claimed he had "saved lives" by having Lingo and Clark and their men stop us that Sunday afternoon—the counties ahead, the places we would have to pass through to get to Montgomery, said the governor, were much more dangerous than anything we faced in Selma. Those same dangers, he now claimed, were too great to allow us to march on this day.

Dr. King and the others were up until 4 A.M. trying to work out some sort of compromise with government officials in the face of a restraining order against this march issued by Judge Johnson. King spoke by phone early that morning with Attorney General Katzenbach in Washington. Then, after a few hours' sleep, King met with several federal officials, including John Doar and former Florida governor LeRoy Collins, who was now director of the Justice Department's Community Relations Service and who had been sent by President Johnson to mediate this situation. After Collins met with King that morning, he went to talk to state and local officials, including Lingo and Clark, who were once again stationed with their troops at the east end of the bridge.

No one besides Dr. King and a few of his closest staffers knew exactly what was decided by those early-morning phone calls and meetings. When a column of two thousand marchers led by Dr. King left Brown's Chapel early that afternoon, walking the same route toward the same bridge we'd tried to cross that Sunday, they all assumed they were headed for Montgomery. When they were stopped at the bridge by a U.S. marshal who read aloud Judge Johnson's order against this march, they assumed this was just a formality. And when Dr. King then led the column over the crest of the bridge to the bottom of the other side, where the armed troopers were massed once again, the marchers steeled themselves for another attack.

This time, though, the troopers stood still and simply watched as Dr. King brought the column to a halt and led the marchers in prayer. Then they sang "We Shall Overcome." And then, as the troopers moved aside to open the way east to Montgomery, Dr. King turned around and headed *back* to the church.

The marchers were shocked and confused. They had no idea what was going on. They had come to put their bodies on the line, and now they were backing down, retreating, going home. They followed Dr. King—what else could they do? But they were disappointed. Many were openly angry.

Jim Forman was absolutely livid. When he—and everyone else—learned that Dr. King had made an agreement with federal officials that morning to march only to the bridge, as a symbolic gesture, and then to turn back and await Judge Johnson's hearing later that week, he exploded, denouncing Dr. King's "trickery" and saying that this was the last straw. SNCC had had enough. There would be no more working with the SCLC. There would be no waiting for any judge's injunction. SNCC was finished with waiting, finished with Selma. It was time to do something on our own, said Forman. Within twenty-four hours he shifted our manpower and focus from Selma to the streets of Montgomery, where SNCC-led student forces from Tuskegee Institute and Alabama State University began laying siege to the state capitol with a series of demonstrations more overt and aggressive than anything seen in Selma. Taunting, provoking, clashing with mounted policemen—the SNCC protests that week in Montgomery would prove to be nothing like our nonviolent campaign in Selma.

All this news hit me like a windstorm when I was released from the hospital that Tuesday night. I was still in great pain—my head was pounding. My skull was fractured. I'd had a serious concussion. The doctors told me I needed more treatment and suggested I see some specialists up in Boston. But there was no way I was going to Boston. There was no time. I'd already lain in that hospital long enough. It was driving me crazy.

One good thing about the three days I spent in that hospital bed was that it gave me a lot of time to think, to reflect. I had every reason to be discouraged. My feelings and philosophy about the movement, about our strategies and tactics, my commitment to nonviolence, my loyalty to Dr. King were all increasingly putting me at odds with many of my SNCC colleagues. We even differed about the events of that Tuesday, about Dr. King's "double-dealing," as some of them called it. I had no problem with what Dr. King did. I thought it was in keeping with the philosophy of the movement, that there comes a time when you must retreat, and that there is nothing wrong with retreating. There is nothing wrong with coming back to fight another day. Dr. King knew—we all knew—that Judge Johnson was going to give us what we were asking for if we simply followed procedure, followed the rules.

But I was in the minority. Most of the people in SNCC were sick of procedure, sick of the rules. Some were sick of me. By all rights, I should have been despondent when I came out of that hospital, but I wasn't. Quite the opposite. I guess I've always been a person who looks at the big picture rather than focusing on little details. That's probably a curse as much as it is a blessing. But that's what I saw that Tuesday night as I emerged from that hospital—the big picture. And it looked wonderful. I was convinced now more than ever that we would prevail. The response we had gotten nationally in the wake of that Sunday attack was so much greater than anything I'd seen since I'd become a part of the movement for civil rights. It was greater than the Freedom Rides, greater than the March on Washington, greater than Mississippi Summer. The country seemed truly aroused. People were really moved. During the first forty-eight hours after Bloody Sunday, there were demonstrations in more than eighty cities protesting the brutality and urging the passage of a voting rights act. There were speeches on the floors of both houses of Congress condemning the attack and calling for voting rights legislation. A telegram signed by more than sixty congressmen was sent to President Johnson, asking for "immediate" submission of a voting rights bill.

Yes, we had serious problems within SNCC. They would have to be worked out, and I had no doubt they would be. But meanwhile, the movement had an incredible amount of momentum. When I came out of the hospital that Tuesday night, despite all the buzz among my SNCC colleagues about the "betrayal" that afternoon, I was exhilarated.

There was a rally that night at Brown's Chapel, and I was overjoyed to be there. People in the press were pushing and pushing about the "split" between SNCC and the SCLC. They asked me openly about it. I told them, no, there was no split. How could there be a split, I said, between two groups that have never pretended to be one?

"I am not going to engage in any public discussion of organizational problems," I stated. "SCLC is not the enemy. George Wallace and segregation are the enemy."

Ivanhoe Donaldson put it a different way. "Within the movement," he told one reporter, "we are a family. Arguments take place in any family."

He couldn't have put it any better. And the wisest families, he might have added, keep their arguments to themselves. Yes, we had problems among ourselves and with the SCLC, but I wasn't about to discuss them with the press.

That night, after the rally at Brown's, I went home with one of the families in the Carver project, the Wests, and slept like a baby. It was not until the next morning that I heard what had happened while I was asleep.

More than four hundred out-of-town ministers—most of them white—had taken part in the march that afternoon. After the rally that evening, three of them went and had dinner at Walker's Cafe, the diner that was such a favorite among movement people. After their meal, as they walked back toward the church, they lost their way and wound up passing through a poor white section of town. As they went by a little bar called the Silver Moon, a crowd from inside the bar came out and surrounded them. Before they knew what was happening, one of the three, a thirty-eight-year-old Unitarian minister from Boston named James J. Reeb, was clubbed in the head by a full baseball-style swing of a bat. He was so badly injured that the local emergency room staff put him in an ambulance and sent him on to Birmingham University Hospital, where he was listed Wednesday morning in critical condition with a large blood clot in his brain.

Thursday, with the Reverend Reeb's condition headlined in the newspapers, I went to Montgomery for the beginning of the federal court hearing on the SCLC request for an injunction to block state interference and allow a Selma-to-Montgomery march. Walking back into Frank Johnson's courtroom, where I'd testified four years earlier during the Freedom Ride, felt familiar in some ways, but different in one hugely important one. Four years earlier, the governor of Alabama was John Patterson. He was the figure of state authority who was squared off against the federal figure, Judge Johnson. Now the governor was George Wallace, a man whose clashes with Judge Johnson went back for years and years.

Frank Johnson and George Wallace had been classmates at the University of Alabama in the 1930s, but other than that they had next to nothing in common. While Wallace was from the same southeastern, deeply Confederate part of the state as I, Johnson grew up in north Alabama, near Tennessee, in a county that had actually sided with the Union during the Civil War. Early in his career Johnson established a reputation for fairness and reason in the face of racists. During the Montgomery bus boycott he was a member of a three-judge panel that handed down a decision in favor of desegregation. Later, he sat on another panel that struck down Alabama's poll-tax law. In 1958 he ordered the voter registration records of Barbour County to be turned over to the U.S. Civil Rights Commission. The Barbour County circuit judge who held those records refused to give them up. Only after Johnson threatened him with a contempt charge did the circuit judge relent and give up the records. That judge was George Wallace.

In the wake of that episode, Wallace famously called Johnson an "integrating, carpetbagging, scalawagging, race-mixing, bald-faced liar." Now, seven years later, the two were squaring off again, this time with Wallace sitting in the governor's mansion.

We had spent several days meeting with our lawyers—Fred Gray, Arthur Shores, Orzell Billingsley and J. L. Chestnut—preparing our case, which was to establish that our rights had been repeatedly violated during our two-month campaign in Selma, often through violent means, and that this march, as a method of demonstrating our *right* to those rights, should be allowed.

We expected the hearing to extend over several days, which it did. I testified, describing in detail my experience the Sunday of the attack on the Edmund Pettus Bridge. The FBI agents who witnessed that attack also testified. A film clip of the attack—three minutes of footage shot by Larry Pierce for CBS—was shown, and when the courtroom lights were turned back on, Judge Johnson stood silently, shook his head, straightened his robe and called for a recess. He was visibly disgusted.

On the third day of the hearing Colonel Lingo testified and indicated that the order to use force that day came straight from George Wallace. He didn't come right out and say it then, but years later, when Lingo was running for sheriff of Jefferson County, he was explicit. "I was ordered to cause the scene that the troopers made," he said. "Who ordered me? The governor! Governor George C. Wallace ordered me to stop the marchers even if we had to use force, to bring this thing to a halt. He said that we'd teach other niggers to try to march on a public highway in Alabama. He said that he was damned if he would allow such a thing to take place."

Whether Wallace actually ordered it or not, he certainly condoned the attack that took place that Sunday. And he never criticized it. In fact, even as Judge Johnson's hearing was moving into its third day, Wallace was on his way to Washington to meet with President Johnson and try to convince the President to step in and stop us from marching. That meeting wound up backfiring on Wallace. Not only did Johnson not agree to help Wallace, but he emerged from the meeting and made a stunning announcement to the reporters waiting outside:

> The events of last Sunday cannot and will not be repeated, but the demonstrations in Selma have a much larger meaning. They are a protest against a deep and very unjust flaw in American democracy itself.
>
> Ninety-five years ago our Constitution was amended to require

that no American be denied the right to vote because of race or color.
Almost a century later, many Americans are kept from voting simply
because they are Negroes.

Therefore, this Monday I will send to the Congress a request for
legislation to carry out the amendment of the Constitution.

That was Saturday, March 13. The Reverend Reeb had passed away two
nights earlier, prompting even more demonstrations across the country in
support of our efforts in Selma. That Sunday, Forman and I flew to New York
for a march in Harlem protesting the events in Alabama. Several thousand
people, most of them black, a great many dressed in white Masonic uniforms,
paraded, then listened as I told them what had happened and what was *going*
to happen in Selma.

Meanwhile, down in Montgomery, as well as in cities across the country,
SNCC-led demonstrations were heating up. There were sit-ins at the Justice
Department and protests outside the White House. I heard later that President Johnson actually complained at a meeting that Sunday night that his
daughter Luci couldn't study because of all the noise outside.

The next day, Monday, I was back in Montgomery for the fourth day of
the hearing. It was clear now that Judge Johnson was going to give us the
injunction we wanted. He asked us that day to submit a plan for the march
we wanted to make. We went back that afternoon—Andy Young, Hosea
Williams, Jack Greenberg, who was head of the NAACP's Legal Defense
Fund, several other SCLC people and I—to the Albert Pick Motel in Montgomery and drew up details of the number of people we expected to march,
the route we would follow and the number of days it would take.

Then I headed back to Selma, where a rally was held that afternoon in
honor of the Reverend Reeb. More than two thousand people marched
through downtown Selma to the courthouse steps, where Dr. King led a
twenty-minute service, with Jim Clark's deputies looking on but doing nothing to stop it.

I was in Selma that night when I got word that there had been an outburst
of violence earlier that afternoon in Montgomery, where several hundred SNCC
demonstrators—mainly the Tuskegee Institute and Alabama State students organized by Forman—had clashed with police and mounted deputies who tried
to stop them from demonstrating. When the police began pushing in and physically shoving the students aside, some of the students responded by throwing
rocks, bricks and bottles. That brought the mounted possemen forward, swinging clubs and whips. When the students ran, the possemen chased them on
horseback, actually riding up onto the porches of private homes. At least one
glass door was broken by the charge of a deputy on horseback.

I was horrified to hear this. It was almost surreal. The violence seemed to be getting wilder and wilder each day. I talked to Forman early that evening on the phone and agreed that we should stage a march the next day to protest the extremity of the possemen's attack. I had the final day of Judge Johnson's hearing to attend in the morning, but I would be there for the march after that.

After talking with Forman, I settled in that night at the home of Dr. Jackson, the Selma dentist, to watch President Johnson make a live televised address to Congress. Dr. King and several SCLC staffers were also squeezed into Dr. and Mrs. Jackson's small living room. The President had invited Dr. King and me to come up to Washington that night and join the audience for his speech, but we decided the place for us to be was Selma.

And so, along with 70 million other Americans who watched the broadcast that evening, we listened to Lyndon Johnson make what many others and I consider not only the finest speech of his career, but probably the strongest speech any American president has ever made on the subject of civil rights.

It began powerfully:

At times history and fate meet at a single time in a single place to shape a turning point in man's unending search for freedom. So it was at Lexington and Concord. So it was a century ago at Appomattox. So it was last week in Selma, Alabama.

It moved toward a climax with a focus on voting rights:

Rarely in any time does an issue lay bare the secret heart of America itself.... The issue of equal rights for American Negroes is such an issue. And should we defeat every enemy, and should we double our wealth and conquer the stars and still be unequal to this issue, then we will have failed as a people and as a nation.

And it peaked with the President citing our favorite freedom song, the anthem, the very heart and soul, of the civil rights movement:

Even if we pass this bill, the battle will not be over. What happened in Selma is part of a far larger movement which reaches into every section and state of America. It is the effort of American Negroes to secure for themselves the full blessings of American life.

Their cause must be our cause too. Because it is not just Negroes, but really it is all of us who must overcome the crippling legacy of bigotry and injustice.

And we *shall* overcome.

All told, the speech was forty-five minutes long. It was interrupted forty times by applause, twice by standing ovations. I was deeply moved. Lyndon

Johnson was no politician that night. He was a man who spoke from his heart. His were the words of a statesman and more; they were the words of a poet. Dr. King must have agreed. He wiped away a tear at the point where Johnson said the words "We shall overcome."

Predictably, not everyone was so moved. I was not surprised to hear Jim Forman attack the speech. The President's reference to our anthem was a "tinkling empty symbol," Forman told one reporter. "Johnson," he later said to another writer, "spoiled a good song that day."

We never did have time to discuss the speech, Forman and I. Events were tumbling much too swiftly. The next morning I was back in Montgomery, watching our attorneys hand Judge Johnson the plans for our march. The hearing was now over. Johnson would make his decision by the following day.

That afternoon—gray, overcast, with a steady rain drizzling down—I joined Forman, Dr. King and others at the front of a group of six hundred people marching from the state capitol to the Montgomery County Courthouse to protest the violence of the day before. To this day, photos from that day's march, showing us wearing ponchos and raincoats, are mistakenly presented as if they were taken during the march from Selma to Montgomery, which they were not. That march was yet to come.

That evening, at a rally called by SCLC officials, with Dr. King and Abernathy in the audience, along with dozens of middle-class, mainstream black ministers, Forman stunned everyone with one of the angriest, most fiery speeches made by a movement leader up to that point.

> There's only one man in the country that can stop George Wallace and those posses.
>
> These problems will not be solved until the man in that shaggedy old place called the White House begins to shake and gets on the phone and says, "Now listen, George, we're coming down there and throw you in jail if you don't stop that mess."...
>
> I said it today, and I will say it again. If we can't sit at the table of democracy, we'll knock the fucking legs *off!*

The fact that he quickly caught himself and muttered the words "Excuse me" was lost on almost everyone there. This was a church. Not only were those pews filled with ministers, but there were women and children in the audience, too. They were shocked. I was not. I'd heard Forman use that kind of language many times at SNCC meetings. But I was dismayed. That was not the language of the nonviolence movement. That was not the *message* of the movement, at least not of the movement I was a part of. And that was what was most significant to me about that speech, not the fact that Forman's words were so bold and profane, but the fact that they pointed the way down a road SNCC was headed that I knew I would not be able to travel.

Even Dr. King, when he stepped to the podium after Forman was finished, had trouble restoring calm. People were visibly upset. Several had already gotten up to leave. Then, as if on some sort of cue, one of Dr. King's staffers arrived, approached the podium and had a word with King, who nodded, smiled and waved everyone quiet.

Judge Johnson, Dr. King announced, had issued his ruling. The march from Selma to Montgomery would be allowed.

The judge's written order, officially released the next morning, beautifully and succinctly summarized what we had been through in Selma, and *why* we had gone through it:

> The evidence in this case reflects that... an almost continuous pattern of conduct has existed on the part of defendant Sheriff Clark, his deputies, and his auxiliary deputies known as "possemen" of harassment, intimidation, coercion, threatening conduct, and, sometimes, brutal mistreatment toward these plaintiffs and other members of their class....
>
> The attempted march alongside U.S. Highway 80... on March 7, 1965, involved nothing more than a peaceful effort on the part of Negro citizens to exercise a classic constitutional right: that is, the right to assemble peaceably and to petition one's government for the redress of grievances.
>
> ... it seems basic to our constitutional principles that the extent of the right to assemble, demonstrate and march peaceably along the highways and streets in an orderly manner should be commensurate with the enormity of the wrongs that are being protested and petitioned against. In this case, the wrongs are enormous. The extent of the right to demonstrate against these wrongs should be determined accordingly.

We had told the judge the march would begin on Sunday, March 21. This was Wednesday. That gave us five days to prepare. And this time, as compared to our small, spontaneous effort on Bloody Sunday, there would *be* preparation, as well as the full participation of SNCC, the SCLC, the NAACP, the Urban League and every other civil and human rights organization in the United States. In many ways, this event promised to be as big as the March on Washington. The numbers would be nowhere near that many, of course, but unlike the demonstration in Washington, which was a rally more than an actual march, this was literally going to be a mass *movement* of people, thousands and thousands of them, walking down a highway, cutting through the heart of the state of Alabama.

The next five days were a swirl of activity, much like preparing an army for an assault. Marchers, not just from Selma but from across the nation, were mobilized and organized, route sections and schedules were mapped out, printed up and distributed, tents big enough to sleep people by the hundreds were secured. Food. Security. Communications. There were thousands of details to take care of, and thousands of dollars, most of it raised by the SCLC, to be spent. Just a quick scan of the records from that week indicates both the enormity and the tediousness of this undertaking:

- 700 air mattresses at $1.45 each
- 700 blankets donated by local churches and schools
- Four carnival-sized tents rented for $430 apiece
- 17,000 square feet of polyethylene for ground cloth, at a cost of $187
- 700 rain ponchos
- Two 2,500-watt generators for lighting campsites
- 2,000 feet of electrical wiring

Walkie-talkies, flashlights, pots and pans and stoves for cooking... the list went on and on. And so did the manpower. A crew of twelve ministers—we called them the "fish and loaves committee"—was responsible for transporting food to each campsite each evening. Ten local women cooked the evening meals in church kitchens in Selma. Ten others made sandwiches around the clock. Squads of doctors and nurses from the same Medical Committee for Human Rights that had provided the physicians who tended the wounded on Bloody Sunday now geared up for a different kind of casualty, with dozens of cases of rubbing alcohol and hundreds of boxes of Band-Aids, for the marchers' sore muscles and blistered feet.

Meanwhile, state and federal authorities were doing their part to prepare. The two westbound lanes of Highway 80 between Selma and Montgomery would be closed off for the five days of the march—all traffic in both directions would be routed onto the eastbound lanes. At the order of President Johnson, more than 1,800 armed Alabama National Guardsmen would line the fifty-four-mile route, along with two thousand U.S. Army troops, a hundred FBI agents and a hundred U.S. marshals. Helicopters and light planes would patrol the route from the air, watching for snipers or other signs of trouble, and demolition teams would clear the way ahead of us, inspecting bridges and bends in the road for planted explosives.

That Saturday night, the evening before the march would begin, more than two hundred people came to spend the night in Brown's Chapel. We all made short speeches—Bevel and Diane, Andy Young and I. Dick Gregory couldn't help working a little routine into his speech. "It would be just our luck," he said, looking ahead to our arrival in Montgomery, "to find out that Wallace is colored."

When we awoke Sunday morning, more than three thousand people had gathered outside the church. Dr. King greeted them with a speech intended to make the local Selmans among them comfortable with the middle-class professionals and out-of-town celebrities who had arrived to join them. We were all very sensitive about this, about keeping the focus as much as possible on the people who had brought this historic day about, the everyday men and women of Selma. We made a point to put them at the front of the march, right behind the row that led the way.

That row included Dr. King and his wife, Coretta, A. Philip Randolph, Ralph Bunche, Ralph and Juanita Abernathy, Andy Young, Hosea, me, Forman, Dick Gregory and Rabbi Abraham Heschel of the Jewish Theological Seminary of America, a biblical-looking man with a long, flowing white beard. When he walked up to join us, one onlooker shouted out, "There goes *God!*"

Someone arrived with an armful of Hawaiian leis, which were placed around each of our necks. Abernathy stepped forward and announced, "Wallace, it's all over now."

And then we stepped off, 3,200 people walking in a column that stretched a mile long.

Ahead of us rolled a television truck, its lights and cameras trained on Dr. King's every step.

Behind us walked an unimaginable cross section of American people.

There was a one-legged man on crutches—Jim Leatherer, from Saginaw, Michigan—who answered each person who thanked him for coming by thanking them in return. "I believe in you," he said over and over again. "I believe in democracy."

There was a couple from California pushing a baby in a stroller.

Assistant Attorneys General John Doar and Ramsey Clark were both there, walking among the crowd like everyone else.

Cager Lee, Jimmie Lee Jackson's elderly grandfather, who had been wounded the night Jimmie Lee was killed, was with us. It was hard for him to do even a few miles a day, but Mr. Lee was bound and determined to do them. "Just got to tramp some more," he said, nodding his head and pushing on.

Ministers, nuns, labor leaders, factory workers, schoolteachers, firemen—people from all walks of life, from all parts of the country, black and white and Asian and Native American, walked with us as we approached the same bridge where we'd been beaten two weeks before. The same troopers were there again, but this time National Guardsmen were there as well, and we passed over the river without incident, trailed by two truckloads of soldiers and a convoy of Army jeeps.

And now we were out of the city, the pebble-and-tar pavement of Highway 80 carrying us on into the countryside, through swampy marshland, past mossy Spanish oaks, rolling red clay farmland, and small, twisting creeks and rivers.

There was some jeering from occasional white onlookers gathered here and there along the shoulder of the road. Profanities from passing traffic were pretty constant. A man in a car with the words "Coonsville, USA" painted on its doors drove beside us for several days. And a private plane passed over the first day, dropping a small snowstorm of hate leaflets. But other than a couple of small incidents—one white marcher was hit in the face when he walked over to a filling station for a Coke, and bricks were thrown into a campsite one night, injuring several sleeping marchers—there was no actual violence.

We covered seven miles the first day, accompanied by the constant clicking of cameras as dozens of photographers and reporters circled us all the way. We stopped that night at a prearranged site, as spelled out in the plans we had given Judge Johnson. A man named David Hall, who worked for the Carver housing project as a maintenance manager and who owned an eighty-acre farm at the east edge of Dallas County, offered his land for us to pitch our tents that first night. The father of eight children, Mr. Hall, who was black, was asked whether he feared retaliation from the white community for doing us such a favor. "The Lord," he answered simply, "will provide."

That was basically the same answer a seventy-five-year-old woman named Rosa Steele gave when asked how she felt about letting us stay our second night on her 240-acre farm in Lowndes County. "I'm not afraid," said Mrs. Steele. "I've lived my three score and ten."

It was cold that first evening, below freezing as a matter of fact. More than two thousand of the marchers bedded down beneath three large tents. In the morning they would have to head back to Selma—Judge Johnson's order included a stipulation that we limit the number of marchers the second day to three hundred, since we'd be passing through a section of Lowndes County where the road narrowed from four to two lanes. The marchers that night made the most of their evening together. They clapped hands, built huge fires, sang and soaked in that Freedom High until they finally fell asleep.

The other thousand or so people who had walked with us that day were driven back to Selma that night in a caravan of cars and trucks. I was among them. Before allowing me to make this march at all, my doctors insisted that I sleep in a bed each evening. They did not want me spending the nights on hard ground, out in the cold. My head was still bothering me badly enough that I agreed with them. I would walk that entire fifty-four-mile route, but I spent each night back in Selma, with a doctor nearby in case something went wrong with my head.

That Monday, the second day, I rejoined the group and put on an orange vest, which we had decided each of the three hundred people chosen to march that day would wear for identification. We moved much more swiftly that day, covering sixteen miles by nightfall. Dr. King left that evening to fulfill a speaking engagement in Cleveland. He would be back two days later for the last leg of the march.

Tuesday the number of marchers swelled back to three thousand as the road widened back to four lanes and we were allowed to lift the limitation. The skies darkened early, and a torrential downpour began that lasted all day. To beat back the rain, we started a song, a little chant written by a guy named Len Chandler:

> Pick 'em up and lay 'em down,
> All the way from Selma town.

The weather was miserable, but no one complained. No one got tired. No one fell back. To me, there was never a march like this one before, and there hasn't been one since. The incredible sense of community—of *communing*—was overwhelming. We felt bonded with one another, with the people we passed, with the entire nation. The people who came out of their homes to watch as we passed by—rural people, almost all of them black, almost all of them dirt poor—waved and cheered, ran into their kitchens and brought us out food, brought us something to drink. More than a few of them put down what they were doing and joined us.

We covered eleven miles that day as well, and sixteen the next. And now we were just outside Montgomery. We were sunburned, windburned, weary, looking like the "last stragglers of a lost battalion," as one reporter described it. Our final stop was a place called the City of St. Jude, a Catholic complex of a church, a hospital and a school located two miles from Montgomery, operated through charity to serve the black community. Dr. King was there when we arrived, along with a crowd of 1,500 people that swelled by the hundreds every hour, as night fell and the scene turned into a celebration, a festival.

Dozens of celebrities arrived for a massive outdoor concert organized by—whom else?—Harry Belafonte. The entertainers included Tony Bennett, Sammy Davis Jr., Billy Eckstine, Shelley Winters, Ossie Davis, Leonard Bernstein, Nina Simone, Odetta, Johnny Mathis, Nipsey Russell, Peter, Paul and Mary, the Chad Mitchell Trio, Anthony Perkins, Elaine May, George Kirby, Joan Baez and Dick Gregory. They all performed that evening on a makeshift stage fashioned from stacks of coffins loaned by a local black funeral home. Yes, *coffins*.

It was a spectacle, a salute to Selma, with more than 20,000 people gathered under the stars for four hours of songs, speeches and sketches. At one point a reporter asked Elaine May if she thought this show and all these celebrities were turning this serious march into a circus. She snapped back, "The only real circus is the state of Alabama and George Wallace."

The next morning—a spectacularly sunny day—we went to see Governor Wallace, 50,000 of us. It was six miles from St. Jude's to the state capitol building. There had been yet another death threat made on Dr. King, and so, as a precaution, several ministers were dressed in the same blue suit he wore that day and marched beside him, to confuse any would-be snipers.

Into downtown we came, around the fountain on Court Square, where slaves had watered their owners' horses in antebellum times, up Dexter Avenue past the church where Dr. King preached when he was a minister in Montgomery and finally out onto the open square in front of the sun-drenched silver-and-white state capitol building. I could see the Alabama state flag flying high above the rotunda dome, along with the flag of the Confederacy. But the American flag was nowhere in sight. Neither was George Wallace, though we learned later that he watched the entire afternoon, peeking out through the drawn blinds of the governor's office.

A podium had been set up on the trailer of a flatbed truck, along with a microphone and loudspeakers. Peter, Paul and Mary sang. Then came the speakers: Ralph Bunche, Roy Wilkins, Jim Farmer, Whitney Young, Rosa Parks, Ralph Abernathy, Fred Shuttlesworth, Jim Bevel, Bayard Rustin and I. And then, finally, Dr. King stepped up to deliver one of the most important speeches of his life. Again, as in Washington, he rose to the occasion:

> I know some of you are asking today, "How long will it take?" I come to say to you this afternoon however difficult the moment, however frustrating the hour, it will not be long, because truth pressed to the earth will rise again.
>
> How long? Not long, because no lie can live forever.
>
> How long? Not long, because you will reap what you sow.
>
> How long? Not long, because the arm of the moral universe is long but it bends toward justice.
>
> How long? Not long, because mine eyes have seen the glory of the coming of the Lord, trampling out the vintage where the grapes of wrath are stored. He has loosed the faithful lightning of his terrible swift sword. His truth is marching on.
>
> Glory hallelujah! *Glory hallelujah!*

Four and a half months after that day, on August 6, after a long, weaving journey through both houses of Congress, the 1965 Voting Rights Act was signed into law by Lyndon Johnson during a nationally televised midday ceremony at the U.S. Capitol. Earlier that morning I was invited to meet privately with the President in the Oval Office. Jim Farmer was there, along with a military officer—a black Army major named Hugh Robinson. This was my first visit to the White House since the March on Washington, and my first one-on-one visit with a president.

Johnson dominated the conversation, his legs propped on a chair, his hands folded back behind his head. We talked for about twenty minutes, and near the end of the meeting the President leaned forward and said, "Now John, you've got to go back and get all those folks registered. You've got to go back and get those boys by the *balls*. Just like a bull gets on top of a cow. You've got to get 'em by the balls and you've got to *squeeze,* squeeze 'em till they *hurt.*"

I'd heard that Lyndon Johnson enjoyed talking in graphic, down-home terms, but I wasn't quite prepared for all those bulls and balls.

The signing that afternoon in the President's Room of the Capitol—the same room in which Abraham Lincoln signed the Emancipation Proclamation—was a powerfully moving moment for me. This law had teeth. Among its provisions were:

- the suspension of literacy tests in twenty-six states, including Alabama, Georgia and Mississippi, which had been the focal points of so much of our work
- the appointment of federal examiners to replace local officials as voter registrars
- authorization for the attorney general to take action against state and local authorities that use the poll tax as a prerequisite to voting

"The vote," President Johnson declared that day, "is the most powerful instrument ever devised by man for breaking down injustice and destroying the terrible walls which imprison men because they are different from other men."

After signing the bill, Johnson gave pens to Dr. King, Rosa Parks and several other civil rights "leaders," including me. I still have mine today, framed on the wall of my living room in Atlanta, along with a copy of the bill itself.

That day was a culmination, a climax, the end of a very long road. In a sense it represented a high point in modern America, probably the nation's finest hour in terms of civil rights. One writer called it the "nova of the civil rights movement, a brilliant climax which brought to a close the nonviolent struggle that had reshaped the South."

It was certainly the last act for the movement as I knew it. Something was born in Selma during the course of that year, but something died there, too.

The road of nonviolence had essentially run out. Selma was the last act. Even that climactic day at Montgomery, at the end of the march from Selma, was darkened a few hours after Dr. King spoke by the murder of Viola Gregg Liuzzo, a thirty-nine-year-old white housewife from Detroit who had come down as a volunteer for the march. She was driving her Oldsmobile sedan back to Montgomery that night after transporting some marchers home to Selma after the march when she was shot to death on a lonely stretch of Highway 80 in Lowndes County—a stretch of road we had triumphantly walked over just days earlier. Four Klansmen were eventually arrested, tried and, not surprisingly, found "not guilty" of Mrs. Liuzzo's murder. The same four men were later tried on civil rights charges in Judge Johnson's courtroom and were convicted and sentenced to ten years in prison, but that was little consolation to Mrs. Liuzzo's family or to the many people in the movement—especially the younger ones—who saw her death as just one more reason to give up on this notion of nonviolence.

How could I blame them? As I later explained to a writer from *The New York Times* who asked me how I felt looking back on the campaign at Selma:

We're only flesh. I could understand people not wanting to get beaten anymore. The body gets tired. You put out so much energy and you saw such little gain. Black capacity to believe white would really open his heart, open his life to nonviolent appeal, was running out.

It had been Selma that held us together as long as we did. After that, we just came apart.

*L*ess than a week after the Voting Rights Act was signed, six days of terrible rioting began in the Watts section of Los Angeles. By the time the smoke above that black section of the city had cleared, thirty-four people were dead, more than eight hundred were injured and over three thousand had been arrested. The day after those riots began, a similar explosion of violence broke out in Chicago, with flare-ups as well in Cleveland, New York, Jacksonville and South Bend.

There had already been many race riots during the decade, but none on this scale. And this frightened me. Rioting is not a movement. It is not an act of civil disobedience. I think it is a mistake for people to consider disorganized action, mayhem, and attacks on other people and property as an extension of any kind of movement. It is not. It is simply an explosion of emotion. That's all. There is nothing constructive about it. It is only *de*structive.

Those riots in the late summer of 1965 bothered me, but they were not surprising. I predicted as much earlier that year, just after the Selma-to-Montgomery march, in an essay I wrote for the *New York Herald Tribune*. The issue I was asked to address was what happens now. What comes after the right to vote? The words I wrote at that time could easily be written today:

> People ask what will happen in Chicago and in Harlem this summer. When will the next Selma take place? The civil rights movement cannot give an answer. The lack of concern on the part of the American public and the lack of concern and courage of the federal government breed bitterness and frustration.
>
> Where lack of jobs, intolerable housing, police brutality, and other frustrating conditions exist, it is possible that violence and massive street demonstrations may develop....
>
> Reality now is what happens in the streets of Selma, Ala., and McComb, Miss., and hundreds of Negro communities, north and

south, where fear and deprivation form an integral part of daily life. If
the government cannot answer our questions and help us to solve
some of these problems, I can only see many long, hot summers
ahead.

We now had the right to vote. We now had the right to eat at lunch counters. We could order that hamburger now... *if* we had the dollar to pay for it.
Far, far too many of us, unfortunately, did not have that dollar. That was the
challenge ahead of us now. Now that we had secured our bedrock, fundamental rights—the rights of access and accommodation and the right to
vote—the movement was moving into a new phase, a far stickier and more
complex stage of gaining equal footing in this society. The problem we faced
now was not something so visible or easily identifiable as a Bull Connor
blocking our way. Now we needed to deal with the subtler and much more
complex issues of attaining economic and political power, of dealing with attitudes and actions held deep inside people and institutions that, now that
they were forced to allow us through the door, could still keep the rewards inside those doors out of our reach. Combating segregation is one thing. Dealing with racism is another. The Mississippi Freedom Democratic Party learned
that painful lesson in Atlantic City. In the late summer of '65, black people
everywhere in America continued to be confronted with that lesson every day.
Unfortunately, as far as we have come in the thirty-three years since then, that
lesson is still being learned by too many black Americans today.

It was that reality that produced the rage and frustration that exploded in
the streets of Watts. That same anger and futility was seething in SNCC, too.
The behind-the-scenes rumblings that had begun at Waveland in late 1964
continued to develop throughout the months of the '65 Selma campaign. At
the same time as all those marches and beatings and arrests and deaths were
dominating the nation's newspaper headlines, the membership of SNCC
was behind closed doors, laying its soul bare and trying to figure out who we
were and where we were going. And even more specifically, who *I* was, and
whether or not the time had passed for a person like me to remain as the
chairman of SNCC.

Most of the "old" SNCC members, those who had been with us through
the sit-ins and the Freedom Rides, still respected me. But many of the newer,
younger members, those who had only heard about the early years, but who
weren't actually *there*, really didn't know who I was, what *we* were—or, at
least, what we had been. Some of those newer members saw me at Selma,
crossing that bridge, having my head beaten in, and they just shook their
heads, dismissing me as a "Christ-loving damn fool" and an "anachronism."
They weren't reading Gandhi or Thoreau. They were reading existentialist

philosophers like Camus, and the radical, black separatist writings of people like Malcolm—*Malcolm X Speaks,* a collection of Malcolm's more extreme speeches and essays, was particularly popular—and Frantz Fanon, whose book *The Wretched of the Earth* described Algeria under colonial rule and preached the philosophy of violence, justifiable terrorism and "an eye for an eye."

I read Fanon's book, as well as all the others. I thought his analysis of the situation in Algeria was fascinating and very thought-provoking. But he sanctioned violence and terrorism, and I just could not accept that. I continued to cast my lot with Gandhi and Thoreau. And Thomas Merton. Which is not to say there wasn't room for adjustment, for even more "radicalism," even among these social philosophers. The question of black nationalism, for instance, which had become a front-burner issue for us, was something I addressed directly during a speech I gave at a SNCC staff meeting the weekend of February 12, 1965—the same weekend Sheriff Clark lay in a Selma hospital bed recovering from exhaustion. We were gathered at Gammon Theological Seminary in Atlanta, and I had just been re-elected chairman, despite some opposition, chiefly from Stokely. In my speech I shared a passage from Merton's book, *Seeds of Contemplation:*

> Is it possible for Negroes and whites in this country to engage in a certain political experiment such as the world has never yet witnessed and in which the first condition would be that whites consented to let Negroes run their own revolution, giving them the necessary support, and being alarmed at some of the sacrifices and difficulties that this would involve?

I then answered that question myself. "If the movement and SNCC are going to be effective in attempting to liberate the black masses," I said, "then the civil rights movement must be black controlled, dominated and led."

This was not really that radical a statement to make. I still clung to the belief that we must have white membership in SNCC, that we must remain an interracial organization. I was not calling for the expulsion of white SNCC staffers, as many of our members were beginning to do. But I was reacting to the growing and understandable concern, especially in the wake of Mississippi Summer, that too many of our local organizations were being taken over by outside white volunteers. I was not as alarmed as many of my colleagues about that, but, as chairman, I had to speak to that concern, I had to respond to it, and to remind any of us who might have lost sight of what we were about that SNCC, though its goal was ultimately to bring about a just and utterly free interracial society, had come into existence because of the unjust situation faced by black people in American society, and that it had to be the black members of SNCC who would steer the way of our organization. I would never dream of throwing our white members off the boat, but I could see why, at this point in the movement, we would have to pull them out of the wheelhouse. Too many of our black SNCC members were demanding it, and I could understand why. I didn't share that feeling, but I had to respect it and respond to it.

Much more significant than my speech that weekend was an episode that occurred during one of our singing/prayer/testifying sessions, which were always so openly emotional, everyone unwinding the way they weren't allowed to unwind on the front lines, letting a lot of stuff spill out that they had to keep inside when they were out in the field. For many of us, this was our one chance to pour everything out—our fears, our worries, our doubts. It was always a very cleansing experience.

Well, on this particular evening, as things reached their peak in a whirl-wind of emotions, with about eighty of us gathered in the meeting hall, Bob Moses stood up and made a very impassioned speech. He said that some of us needed to leave, get out now. *Leave*, he said. Leave the movement because we were becoming nothing but creatures of the media. He looked straight at Jim Forman, at me, at Stokely and at several other people. Get out of the SNCC office, he said. Get out of Atlanta.

Moses wasn't about to spare himself. He had been tortured for some time by the attention *he* was getting from the media and other outsiders, and by the awe and adoration he inspired in so many of our members. And so, once he had warned the "leaders" among us that we needed to leave, he set his sights on himself.

"My name," he announced, "is no longer Robert Moses or Bob Moses."

The room was already silent. Now people looked puzzled, confused. No one knew where this was going.

"I am Bob Parris now," he said.

Parris was Moses's middle name.

"Bob Parris," he said again. "That is who I am."

Then he left. Just walked out of the room.

People were stunned. Dead silent. No one knew what exactly to make of this. But everyone knew it was hugely significant, that something had just happened that spoke to all that we were going through. Very spontaneously, without any direction at all, we came into a circle, a ring around the room, and sang "Will the Circle Be Unbroken?"

And then we left.

Moses's name change was all people could talk about for weeks after that meeting. What did it mean? I have heard, in the years since, that Moses was trying to avoid the Selective Service, that they were trying to track him down, and this was a way of delaying them, of avoiding going to Vietnam. I knew nothing about this at the time, and even if it's true that his draft board was trying to find Moses, I don't believe that was behind his name change. Bob Moses had much, much deeper concerns inside his soul than simply saving his skin. He did have growing concerns about American involvement in Vietnam, and he would eventually share those concerns in a very public way. I don't think he was hiding from anyone, at least not then.

Not long after that meeting in Atlanta, soon after the march from Selma to Montgomery, our executive committee decided to put SNCC's resources into supporting a congressional challenge on behalf of the Mississippi Freedom Democratic Party. In the wake of the convention in Atlantic City and the subsequent elections of 1964, the MFDP filed a suit challenging the seating of Mississippi's regular Democrats in Congress. We helped gather more than six hundred depositions giving evidence of illegal practices in the election of those Democrats. We went to court and also up to Washington to testify before congressional committees to support the nomination of three MFDP members—Fannie Lou Hamer, Victoria Gray and Annie Devine—to take the place of those regulars. I made several trips up to Washington myself, button-holing individual legislators, trying to convince them to support us. One hundred forty-three of them did support us, voting in favor of our challenge, but 228 did not. After that vote Fannie Lou was shaking with sobs as reporters gathered around her. "I'm not crying for myself alone," she said. "I'm crying for America. Because it's later than you think."

That April we had another stormy SNCC gathering, in a place called Holly Springs, near the northern border of Mississippi, not far from Memphis. The agenda was to focus on how to react and respond to President Johnson's newly announced War on Poverty, part of his sweeping anti-poverty domestic program, which he'd dubbed the Great Society. But the weekend had hardly begun when internal issues again erupted. This time the concern was the role in SNCC of what had come to be called floaters—staffers and volunteers who had no specific assignment or designated site but who were free to go from place to place as they felt fit, filling whatever need might be calling. The emergence of floaters fit right in with the Freedom High philosophy, and now there was a growing backlash against it. People, especially many of our entrenched Southern-rooted staffers, were complaining that too many of the floaters were undisciplined, disruptive and unfocused, that they took advantage of their freedom in the field, and that they disturbed the flow of meetings such as this.

I had no problem with those complaints. I was all for tightening discipline and direction, and I said so at that meeting. People should "shape up or ship out," I said. Unfortunately, that edict got taken too far. The decision was made to evaluate and scrutinize the work of more than one hundred staff members, person by person. It was a purge, in effect, and it had that effect. Several staff members were actually dismissed, but worse than that was the growing climate of suspicion and mistrust within our ranks. The "band of brothers" was becoming a distant memory.

I spent that summer traveling to Gary, Indiana, Jackson, Mississippi, and Americus, Georgia, where I was arrested two days after the Voting Rights Act was signed. The Sumter County Courthouse in Americus had continued to violate the law by having two voter registration lines, one for whites and one for blacks. When two black women tested the law by taking a place in the white line, they were arrested. When I arrived and led a rally at a local church in support of the women, I was arrested, too. As always, when it came to the Deep South, passing laws was one thing; enforcing them was another.

But the new voting laws did have a significant effect that year in Lowndes County, the place through which we had marched on our way from Selma to Montgomery and where Viola Liuzzo was murdered after that march. During that summer a core group of our people—Stokely, Bob Mants, Scott Smith, Willie Vaughn and Judy Richardson, among others—dug in and began working hard at registering voters in Lowndes, where four fifths of the population was black, and, as of the beginning of the decade, not *one* black county resident was registered to vote. In the wake of the surge created by the Selma march, our SNCC people there helped guide the Lowndes County residents through the process of creating an independent political party, in much the same way that the MFDP had been formed in Mississippi. This party was called the Lowndes County Freedom Organization. Alabama law had a requirement that all local political parties have a visual symbol because of the large number of illiterate voters. Alabama's regular Democratic Party used a white rooster above the words "White Supremacy for the Right"—"the white cock," some of us used to call it. Courtland Cox contacted a designer in Atlanta to come up with a symbol for this new group in Lowndes. She first came up with a dove, but Courtland and the others thought that was too delicate, too soft. The designer then looked at Clark College's emblem, a black panther, and they had the symbol.

And the Lowndes County Freedom Organization had a new name: the Black Panther Party.

Soon thereafter, Black Panther political parties began popping up everywhere, not necessarily connected to one another in anything but the name and the attitude of open defiance. The most visible, of course, was the Black Panther Party for Self-Defense in Oakland, California, founded by Bobby Seale and Huey Newton.

The Lowndes County Black Panther Party members, some of them SNCC staffers, began openly carrying weapons that summer, prompting Rowland Evans and Robert Novak, the conservative syndicated columnists, to call SNCC the "Nonstudent Violent Coordinating Committee."

I didn't know any of this was coming—the creation of the Black Panther Party, the use of weapons—until it happened. The people working in Lowndes County didn't need our okay. Despite the "purge" after our meeting at Holly Springs, the attitude of Freedom High continued to prevail, and the local organizations within SNCC operated essentially autonomously.

I didn't like the idea of this independent third party in Lowndes County. I have always been a believer in a strong two-party system. In Mississippi, we had worked within the structure of the existing Democratic Party to create a biracial alternative. The MFDP was open to all people. The Black Panthers, on the other hand, were segregated. And the fact that some of them carried weapons violated our most basic tenets of nonviolent action. But we had no means of enforcing those tenets. We never had. SNCC wasn't built that way. It didn't operate that way. We had a constitution, but no one looked at it. I'm not even sure we could have found a copy at our headquarters. We had never needed to. As a group built on the philosophy of consensus, we had never resorted to rules or regulations. We had never needed to. Now that there appeared to be a need, it was impossible. There were too many forces pulling in too many different directions. The same freedom we had thrived on in our early years was now pulling us to pieces.

There were so many issues for us to wrestle with, and by the end of that year there was another: Vietnam.

America had been vaguely involved in Vietnam for some time, but it actually became a *war* on August 4, 1964—the same day the bodies of Schwerner, Goodman and Chaney were found. That day, American warplanes bombed North Vietnamese villages in retaliation for attacks on U.S. destroyers in the Gulf of Tonkin, and with that, U.S. soldiers began flooding into South Vietnam by the tens of thousands. Many of those soldiers were, of course, black. And most of those black soldiers were sent to the front—if you could use such a term in a war like that.

In any event, from the outset, black U.S. soldiers were dying in Vietnam in horrifyingly disproportionate numbers—while 10 percent of the nation's population was black, one out of every four American fatalities in Vietnam was a black soldier. By late 1965, America's front lines in Vietnam were so filled with black men—as many as 60 percent—that the soldiers called it Soulville. Some of these black soldiers had to grapple with the sight of occasional Confederate flags, burnt crosses and Ku Klux Klan costumes showing up among their white comrades.

By the fall of '65, there was a tremendous amount of debate within SNCC over the issue of how we should respond to the war, or whether we should respond at all. There was no question that the subject was hitting close to home. Several young men in SNCC—field secretaries and staff people—had already been drafted, and about 85 percent of our members were eligible and exposed to the draft. Most of our people didn't qualify for student defer-ments—they were out of or away from college—and they certainly couldn't expect their draft boards, most of them in the South, to give them a sympa-thetic ear.

There were SNCC volunteers who were drafted and eventually died in Vietnam. Some were from Selma, young black men who had stood on those courthouse steps with me in '64 and '65. I can't remember their names, but I can remember their faces. They went to Vietnam and they did not return.

Although SNCC as an organization had not taken a formal position on the war in Vietnam by the end of 1965, many of our members, including me, had already come out against the war on an individual basis. Early that year, in April, SDS (Students for a Democratic Society) staged the first antiwar protest of the Vietnam era in Washington, and Bob Parris (Moses) went there to speak to the crowd of 25,000. Comparing the killing in South Vietnam to the killing in Mississippi, Moses told the crowd to ask themselves and their government, "Do you have the right to plot and kill and murder in defense of the society you value?"

A year later, Moses, who had received a student deferment when he was first called up in the late 1950s and who had applied for conscientious ob-jector status in the early '60s, received his draft notice. He had been classified 1-A and was ordered to report to New York City. Instead, he fled to Montreal, where he went underground for two years. Finally, in 1968, he left for Africa, where he settled in Tanzania. I still don't believe this had anything to do with Bob changing his name, but clearly the war confronted many people with an extremely difficult decision. Several SNCC people followed Moses's lead dur-ing this time, some seeking asylum in Canada, others going to Scandinavia. Personally, as opposed as I was to the war, I felt that the principle of nonvio-lence says you should stay and confront the system, battle it head on and face the consequences. Don't run from it. That's what I chose to do. In pursuing my conscientious objector status, I was fully prepared to go to jail and serve the time if necessary. But I would never sit in judgment on people who de-cided to do otherwise. As always, I believe the deep moral decisions that con-stantly confront each of us in our lifetimes are ours alone to wrestle with, and no one has the right to judge another for the decisions he or she makes.

Following that antiwar demonstration in Washington, late in the spring of

'65, a statement titled "Declaration of Conscience Against the War in Vietnam" was circulated by the Catholic Worker, the Committee for Nonviolent Action, the Student Peace Union and the War Resisters League. It was signed by a long list of Americans, ranging from academics and intellectuals like Nobel Prize winner Linus Pauling and psychologist Erich Fromm to civil rights movement leaders including Jim Bevel, Bayard Rustin and me.

I had already thought long and hard about what was happening in Vietnam. Beyond the fact that warfare of any kind contradicts my position of nonviolence—my belief that the means must be consistent with the goal and that that goal must always be, ultimately, the creation of the Blessed Community—this particular war was appalling in many ways. It seemed extremely contradictory to me for President Johnson to be sending tens of thousands of troops to fight this war in Vietnam to "protect the rights" of the people of South Vietnam at the same time as the rights of black people across the nation continued to be violated without protection.

I had no doubt this war was hurting not just the movement but the whole of America. On a practical level, it was taking resources away from the Great Society and spending them on bombs and bullets and battles being fought halfway around the planet. It is extremely difficult to fight a war on two fronts, and in this case it was impossible. Something had to give—either the War on Poverty or the war in Vietnam.

Beyond the practical issues were moral ones. I did not agree with the reasoning behind a "just" war, and this war was not even that. It was not just, and it was not being carried out justly, even at home, where black people and poor people were being selected to do the bulk of the dying. As for what was taking place in Vietnam itself, our actions were illegal, immoral and criminal. The wholesale bombing of villages with innocent people being slaughtered, the use of toxic chemicals to defoliate huge sections of forests, measuring victories by body counts—there was nothing noble or honorable about any of these things. There was nothing that was just.

All of these points and more were included in speeches I made that fall, speeches in which I compared Saigon to Selma and Mississippi to South Vietnam. At our fall SNCC meeting that November, held again at Gammon Theological Seminary, the central subject was Vietnam and our position against the war. I usually listened more than I spoke at most of these meetings. I felt that was part of my job as chairman, to hear the concerns of others. But at this meeting I took a very active role. I felt very strongly that we should come out publicly against the war. I felt we had a moral obligation here, a mandate, that we couldn't talk about what was going on in Mississippi and Alabama and south Georgia and not relate to and identify with the people who were being sent over to Vietnam, as well as the people, American and Vietnamese alike, who were being destroyed there.

Most of the membership agreed with me, though for differing reasons. To me, the principle of nonviolence was paramount. Most of the others were angered more by the idea that black men were being sent to fight a war for a white society that oppressed and exploited them. An extremely popular poster had emerged by that time, and you saw it hanging on the walls of many black organizations, as well as in the rooms of many black college students. We had a copy mounted on the wall of our SNCC headquarters in Atlanta. It read:

"NO VIETNAMESE EVER CALLED ME NIGGER"

Not everyone, though, agreed that we should come out against the war. Marion Barry, for example, had strong reservations about it. He thought it would hurt our ability to raise money. If we took a position against the war, he said, we would lose most of the little funding that we had. I answered that that was all the more reason to take a stand here. If we were going to go out of existence, I said, let's do it standing on principle and not clutching at a few meager and useless dollars.

In the wake of that meeting, Forman, Courtland Cox and I—the same threesome who had worked so much on my speech at the '63 March on Washington—drafted a statement against the war. Throughout November and December the statement was circulated among all members, to get everyone's opinion before we released it. Coincidentally, late that December, my own draft status was pronounced. I had been given my CO classification—1-O.

As that year wound down, I was doing a lot of traveling, literally from coast to coast, working very hard to raise some of those funds Marion was concerned about. Our SNCC bank account had hit rock bottom. We were more than $50,000 in debt. Creditors were calling seemingly every day. We were behind in our rent, our telephone payments, our light and car repair bills, and we were no longer able to send out our own paychecks. My $40-a-week salary was weeks overdue, and I'd taken to writing letters to my landlord asking for extensions of the $54-a-month rent on my apartment on Gordon Road.

I guess I was more tired than I realized. The stress and strain of constant traveling and public speaking were taking a toll I didn't notice. I was shocked when I got back from a trip to California that December and saw a memo to our Atlanta office written by a SNCC volunteer in San Francisco named Penny Bartlett, who had accompanied me during a swing through the Bay Area:

December 11

MEMO
TO: Jim, Nancy, Jimmy, Mary, Julian—everybody else around
        the place
FROM: Penny
RE: Health of John Robert Lewis, Esq.

Be it herewith noted that John Robert Lewis has been traveling extensively for the last month and a half and speaking almost continuously in all parts of these United States on behalf of the Student Nonviolent Coordinating Committee, of which he is chairman.

Be it herewith also noted that John Robert Lewis, having been in the Bay Area this past weekend, discharged his responsibilities with an unusual amount of care, concern and regard for the movement he represents and for the people with whom he came in contact. May his attention to small details and his consideration for each person he spoke to be noted. May his devotion to the ideals of the movement, as expressed in his speeches, be considered. May the responsiveness on the part of his many audiences (approximately 3.5 per day, excluding days of travel) be noted. May his patience in the face of trivia, irritating situations, and long, demanding speechifying be noted.

Speaking as one who acted as chauffeur this past weekend, may I recommend for your observation that John Robert Lewis is *tired* (me, too) and that he needs a Rest. I had the illusion most of the time that I was driving a hearse, because the person contained therein resembled a corpse more than any other thing, so great was his exhaustion.

Hoping that you will consider the above information seriously and act upon it with all judiciousness, I remain

Yours in freedom,
Penny

I appreciated those sentiments, though taking any kind of break or vacation was out of the question. We didn't take vacations in SNCC. But Penny's timing was good. Christmas was around the corner, and I was able to spend a few days with my family at home before turning to the new year, which began, horrifyingly and literally, with a bang.

On the night of January 3, a SNCC volunteer named Sammy Younge left a party at an apartment in Tuskegee to pick up some mayonnaise and bring it back for some tuna sandwiches he and his friends were making. Sammy was one of the leaders of the Tuskegee students who had demonstrated on the streets of Montgomery during the previous spring's Selma campaign. He dropped by our office in Atlanta several times during those months, and we'd talked several times. He was a good-looking young guy, fair-skinned, tall, slim, very engaging. He was only twenty-one, but he'd already served in the U.S. Navy. Now he had returned to college at Tuskegee Institute, where he was both a student and a veteran.

That day he had been helping voters register at the courthouse in downtown Tuskegee. Now he was unwinding at this party with several friends, some of whom were involved with SNCC.

After he got his mayonnaise that evening, Sammy stopped on the way back to the party to buy some cigarettes at a gas station, a Standard Oil station. While inside, he asked the man tending the cash register, a white man, if he could use the rest room in the station. The man, a sixty-nine-year-old employee named Marvin Segrest, told him to go out and around the back, to the rest room reserved for blacks. This one, he told Sammy, was for whites only. Sammy looked at the man and said, "Haven't you heard of the Civil Rights Act?"

The man then pulled out a gun and told Sammy to get off the property. Sammy left, got in his car and pulled it over to the Greyhound bus station next door. When he stepped out, the man was standing outside the station, still holding his gun. More words were exchanged. The man came toward Sammy. There was a bag of golf clubs sitting on the bus platform, waiting to be loaded. Sammy pulled one of the clubs from the bag and waved it at the man. The man stopped. Sammy then turned to run, and the man fired his gun. He missed.

Sammy clambered onto a waiting bus and shouted back at the man, "Would you shoot me on this bus?"

The driver scrambled off and tried telling the man to put down the gun. The man backed off. Sammy then got off the bus and headed for his car. Another shot rang out. This one did not miss.

The coroner's report stated that Sammy Younge was killed at 11:45 that night by a single bullet to the back of his head.

I got the news the first thing the next morning, as soon as I arrived at our office in Atlanta. As many times as I had gotten this kind of news, I was still stunned. I really thought this type of thing was finally behind us. More than three thousand people marched through Tuskegee that day, and the next day Sammy Younge was buried. As I stood there, watching an American flag draped over his casket, the irony hit me very, very hard. Here was a man who had served his country, a military veteran, and what had it gotten him? His killer wasn't even indicted until that November, although the shooting had happened in a public place, in front of several witnesses. When the jury delivered its verdict at the trial that December, in a Macon County courtroom, it found Marvin Segrest, incredibly, "not guilty."

The day after that funeral, Thursday, January 6, we called a press conference, and I read aloud SNCC's statement denouncing the draft and America's involvement in the Vietnam War. The reporters gathered there that day had no idea what they were in for when they arrived. They didn't know what this press conference was going to be about. As I began to read the statement, I could see the stunned looks on their faces. This was real news, big news, national news—the first public statement of opposition to the war by a civil rights organization. And Sammy Younge's death had become part of that statement:

> We believe the United States government has been deceptive in its claims of concern for the freedom of the Vietnamese people, just as the government has been deceptive in claiming concern for the freedom of colored people in such other countries as the Dominican Republic, the Congo, South Africa, Rhodesia, and in the United States itself. . . .
>
> The murder of Samuel Younge in Tuskegee, Alabama, is no different than the murder of peasants in Vietnam, for both Younge and the Vietnamese sought, and are seeking, to secure the rights guaranteed them by law. . . .
>
> We are in sympathy with, and support, the men in this country who are unwilling to respond to a military draft which would compel them to contribute their lives to United States aggression in Vietnam in the name of "freedom" we find so false in this country. . . .
>
> We take note of the fact that 16 percent of the draftees from this country are Negroes called on to stifle the liberation of Vietnam, to preserve a "democracy" which does not exist for them at home. We ask, where is the draft for the freedom fight in the United States?

I went on to call upon all Americans to refuse the draft and to do alternative service with civil rights groups and local poverty agencies throughout the South.

> We believe that work in the civil rights movement and with other human relations organizations is a valid alternative to the draft. We urge all Americans to seek this alternative, knowing full well that it may cost them their lives—as painfully as in Vietnam.

Our statement was the lead story across the nation the next day. Predictably there were reactions of outrage and alarm. The Atlanta FBI office immediately forwarded a copy of the statement to FBI headquarters in Washington. Atlanta congressman Charles Weltner asked the House Un-American Activities Committee to study the matter. And almost overnight I received a notice from my draft board informing me that my status, which had just been assigned the month before, had now been changed from 1-O to 4-F. I was "morally unfit" for service, they explained, because of my long record of arrests.

As for other civil rights organizations, they offered us no more support than they had in the past. Wilkins's NAACP and Young's Urban League predictably rushed to the side of Lyndon Johnson and Hubert Humphrey, shaking their heads at our "outrageous" attacks on the administration. Dr. King refused to join them—a year later he would come out against the war himself. But neither did he openly support us. It bothered me that so many of our own brothers in the movement refused to take this stand with us. I shared that concern with one reporter at the time:

> I think it is a tragedy that the so-called responsible well-established civil rights organizations, the so-called responsible leaders and Negro leaders and civil rights leaders in general, have not taken a position on the war in Vietnam....
>
> I don't know the particular reasons of people like Farmer or Wilkins or Whitney Young. On the one hand I do have a feeling that some of the people cannot understand, or just refuse to understand, that what is going on in Vietnam or in Africa or in Latin America, or in Europe, is part of a much larger struggle; that in a sense what we're doing is part of the whole struggle, a worldwide struggle on the part of people, and that somehow we must be in tune with the mood of the people. And on the other hand I think that some people, some of the so-called Negro leaders in particular, are involved in the whole political game; they're getting involved in things with President Johnson.
>
> They want to get something for keeping silence, for not getting involved.

The most lasting legacy of that SNCC statement against the war, oddly enough, was its effect on Julian. I'd never heard him say much, if anything, about the war, either in our meetings or in private. He wasn't involved in the drafting of the statement. I'm not sure whether he had even read it completely at the time it was released. He had other things on his mind at the time, most notably taking his seat as a newly elected member of the Georgia House of Representatives.

A Supreme Court decision the previous year had created a new, predominantly black district in Georgia very near our SNCC headquarters, and Julian decided to run for that seat as a Democratic Party candidate. Predictably, he was criticized by some SNCC people for "selling out" by joining that party.

Naturally, I was behind him 100 percent. I believed in the two-party system, and I also didn't want his to be a symbolic candidacy. Julian could win, but only if he worked through the system.

This was the first time I ever campaigned for anybody. This new district— the 136th—was 98 percent black, located in the heart of Atlanta. I went house to house knocking on doors, just talking to people. No speeches. I visited barbershops and beauty shops, encouraging people to vote for Julian.

And they did. Julian won by a landslide, drawing 82 percent of the vote against his opponent, a black Republican named Malcolm Dean, the dean of men at Atlanta University. Julian's success in that '65 election inspired several SNCC members to begin involving themselves in politics, including Marion Barry, who moved to D.C. and began his career there as the head of SNCC's Washington office and as director of the "Free D.C." movement.

The day our statement on Vietnam was issued, Julian was less than a week away from being sworn in as a Georgia state legislator. Because he was still our communications director, it was his job to release my statement to the press. Naturally, once the statement got out, Julian was besieged by requests from reporters wanting comments or interviews with me or Forman. It was part of Julian's job to set those up. But in this case, one young reporter caught Julian off guard by asking him what *he* thought of the statement. Did he support it?

"Sure," he said, almost nonchalantly, "I support it."

And then, as the saying goes, the feces hit the fan. Julian's soon-to-be colleagues in the statehouse had been none too eager to welcome him in the first place, and now they had something to chew on. Words like "traitor" and "treason" and "radical" were sprinkled all through the interviews given by the Georgia legislators. It was one thing for me to speak as a member of SNCC; it was another for Julian to speak as a state government representative.

He was really shaken by all this—very nervous, very scared. We were all completely behind him. He had our total support. But it didn't help much. This was the first time he'd been on the firing line, his first taste of what it was like to be in the heat of battle. Up till then, during all our campaigns, while our people were out in the field facing the spitting and fists and paddy wagons and jail cells, Julian was back in Atlanta, relaying the news to the nation's reporters. That was his job. Now, for the first time, *he* was the story, and he had no idea how this was going to turn out. None of us did.

Four days after our statement was released, Julian arrived at the statehouse to take his oath of office. Instead of joining the other new legislators, he was told to stand aside, that the others were going to be sworn in and then they would all debate Julian's antiwar stand and decide whether he should be unseated for violating his oath to uphold the Constitutions of Georgia and the United States.

When the vote came, he lost. His seat was denied, taken away.

I couldn't believe this. It was astounding. It wasn't even legal. Once again, we were getting screwed. Once again, the system was making a mockery of justice. Was it any wonder that people in the movement were bailing out right and left, abandoning all hope of appealing to and working through a system that could do something like this? It was a replay of what had happened to the MFDP in Atlantic City. It was an echo of all the "not guilty" verdicts sneeringly returned in Deep South courtrooms where white men stood trial for the blatant murders of blacks. It was the same government that was on the one hand only too happy to send young black men to die in Vietnam, but on the other hand would not dream of allowing a young black man to hold office.

We immediately rallied to Julian's support, pushing and protesting for some justice. A special election was held and Julian was reelected. And then his seat was *still* denied. "They can keep on electing him till Gabriel blows his trumpet," laughed Denmark Grover, a rural Georgia legislator, "but they ain't ever gonna get him in here."

Now it was time to sue, to take this to court. And that's when things began to snowball. Julian's cause became national, and he was suddenly famous, embraced as, of all things, a champion of the antiwar movement. John Lindsay, by then the mayor of New York, said he wished he was still practicing law so he could come down to Georgia and represent Julian Bond. Dr. King led a march to support Julian. The case went all the way to the U.S. Supreme Court, and in December of that year, 1966, Julian's seating was ordered by the High Court. By then, he was no longer a member of SNCC. And by then, all his fear and doubts had vanished, replaced by the flush of celebrity. He was a star, and he liked it.

As for me, the process of becoming an odd sort of outcast began taking place. Comments like my statement about the reluctance of other civil rights organizations to take a stand on Vietnam did not make me many friends elsewhere in the movement. And, ironically, I wound up being taken to task by my own organization during this time for being too "chummy" with the White House and President Johnson. That happened after I received an invitation from the White House in early 1966 to participate in a conference in Washington in June titled "To Fulfill These Rights." I decided to accept the invitation, to the great dismay of many of my SNCC colleagues. They were entirely against working with the establishment at this point. They wanted to boycott this gathering, to send a message that SNCC had had enough, that the government should come to *us* on *our* terms, no more going to them on theirs. I disagreed. My position was—and has always been—that in any situation where people are prepared to talk about problems, to negotiate, to try to work out solutions, it is imperative to listen, to at least hear what they have to say. That is an essential part of the philosophy of nonviolence, that you are as open to receive as to deliver, that you are willing and able to keep all possible doors open.

That March I went to Washington for a planning session on the conference. I thought the focus would be civil rights, that that was the reason I had been invited. But at this session all President Johnson talked about was the upcoming congressional elections that fall, his fear of Democratic Party losses, and how much he needed our support. "I need your help," he kept saying. "You have to help me, we need a consensus." A consensus. He must have used that word a dozen times. And there *was* no consensus anymore. Not among his own party. Not among Americans. Not among black Americans. The war, the economy, civil rights—all these issues were seething, just tearing the country apart, turning people against one another.

That meeting was the end of my involvement in this conference. But the fact that I had attended at all was held against me by many SNCC members. So was the fact that I continued to serve on the board of the SCLC. The resentment among the SNCC rank and file against Dr. King was almost as strong as the disgust with President Johnson. Both men represented a system that SNCC was fed up with. More than ever, there was pressure put on me— chiefly from Stokely and Courtland Cox—to resign from that board, something I would not dream of doing. I'd been on that board since 1962. I thought it was important to maintain a liaison with Dr. King and the SCLC, based on the same principle of keeping doors open that had brought me up to Washington for that planning session. Beyond that, I had an extremely deep relationship with Dr. King, and I was not going to give that up. Ever.

Beyond the friction over those issues, and our ongoing disagreements over SNCC's shift away from nonviolence toward militancy and black nationalism, I disagreed with the decision that spring for SNCC to set its sights beyond the South by setting up SNCC projects in Northern urban ghettos. I felt our mission and primary responsibility was in the South. We knew the South. That was where we had established our organization. That was where we'd been effective. And there was still a great deal of work to be done there, a great deal of unfinished business. In the same way that America could not afford to spread its resources from domestic programs to Vietnam, I believed we would be spreading ourselves too thin by moving north.

All these issues were simmering that spring as I traveled around the country making speeches on behalf of SNCC to many peace groups. I had cofounded an organization called the Southern Coordinating Committee to End the War in Vietnam, but the talks I gave were not focused just on that war. I spoke much more generally, sharing my personal attitude and philosophy about U.S. military involvement all around the globe. I talked with one reporter about it in an interview early that year:

> I think there's a myth, some type of fever or something, that's running wild on the American scene that gives us the idea that we are so right, and that we are so powerful that we should emerge as the keeper of the world's record, as the big cop. We are more and more going to different places around the world, and we're going in the name of peace, and to stop the spread of communism. We're going to the Congo and to the Dominican Republic and Vietnam, and after Vietnam no doubt we'll be going someplace else, saying that this is part of a peacekeeping effort.
>
> And one of the real problems is that our whole economy in this country in my own estimation is built around war and conflict. We have a war economy and we hate to do any serious thinking or contemplation about peacetime economy....Somehow the American people must force the government to do some serious thinking, some serious planning, about a peacetime economy and of absorbing the millions of men that we have in uniform into our economy.

I believe those words are as true today as they were then. From Beirut to Bosnia we have continued to mire ourselves in "peacekeeping" military efforts, and our economy continues to be dependent on the vast military-industrial complex that Eisenhower warned us about forty years ago. We continue to spend billions of dollars on bombers and warships based on a model of international relations that is long outdated and counterproductive.

I talked about all this that spring in speeches around the country and overseas as well, including a trip to Norway arranged by a student group there. I returned from that trip just in time for our annual SNCC meeting in Nashville—the last SNCC meeting I would ever attend.

As soon as I got back from the airport, I learned that Stokely had been mounting a campaign for the chairmanship. This was not something we ever did. No one in SNCC had ever campaigned for a position before. All elections were conducted by acclamation at general meetings, in keeping with our spirit of utter openness. No behind-the-scenes campaigning was supposed to take place. But it was taking place now. This was politicking, and I didn't want any part of it.

At first I was not going to run for reelection. I didn't like what was happening here. I'd been chairman for three years. Maybe it was time to give someone else a chance.

But then I thought hard about the direction SNCC was moving, the issues that were splitting it apart. Were we going to be an interracial movement or a separatist movement? Violent or nonviolent? Moving toward community or toward conflict? The very future of SNCC was on the line, and I still believed it was possible to salvage our basic principles while still adjusting to the American realities of 1966, which were far different from the realities of 1961. I could see room for us to become more radical, to meet the emotional demands of the people, without crossing the line of nonviolence.

I finally decided that I had an obligation to stay, to stand up for the SNCC I believed in and for the vision of America that I could still see. Maybe if I stayed around for another year, I could hold the group together and we could stay on course.

The conference began May 8 at a rustic, forested church retreat in a place called Kingston Springs, near Nashville. More than two hundred people arrived, bunking down in bare-bones, dormitory-style cabins and gathering for our meals and meetings in a central mess hall, a large wide-open shelter with pine floors, pine walls and windows opened to the Tennessee woods outside.

For nearly a week we held meetings and discussions and song and prayer groups. The major issue of discussion that entire week, the subject we kept coming back to again and again, was the relevancy and even the possibility of an interracial democracy.

Earlier that year, the staff in our Atlanta Project, under the direction of a SNCC member named Bill Ware, had developed some extreme ideas of black separatism. Ware was from Mississippi, had gone to college in the North (in Minnesota) and had spent a year in Ghana with the Peace Corps before joining SNCC in 1964. He was very well read, very articulate, with well-developed ideas that corresponded in many ways with Malcolm X's philosophy of blacks controlling their own fates without the involvement of whites. That January, the same month we issued our statement on Vietnam, Ware recruited several young women from Spelman College and, with their input, published a position paper that expressed their views that black people needed all-black organizations to establish their own identities and develop their own direction.

This idea caught fire with many SNCC members, who felt that black Americans were no longer any more willing than whites to respond to the concept of an interracial democracy. They *would,* however, respond to programs based on racial separatism. Ware's own Atlanta Project had been successful with urban organizing based on a model of exclusively black involvement. Down in Lowndes County, where Stokely's group had been successful in mobilizing people with the concept of black identity, the argument could be made that this approach worked as well, although there the intent had not been to create an exclusively black organization. That was just the way it worked out in a place where whites had nothing whatsoever to do with blacks other than to occasionally attack or try to kill them. Stokely, as a matter of fact, was not as anti-white as many of our membership. His views on this subject were not nearly as extreme as those of Bob Ware and his people.

As for me, the notion that blacks needed to do for themselves, to develop independence and self-reliance, was fine. But I wasn't ready to separate us from the community around us. The future of this nation depended on us learning to come together, not pushing ourselves apart. I was not willing to be a part of any community that excluded other human beings from its membership. Neither was I ready to be part of an organization that did the same thing. Many of our white members had seen just such a movement forming over the past year and had, sadly, left SNCC behind. I was not about to throw out the twenty or so white staffers who were left. Neither was Stokely, though he wasn't as clear about it.

Thanks mostly to Bob Zellner's work that week, a motion was passed to keep whites in SNCC but to have them work only in white communities. Everyone could see it would be only a matter of time before they were ousted entirely, and that was painful, for these young white people who had come of age in SNCC, who identified themselves with this group, who had developed personal relationships with black members that were as close as family ties. That's what we had been, a family, and now some of us were being told to leave the family, to get out. That hurt a lot of people, white and black alike. It hurt me terribly. Bob Zellner, Bill Hansen, Sam Shirah, Betty Garman, Mary King, Casey Hayden and Danny Lyon—these were my brothers and sisters, not just my friends.

Finally, that Saturday, our last evening before leaving, it was time for the election. We arranged ourselves in a huge semicircle several people deep. Some were sitting on the floor, others in chairs. Most preferred to stand. As expected, I was opposed by Stokely and a couple of other staffers. Lafayette Surmey was one of them, but I can't remember the others. None of them were serious about it. It was almost a joke. But for Stokely, this was no joke.

We began with a very emotionally charged open discussion, with people standing up and speaking out about changes we needed to make. I again spoke my piece about keeping whites among our membership and got some backlash about that from some of the more strident voices in the room. I was criticized for spending so much time visiting college campuses around the country—"white" college campuses. I was also criticized for going to Washington for that planning session in March. I was attacked for my SCLC affiliation and my allegiance to Dr. King. Even my religious orientation was attacked.

It got very low and nasty, very bitter and mean. People stood up and said we needed someone who could grab Lyndon Johnson by his balls and tell him to kiss our ass. We needed someone who would stand up to Dr. King and tell him the same thing. That was a phrase I heard several times—"kiss our ass."

I wasn't about to tell Dr. King—my friend, my hero— to kiss my ass. I wasn't about to turn my back on him or on our white members, or on any segment of our society, including the federal government. No matter how many times our hopes and dreams seemed dashed, I continued to believe that the American government, along with American society at large, would ultimately respond and open itself up and embrace *all* of its people.

But that was not what this discussion was about. What it was about, in the end, was who was "blackest," and it was hard to tell where the lines were drawn. The people who spoke out were very loud, but the vast majority simply listened. It was hard to tell what they were thinking.

And then, close to midnight, came the vote.

Forman had resigned as executive secretary earlier that week, and Stokely had been nominated for that position but refused to accept it. Ruby Doris Robinson wound up being elected to replace Forman. Cleve Sellers was elected as program secretary. And finally, by a vote of 60 to 22, with a lot of abstentions, I was reelected as chairman.

With that, people began moving out, drifting back toward their cabins for some sleep before packing and leaving the next morning. It was late. Everyone was exhausted.

More than half of them were gone when Worth Long stood up and made an announcement.

He wanted to challenge the election. We had violated the constitution, he said. He said something about not following procedure. No one was sure what exactly he was talking about. Very few of us had even looked at our constitution in years, if ever. Worth wasn't even a staff member at this time, which might have raised the question of whether he had any basis for making any objection at all, or even for participating in the meeting.

But no one asked that question. In the climate of the times, with everyone's emotions at such a high pitch, and with our lack of structure for these meetings, the door was quickly opened to another discussion. Suddenly, the election was on the table again. Everything was on the table again.

I've thought a lot over the years about why Worth Long did what he did. What was behind it? And long ago I came to suspect that Jim Forman was in part responsible. I think Forman wanted me out. He'd wanted me out for a long time. He was in sympathy with this new wave of militance and separatism. He had never accepted the philosophy of nonviolence. He'd never accepted the concept of an interracial democracy, of a truly biracial society. It always irked him to hear me preaching love and tolerance and nonviolence, to see me offering respect and admiration for Dr. King, to watch me stick up for Bobby Kennedy and defend John Kennedy and try to work with Lyndon Johnson.

There may have been the factor of ego at work here as well. From the beginning, Jim Forman had appeared to have a deep-rooted envy of Dr. King. It just ate at him to see King and the SCLC constantly getting the spotlight and the adulation, often receiving credit he felt rightfully belonged to SNCC and other groups.

Beyond that, Forman was obsessive about control. When he joined SNCC, people deferred to him because of his age and his forceful personality. Then, over time, a fear factor developed as well. Forman gathered as much power as he could, primarily by controlling the purse strings of our organization. That mattered a lot to the people in the field. He was the one who decided whether you'd get a staff car or not, whether you'd get expense money to go from Atlanta to Cambridge, whether your office would be assigned the number of members you needed to get the job done that you had in mind. Forman had total control over all these things, and he seemed to like it that way. I suspect that's why he arranged back in 1963 for nice, quiet, young John Lewis to become chairman—because, in his eyes, I wouldn't be a threat.

Unfortunately, as people have done throughout my life, Forman misjudged me. He mistook my demeanor for meekness. He had no idea in the beginning how committed, how forceful in my own way, I can become once I have made my mind up to do something. He learned this about me over the years, and it was maddeningly frustrating for him.

Now, finally, Forman was ready to leave, and I have little doubt that he wanted to make sure he took me with him when he went. Even Stokely's ascent, in large part, was, I believe, due to Forman's engineering behind the scenes. Putting Stokely out there, with all his fireworks and histrionics, was a good cover for Forman to see me removed. I've always believed that.

And I have to say it hurt. We had been through a lot together, Jim Forman and I. I had always understood his ego, but I had never thought he would turn on me. Nor did I imagine my own family, the SNCC organization as a whole, would do the same. But that's what happened as that night moved into early Sunday morning, and the discussion quickly veered away from the legitimacy of the vote just taken to a wider-ranging debate over what SNCC stood for and what I stood for and whether the two were a good match.

Fewer than half the people who had been there at the beginning of the evening were still around. Most of my friends, the people who supported me, were back in their cabins asleep. Charles Sherrod and his southwest Georgia group; Bill Hansen and the people from Arkansas; the Peacock brothers,

James and Willie, along with their rank-and-file colleagues from Mississippi; Bob Mants—they were all gone. They did not find out until the next day what happened late that night. Some of them left so early the next morning that they didn't hear the news until they got back to their homes.

It went on for several hours, people raising their voices and shouting, all these feelings bursting out, just a torrent of pent-up frustration and anger. It was almost like a mob, people swept up by the emotions around them. I could see this was a wave no one could stop. I just sat and listened. I didn't speak. I certainly didn't protest. What was I going to protest? With what authority? There was no higher authority to appeal to now. It was anarchy. Everything was gone. This was the end.

Finally, at five-thirty that morning, Ruby and Cleve "resigned" their positions in order to allow the vote to be retaken. I refused to join them, but it didn't matter. I could have just left, but that would have been wrong. I wasn't going to run away. I stayed and took the pill. The "election" was a foregone conclusion, an exercise in going through the motions.

And that was it. Stokely Carmichael was the new chairman of SNCC.

I went back to my room drained, exhausted, dazed. The sun was coming up. I was so tired I couldn't think or feel. It wasn't until I woke up late that morning that I realized what had happened. It was true. It was over.

I thought about the fact that no one had spoken up for me. Not one person. I didn't get upset, maybe because I *couldn't* let myself feel it. If I had, it would have hurt too much. I just couldn't have gone on. So I locked my feelings away.

I went to the cafeteria to get something to eat, and some of my friends gathered around—Mants, Hansen, Sherrod. They were stunned. Outraged. But no one knew what to do. And I didn't want them to do anything. This had been coming a long time. It was supposed to happen, and so it did. It wasn't as if we hadn't done all we could to try to stop it.

By the time I got home to Atlanta, my phone was ringing off the hook. There was a lot of emotion coming through those lines, a lot of crying. My mailbox filled up with notes and letters. Julian, who was out of town a lot during this time, wrote me often, telling me it wouldn't be long before he'd be leaving, too. "The crazies are taking over"—that was the way he put it.

As much as I tried not to feel it, this was a serious blow, a personal thing, and it affected me very much. My life, my identity, most of my very existence, was tied up in SNCC. Now, so suddenly, I felt put out to pasture. I was able to reason it out, to rationalize and understand it, especially with other people around, but when I was alone, it hurt. It hurt more than anything I'd ever been through. I had always told myself and others that whatever the setback, we had to keep going, that the road was a long and winding one. But nothing had tested that belief like this. I intended to stay true to it, but I honestly didn't know if I could.

What happened that night was devastating for me, yes, but even more so for SNCC. Breaks were created; wounds were opened that would never heal. I didn't consider it so much a repudiation of me as a repudiation of ourselves, of what we *were,* of what we stood for. We denied and denounced ourselves that night. It was a very sad thing, very tragic.

When I next walked into our Atlanta headquarters, it was with a new assignment—director of SNCC's recently formed Committee for International Affairs, a branch of the organization which I had created as chairman to strengthen our ties with black struggles in Third World countries. This was clearly a throwaway, a consolation. But I accepted it. I didn't resign, not at that point. Quitting then would have seemed small.

In the aftermath of my "de-election," I was naturally besieged by the press. I shared none of my feelings and thoughts with them. Even with all that had happened, I still cared about SNCC, I still wanted it to have every chance to succeed. And so I went along with our strategy for dealing with this change, which was described in minutes from a meeting that took place as soon as we got back to Atlanta from Nashville:

> Julian Bond, Joanne Grant and Bill Mahoney will write and release a statement on the change of officers; there will be a closed meeting to deal with John Lewis' ideas about the change of power....
>
> The statement will be released at a press conference on...May 24, 1966. There will be an attempt to cultivate the Negro press.... John Lewis and James Forman will be at the Atlanta press conference to avoid any interpretation of there being a split in the organization.

There was no "closed meeting" to deal with my "ideas about the change of power." There was nothing left for anyone to say about that. The press conference in Atlanta did take place, and I even attended a fund-raiser with Stokely in Washington as a show of solidarity. It felt sort of odd sitting there watching him take charge. I had to swallow some pride, some self-respect, some dignity. I was fully aware that I was compromising those things, but I told myself it was toward a greater good, toward some sense of peace.

I didn't truly believe that, but I told myself it was so. Looking back at the way things turned out, if I had it to do over again, I would have resigned the night of that election. Then everything would have been over much sooner, at least for me. I chose to hold on, hoping that somehow, something good could *still* emerge from all this.

I was so wrong.

One month after that SNCC conference in Kingston Springs, James Meredith, who in 1963 had become the first black student to graduate from the University of Mississippi, began what he called a March Against Fear through that state, to "tear down the fear that grips the Negroes in Mississippi" and inspire some of Mississippi's 450,000 black citizens eligible to vote to register. Meredith began his 220-mile march from Memphis to Jackson alone, wearing a pith helmet and carrying an ivory-headed African cane.

I had heard something about this march, but like a lot of other people, I did not consider it that big a deal. Meredith was never really a part of the movement. He was a strange bird from the beginning, always going here and there, acting on his own with no real direction or agenda. One day he'd be in Hawaii, and the next he'd announce that he was going to run for president. There was something about him that was kind of strange. But then you could probably say that about all of us. You'd have to be a little strange to do some of the things we did.

Few people paid that much attention when Meredith set out on his march on June 8, but the next morning he was, incredibly, wounded by three blasts from a sniper with a shotgun, an unemployed clerk waiting in ambush in the woods. I was shocked when I heard the news, but I was not surprised. I knew that part of Mississippi. I knew what some of those people were like.

No sooner had Meredith arrived at a hospital in Memphis than people from all corners of the movement began rallying to the scene, first to visit Meredith, who, amazingly, survived the shooting, then to the road to pick up and carry on the march Meredith had begun. Dr. King came. So did the new director of CORE, a man named Floyd McKissick, who had replaced Farmer on much the same grounds as Stokely had replaced me—by rejecting non-violence. McKissick called it a "dying philosophy" that had "outlived its usefulness." Stokely, too, was there, as chairman of SNCC.

I did not join them, not at first. There was no real place for me in this march, and beyond that I wasn't clear about its purpose. This situation was different from Selma, where the march was a culmination of a long campaign with a particular focus. This was a spontaneous reaction to a specific incident. It took place in a vacuum, more or less, with no unity of purpose—with no unity at all, for that matter. That became clear as it developed. It became almost a contest among the different factions of the movement, with lots of speeches each night, during which the three main leaders—King, McKissick and Carmichael—jockeyed for control of the crowds, sharing their different positions on black nationalism and nonviolence and arguing among themselves. All the cracks and fissures and divisions within the movement were literally put on-stage for everyone to see. The reporters covering that march had a field day.

Their third day out, June 11, I was at my desk in our Atlanta headquarters when I overheard Cleve Sellers talking to Stokely on the telephone, discussing plans to "take over the march." I could only pick up snippets of the conversation, but it revolved around doing something to "set up" the SCLC people.

That was the last straw. There was nothing left to hold on to here. Until then I had held on to a thin thread of hope that SNCC could still turn itself around. But this was too much. I could never be a party to anything that involved deviousness or deceit. That afternoon, I submitted my resignation, effective July 22.

Meanwhile, the march in Mississippi made news once again, with the introduction of a phrase that reflected the shift of the entire civil rights movement:

"Black Power."

It was a SNCC staffer named Willie Ricks who brought this about. Ricks was twenty-three, three years younger than I. He had come out of Chattanooga, Tennessee, as a high school student in the early '60s. He was brash, aggressive and understandably angry—early on, a close friend of his was killed during a demonstration.

Ricks was a good agitator. He knew how to stir up a crowd. He termed himself a black nationalist, and he was not at all interested in the philosophy of nonviolence or the concept of a biracial community. He used phrases like "white blood flowing" in his speeches.

He began speaking often during the Meredith march, to small audiences in churches and meeting halls, and midway through the march he began using a new phrase in his speeches. We had a slogan we had used during our Alabama campaigns: "Black power for black people." Ricks shortened it to "Black Power" and began sprinkling it into his speeches. This was not a new phrase. It had been used by black writers and politicians for years. The novelist Richard Wright used it. So did the congressman from Harlem, Adam Clayton Powell. Actor Paul Robeson used it in response to the Little Rock crisis of 1957. But Willie Ricks's timing was perfect. People were ready for a notion like this, and they really responded. A nerve was struck. When Stokely heard that Ricks was really whipping the crowds up, he went to see for himself one evening what was going on. He saw how the people just went crazy over that phrase and he decided to adopt the term himself.

The night of June 17, after he'd been arrested and released in Greenwood, Stokely stepped before a heaving, upset crowd and said, "This is the twenty-seventh time I have been arrested. I ain't going to jail no more.

"The only way we gonna stop them white men from whuppin' us," he continued, "is to take over! We been sayin' 'Freedom Now' for six years and we ain't got nothin'. What we gonna start sayin' now is 'Black Power'!"

With that, Willie Ricks jumped up beside Stokely and yelled, "What do you *want?*"

The crowd roared back, *"Black Power!!!"*

Back and forth went that chant, sweeping up everyone there, including the reporters and cameramen who recorded it and showed it to the nation. That's how I heard about it, the next day.

Mainstream America, as well as the heads of the other major civil rights organizations, were appalled. Here went SNCC again, first condemning the war in Vietnam and now trying to incite a race war. Dr. King called the phrase "an unfortunate choice of words." Roy Wilkins equated it with Nazism, calling it "the father of hate and the mother of violence." Bayard Rustin said the phrase "lacks any real value for the civil rights movement." Hubert Humphrey called it "reverse racism."

A young Associated Press reporter named Don McKee talked to me soon after that speech and asked me what I thought about it.

I had so many thoughts about this concept. The way I had always understood the phrase, it had more to do with self-reliance than with black supremacy, though that distinction was hard to see, especially through the fire and spit with which Stokely and some of the others tended to deliver their message. The way he was using it, I thought it tended to create a schism, both within the movement itself and between the races. It drove people apart rather than brought them together. But at that time Stokely was not interested in bringing people together. He was out to stir things up. He delighted in scaring white people, and this did the trick.

I didn't say all that to Don McKee. What I told him was more succinct. I said I thought this phrase frightened people, that it created a gulf. "As an organization," I said, "we don't believe in sloganeering. We believe in programs."

That was enough. McKee's story went out over the wires, and the next day's headlines read "JOHN LEWIS BREAKS WITH SNCC OVER PHRASE BLACK POWER."

A week later came my last public appearance as a member of SNCC. The march in Mississippi was nearing its end, and the marchers had arrived at the town of Canton, where they began setting up tents on a schoolground there to spend the night. They were immediately confronted by a battalion of Mississippi state troopers who told them they were trespassing. Within minutes the troopers were wading into the crowd with clubs and tear gas. It was very brutal, some said as brutal as Bloody Sunday. When I got the news, I told myself I had to go there for the people who were hurt. This was not about speeches and politics. It was not about SNCC. This was, as in Selma, about the people.

When I got there, plans had been made for a rally protesting the attack, and I was put on the schedule to speak. Paul Good, a writer for *The New York Times Magazine,* described the scene:

> The knowledge of disunity was in the dark air as people stood and waited for their leaders on ground made soggy by state troopers who had opened water pipes in a final act of petty harassment.
> The people wanted to do something, but no one knew what. The chunky form of Lewis rose on a shaky box. "Fellow freedom fighters," he said. "The whole man must say no nonviolently, his entire Christian spirit must say no to this evil and vicious system...."
> Even as he spoke, listeners sloshed away. The speaker's credentials were in order, but his time was out of joint. He spoke the old words of militant love, but the spiritual heart of the movement that for years had sent crusaders up and down American roads, trusting in love, was broken and Lewis had become that most expendable commodity, a former leader. It was not so much that he was losing his audience; the audience was already lost.

I remember talking to Good and telling him that I felt like an uninvited guest that night, that things had been much simpler in the earlier days, that we really believed it would be enough just to offer up our bodies, and that that had turned out not to be so. Everything had become much more complicated than that. Everything had become much messier.

Even Dr. King was losing his faith after that march. "The government," he told Good, "has got to give me some victories if I'm gonna keep people nonviolent. I know I'm gonna stay nonviolent no matter what happens. But a lot of people are getting hurt and bitter, and they can't see it that way anymore."

Was my own faith shaken? No. I'd adopted a slogan along the way, something I read in a magazine article and cut out and kept with me at all times. It was the rallying cry of native Africans resisting Portuguese colonialists in Mozambique and Angola: *Aluta continua*—"the struggle continues."

Frederick Douglass said essentially the same thing back in 1857: "There must be a struggle." I have always embraced the idea that the pursuit of a worthy, deep goal is never for a day or for a year, that the journey is long and hard, and no one can say how long it will take. You take in all the information you can, you decide what is right, and once you make that decision, you pursue it. You commit, with perseverance, steadfastness and faith.

I still had faith in the principles we had applied to the formation of SNCC. But SNCC itself had now abandoned them. The organization was riddled with bitterness and talk of retaliation and violence, actions that might deliver some quick comfort but that in the long run were debasing. I felt I owed an allegiance to a higher principle than SNCC, and so it was time for me to leave. A month after that rally in Canton—July 22—I cleaned out my desk and left SNCC for good.

It hurt. It hurt to leave my family, so many good brothers and sisters with whom I had shared so much. My ego was hurt as well. My feelings were hurt. I felt abandoned, cast out. I'm a very forgiving man, and I was able to forgive this. But it was probably the hardest thing I've ever done. And though I was able to forgive it, I have never forgotten it. The pain of that experience is something I will never be able to forget.

So there I was, twenty-six years old and starting my life over, broke, with no job, no skills, no wife, no children, no place even to call home. Going back to my family in Alabama was not an option. They didn't even know what had happened, that I was no longer chair of SNCC. None of this was a part of their world. My family had never really been connected to or understood my involvement in the movement. To them, it was as if I was living in a foreign country. Their lives were very simple, very insular, very close to the earth. They didn't look too far beyond their immediate surroundings. Getting up and going to the fields every day, struggling to make ends meet, going to church on Sundays—that was their world. And I, Robert, was out there *somewhere,* doing all these things they didn't understand, didn't know about or didn't *want* to know about. Maybe they were scared. Maybe it was just too big, too overwhelming. "Put it in the hands of the Lord" was my mother's attitude toward anything she couldn't get her hands around.

Whenever I did go home during the six years I was a member of SNCC, all my mother wanted to know was whether I was okay, whether I was well. We never discussed the marches or the arrests, the ideas of Malcolm X or the war in Vietnam. None of that. We would talk about Pike County, about the farm, about how my brothers and sisters were doing. Sam, my younger brother, wound up being drafted, was sent to Vietnam, got wounded in the thigh and received a Purple Heart, but we never talked about it. Sam was home, and that was that. The same with me whenever I went back. Robert was home, and that was that.

No, there was nothing for me in Pike County. Nothing for me in Atlanta either. I thought about maybe going back to school, to finish that philosophy degree at Fisk, but first I needed to find a job. I needed to make a living.

That's when I got a call from a man named Carl Holman. He was a black journalist with a little paper called the *Atlanta Inquirer,* a weekly that was started during the Atlanta sit-in movement of 1960. Carl had been a professor at Clark College, and was now on the board of directors of an organization called the Field Foundation, a New York City–based group that supported civil rights and child welfare programs around the country.

Carl told me he had talked to the director of the Field Foundation, a man named Leslie Dunbar. Les was a political scientist with a tremendous interest in race relations, just a good, decent human being. He had been head of the Southern Regional Council and he was well aware of me and the work I'd done with SNCC. He said he might have something for me to do in New York if I was willing to leave the South.

I didn't exactly have a lot of options. Leaving the South would be difficult, no question, but maybe it would be good for me to put some space between what was behind me and what lay ahead. Besides, I needed a job. And so, on the first day of August 1966, I went to work as the associate director for the Field Foundation in New York City.

As I rode the train up from Atlanta, I felt more lonesome than I had ever felt in my life. I had lived a lifetime in the past six years, and now the rest of my life lay ahead of me, without a map, without a blueprint.

All I kept thinking was, Where am I going?

And why?

Why?

*I*t was the summer of '67, the "Summer of Love," according to the newspapers and magazines displayed at the corner newsstand just up the street from the plain brick apartment building where I lived, in the Chelsea section of Manhattan. Each evening, on my way home from work, I would stop and leaf through the pages of this publication or that, searching for news from back home, from down south. Maybe I would find something, maybe not.

My place was on West Twenty-first Street, between Eighth and Ninth Avenues, kind of a bohemian area, a blend of urban renewal and decaying slums. It was a racially mixed neighborhood, mostly white, with a good number of blacks and a few Puerto Ricans. I didn't know any of my neighbors, and they didn't know me. I was like Ralph Ellison's "Invisible Man," walking home from the subway station each night, hearing Motown music drifting down from the open windows of the buildings I passed, the drumbeat of new rock groups with names like the Doors throbbing out of car radios, all that noise trailing behind me as I climbed the echoing stairwell of my building and let myself into my fourth-floor studio flat.

Love? A better word for the way I felt that summer was lost. But it wasn't the kind of lost that makes you sad. It actually felt good, in an odd, liberating kind of way. This was a time of transition for me, a time when I needed to be lost for a while. And there is no way better for a boy from the rural South to be lost than to pick him up and put him in a place like Manhattan.

My apartment was sparsely furnished. One photograph hung on one wall—a shot Danny Lyon had taken of two water fountains in the Albany, Georgia, courthouse. One of the fountains, a large, stainless steel water cooler, was marked WHITE; the other, a tiny porcelain basin below a spigot sticking out of the wall, was marked COLORED. The picture seemed linked to another lifetime.

My space was small—a single room, with a daybed against one wall and a tiny kitchen area in the corner. I cooked simple stuff—toast, mostly, maybe a chicken once in a while and a lot of those little pot pies.

Sometimes I would open a can of Rheingold beer and sip it while I looked through *The New York Times* or read and reread the long letters Julian wrote me from Atlanta. He was the one who stayed in touch, sending updates on himself and the movement, snippets of behind-the-scenes stuff that wasn't included in the stories I read in the *Times*, the *New York Post* or the city's black newspaper, the *Amsterdam News*.

It was strange to watch from a distance as SNCC shrank and withered. Internal conflicts over philosophy and methods and direction were ripping it apart. The last five remaining white members were fired in December '66, and the shrinking ranks were now filled with people I hardly knew, people like Julius Lester, who joined SNCC after Stokely took my place and was now getting a lot of attention for an essay he wrote called "Look Out, Whitey! Black Power's Gon' Get Your Mama!," which included statements such as "It is clearly written that the victim must become the executioner" and "We must fill ourselves with hate for all white things."

I knew Julius Lester back in my Nashville days, when he was a student at Fisk. He was not involved in the movement then, but when Guy Carawan and his wife, Candie, came to campus to play a concert of their folk and freedom songs, Lester was one of the few black people who picked up a guitar and played along with them.

I hadn't heard of him for years, and suddenly he sort of emerged as this new voice within SNCC. I didn't take him or his ideas too seriously. It seemed to me that, like so many people during this period, he was swept up in the times and had caught a wave, kind of like getting religion. I didn't see much that was heartfelt or deeply thought out or consistent in his ideas. It seemed more like a phase he was going through. First he had been the drifting, folksinging college student. Now he was a radical activist. Later, he converted to Judaism. Julius was a searcher, a lost soul, and I think he symbolized what a lot of people were going through at that time—a kind of groping lostness.

Some were louder in their lostness than others, especially some of the people in SNCC. By the summer of '67, Stokely had been replaced as chairman by a guy named H. (for Hubert) "Rap" Brown. I knew him through his older brother, Ed Brown, who was part of the Howard University contingent of activists and intellectuals up in Washington. Rap had grown up in Louisiana, attended Southern University, gotten involved in the Cambridge movement in '63 and joined SNCC in early 1966. He didn't have the most developed, thought-out ideas in the world, but like Stokely, he knew how to work a crowd. With his black beret and dark sunglasses—the standard look of the new SNCC, which had replaced our old overalls and T-shirts—Rap Brown grabbed headlines with quotes like "Violence is as American as cherry pie."

I would actually agree with that statement. Violence has always been endemic to American culture. Dr. King said the same thing. We are, and have always been, a very violent society. But that doesn't mean we have to accept it. It doesn't mean that we have to respond to the worst of America with the worst of ourselves. We have something better to offer. I have always believed that. I have always believed it is possible to show ourselves a different way, a better way to solve our problems. This is what Gandhi tried to do in India. It is what Dr. King tried to do here, and it goes far beyond civil rights alone. It extends to all of the conflicts we face among ourselves and among other nations. There are simply other and better ways to solve our differences than through violence.

It was this theme that brought Dr. King to New York City that April 1967, where he delivered what I consider the greatest speech of his life.

The event was an antiwar rally organized by a group called Clergy and Laymen Concerned About Vietnam. It was held at the Riverside Church in Manhattan, and I made sure I was there. I hadn't seen Dr. King since leaving SNCC, and I was eager to hear what he was going to say about Vietnam.

It was a cool, clear evening, and more than three thousand people showed up. The scene was loose, boisterous, colorful, almost like a happening, with dozens of religious leaders of all denominations streaming into the church. There were several speakers on the agenda, but the one everyone had come to hear was Dr. King. This was the night he would finally take a stand on the war.

He began by acknowledging that he had shared the same feelings we in SNCC had made public a year earlier. It was time, he said, to "break the betrayals of my own silences and to speak from the burnings of my own heart." He then spelled out the divisive, destructive effects of America's involvement and investment in Vietnam. He called America "the greatest purveyor of violence in the world." America is a great nation, he said, but she would be greater if she would turn herself away from violence, away from war and all that comes with it. "A nation," he said, "that continues year after year to spend more money on military defense than on programs of social uplift is approaching spiritual death."

He urged the young men of America to become conscientious objectors and offer themselves for alternative, productive service. It was essentially the same message I'd delivered on behalf of SNCC a year earlier—the same message I deliver today.

I had heard Dr. King speak many, many times, and I had no doubt that

this speech was his finest. It was deep, comprehensive, thoughtful and courageous. It was about what we were doing in Vietnam, but beyond that it was
about what we were doing on this *earth*. He was saying that those bombs that
were being dropped in Vietnam would detonate here, that they were being
dropped on the hopes and dreams of the American people. And he was
so right. We are still recovering today from the spiritual wounds inflicted by
that war.

I came away from that evening inspired. I still believed, in the face of so
much that seemed to be falling apart, that slowly, inexorably, in ways I might
not be able to recognize or figure out, we were continuing to move in the
direction we should, toward something better. I wasn't in the midst of the
movement anymore, not at the moment, but I knew I would get back to it.

Meanwhile, I went to work every day, up before dawn to shower and
shave, then a short walk to the Twenty-third Street station, where I'd catch the
subway to Times Square. Then the shuttle train from there to Grand Central
Station, a short walk over to Park Avenue—250 Park Avenue—and five floors
up on the elevator, to the offices of the Field Foundation.

The Marshall Field Foundation was created by the late department store
magnate to make grants available to organizations working in the area of child
welfare and race relations. Most of those organizations were in the South, in
many of the same places where I had worked as a member of SNCC. In a
sense I was continuing the work I'd done then, on a different kind of playing
field, from a different position. Before I had helped many of those local community organizations apply for grants to help them with their efforts. Now I
was literally on the other side of the table, digesting, evaluating and deciding
on grant applications from all across the nation.

Our staff was small—five people, including Les and me. I had a little office looking out over Forty-fifth Street. My salary was $200 a week, five times
what I'd been making with SNCC. Of course, none of us in SNCC had paid
attention to our salaries. No one was in SNCC to make money. And no one
was paying $150 a month rent for an apartment, as I now was in New York.
This was altogether a different life than the one I'd been living before.

I did a good amount of traveling, visiting many of the locations and organizations that requested money from us. I'd go up to Syracuse, or over to the
Bronx or Brooklyn, but primarily I went down south. A group in Hattiesburg,
Mississippi, might file for a grant and Les would ask me if I knew these folks,
then send me down to see what they were doing.

But I spent more time in the office than I did on the road, often receiving
visits from representatives of various groups. On one occasion Andy Young
and Dr. King came by to talk about an SCLC citizenship education program.
It felt odd, to say the least, to be facing them across a table and hearing them

describe what they needed to me and to Les. I never imagined I'd be in a situation like that. It was just another sign of how much times were changing for all of us.

Every now and then I'd run into someone from what were rapidly becoming the old days. One weekend, Bevel came up to attend a meeting against the war organized by Tom Hayden and a man named Dave Dellinger. Dellinger was a New Englander a generation older than we were, a lifetime pacifist, a disciple of nonviolence and a leading activist against the war. He and Hayden were two of the architects of a group called the National Mobilization Committee to End the War in Vietnam.

Bevel spent the night at my place, and we reminisced a little about the movement. He was still with the SCLC, but the issue he was on fire with now was Vietnam. That's what he really wanted to talk about. He was urging the SCLC leadership to send a group of demonstrators, including him, over to the Mekong Delta to put their bodies between the Viet Cong and the American troops and force a cease-fire. A sit-in on the battlefield—that was Bevel's newest idea. He was still the Bevel I'd always known.

He told me I needed to join the SCLC, work with them. But there was no way I would ever consider that. First of all, I still needed time, time to separate myself and reflect. Beyond that, I could never go back and play a smaller role with another civil rights group than I had played with SNCC. I had been the national chair of a major organization. I'll admit it—it was a matter of pride, to a large degree. I had been the national chairman for the Student Nonviolent Coordinating Committee. How would I have looked if I returned as an Alabama field secretary for the SCLC? That would have been too much for me to take.

The one friend I saw a lot of during that time was Don Harris. He'd gotten married in '65 and had moved to Boston to attend Harvard Law School. His wife, Kate, was the daughter of social psychologist Kenneth Clark, whose 1950 study of black children in segregated schools had become a landmark in civil rights history. Dr. Clark's study showed that black children in segregated schools had lower self-esteem than those in integrated schools, and it became an important factor in the Supreme Court's '54 *Brown* v. *Board* decision.

Dr. Clark occasionally came by our Field Foundation offices to talk with Les, and he was always very warm, very gracious—just a wonderful man. He had a house on the Hudson River just outside the city, a spacious, beautiful home, and Don and Kate would often come down from Boston to visit him. When they did, they'd invite me up, and the three of us would sit outside and just relax. Sometimes they went out to Martha's Vineyard, and I joined them there once as well. I'd never seen a beach setting like that. It was everything I imagined the New England seaside would look like—grassy dunes and wild roses and steep cliffs on the south side of the island. I couldn't swim—I still can't—so I stayed away from the water and contented myself with strolling on the sand and sitting with Don and Kate.

My time in New York actually passed pretty quickly that year. By the time August rolled around—the anniversary of my arrival—I was starting to feel that I'd been there long enough. The work was fulfilling, but I'd never intended it to be a long-term thing. Les knew that. This was a time of transition for me, and now that time was just about done. I felt that the shadow of my SNCC experience—especially how it ended—had passed, and now I was ready to confront the South as it was, not as it had been, and as who I was, not who I had been. People were beginning to talk about the South as being the stage for the next big wave of change in America. I believed that the next decade would see the whole nation looking to the South for direction and leadership. I wanted to be a part of that.

Besides, New York was just too big for me. I didn't feel as if I could get my hands around it. In the South, communities seemed comprehensible, manageable, workable. You could see where things started and ended. You could get a grasp of the place and the people, as well as their problems. And you could respond to those problems with solutions that might work. I felt lost in New York. Overwhelmed, really. For many reasons, both personal and practical, I knew that the South was where I belonged. I needed to go back.

One of the people who often visited our Field Foundation office looking for funding was the young director of the Southern Regional Council, a young man named Paul Anthony. The SRC had been created back in 1919 in response to a wave of race riots that erupted across the country that year. It was an interracial organization committed to social justice and the elimination of racial discrimination. It had been at the forefront of the fight against Jim Crow laws in the 1930s. In the '40s it had led the campaign to repeal all-white primary elections in the South. By the 1960s, it had shifted its primary focus to voter registration, labor organizing and community organizing.

Early that fall of '67, Paul Anthony stopped by the Field Foundation not to talk about a grant application, but to talk with me about a job. He'd heard I was looking to return to the South, and he said he was looking for someone to direct the SRC's Community Organization Project. I didn't even need to think about it. That October, I thanked Les Dunbar, handed him my resignation and, with his best wishes, headed back to Atlanta.

The SRC headquarters were located in the heart of downtown, just across the street from the *Atlanta Journal-Constitution* building. Our staff of about forty men and women occupied an entire upper floor. These were some of the most progressive, well-meaning, highly respected black and white people in the nation in terms of research and programs in the area of race relations. They were the bane of a man like Lester Maddox, who contemptuously called us a bunch of "do-gooders," and noted in one interview that, with all of us located on the same floor in that building, "one bomb could wipe all the do-gooders and liberals out." This was the governor of Georgia's idea of a little joke. But I'd seen enough real bombs in my time to be not only sickened but also a little bit frightened by his weak stab at humor. It wasn't too hard to imagine someone taking the governor's words as a license to go ahead and do it.

Although the SRC's staff was fairly large and its work extensive, its budget was minuscule—that's one reason why Paul Anthony paid so many visits to the Field Foundation. I had no office of my own here, just a desk in a large open room, which was fine. On this job I wouldn't be spending much time at my desk.

The Community Organization Project was aimed at establishing cooperatives, credit unions and community development groups in rural and urban neighborhoods in towns and cities throughout the Deep South. This was grassroots work, very much in keeping with the War on Poverty. My partner was a young, energetic white man from North Carolina named Al Ulmer, a former SRC staffer who now worked for the agency as a consultant. He had not been involved in the civil rights movement, but he had spent time in the Peace Corps, and he was a big believer in community organizing from the bottom up, a big believer in the concept of self-help.

We traveled all over the South, Al and I, into little towns and farming areas, many of the same places I'd spent time in during the first half of the decade. Selma, Greenwood, Americus—they were the same, but they were different now, too. Sleepier, sedate, calmer, quieter. No marching, no battalions of troopers, no press. The press had moved north now, following the movement and the action into the cities. The "revolution," riots, Black Panthers, campus unrest, Vietnam—these were the big stories now. The civil rights movement was old news. There were no more stories down south, at least not the kinds of stories that make front-page headlines.

Little towns like McComb and Ruleville and Andalusia had problems now that wouldn't be helped by marching or singing. The people living there could finally vote, but other needs—food and shelter and jobs—were wanting. My job was about helping these people join together, helping them help one another to fill those needs. It was about showing people how to pool what money they had to form a bank of their own, a credit union. Or how to band together to buy groceries, or feed, or seed, in bulk amounts at low prices—how to form cooperatives.

Sweet potato cooperatives.

Okra cooperatives.

Hog cooperatives.

We even helped organize quilting cooperatives, where farmers' wives made quilts and sold them all over the country, then used the money to buy a refrigerator for one family, or a stove for another, or a washing machine.

This was hands-on work, and I loved it. I felt at home again, literally. Once again I was often sleeping in the homes of families who would invite me to spend the night—me and Al and a staff member named Charles Prejean, who accompanied us on many of our trips. More than once the three of us would bunk down in a back room of a small shotgun home, sometimes with two of us sharing the same bed. Or we'd stay in an empty dormitory room at a college like Tuskegee or Jackson State. Anyplace to lay our head, and anyplace felt good.

I finished my schoolwork during this time, earning my degree in philosophy from Fisk by writing a paper on the impact of the civil rights movement on organized religion in America. My central thesis was that the movement essentially amounted to a religious phenomenon. It was church-based, church-sanctioned; most of its members and its activities flowed through and out of the black church, in small towns and rural communities as well as urban areas. The church, in a very real way, was the major gateway for the movement. It was the point of access in almost every community. By giving its blessing to movement organizers, the church leadership opened the door to its membership, who may not have known or understood at first what we were about but who had complete faith in what their church elders told them. No matter what it was, if it was coming out of their church, then the people were ready to climb aboard. If the church said it was all right, then it must be all right.

That was what the church had come to mean to me. I felt the spirit, the hand of the Lord, the power of the Bible—all of those things—but only when they flowed through the church and out into the streets. As long as God and His teachings were kept inside the walls of a sanctuary, as they were when I was young, the church meant next to nothing to me.

My work, my commitment to community, had become my church, both during the movement and now, as I was making my way on my own. My work was my religion, my entire life. I once again had an apartment in Atlanta, on the same road, in fact, where I had lived during my SNCC years—Gordon Road. But this place was farther out from the center of the city, a little bigger and twice as expensive—about $100 a month. It was the nicest place I'd ever lived in at that point—two huge bedrooms, a kitchen, a living room and a bathroom, all up on the second floor of a brand-new building. Julian had helped me find it.

I saw Julian only occasionally. From time to time we'd meet over at Paschal's and have something to eat. He and Alice had children now, and I was still single, still married to my job, still spending far more time sleeping in someone else's spare bed than in my own. I socialized a little with a few friends, people like Bobby Hill, one of Julian's fellow black members of the House, and Stanley Wise, an old friend of mine from SNCC who was now working for the National Sharecroppers Fund.

I rarely, if ever, went out on a date. Friends would occasionally try to fix me up with someone, but nothing ever developed. I didn't have the time or the room in my life for a relationship. So when I got a phone call late that December from Bernard LaFayette inviting me to a small New Year's Eve gathering at a friend's house and hinting that a particular young woman would be there whom I might enjoy meeting, I didn't expect much to come of it.

Bernard was working for the SCLC in Atlanta at that time. He and Colia had divorced and he had returned to school. A friend of his in Atlanta, a woman named Xernona Clayton—whose husband had been the public relations director for Dr. King at the SCLC—was hosting this party. It was a friend of Xernona's, Bernard explained, that he thought I ought to meet.

"You'll like this young lady," he said. "She's very pretty. And she can *drive.*"

I always, he reminded me, needed someone to take me to the airport.

It was a pleasant little dinner party, about eight people. Xernona's friend's name was Lillian Miles. She was the assistant circulation librarian at the Atlanta University library. One of her coworkers was Julian's mother, Julia Bond, who was the university's circulation librarian.

During the course of the evening Bill Rutherford, who had worked for the SCLC, began a friendly discussion about what happened to resources in the movement—money, in particular. The conversation soon turned into an argument, with criticism and blame leveled at the movement leadership in general and at Dr. King in particular. Lillian hadn't said much at all up to that point, but when Dr. King was attacked she rose to his defense, speaking strongly and very surely. I was extremely impressed. She not only had feelings about this, but she knew her facts as well.

Bernard was right. She *was* very pretty, but beyond that she was smart. I didn't know it at the time, but she had graduated cum laude from California State College at Los Angeles and had then gotten her master's degree in library science from the University of Southern California. She had spent some time after college working with Operation Crossroads Africa—the same program Don Harris had been a part of. And she taught for two years with the Peace Corps in Yaba, Nigeria, before being hired by Atlanta University and moving to Georgia in the fall of 1965.

Sparks did not fly that New Year's Eve. This wasn't a head-over-heels kind of thing—I'm not sure I have that in me. But we had a nice evening, and she

did stay on my mind. I didn't see her again until February, when I invited
her to a birthday party I was throwing for myself. It wasn't like me at all to
have a party for myself, but I wanted to see Lillian Miles again, and this was a
good way to do it. I wanted my friends—Julian, Alice, Stanley—to meet this
woman and to get their approval. There was something going on here that deserved more than just a simple date or two, something that perhaps might be
serious.

So I pulled out the stops—in classic bachelor fashion. I invited about
twenty people, went out and bought a very new, very inexpensive turntable,
got some records, some soft drinks and beer, dips and chips, and for the coup
de grâce, I cooked up several pans of my famous barbecued chicken wings—
the only thing I could cook with any confidence. My sister Ora had taught me
how to make them years before, and they were always a big hit whenever I had
company.

I was making my move. I'd never made my move like that, but I really
wanted to impress Lillian Miles.

Almost everyone was there by the time she and Xernona arrived, and I
couldn't believe my eyes when they came through the door. Lillian was wearing this short dress, green and beige, very '60s, a minidress, and all over it
were these little peace symbols. I mean, they were *all* over it, even on the
straps. I said to myself, This woman is really something. She's really hip. She
not only believes in peace, but she wears it on her sleeve.

Lillian told me later that she'd never actually given much thought to
those symbols when she bought that dress, that it was the design, not the politics, that caught her eye. But she did say she wanted to impress me that night
as much as I wanted to impress her. She told me she liked the fact that I
seemed to have a commitment to something beyond myself. She said she
hadn't seen much of that among the men she'd known in Los Angeles.

So we started dating. Lillian always drove, naturally, and we began getting
together a lot with Alice and Julian. Almost every weekend we'd go to a
movie, or have an early breakfast at an all-night club, or have dinner and play
Scrabble at one of our homes.

It was nice to have another person as a part of my life. It made everything
feel a little fuller, a little richer. And it was wonderful to be spending time with
Julian and Alice now in a way I hadn't been able to before, when I was a single
man.

So now it was 1968, and my life was moving ahead. I was in a relationship, I had a fulfilling job, and I was still paying close attention to the movement, although I was dismayed by what I was seeing. On almost every front,
the attitude of nonviolence and the belief in a biracial democracy, in the
Beloved Community, were being abandoned. Dr. King was doing his best to

stay the course, but even his efforts were beginning to falter. Along with everyone else, he had shifted his sights to the North, mounting a campaign in Chicago that was a disastrous failure and mobilizing a Poor People's Campaign that couldn't seem to quite get off the ground. A sanitation workers' strike in Memphis had recently become his latest focus, his next Birmingham or Selma, the place where he hoped to strike yet another chord and right the direction of a movement that seemed to be teetering toward collapse.

There was no place for me in that movement, not as it had become. But when it began to appear that spring that Bobby Kennedy might make a run for the presidency, on a platform focused on his opposition to the Johnson administration's war policy in Vietnam, and on Kennedy's concern for America's "invisible" poor, as he called them, and on his commitment to confront and to close the racial rifts that were turning the streets of the nation's largest cities into battlefields, I became excited. The America Bobby Kennedy envisioned sounded much like the Beloved Community I believed in. In mid-March, as I was leaving a community organizing meeting in Jackson and saw a crowd gathered around a small television, I heard Bobby Kennedy's voice coming from the screen, announcing that he was indeed entering the presidential race. I immediately sent him a telegram offering my support. I told him I wanted to help in any way I could.

When I got back to Atlanta two days later, I received a telephone call from Earl Graves, Kennedy's chief black assistant. He told me that Senator Kennedy would like very much for me to come work with the campaign, if I could take time off from my job. That was no problem. They would take care of my expenses, Graves said. The SRC gave me its blessing, and late that March I left Atlanta and flew to Indiana, where Kennedy would face his first primary election of the campaign.

I was there to help get out the black vote. There were several other people doing the same thing in other sections of the country, most notably Charles Evers, Medgar Evers's brother. But I was the only major figure from what was left of the movement to come out for Kennedy. There was still a lot of resentment among a lot of people about the Justice Department's actions and inactions during the time Bobby Kennedy had been the attorney general. I still had problems with that myself, but I believed Kennedy had dramatically changed, that he had grown. And I had no doubt, compared to the other Democratic Party prospects for this presidency—Johnson, Eugene McCarthy, perhaps Vice President Humphrey, if Johnson chose not to run—Kennedy was the man for the task, the man for the moment. As I told one reporter soon after I arrived in Indiana, "He is the one guy who can bring people together."

That was the message I brought to Indianapolis, where I dug in with the campaign staff there, meeting with and helping local black community leaders and organizations mobilize the black voters in that city. On March 31, President Johnson stunned everyone by announcing that he was not going to seek reelection. Now, with no incumbent to struggle against, the race was truly wide open.

The first week of April, with the Indiana primary election a month away, we geared up for Bobby Kennedy's first visit to Indianapolis since I'd arrived there. We had a mass rally arranged in a downtown black neighborhood—a poor, inner-city section of the community. The date set for the rally was Thursday, April 4, 1968—exactly one year to the day after Dr. King had made his speech at Riverside Church, the one in which he had denounced the war.

The night before Kennedy's arrival in Indianapolis, history was unfolding nearly four hundred miles south of us, in a Masonic temple in downtown Memphis, where Dr. King stepped in front of an audience of two thousand people to deliver a speech that would turn out to be the last of his lifetime.

A week earlier he had led a march in that city that had erupted into violence and left a fourteen-year-old boy dead. Dr. King was devastated by that death, by the unsteady swirl of ugliness and killing that was rising up all around him. He could feel it closing in. He was receiving constant threats on his life these days, including an anonymous warning that he had best not deliver the speech he had come to make that night.

But he had come, and now he was making it. Against a backdrop of tornado warnings and a driving rainstorm outside, he told that standing-room-only crowd that he'd been cautioned not to come back to Memphis, but that he was not going to let "some of our sick white brothers" keep him away. Then he unloaded his heart, with words that sounded almost like a farewell, like a eulogy:

I don't know what will happen now. We've got some difficult days ahead. But it really doesn't matter with me now. Because I've been to the mountaintop.

Like anybody, I would like to live a long life. Longevity has its place. But I'm not concerned about that now. I just want to do God's will. And He's allowed me to go up to the mountain. And I've looked over. And I've seen the Promised Land.

And I may not get there with you. But I want you to know tonight that we, as a people, will get to the Promised Land. So I'm happy tonight. I'm not worried about anything. I'm not fearing any man. Mine eyes have seen the glory of the coming of the Lord!

It was as if he knew.

Late the next afternoon, near sunset, we were gathered at the rally site, a large open lot in the shadows of several tall, run-down brick buildings. The weather was brisk, overcast, but a large crowd had turned out, a good crowd, about a thousand people, almost all of them black, all of them upbeat, eager and excited to see the man who might well be the next president of the United States.

It was about half past six, an hour or so before Kennedy was due to arrive, when Walter Sheridan, one of Kennedy's advance men, came rushing up to me, very nervous, visibly upset. He took me aside and said, "John, we just got word that Dr. King has been shot in Memphis."

Oh my God.

I can say those words today. They are what I feel when I think of it now, thirty years later. But at that moment I had no feeling. No thoughts. No words. I was obliterated, blown beyond any sensations whatsoever. I was numb. Frozen. Stunned stock-still, inside and out. I just stood there, not moving, not thinking, as the cold Indiana wind stirred the dirt around my feet.

I have my own way of responding to grief. I never let it in immediately. I never answer to it right away. I set it aside, push it into a drawer, in effect, and turn to the matter at hand, whatever it is. Later, when I'm by myself and the job is done, I open the drawer and pull out the pain and allow myself to feel it. That's when I grieve.

That is what happened here. I don't know how long I stood there. Sheridan had moved on to tell some other people, but the crowd, the thousand people who had come to hear Kennedy, knew nothing. They hadn't gotten the word yet. Today, in this age of instant information, with CNN and all-news radio stations and the Internet, the people in that crowd would have known as soon as we did—maybe sooner. But this was 1968. News traveled more slowly, and no one knew a thing. Kennedy was coming, that's all they knew.

That was the matter at hand. This was to be the biggest moment in his campaign so far, at least as far as I was concerned, and now we had to decide how to deal with it. We had to decide what to do about these people, about the candidate—who was in the air now, en route from Muncie—and even about ourselves. A half dozen of us—Sheridan, Graves, two or three of Kennedy's staff people and I—huddled in a small circle and debated whether the event should be canceled. I had no doubt that it should not.

"Somebody has to speak to these people," I said. "You can't have a crowd like this come, and something like this happen, and send them home without anything at all. Kennedy has to speak, for his own sake and for the sake of these people."

The others agreed. And we agreed that it should be Kennedy who would break the news to this audience of men and women and children, who would tell them that Dr. King had been shot.

By the time Kennedy's plane touched down at the Indianapolis airport, word had come that Dr. King was dead. To this day I can't recall how I got that news, or when, or exactly where. I think I was too much in shock to store anything in my memory. I was completely immersed in the present, moving from minute to minute, completely focused on getting one foot in front of the other.

I do know that it was getting dark now, and that I had a word with Kennedy on a two-way radio in one of his staff member's automobiles. He was on his way from the airport. His voice coming over that radio was crackly and strange. "I'm sorry, John," he said. "You've lost a leader. We've lost a leader."

By the time Kennedy's entourage pulled up—several cars, including the black sedan in which he was riding—it was nighttime. The crowd was laughing and cheering. They still had no idea what had happened.

Kennedy looked pretty awful. He was exhausted from the grind of round-the-clock campaigning, and the shock of this news had really hit him hard. You could see it in his face.

But few people in that crowd were close enough to see him that clearly. We had a stage set up, but Kennedy decided to speak right there. He climbed up on the back of the car and stood on the trunk so the crowd could see him. He was wearing a black trench coat. The wind, turned even colder by the darkness, whipped at his hair.

"I have bad news for you . . . ," he began.

Half the crowd was still talking and laughing and letting out little cheers. They hadn't quieted down enough yet to hear what he was saying.

". . . for all of our fellow citizens, and people who love peace all over the world . . . ," he continued.

And now you could see the faces beginning to drop in the front section of the audience, as the sobriety of Kennedy's tone moved through them like a wave.

". . . and that is that Martin Luther King was shot and killed tonight."

You could hear gasps. Shouts of *No!* People broke down and wept. Some dropped to their knees. Others, far in the back, where the wave had not yet reached, continued cheering and clapping.

It was so weird, that contrast. So unreal.

But within seconds the message had spread all the way. Everyone knew. And Kennedy continued, standing there in the harsh glare of some makeshift spotlights.

He had no notes. He spoke simply and honestly, completely extemporaneously, straight from his heart. And the crowd hung on his every word. It didn't matter that he was white or rich or a Kennedy. At this moment he was just a human being, just like all of us, and he spoke that way. And everyone listened:

Martin Luther King dedicated his life to love and to justice for his fellow human beings, and he died because of that effort.

In this difficult day, in this difficult time for the United States, it is perhaps well to ask what kind of a nation we are and what direction we want to move in.

For those of you who are black—considering the evidence there evidently is that there were white people who were responsible—you can be filled with bitterness, with hatred, and a desire for revenge. We can move in that direction as a country, in great polarization—black people amongst black, white people amongst white, filled with hatred toward one another.

Or we can make an effort, as Martin Luther King did, to understand and to comprehend, and to replace that violence, that stain of bloodshed that has spread across our land, with an effort to understand with compassion and love.

For those of you who are black and are tempted to be filled with hatred and distrust at the injustice of such an act, against all white people, I can only say that I feel in my own heart the same kind of feeling. I had a member of my family killed, but he was killed by a white man. But we have to make an effort in the United States, we have to make an effort to understand, to go beyond these rather difficult times. . . .

We've had difficult times in the past. We will have difficult times in the future. It is not the end of violence. It is not the end of lawlessness. It is not the end of disorder.

But the vast majority of white people and the vast majority of black people in this country want to live together, want to improve the quality of our life, and want justice for all human beings who abide in our land.

Let us dedicate ourselves to what the Greeks wrote so many years ago: to tame the savageness of man and to make gentle the life of this world.

Let us dedicate ourselves to that, and say a prayer for our country, and for our people.

It was an amazing speech. I knew he had to have thought of his brother when he got this news, but I never dreamed he would talk about him. That was something Bobby Kennedy never, ever did in public—he never talked about the murder of his brother. To do it that night was an incredibly powerful and connective and emotionally honest gesture. He stripped himself down. He made it personal. He made it real.

We went back to the hotel after that—Kennedy and his staff, all of us. As soon as we got to the room—I can't recall whose room it was—Kennedy broke down on a bed, lay there on his stomach and cried. A lot of people were crying.

After a short while he got up and talked briefly and softly with several people in the room. He told me again how sorry he was. Then he phoned Coretta King and offered his condolences. He asked what he could do to help. She asked him to help get her husband's body back from Memphis to Atlanta as soon as possible. He said he would. Then he hung up.

Then the whole room began talking about getting back to Atlanta as soon as possible. Earl Graves and I tried to make arrangements for a flight that night, but everything was booked. Press people, ordered by their editors to drop off the campaign and get to Atlanta immediately, had already filled every available seat.

The next day Earl and I finally boarded a flight. Kennedy went on to Cleveland to make a speech. He'd be back in time for the funeral.

I began opening my emotions a little on that flight. I'd learned some of the details of the assassination by then, how at a minute past six, as the sun was beginning to set on the mugginess of that late afternoon in Memphis, Dr. King had stepped out on the balcony of the Lorraine Motel, ready to go out for some dinner with a group of his staff. Suddenly there was a crack. A single bullet, from an unseen sniper. Dr. King was shot in the side of the neck and the jaw. A little more than an hour later, in the emergency operating room at Memphis's St. Joseph's Hospital, he was pronounced dead.

When we arrived in Atlanta, the city looked orderly and calm, which was surprising, considering the fact that riots had broken out from coast to coast during the past twelve hours, a shock wave of rage that swept through the streets of more than seventy towns and cities. Seventy thousand federal troops and National Guardsmen had been called out, and before it was over, forty-six people would be dead—all but five of them black. More than 2,500 people would be injured. Twenty-eight thousand people would be in jail. And property damage would be estimated at a total of more than $50 million.

At a SNCC press conference held that morning, Stokely Carmichael declared, "When white America killed Dr. King, she declared war on us.... Black people have to survive, and the only way they will survive is by getting guns."

I didn't even want to think about Stokely, about how his words flew in the face of everything Dr. King stood for, and about how this surge of rioting did the same thing. What way was this to respond to the death of one of the most peaceful leaders of our time, a man completely opposed to violence in any form?

Then again, I could understand that it wasn't just the death of Dr. King that people were crying and shooting and burning for. It was the dying in their own lives, the little deaths they felt every day, of hope and opportunity and belief. This rioting and rage was the language of a frustrated people, the only language they could speak in, the only way that their voices could be heard. Whether they were heard or not didn't even matter to them anymore. What mattered was that they let it out, let it all out—the pain and the despair and the rage.

That's what a riot is—just letting it out. Nothing is held back. Anything goes. Burning. Looting. Killing. Even one another. Part of the effort of the movement was to tame the madness of men, to take the beast that lives in all of us and turn it toward love, to show humankind a different way, to teach the way of compassion, of connection and community, of peace and nonviolence. Yes, we are human, and yes, there is a savage side in all of us. The first impulse of man has always been to react like an animal, to respond to attack in a like manner. If someone hits you, strike back. If someone bombs you, bomb back. But there have been teachers, men and women throughout history, who have stood and said, No, you can't take an eye for an eye. If you do, we will all be blind. At some point we have to lift ourselves to a higher plane. And it is possible. Men have shown throughout history that it is possible.

But that April of 1968, it began to seem that it might not be possible. And little did I know how much worse it was going to get before the year was through.

It was five days before Dr. King was buried. During that time I took part in a series of emergency board meetings of the SCLC, with the issue being the question of who should succeed Dr. King. There were several people jockeying for position. Most of the rank and file felt that the Reverend Abernathy was the natural choice, that he had been the man closest to Dr. King, the person Dr. King would have chosen himself, were he here to have his say.

Others felt that Coretta King, who had been much more than a silent partner in Dr. King's career, should be his successor.

One man who pushed hard for the position was a minister named Sam Williams, the pastor of one of Atlanta's most important churches, Friendship Baptist, and a professor of Dr. King's at Morehouse College. Williams had the black middle- and upper-class power structure of Atlanta behind him—doctors, college administrators, lawyers. He had long been very active with the local NAACP and had sat on the board of the SCLC for some time. He felt he was better prepared than anyone else to head the organization, and if it depended on pure intellect and political connections, he might have been right. Sam Williams was one of the most scholarly, distinguished men I had ever met.

The problem was that he knew it. In any meeting, even in simple conversation, he always gave the impression that he considered himself the smartest person in the room. He assumed everyone else was there to listen and learn from him. He didn't speak so much as he lectured. I don't know if he was even aware how he came across. But it rubbed a lot of people the wrong way. Many of the less elevated ministers and activists in the SCLC, those who weren't as well connected or as well-to-do as Dr. Williams and his circle of friends, did not take too kindly to his condescending attitude.

It took several meetings to work this all out. There were a lot of egos at stake, and the stakes were high. I felt that Abernathy should be the choice. He was the person closest to Dr. King—besides Coretta, of course—and the philosophies of the two men were almost identical. In the end, at a meeting held the very morning of Dr. King's funeral, April 9, the decision was finally made by the board to name Ralph Abernathy as the new president of the SCLC.

I was very tired by the time of that meeting. The night before, I hadn't gotten to bed until nearly 5 A.M. Earlier that evening, around midnight, I had attended a meeting in Bobby Kennedy's suite at the Hyatt Regency Hotel. It was up on the twenty-second floor. Andy Young was there, as was Harry Belafonte, Kennedy, and a handful of SCLC and Kennedy staff members. The senator had called us together to talk about where we should all go from here. We discussed the remainder of his campaign and its thrust in terms of the civil rights movement in general and Dr. King's legacy in particular.

"I know we must bury Dr. King tomorrow," Kennedy said. "I don't want to talk politics, but I do want to ask, what can I do? What *should* I do?"

Some general issues were discussed, and when the meeting wrapped up, about two that morning, Earl Graves took me aside and asked if I'd meet Bobby and Ethel Kennedy over at Ebenezer Baptist Church, where Dr. King's body lay, waiting for the next day's funeral.

I had seen the body earlier, on display in the Sisters Chapel on the campus of Spelman College. I had joined the crowd of tens of thousands of people who had paraded past to view it—more than 1,200 people an hour, according to the official count. The funeral and procession scheduled for the next day would draw a crowd many times that size, and on this last night before the body was to be buried, as Dr. King's casket sat in the sanctuary of Ebenezer, Bobby and Ethel Kennedy wanted to visit it by themselves. And Earl asked if I might take them there.

We arrived at the church in two sedans, six of us, including a couple of Kennedy's staff and security people. It was three in the morning. The inside of the church was pitch dark and empty. Our footsteps sounded loud on the bare floor as we entered the door. I led the way, through the education building, up some stairs, down some stairs. It was hard to see, but I knew my way through this church. I had been there so many times I could find the way with my eyes closed.

There was a faint glow as we stepped into the sanctuary, the flicker of candles throwing shadows against the walls. Flowers were everywhere. And the casket was open, with Dr. King lying inside. An honor guard and some security people stood quietly by the doors.

Bobby and Ethel approached the casket while we stayed back. They made the sign of the cross, knelt, prayed and spent several long minutes in silence.

When they were finished, I went forward myself. In my own way I wanted to say farewell to my friend.

The body looked as if it were sleeping. The morticians had worked hard to reconstruct the part of his face that had been shot away, and they had done a good job. It looked like his face. But it didn't look like him. It couldn't. It was not him anymore. This was just a shell, his body. *He* was dead.

I felt a wave of discomfort. It felt unreal.

And that was the last time I saw Martin Luther King.

The next day, after our SCLC board meeting, I walked to Wheat Street Baptist Church, a door or two down from Ebenezer. It was all I could do to get through the ocean of people thronged outside. More than 60,000 people had gathered on the sidewalks and the street. The sanctuary could seat only eight hundred, and those seats were reserved for Ebenezer members, dignitaries, politicians, and other VIPs. The Kennedys, Richard Nixon, Hubert Humphrey—they were all there. So were Diana Ross and Mahalia Jackson, Bevel and Belafonte, Roy Wilkins and Whitney Young and Jim Forman. Stokely showed up with six "guards" and caused a small uproar when he was told that just he, and not his entourage, would be allowed inside.

Earlier in the day, knowing how few seats were available, I offered to give mine up, which was why I was walking to Wheat Street now. The service would be broadcast there on loudspeakers, just as it was to the people gathered out on the street. That is where I listened to Abernathy pronounce this "one of the darkest hours in the history of the black people of this nation, one of the darkest hours in the history of all mankind."

A tape was played of a sermon Dr. King himself had delivered once at Ebenezer, a sermon that included instructions for his own funeral. It was eerie to hear his voice coming from those speakers as his body lay in that casket.

"I don't want a long funeral," the voice said. "If you get somebody to deliver the eulogy, tell him not to talk too long...."

People smiled through their tears. Dr. King always knew how to meet the moment, even at the end.

When the service was done, a lady I knew from Virginia, a prominent black attorney from Danville named Ruth Charity, fell in step with me, and we walked together to the mule-drawn wagon that would carry King's casket through the center of the city, down Auburn Avenue—"Sweet Auburn," as it's still called today by the black Atlantans who live and work along its length—to the campus of Morehouse College, where a second service was to take place.

The day was hot and humid. There were no clouds in the sky, nothing between us and that fierce sun as we walked just behind the wagon, with 50,000 people behind us. Many of those people had marched with Dr. King in one city or another, here in Atlanta or in Montgomery or Birmingham. That was as close as many of them had come to King, by walking with him. And now they were doing it one last time.

It was five miles from Ebenezer to Morehouse, and midway there Ruth Charity shook a little, then slumped to the ground. I thought she had stumbled, but it turned out the heat had gotten to her. She had fainted. I stayed with her while someone went to get help. Then I went on, alone.

At Morehouse, the casket was set outside, in the center of campus, with the crowd stretching across the lawn, under the trees, listening as Benjamin Mays, Dr. King's teacher and mentor and the president emeritus of Morehouse College, delivered the second eulogy of the day. Dr. Mays pointed out that Dr. King had always been for the common man, the everyday man:

> He believed especially that he was sent to champion the cause of the man farthest down. He would probably say that, if death had to come, I'm sure there was no greater cause to die for than fighting to get a just wage for garbage collectors.

Lillian and Xernona saw me standing alone and came over to join me. When the service was done, they took me with them in their car to South View Cemetery, where the burial would take place. We were allowed through to get close to the grave, and we stood by the King family and watched with them as the casket was lowered into the ground.

It really was a beautiful day. Dogwoods were blooming, and spring was in the air. The beauty made the sadness hurt that much more.

We went over to Paschal's afterward for a little food, and then I went home and dropped out for several days. Now had come my time to grieve.

Dr. King was my friend, my brother, my leader. He was the man, the one who opened my eyes to the world. From the time I was fifteen until the day he died—for almost half my life—he was the person who, more than any other, continued to influence my life, who made me who I was. He made me who I *am*. To this day I owe more of myself to him than to anyone else I have ever known. It's difficult to express in words. I have never believed in any man as much as I believed in Martin Luther King. When he was killed I really felt I'd lost a part of myself.

It took several days for me to make my way through the sorrow. When I finally began coming out, it was with the thought that, Well, we still have Bobby Kennedy. We still have hope.

Dr. King's death made it all the more important for me to put everything I had into Kennedy's campaign. I saw this as the final extension of the movement. I transferred all the loyalty I had left from Dr. King to Bobby Kennedy.

I went back to Indiana, watched Kennedy win there, then moved on to Oregon, where we focused on the young people, the students. At a rally at Oregon State, I introduced Kennedy to an audience that roared so loudly I couldn't hear my words as I spoke them. Neither could they, I'm sure, but who cared? Those kids were crazy about Kennedy.

But he was concerned about Oregon. We all were. Despite the support of young people and liberals, the polls heading into the May 28 primary there showed him trailing McCarthy. The day before the election, we were in a hotel room in Portland—Pete Edelman, who was Kennedy's chief advisor, Adam Walinsky, who wrote most of the senator's speeches, and I. Kennedy came out of the shower, in a bathrobe, staring at the floor, as if he was in another world. Then he suddenly snapped his head up, as if he had just noticed us.

"What are you fellows doing still here?" he said. "You could be outside, knocking on doors, getting me some more *votes.*"

He was serious. So we went out and knocked on some doors.

Kennedy lost in Oregon, but it was California that mattered most. If he won California, the nomination would be his. After that, no one doubted, so would the presidency. Richard Nixon had lost to a Kennedy once, and few people questioned that he would lose again, if it came down to him and Bobby.

I had spent only four or five days in Oregon, but I worked for nearly two weeks in California. During that time I phoned Julian back in Atlanta several times and told him to come out and endorse Kennedy. He was sort of toying with the idea of going for McCarthy, but hadn't committed himself either way. That was something Julian had always had a problem with, committing himself. He was always hesitant to make a big move, always reluctant. He was never the first to step out front. I kept telling him if he thought about it too long, he would make the wrong decision, or it would be made for him. Later on he told me that I had been right about this one, that he should have endorsed Bobby Kennedy. But he didn't. He waited, and then circumstances took over, the hand of history, and he never got his chance.

I spent a lot of time during those two weeks with Cesar Chavez, the Chicano labor leader and activist, with whom Kennedy had hooked up very early and who was a tremendous supporter of the senator. Chavez was a humble guy, very religious, a ground-level worker who was just like the people he led, which was why they loved him so much. He was one of them, and he never forgot it.

During the days we went deep into some of the poorest neighborhoods in the city, both Hispanic and black, meeting and talking to people, one by one or together at rallies. Each evening we would go out to wealthy homes in areas like Hollywood and Beverly Hills to speak to small gatherings of locally influential people. John Kennedy's campaign had used these little coffee klatches to great effect all across the country back in his 1960 campaign. "Coffees for Kennedy"—that's what they called them, and Bobby was using them now in Los Angeles. A large section of the mostly liberal entertainment industry put everything it had behind Bobby, including my old friend Shirley MacLaine, whom I saw at several of those functions.

The day before the primary we took a motorcade through the same black and Hispanic neighborhoods we'd been working so hard for the previous two weeks. The outpouring of emotion as we passed through those streets was much more than mere support for Kennedy. It was love. It was adoration. People, especially young people, just mobbed us, climbing all over the cars, trying to get close to Kennedy, to touch him. It was amazing, that Kennedy magic.

Then came June 4, Tuesday, primary day. We went back into the neighborhoods one more time, walking door-to-door, nailing up signs near polling places, doing everything we could to get out the vote.

That night, all that was left was to watch and wait. A large group of us were gathered in a fifth-floor suite at the Hotel Ambassador, across the hall from Kennedy's private room. Celebrities, authors, journalists and friends of the Kennedys filled the suite. Jimmy Breslin; Loudon Wainwright; Teddy White; who was working on his book The Making of the President, Jack Newfield of The Village Voice, who was a big admirer of Kennedy's; George Plimpton; Charles Evers; Milton Berle; John Glenn.

Some stood around the bar laughing and drinking; others sat by the television, watching the early returns. That's where I was, watching the TV and nursing a glass of orange juice.

Close to nine o'clock, Kennedy was projected as the winner. The mood shifted from upbeat to jubilant. Everyone was in high spirits. The bar was really crowded now.

By ten-thirty the returns from those Hispanic and black precincts came in and pushed Kennedy over the top. Cheers and applause swept through the room.

Close to midnight, Bobby ducked in on his way downstairs to make his victory speech.

"John," he said as he shook my hand, "you let me down today. More Mexican-Americans voted for me than Negroes."

We all laughed, including Bobby. Then he turned to the room and said, "Wait for me. I'll be back in fifteen or twenty minutes."

He looked as if he could have floated out of the room. He was in such wonderful spirits

We crowded around the TV to watch the speech. A lot of people sat on the floor, some in the chairs, but most of us stood. I was standing.

The room broke into a little cheer when the screen showed Bobby stepping up to speak. He made a joke about Don Drysdale pitching a shutout that day for the Dodgers and how he hoped he'd do as well from here on out. He thanked Ethel, and Cesar Chavez and others for their support. Then he wound it up.

"My thanks to all of you," he said, "and on to Chicago, and let's win there."

On to Chicago, to the Democratic convention.

And from there to the White House.

We were all just soaking it in, waiting for Bobby to come back upstairs. The TV was still on, in the background now as most of the room had moved away, over to the bar or off into groups to laugh and talk.

And then...

"Oh my God!" came a woman's voice.

I turned and looked at the television, and there, in black and white, was a grim-faced commentator saying the senator had just been shot. The voice went on, while the screen showed film of Kennedy moving through a crowd with lights and people all around him, then a burst of movement, and Kennedy falling to the floor.

I dropped to my knees, to the carpet. I was crying, sobbing, heaving as if something had been busted open inside. All around me the room was filled with groans and shock. The television was still on, replaying Kennedy's victory speech.

I sat on the floor, dazed, rocking back and forth as if I were autistic, saying one word out loud, over and over again.

"Why? Why? Why?"

Eventually, after I don't know how long, I pulled myself up and wandered out of the suite, down to the ballroom, where Kennedy had made his speech. People were scattered around, in ones and twos, slumped on chairs or sitting on the floor, crying, comforting each other. Red and blue streamers hung from the stage and the chandeliers. They looked horrible, chilling.

I kept walking, out of the hotel, into the night. My room was a couple of blocks away, up Wilshire Boulevard. That's where the staff was headquartered, where most of us were staying. When I got to the staff suite, the scene was the same as in the room I'd just left. People were standing in shock, in silence, staring at the TV, which was now updating Kennedy's condition with live reports from Good Samaritan Hospital. The senator was still alive, but he was also still in the operating room, which was not good.

It was now three in the morning. I felt dead. I couldn't think anymore. I went to my room, lay down on the bed and in seconds fell fast asleep.

When I awoke in the morning Kennedy was still alive. But there was no hope. It was just a matter of time, hours now, until he would be dead.

I packed my bag and caught a plane early that afternoon back home to Atlanta. That was the loneliest, longest flight of my life. Coming over the Rockies, I looked down and could see snow. Snow in June. I cried some more. No sound. Just tears coming up from inside, washing out of my eyes and down my face.

Bobby Kennedy died early the next morning, June 6, a Thursday. I was home when I heard the news, and later that day I received a telegram from his family, asking me to come to New York and serve as part of an honor guard at the funeral. I flew up the next day, landed as evening was falling and went straight to St. Patrick's Cathedral. Tens of thousands of people stood outside, waiting in a long line to pass into the church and up past the casket. The viewing had begun at five-thirty that morning and would continue on through the night and into the next day.

Pairs of people, ranging from personal friends to Kennedy staffers to members of the various movements he had come to embrace—the antiwar movement, the civil rights movement—took turns standing vigil by the senator's body as the public walked past. I stood my shift with the Reverend Abernathy, the two of us flanking the casket like soldiers. We stood that way for an hour, then stepped down to allow the next pair to take our place.

The following morning, Saturday, June 8, I attended the mass for Kennedy. His brother Ted gave the eulogy.

"My brother," said Ted Kennedy, "saw wrong and tried to right it, saw suffering and tried to heal it, saw war and tried to stop it."

It was that simple. That was all Bobby Kennedy wanted to do. It was all any of us wanted to do.

After the mass I boarded one of thirty buses lined up to take invited guests to Penn Station, from where we would travel by rail with the body to Washington. The funeral train was twenty-one cars long, including a special car with large plate-glass windows on each side, so the crowds lining the tracks could see the casket inside. I walked back to take a look, and saw that the casket had been raised, placed up on chairs to give the people outside a better look. I thought that was so nice, so thoughtful, to consider the people that way.

All the way down, through New Jersey, Pennsylvania, Delaware, Maryland, I could look out the window and see crowds standing along the tracks, waving, holding signs, crying. "We Love You, Bobby" and "Goodbye Bobby"—the signs looked so sad, so moving. I felt as if it was a dream, as if I was floating. I didn't want that train to stop in Washington. I wanted it to just keep going, keep going forever.

The burial was that evening, at Arlington National Cemetery. I had never been there before. We—my SNCC colleagues and I—had decided against visiting JFK's grave back in '63. So now, in a way, I was paying respects to both of them, to Bobby and to John.

An odd thing happened late that evening, just a little thing, but very striking. I'd returned from the funeral to downtown D.C., where I had a room at the Statler Hilton—the same hotel we'd all stayed at during the March on Washington. I was heading toward the front doors when I looked across the street. There was a little White Tower restaurant there, one of those all-night hamburger cafes. Inside, right by the front window, sitting all alone in a booth, was a man I swore had to be Sargent Shriver, the brother-in-law of the Kennedys. I thought to myself how strange that was, that he was there by himself instead of with the family, sitting under the harsh, lonely glare of that diner's fluorescent lights, in the middle of this dark, dark night.

He looked the way I felt. That whole scene captured the way I felt—bare, hollow, empty.

I sleepwalked through the next few weeks, wondering if I could ever put my belief and faith and trust in someone again. First Dr. King, then Bobby Kennedy, both shot dead within weeks of each other. It hurt so incredibly much when they were taken away. It was like trusting yourself to fall in love again after you've given your heart once and had it broken. Here, it had happened twice, and I knew that what I was feeling was the same thing millions of Americans felt. What could we *believe* in now? How much more of this could we take? I didn't know if I could take this anymore. The murders of innocent people. Of young men and little girls. What had we come to as a nation, as a people?

I don't have any doubt that we lost something with the deaths of those two leaders that year—in the wake of the death five years earlier of John Kennedy—that as a nation we will never recover. Call it innocence or trust. The willingness to follow and believe, to *love* the man who stands before us— a King or a Kennedy—I don't think has ever been regained. I don't think we will ever be able to love our leaders like that again, not after what it came to that year, and not with all that has happened since.

But still, we do what we can. We do our best, which I resolved to do late that summer, when I was called to attend a meeting in Macon. A man named

E. T. Kerher, head of the civil rights division for the AFL-CIO's regional office in Atlanta and a very involved, very progressive Democrat, had arranged for the gathering. The subject was the upcoming Democratic National Convention in Chicago, and the question was whether a challenge should be mounted to the Georgia delegation, which was controlled and guided by our governor, Lester Maddox, whose name was synonymous with extreme segregation and right-wing groups like the John Birch Society. Kerher felt strongly that the delegation Maddox was sending to Chicago was more a reflection of his political power than of the people of Georgia whom they were supposed to be representing.

We came away from that meeting committed to mobilizing enough people like ourselves—labor activists, civil rights activists, people against the war—to send a strong delegation to Chicago to challenge Maddox's group. One of the people who helped organize this effort was a young college student, a McCarthy supporter named Taylor Branch—the same Taylor Branch who would go on to write *Parting the Waters,* the Pulitzer Prize–winning account of the early years of the civil rights movement.

By August we were ready to go, nearly sixty of us. We called ourselves the Georgia Loyal Democrats, and Julian was drafted to be our chairman. The last week of that month we left for Chicago.

The city was in a state of near war when we arrived there. The parks downtown—Grant Park and Lincoln Park—were filled with thousands of antiwar protestors who had been streaming into the city all week, readying themselves for the start of the convention that Monday night, the twenty-sixth. The war had gone over the edge that summer, with huge step-ups in troops and bombings. More than a half million U.S. soldiers were now stationed in South Vietnam. These protestors, the vast majority of them young and white, a large number of them college students, many of them veterans of our civil rights movement in the South, had come from across the country to show themselves to the convention and to the nation.

"Hey, hey, LBJ! How many kids did you kill today?"

That chant, which went on all week, was directed more at the party of the sitting president than at the President himself. These tens of thousands of kids, swarming the streets of the downtown Loop section of the city, where the delegates were staying in some of Chicago's most expensive lakeside hotels, wanted to make sure their voices were heard. We, the Georgia Loyal Democrats, were not staying in one of those hotels. We couldn't afford to. Some of us got rooms at the YMCA; others were scattered in cheaper, smaller, rinky-dink hotels and motels far from the Conrad Hilton, where most of the chaos was taking place.

But we saw it as soon as we got there, and we passed through it every day.

It was like a battlefield downtown, along Michigan Avenue and around those park areas. The smell of tear gas and stink bombs and marijuana, and the thumping of helicopters passing overhead, filled the air, along with the chants and shouts of the protestors. Richard Daley, the bulldog-like mayor of Chicago, had responded to these kids the way Bull Connor and Jim Clark responded to us in Birmingham and Selma. Daley called out all 11,000 of his city's police force and put them on twelve-hour shifts around the clock. More than 5,000 National Guardsmen were called up, and another 7,000 Army troops were placed on standby alert. By the time we arrived that Sunday, clashes had already broken out between demonstrators and police, and the convention hadn't even begun yet.

I was very sympathetic to those young people. They were trying to do exactly what we had done down south—dramatize the issue, put it in front of the politicians, put it in front of the nation, make their voices heard. They were not violent. It has been shown beyond a doubt, by numerous studies and reports produced since then, that the rioting and violence that took place that week were not caused by the demonstrators but by the Chicago police, who reacted swiftly and brutally and without discipline or restraint, lashing out at the slightest provocation, or even with no provocation at all.

These people had a right to protest, as all Americans do, and that right was being denied them in a nightmarishly brutal way that was only too familiar to me.

The convention itself was held several miles south of the Loop, in a huge hall—the International Amphitheatre—near the city's old stockyards, not far from the ghettos of South Side Chicago. When we got there Monday night, we had to pass through barbed-wire fencing and dozens of Chicago policemen, dressed in their blue shirts and blue-checkered caps, who stopped each of us, one by one, to check our credentials before letting us inside. While thousands and thousands of protestors were battling police a mere couple of miles up the lakefront, I saw none of them outside the convention center. None would get close to there that entire week.

We had the necessary credentials to allow us into the hall, but the fight to earn our seats still lay ahead. We began that evening up in the balcony along with hundreds of spectators. The scene down on the floor was chaotic, with Daley using his welcoming speech to pronounce that as long as he was mayor, there would be "law and order in Chicago." That brought hoots and whistles from some of the crowd, many of whom were, like me, in sympathy with the protestors outside. Later during the week, when Senator Abraham Ribicoff of Connecticut stood to nominate Eugene McCarthy for president and during his speech pointed to the chaos outside and said that it amounted to a police state, Daley gave him the finger from the floor, sputtering with fury and saying—according to witnesses sitting near enough to hear, and to professional lip-readers who have studied the videotapes in the years since—"Fuck you, you Jew son of a bitch." Daley denied until his death that he said any such thing, but I don't doubt he could have. He certainly had it in him.

That opening night we were the center of attention, as a motion was put on the floor to split Georgia's votes between the regular delegates—Maddox's group—and us. We made the case that our group better reflected the state in terms of our mix of men and women, black and white. The Maddox delegation had one black member, a woman named Mamie Reese, who taught at Albany State College.

We were eventually allowed to move down to an aisle on the floor, to wait while our fate was decided. No decision was made that night, but the next day we were seated and each given a half vote, as we had requested. Twenty of the regulars walked out in protest, just as the entire Mississippi delegation had done in Atlantic City four years earlier.

As our chairman, this became Julian's moment to shine. The press, many of whom already knew him through his work as SNCC's communications director, was all over him that week. When McCarthy was nominated, Julian stepped up and gave the speech to second the nomination. When a group of antiwar delegates led by Wisconsin's Don Peterson gathered to try to get Al Lowenstein up on the podium to make a statement against the war, they decided the way to do it was to nominate someone for vice president and have Lowenstein make a speech seconding that nomination. Julian had by now become very visible as an opponent of the war. Nearly three years had passed since I had read that SNCC statement condemning America's involvement in Vietnam and Julian had been drawn into that whole mess. Now it had become his claim to fame. Now he was Julian Bond, an outspoken activist against the war and a perfect choice for this nomination.

Which is how his name wound up being placed on the floor of the 1968 Democratic National Convention as a candidate to become the next vice president of the United States.

No one thought to point out that Julian was only twenty-eight years old, seven years too young to meet the constitutional minimum age requirement for the job. It all moved very, very fast. It was a protest, a maneuver. And Julian went with the flow. He was enjoying it. He wound up refusing the nomination because of his age, but the fact remained that he *had* been nominated, and that was enough, at least for posterity. In the same way that he had come to be known as an antiwar leader, he was now suddenly in the national spotlight as a political force to be reckoned with—young, black and already nominated for vice president before he had even turned thirty.

Julian handled it extremely well—very low key, very reasonable, very impressive. He was a national symbol now, both of the opposition to the war and of the new generation poised to inherit the nation's political mantle, the "radical chic," as magazines were calling it. *The New York Times* came out and labeled Julian "the leader of the New Politics."

It was an incredible experience to watch my friend become a superstar. It was fun. We loved each other like brothers. And we knew each other very, very well. I could see that he could hardly believe what was happening to him. It was all pretty dizzying, at least at first.

So for us, the Georgia Loyal Democrats, and for Julian, the convention was a success. But for the Democratic Party itself, and for the nation, it was a disaster. The madness and chaos beamed each night into televisions around the nation became identified with the Democratic Party. If we couldn't even control a convention without having everything fall apart, how could we be trusted to control the country?

By that fall of 1968, the American people were frightened. Violent protests on college campuses, race riots in the cities, the war in Vietnam going more badly every day—the nation looked as if it was losing its senses, coming apart at the seams. Hubert Humphrey, who came out of Chicago as the Democratic candidate for president, had little to offer in terms of soothing those fears. He stood strongly and in the right place on almost every specific issue—at least as far as my politics were concerned. But the issue that mattered most was simply how to make Americans feel safe and secure. That's the issue Richard Nixon spoke to during his campaign, with his promise of "law and order"—the same phrase Daley had used at our convention. And that's one reason Nixon narrowly defeated Humphrey in that November's election—because he assured Americans that he would make them safe.

That was the first time I ever voted in a presidential election—I'd been in Africa in '64. I wasn't crazy about Humphrey—he had worked hard against us in Atlantic City—but I liked his stand on civil rights, and if he had only broken earlier with Johnson on the war, I really think he would have won.

And Nixon? I didn't like him at all. I didn't like his red-baiting back in the '50s. I didn't like him when he ran against Kennedy in 1960. And I liked him even less now. He just didn't seem like a person who thought the way I did at all. I know it's something that's said so often today, but I was saying it back then—I just did not trust that man.

So that was the way that awful year ended, with Richard Nixon about to move into the White House. The flame of faith and hope—mine, the nation's—had been barely flickering at the beginning of that year. By the end, it really felt as if it had gone out. Something in the civil rights movement died for good in 1966, but something died in all of America in 1968. The sense of hope, of optimism, of *possibility*, was replaced by horror, the worst of times, the feeling that maybe, just maybe, we would *not* overcome.

It was a dark, dark time.

There was a quote Ted Kennedy used to end the eulogy for his brother that June. It was a quote from Bobby himself, a phrase I have always kept at hand at all times:

"Some men see things as they are and say, 'Why?' I dream things that never were, and say, 'Why not?'"

I had dropped to that hotel room floor the night Bobby was shot, crying out, "Why? Why? Why?"

I had managed to pick myself up and move on, once again daring to hope and ask, "Why not?"

Then had come the convention.

And then Nixon.

The question now, for both me and the country, was, could we pick ourselves up yet again?

Part VII

HOME

There was one good thing about the end of 1968 beyond the fact that that horrific year was finally over:

Lillian and I became man and wife.

I had come home from the convention in Chicago feeling pretty low, very tired. I imagine I looked much the way Penny Bartlett had described me in that SNCC memo in late 1965. I didn't normally *get* tired. Energy was one of my greatest attributes; I could go two days without sleep, if necessary, and often I did. A few hours' rest at that point and I'd be ready to go again. So this fatigue worried me enough that I went to see my doctor in Atlanta, an internist named James Palmer, who counted many SNCC and SCLC people—including Dr. King—as his patients. Dr. Palmer took one look at me and checked me into the hospital. "That's the only way," he said, "that you're going to sit still and get any rest."

I was there a couple of days, and each morning Lillian came by with the daily newspaper and my mail. We watched the Republican convention together on television, which made me feel even lower than I'd been when I checked in. I can't say exactly what precipitated it—Lillian always says I simply got caught at my weakest moment—but while I was lying in that hospital bed, I said to her, "Why don't we get married?"

And so we did, four days before Christmas, at Ebenezer Baptist Church. Daddy King—Martin's father—performed the service. A cross section of my SNCC and SCLC friends were there, as well as Lillian's friends and family—about three hundred people, all told. Don Harris was my best man. Julian was an usher. My mother, my brother Grant and my sister Rosa were there—the first time any of my family had ever come to Atlanta to see me. Atlanta was a frightening place for them. Too big. Too far away from the farm. That's the reason my father wasn't there that day—he had too much work to do and couldn't afford to leave.

Once we were married, Lillian and I leased a house near Emory University, where we stayed until the next autumn, when we bought our first home. We still live there today. It's a California-style ranch with three bedrooms and a nice wooded yard, purchased at a 1969 price of $35,000.

The neighborhood is called Venetian Hills, a comfortable, middle-class community of established homes and rolling, tree-shaded streets. It was racially mixed when we moved in, but it didn't stay that way long. We were the first black family to move onto our block, and within two years we were flanked by black neighbors, both renting and buying, as the white owners began moving out.

Some sections of the neighborhood tried digging in, doing their best to keep black buyers out. I saw signs appear in yards that announced, "THIS IS OUR HOME: IT IS NOT FOR SALE." The signs would come down only when a white buyer appeared. Real estate agents complied, "steering" black buyers away while inviting white buyers in.

This was happening in neighborhoods all around Atlanta, sections of the city committed to keeping themselves racially segregated. Banks and other lending institutions cooperated as well, making mortgages available to white home buyers in these neighborhoods while discouraging or simply turning away black applicants. Insurance companies did the same. The process is called redlining. It is blatantly illegal. In 1989, the redlining going on in Atlanta was finally exposed in a series of investigative stories in the *Journal-Constitution* that won the newspaper a Pulitzer Prize. In 1970, though, this was one of those things that everyone knew about but no one addressed.

The '60s were over, but many of the problems we had confronted with the movement remained. We had made remarkable progress, we had forced the side of segregation and discrimination to retreat on many fronts. But they did not surrender. Far from it. They simply retrenched in different, more subtle ways. Redlining was just one example of the kinds of strategies we now faced.

As for the civil rights movement—at least the movement I had been part of, the massive organization and mobilization of people of conscience, black and white together, gathered to confront racism and segregation in an aggressive, disciplined, nonviolent manner—that had all but vanished.

By 1970, SNCC was a shell of its former self. Many of the people who had been most involved in SNCC, who had come of age in SNCC, who defined themselves in terms of SNCC, found themselves lost and adrift—not too different from the way America as a whole was feeling. Things had gotten out of control. It was if a bomb had exploded, the house had blown up, and the people inside had come to, shaking their heads, gathering their senses and trying to figure out where to go from here. Some turned inward, others went off by themselves, and a fortunate few were able to figure out a way to carry on somehow. Like Vietnam vets, they stepped into a society that offered them no welcome-home parade. But unlike the military veterans, the veterans of the civil rights movement had no hospitals or support groups or government programs to help them out. They were on their own. Many took off in strange directions, down paths no one could have imagined a half dozen years earlier.

Jim Forman joined the Black Panthers, as did Stokely, who married the South African singer Miriam Makeba, then moved to Conakry, Guinea (which our SNCC delegation had visited in 1964), where he changed his name to Kwame Toure and began shuttling back and forth from Africa to the United States as director of a group called the All African Peoples Revolutionary Party, working for the unity of African nations as a step toward black liberation around the globe.

Rap Brown got caught up in several firearms violations, and in March 1970 was at the center of a bizarre, tragic incident involving a SNCC staffer named Ralph Featherstone, a wonderful young man. Ralph had been director of a Freedom School in McComb and was a SNCC central committee member. He had become a close friend of Brown's, and on this particular afternoon in March he was driving to a small town called Bel Air, north of Baltimore, where Brown was to go on trial the following day on a federal firearms charge.

Just outside Bel Air, Ralph's car exploded. Two bodies, burnt beyond recognition, were found inside. One was identified as Ralph's. The other, at first report, was Rap Brown's. Soon, the second body was identified as a friend of Ralph's named "Che" Payne. No one knew where Brown was. He didn't show up for that trial.

FBI investigators concluded that Ralph and his friend had made a bomb and planned to bring it to the courthouse in Bel Air. Something went wrong, they speculated, and the bomb blew up early.

That didn't make sense to me. I still find it difficult to believe. Ralph Featherstone would be the last person to ever consider doing something like that. But then, during this time, at the turn of that decade, people were becoming so strange, so desperate, that you didn't know what to believe. Anything was possible. Look at George Jackson and the brazen shoot-out at the Marin County courthouse in 1970, and Jackson's own shooting death a year later on the yard at San Quentin Prison. And the bizarre murder trial of the Manson "family." And the killings at Kent State. The dawn of the '70s was a disturbed, disturbing time in America, an unsettlingly violent time.

Ralph Featherstone's funeral that March was like a SNCC reunion. It was held in Washington, and it was the first time many of us had seen one another since 1966. I didn't mingle much with many of the people there. My feelings were still too raw. It hadn't been that long since I'd left. But I wanted to be there for Ralph, and we all shared the sorrow about his death. During the wake they kept playing one song over and over—Ralph's favorite, just out that year from Aretha Franklin—a song titled "Call Me":

> *Baby, will you call me the moment you get there?*
> *...I know we've got to part,*
> *...It really doesn't hurt me that bad,*
> *Because you're takin' me with you,*
> *And I'm keepin' you right here in my heart.*
> *Call me the minute, the second that you get there.*

Everybody was just crying, really weeping.

Rap Brown did not surface until a year later, when he was wounded in a shoot-out with police during a holdup attempt at a bar in Manhattan. It turned out he had been hiding in Canada since skipping his trial in Maryland. Now he was in court for robbery as well, and wound up in prison.

And then there was Bevel. The last time I'd seen him was at Dr. King's funeral. He had always been an intense, on-the-edge person, but the shooting of Dr. King sent him over the edge. By the summer of 1970, he was still with the SCLC, but his behavior had turned more emotionally erratic than ever. He and Diane had divorced by this time. Their two children were living with her, and Bevel was just floating, aimless. I'd hear about him here and there, when he was in and out of Atlanta, but what I heard early that summer was hard to believe, even by Bevel standards.

It happened in one of the hotel rooms above Paschal's. Bevel had gathered around him a number of students from Spelman College, along with several SCLC staffers—about a dozen people, all told—and sequestered the group and himself there above Paschal's for several days, with the door locked, never leaving, ordering food from downstairs. Bevel was convinced that he had become a prophet of some kind, and he spent those several days preaching to the group, writing on the walls with Magic Markers, telling them they had to believe in him. He had enough influence and charisma to keep these young people there. But when, according to later reports from some of the participants, he urinated in a glass and told them they had to drink it to prove they were true followers, they'd had enough.

When word got out, the SCLC held a board meeting to decide what to do about this incident, whether or not to expel Bevel. Almost everyone wanted to put him out, especially Ralph Abernathy—he and Bevel did not get along, especially after Dr. King's death.

I took the position that Bevel should not be expelled. He's sick, I said. We need to help him. But only Andy Young agreed. When it was time to decide, ours were the only votes for allowing Bevel to stay. And so he was put out, banished from what was left of the movement.

Later that day I met with Andy. I had a letter I wanted to show him, a letter I'd written the previous November to Julian.

Ever since I became involved in Bobby Kennedy's campaign, I'd been convinced that politics was the road we must now take to achieve the goals we had pursued until then through direct action. Now that the primary purpose of those years of action—securing the right to vote—had been achieved, it was time to show black Americans in the South not only that they could select their political representatives but that it was possible to *become* those representatives. The MFDP had taken a stab at it, but the time had been too soon. That failure, far from inspiring black voters, discouraged many of them. Any belief they might have had in the political system was destroyed.

But six years had passed since then. Local and state governments throughout the South had become sprinkled with black elected officials, people like Julian. Now it was time to send somebody to Washington.

No black congressperson had been elected from the South in this century, not since Reconstruction. If there was a place for it to happen now, I believed that place was Atlanta. The city's population was 60 percent black. With its six black universities, the city had an extraordinary concentration of well-educated, progressive black men and women. The local black religious, educational and business communities were heavily entrenched and well organized. We had a black vice mayor—Maynard Jackson, elected in 1969—and five black aldermen on the city council. Although the congressional district that included Atlanta also included enough surrounding suburban communities to give white voters an overall majority, a black congressional candidate in Atlanta stood a good chance of making a serious run.

And the man who should make it, I had no doubt, was Julian.

It seemed pretty obvious to me. Julian had been in the statehouse for three years now. And ever since the '68 convention, his national reputation had ballooned. He was in great demand as a speaker on college campuses around the country, where he was often introduced as the "future president of the United States." He continually wrote me notes and postcards from the road, little bits of news about whom he came across on this campus or that, whom he ran into at the airport.

Now, in November 1969, it was time for *me* to sit down and write *him*. I had no idea at the time how the issues and specifics set forth in that letter would reverberate over the course of Julian's career through the next two decades and would finally collide with the course of my own life. Some of the names mentioned in the letter have since risen to national recognition (Vernon

Jordan, Ivan Allen); others are largely unknown today beyond the bounds of Atlanta (Ben Brown, Lonnie King, Leroy Johnson, Horace Tate, Fletcher Thompson, Sam Massell). But it is fascinating to look back at this letter, both for the picture it paints of black politics in a Southern city at that transitional time, and for the light it throws on so much that would happen in Atlanta's black political community over the next twenty years:

November 12, 1969

The Honorable Julian Bond
House of Representatives
District 111
162 Euharlee Street, S.W.
Atlanta, Georgia 30314

Dear Julian,

I don't quite know how to begin this letter because it might seem a little presumptuous on my part to write such a letter to a friend.

As you know, I have a deep interest in seeing what I call "good men" elevated to higher positions in the political arena. Those men who act on principles and their own convictions and not according to political expediency. Those who are willing to inject into the body politic a degree of the honesty and morality that we witnessed in the early days of the Civil Rights Movement.

Some of us have said many times in private discussions, interviews and even speeches, after the deaths of Martin Luther King and Robert Kennedy, that you arose as the political leader of many. Your presence filled a vacuum and you became the hope of millions who had previously identified with these two great men. Many blacks and whites who were committed to humane political leaders in the past placed their future in your hands. On the other hand, there are hundreds of thousands of young people, both black and white, who are dissatisfied, disillusioned, disappointed, frustrated and bitter, who have given up on the political system. Julian, you have an obligation to the youth of today to use your influence to let them know that there are some basic changes that can be made through the machinery of politics.

Now, the preaching is over! Let's consider the matter at hand. As you know, during the past few days and especially since the recent election, there have been rumors and speculations about who will run for Congress from the 5th Congressional District. In addition to yourself, Senator Leroy Johnson, Representative Ben Brown, Vernon

Jordan, Lonnie King and Horace Tate have all been mentioned as likely candidates.

I have no idea what you have decided to do, for the last time I talked to you, I got the feeling that you were seriously contemplating a decision. Personally, I think you should seriously consider running and run like you have never run before! If you do decide to run, you cannot afford to let the luxury of being a political celebrity and in demand throughout the country keep you from tackling the "nitty-gritty" and difficult problems of planning and building a political organization.

Julian, you know for the most part that things don't just happen in the world of politics. One has to work and get the people behind him. I have a few suggestions that I wish you would consider. (1) Spend more time in Georgia, and particularly in your own district, speaking and just being visible; (2) Become more involved in the Fulton County Democratic Party; (3) Work more closely with the black community and neighborhood groups in your district and other parts of the city and state; (4) Work with the students in the Atlanta University complex; (5) Accept more speaking engagements within the state, schools, colleges, both black and white, teas, clubs, PTA's, churches and other civic groups; (6) Start developing your campaign platform and an organization for your next election.

Vernon Jordan is operating on the theory that if he makes what he considers the right move, that is, touching base with certain forces in both the black and white liberal community and announces his candidacy early, he would pre-empt any other black candidates from entering the race. I cannot accept this theory, for the time is always right for the right man to run.

Vernon has said to me on several occasions during the past few days that he has "got to run, for it's in my blood." He is campaigning now. All he has to do is make it official. He is aware of the fact that he is not well-known in the city and that he must become highly visible in the black and white community. He sees you as unbeatable in the Democratic Primary if you do decide to run. He even asked me to talk you into not running. Vernon is also operating on the belief that if he runs and loses to Fletcher Thompson in 1970, he would be the natural black candidate for Congress in 1972 when the redistricting takes place. With this rationale, he is maintaining the idea that he can afford to be defeated. It is obvious that I disagree with his conclusion, for if any politician can afford to lose an election as a step toward winning one, it is you. Vernon is attempting to project himself as the black sacrificial lamb of 1970, to do battle with the bad white wolf, Fletcher Thompson, in order that the black voters will remember him in 1972.

Now Leroy Johnson is a sure-safe politician. He is not going to get out on the limb if there are some questions about the capacity of the limb to sustain him. I don't think there are any doubts that Senator Johnson's political stock did go up with the recent election. This is due to his early endorsement of Sam Massell for Mayor and his efforts to turn out the black votes for Massell even in greater numbers after Allen's statement. (Julian, I think you made a mistake in not returning to the city to assist in getting the black votes out for Massell. You would have emerged as the "great deliverer" of black votes in Atlanta. This sounds like a joke, but I am serious.) So many political observers tend to credit Senator Johnson for the overwhelming black support of Massell. However, I believe Senator Johnson will not run for Congress.

Representative Ben Brown has been sending up and out some trial balloons. Apparently they returned without a message. I don't think he will run, for he was just engaged in political masturbation.

Dr. Horace Tate is out of the running for anything for quite a while. I don't think he would run for Congress next term.

I ran into Lonnie King last Friday outside Paschal's and I was surprised to hear him say that he was considering running as an independent. I am not sure, but I would like to believe that he said or implied that he would run only if you decided not to run. I cannot conceive of Lonnie King running against you!

Julian, out of all the possible candidates, you are the only one that could get 300 or more students to work in your campaign as volunteers. In addition, you are the only one that people throughout the nation would contribute the necessary funds to to conduct such a massive campaign, and you would have the support not only of the black votes, but the white liberals and young people. Your position on the war in Vietnam and the Urban Crisis is clear. I am not sure where the other possible candidates stand on these issues. I am positive that the war in Vietnam and the problems of the cities will be the issues in next year's election.

Julian, if you decide to run, I don't think it is necessary for you to announce it early. However, during the period between reaching your decision and the announcement of your candidacy, you should have put together an effective organization and begun raising funds for your campaign. On the other hand, if you reach a decision and decide not to run for Congress, I don't think you should be quick to announce it. I just think you have to keep all the possibilities open.

I realize that you must be under a great deal of pressure, for I am receiving all kinds of suggestions and proposals from other people.

Whatever you decide to do, you have my support.

Sincerely,
John Lewis

I hand-delivered that letter to Julian over lunch at Paschal's. He read it right then and there, in silence. When he was done, there was more silence. Finally he spoke.

"It's a good letter, Mr. Chairman," he said.

He had questions about money, he said. And time.

"Let me think about it," he said.

And that was the last I heard from him on the matter.

Now it was the summer of '70, and it was time, I felt, to talk to Andy Young. I liked Andy, I respected him, he'd been an active participant in the movement, and we seemed to think alike on many of the issues that arose whenever the board of the SCLC came together.

I handed him a copy of the letter I'd written to Julian and asked him to read it, to see what he thought. He said he had a plane to catch for New York, where he was meeting that evening with Harry Belafonte to plan some SCLC fund-raising events. He would take the letter with him, he said, and read it on the way up. Late that night my telephone rang. It was Andy, calling from Belafonte's home.

"If Julian fails to do it," he said, "I will."

Julian had already failed to do it. And so, not long after Andy returned from that trip, he announced his candidacy for Georgia's Fifth Congressional District seat.

Despite the city's heavily concentrated black population, the district as a whole contained twice as many white registered voters as blacks. Andy's challenge was to pick up enough of those white votes to win. Ivanhoe Donaldson, my old colleague from SNCC, signed on to manage Andy's campaign. I couldn't afford to take a leave from the SRC, but I helped out all I could, as did Lillian.

Andy's opponent for the Democratic nomination was Lonnie King, Julian's old buddy from their student movement days at Morehouse. When Andy won that nomination, our hopes were high, especially because Republicans so rarely were elected anywhere in the overwhelmingly Democratic Deep South. But with a black candidate on the ballot that November, an amazingly high number of Fifth District white voters—many of them blue collar and conservative—turned out to vote Republican, and Andy lost to the white incumbent mentioned in my letter, Fletcher Thompson.

That was the same election in which Jimmy Carter was elected governor of Georgia. I had never met Carter, though I knew of him, of course. He was not a favorite among black voters, for several reasons. First, he was from rural south Georgia—the town of Plains, in Sumter County—the region of the state where we had fought so many of our battles, mostly around Albany and Americus. Jimmy Carter was a local political leader and an influential businessman during that time, but we never heard from him. He never spoke up or spoke out about what his black neighbors were going through. Not a word.

So it was not surprising that his black support was not overwhelming when he ran for governor. Personally, I supported attorney C. B. King in that election—the same C. B. King who had been beaten bloody in Albany back in '62, the same C. B. King I referred to in my '63 speech at the March on Washington.

When King lost, we knew we would now learn where Jimmy Carter stood on the issues that mattered most to the black citizens of Georgia. He would no longer be able to stay silent.

Earlier that same year, 1970, I took a new position with the SRC. Vernon Jordan, who had been executive director of the organization's Voter Education Project (VEP), resigned to become head of the United Negro College Fund, and I was chosen to take his place. The job was a perfect fit, a direct extension of the work I'd done during all those years with SNCC.

The VEP had, up to that point, helped register more than 1.5 million Southern black voters since its inception in 1962. But there were many millions more still unregistered. And so far, there were only small stirrings of political involvement among blacks seeking elected office, despite the fact that there were 102 black-majority counties in the Deep South at the time.

I headed a staff of thirty-eight, much larger than what I'd worked with in the Community Organization Project. We covered eleven Southern states, from Virginia to Texas, spearheading get-out-the-vote drives, presenting seminars for young black people interested in politics, and offering technical and financial assistance to black community groups interested in political education.

One of the first things I did after taking that job was to commission a poster, something we could use out in the field to inspire people and stir them to action. A young local artist in Atlanta named Herman "Kofi" Bailey drew it. It depicted two strong black hands, one pulling cotton from a boll and the other putting a ballot in a box, with the words "HANDS THAT PICK COTTON NOW CAN PICK OUR ELECTED OFFICIALS" emblazoned at the bottom. More than 10,000 copies were made and distributed all through the

South, where they wound up on the walls of beauty parlors and barbershops, schools and churches. I framed and hung Kofi's original drawing in my VEP office. Today, it hangs in the front foyer of my home in Washington. It's the first thing visitors see when they step through the door.

It was good getting back to the kind of hands-on work that the VEP was all about, where success could be measured in tangible terms, vote by vote. It was very therapeutic for me after the vagueness and theorizing and lostness into which the movement—at least the SNCC section of it—had stumbled in its last years.

Julian became very involved. He joined my board of directors, and he was enthusiastic about the idea of the VEP getting visible public figures, black leaders and politicians, to go out into these little villages and hamlets, places where people had never *seen* a black elected official, and give them a chance to meet a Julian Bond; or a state senator like Doug Wilder from Virginia; or Tom Reed, a state representative in Alabama; or Fred Gray, who was now a member of the Alabama legislature. We gathered local elected officials as well, along with visible, influential figures like Coretta King and Ralph Abernathy.

One by one, sometimes two or three at a time, we took these people all over the South, to Texas, Tennessee, Arkansas, Louisiana. It was almost like a political campaign, with our VEP staffers doing the advance work, preparing as if for the arrival of a candidate—though this had nothing to do with partisan politics; being a nonprofit agency, we were forbidden to make any such endorsements.

On a given day, we might make ten or twelve stops in one county. Or we might cover ten counties in one day. And no one made more of those trips than Julian. Mississippi remained, as always, a prime target in need of this type of effort, and I went there more than anyplace else. Often it was with Julian. Often we were met by Fannie Lou Hamer, who was still fighting the good fight, working for VEP now as a local coordinator and grant administrator. During one eight-day stretch in 1971, the three of us—Julian, Mrs. Hamer and I—made thirty-nine speeches in twenty-five counties. That same year, Fannie Lou ran for a seat in Mississippi's state Senate. Her campaign received national attention as much for the fact that she was a woman as that she was a black. Betty Friedan came down and campaigned for Fannie Lou. I came down, too, but she lost, to an incumbent with the unfortunate name of Crook.

That didn't slow her down, however. Nor us. We continued walking out into the cotton fields together, Fannie Lou, Julian and I, convincing people chopping cotton to vote. We'd move on to an evening meeting, which Fannie Lou would begin by breaking into a song, "This Little Light of Mine," the sweat just popping out of her forehead, the people mesmerized by the power of her incredible voice.

I was on the go—and loving it—from my first day on that job. People would see me out and around so much, and they'd tease me, saying, "John, are you *running* for something?"

No, I was not. But I was paying close attention now to my friends who were. In 1972, Andy ran again for that Fifth District Congressional seat. Again he won the Democratic nomination, defeating a young white attorney, Wyche Fowler. Fletcher Thompson decided not to run this time, so, in that November election, Andy faced a moderate Republican, Rodney Cook, and won.

I was ecstatic. Barbara Jordan of Texas also won a congressional seat that year, but Texas is not really the South, not the way Alabama, Mississippi and Georgia are. Andy's ascension was cause for us all to celebrate, something to hold up to the people we were working with through the VEP—the Deep South's first black U.S. congressman of the century.

I could not campaign for Andy in that election because of my VEP position. But I hailed his success. And I attended both national party conventions that year in Miami Beach as an observer. Lillian went, too, as a delegate to the Democratic convention as a Shirley Chisholm delegate.

For the next several years I dug in deep with my VEP work, doing door-to-door canvassing in places like Dawson, Georgia; Ville Platte, Louisiana; Soul City, North Carolina. In the 1970s, I visited a town called Waterproof, Louisiana, with Julian, and the meeting hall looked like a nineteenth-century one-room schoolhouse that was about to fall over. About 150 people showed up, most of whom were not registered to vote, many of whom were nervous about even being seen at a gathering like this. This was the 1970s, but Waterproof was still a segregated community. Not one of its elected officials was black.

Three years later I came back and was greeted by the town's new mayor—a black man. The majority of the city council was now black as well. Waterproof had done a lot of catching up in three short years.

That was the basis of the VEP's efforts, to allow people who had been left out and left behind to catch up. If you boiled it down, that was the basis of the civil rights movement as well.

In 1975 we faced a major setback. The Voting Rights Act of '65 expired that year. Our funding plummeted, along with our staff, which shrank to nine. My priority that summer was providing documentation and testimony in Washington supporting a renewal of the act. What I preferred was to see it become permanent and to extend it to the entire nation, not just the South. We constantly received appeals from all over the country for assistance— from New York, Philadelphia, Boston, Detroit.

I noted during my testimony at those congressional subcommittee hearings that at the time the 1965 act was passed, only 2 percent of the eligible black population in the South was registered to vote. Now, a decade later, that number was close to 60 percent. During that time the number of black public officials elected in the region had rocketed up from fewer than twenty to more than a thousand.

Congress did not vote to make the act permanent nor to make it national, but it was extended and signed into law once again on August 6—the tenth anniversary of Lyndon Johnson's original signing. This time it was President Gerald Ford who gave it his signature.

That year began and ended with a pair of personal honors. First, in January, I was given the Martin Luther King Jr. Peace Prize. It was presented at Ebenezer Church on Dr. King's birthday, January 15. Created to honor the philosophy and principles that Dr. King believed in, the prize was first presented in 1973, to Andy Young. Cesar Chavez was awarded the second prize, and subsequent honorees have included Bishop Desmond Tutu, Mikhail Gorbachev, Sir Benjamin Mays, Jimmy Carter, Rosa Parks, Sir Richard Attenborough and Harry Belafonte. I received a medal and $1,000. I donated the money to several organizations; the medal remains one of my most treasured possessions.

Eleven months later, in its final issue of the year, *Time* magazine came out with a cover story titled "Messengers of Love and Hope: Living Saints." On the front of the magazine was a drawing of Mother Teresa. Inside were interviews with various religious scholars and theologians on what constitutes a "saint" in modern times.

"Love, self-denial, sacrifice and grace," said one expert.

"A certain personal serenity," said another.

"A saint," said yet another, "has to be a misfit. Saints tend to be on the outer edge, where maniacs, idiots and geniuses are."

Finally, noted one observer, a contemporary saint must be an activist, "a person who is willing to spend his whole life in a struggle for justice."

The story then went on to describe the work of various such activists around the world, ranging from a Norwegian nurse working as a medical missionary in China to a Dutch minister agitating against apartheid in South Africa. The list included Dom Helder Pessoa Camara, who had devoted his life to working with the poor in Brazil, and Dorothy Day, a tireless activist whose causes ranged from Mexican migrant workers to the homeless in Manhattan.

"The best things to do with the best things in life," Day told the magazine, "is to give them up."

And then there I was, "the young apostle of nonviolence," as the magazine put it. I was embarrassed, needless to say. Friends took to calling me

St. John. Julian teased me about it. This was during the Christmas season, and when I arrived at parties, people would straighten up and hide their drinks. Then I'd hear this little chant: "Here comes the saint."

But I was moved as well by this honor, to be in the company of the people described in that article. I imagine each of them felt much the same way—ill at ease, humbled and honored, all at once.

The following summer Lillian and I became parents. We had wanted a child for some time, but were not able to have one naturally. So we began the process of searching for an infant to adopt. We started with a private agency, then contacted the social services agency in Fulton County. That May they let us know that they had located a newborn baby for us, a little boy. We went to see him for the first time at the agency's offices on Martin Luther King Drive. We were allowed to be alone with him. We held him, played with him. And we loved him immediately. We knew nothing about his background, only that his mother was a single parent, a schoolteacher.

Two months later, on Friday, August 6, 1976, we brought John-Miles Lewis, our son, home with us. That day happened to be the anniversary of the Voting Rights Act, a beautiful coincidence.

The 1976 presidential election was around the corner by then, and it looked as if Jimmy Carter would be the Democratic nominee. I was happy about that. During his time as governor he had earned my respect, responding to issues of race in ways that won the confidence and support of many black Georgians. I saw him as a symbol of the New South—progressive, socially sensitive and racially responsive.

During that summer we staged a VEP dinner at the Hyatt Regency Hotel in Atlanta to raise funds for our "Get Out the Vote" campaign. We invited Carter, who'd just been nominated at the convention, to be our keynote speaker, and he accepted. The event was a sellout, about 1,500 people, and it was the first opportunity I'd had to meet him one-on-one. He was well aware of the fact that the swelling number of minority voters in the South—including Hispanics in Texas and Native Americans from Florida to North Carolina, as well as hundreds of thousands of black men and women every year—had become a force to be reckoned with. In the six years since I'd joined the VEP, we'd added nearly 2 million voters to the registration rolls. The total of black registered voters in the Deep South was now more than 4 million. Both Carter and Ford wanted those votes, but Carter, who in the past would have been hurt among black voters by the simple fact that he was a white man from the South, now had an advantage among the formidable black electorate of the South, most of whom gave him credit for the work he had done as governor. Coming to that fund-raising dinner, whether consciously or not, was his way of saying thank you to the VEP for helping nurture that electorate.

When Jimmy Carter was elected president that November, I cried. I sat in front of the television set with tears streaming down my cheeks. Lillian was shocked. She didn't know why in the world I was so emotional. I wasn't *that* crazy about Carter.

But those tears weren't about him. They were about the fact that the hands that picked cotton had now picked a president. The black vote in that election was decisive, not just in terms of the numbers, but because black Southerners, black Georgians, had said to the rest of America, both by word and by their votes, that this man was all right. If the nation was skeptical about this white Southerner in terms of the race issue, it needed to look no further than the black support he received right there in the South to set its doubts aside.

My mind drifted back that night to Dr. King. I wished he could have been there to see a native son, a *Georgian,* elected president. He would have been so satisfied, to see a candidate from the heart of the Deep South stepping forward to lead the nation, laying down the burden of race—or at least easing it. It wouldn't have happened without the years of struggle in Montgomery and Nashville and Birmingham and Selma. If it hadn't been for Martin Luther King Jr. and the civil rights movement, Jimmy Carter would never have gone to the White House.

The weekend after that election, a SNCC reunion was held in Atlanta, at the Hotel Internationale, near Fulton County Stadium. It had been ten years since I'd left SNCC, six years since Ralph Featherstone's funeral, and I was much more relaxed around my former SNCC colleagues now than I had been then.

It was a pleasant evening, very informal and stretching late into the night, about 150 of us gathered in the hotel's main ballroom. There was singing, including a lot of the old freedom songs. At one point we went around the room, and people talked about what they were doing now. Julian was there. Stokely was not. Marion, who was now a member of the D.C. Board of Education, was there. Don Harris, who had been as dismayed as I by the direction things went at the end and had completely cut his ties with SNCC, was not there. Neither was Bevel. Nor Diane. Nor Bernard, who like Bevel had become more connected early on with the SCLC than with SNCC.

Bill Hansen flew in from Europe, where he was now working for the military's *Stars and Stripes* newspaper. It surprised all of us when we heard that this was what he was doing. Bob Zellner was not there—he was working in New Orleans now as a labor organizer. Bob Moses, like Stokely, was in Africa and did not attend. Jim Forman was there, down from Cornell, where he had returned to finish his graduate work in Pan-African studies. Rap Brown had just been paroled from prison, but he did not come to the reunion.

We all looked different. We weren't kids anymore. I guess it was like any reunion—a lot of graying, a lot of balding and a lot of added pounds. The last two had certainly happened to me.

A couple of people that evening asked me a question I'd been hearing often lately: John, when are you going to run for something? You've got to *run* for something.

Well, the fact was, I was considering it. I hadn't even thought about myself back in '69 and '70, when I passed that letter to Julian and Andy. I was nowhere near ready at that time to try my own hand at politics. But I'd learned a lot in the ensuing six years. Through my positions both with the Field Foundation and the Southern Regional Council, I'd worked closely with politicians at all levels. I understood the political process much more than when I had been an activist in the '60s, on the outside looking in.

And there was now a spot open. Andy had been reelected to Congress that November, then made the stunning announcement that he was stepping down to take a position as United States ambassador to the United Nations. There was a lot of controversy about that decision. A lot of people who had worked and voted for Andy felt used, let down, abandoned.

The move seemed strange to me, very unusual. Andy didn't ask my advice about it, but if he had, I would have told him to stay in the House. Yes, it was a great honor to be asked by the President to go to the United Nations, but I thought he could have been much more effective for the causes of social justice and progressive politics if he had stayed in Congress. I don't think there's any question that Andy lost a lot of influence by leaving Congress. On the other hand, he felt that he could make a contribution by serving in the Carter administration, and with his interest in Africa, he would be in a position to put many of the concerns and interests of that continent on the table. I didn't agree with Andy's decision, but I didn't pass judgment either.

The immediate effect of Andy's decision was to create a scramble to find his successor. A special election would have to be held, and the black community in Atlanta set about trying to find the best consensus candidate. A local organization called the Bipartisan Voters League, led by the publisher of the *Atlanta Daily World,* C. A. Scott, held a series of meetings that November and December, inviting various local black leaders to attend. Scott had made it his personal crusade to do all he could to see that the next congressman from the Fifth District was black. I was invited to several of those meetings, as were the Reverend Abernathy, state representative Billy McKinney, and another state representative, Henrietta Canty.

Julian was not interested. If he had been, I would not have entered the race. I would not have considered running against one of my closest friends— not at that time.

But when I told him he should run, he said, "No, Mr. Chairman, I'm not going to. But why don't *you* consider doing it?"

Julian knew I was interested. But I still had several reservations, several reasons to wonder if I was really ready for this. First, I had no background or experience whatsoever in politics at any level, not on a school board, not on a county commission, not on a city council—nothing. And I was not charming or charismatic in the way that, say, a Julian Bond was. I always preferred to walk the walk rather than talk the talk. But politics is about walking *and* talking. Give me the room to talk, to actually spend some time with people—whether it's making a speech or having a real conversation—and I can make the points and have the effect I desire. But the same qualities that can come through so strongly in that kind of setting—earnestness, sincerity, substance—can come across in ten-second sound bites on the evening news as just plain dull. And as everyone knows, modern political campaigns are, unfortunately, steered largely by sound bites.

Finally, and this was no small consideration, if I was going to run for this office I would have to give up my position with the VEP. If I lost, I would be unemployed. Lillian would still be working, but it would not be easy. Add to that the fact that we had a brand-new baby, with whom I would not be spending as much time as I'd like if I was immersed in a political campaign, and this was a difficult decision to make.

Lillian and I talked it over at length. She had always been very involved in politics, much more than I. She had been a delegate to the Democratic National Convention in '72, and she was constantly active in a variety of local circles and organizations. She was outgoing, involved, intelligent and great in front of an audience—she could *make* a speech. She also knew how to organize, how to chair a meeting, the nitty-gritty stuff. When she finally said, "Let's do it. Let's go for it," that was enough. We were in.

I resigned from the VEP that December and immediately began my campaign for the vacant Fifth District congressional seat. Oddly enough, I was nowhere near as well known in Atlanta as I was in Mississippi and Alabama and south Georgia—the places where my presence had been felt during the movement. My name recognition in Atlanta was almost nil, and I was up against a large field of locally well known, established politicians.

This was a "fusion" election, Democrats and Republicans all running together in one big horse race. There were twelve candidates in all, ranging from state senator Paul Coverdell—who is now a U.S. senator—to Wyche Fowler, who had been president of the city council and had lost the Democratic primary election to Andy Young earlier that year. It appeared at first that Maynard Jackson would run, but he took himself out early. Ralph Abernathy, on the other hand, did enter the race, which made me a little uncomfortable. I didn't like running against a colleague, a friend. But I had a lot of friends. If I was going to enter politics, I was going to wind up running against some of them.

My chief advisor was Lillian—she was in on every major decision I made, every key strategy meeting. Lonnie King also became a close advisor, along with a local political activist named Russ Marane, a real roll-up-the-sleeves kind of guy.

My support included a number of local labor leaders, as well as the Bipartisan Voters League, which endorsed me against the other black candidates.

Julian was a big supporter. He wrote letters, appeared at fund-raisers, made telephone calls, put me in contact with people and came by my campaign headquarters often, giving advice when I needed it.

Daddy King backed me in a very visible, very vocal way, as did Georgia lieutenant governor Zell Miller. I had some strong support in the local white community, which was critical in a district whose population was 60 percent white. I made numerous appearances at breakfasts and brunches in wealthy northside neighborhoods, a section of Atlanta I had never been in before. I figured I needed about 30 percent of the white vote in order to win this election. Early polls gave me 9 percent of the *total* vote. I knew this was going to be an uphill battle, but I had not realized how steep that hill was going to be.

The campaign lasted two months, leading up to the election in March—two months of mass meetings and discussions and debates, often with all twelve candidates taking the stage together. It was a sea of confusion, and I found it very hard to make myself stand out.

It might have seemed that Abernathy would have a big advantage in the black community, with his visibility as head of the SCLC and his identification with Dr. King. But there has long been a history in Atlanta of the black electorate drawing a line between its ministers and its political representatives. I think people in the black community feel that the church is one place and politics is another. It's okay to talk politics in the church, and it's fine for politicians to come into a church to rally support or push for a cause. But it is not okay for a minister to leave the church and run for office. A pastor is supposed to be a pastor, and a politician is supposed to be a politician.

Some people might ask, Well, what about Dr. King? Dr. King was different. From the beginning he was never seen as a pastor per se. He was seen as a social leader who happened to be a minister. He was in a category by himself.

It wasn't Abernathy who was my chief concern in that race. Wyche Fowler was the one everybody was chasing. I did my best to catch up to him. I worked my butt off—got up and out on the streets before dawn and was downtown by five-thirty in the morning to pass out leaflets to black women, maids getting on the bus to go out to their jobs in the suburbs. Then I'd move to a factory and meet the 7 A.M. shift change at the front gate. I didn't have the money or the connections some of my opponents did. But I had energy and desire. No one was going to outwork me.

The day before the election, the *Atlanta Constitution* endorsed me, with an editorial headlined "JOHN THE UNKNOWN":

> It is true that Lewis' mouth does less work than his mind. And it is true that he seems to take more pride in, gain more satisfaction from, accomplishing deeds than in speaking of them.
>
> If the reverse were true, would that make him more "known"? Perhaps.
>
> But we prefer John the Unknown, who is known by millions as a hardworking, dedicated man, sensitive to human problems, capable of helping to solve those problems.
>
> In short, John Lewis is a man the U.S. Congress needs.

That night, Monday, March 14, I got word that Fannie Lou Hamer had died. She had been bedridden for some time with cancer, diabetes and heart disease. That afternoon her heart had finally given out—that enormous heart. I was going to miss her. We all were.

The next day came the election. As expected, Fowler ran away from the rest of us, with 40 percent of the vote. The good news was that my second-place finish, with 29 percent, was enough to force a runoff election between just Fowler and me. I was still standing. That in itself felt like a victory.

If I had any hope of defeating Fowler in the runoff, however, we would have to figure out some way to get more people out to vote. Only a third of the district's 300,000 registered voters had turned out for that March 15 primary, a very low number. Barely more than a fourth of the eligible black voters cast their ballots. We would have to double that figure for the April 5 runoff to have any hope of winning.

Now, with the way cleared for just Fowler and me, endorsements and contributions to my campaign began to flow in. Andy Young was behind me. Abernathy, who finished far back in the primary, came on board, as did almost every minister and religious leader in the black community. More white support came my way when Herb Mabry, a local labor leader and state head of the AFL-CIO, went all-out and endorsed me. Mabry lived in a lily-white, conservative, heavily Republican northside community, and he took a lot of heat for that endorsement, including telephone calls to his home attacking him for supporting the "nigger," John Lewis.

Unfortunately, the issue of race rose to the top during that runoff campaign. Wyche didn't raise it at all—he was, and is, an incredibly decent, wonderful human being. But there were cries from some sections of the community that my candidacy was intended to keep this a "black seat."

I tried convincing people that this seat had no color as far as I was concerned. I had never appealed to race. My perspective had always been a biracial one. My life's path had proven that. Indeed, I had suffered among some of my black brothers and sisters for it. Never during that campaign did I mention the fact that the black citizens of Georgia were vastly underrepresented by their government leaders—a fourth of the state's population was black, but only 3 percent of its elected officials were "colored." I never pointed that out. I wanted the voters to look beyond race and simply, truly consider who would represent them best in Washington.

Support came in from around the nation as I headed for that runoff. Marion Barry came down from D.C. Maxine Waters, the state assemblywoman from California, arrived to lend a hand, as did Earl Graves, Bobby Kennedy's former assistant.

Ted Kennedy came down as well. We had met only in passing up until then—during Bobby's campaign and during my visits to Hickory Hill, Virginia, the Kennedy estate just outside Washington, where I attended meetings as a member of the Robert F. Kennedy Memorial Foundation board of trustees.

I admired Ted Kennedy for his willingness to carry on, to get out there in the public arena even after what happened to his brothers. His name had been pulled from consideration for the presidency in '68 because people were afraid, in the crazy climate of that time, that he might be assassinated. Why put him through that? went the reasoning. Why do it? But here he was, carrying on, making trips like this, traveling down to Georgia to speak on behalf of a fellow Democrat.

Having the support of a Kennedy was still a political liability in most of the Deep South—John and Bobby's Catholicism and their sympathy for the cause of civil rights made them pariahs in most of the places where the movement had done its work. They were as despised by white segregationists as Martin Luther King. But Atlanta was different. It was a pocket of relative progressiveness, not like the rest of the Deep South, certainly not the rest of the rural South. Ted Kennedy's endorsement would help me, and I welcomed it.

But in Wyche Fowler I faced a formidable opponent. He had deep roots in Atlanta, a strong political base developed over years on the city council and great charisma. He was likable, tireless, a bachelor whose youth—he was thirty-six, the same age as I—and boyish good looks carried a Kennedy-like appeal. He could charm a room full of college coeds, then turn around and pick up a guitar and sing hymns with a gathering of senior citizens.

The night before the election, the Reverend Abernathy stood before the congregation at Ebenezer Baptist, gathered for the anniversary of Dr. King's death, and pointed out that only eighteen of the nation's 435 congressmen were black. My victory the next day, he declared, was "part of God's plan."

Not quite.

Fowler destroyed me, 62 percent to 38. I received 90 percent of the black votes, but barely 30 percent of the eligible black voters turned out—nowhere near the 50 percent we figured I'd need to win. The white turnout was no better, but those who did vote went overwhelmingly for Fowler.

The only explanation I could find for the remarkably low turnout that day was that people were simply "electioned out." They had gone through state, local and national campaigns the previous fall, then a bond issue that spring, then the special election and now this one. I think the people of Atlanta were just tired of voting.

I was tired, too. Exhausted. But I felt good. I said so in my concession speech that night, with Lillian and Coretta King by my side. "Two months ago," I declared, "nobody knew who John Lewis was. This is only the beginning. This is only the beginning."

The *Journal-Constitution* echoed that feeling in an editorial about the race I'd just run:

> He has, even while losing his first political campaign, established himself as one of the few remaining serious black politicians in Atlanta....
>
> He moves into the limelight of Atlanta politics at a time when there is a glaring and extremely serious void in high level, responsible black political leadership here....
>
> Ask any citizen of any race in Fulton County, outside the state Senate district level, to name a serious local black politician, and chances are that Maynard Jackson, John Lewis, and perhaps Julian Bond—who is no threat to anybody—will be the only names mentioned.

That comment about Julian—"no threat to anybody"—did not go unnoticed in the city's black community. No one was surprised by that criticism. Julian had by now developed a reputation for reluctance. The same issues I had advised him to pay attention to in the letter I had written to him back in 1969—spending more time in Georgia; becoming more involved in political activities close to home—had now become liabilities for him because he had largely neglected them. He was now drawing a lot of criticism for his lack of leadership and even participation in the state senate. He missed more than his share of votes and was involved in very few bills, largely because he spent so much of his time traveling around the country, making good money—very good money—on the speaking circuit. There was no question that he faced a difficult challenge in the Georgia statehouse, where any bill he introduced was bound to be treated by the majority of his white colleagues as if it were radioactive. But rather than dig in and confront this challenge, Julian seemed to prefer avoiding it. He was a national figure, well respected and much in demand, so he spent much of his time traveling around the country while the people back home were wondering whether he really cared about the job he was supposed to be doing for them.

I had faced that same kind of criticism during the tail end of my time at SNCC. I understood what Julian was facing. What role should a person play? Can you play a dual role? Can you manage the store, make the trains run on time and at the same time be a carrier of a message to a much larger community, to society as a whole?

It's a difficult issue, one that congressmen have to wrestle with all the time. They have two roles to play, one back home—where they must see that their elderly constituents get their social security checks, that roads and bridges are built, that veterans receive their benefits—and one with society at large, in which they work to create a complete community, a society at peace with itself, just and humane. Can you do both? It's an eternal question, an ongoing struggle.

I knew after that 1977 campaign that I wanted to be a congressman someday. But at the moment I had more immediate matters to deal with, the foremost being finding a job. The race was over, I had a campaign debt of roughly $50,000, and I was not sure which way to turn next. It was a little like going back to my situation in 1966. What would I do next? Where would I turn?

There was the possibility of a position with the Carter administration. I knew I was being considered for a position with ACTION, the federal agency for volunteer service, which directed both the Peace Corps abroad and several other agencies domestically. But I didn't know if anything would come of that.

A month after the election I got a phone call from a guy named Sam Brown. I knew of Sam, that he had been a divinity student at Harvard and was active in the "Dump Johnson" campaign during the height of the antiwar movement, that he had worked for the McCarthy campaign during the same 1968 presidential race that I had worked for Kennedy, that he had gone on to become a successful young politician in Colorado, where he had won a statewide election as treasurer, and that he had given up that position to join the Carter administration to direct ACTION.

What I did not know was that earlier that year he had discussed my situation with his assistant director, Mary King—the same Mary King who had been Julian's assistant in the communications department of SNCC. The two of them had decided that if I did not win that congressional seat, they would recommend to the President that he nominate me as associate director of ACTION for domestic operations. That meant running the VISTA (Volunteers in Service to America) operation, often referred to as the domestic Peace Corps, and two national programs for elderly volunteers: RSVP (Retired Senior Volunteer Program) and FGP (Foster Grandparent Program).

Sam seemed very outgoing on the phone, warm and engaging. When he offered me the job, I told him I needed to think about it. But I knew I was going to take it. First, I had no other offers. Beyond that, it was quite an honor to be nominated by the President of the United States for such a high-ranking position in the federal government. I talked it over with Lillian, and she was excited. We had set our eyes on my going to Washington as a member of Congress. This would be another way of getting there—if I were confirmed.

That June, on Father's Day, my father died. He had had a serious stroke the year before, and he never fully recovered. He had recovered to the point where he could get up and walk around, but he couldn't work anymore, and that just about killed him right there. It was very difficult for him to work as hard as he had all his life and then to suddenly be able to do nothing at all.

When my brothers called that Sunday to tell me he had died, I was shaken. For my mother, however, it was devastating. She and my father had totally depended on each other almost their entire lives. Together they had raised ten children, made ends meet with the farm, and faced all that came with being poor and black in rural Alabama through the middle of this century. They were inseparable. With so many couples like that, when one dies, the other often follows shortly thereafter, as much out of grief and surrender as anything else. I wondered what would happen to my mother.

She was distraught, but she had a lot of support—her brothers and her sister, we children, her church and the community, too. My father had become one of the most well known men in Pike County, both through his decades of farming and through his years of driving that school bus. Everyone knew Eddie Lewis, and they all turned out for his funeral, held at little Antioch Baptist Church, near our home. I spoke, and then we buried him down the slope behind the church, near the edge of the woods he had worked in so hard all his life.

A month after that funeral, I was formally nominated for the ACTION position by President Carter. In my testimony before the Senate Human Resources Committee, chaired by Alan Cranston, I was asked to discuss how I planned to approach volunteerism in America. I told the senators I intended to tap into the spirit of the civil rights movement, to direct the agency's programs at a grassroots level, bringing our services to the disadvantaged and disabled as well as to minorities, going out into neighborhoods and communities and building a better society, a Beloved Community, literally block by block.

When I was done, Senator Cranston said, "Mr. Lewis, it's been a long time since we heard the word 'love' used in this hallowed place. We're glad there's someone in this administration who believes in love."

I was confirmed, and that November, Lillian and I and John-Miles put our house up for rent and moved to Washington, first to an apartment on New Hampshire Avenue and then into a house on Logan Circle, in the same predominantly black neighborhood where Daddy Grace, the prophet and religious leader of the 1930s and '40s, and Adam Clayton Powell had lived.

It was not far to the ACTION headquarters, on the tenth floor of a building on Lafayette Square. I had a corner office looking down on the White House two blocks away. The view was a good one—so good, in fact, that when Menachem Begin and Anwar Sadat came to sign the Camp David accords in 1978 on the lawn of the White House, the Secret Service ordered my windows closed and my blinds drawn, then asked me and everyone else working on that side of the building to leave until the ceremony was over.

My position with ACTION was the biggest job I had ever had in terms of budget, personnel and scope of services. My staff included roughly 125 people, divided among ten regional offices around the nation, including our headquarters there in Washington. Those staff people oversaw about 5,000 VISTA volunteers and a total of more than 230,000 elderly volunteers working through RSVP and FGP.

Beyond directing the volunteers we already had, my staff and I were responsible for recruiting additional volunteers, both for the Peace Corps and for our domestic agencies. I discovered that there was a severe shortage of young black Americans—especially young black men—willing to do this kind of work, especially for the Peace Corps. A large number of young black Americans had essentially given up on a society that they felt had given up on them. This was a low, hard time for volunteerism in America in general, but it was especially so in terms of black American volunteers.

I traveled almost a quarter million miles in my two and a half years with ACTION. I visited forty-two states and tried my best to follow through on the vision I had shared during my confirmation hearings. We had our volunteers apply many of the same techniques and tactics that had been used so effectively to mobilize people during the peak years of the movement. Across the nation my staff and I went into the homes and communities of the poorest of the poor, Americans who were living in conditions that were unthinkable, obscene and largely unseen by mainstream society. I saw people who refused to give up, who kept their faith in the face of horrifying circumstances and adversity. We tried to help them through a range of programs similar to those I had directed with the Southern Regional Council.

We helped form cooperatives in rural communities. In urban areas, we worked on rehabilitating worn-out inner city neighborhoods not by simply renovating, raising the rents and pushing out the people who could no longer afford to live there. That process of gentrification is, in my opinion, selfish opportunism. We searched instead for ways to maintain and improve older urban neighborhoods without displacing the people who live in them, people who in most cases are black.

We opened medical clinics in remote regions. We worked to improve nursing homes, homes for retarded children and orphanages. We directed sites and centers where foster grandparents worked with troubled children, many of whom had no parents to speak of in their own homes. We recognized the immense untapped resource of elderly Americans in this nation. Applying their eagerly offered talents and energy was a large focus of my job.

My vision of poverty in this country was incredibly broadened and deepened by this job. I was well aware of the kinds of conditions faced by the poor of the Deep South, both black and white. But I had never before been so exposed to the isolation and impoverishment of Native Americans on reservations in the Southwest, where I would visit not for a day but for a week at a time; or of Hispanic people in the poorest sections of cities like El Paso and San Antonio; or the utter hopelessness of out-of-work coal miners in Appalachia. The alcoholism, the homelessness, the humanity that was excluded, denied, left behind and treated like so much refuse in these places was heartbreaking to see.

Particularly devastating was a trip I took to West Virginia in the fall of 1979. That was the first time I'd ever been down into a coal mine, met miners in their homes, spent time with families that couldn't afford the coal they were digging, seen children so filthy and unclothed and fathers with black lung disease. And with all that, I also saw the pride and hope that these people held on to, even in such hopeless circumstances. Their tenacity and their indomitable spirit both shamed and inspired me.

I was so shaken by what I saw on that trip that I called a staff meeting as soon as I returned, to brief everyone on what I'd just seen. I was very emotional at that meeting. Some of the staffers weren't used to that. No one gave "briefings" like this.

I followed it up with a long letter to President Carter, telling him he needed to take a trip like this himself, to see what I had just seen. Don't just do the ordinary, presidential things, I said. Be daring. Don't go to just the politically safe, politically advantageous places. Go to the difficult places. Make it *real*. When, I wanted to know, was the last time that an American president—not a candidate, but a president—visited a Sioux reservation, or the ghettos of South Side Chicago, or a coal-mining village in eastern Kentucky?

I got no response from that letter. By then, I was feeling very frustrated and disheartened. The President had made campaign promises specifically to the poor, and he was not following through on them. The people I encountered all across the country during my two years on that job felt the same way. They felt ignored by the federal government, forsaken. I knew that feeling so well. We had felt it acutely in the South during the civil rights movement.

Beyond that, I was seeing too much bureaucratic and political infighting all around me. An example was the case of Carol Payton, who was director of the Peace Corps during the time I was with ACTION. Sam Brown wanted the Peace Corps to break out of its traditional mold, to move beyond what he called "make work"—such as building a school or a bridge. He wanted the organization to break away from local political control and get more involved in teaching skills to the people themselves, "empowering" them, in the phrase of today. Payton resisted. She preferred to continue running the agency as it was. Their dispute wound up going public, with Payton, who is black, claiming that Brown, who is white, was essentially racist.

I didn't see it that way at all. Sam Brown was one of the last people in the world who could be called a racist. This was an issue of philosophical differences. Payton tried to turn it into a racial issue, and when I didn't stand up and defend her, I was attacked for not being a "team player," for not being "black" enough. This wasn't the first time I had faced that kind of criticism, and it would not be the last.

The last straw came during congressional hearings in late 1979 on renewing several ACTION programs. During one fourteen-hour session we were accused by several conservative congressmen on the Appropriations Committee—most notably Bob Michel, a Republican from Illinois—of funding "subversive groups." As an example, they pointed to our support of an organization in Chicago connected with Saul Alinsky, the longtime activist.

I had been through this kind of "red-baiting" before. Michel and his conservative colleagues knew all about Sam's activities against the war in Vietnam, and they knew all about my chairmanship of SNCC. These men had long memories, and they were not comfortable with us. They considered us in the pocket of the liberal left. Their opposition was about ideology, period, and it was affecting hundreds of thousands of people who depended on our agency to give them the only help they had ever had.

After that Congressional hearing, I said it was time for me to go. I had listened to too much talk, waded through too much paperwork, battled over too many budgets and seen too few tangible responses to real, human, heart-breaking problems—problems the government was fully capable of dealing with directly if it could only move beyond political haggling and turn to the task of serving the people. Not just the people with power, or the people with influence, or the people with money, but *all* the people.

Washington, unfortunately, is a city filled with ambition, with individuals whose first instinct when faced with a decision is to look over their shoulders and calculate how this might help or hurt *them*, who are unwilling to take a chance, to take a risk, to think of anyone or anything else besides themselves and their own careers.

I was not naive. I knew how Washington works. I understood what could be done, and I tried to do it. I was convinced now more than ever that I had to find a way to get elected to a position where I would have more control over the things I thought ought to be done, where I wouldn't have to go up to Capitol Hill and answer to some committee chair who was simply using this agency or that to score political points. I wanted to get on the other side of that table. I wanted to be one of those people doing the listening and the deciding.

But I had to leave where I was if I was going to get there. And I had to leave soon. The 1980 presidential election was coming up. I knew Kennedy was going to run. So was Carter. And I did not want to get caught in the middle of that.

I knew what I needed to do, and I needed to do it now.

I needed to come back to Georgia.

In November of 1979—a month before I submitted my resignation from ACTION—I was at a staff retreat in the mountains west of Denver when I received a call from the White House.

Louis Martin was on the line. Martin was a man who had been deeply involved in national Democratic politics since the Kennedy/Johnson years. He was now a special assistant to the President, Carter's chief black advisor, and he was calling to tell me the President was concerned about a rumor he'd been hearing—not that I was leaving Washington, but that I was doing so to join the Kennedy campaign for 1980. A *Newsweek* story out that week referred to "another administration official who is about to jump ship to support Ted Kennedy." The word going around Washington was that I was that official.

I had no intention of working for Kennedy's campaign—or for Carter's. It bothered me, though, that it was not the fate of the ACTION agency nor of my services there that seemed to concern the President. It was simply his fear that I might get in the way of his bid for reelection.

As soon as I returned to D.C., I was invited to the White House. President Carter and I sat together on a sofa in the Oval Office. I had a terrible cold that I'd picked up in the Colorado mountains. I really didn't feel like meeting with anyone.

Our conversation was friendly, very civil, very polite. Carter did not mention the upcoming campaign, but I knew that was the only reason I was there. So I broached the subject.

"I am resigning, Mr. President," I said. "But I will not be campaigning for Senator Kennedy. I simply want to return to Atlanta."

I left him with my letter of resignation, and that was that. Or so I thought. In the years since then, I have repeatedly been surprised—and dismayed—to hear Jimmy Carter refer to my lack of loyalty, saying that he has "never been able to get anything out of John Lewis," and pointing as proof to my support of Kennedy in that 1980 campaign. Apparently, the President did not hear what I said in that meeting, or he didn't believe it.

As a matter of fact, Ted Kennedy's people did call me *after* I resigned, and I told them the same thing I told Carter—that I was moving back to Atlanta and would not be involved in either candidate's campaign for the Democratic nomination.

Julian called me several times during this period as well, trying to convince me to support Kennedy, whom he was strongly behind. Julian and I had not seen a great deal of each other since I'd left for Washington. I had become a member of the Carter administration, and Julian was not fond of Jimmy Carter. He had no love, absolutely *none,* for the man. Back in 1972, Carter had had some designs on seeking the Democratic vice presidential nomination as George McGovern's running mate. Julian was close to the McGovern forces, and apparently he spoke out strongly against Carter during those deliberations. He felt that Carter was too conservative as governor, that for all the praise Carter was receiving for improving race relations in Georgia, he was not doing enough. I think the real problem between the two was simply a personality clash. Julian just never liked the guy.

So now he was pressing me hard to come work for Kennedy. I told him no. I'd said no to everyone else and I was saying the same thing to him. The fact was that I really had no strong feelings about either Carter or Kennedy. I was certainly never as enthused about Ted Kennedy as I had been about Bobby. I never really worked with him. I didn't know him the way I knew Bobby. As for Carter, I was extremely dismayed that he had let me down during my time with ACTION, and by letting me down, he had let down many, many good, decent Americans who needed his help and had believed him when he said during his '76 campaign that he was going to give it.

What I *did* care about was the Democratic Party. I did not want to see a bloodbath at that year's convention. I thought Carter would probably be renominated, and he was. At that point, when the contest became Jimmy Carter against Ronald Reagan, I certainly did campaign for Carter. I campaigned hard, and I would have done the same for Kennedy if he had been the Democratic nominee.

I finally returned to Atlanta early that summer, and I considered running for the Fifth District seat again. There was talk that Wyche Fowler might leave to run for the Senate against Herman Talmadge, who had been troubled by the discovery of a large amount of cash stuffed in one of his overcoats. I met with Wyche, and when he told me he was not going to run against Talmadge, that he had decided instead to run for reelection to the House, I set my sights on the local level. In 1981, Atlanta's political landscape would be opening up, with Maynard Jackson vacating the mayor's office—he had already succeeded himself once and so was ineligible to run again—and with the city council elections taking place.

I never considered running for mayor. People still ask me to come back and run for that position, but it's not a role I could see myself playing. I just don't have the feel for being the chief executive officer of a city. I prefer being a legislator, making laws, influencing policy. City council was what I had my eyes on. Meanwhile, I needed a job.

I worked for a couple of months that summer closing out grants for the Field Foundation, which was preparing to go out of business. This was kind of a mop-up operation, and I went around the country taking care of some of that. Then, at the end of that year, I took a job as director of community affairs for the National Consumer Cooperative Bank (NCCB) in Atlanta.

The bank was based in Washington, with regional offices all around the country. It was a lending institution that made resources available not to individuals but to nonprofit organizations and cooperatives, with the purpose of stimulating economic development in low-income, underdeveloped communities. We primarily made loans, but we also offered technical assistance to local, regional and national cooperatives—housing cooperatives, farming cooperatives, all kinds of cooperatives. I spent a great amount of time in D.C., reviewing and analyzing applications for loans and getting background information on organizations and groups seeking our assistance.

I wasn't with the NCCB long—they understood when I took the job that I'd be seeking a city council spot in 1981. But I was there long enough to be drawn into yet another situation in which I was attacked for my color-blindness, for betraying my race.

The bank had foreclosed on a neighborhood co-op grocery store in Atlanta. The store was located in the heart of the city, in a solid black neighborhood. There had been questions about the co-op's operation, and when the bank investigated, it didn't like what it saw and decided to withdraw financing. I wasn't involved in the decision, but I supported it. After I looked over the information we had, it was clear to me that the co-op was not being run for the benefit of the people in that community so much as it was a private domain for the interests of one of the people involved in it.

This person's response to the bank's decision was to say that it was "racist," which was ridiculous considering the fact that almost all the bank's activities involved assistance to black communities. This person was doing what too many people in this kind of situation do when they have nothing left to fall back on—playing the race card. I'd seen it before, and I've seen it since. What Johnnie Cochran did to defend O. J. Simpson was nothing new. It happens, unfortunately, all the time.

I judged the grocery case on its facts and merit, not through the lens of race. I've always believed that the only way we will ever move beyond the barriers of race is to stop seeing everything through that filter. We have to be fair, consistent and accountable to standards higher and more universal than what particular race, age, gender, community, culture or country each of us belongs to. There are standards of honesty, decency and humanity that arch above all the differences that keep us apart. To appeal to those differences only *continues* to polarize us.

I was, of course, roundly criticized in some sections of the community for standing with the bank, for taking sides against a "brother." Never mind that this was, and should have been, a case of right and wrong. To some people— on both sides of the fence unfortunately—any issue or conflict in which race can be invoked quickly becomes a case of black and white.

Late that spring the campaigns for Atlanta's city council began. There were a total of eighteen seats—twelve filled by members elected by each of their local districts, and six members elected at large.

Bill Campbell, a young attorney and a good friend of mine—he's now mayor of Atlanta—asked me to chair his campaign for one of those twelve district seats. I told him I'd be glad to, and began making the rounds of fundraising dinners and events. Everywhere I went, people came up and said, "*You* should run. Why aren't *you* running?"

I planned to. Bill knew that. I hadn't yet pulled together my organization enough to announce. In the meantime, I was glad to help Bill, and that gave me a chance to get a sense of the situation, the lay of the land. The at-large seat I'd be aiming at was held by a man named Jack Summers, who had been on the council for nearly a quarter century. Daddy King told me Summers would be tough to beat. "This man goes to all our funerals," he said. "He comes to all the weddings, supports the church, his brother is a supplier for all the barbershops and beauticians." Summers was, in other words, connected.

But there were problems in the two districts he represented. The schools in those districts had, of course, been desegregated, but 90 percent of the students in them were black. Most of the white students, along with their families, had fled to the suburbs. All the consequent problems created by white flight—abandoned housing and businesses, a depleted economy, a shrinking tax base, increased street crime—were plaguing this part of Atlanta. Despite the city's progressiveness in many areas—Atlanta was far ahead of most of the nation in terms of its commitment to economic empowerment of the black community, notably by including minority hiring provisions in city construction contracts—it was still segregated, with 80 percent of the black residents living in the area below North Avenue and most whites living above it, or beyond in the subdivisions outside the city limits.

When I announced my candidacy that July, it was with a platform based on the nurturing of an ethical, fair and just biracial community. I promised to raise my voice, as I always had, for the voiceless, the dispossessed, those outside the walls of power. I campaigned all over Atlanta—although each at-large seat represented only two districts, everyone in the city voted for each position. From Buckhead—an upscale financial, retail and entertainment section of the city, very wealthy, very white—to Vine City—a southside area of low-income housing projects, as well as established middle-class neighborhoods, all very, very black. From dawn to dusk I went door-to-door, not taking anything or anyone for granted. Early evenings I would attend dinners or meetings, give a speech, meet the people. Then, late at night—ten, eleven, midnight and beyond—I'd plant myself like a lamppost in front of an all-night grocery store, or a discotheque, catching the crowds as they came and went, passing out leaflets, letting them know who I was. I didn't count on radio or television. I counted on my feet. I wanted to meet people in the flesh and give them a chance to meet me.

An odd thing about that campaign was that there were *two* John Lewises on the ballot. The other John Lewis was an older man, a longtime cabdriver and horse-and-buggy operator downtown. He was running in a different district, but the name still caused some confusion. This John Lewis did not win his race, but he wound up taking enough votes away from the incumbent, a Republican named Q. V. Williamson, that a woman named Myrtle Davis won that seat in a big upset. There were complaints that the "John Lewis" factor cost Williamson that race. Meanwhile, the other John Lewis claimed during his campaign that *I* was getting votes because of *him,* that he'd been around Atlanta a lot longer than I and was better known to the people.

In any event, I won, as did Bill Campbell and Myrtle Davis, giving the city the first black-majority city council in its history. In that election Andy Young returned from New York and won Maynard Jackson's vacated mayor's seat— the first time in American history, in a city of any size, that one black mayor succeeded another. Andy and I were still good, warm friends. But that would soon change.

We were all sworn in that January of 1982, at an inauguration that seemed like a celebration of the civil rights movement—a black mayor, a black city council, elected by a Southern city that was looking to the future rather than the past. There were a lot of old SCLC people there, though not many from SNCC—hardly any at all, in fact. Besides me, Julian was there, and Stanley Wise, who was now an insurance executive in Atlanta. That was about it.

The black-tie affair that night was a truly gala event. But the honeymoon didn't last long. During my campaign I didn't talk specifically about cleaning up the city council, but I did talk about ethics in government. And I was thinking about Atlanta. Over the years I had seen too many local elected officials represent too many questionable interests, including their own. There had long been people on the city council who received benefits ranging from consulting work to development contracts from businesses that had benefited from the votes these individuals had cast. When it came to issues of zoning, for example, a developer or his attorneys would come before the zoning committee or before the council as a whole and get someone to carry water for him, to deliver the goods. In return, that council member would receive something nice, maybe a campaign contribution or maybe something more direct than that, like a generous consultant's fee.

This was certainly nothing new or rare. I could be talking about any city in America. Politicians typically form parternships on their way to office. They make friends. They make deals. Some people might say it's the American way. Call me naive, but I've never agreed with that. When I ran for that city council seat, I was not beholden to anyone. I think that's what a lot of voters liked about me—they respected my sense of independence. When I arrived on the council, I was in nobody's pocket. And I think that made some of the council members, especially those who were more entrenched, uncomfortable.

My outspokenness certainly did not endear me to Marvin Arrington. Arrington had been on the council since 1969 and had worked his way up to its presidency. He was a very savvy, very street-smart lawyer, one of those back-slapping guys who always has his eye out for a deal. Over the table, under the table, around the table—anywhere he could make it, Arrington enjoyed nothing more than to work out a deal. He was great at deals. That's what made him such an effective and powerful politician. But it also raised questions about whom he was dealing with behind the scenes.

This was one of the first issues I addressed upon becoming a member of the council—conflicts of interest. Several council members, including Arrington, acknowledged that they were involved in businesses that sometimes benefited from council decisions. They took the position that they had "a right to earn a living," as Arrington put it, and that they kept their business and political interests separated. But that line between the two was vague, as were the regulations concerning this issue. On the several occasions that the city's ethics board had reviewed Arrington's practices, it had ruled that they were within the law, but I felt that the law was too loose. I pushed for legislation requiring public disclosure of sources of income of city council members. I also wanted to give the board more power in its investigations.

Predictably, my proposals brought cries of protest. One council member anonymously told a reporter that the standards I was suggesting would turn the council into "a bunch of secretaries, unemployed people and third-level people that don't have any business acumen, and it's going to affect the way your city is run."

Council members complained over and over again that I was not a "team player." I answered that "team player" was code for "He can't be bought."

"John's approach," warned a council member, again speaking anonymously, "is not going to help him in anything else he wants to do."

That was certainly true. In my first year on the council there arose probably the largest, most painful struggle of my five-year career there. The press dubbed it the "Battle of Great Park."

During the campaign of 1981 a plan had been announced to build a Jimmy Carter library and research center in Atlanta's downtown Great Park. Included in the plan was a four-lane highway to bring visitors and out-of-town tourists to the center. Almost every person running for office that fall, including Andy Young, came out in opposition to this road for basically the same reasons I was against it—namely, that it would further congest our already overly congested downtown traffic; that it would provide an expressway for white flight; that in a city which already fell short of environmental standards for clean air, it would cause further pollution; and that it would divide and do damage to several old, established downtown neighborhoods and historic homes, black and white. Any short-term benefits of building this parkway— chiefly the jobs it would provide—would be far outweighed, I felt, by the long-term damage that would be done.

Almost all my fellow candidates agreed, but once they took office, several of them switched positions, including the mayor. The jobs offered by this highway construction were extremely enticing, especially at a time when the city's budget was being squeezed by massive federal and state cuts in funding. Andy Young began pushing hard for this road, and I became one of the few council members who stood their ground and resisted.

I began hearing from some of Andy's staff people. One of his assistants came to me and suggested that my campaign debt (which was about $10,000 or $15,000, not much) would be "taken care of" if I supported the mayor. Friends and people I respected delivered messages from Andy's camp. "This is going to hurt you if the mayor loses," they said. Joe Lowery, now president of the SCLC and one of Andy's biggest supporters, told me I should back off on this one.

Pressure began rising from some sectors of the black community as well, and that old bugaboo of racial loyalty was once again raised. A group of black ministers issued leaflets proclaiming that a vote against the park plan was "a vote against the mayor and against the black community." Trucks with mounted loudspeakers actually rolled through some of the city's black neighborhoods, blaring the message that some council members were betraying our black mayor and our black community.

I had never faced anything as intense as the anger that came my way over this road. It was in no way a racial issue, but that's what it became for many people. Once again I was accused of not being black enough. A friend pointed out to me that I had spent my entire life fighting blurred vision and self-interest in the white community. Now I was facing the same problems among the *black* community.

The Saturday morning before the vote on this issue, which was scheduled for Monday, a fellow councilman named Ira Jackson asked me to join him for breakfast at a little place called the Canopy Castle, just up the street from Paschal's. When I got there I was greeted not just by Ira, but also by Andy and several of his staff people, along with some other members of the city council. Andy knew where I stood on this thing. We'd talked privately several times. Now, over eggs and grits, he asked me publicly to abstain from the vote.

"If you can't vote for this," he said, "will you consider not voting at all?"

He should have known better. Anyone who knows me knows how I am about following through once I've taken a position.

"There's no way I can do that," I said. "No way. If I'm there, I'm going to vote."

And, of course, I planned to be there.

The next night, Sunday evening, the phone rang and John-Miles answered it. He was six years old now.

"Daddy, Daddy!" he called, running into the room. "A man's on the telephone and he says he's President Carter. But I don't believe it."

John-Miles was laughing. So was I. And so was Jimmy Carter when I got to the phone.

We exchanged pleasantries. Then he quickly came around to the reason he was calling.

"John," he said, "it's about that vote that's coming up."

I was listening.

"I don't believe that you love me anymore," he said, half joking, half serious.

"I need your help here," he said. "I gave you a job, and you came up to Washington and took it. And then you left and went and worked for Ted Kennedy."

I couldn't believe it. He was still stuck on that old *Newsweek* story about me jumping ship to go with Kennedy.

"Mr. President," I said, "nothing could be further from the truth. I didn't support Kennedy. As a matter of fact, after the convention, I campaigned for *you.*"

I don't think he was listening. He hadn't called to talk about the past.

"I need your help," he said again. "I really need you to vote for this road."

"I'm sorry, Mr. President," I said, "but I don't think the road is needed. I made a commitment during the campaign, and I have to stay with that commitment."

And that was that. My conscience was clear. I felt I was on the side of the angels. I was doing what I thought was fair and right. It might hurt me politically. It might destroy me. But it was the right thing to do. There is no more solid ground a man can stand on than that.

I know I pissed Andy off the next day when I pointed out during my speech prior to the vote that he had been against this road during his mayoral campaign. "He changed his mind," I said. "He has a right to change his mind. But I made a commitment to the citizens of this city. I'm not going to change mine."

My vote, along with Bill Campbell's and Myrtle Davis's, turned out to be the only black votes against the project. It was passed, but in a compromised form—the parkway would now be two lanes, not four. Later, after it was built and the center was finally opened in 1986, it came out that among the many contractors and subcontractors brought in to construct that road had been a trucking firm hired to haul away some of the dirt and refuse from the sites— a trucking firm owned by Marvin Arrington.

No question it hurt me politically to stand against the mayor on that issue. During the time I was on the city council, I was kept off any of the important committees. The people in control also made sure that I did not become a chairman of any committee I served on during my five years on the council. That's unheard of. Every council member becomes a chair of *something*. But not I. After I was reelected in 1985, I saw first-term members named chairs of committees all around me, while I still chaired nothing. It was almost funny.

By the time of that reelection, some people were saying that I didn't belong on the city council, that I thought too large, too big, too universally for a job like this, that I wasn't cut out to be dealing with water systems and sewers and roads, that I was a "visionary" and visionaries don't make good local officials. Maybe they were right. I do know that the people of Atlanta appreciated my independence, the fact that I did not follow lines of political alliance or convenience or race, that I acted according to the facts and circumstances of each individual situation. Other politicians might not have liked that, but most voters did. And that's whom I was there for. When I was reelected in the fall of 1985, it was with 85 percent of the vote, a pretty strong mandate for my approach to the job.

Soon after that election, plans began to take shape for my second run at Congress. Throughout that fall I had been in constant contact with Congressman Fowler, who was considering a run for the Senate in '86. He told me I'd be the first to know if he decided to do it because he wanted me to succeed him in the House. Early that October, Wyche and I had lunch, and he told me he was going to do it, he was going to go after the Senate seat held by Republican Mack Mattingly.

Word was already out and around by then that Wyche was going to step down. Speculation was already rampant as to who might run to replace him. None of the names I heard surprised me. But one troubled me a great deal. I had hoped this day would never come, that our paths would not have to cross this way, but now it looked inevitable:

Julian was going to go for this seat as well.

Things were different now than they had been in 1976, when I had consulted Julian before deciding to run. Ten years had passed. I had changed. I had grown. I had run for office and tasted defeat. I was stronger, more seasoned. I'd been in the arena, both in Washington, where I'd seen the workings of Congress and the federal government, and in Atlanta, where I'd learned about politics on the local level. I had worked my way up; I'd paid my dues.

And Julian? He was different now, too. Our relationship was different. During the time I was in Washington, something of a gap grew between us. Part of that was the geographic separation—out of sight, out of mind. But we had grown apart in other ways as well. We had always been different in our lifestyles and personalities, but that had never affected our friendship. In fact, our differences were part of what we appreciated in each other, part of what attracted each of us to the other. Now that we were in the same line of work, however—politics—the differences in how we saw the role of government, and, more importantly, in how we saw our own roles as elected officials—how we approached our *jobs*—could not be ignored.

Julian enjoyed being a star. He approached his work as if it were an inconvenience. Everything had always come easily for Julian; sweating was not something he liked to do.

And yet now he wanted to be a congressman. And everyone assumed he would be a shoo-in. And *that* bothered me a great deal. I had long resented the accepted tradition in the city of Atlanta of a select few leaders, black and white, handpicking and determining who went to Washington. I didn't like the idea of someone being anointed. That goes back to the SNCC ethos, I guess—the belief that the masses should truly decide their fate and be able to choose their representatives rather than be controlled by a chosen few. The assumption that this job was Julian's if he simply wanted it just rubbed me the wrong way.

This attitude—that some individuals, because of pedigree or connections or wealth or class, are somehow *meant* to be leaders, while others are meant to follow—has, of course, always pervaded much of politics in America, at all levels. Jesse Jackson embraced this attitude, with his slogan "Some people are meant to plant the tree and others to shake the tree." I couldn't disagree more. I feel that people who plant the trees are fully capable of shaking them—maybe more so than those who haven't gotten their hands dirty.

This idea that some people are born for one thing and some for another violates one of the cornerstones of the American ethos: that we all are on equal footing in this society, and that we make our way depending not upon status or wealth or image or influence, but upon effort and merit and imagination and achievement—and sometimes even compassion. I know this sounds idealistic, maybe foolish, and I know we are far from actually living in such a society, but it is something we must always aim at and move toward as best we can.

I had worked hard to get to the place I had come to that autumn of 1985. I thought I deserved at least to be considered seriously. But all I heard was how unbeatable Julian Bond would be if he decided to run, simply because he *was* Julian Bond. Talk like that made me even more determined to fight this fight, if that's what it came to.

Late that October, Julian called and invited me to lunch. We met at the Marriott—now it's a Radisson—in downtown Atlanta, on Courtland Street. He brought his son, Michael Julian, who was a teenager now, a young man. The three of us sat down. We ordered our food, then got right to the point.

"Senator," I said, "what are you going to do?"

"I'm going to run for Congress, Mr. Chairman," he said. "What," he then asked, "are *you* going to do?"

"I'm running, too," I said.

Julian has always had a habit of shaking his leg when he's nervous, just a slight little twist back and forth. His leg was shaking now.

"Well," he said, rubbing his hand across his mouth, "I'll see you on the campaign trail."

At that moment we knew we were not on the same team anymore. Our friendship, as it had been, was over.

I made my formal announcement the first week in February. A lot of people outright laughed. They couldn't believe I was dreaming of making a run against Bond. The newspapers were filled with quotes from unnamed observers of Atlanta's political scene.

"He hardly knew what to do on the City Council," said one. "Now he's talking about Congress!"

"John's too nice," said another. "He's not ready for D.C. He's got too much goodness in his heart. They might blow him over. But Julian can handle it."

The media was drooling. Here was a story made in heaven—two black brothers-in-arms from the civil rights movement, both exactly the same age, mirror opposites of each other, squaring off in the heart of the Deep South. Magazine and newspaper editors across the nation sent their star writers to let loose their imagery on this one. And the images abounded.

First there was Julian:

"Tall, slim, handsome"... "light-skinned, dashing, erudite, articulate"... "nonchalant, glib, charming"... "a silver-tongued orator"... "a blue blood, son of a college president"... "guest host of *Saturday Night Live*"... "dresses and speaks like a banker"... "SNCC's scholar in residence"... "the cool poet and wordsmith, the philosopher"... "once declared by *Cosmopolitan* magazine one of America's 'Ten Sexiest Men'"... "a state senator with a national profile"... "still preppified at 46"... "he has money, identity and the buppies"... "the walking embodiment of the phrase 'young, gifted and black.'"

And then there was me:

"Short, squat, thick-necked"... "balding, dark, scowling"... "a sharecropper's son"... "dogged, determined, pugnacious"... "wooden"... "humorless"... "built like a bulldog"... "looks like a club fighter who would be tough on the ropes"... "an anachronism—a man of almost painful sincerity"... "a paragon of Calvinist rectitude"... "as real as a pine knot"... "a lousy speaker."

Cain and Abel.
David and Goliath.
The Prince and the Pauper.

This wasn't just a local or a state story. This was national news, and it wasn't just about politics. The *Washington Post* called it "a race featuring money, good looks, smooth talk, old ghosts, guilt trips and civil rights revisionists in the dawn of the black yuppie... a litmus test of conscience in the black community."

And I didn't stand a chance, not according to the experts, not according to anyone. My own staff was doubtful. During the early planning meetings we held at my house, my campaign chairman, a determined, energetic friend of mine named C. T. Martin, said over and over, "If you want to do this, we can do it," in a tone that sounded as if I was considering leaping off a cliff. Other staffers were more straightforward. "Maybe you shouldn't do this," they said. "Maybe you should wait."

Phone calls began flooding in, both from friends and from strangers, telling me to quit, that this was political suicide. The oddest of those calls came late one evening from, Stokely Carmichael—or Kwame Ture, as he was now called.

At first, I didn't believe it was he on the line. I hadn't spoken to Stokely since 1966. I had no idea where he was calling from—New York, Washington, someplace in the United States, that's all I knew.

"John," he said, "one of you should drop out. You're just dividing the Atlanta community."

Where did *that* come from? What did Stokely Carmichael possibly care about the Atlanta community? The only explanation, it seemed to me, was that someone in Julian's camp had put Stokely up to this, but who? Whoever did must have been crazy. Stokely Carmichael would be the last person on this planet who could have influenced my decision, the last person I'd respond to, the last person I'd respect. His phone call that night made me more determined than ever to see this thing through.

But I had to admit that on every front, from fund-raising to endorsements, things looked bleak. People were flocking behind Julian right and left, many because they believed in him, and just as many, I'm sure, because they wanted to back a winner. If Julian Bond was going to Congress, they wanted to be on that train.

Support for Julian cascaded in from across the country. Los Angeles mayor Tom Bradley went for him. New York's Ed Koch gave him his endorsement. So did Marion Barry, who was now the mayor of Washington, D.C. Ted Kennedy endorsed Julian, which did not please some members of the Kennedy family, especially on Bobby's side. But I was not surprised. To his credit, loyalty counts for a lot with Ted Kennedy. Julian had supported him against Carter in 1980 while I stood aside. He hadn't forgotten that, and I understood. I was not happy when someone on my staff, upon hearing of Kennedy's endorsement of Julian, fired off an angry telegram to Kennedy's office. My staff—who knew the meaning of the word "loyalty," too—were much more upset than I was.

Locally, the only endorsement I received from a major civil rights figure was from Ralph Abernathy. I met with Andy Young early on and told him if I did not have his support, I hoped he might remain neutral. His answer was sphinxlike.

"The seed of the righteous," he said, "shall not founder."

This was the same biblical phrase my mother had repeated throughout my childhood, the same phrase that echoed for me during the lessons of "redemptive suffering" that Jim Lawson had taught. I understood the meaning of the phrase, that the good, the worthy, would persevere, that they would eventually triumph. But whom did Andy consider the worthy one here—Julian, who had never squared off against him the way I had when I was on the city council, or me? And if it was I, was he telling me he believed I would win this struggle right now, or was he assuring me that I'd be okay in the long run, somewhere down the line, after this was all over?

To this day I'm not sure what Andy meant by that answer. He never openly endorsed Bond, but I knew that every one of his staff people was in Julian's camp.

Coretta King took no side either—not openly. But just before the primary, when Ed Koch came down in an attempt to rally the Jewish support that Julian was losing, Coretta joined them for a tour of the King Center. A photo of the three of them that ran in the next day's newspapers showed Coretta beaming at Julian with the kind of adoration a mother gives to her newborn baby. Mrs. King didn't endorse either of us publicly, but who knows what was going on behind the scenes?

Marvin Arrington, of course, threw his considerable local influence in the black community completely behind Bond. One afternoon Arrington hosted a big fund-raiser for Julian at his home on the same day and at the same hour as a nearby neighbor held a reception for me. This was in the heart of a middle-class black neighborhood called Cascade Heights. It was an amazing scene: people parking in front of one house and walking to the other, neighbors and friends giving each other the evil eye as they strolled up the front sidewalks toward each door.

Julian had the big names in his camp, no question. And his coffers overflowed with contributions from across the country, much of it raised by celebrities and entertainers who staged benefit performances on Julian's behalf. Miles Davis, the Temptations, Bill Cosby, Cicely Tyson, Hugh Hefner—Julian's list of contributors looked like an issue of *People* magazine.

Pulling most of that money together for Julian was Morris Dees, the Alabama attorney and activist who co-founded the Southern Poverty Law Center in 1971. The center, located in Montgomery, was created to combat race crimes through legal means. It has continued its work over the past quarter century, broadening its targets to include hate groups and militia organizations and offering educational programs intended to teach tolerance to schoolchildren.

I was on the center's first advisory council in the early '70s, and Julian was its first president. Dees went on to establish himself over the years as one of the national Democratic Party's most capable fund-raisers. He spearheaded McGovern's fund-raising in 1972, Carter's in 1976, Kennedy's in 1980... and now he was running the national campaign for Julian Bond.

And the spigots were flowing. Julian was bringing in three and four times as much money each week as I. His campaign headquarters was a palatial auto dealership, which he spent nearly $40,000 in campaign funds to renovate. Mine was an old shabby storefront which we rented for $400 a month and furnished with borrowed tables and lamps and used chairs and desks bought from a secondhand store. We planned to rent a TV for election day. Until then, we went without one.

A lot of my friends were concerned about how I was going to make it financially. Lillian and I had our house, and that was about it in terms of assets. She made less than $30,000 a year at the library. My city council salary, which I had given up, was only $18,000. We weren't starving poor, but we weren't shaking money out of any trees either. I had no fallback job or appointment lined up in case I lost. No parachutes. In terms of our financial security, Lillian and I were really rolling the dice on this one.

But I honestly wasn't worried. Throughout my years in the movement and throughout this new political career of mine, people had always underestimated me. With my background—the poor farm boy from the woods— and my personality—so unassuming and steady—people tended to assume I was soft, pliable, that I could be bent to meet their needs. They were always amazed, those who didn't know me, to see me dig in and stand my ground. Independence and perseverance—people had shortchanged me on those qualities all my life, often, in the end, to their dismay.

I was counting on the same thing happening here.

My strategy was essentially the same one I had used in 1977—a biracial appeal aimed at all segments of the community. But the setting and circumstances were dramatically different now than they had been then. Julian's presence, of course, was the major factor. But beyond that was the makeup of the district. The voters, who had been predominantly white in '77, were now predominantly black—a realignment in 1982 had changed the boundaries of the Fifth District, creating a two-to-one black majority population. One of the architects of that realignment had been state senator Julian Bond.

My first priority was simply to prevent Julian from winning straight out in the primary. If I could keep him from getting 50 percent of the vote in that election, a runoff would then be required. And I knew that if it was just Julian against me, in a field undiluted by other candidates, I would win.

So I decided to save some of my punches, to keep my sleeves rolled down in the first round and hold back my best shots in terms of Julian—as well as the bulk of my funds—until that second-round showdown. It was a gamble, saving myself like that, but my resources were too limited to go all-out all the way. Like a boxer, my plan was to set up my opponent early, maybe lull him a little, allow him to become complacent, then come on strong at the end.

First, of course, I had to beat the others, and that would be no small task. An impressive field of candidates had entered this race—twelve in all. They included a community activist named Jan Douglas; an attorney named Charles Johnson, whose grandfather was once president of Fisk University; former state representative Alveda King Beal, who was a niece of Dr. King's; and another former state representative and college professor at Atlanta University named Mildred Glover.

All of us were chasing Julian. But I focused neither on him nor on them. Instead, I focused on myself, on telling my story, letting people know where I'd been and what I stood for, reaching out to as many of them as I possibly could. There were still a good number of Atlantans who did not know who I was. And there were many more who had no idea of my politics, my philosophy, my beliefs.

I went after every constituency. Unlike in the past, a candidate could no longer get elected in this district without strong support from every segment of the community—blue collar, white collar, gay, Jewish, female, labor, environmentalist—I sought the support of them all. Jesse Hill, a black business leader. Herb Mabry, a labor leader. Members of the Buckhead Business Coalition. And a group of black doctors and ministers.

The Jewish vote was particularly interesting. The Jewish community in Atlanta is relatively small in number, but they are a significant factor in elections because they tend to turn out in higher numbers than most other segments of the community. When I began courting their votes, there were grumblings of disapproval from some sections of the community, both black and white, which did not surprise me. I'd seen that kind of response all my life.

I've always felt an affinity with the Jewish community, ever since I was a boy growing up near Troy. As long as I could remember, I heard many white people in the South pronounce the word "Jew" in the same way they used the term "nigger." They would spit the word out, like a bad piece of food. There was a small department store in downtown Troy operated by a Jewish merchant. I remember how it stung me when I heard people say things about him—the same kinds of things they said about us. I grew up singing songs in church such as "Go Down, Moses." I grew up studying Bible stories about the Jewish people. I identified with those stories. I felt a kinship with the children of Israel. I could see that their struggle was very similar to ours.

I never lost that feeling. During the movement there was a strong alliance between the black and Jewish communities. In Nashville, Birmingham, Montgomery—in almost every large city we went into—we found some of our strongest white support among the Jewish people who lived there. I was always aware of that, and I never forgot it.

The gay community, women—my connection with them and their issues sprang from that same affinity I felt with Jewish people, the understanding of what it means to be treated unequally, to be treated as less than, simply because you are different from the long-entrenched white Anglo-Saxon Protestant standard that defined and controlled our society for its first two hundred years.

We have come a long way in recent decades in terms of our treatment of blacks and women and gays in America—and Hispanics, and Native Americans, and the poor. But we still have a good way to go. And we must not tolerate the kind of backlash that has gathered in recent years against each of these movements—the attempts to repeal affirmative action, the hardheartedness of wholesale welfare reform, the rising complaints of that newly emerging "oppressed" class of Americans, white males. Those complaints might well be, to a certain extent, justified. But there is a difference between fixing something and throwing it out. We must never lose sight of the distance we have traveled in recent decades in pursuit of a just, fair and inclusive Beloved Community, and we must not let the kinks in the programs we have created along the way blind us to the worthiness of what those programs aim to achieve.

That was the message I took all over the city of Atlanta that summer of 1986. From the morning in June that I walked downtown to pay my qualifying fee and officially enter the race—*walked* eight miles from the northernmost point of the district to the capitol, with two dozen supporters and a red-white-and-blue "John Lewis for Congress" hot air balloon floating above us—until the primary election day that August, I worked harder than I ever had in my life. No speaking invitation was too insignificant to accept. Civic groups, firefighter units, family reunions, church picnics—sometimes I'd appear at as many as five or six of these gatherings in a single hour.

Again I began each day at 5 A.M., as I had when I ran for the city council. Again I planted myself at bus stops and factory gates and grocery store doorways, handing out leaflets and brochures describing my stand on specific issues: more resources and federal involvement in education; support for universal and single-payer health care; more resources for a rapid transit system; creating jobs, of course; and protecting the environment—I said it over and over, that people have a right to know what's in the water they drink, the food they eat and the air they breathe.

And whenever I had the chance, I'd tell my story, of my childhood and of the movement. When you needed someone to sit in, I would say, I was there. When you needed someone to ride, I was there. When you needed someone to march, I was there. And now, when you need someone with vision and strength to represent you in Washington, I will be there.

Many people, especially the young ones, didn't know their history, didn't know the story of the movement, didn't know *my* story. So I told it, over and over and over again.

Jan Douglas, whose base of strength was the black female community, got sick of it. We'd share the stage at a function, I'd get up to speak, and she'd mutter under her breath, "Not that *chicken* story again." She'd tell audiences they "don't need another hero."

Midway through the campaign Mildred Glover made headlines by raising an issue that would remain in the race long after she dropped out.

The newspapers labeled it "Jar Wars."

It began with a debate arranged by the local League of Women Voters. The league wasn't prepared to invite all twelve candidates, so they drew the line at those individuals who had at least $5,000 in their campaign account. That was the league's way—certainly debatable—of measuring who the serious contenders were.

Mildred Glover did not qualify. I don't think she even had a formal campaign headquarters. But she was not about to take this snub sitting down. She organized her supporters, who came out the night of the debate and put a picket line in front of the auditorium where the event was to be held. I honored that line. I refused to cross it. My people begged me and begged me to go on in. I needed this exposure, they said. I needed this publicity. But I said no, I had never crossed a picket line in my life, and I was not about to cross one now. To me, a picket line—any picket line—is sacrosanct. Period.

Two of the four other candidates invited that evening also stayed away, leaving Julian and Charles Johnson to debate each other.

After that debate, Glover surprised us all by challenging the entire field of candidates to take a drug test. This came totally out of the blue, but then again it was not surprising. Mildred was peeved. She was being left behind, ignored. She needed to do something to get some attention. Raising the issue of drugs would certainly do the trick.

And it was not an entirely unreasonable request. This was the height of the '80s, when power and money and cocaine went hand in hand. Nancy Reagan was in the White House just saying no while drugs were flowing through the halls of power—including the halls of Washington—like water.

I knew drugs were around. They'd been around a long time. I'd never actually seen anyone using cocaine, but I'd been around plenty of marijuana in the '60s and '70s. It was routine for some people to relax at the end of the day by lighting up a joint. I was never interested in trying it myself, and by the early '70s it made me nervous. If I was around someone who lit up a joint, I'd push a towel against the bottom of the door and spray the room with Right Guard.

Glover wasn't thinking about me with that test. She was clearly sending a message to the front-runner. For years there had been whispers and rumors about Julian and drugs—not just about Julian, but also about the people on his staff. They were never substantiated, but the rumors persisted. I suspected Glover wanted, in part, to put them to the test.

As a rule I don't believe in drug testing. I think it violates our basic constitutional rights in terms of civil liberties. I can accept the need to screen people who work in sensitive positions involving public safety—airline pilots, people who drive buses, rail engineers. But generally I am opposed to it.

I did, however, answer Glover's call. I stated that while I was against testing in principle, I would submit to it in this case. I didn't want this issue hanging out there and clouding anyone's mind. My campaign staff agreed.

Julian did not. He adamantly refused to take the test, and his refusal would wind up hanging over his head during the remainder of the campaign. This was not the last we would hear of Jar Wars.

In the final days before that primary election I was worried. My own polls showed Julian with well over 50 percent of the vote, compared to my 20-something. Julian and his staff were confident, cocky. A guy named David Franklin—a fast-lane entertainment lawyer whose list of clients included names like Roberta Flack, Miles Davis and Cicely Tyson—was a big Bond supporter. He was the one who had lined up many of those celebrities early in the campaign. He was so sure Julian had this thing wrapped up that he dropped out before the election and went across town to help Martin Luther King III— Dr. King's son—who was running for county commissioner. Franklin explained to the newspapers that he was "bored" with the Bond campaign. It was in the bag.

The day before the election, the *Journal-Constitution* again endorsed me, as it had in 1977:

> John Lewis is not the snappiest talker in this amazingly articulate field.
> He may not always be the first on the scene of a trendy new issue, but
> he is a thoughtful, dedicated, dead-honest man who steadily works
> himself toward positions that are both reasonable and, precisely be-
> cause he has thought them out with care, usually durable.

I hoped that endorsement might help. Anything would help. I was not aiming to win here. I just needed to keep Julian from getting more than 50 percent of the vote. That was all. I was rooting for the rest of the field as well as for myself. Every vote against Julian was a vote for me—as long as I finished second.

It didn't look good that election evening. The early returns showed Julian running away from the pack, as expected, with well over half the vote. But a surge of support for me at the end, much of it coming from the white neighborhoods on the north side of the city, pulled Bond back down. Late that evening the final results were tallied. Julian finished first, with 47 percent; I was second, with 35.

My staff and supporters went wild. You would have thought we had won. Amidst whoops and cheers I climbed on a chair and pronounced to my friends and to the reporters scribbling madly in their notebooks, "Go and tell Andy Young! Go and tell David Franklin! Go and tell Maynard Jackson! Go and tell Julian Bond! Here we *come!* Here we *COME!*"

Now it was just Julian and me. I had three weeks—the time until the runoff election would be held—to work what the press was saying would be a miracle. Yes, I had surprised them all by forcing a runoff. That was nice. It made for a good story. But the fact remained that Julian had beaten me by twelve points—a margin of landslide proportions. No one gave me much chance of closing a gap like that.

But things were changing now, and fast. Resources I hadn't had before began pouring in—money, volunteers, endorsements. What had been a trickle had now turned into a steady stream—not a gusher, but better than I could have imagined.

Bill Campbell, my colleague on the council, came in as a member of the campaign's steering committee. Kevin Ross, a young black attorney, signed on as a senior advisor. Together, we rolled up our sleeves and mapped out our plan. Julian had doubled my count among black voters. I had doubled him among whites. If that pattern stayed the same, with 58 percent of the city's voters being black, I would lose.

We knew where my support in the white community had come from. Those who were concerned about having a black representative were more comfortable with a down-to-earth, hardworking candidate concerned with ethics and results than they were with a candidate whose campaign—and career—seemed largely based on image. For most white Atlantans, I really believe race wasn't an issue at all in this election. What they saw were two distinctly different men, two drastically different personalities and approaches to the role of a government representative—and most of them preferred mine.

As for the black community, Julian had gathered a lot of votes during the primary race by the sheer size and momentum of his visibility and presence. No one took him to task in terms of his past record, of what he had and hadn't done both during the civil rights movement and during his years in the statehouse. Or if they did, it was lost in the din and swirl of that twelve-candidate field. Now, however, with just he and I taking the stage, people were ready to look closer and to listen. I was counting on that.

There were a lot of experts and observers who said that I would only hurt myself by attacking Julian, that by attacking him I would implicitly be attacking his supporters, who included most of Atlanta's black political establishment—Young, Jackson, Arrington and the others. It would appear that I was betraying my own people. Once again I could hear echoes of that old, familiar phrase: "Uncle Tom."

But once again I refused to buy it. I wasn't criticizing or attacking *blacks*. I was criticizing *politicians*, based not on their race or any other personal criteria, but on how they did their jobs. As simple as that. I had faith the voters would appreciate that. I respected the public's intelligence and decency, and its ability to see through the kinds of smoke screens being thrown up in the name of race. The Bond camp might try to write me off as a "white" candidate, but anyone who knew or learned about my past, and who met and saw and listened to me, would see how absurd, how ridiculous, how stuck in the past a charge like that was. Frankly, I believed that tactic was going to turn a lot of people off. The fact was that black Atlantans had become tired of the "polished" politicians in their community. That was exactly the word used by many voters interviewed in the torrent of stories that began appearing in local newspapers each day as the runoff race began. Atlanta's black community had seen a black majority on the city council for well over a decade, with not a lot to show for it. The voters had not forgotten that I had stood so often against that majority, and now they were ready to give me credit. They wanted something different. They wanted some changes, some results. And more than a few resented the power play Julian seemed to be pulling with his impressive array of spotlighted, celebrity backers. "I don't want anyone telling me how to vote," one woman told the *Washington Post*. I counted on that feeling to grow.

Julian and I did not differ greatly on issues. Our differences were in character, leadership and attitude. During the primary I had largely left it to others—mainly the press—to point those differences out. Now it was time for me to take the offensive.

In speeches and interviews, I began taking Julian to task for his tendency to always play it safe, to hang back from acting or deciding on something until he was sure he would not be hurt.

I had always known this about Julian, but I had always accepted it. When you have a friend, you accept him or her without judgment. You take the good with the bad, the chaff with the wheat. And Julian was my dear, dear friend.

Now, however, the situation demanded that I point these things out. I had never had a reason to do so before, but I did now. These things mattered now in a way they did not matter before. The questions they raised pointed directly to the decision the voters faced in deciding whom they should send to Congress to represent them. It wasn't pleasant to point these things out, but it was necessary. And it was the truth. It had always been the truth.

Julian's record in the statehouse, his starstruck attraction to TV and Hollywood, sometimes at the expense of time and energy spent on his job (besides his *Saturday Night Live* appearance, he appeared in a film called *Greased Lightning* with Richard Pryor, and in 1978 he auditioned to become a correspondent for a new ABC television program called *20/20*—he was not hired), and the fact that more than 80 percent of his campaign contributions came from outside the district while 90 percent of my funding was local—all these facts were put on the table as my runoff campaign picked up steam.

Any trace of our friendship was gone. The days when Julian and Alice and Lillian and I had been inseparable, when we would vacation together at Disneyland or in Barbados, when we would stay up till three in the morning playing Scrabble, when we filled our scrapbooks with photos of the four of us laughing and sharing our lives together—those days were now behind us. And that hurt. It was heartbreaking. But it had to happen. This was about something beyond friendship. As painful and unfortunate as it was to cut our personal ties, this was about something bigger.

And it had an effect. During that three-week stretch run, I pounded the pavement not from dawn to dusk but from dawn to *dawn*. My beat-up blue Nikes gave out the first week. I went through two more pairs before it was over, jogging from door to door in neighborhood after neighborhood, my white shirt soaked with sweat, my tie loosened, my sleeves rolled up. I was literally "running" for office, going into the black business districts, working both sides of Martin Luther King Drive and Auburn Avenue, searching out every beauty shop and soul food restaurant, and when they closed I'd move to the Midtown and Stewart Avenue sections of the city, into topless bars and gay clubs and all-night supermarkets, shaking hands at three in the morning, shaking so many hands I developed a condition called trigger thumb, something most politicians are painfully familiar with. The tendons and ligaments at the base of the thumb become strained and swollen. The muscle becomes uncontrollable. The thumb closes against the palm of the hand and sticks there. You have to pull it back with your other hand. Sometimes you hear a pop. Mornings are the worst. It's a struggle to button your shirt or zip up your pants, or put your wallet into your pocket. So you learn to use both hands when working a crowd, reaching out first with the left and then with the right, alternating to ease the load.

Looking back, I don't know how I did it. Covering that much ground, at that kind of pace—I was operating on something I didn't know I had.

The question was, did I have time to catch up in the mere handful of days that were left? Despite all my work and ground-pounding, there were a lot of people who just didn't know me. The race was exhaustively covered by the local press, primarily by a young reporter with the *Journal-Constitution* named Nathan McCall—the same Nathan McCall who went on to the *Washington Post* and then wrote a best-selling memoir titled *Makes Me Wanna Holler* about his life growing up in the urban projects of Portsmouth, Virginia. I knew nothing at the time about McCall's past. All I knew was that he was an eager, hardworking journalist who always wanted to get the story, always wanted to get beyond the bullshit. "John," he'd say, "what's *really* happening here? Tell me. Come on, come *clean* with me. Be *straight* with me."

Reporters like McCall did a good job, but sad to say, newspapers are one thing in terms of exposure in a contemporary political campaign, and television is another. We were able to afford a few small TV ads, but it wasn't close to what we would have liked in terms of getting my face and my message out in front of the public.

We needed more airtime, we knew that. But we couldn't see how we might get it.

And then came a godsend.

Julian issued a challenge to debate me.

To this day I'm not sure why he did it. My guess is that it was the people around him—his staff and close friends—who convinced him, who told him he needed to crush me, punish me, teach me a lesson for daring to challenge him this way. Call it ego or hubris. But it was exactly what I needed, a chance to stand side by side with Julian, an opportunity for people to size up the men, not the images, to see us for who we were and to make their own comparisons. Julian had everything to lose by this decision. And I had everything to gain.

I leaped at the opportunity. A series of five debates was scheduled—four on television, one on radio. As soon as the dates were set, I called the one person outside my immediate staff who needed to know this was happening, the one person whose role would be greater than anyone else's in helping me prepare for this face-off.

Her name was Shawn Reed. She had appeared out of the blue toward the end of my primary campaign. The wife of a political reporter at the *Journal-Constitution* had called one afternoon and recommended her, saying she was an expert in media relations, a professional who could help us deal with the growing onslaught of television and radio attention.

During the early part of the primary campaign, I had enrolled in a program offered by SpeakEasy, a firm based in Atlanta that specializes in training clients—primarily businesspeople, but occasionally politicians—to deal with the press, to give an effective interview, to come across convincingly in front of a camera. I picked up some basics there—what color shirt works best in a studio (light blue rather than white), what style tie to wear (something subdued, not loud). But I was now offered something more, and I accepted it. I immediately made arrangements to meet Ms. Reed at her home northeast of the city, beyond Emory University.

Shawn was in her late forties, very professional, a no-nonsense kind of person. As soon as several of my staff members and I arrived, she invited us into her living room and we got right down to business. She pushed and prodded me on my ideas, made me answer every question she had—which was every question a reporter or an opponent might have. We role-played: She and three or four of my staff people played the part of different candidates, each of them grilling me, debating me, pushing me in every possible direction. It was intense. It reminded me of the nonviolent workshops we went through in the early days of SNCC.

We met several times like that, Shawn and I, during the primary campaign. But now, with just Julian and me facing off, it was time to focus even harder. Now it was just Shawn and I, spending an hour or two at a time, going one-on-one. She was relentless, like a trainer working with a boxer. "Julian's good," she'd say. "He's so fast. He's quick." There was no way I was going to beat him at his game, she said. I was not going to out-Julian Julian. The key for me was to emphasize our differences, to be myself as totally and completely as I could. Look straight into the camera, relax, don't worry about slurring a word here or there. *Tell* the people that I grew up in rural Alabama, that I came off a farm, that I may not be able to speak 120 words a minute like some of my friends, that I may leave an s off a word here or there, but that I think people can understand what I have to say.

Don't try to be anything other than who and what you are was Shawn's biggest piece of advice. She sharpened me on all the specifics I'd have to be ready for in these debates, but the foundation on which everything stood was the necessity to relax and stay grounded in my self.

The night of the first face-off Shawn had me come over an hour or so before I was to be at the studio. I assumed we'd be making a last-minute run-through. But when I got there, she told me to go out and get in her hot tub. Meditate, she said. Just relax. Which, for the next twenty-five minutes, I did. Then I dried off, dressed and left for downtown.

Julian and I had made several joint appearances before, both with other candidates during the primary and one-on-one before various live audiences. But this was our first square-off on television, and I felt remarkably calm, very relaxed. Almost as soon as the cameras came on, Julian took me to task for taking *him* to task.

"We've been friends for twenty-five years," he said. "We went to Africa together. We were in Selma together. . . .

"But never in those twenty-five years did I ever hear any of the things you are saying about me now. Why did I have to wait twenty-five years to find out what you really thought of me, to find out that you really don't think I amount to much?"

Shawn had asked me the same question during our sessions. My response then was the one I gave now.

"Julian, my friend," I said, "this campaign is not about the past. It's not about our friendship. This is a referendum on the future of our city, on the future of our country."

There was nothing he said that evening, nor was there anything that was asked by the moderator, that surprised me. There were no knockout punches for either of us. And that in itself was a shock to Julian's staff. They had expected to destroy me, to see me fall apart under the heat of those lights. When I didn't, they were amazed. They could see they were going to have to *work* here. Just showing up was not going to be enough. Now they were no longer angry and insulted. Now they were feeling a little bit of fear.

The next day Julian's lead had slipped just a little bit more. I was continuing to cover the city on foot, running from speech to speech, still standing outside concert halls and theaters, handing out leaflets and shaking hands. That, combined with this TV exposure, was building a wave now, a wave that had Julian's camp clearly concerned.

Before the start of the second debate, just before we went on the air, Julian turned to one of his staff members and asked loudly, making sure I could hear, "Do you have the book? The Shirley MacLaine book? Is the page marked?"

Someone on his staff must have dug up the chapter describing the SNCC party that Shirley had visited back in 1964, the one in which she had danced with me, then watched me drop "stoned" into an easy chair. Julian knew full well that the word "stoned" meant something far different in 1964 than it did in 1986. Shirley was referring to the two beers that had put me out. Julian was playing on the modern drug-related use of the term—maybe a little payback for the "Jar Wars" questions that continued to nag him.

He never did actually pull that book out that night. I don't think he ever intended to. I think he just wanted to shake me up a little. But I wasn't worried. Actually, I thought it was pretty amusing. I hadn't looked at that book in almost twenty years. It brought back some nice memories, which I would have been happy to share with the viewers.

You could sense something close to desperation growing now. Though he was still ahead in the polls, Julian's lead was crumbling, evaporating. The third debate, held the Friday before Tuesday's election, was critical. It took place in the same city council chambers where I had served for five years.

Every seat was taken, with standing room only—a live audience of about two hundred people, plus those tuned in at home.

Midway through, a question arose about campaign contributions and conflict of interest. I'm not sure where the interviewer got his information, but he wanted to know about a contribution of $200 made to my campaign by a lawyer who worked for a firm that represented a local cable television company and a contribution of $50 by a young woman who was a lobbyist for that company. I had voted as a city council member to award a franchise to this company. The question now asked was did this constitute a conflict of interest.

It clearly did not. Both the lawyer, a man named Clay Long, and the lobbyist, a woman named Sharon Adams, had been friends of mine for years, since I had first come on the city council, long before the issue of this franchise arose. And the franchise was voted on long before these people made a contribution to my campaign. After all the work I had done with the city council on the issue of ethics, it was surprising to be asked to answer for my own honesty.

But I was glad to. I said this was in no way a case of a conflict of interest.

The interviewer then turned to Julian, who knew as well as I did that I wouldn't be involved in something unethical.

"If it looks like a duck," he deadpanned, "and quacks like a duck and waddles like a duck, then it must be a duck."

I was stunned. I could not believe he was questioning my integrity, of all things. And he *knew*, he *knew* this was not true. My immediate reaction was "I'm not gonna let this Negro get away with this." I said that to myself.

My advisor Kevin Ross had told me over and over in preparing for these debates, "If they try to set you up in any way, don't back down. Go for it. Do whatever you think you should. Strike back."

It's not in my nature to let my emotions rise up. It's not in my nature to strike out. But this was a time when it happened. This was a time when I hit back.

"Mr. Bond," I said. "My friend. My brother. We were asked to take a drug test not long ago, and five of us went and took that test. Why don't we step out and go to the men's room and take another test?"

The room was dead silent. You could have cut the tension with a knife.

"It seems," I went on, "like *you're* the one doing the ducking."

Julian was flabbergasted. He gathered himself and responded with a nervous joke about "Star Wars" and "Jar Wars." But no one was laughing.

There's no telling exactly how much that exchange hurt Julian, but it didn't help. His lead continued to shrink, but time was running out now. I spent that Labor Day weekend running myself ragged with one last round of picnics and festivals.

And then it was Tuesday, September 2. Election day.

It was raining when I awoke, not a good sign. One key we were counting on was a larger turnout than there had been for the primary. Rain might keep some people away from the polls.

And it did. Throughout the day my people went from precinct to precinct, reporting back what they saw, and what they saw was a voter turnout even lighter than it had been for the primary. That was partly due to the weather. It was also partly due to the absence of many voters who would have turned out if there had been a runoff for the Senate nomination as well. There was not because Wyche Fowler had won more than 50 percent of his vote in the primary. Julian's camp had been glad to see that, knowing that most of the voters who would have turned out for Wyche would have voted for me as well.

One last reason for the light turnout this day was the fact that, despite the momentum I'd picked up in the last days of the campaign, Julian was still the heavy favorite, and a lot of voters didn't bother showing up simply because they figured Julian's victory was a done deal.

It looked early on as if they were right. When the first returns began coming in that evening, we were crowded around our rented TV, watching the numbers build, much more for Julian than for me. Midway through the evening Andy Young was interviewed, and he felt confident enough in Julian's lead that he made an admission.

"Well," he said, "the election is over. I guess I can tell you how I voted. I voted for Julian Bond.... If anyone was going to run against Julian, they should have started twenty years ago."

Dewey defeats Truman. The delight on Harry Truman's face as he held up that headline the morning after his presidential victory in 1948 was an image I always held close to my heart. The underdog coming through against all odds. Maybe it could happen again, here, on this night.

I was still trailing late in the evening, well past midnight, when I left to go downtown to a local TV station to do a live interview. On my way back I looked over the two statements Shawn and I had prepared, one in case I won, the other in case I lost.

It was two-thirty when I came through the doors of my headquarters. And the place was exploding. People were shouting, hugging, crying, climbing on chairs and tables, leaping all over each other screaming, "We *won!* We *won!* We *won!*"

We . . . won?

I had still trailed when I left the TV station, but not by much. And the returns had not yet come in from the last precincts to report—the northern precincts, which were predominantly white. I had taken nearly 90 percent of the white vote all evening. Those last precincts had come in even higher and, along with a surge of votes in the poorer black neighborhoods, had pushed me over the top.

The final count: 52 percent for me, 48 for Julian.

Everything began swirling around me. We had reserved the ballroom of the downtown Westin Hotel for our victory celebration—if there was one. Now it was time to go there.

As we came outside, a long white limousine pulled up to the curb. Out stepped a young man, one of my campaign supporters, a very optimistic soul who earlier that day had convinced the company he drove for to allow him to borrow one of their limos for my victory ride. Now he was holding the door open, beaming as if *he* had just won this election.

John-Miles and one of his friends began to climb in, but I told them no. I appreciated more than I could say the fact that this young man had gone to such great lengths to help me celebrate, but I hoped he would understand that arriving at the Westin in a limousine just didn't feel right. We needed to *walk*.

And so we did, forty or so of us setting off in the black of night, just the streetlights above us. No one else around. It was three in the morning and the streets were deserted. But as we began the mile-and-a-half walk to the Westin, people began coming out of the darkness, seemingly from nowhere, to join us—people who had stayed up to watch the results and had now rushed downtown to be part of the jubilation.

Soon there were a hundred of us. Then two hundred. Then three and four hundred, our shouts and singing and laughter echoing off the empty buildings. As we came near the hotel, passersby blew their car horns and waved. Police officers stood at intersections and opened the way for us. We had no permit for this parade, but we didn't need one. I knew just about every one of those policemen—Marvin Arrington had probably thought he was punishing me when he assigned me early on in my city council career to the public safety committee, an unglamorous position but one that allowed me to meet and become friends with almost every fireman and policeman in the city. They were out there now, holding back traffic, their smiles as broad as mine.

I looked behind me, at the hundreds of ecstatic faces, and beyond, at the darkness out of which we had come. And then I looked ahead, at the bright gleaming lights of the Westin, and I thought to myself that with all the walking I had done in my life, with all the marches I had ever made, this was the sweetest.

This was the best. I was walking with the wind.

There is a rhythm to the life I lead today that is hardly different from the schedule I followed as a boy on my family's farm—except that my duties now are those of a United States congressman.

I still rise between five and five-thirty each morning, though my bedroom now is in a District of Columbia row house rather than the wooded Pike County home in which I grew up. I'm usually out the door by six, but instead of heading for a day of picking in the fields I walk two blocks to the Capitol, where I join several of my colleagues—Dick Durbin and Glenn Poshard of Illinois, and Peter DeFazio of Oregon—for a workout on the treadmill and weight machines in the House gymnasium.

By eight I'm in my office, along with my staff, to begin what is typically at least a twelve-hour day. Committee and subcommittee meetings, visits from constituents and lobbyists, a steady stream of receptions and fund-raisers, breakfast, lunch and dinner meetings, television and radio and newspaper interviews and press conferences, and, of course, my duties on the floor of the House itself—these responsibilities fill my days when Congress is in session. On weekends, as often as I can, I fly back to Atlanta to spend time with Lillian and John-Miles, and to connect with the people I represent.

Some of those people never dreamed I would still be in office today. When I was first elected in 1986, there were more than a few skeptics who predicted that I would, as one observer put it, "be ground into paste by Washington's Capitol Hill glue factory." Twelve years later I've been reelected five times and am fortunate enough to have risen to the position of chief deputy Democratic whip, making me one of the highest appointed or elected black officials in the country.

It really does seem like only yesterday that I was sworn in as a freshman member of the 100th Congress. I remember looking around at the inauguration ceremony, at some of my fellow first-term colleagues—former professional basketball star Tom McMillen; a lawyer from Mississippi named Mike

Espy; Bobby Kennedy's son Joe; Ben Nighthorse Campbell, who likes to call himself a "half-breed Indian from Colorado"—and I marveled at the fact that only in America could you have an Indian, a black man and a member of the Kennedy family standing together to take the oath as newly elected members of the U.S. House of Representatives.

I was overwhelmed during those first days by the mailbags of résumés—more than three thousand—that came to my office from people seeking one of the eighteen staff positions I had to fill. The New York Times applied a little tongue-in-cheek pressure to my arrival in Washington by calling me "one of the few members of Congress who must deal with the sainthood issue." But the business at hand was no joke to me, and I approached it as if the world depended on it—which, as far as I am concerned, it does. I hit the ground running, attending every caucus meeting and every briefing session, accepting every invitation to speak, and never, not once, missing a vote during that first term. I was one of only twelve out of the 435 members of the House to compile a perfect voting record that session, and I've continued close to that pace during the ensuing decade, casting my vote more than 95 percent of the time. My constituents might not agree with every vote I make, but I make them. I'm there. And they appreciate that fact.

They have also appreciated my ability to build the foundation that every congressman must have, positioning myself to take care of the bread-and-butter needs of my district as well as helping to steer and govern the nation as a whole. It was dealing with this nitty-gritty end of politics, the intricate process of connecting with the right coalitions and getting on the right committees to be able to bring a fair share of federal dollars and resources back to my district, that my detractors doubted I would be able to do. When I wound up that first term with seats on both the Interior and the Public Works and Transportation Committees, and was able to secure hundreds of millions of federal dollars for the sorely needed expansion of Atlanta's rapid transit system, as well as federal funding for new highway construction and water projects around the city, most of those critics were silenced.

I have continued to tend to the hands-on needs of my constituents. But beyond that, my overarching duty, as I declared during that 1986 campaign and during every campaign since then, has been to uphold and apply to our entire society the principles which formed the foundation of the movement to which I have devoted my entire life, a movement I firmly believe is still continuing today. I came to Congress with a legacy to uphold, with a commitment to carry on the spirit, the goals and the principles of nonviolence, social action and a truly interracial democracy. These are principles that continue to be crucially relevant. Dr. King, were he still alive, would be in the forefront of reminding the government that its first concern should be the basic needs of its citizens—not just black Americans but *all* Americans—for food, shelter, health care, education, jobs, livable incomes and the opportunity to realize their full potential as individual people.

I have sponsored during my years in Congress legislation that has ranged from funding for breast cancer research to laws ensuring environmental protection and safety. I have stood in picket lines, supporting laborers ranging from workers at a poultry processing plant in North Carolina to employees of Eastern Airlines. I have spoken at countless union rallies across the country. I was arrested—yes, again—in 1988 outside the South African Embassy in D.C. for joining demonstrators protesting the racial repression mounting in that nation at the time. That same year I traveled to Moscow to meet with "refuseniks"—Soviet Jews who had been denied permission to leave for Israel—and to address members of the Supreme Soviet on the subject of human rights.

The struggle for such rights is a global one, and we must approach it that way. Just as we must recognize that as Americans we are all part of a connected community, so must we see that America is inextricably linked to the rest of the world as part of a global community. Simply put, we are all in this together. The principles we apply to ourselves we must apply to others—including the principles of nonviolence. That is why I stood on the floor of the House in January 1991 to oppose the Gulf war resolution.

"Death and destruction," I said at the time, "diminishes us all." I quoted the old spiritual: "I'm going to lay my burden down...Down by the riverside...I ain't gonna study war no more." War is obsolete as an instrument of foreign policy, I explained. Negotiation, sanctions, the way of nonviolence—these options must be exhaustively pursued before we even consider the use of weaponry. As a politician I can understand and accept the need for a certain amount of military strength as a deterrent, even though as an individual I believe that nothing, but *nothing,* justifies the use of violence between people or nations. But there is no excuse for the waste of the resources our nation spends on a military force that is far more massive than is necessary to maintain a margin of safety in this world. Iraq supposedly had the fourth largest army in the world at the time of the Gulf war, and look what our might did to them. Do we need that much? I don't believe in killing at all. But as bad as killing is, *over*kill is even worse.

Naturally I was criticized in many quarters for taking a stand against that war, just as I've been criticized for my opposition to capital punishment. My feelings about the death penalty stem from essentially the same beliefs as my feelings about combat. Capital punishment, as far as I am concerned, is simply barbaric. It is backward, outdated and not worthy of a great nation. It should have been outlawed years ago. This belief was at the root of my vote to block the 1994 crime bill that greatly broadened the number of federal offenses that would be subject to the death penalty—a bill that was supported by President Bill Clinton. Standing against my own party and president was a politically difficult decision to make, but I simply cannot condone killing of any kind, especially when there are other options, which I believe there always are in the case of capital punishment.

We don't have the right to play God. No government has the right to kill another human being. That responsibility should be reserved for the Almighty, a power greater than humankind. I happen to believe that in the bosom of every human being there is a spark of the divine. When we kill another human being, we are killing a reflection of the divine.

I've worked hard during my time in Washington to have the government commemorate in various ways what was achieved by the civil rights movement, so that people do not forget. Among the initiatives I've pushed have been the creation of a National African American Museum in Washington, D.C., and the designation of the route from Selma to Montgomery as a National Historic Trail—making it one of only six such routes in the nation, including the Natchez Trace and the Santa Fe Trail.

My interest in saving and preserving the past extends to just about every aspect of my life, personally as well as politically. Maybe it's in my genes, for I have a hard time throwing anything away. Not only that, but my only hobby, if you want to call it that, is combing flea markets and antique stores during my travels, searching for old posters, artifacts and books—*especially* books. The back room of our home in Atlanta is so crammed with old volumes of history and biography that they're spilling out onto the living room floor. My house in D.C. is almost as crowded.

The books I especially treasure are first editions by or about black people, as well as old autographs. Over the years I've collected the writings or signatures of Frederick Douglass, Booker T. Washington, Ralph Bunche and Langston Hughes, to name a few. But the one I treasure most is a book I found back when I was working in D.C. for the Carter administration in the late '70s. I was rambling through an old flea market in Alexandria, Virginia, one weekend, a cobwebbed little shop full of dust and dirt, when I came across a familiar title on a back shelf—*Stride Toward Freedom*, by Martin Luther King Jr. I pulled it out, wiped the dust off the cover—the original dust jacket—opened it and saw that it was a first edition. Stuck in its pages was a program from a Sunday service at the Shiloh Baptist Church, a black church in downtown Washington. The program was dated June 21, 1960, and it listed Dr. King as the speaker at two services that day, one at 11 A.M. and the other at four. Inside the cover of the book was the inscription "Best Wishes, Martin Luther King Jr."

I had never bothered collecting or saving anything from Dr. King back when we worked together. The thought never occurred to me. I always imagined we would both grow old, that the time for reminiscence and nostalgia would come much later, and that we would somehow share it. I just never thought to save anything. I was too much in the present during that time to think that it would someday be the past. The only item I ever owned that bore Dr. King's mark was a copy of his book *Where Do We Go from Here?*, which he gave me just before I left for my 1964 trip to Africa. In it he had written a long personal inscription, covering an entire page. I left the book in my SNCC office, and when I got back from that trip, it was gone. I don't know what happened to it. Every now and then I still pray that someone will call me up and tell me he or she found it.

Naturally I thought about that loss as I carried the copy of *Stride Toward Freedom* up to the counter in that Alexandria shop. I was so nervous my hands were shaking. I couldn't imagine how much they were going to ask for it. I wasn't sure if I was going to be able to afford it. "Ma'am," I asked the cashier, "how much do you want for this book?" She took it, looked it over, then handed it back to me and said, "Fifty cents."

Fifty cents.

I gave her a dollar, she gave me my change, and I rushed out as fast as my legs could carry me. Today that book is locked in a safe in Atlanta, one of my most prized possessions.

Beyond merely commemorating the movement, I believe it's absolutely essential that we carry it on, in small ways as well as large. It's vitally important that each of us reaches out and actually *does* something, which is why I proposed legislation in 1994 making the Martin Luther King holiday a day of community service and action rather than just a day off from work. Dr. King was more than just a teacher or a preacher. He was a man of action, and I suggested that we could honor his memory best by making this a day of sharing and caring and acting on the principles of community and connection. Create one-day projects of reaching out to those in need—pitch in to paint or renovate homes or buildings in need of repair; spend the day volunteering in a homeless shelter, or feeding those without food, or working with the elderly, or assisting in a day care center; clean up a park or a roadway. In an era in which we seem as a society to be recognizing the emptiness between and within so many of us, the void that material possessions and leisure time and mind-spinning technology do not fill, the feeling of disconnection that has risen as families and communities and personal spirituality have waned, a good place to start addressing those feelings might be right in our immmediate neighborhoods. By stepping outside our own small, familiar circles and reaching out, touching and connecting with people and lives that are different from ours and that are in need, we may begin filling that empty place in our own souls, both collectively and individually. Volunteerism and action—see what *they* do to the sense of aimlessness and cynicism and despair and anger and frustration that fills so many of our lives.

This is where we can start, in our own backyards, on our own blocks, down our own streets, from one section of a town or city into another, from white neighborhoods into black, or vice versa. This is where integration truly begins, not by government mandate, but by literally reaching over the fences around our own homes. Folksinger Tracy Chapman put it succinctly in a song of hers that came out a few years ago:

> *Across the line,*
> *Who would dare to go?*
> *Under the bridge,*
> *Over the tracks*
> *That separate whites from blacks.*

The alternative to reaching out is to allow the gaps between us to grow, and this is something we simply cannot afford to do. We live together in the same house—in different rooms perhaps, but under the same roof and within the same walls. If one section of our house begins to rot—a basement, a back room, a closed-off closet—the entire structure is in danger of collapsing.

I go home to Atlanta almost every weekend, as well as during recesses and between congressional sessions. When I do, I go into the streets, into the neighborhoods, into the projects. I see the homeless, the helpless, the anger and the violence, the drugs and the despondency. It is real, it is pervasive, and it cannot be ignored. Some people were shocked by the explosion of rioting in Los Angeles in 1992. They asked aloud, "Where did *that* come from?" It came from the same place as the rioting in Watts in 1965 and in dozens of other urban neighborhoods in the quarter century since then. The stew of poverty and despair simmers and cooks in the grimmest parts of our cities, and it will not go away. We who do not live in these places might close our eyes or our hearts, we might pretend it does not exist or that it has nothing to do with us, but it will not simply go away. And it has *everything* to do with us. We have a choice. We can look and listen and respond in constructive, creative ways to our places of poverty, or we can be *forced* to respond by outbursts of violence such as these riots.

The path that remains to lead us to the Beloved Community is no longer racial alone. It is one, I believe, marked by the differences, divisions and canyons created by class. There hasn't been a time in America—certainly not since World War II—that the classes have been pushed as far apart as they are today, with vast numbers of poor at one end, a small number of wealthy at the other and a middle class in danger of completely disappearing as most of it is pushed toward the lower end of the spectrum. Measurements of economic well-being are misleading. The overall economy might be healthy, but where is most of that wealth going? Vastly and disproportionately, it is funneled to the relatively few at the top. America's total wealth, jobs and productivity might be growing, but the benefits are being enjoyed primarily by a small minority.

We cannot let this continue. We cannot have a very few people visibly and luxuriantly living in excess while the rest of the nation lives in fear and anxiety. We cannot afford to have two societies, moving further apart. The famous 1968 Kerner report warned that America was in danger of becoming "two societies... separate and unequal." At that time those societies were defined by race. Now, I believe the division is both class and race.

And such disparity is a recipe for disaster. It creates a climate of cynicism and discouragement. It encourages people at all ends of the spectrum to turn away from one another, to insulate themselves and, yes, even to arm themselves, for both defense and attack. It makes the political system seem distant, incomprehensible, irrelevant, monolithic and insensitive to the needs of the people. If we are going to begin turning back toward one another, to *humanize* one another, we need to humanize the political system, we need to make it respond directly to the problems of the people—not just to the people in power, or to the people who are loudest, but to *all* of the people, including, crucially, those who have no power, those who have no voice.

The poor, the sick, the disenfranchised. We cannot run away from them. We're all living in this house. When we move away from community and connection and live instead in a climate of "every man for himself," we are sowing the seeds that will lead to the destruction of American society as we know it. If we are not going to become divided and balkanized, like Northern Ireland or Lebanon or Rwanda or so much of Eastern Europe, we must push and advocate and make real the policies and decisions that can pull us together, that recognize our dependence on one another as members of a family. If we continue to allow hundreds of thousands of our young people—black, Hispanic, Asian, Native American, white—to grow up without a feeling that they have a stake in this society, if we let them come into young adulthood without ever holding a meaningful job, without any sense of hope, I think we are asking for trouble. We can't retreat from them. We can't turn our backs on them. We can't circle the wagons in suburban developments with armed guards at the gates and believe that we are safe. The people, the masses, will eventually arrive at those gates, angry and upset, and then it will be too late. We must reach out to one another *now*. We must realize that we are all in this together. Not as black or white. Not as rich or poor. Not even as Americans or "non"-Americans. But as human beings.

I believe in America. I love this country. That's why I've tried so hard over the years to make it better. This is unquestionably the greatest nation on earth, a land of limitless opportunity and possibility, not just in material terms but in moral, ethical and spiritual terms. I believe the next frontier for America lies in the direction of our spiritual strength as a community. This is the place where we must move if we are to continue to lead the rest of the world. It is not just materially or militarily that we must measure our might, but morally.

Somewhere, sometime—and I hope in the not too distant future—someone must take the lead. At the highest level—in the White House, in the Senate, in the House of Representatives—somebody needs to say, forcefully and with complete conviction, that we are one nation, we're one society, we're one people. We're one house, the American house. We're one family, the American family. We don't speak that way anymore. I'm not sure we even *think* that way.

But we must. And those of us in government must lead the way. It must create the climate, create the environment and set the agenda for these changes. We must insist that the government form policies, legislation, programs—whatever is needed—to nurture the environment in which we can narrow that gap instead of allowing it to continue to grow. We must develop a just and sensible way of redistributing our resources so that no one, but no one, will be left out of society.

The resources are there. We are a wealthy nation, a bountiful nation. Unfortunately, much of that wealth and bounty has been gathered by a very few, who have then used that wealth and power to shape the political system to benefit them. A lot of people made a lot of money during the 1980s, and those same people are now enjoying massive tax breaks. I think they should be required to pay up, to contribute their proportionate share, to invest in the areas of our nation that are falling down—the inner cities, the rural communities—providing the resources for large numbers of their fellow Americans to begin building meaningful lives.

That is one thing that can be done with the people inside the walls of power. As for those on the outside, they need to push, to agitate, to create a climate in which the government cannot ignore them. This is what we did during the movement. We *made* the government listen. We *made* the government respond.

I really don't think that many political leaders are genuinely concerned about the problems of the poor, of blacks, of Hispanics, of the people in the inner cities. Yes, all politicians love people in *general*. They love humanity. But many of them are very uncomfortable with people in *particular*—especially up close. They are very uncomfortable with the poor or the rough or the dirty. They are hesitant to get their hands messy, to confront and come in contact with the sticky stuff of real life—the life that's lived day in and day out by more Americans than they would like to believe, by more Americans than they can afford to ignore.

I think too many of our elected officials look at what is happening in our inner cities, especially to young black people, *especially* to young black *males,* and they shrug and turn away and treat it as a *fait accompli*—business as usual. Or worse, I think some say, "We can't solve it. It will never change." The people in those communities must not allow that to happen. They should not stand for it. What is happening right now in the poorest communities in America—which are largely black communities—is the worst situation black America has faced since slavery.

The way out must begin by the people in these communities taking matters into their own hands. They are not powerless. They are not voiceless. They must demand to be valued by the society that surrounds them. They must demand to be respected. At the same time they must value and respect themselves. Too many of our young people in these communities have little or no respect left for one another or for life itself. They fight, they shoot, they kill one another over nothing but crumbs—material crumbs like a pair of over-priced basketball shoes, or territorial crumbs like the loyalty of a neighborhood gang. They kill over these trivialities because crumbs are all they know, all they believe they can have. These tiny flakes of life are all they see, and so those flakes seem large. The models of success become the pimps and the drug dealers.

I truly believe that if we don't invest more in our young people, we are headed for disaster. And this is where the revolution must begin. A revolution of values. A revolution of attitude. A revolution that instills the sense of *possibility* in these young people's minds and hearts, a belief that this nation does indeed offer to them the opportunities of life, liberty and the pursuit of happiness.

The people, young and old alike, in these communities need to organize, to form a movement, a movement fueled not just by anger and rage, but by moral *authority,* by a sense of human righteousness fueled by the spirit. First, however, that spirit must be kindled within and among these communities— in these homes, in these neighborhoods, among the poor and the outcast themselves. I have been poor. I know what it is like. And I know that it is possible to pool our interests, to gather our resources, as scant as they might seem. And I am not talking just about money. I am talking about courage and strength of character, about stepping back and deciding what is important and valuable about life in the long run, not just how to make ourselves happy today, or maybe tomorrow. We need to think twice about wasting ourselves and what money we have on alcohol and clothing and jewelry and cars, on having a good time. There is nothing wrong with any of these things, but at a time of crisis there need to be priorities. These things are sedatives, they are seductive, and they turn our attention and effort and strength away from the work that is necessary if we are to survive as a society.

This mobilizing, organizing, sharing the sense of purpose of a movement has an immediate effect on a community. You could see it with us back at the height of the movement We were involved in something bigger and beyond just ourselves, and so we were *good* to ourselves. Studies of that time have shown that wherever there was a strong nonviolent movement taking place, the crime rate in that community went down. In Montgomery or Birmingham or Selma, during the early to middle 1960s, there were very few violent crimes in black communities, very few people coming into hospital emergency rooms on a Friday or Saturday night with a gunshot wound or a cut from a knife.

The movement must begin inside each of us, individually and as families. Then it must spread into the community, through civic groups and organizations, through social clubs, fraternities and sororities, through our schools and our churches, and from there to our elected officials, who can make the movement tangible through government action and programs that turn resources back toward these communities, supporting what has already begun in the hearts of the people. If those resources are not provided, if the government does not respond, then the people must remove it. Remove those elected officials from office. Vote them *out*. Replace them with people who will do what is demanded, what is needed. People are too quiet, too patient. In the great words of a nineteenth-century civil rights fighter, Frederick Douglass, we need to "agitate, agitate, agitate."

The government can respond. We proved it with the civil rights movement. The changes we brought about have been enormous. No one, but no one, who was born in America forty or fifty or sixty years ago and who grew up and came through what I came through, who witnessed the changes I witnessed, can possibly say that America is not a far better place than it was. We live in a different country than the one I grew up in. The South is different. There is no way to describe how palpable the fear was among black people living in the South just thirty and forty years ago. I'm talking about raw *fear*. You could see it in people's eyes. The fact that James Meredith could be shot in broad daylight, that a boy like Emmett Till could be dragged from his home and beaten to death, that three young men such as Mickey Schwerner, James Chaney and Andrew Goodman could be murdered and buried with the complicity and cooperation of law enforcement officials, that a church in the middle of a city as large as Birmingham could be blatantly bombed on a Sunday morning makes it easy to understand the fear people felt when we asked them to rise and act. But they did. And that level of fear is gone. Racism is not gone. Violence between blacks and whites is not gone. But no one could suggest that the situation today, especially in the Deep South, is anything like it was a generation ago.

So many things are undeniably better. More than three out of four black families in America today live above the poverty line, compared to one out of two in 1960. The number of black students attending college today is thirty times as large as it was a half century ago. By the turn of this decade, nearly 7,000 black men and women across the nation held elected office, and the mayors of more than thirty major cities were black.

Joe Smitherman is still the mayor of Selma. He recently presented me with a key to the city as part of a ceremony commemorating the thirtieth anniversary of the march to Montgomery. "We were wrong," he said during that celebration. "All Americans should have the right to vote." They have voted in Selma, which today has a black majority city council and is represented in Washington by a black congressman, Earl Hilliard. Selma now has a black chief of police.

There is no denying the distance we have come. But there is a mistaken assumption among many that these signs of progress mean that the battle is over, that the struggle for civil rights is finished, that the problems of segregation were solved in the '60s and now all we have to deal with are economic issues. This is preposterous. Yes, we now have the laws. In terms of establishing formal equal opportunity, we have done well. But in terms of actually bettering the lives of poor people, and the disabled—of actually seeing them take their rightful place in society—we still have a long way to go. And we are still far too segregated. We need look no further than our schools and our neighborhoods to see that segregation still exists on a massive scale in this country. With the highly organized, well-financed attack on affirmative action, our colleges and universities will become resegregated.

And while the lives of the poor are better in many ways than they were thirty years ago, those lives are still alarmingly in distress, especially among people who are black. The statistics are numbingly familiar. The proportion of poor blacks is still three times that of poor whites. Unemployment rates for black males are double that of whites. The rate of death from homicide is six times higher for black males than for whites. Two thirds of all black infants are born to unmarried mothers.

These are critical problems. Where are they rooted? How do we respond to them? Certainly not by turning our backs on the people who suffer from them, certainly not by punishing these people. We need to look hard at the circumstances surrounding these statistics. We need to probe the soil from which these problems spring, and we need to go *there* with our resources and energy.

There are strong forces within our government that would have us go in the other direction, *away* from the places where these problems exist. During the past decade there has been a rising wave of reaction and backlash against the principles that formed the basis of the civil rights movement. We have seen since the early 1980s a rising political wave based on a philosophy of exclusion, of divisiveness and of selfishness. That wave culminated in 1994 with the so-called Republican Revolution that saw large numbers of conservative congressmen and senators take office with a self-professed mandate to "give the government back" to the people. Their spiritual leader is the congressman from the district abutting mine, the Sixth Congressional District of Georgia—Newt Gingrich.

Newt and his followers represent a different breed of politician, one that is mean, angry, vindictive and harsh. Compassion is not a term that seems to matter much in their vocabulary. They argue that Lyndon Johnson's Great Society was a dismal failure, that it set the country back, made people dependent, misallocated precious resources and sowed the seeds of most of the problems society faces today. They argue that those problems stem from "big government." Their mandate—their "Contract with America"—is to dismantle that government, to pull apart the federal system and put control back in the hands of states and localities, back, as they put it, "in the hands of the people."

Many of these men and women hark back to a better day, somewhere in the past, somewhere back before John Kennedy and Lyndon Johnson and all the "liberalism" of the '60s supposedly undid our society. They point to "traditional values" in the time of their parents, before the upheavals of the '60s.

Well, we must not forget what that time was like for many of us—for blacks, for the underprivileged, for women, for the disabled. Ask *these* people if they want to go back to that time. Ask *them* about the "values" they faced during that time. Ask them how "valued" they felt. Do we really want to go back to that?

Yes, power should absolutely be put in the hands of the people. But when some of the people choose to use that power to deny the rights and opportunities of those who might be ill or poor or weak—or black or yellow or brown—that is precisely when a strong federal government is needed, as a steward of freedom and justice for *all*. It took a strong central government to give us Social Security, civil rights, the minimum wage, medical care, the GI Bill, and the environmental and civil liberties protections we enjoy today. We can't allow ourselves to forget that. And we can't allow political revisionists to rewrite our history.

Sometimes I feel that I'm reliving that history, that I'm reliving that part of my life. I hear talk of "states' rights," of the evils of a powerful federal government, and I swear I can see George Wallace standing again in that schoolhouse door. I feel that I'm passing down a road I've walked before. The anger, the militancy, the separatism, the schism both between whites and blacks and within the black community itself—it's all so familiar. It is eerie.

In terms of the climate in Washington, however, the situation now is worse than it was then. Back then, it was essentially the states we were fighting. We could look to the federal government and the Supreme Court for redress, for hope and optimism, for justice. The response of that government was slower than it should have been, but it did come. Laws were passed. Promises were kept.

Today, however, we have people in those places—in Congress and on the High Court—who are not at all sympathetic to the principles of fairness. By its actions and its statements and its votes and decisions, our government is destroying much of the hope and belief that are holding the most tenuous sections of our society together.

The backlash against affirmative action programs is, of course, a prime example. Several states have recently passed laws forbidding the use of affirmative action in state programs. A number of law schools have ended preferences for admitting students altogether. There is a movement afoot in Congress to pass federal laws forbidding such preferences in schools and in the workplace. And soon the Supreme Court will probably consider a case that could abolish affirmative action outright.

To all these determined critics of affirmative action: I agree with President Clinton. I say, "Mend it, don't end it." Yes, there are problems with some aspects of affirmative action programs. Adjustments can be made. Solutions can be found. But we should not end affirmative action simply because the system has problems. Its principles are sound. They are healthy. They are healing. We should not throw the baby out with the bathwater.

The recent movement toward school choice and the dismantling of court-ordered desegregation is causing schools and communities to coalesce into separate enclaves of blacks, whites and Hispanics. The people supporting the notion of school "vouchers" are primarily people who have already pulled their children out of public schools and who now want to drain the public coffers for the privileged few. I think it is cynical and self-serving of them to pretend that their concern is for the quality of education of the students who have been left behind in those neglected, decaying schools. Pretty transparently, their concern is to stop paying taxes for a system they have already abandoned. This is just one of many paths leading to resegregation, and we cannot afford to let it happen.

Another area in which there has been a recent push in what I believe is the wrong direction is, of course, welfare reform. From the day they arrived in Washington, Newt Gingrich's army of Republican "revolutionaries" vowed to balance the budget and promised to do so in part by cutting federal programs for the poor. Their welfare reform proposals, which were rejected initially by President Clinton but were then accepted in revised form during his 1996 reelection campaign, leaving us with the sweeping cutbacks and drastic limitations now being implemented in communities across the nation, are heartless, mean-spirited, low-down and dangerous. I've said this many times: It does not profit a nation to gain the world if we must lose our soul—which includes our compassion. That sense of caring and sharing that makes us a society and not just a collection of isolated individuals living behind locked doors must never be lost, or it will be the end of us as a nation. Franklin Roosevelt recognized this sixty years ago, when the New Deal welfare safety net was established to protect and provide for what he called the "ill-housed, ill-clad, ill-nourished" Americans among us. Lyndon Johnson's Great Society reforms continued that legacy.

Now those sentiments are rejected, those commitments discarded. At a time when we most need to be turning toward one another, we are turning away. The nation's anti-poverty system needs reform, no question. I absolutely believe that every able-bodied person should work and pay his or her fair share, that all men and women should be as fully responsible for themselves as possible. But the fact is that there are millions of people in this society who, through no fault of their own, need our help. They need our assistance, and we have the resources to offer that assistance. Welfare represents only about 4 percent of the federal budget. It is not the place where we are going to fix America. It is morally wrong to attempt to balance the budget on the backs of the poor.

We must not turn away from one another. We must not retreat into separate tribes of like-minded, like-looking people who worship the same god, wear the same clothes, read the same books and eat the same food as one another. This is the way of exclusion, not inclusion. We cannot afford to keep going this way. If we are to survive as a society, as a nation, we must turn toward one another and reach out in every way we can. It is not a choice; it is a necessity. We need to listen to one another, to look, to open our minds as well as our hearts. Don't turn away from rap music simply because it's loud or violent or sexist or lewd—which so much of it is. Don't turn away from the damage and destruction of drugs by simply declaring "war" on them and filling our prisons with the people who use them. Look hard at where the *need* for those drugs is coming from. Look hard at what's behind the anger and rage of that rap music. Pay attention. These are symptoms. They are responses. It is not the heroin-filled syringe of the addict that is the problem. It is not the hateful verses of the gangsta rapper that we must outlaw. It is the conditions and circumstances out of which the user and the gangster spring that must be looked at, understood and addressed. Change the world in which the addict lives and you'll change his need for the drug. Change the world about which the rapper chants and you will change his words and his music.

We have problems. We will always have problems. A free and open society—a democracy—is by definition an eternal work-in-progress. As someone once said, democracy is ongoing conversation. It will always be altering, shaping and defining itself for the better. That is the way we move forward, by responding to problem after problem, step-by-step. We will never reach the top of the mountain. The summit will always recede. It is not there to be reached. It is there to give us a direction, a goal. It is there to lead us higher.

Going backward will not take us where we need to go. We must push ahead, and it is not easy. We must struggle with *creating* solutions and *creating* a better society, rather than pulling down what we have built. We cannot run away, not from our problems and not from one another. This is the true meaning of integration—*integrating* all that we encounter around us, from problems to people, folding it all in to make us larger and stronger, rather than throwing it out, which only makes us small and weak.

It's not fashionable to talk about integration today. Not long ago, a national magazine ran a cover story about me and my politics titled "The Last Integrationist." Even the black community has grown weary of that struggle. When you talk about integration today, many black Americans dismiss it as old-fashioned and out-of-date. It's weak, they say. It's passive. The same polarization taking place in society at large is taking place within the black community. A new wave of conservative blacks—both academic intellectuals and politicians—has arisen who mock beliefs like mine, the beliefs that were at the core of the civil rights movement. They echo the ideology and even the terminology of Newt and his Republican army. I read columns in national magazines written by young, smug black pundits decrying a "dependency" on a "welfare state" and the "largesse" of big government, criticizing recipients of government aid for a "self-imposed isolation from the growing opportunities all around them." These are the phrases one black columnist used in a recent issue of *Time* magazine.

I think this kind of attitude is an affront to the struggle of hundreds and thousands of people, black and white, who devoted and in many cases even sacrificed their lives for the principles it is now so fashionable to dismiss. Each generation stands on the shoulders of the previous one. This is the way we move ahead, as individuals, as families and as a nation. Without the years of struggle of the civil rights movement, without people like Dr. King, without the unsung heroes of the movement, without the people who came before them and the people who came after, we would not be where we are today. The barriers that have fallen down would still be up. And those young commentators who so casually dismiss the principles of the movement would have no stage to stand on, no platform from which to speak. Their stage and their platform were earned largely by the bravery, the sweat, and even the blood of people they never knew, people they would now urge us all to forget.

This was why I strongly opposed Clarence Thomas's 1991 nomination to the U.S. Supreme Court. The fact that he is black did not matter to me. The fact that his politics are conservative was not the issue. But like most of the black conservatives I know, he is a direct beneficiary of the civil rights movement, and the fact that he now stood poised to deny to others the kind of opportunities he enjoyed was appalling to me. Without the commitment of the federal government to equal employment opportunities, there would have been no Equal Employment Opportunity Commission for Clarence Thomas to chair—the position that catapulted him to his nomination to the Supreme Court. Without the *Brown* v. *Board of Education* decision, which he had come to call "misguided," he would not have been able to pursue the career path in law that he enjoyed, and he certainly would not ever have been considered for a seat on the Supreme Court.

No one in the movement ever asked the government for a handout. No one wanted or expected a welfare state. What we wanted was simply a fair shake. We wanted justice and opportunity. We wanted a place at the table. And we insisted that the national government recognize that it had a role to play, a responsibility to the American people—to *all* American people—to open the doors of business and government and education, to open the way, to provide the freedom and fairness that our forefathers envisioned in creating this country.

My stand against Clarence Thomas brought an incredible amount of heat from the black community. I had turned on a "brother," a fellow Georgian. I had betrayed my race. I had not done "the black thing."

That is true. I am and have always been focused on and dedicated to doing the *right* thing—which does not always mean doing the "black" thing. This kind of attitude did not sit well back in the '60s with some of my colleagues in SNCC, and it has not sat well in the '90s with some of my black colleagues in Congress. I have often been accused of marching to my own drummer. There is nothing wrong with that. In fact, I have often taken the road less traveled because of the dictates of my conscience. I arrived in Washington with a commitment to addressing issues in terms of what's best for America, not in terms of what's best for this group or that group. I'm a coalition builder. I will never compromise my belief in interracial democracy, and I do not ascribe to a narrow, rigid race-based orthodoxy. I don't pass my politics through the lens of race. Neither do I pass my friendships through that filter.

When then–Speaker of the House Tom Foley selected me in 1991 to become a chief deputy whip for the Democratic Caucus, Foley was impressed by my stand against the Gulf war. He liked my independence, my willingness to listen and consider all views, regardless of special interests. He liked my willingness to buck large House majorities of any sort and consider all sides of an issue, a quality that is needed in a whip, whose job is gathering votes, forming coalitions and consensus on key issues.

Some Black Caucus members lobbied hard for another black member, Alan Wheat of Missouri. Alan was on the Rules Committee and was senior to me. I'm still an active member of the Black Caucus. I still attend meetings. But I still continue to go with my conscience, not my complexion.

I did so with the Million Man March, again to much criticism. I supported the idea and goals of that march. I did not march because I could not abide or overlook the presence and central role of Louis Farrakhan, and so I refused to participate. I believe in freedom of speech, but I also believe that we have an obligation to condemn speech that is racist, bigoted, anti-Semitic or hateful. Regardless of the race of the speaker, I won't be a party to it. The means by which we struggle must be consistent with the end we seek, and this includes the words we use to pursue those ends. It wasn't just Farrakhan's remarks made shortly before the march about Jewish people being "bloodsuckers" that turned me away; it was his long history of similarly hateful, divisive words and ideas. I am committed to bringing the people of this nation together, not pushing them apart.

Not long ago I was at the Atlanta airport, on my way home, when I stopped in a men's room. As I stood at a sink washing my hands, a man several faucets away turned and looked directly at me. We were the only people in the room. He was dressed entirely in black—black shoes, black socks, black slacks, black shirt. He wore an African kente cloth scarf draped over one shoulder. His head was clean shaven.

"I need to talk to you," he said. No salutation. No greeting. The statement was a demand, not a request. "I need to talk to you," he said again, "about how you attacked me on the floor of the House."

Now I realized who this man was. His name is Khalid Muhammad. He is—or was—an aide to Minister Farrakhan. Two years before the Million Man March, he made a speech at Kean College in New Jersey, in which he graphically and violently denounced Jews and Catholics, disparaging the Pope in filthy terms, praising Hitler and calling for the extermination of all whites in South Africa. In the wake of his remarks, I stood on the House floor to speak for a resolution condemning these violent, sick and poisoned words. Now, four years later, I was confronted by this "man in black" in an airport rest room.

"I'll be happy to sit down with you anytime," I told him. And I meant it. "Just call my office. Let me know."

The rise of a man like Louis Farrakhan speaks to both the hunger of the people of this nation to be led as well as to the lack of leaders to step in and fill that role. It's not just black people, but whites as well who are looking for a human symbol, who are hungry for heroes. There's a need there. People are starving for someone to believe in.

But we're at a point in our history where we're not sure we *can* believe in anyone. I believe great leaders can still emerge. I believe that will always be possible. But this is probably as difficult a time as there has ever been for it to happen at a national level in America. There are so many factors conspiring against it.

First, I believe, there is a general fear, a mistrust of putting our faith in any individual in an era in which everyone has disappointed us, everyone has let us down, no one has turned out to be who we thought he or she was. The past thirty years have seen so much betrayal, so much deceit, so much disappointment, not just among our elected officials, but among our religious leaders, our sports and celebrity icons—among all those figures who have traditionally been a focus of our hopes and beliefs and respect. There has even been an erosion of respect within our families, as too many families have sadly lost the qualities of cohesion and commitment that form the basis of belief. It's not surprising to see the phenomenal outpouring of universal grief over the recent passing of Princess Diana and, to some degree, of Mother Teresa. People are desperate for a place to put their beliefs and respect. And they find so few figures anymore who seem to deserve it.

A huge factor in this loss of faith in our leaders is the media. Never has there been such a collective microscope put on people of prominence in our society as there is today. We have a voracious mass market of hundreds and hundreds of newspapers, magazines, network and cable television programs, radio, *talk* radio, the emerging technology of the Internet—all of it demanding a ceaseless torrent of material to feed its bottomless pit of programming and pages.

And so we learn everything about the people who would be our leaders, everything about their personal character, their personal tastes, their parents, their personality, their past. We dissect them. They step into the spotlight and we eat them up, just chew them up and spit them out, almost as sport, as an end in itself. Anyone who emerges on the national landscape becomes a target of this feeding frenzy, not because there is necessarily cause, but simply because he or she stands out. I'm not condemning the right nor the need of the press to search for and share the information and analyses that provide the public with the knowledge necessary to make informed decisions. And there is no denying the natural desire and delight of people to peek into the lives of larger-than-life figures—the stars and celebrities of the sports and entertainment industry, for example. But we need to ask ourselves where lines might be drawn. On the celebrity side of things, the death of Princess Diana certainly prompted a serious international dialogue on this issue. In terms of our elected officials, I think we need to ask some of the same questions: How far should we go with our need to know before we completely veer off into the personal and the private and leave behind any chance of having a legitimate debate or discussion or discourse about the issues at hand?

Those lines are difficult to draw, and they are made even more difficult by the lack of *listening* going on in America right now. This is another result of the polarization and segmentation of our society, combined with the explosion of the media. Everyone's got an agenda. And everyone's got a platform. Turn on the television and you'll see a roundtable of "experts" shouting each other down in a "discussion" of the day's hot topic. Turn on the radio and you'll hear callers arguing endlessly about the same subjects the experts on TV are shouting about.

But none—or very few—of these discussions lead anywhere because no one is actually listening, no one is considering and possibly absorbing anyone else's ideas but their own. It's as if people's object is to stand behind the walls of their own opinion and hurl bombs at one another, to see whose make the loudest bang. There is nothing constructive about that. And that kind of behavior has crept into the political arena as well, with blanket statements, finger-pointing and attacks replacing reasoned discussion and debate.

I think it's time, both individually and collectively, for us to step back and consider whether we want to keep going in this direction. When opinions and information become ends in themselves rather than means to an end, we need to stop and ask ourselves what's the point? Where is it taking us?

It's no wonder that many people are simply turning away from it all—from the newspaper, from television, from radio, from politics, from the whole loud, noisy mess. They're disgusted. They're weary. They want to believe in something—that need never goes away—but they don't believe they'll find what they're looking for in any public arena.

Is it possible for government to ever fill that need again? Is it possible for a leader to emerge of the kind we have had in the past? Is it possible for some force or some figure to come forward who can restore our faith in the system of government that has gotten us to this point in our history? Can we ever have another King, or another Kennedy?

I don't know. I really don't know.

But I can say this. If a leader is to emerge, he or she will have to come from a place beyond race. I honestly don't believe we can have a national leader today who appeals to just one or two or a few segments of this vast and diverse nation we call America. I believe the power and the endurance of Martin Luther King Jr.'s vision and leadership was the fact that it extended to all people, regardless of class or race. Most of the American people, black and white alike, understood and *believed* his message of brotherhood and justice, a message that cut across all lines of wealth, or color, or gender, or age. They understood it and they *felt* it when he spoke of the Beloved Community.

Consider those two words. "Beloved"—not hateful, not violent, not uncaring, not unkind. And "Community"—not separated, not polarized, not adversarial.

People are dying to embrace these feelings, if only they could trust, if only they could dare to believe, both in one another and in their leaders.

That belief must be earned. It cannot be bought. It cannot be elected. It cannot be legislated. A person does not become a leader simply by assuming a position, filling a chair or earning a title. A real leader doesn't see himself as standing out in front of the people. He sees himself as standing *beside* them, *among* them. He doesn't tell people to dig a ditch; he gets down in the ditch with them and helps dig it himself. That's why people believe so strongly in and follow so faithfully a figure like Mother Teresa, Gandhi, Cesar Chavez, or Nelson Mandela—because they spent their entire lives getting down in the ditch and digging.

Our future is in the hands of the young, as it always has been. One generation hands off to the next, and each new generation has its own vision, its own ideals, its own beliefs. That is what it means to be young: You believe. Your focus is on the future, not the past. But at this juncture in American history, perhaps more than any other, it is critical that our young people be aware of and understand the past. I try my best to keep in contact with the young, both by going out into the communities and the schools and by meeting students in Washington when they come to visit. And I can say with certainty that there is a feeling of despondency, of cynicism, of utter disbelief among a large majority of them that the system can respond to their needs and beliefs at all. Many young black people, because they have never experienced the old discrimination, the old order, have a hard time believing that there has been any progress at all. As for young white people, many of them either aren't aware of or refuse to believe what it was really like to be black in America just forty years ago; they perceive black demands for justice today as special pleadings for unfair advantage.

Black and white alike, a large number of our younger generation are caught up, like the larger society, in getting their piece of the pie. A large number of them no longer speak in moral terms. They are not asking what they can do to help the total society, including that large segment of the society that is still left behind. Instead they are simply asking what they can do to help *them*selves.

What I tell them is that the best way to help themselves is to help each other. To work for each other. To *push* for each other. To *pull* for each other. Yes, it's a different setting, a different situation, a different world we live in today than the one in which I came of age. A generation ago we were eighteen, nineteen, twenty years old, and we were actually holding entire cities, states—an entire *nation*— at bay over what we believed. It was easier for us to stand up and confront blatant segregation then than it is for young people today to deal with the more insidious and subtly deep-seated dynamics of racism, or sexism, or greed and exclusion. But that doesn't mean they can't do it. In fact, I tell them, they must. They have a moral obligation and mandate and mission to do it.

There are still visible targets out there. There are specific issues on which to focus. Look at college education, for example, the price of the young generation's own future. Those doors are being shut tighter every day, with costs skyrocketing out of sight. Fewer and fewer young Americans, black or white or any other race, are going to be able to see college as a real opportunity in their lives in the next decade unless drastic changes are made. There are people within the higher education system and within the government working on those changes, but where are the students themselves, the young people? Why aren't they out in the street and up on the ramparts *demanding* these changes? This is *their* future we are dealing with here. Why don't they take it into their own hands?

You cannot wait for someone else to do it. This is what I tell the young people I meet. You cannot wait for government to do it. You must *make* it happen through your own efforts and action and vision and resourcefulness.

And unity. A people united, driven by a moral purpose, guided by a goal of a just and decent community, are absolutely unstoppable. We proved that a generation ago. There is no reason it cannot continue, today and on into the dawn of the coming century. Know your history. Study it. Share it. Shed a tear over it. Laugh about it. *Live* it. Act it *out*. Understand it. Because for better or for worse, our past is what brought us here, and it can help lead us to where we need to go.

And where do we need to go? It's not about who wins. It's not even about who is right. It's about *what* is right. What is *right*—that never changes. It's not about political parties. It's not about personalities. It's not about nations.

It's not owned by the Bible, or by the Koran, or by the Bhagavad Gita. It's not just about today, 1998, or 1968, or 1868. It is timeless and it is eternal.

What...is...right?

If we keep our hearts and minds constantly focused on that single question, and if we act on the answer with courage and commitment, we will overcome all that stands between us and the glory of a truly Beloved Community. We *will* overcome.

I had the privilege of attending Mother Teresa's funeral last September in Calcutta with the First Lady, Hillary Clinton. The caisson that carried her casket through that city's monsoon-soaked streets reminded me of John Kennedy's and of Dr. King's. The carriage that bore Mother Teresa's body was the same one that carried Gandhi to his funeral pyre in 1948.

The funeral itself was held in a large stadium. The Vatican secretary of state, a man named Angelo Sodano, led the Mass and delivered the eulogy on behalf of the Pope. His words were direct, and they spoke to a truth that Mother Teresa understood, a truth that is timeless, and that we in America—especially those of us in government—would do well to remember. "The beggar, the leper, the victim of AIDS," said Sodano, "do not need discussions and theories. They need love. The hungry cannot wait for the rest of the world to come up with the perfect answer."

The hungry cannot wait. Talk is fine. Discussion is fine. But we must respond. We must act. Mother Teresa acted. She reached out to those who were left behind—the forsaken, the poorest of the poor, the sickest of the sick.

And where did she find her strength, her focus, her fuel? She was asked that question back in 1975, for that *Time* magazine story on "living saints." Her answer was succinct. The fuel, she explained, is prayer. "To keep a lamp burning," she said, "we have to keep putting oil in it."

Prayer.

I was asked several years ago to write an essay on what prayer means to me, on how I pray. Each of us has our own answer to that question. Here is mine:

On the one hand prayer to me is an attempt to communicate with a power, with a force, with a being much greater than I am. On the other hand it is a period of simply having an executive session with yourself. It's a period of being alone, a period of meditation, a period of quiet and just being you.

It can happen in a public setting. It can happen in a meeting. It can happen while you're flying in a plane or riding in a car or waiting to make a speech or at almost any time. You hear people from time to time say, "I need to steal away and pray." In my own case I can steal away almost anytime. I can be on the elevator. I can be involved in a march, a sit-in, some type of nonviolent protest, and still be engaged in prayer. And sometimes I pray when I have something very difficult to deal with. You're constantly in prayer to some spirit or some force to help you make the right decision, to give you the courage to follow through or to stand your ground.

I don't as a rule engage in formal prayer. When I first came to Congress, I attended the Thursday-morning prayer breakfast on a regular basis. A conflict of meetings makes it impossible for me to go now. But that doesn't keep me from praying. When I go home in the evening, I pray just like when I was growing up. I don't necessarily get down on my knees and say a prayer before going to bed, but sometimes I'm in bed and I say a prayer. I'm always asking somebody, some force, some power—whether it's God Almighty or what I sometimes refer to as the Spirit of History—to take care of me, to help me make the right decision, to see me through something. Sometimes when I have a major statement to make on the floor, I call on that force, that source, to help me, to guide me.

...When I look back on my own life and what I've come through, I can say that it was the prayers of the true believers, the prayers of an involved community of similar minds, that made it possible for me to still be here. Sometimes when I look back at the film footage of that civil rights fight and see what happened to me at Selma or on the Freedom Rides, I have to believe that it was the prayer of the faithful that made it possible for some of us to still be here.

From time to time I feel the presence of that power, that force that I call the Spirit of History. Sometimes you're guided by it, led by it. Other times you're in tune with that force and you can communicate with it. You have to be in tune, and you have to allow yourself to be used by this Supreme Being. That's what made me feel when we were at the height of the civil rights movement—whether it was the march from Selma to Montgomery, or going on the Freedom Rides— that we were involved in something like a Holy Crusade. It was an extension of my religious convictions, of my faith. We would sing a song or say a prayer, and it was an affirmation that it was the right thing to do. At that time we were communicating with a Supreme Being, with this force.

Prayer is one of the most powerful—well, I don't want to call it a weapon, but it's a tool, an instrument, a way of reaching out that humankind has. We can and do use it to deal with problems and the things and issues that we don't understand, that we don't quite comprehend. It's very hard to separate the essence of prayer and faith. We pray because we believe that praying can make what we believe, our dreams and our visions, come true.

Amen.

There is an old African proverb: "When you pray, move your feet." As a nation, if we care for the Beloved Community, we must move our feet, our hands, our hearts, our resources to build and not to tear down, to reconcile and not to divide, to love and not to hate, to heal and not to kill. In the final analysis, we are one people, one family, one house—the American house, the American family.

INDEX